Yale Book Store
New Haven, Ct.
Dec. 30, 1989
@ Christopher —
"my first visit"

[signature]

MAYHEW'S LONDON

HENRY MAYHEW

MAYHEW'S LONDON

Henry Mayhew
Edited by Peter Quennell

Bracken Books
LONDON

This edition published 1984 by Bracken Books,
a division of Bestseller Publications Ltd,
Princess House, 50 Eastcastle Street, London W1, England
under licence from the proprietor.

Reprinted 1987

ISBN 0 946495 03 3

Printed and bound by Grafoimpex, Yugoslavia

CONTENTS

CONTENTS

CONTENTS

CONTENTS

CONTENTS

CONTENTS

CONTENTS

CONTENTS

LIST OF
ILLUSTRATIONS

INTRODUCTION

DURING the fourth and fifth centuries after Christ, the ordered landscape of the Roman world suffered a process of transformation, no doubt gradual in its development but, as regards its ultimate effects, certainly disastrous. The imperial system was slowly breaking up; and, while the great landowners withdrew to remote fortified demesnes (where, if they were originally of Roman descent, they soon took on the manners and costume of outlandish barbarian neighbours), the huge open cities, which had expanded under the sun of *pax romana*, with their libraries and their baths, their market places and their temples, shrank into smaller and meaner compass, behind massive walls often constructed from the debris of demolished shrines and palaces. Aqueducts had been breached, flooding the farm-lands: as travel grew more dangerous, the postroads were neglected. Fugitives thronged into the safer townships: · the mediaeval city began to appear, picturesque, squalid and overcrowded, with its girdle of crenellated ramparts, its narrow, tortuous streets, its confusion and its poverty.

For more than a thousand years, almost up to the dawn of the Industrial Revolution, most European cities belonged to the Middle Ages, both in their design and in their outlook. Many of them preserved their gates and walls; and through the gates a citizen could walk without hindrance into the unpolluted countryside. As late as the opening of the nineteenth century, Londoners, though they might grumble at the stink an congestion and noise of their immense metropolis, were never far separated from country sights and sounds. Three windmills could be viewed from the Strand; and even the most sedentary inhabitant of the thoroughfares between Oxford Street and Piccadilly had only to stroll west beyond Hyde Park Corner, or northwards through the fields behind Portland Place, to lose himself in some rambling lane among meadows and market-gardens. But already the speculators were hard at work; waves of brick advanced upon farm and garden; Cockney terraces and squares and crescents sprang up with bewildering rapidity on London's urban outskirts, filling the green space between the nucleus of the city and its small surrounding villages. A new type of city was being born: a new civilization was emerging, from which would spring a potent and incalculable force in modern European literature.

Henceforward, the majority of writers, by necessity or habit, would be first and foremost city-dwellers; and urban life would give their work a very definite, at times harsh, but extremely individual colouring. They would love the city as much as they hated it. Among French writers we think immediately of Charles Baudelaire, whose imagination was deeply stirred by the spectacle of mid-nineteenth century Paris, in which the ancient and intimate metropolis of his boyhood was dissolving and disappearing; and, on this side of the English Channel, London was at once the nursery and the forcing-house of Charles Dickens's utterly dissimilar and completely Anglo-Saxon genius. Though it may be wrong to assert that, without London, there would have been no Dickens, it is undoubtedly true that, had he been brought up in any other city or any other period, his novels would have lost something of their peculiar strangeness. Eighteenth-century London was still small enough to be compact and personal; its industries were localized; the structure of its social life was relatively uncomplicated. During Dickens's lifetime, however, a tremendous influx of population brought with it a corresponding loss of freedom, health and dignity. The individual was submerged in the mass of anonymous toilers, whose whole world was circumscribed by the bricks-and-mortar of whatever nook or cranny they had been shoved into by circumstance. From the ranks of these little people, these waifs and oddities and misfits, human rubbish thrown up by the struggle for existence conducted on principles of economic *laissez faire*, the novelist drew the raw material of those fascinating minor personages who constitute the all-important background of any Dickens story—the creepers and the climbers, the grovellers and the schemers, scrambling over one another in the dark confusion of their pestiferous urban ant's-nest.

With every decade their number increased. During the first thirty years of the century the population of the Greater London area rose from 865,000 to 1,500,000; and in the next twenty years another million inhabitants were somehow piled in. They were housed (writes a contributor to that valuable compilation, *Early*

Victorian England) 'by overcrowding, and by lateral expansion in houses, mainly two-storied, built on estates it was desired to develop, and ribboned along roads. That is why, in the *Pickwick Papers*, Mr. Wicks, of Dodson and Fogg's, found it was "half past four before he got to Somers Town" after a convivial evening... and Mr. Jaggers cultivated the family affections behind a ditch in Walworth.' As the population thickened, so did its occupations grow more and more miscellaneous, its character more amorphous. Parasites fastened on parasites; the refuse and leavings of one class helped, literally as well as figuratively, to provide a means of livelihood for the class immediately beneath it; and, while the poor but 'respectable' members of commercial society, the clerks and small employees, tended to gravitate towards pretentious gimcrack suburbs pullulating uncontrolled upon London's shabby outer edge, the lowest and weakest of its citizens, the scavengers, ragpickers and pedlars, drifted into its noisome central slums, into one or other of the many 'rookeries', clusters of dilapidated ancient houses—such as 'Tom All Alone's,' under the shadow of Westminster Abbey, scathingly described as *Bleak House*.

The first chapters of that novel—together with *Our Mutual Friend*, probably Dickens's most ambitious attempt to delineate the London landscape—were published in periodical form during the Spring of 1852. But the public conscience was already aroused, for the Victorian Age, in spite of its numerous detractors, was neither self-complacent nor insensitive; and throughout the 'thirties and 'forties repeated plans had been made for the delivery of at least a preliminary attack on the gigantic Augean stable that London, at its then rate of development, was in danger of becoming. There were sanitary commissions, inquests on water-supply, while a vast and compendious *Report on the Sanitary Condition of the City of London* for the years 1848-49 provoked the indignation and excited the alarm of every thoughtful Londoner. Though 'rookeries' still bred disease, their existence was threatened, if not by the moral scruples of the English upper classes, at all events by the practical necessity of opening up new thoroughfares; and, to clear the approaches to New London Bridge, a million and a half pounds' worth of old property had been purchased and demolished. The spirit of reform and philanthropy was omnipresent; and by a singular stroke of good fortune an enterprising philanthropist of the period happened at the same time to be an extremely able journalist. Two volumes of articles, which had originally appeared in the London daily press, were collected by their author, Henry Mayhew, and published under the title *London Labour & the London Poor* in 1851.

Considering the scope of his works on London and the remarkable quality of their content, it seems odd that Mayhew's name should be so little known to the ordinary modern reader. On the career of this gifted and industrious man the *Dictionary of National Biography* is concise and informative but somewhat unenthusiastic. Born in 1812, the son of a London attorney, he survived till 1887, dying at a house in Charlotte Street, to which, so far as the present writer is aware, the London County Council has not yet contemplated attaching its commemorative blue tab. His activities during that time were numerous and varied. He began his working-life as a dramatist, his first production being a one-act play entitled 'The Wandering Minstrel' in which he introduced the celebrated Cockney song, 'Villikins and his Dinah', and was the author of many other successful comedies and farces. As a middle-aged journalist, he attended at the birth of *Punch*, of which for a while he acted as joint-editor; and, in addition to his dramatic, journalistic and philanthropic efforts, he found time to turn out travel-books, biographies, novels and stories and treatises on popular science. The bulk of his work was ephemeral; but there can be no doubt that *London Labour & The London Poor*, reissued in 1861, 1862, 1864 and 1865 with copious additions and supplementary volumes, is an achievement that deserves the respectful attention of posterity. Not only was Mayhew a pioneer in this particular type of sociological record but, thanks to the original cast of his mind and to his extraordinary gifts both as an observer and as a reporter, he left behind him a book that one need not be a student of history or a sociologist to find immensely entertaining.

The plan is ambitious. Disregarding the strongholds of wealth and privilege, Mayhew's intention was to plumb to its depths the dark ocean of poverty or semi-poverty by which they were encircled, to discover how the poor lived—the hopelessly poor, as well as the depressed and struggling—and to examine the means, ignoble and commendable, furtive and above-board, by which the majority of London's unorganized millions precariously scraped a livelihood.

Had he been exclusively concerned with economics, Mayhew's *magnum opus* might make useful but tedious reading. In fact, his interests were many-sided; and no less than three persons appear and re-appear as we turn the pages of his survey. First, there is the impassioned *Statistician;* but in this guise, it must be admitted, Mayhew with the best intentions in the world is often slightly ludicrous. He loved figures for their own sake, and welcomed every opportunity of drawing up vast ingenious tables, all of which, for the sake of brevity and clarity, have been omitted from this reprint. A single specimen may be sufficient. Mayhew is engaged in an enjoyable tussle with the problem of London street-cleaning and street-cleaners, evidently a subject he found extremely stimulating; and, besides classifying the sweepers themselves, analyzing their economic position and depicting their personal habits, he catalogues the different types of refuse that befoul the London pavements:

FOOD CONSUMED BY AND EXCRETIONS OF A HORSE IN TWENTY-FOUR HOURS

	FOOD			EXCRETIONS	
	Weight in a fresh state in grammes	Weight in a fresh state in pounds		Weight in a fresh state in grammes	Weight in a fresh state in pounds
		lb.　oz.			lb.　oz.
Hay ..	7,500	20　0	Excre-ments	14,250	38　2
Oats ..	2,270	6　1	Urine	1,330	3　7
	9,700	26,1			
Water ..	16,000	42.10			
Total ..	25,770	68.11	Total ..	15,580	41.9

Nor is the above table allowed to speak for itself. Mayhew follows it up with the results of an investigation into the metabolic processes of a 'Brown horse of middle size', conducted at the Royal Veterinary College on September 29th, 1849, and goes on to discuss the trouble caused to London street-cleaners by the passage through the streets of horned cattle, calves, sheep and pigs, till the reader, overwhelmed and exhausted, has squeamishly pulled out his handkerchief.

Luckily, another aspect of Mayhew's personality is very soon in evidence. As the philanthropic *Social Investigator*, he feels a deep concern with the material needs and financial vicissitudes of his fellow human beings. He is intensely preoccupied with the lives of others; and no detail is so trifling that it can slip through the meshes of his inquisitorial drag-net. We are informed, for example, that a working scavenger of the 'fifties, having earned fifteen shillings by his week's labour, had spent, in the instance selected, the sum of exactly thirteen shillings and twopence-farthing—one-and-nine-pence being the rent of an unfurnished room, sevenpence going on tobacco, two-and-fourpence on beer, one-and-a-penny on gin, a penny-three-farthings on pickles or onions, and two-and-fourpence on boiled salt beef. A journeyman sweeper was maintained by his master at the cost of approximately sixpence-half-penny. His week-day diet was as follows:

	s.	d.
Bread and butter and coffee for breakfast	0	2
A saveloy and potatoes, or cabbage; or a 'fagot', with the same vegetables; or fried fish (but not often); or pudding, from a pudding-shop; or soup (a two-penny plate) from a cheap eating--house; average from 2d. to 3d.	0	2½
Tea, same as breakfast	0	2

But we learn, with relief, that 'on Sundays the fare was better. They then sometimes had a bit of "prime fat mutton taken to the oven, with 'taturs to bake along with it"; or a "fry of liver, if the old 'oman was in a good humour", and always a pint of beer apiece.' But Londoners had not only to be fed; they must also be clothed; and in certain callings a decent appearance must be carefully kept up:

'A prosperous and respectable master green-grocer (writes Mayhew), who was what may be called "particular" in his dress, as he had been a gentleman's servant, and was now in the habit of waiting upon the wealthy persons in his neighbourhood, told me that the following was the average of his washing bill. He was a bachelor; all his washing was put out, and he considered his expen-diture far *above* the average of his class, as many used no night-shirt, but slept in the shirt they wore during the day, and paid only 3d., and even less, per shirt to their washer-woman, and perhaps, and more especially in winter, made one shirt last the week.

	s.	d.
Two shirts (per week)	0	7
Stockings	0	1
Night-shirt (worn two weeks generally, average per week)	0	¾
Sheets, blankets, and other household linens or woollens	0	2
Handkerchiefs	0	0¼
	0	11 '

These extracts (two of which we have been obliged to omit from the present abridged edition of *London Labour*) have been chosen more or less at random, but may serve to illustrate the meticulous humanity with which Mayhew pursued his subject. And now a further facet of his character emerges. It would be presumptuous, no doubt, to call him the nineteenth-century Defoe; but, if he had none of Defoe's imaginative genius, he had the same devotion to the literal fact, the same grasp of detail and the same observant eye, that makes Defoe the most poetic of the great European realists. Mayhew's notes on economic conditions were accompanied by brilliant portraits of individual men and women. One would like to know what were his methods of work. This Victorian Mass-Observer would appear to have spent long hours of conversation in attics, pubs and back-streets, asking innumerable questions and patiently noting down the answers. Here he reveals his third facet—perhaps the most important—the dispassionate *Literary Portraitist*, who bore some resemblance both to Daniel Defoe and to Restif de la Bretonne. Like them he browsed and botanised; but he had a knack of recording living speech which was peculiarly characteristic of the period he lived in. Take, for instance, this speech by an old soldier:

'I'm 42 now (he said), and when I was a boy and a young man I was employed in the *Times* machine office, but got into a bit of a row—a bit of a street quarrel and frolic, and was called on to pay £ 3, something about a street-lamp; that was out of the question; and as I was taking a walk in the park, not just knowing what I'd best do, I met a recruiting sergeant, and enlisted on a sudden—all on a sudden—in the 16th Lancers.... Well, I was rather frolicsome in those days, I confess, and perhaps *had rather a turn for a roving life,*

so when the sergeant said he'd take me to the East India Company's
recruiting sergeant, I consented, and was accepted at once. I was
taken to Calcutta, and served under General Nott all through the
Affghan war. The first real warm work I was in was at Candahar.
I've heard young soldiers say that they've gone into action the first
time as merry as they would go to a play. Don't believe them, Sir.
Old soldiers will tell you quite different. You *must* feel queer and
serious the first time you're in action; it's not fear—it's nervousness.
The crack of the muskets at the first fire you hear in real hard earnest
is uncommon startling; you see the flash of the fire from the enemy's
line, but very little else. Indeed, oft enough you see nothing but smoke,
and hear nothing but balls whistling every side of you. And then you
get excited, just as if you were at a hunt; but after a little service—I
can speak for myself, at any rate—you go into action as you go to
your dinner.'

'Something about a street-lamp'—how admirable the phrase is!
Mayhew's pages are illuminated, again and again, by these sudden
vivid flashes in which the essentials of a situation or character—
here the headstrong young man on a spree; the tinkle of broken
glass; the mood of exhilaration passing into the mood of angry
desperation during which he meets the sergeant—seem concisely
summed up. As memorable are his impressions of interiors; for
his omnivorous curiosity was not confined to street-life; and, bound
on a visit to an impoverished coster-monger, he had climbed a
flight of tottering and broken stairs, and entered a room thick with
smoke that was pouring from the chimney:

'The place was filled with it, curling in the light, and making everything so indistinct that I could with difficulty see the white mugs
ranged in the corner-cupboard.... On a mattress, on the floor, lay
a pale-faced girl—"eighteen years old last twelfth-cake day"—her
drawn-up form showing in the patch-work counterpane that covered
her. She had just been confined, and the child had died!.... To shield
her from the light of the window, a cloak had been fastened up slant-
ingly across the panes; and on a string that ran along the wall was
tied, amongst the bonnets, a clean nightcap—"against the doctor
came", as the mother, curtsying, informed me.... The room was
about nine feet square, and furnished a home for three women. The
ceiling slanted like that of a garret, and was the colour of old leather,
excepting a few rough white patches, where the tenants had rudely
mended it. The white light was easily seen through the laths, and in
one corner a large patch of the paper looped down from the wall....
They had made a carpet out of three or four old mats. They were
"obligated to it for fear of dropping anything through the boards
into the donkey stables in the parlour underneath. But we only pay
ninepence a week rent", said the old woman, "and musn't grumble".'

Mayhew's impressions, however, are not of gloom unmitigated or poverty unrelieved; and many have the cheerfulness and distinction of a Dutch or Flemish *genre* picture. He describes, for example, his visit to the home of a thriving coster-monger, where 'the floor was as white as if it had been newly planed', and 'the wall over the fire-place was patched up to the ceiling with little square pictures of saints. ... On the mantel-piece, between a row of bright tumblers and wine glasses filled with odds and ends, stood glazed crockeryware images of Prince Albert and M. Jullien. ... In the band-box, which stood on the stained chest of drawers, you could tell that the Sunday bonnet was stowed away safely from the dust.' Even the room occupied by a family of struggling costers was not entirely squalid:

'The man, a tall, thick-built, almost good-looking fellow, with a large fur cap on his head, lived with his family in a front kitchen, and as there were, with his mother-in-law, five persons, and only one bed, I was somewhat puzzled to know where they could *all* sleep. The barrow standing on the railings over the window, half shut out the light, and when any one passed there was a momentary shadow thrown over the room, and a loud rattling of the iron gratings above that completely prevented all conversation. When I entered, the mother-in-law was reading aloud one of the threepenny papers to her son, who lolled on the bed, that with its curtains nearly filled the room. There was the usual attempt to make the fireside comfortable. The stone sides had been well whitened, and the mantel-piece decorated with its small tin trays, tumblers, and a piece of looking-glass. A cat with her kittens were seated on the hearth-rug in front.... By the drawers were piled up four bushel baskets, and in a dark corner near the bed stood a tall measure full of apples that scented the room.... On a string dangled a couple of newly washed shirts, and by the window were two stone barrels, for lemonade, when the coster visited the fairs and races.'

Still more vivid, in its extremely Dickensian way, is Mayhew's account of his meeting with Jack Black, 'Rat and mole destroyer to Her Majesty', whom he discovered at his house in Battersea, and whose expression radiated a kindliness that did not 'exactly agree with one's preconceived notions of rat-catchers. His face had a strange appearance, from his rough, uncombed hair being nearly grey, and his eyebrows and whiskers black, so that he looked as if he wore powder'. He, too, lived surrounded by the apparatus of his daily work—he was, incidentally, taxidermist and bird-fancier as well as rat-catcher; his parlour was 'more like a shop than a family apartment. In a box ... like a rabbit-hutch, was a white ferret, twisting its long thin body with a snake-like motion up and down the length of its prison, as restlessly as if it were a miniature polar bear. When Mr. Black called "Polly" to the ferret, it came to the bars and fixed its pink eyes on him. A child lying on the floor poked its fingers into the cage, but Polly only smelt at them ...'

Nothing is more remarkable about Mayhew's book than the fantastic diversity of trades and occupations that came beneath his survey. Besides street-sellers innumerable, vending every kind of object from nutmeg-graters and tracts to dogs and birds-nests, there were (in addition to sweepers and scavengers) a considerable class of 'finders' who existed, from hand to mouth, on the material they picked up. In the first class—the itinerant street-merchants— the London coster-mongers were probably the most vigorous and independent. They had their own dress, which Mayhew describes at length, their own public-houses and slang and round of social gaieties: they patronised 'the Vic Gallery', frequented 'two-penny hops', were fond of gambling, singing, fighting but, in spite of brutal and pugnacious habits, were devoted to their donkeys. Such were the chivalry of London back-streets. On a lower level— physically and morally, if not always financially—was the section of the populace that dealt in London's ordures. This section was sharply subdivided. At one end of the scale were 'mud-larks' and 'pure-finders', the poorest of the poor, destitute children or aged men and women, some of whom, like the 'mud-larks', gathered lumps of coal or fragments of old iron from London's slimy river-side, where they spent their days wading and grubbing among the refuse of the mud-banks; while others—the 'pure-finders'—scoured the pavements for the droppings of dogs, which they then sold by the pailful to some local tannery. Their earnings were as meagre as their method of livelihood was nauseous. But this branch of commerce had its aristocracy; and Mayhew devotes one of his most curious and entertaining chapters to the 'toshers' or sewer-hunters, whose business it was, before the building of the Thames embankment, to explore the urban sewer-system which still opened on the fore-shore. Their work was profitable but uncommonly dangerous. London's sewers during the 'fifties were ancient, dilapidated and of unknown extent. Some dated from the Middle Ages; the brick-work at any moment might collapse on the explorer's head; he might be stifled by sewer-gas; hordes of ferocious sewer-rats might attack and overwhelm him, and, before help came, pick his bones clean; or he might be drowned by an unusually high tide gurgling up unperceived through the labyrinthine passages of his mephitic under-world. But on the proceeds of what they discovered—old iron, copper coins, even sovereigns and silver tea-spoons—the 'toshers' could expect to clear a far bigger profit than often came the way of the ordinary industrious above-ground London artisan. Nor did their health suffer. Though it was a 'roughish smell at first' (as one of them admitted), the atmosphere of the sewers soon ceased to incommode them; and the 'toshers', as a class, were 'strong, robust, and healthy men, generally florid in their complexion'. Their personal habits were regrettably intemperate '. . . Like all who make a living as it were by a game of chance, plodding, carefulness, and saving habits cannot be reckoned among their virtues... The shoremen might, with but ordinary prudence, live well, have comfortable homes, and even be able to save sufficient to provide for themselves in their old age. Their practice, however, is directly the reverse. They no sooner make a "haul", as they say, than they adjourn to some low public house in the neighbourhood, and seldom leave till empty pockets and hungry stomachs drive them forth to procure the means of a fresh debauch. It is principally on this account (writes Mayhew, who had visited an intelligent 'tosher' in an abominable slum-yard off Rosemary Lane) that, despite their large gains, they are to be found located in the most wretched quarter of the metropolis'.

* * *

The present abridged edition of *London Labour & the London Poor* has been designed for the convenience of the general reading public. Much interesting material—including all the longer passages quoted above—has necessarily been sacrificed. Our intention was to concentrate on the more graphic and personal side of Mayhew's massive survey, and, with the help of these extracts, to provide a detailed panorama of London in the 'fifties—of that part of London, at least, which underlay the pompous urbanity of its fashionable streets and squares. Our text is derived from the three-volume edition of 1861; the contents of a fourth volume, published in 1862, on prostitutes, thieves, swindlers and beggars, have been omitted in entirety.

PETER QUENNELL

THE STREET FOLK

OF the thousand millions of human beings that are said to constitute the population of the entire globe, there are—socially, morally, and perhaps even physically considered—but two distinct and broadly marked races, viz., the wanderers and the settlers—the vagabond and the citizen—the nomadic and the civilized tribes.

The nomadic races of England are of many distinct kinds—from the habitual vagrant—half-beggar, half-thief—sleeping in barns, tents, and casual wards—to the mechanic on tramp, obtaining his bed and supper from the trade societies in the different towns, on his way to seek work. Between these two extremes there are several mediate varieties—consisting of pedlars, showmen, harvestmen, and all that large class who live by either selling, showing, or doing something through the country. These are, so to speak, the rural nomads—not confining their wanderings to any one particular locality, but ranging often from one end of the land to the other. Besides these, there are the urban and suburban wanderers, or those who follow some itinerant occupation in and round about the large towns. Such are, in the metropolis more particularly, the pick-pockets—the beggars—the prostitutes—the street-sellers—the street-performers—the cabmen—the coachmen —the watermen—the sailors and such like.

Those who obtain their living in the streets of the metropolis are a very large and varied class; indeed, the means resorted to in order 'to pick up a crust,' as the people call it, in the public thoroughfares (and such in many instances it *literally* is) are so multifarious that the mind is long baffled in its attempts to reduce them to scientific order or classification.

It would appear, however, that the street-people may be all arranged under six distinct genera or kinds.

These are severally:
    I. STREET-SELLERS.
    II. STREET-BUYERS.
    III. STREET-FINDERS.

IV. STREET-PERFORMERS, ARTIST, AND SHOWMEN.
V. STREET-ARTISANS, or WORKING PEDLARS; and
VI. STREET-LABOURERS.

OF THE NUMBER OF COSTERMONGERS AND OTHER STREET FOLK

THE number of costermongers,—that it is to say, of those street-sellers attending the London, 'green' and 'fish' markets,'—appears to be, from the best data at my command, now 30,000 men, women and children.

The costermongering class extends itself yearly; and it is computed that for the last five years it has increased considerably faster than the general metropolitan population. This increase is derived partly from *all* the children of costermongers following the father's trade, but chiefly from working men, such as the servants of green-grocers or of innkeepers, when out of employ, 'taking a coster's barrow' for a livelihood; and the same being done by mechanics and labourers out of work. At the time of the famine in Ireland, it is calculated, that the number of Irish obtaining a living in the London streets must have been at least doubled.

During the summer months and fruit season, the average number of costermongers attending Covent-garden market is about 2,500 per market-day. In the strawberry season there are nearly double as many, there being, at that time, a large number of Jews who come to buy; during that period, on a Saturday morning, from the commencement to the close of the market, as many as 4,000 costers have been reckoned purchasing at Covent-garden. Through the winter season, however, the number of costermongers does not exceed upon the average 1,000 per market morning.

OF THE VARIETIES OF STREET-FOLK IN GENERAL AND COSTERMONGERS IN PARTICULAR

AMONG the street-folk there are many distinct characters of people —people differing as widely from each in tastes, habits, thoughts and creed, as one nation from another. Of these the costermongers form by far the largest and certainly the mostly broadly marked class. They appear to be a distinct race—perhaps, originally, of

Irish extraction—seldom associating with any other of the street-folks, and being all known to each other. The 'patterers,' or the men who cry the last dying-speeches, &c. in the street, and those who help off their wares by long harangues in the public thorough-fares, are again a separate class. These, to use their own term, are 'the aristocracy of the street-sellers,' despising the costers for their ignorance, and boasting that they live by their intellect. The public, they say, do not expect to receive from them an equiva-lent for their money—they pay to hear them talk. Compared with the costermongers, the patterers are generally an educated class, and among them are some classical scholars, one clergyman, and many sons of gentlemen. They appear to be the counterparts of the old mountebanks or street-doctors. As a body they seem far less improvable than the costers, being more 'knowing' and less impulsive. The street-performers differ again from those; these appear to possess many of the characteristics of the lower class of actors, viz., a strong desire to excite admiration, an indisposition to pursue any settled occupation, a love of the tap-room, though more for the society and display than for the drink connected with it, a great fondness for finery and predilection for the performance of dexterous or dangerous feats. Then there are the street mechanics, or artisans—quiet, melancholy, struggling men, who, unable to find any regular employment at their own trade, have made up a few things, and taken to hawk them in the streets, as the last shift of independence. Another distinct class of street-folk are the blind people (mostly musicians in a rude way), who, after the loss of their eyesight, have sought to keep themselves from the work-house by some little excuse for alms-seeking. These, so far as my experience goes, appear to be a far more deserving class than is usually supposed—their affliction, in most cases, seems to have thastened them and to have given a peculiar religious cast to their thoughts.

Such are the several varieties of street-folk, intellectually con-sidered—looked at in a national point of view, they likewise include many distinct people. Among them are to be found the Irish fruit-sellers; the Jew clothesmen; the Italian organ boys, French singing women, the German brass bands, the Dutch buy-a-broom girls, the Highland bagpipe players, and the Indian crossing-sweepers—all of whom I here shall treat of in due order.

The costermongering class or order has also its many varieties. These appear to be in the following proportions:—One-half of the entire class are costermongers proper, that is to say, the calling with them is hereditary, and perhaps has been so for many generations; while the other half is composed of three-eighths Irish, and one-eighth mechanics, tradesmen, and Jews.

Under the term 'costermonger' is here included only such 'street-sellers' as deal in fish, fruit, and vegetables, purchasing their goods at the wholesale 'green' and 'fish' markets. Of these some carry on their business at the same stationary stall or 'standing' in the street, while others go on 'rounds.' The itinerant costermongers, as contradistinguished from the stationary street-fish-mongers and greengrocers, have in many instances regular rounds, which they go daily, and which extend from two to ten miles. The longest are those which embrace a suburban part; the shortest are through streets thickly peopled by the poor, where duly to 'work' a single street consumes, in some instances, an hour. There are also 'chance' rounds. Men 'working' these carry their wares to any part in which they hope to find customers. The costermongers, moreover, diversify their labours by occasionally going on a country round, travelling on these excursions, in all directions, from thirty to ninety and even a hundred miles from the metropolis. Some, again, confine their callings chiefly to the neighbouring races and fairs.

OF COSTERMONGERING MECHANICS

'FROM the numbers of mechanics,' said one smart costermonger to me, 'that I know of in my own district, I should say there's now more than 1,000 costers in London that were once mechanics or labourers. They are driven to it as a last resource, when they can't get work at their trade. They don't do well, at least four out of five, or three out of four don't. They're not up to the dodges of the business. They go to market with fear, and don't know how to venture a bargain if one offers. They're inferior salesmen too, and if they have fish left that won't keep, it's a dead loss to them, for they aren't up to the trick of selling it cheap at a distance where the coster ain't known; or of quitting it to another, for candle-light sale, cheap, to the Irish or to the "lushingtons," that haven't a proper taste for fish. Some of these poor fellows lose every penny. They're mostly middle-aged when they begin costering. They'll generally commence with oranges or herrings. We pity them. We say, "Poor fellows! they'll find it out by-and-bye." It's awful to see some poor women, too, trying to pick up a living in the streets by selling nuts or oranges. It's awful to see them, for they can't set about it right; besides that, there's too many before they start. They don't find a living, *it's only another way of starving.*'

THE LONDON STREET MARKETS ON A SATURDAY NIGHT

THE street-sellers are to be seen in the greatest numbers at the London street markets on a Saturday night. Here, and in the shops immediately adjoining, the working-classes generally purchase their Sunday's dinner; and after pay-time on Saturday night, or early on Sunday morning, the crowd in the New-cut, and the Brill in particular, is almost impassable. Indeed, the scene in these parts has more of the character of a fair than a market. There are hundreds of stalls, and every stall has its one or two lights; either it is illuminated by the intense white light of the new self-generating gas-lamp, or else it is brightened up by the red smoky flame of the old-fashioned grease lamp. One man shows off his yellow haddock with a candle stuck in a bundle of firewood; his neighbour makes a candlestick of a huge turnip, and the tallow gutters over its sides; whilst the boy shouting 'Eight a penny, stunning pears!' has rolled his dip in a thick coat of brown paper, that flares away with the candle. Some stalls are crimson with the fire shining through the holes beneath the baked chestnut stove; others have handsome octahedral lamps, while a few have a candle shining through a sieve: these, with the sparkling ground-glass globes of the tea-dealers' shops, and the butchers' gaslights streaming and fluttering in the wind, like flags of flame, pour forth such a flood of light, that at a distance the atmosphere immediately above the spot is as lurid as if the street were on fire.

The pavement and the road are crowded with purchasers and street-sellers. The housewife in her thick shawl, with the market-basket on her arm, walks slowly on, stopping now to look at the stall of caps, and now to cheapen a bunch of greens. Little boys, holding three or four onions in their hand, creep between the people, wriggling their way through every interstice, and asking for custom in whining tones, as if seeking charity. Then the tumult of the thousand different cries of the eager dealers, all shouting at the top of their voices, at one and the same time, is almost bewildering. 'So-old again,' roars one. 'Chestnuts all 'ot, a penny a score,' bawls another. 'An 'aypenny a skin, blacking,' squeaks a boy. 'Buy, buy, buy, buy, buy, bu-u-uy!' cries the butcher. 'Half-quire of paper for a penny,' bellows the street stationer. 'An 'aypenny a lot ing-uns.' 'Twopence a pound grapes.' 'Three a penny Yarmouth bloaters.' 'Who'll buy a bonnet for fourpence?' 'Pick 'em out cheap here! three pair for a halfpenny, bootlaces.' 'Now's your time! beautiful whelks, a penny a lot.' 'Here's ha'p'orths,' shouts the perambulating confectioner. 'Come and look at 'em! here's toasters!' bellows one with a Yarmouth bloater stuck on a toasting-fork. 'Penny a lot, fine russets,' calls the apple woman; and so the Babel goes on.

One man stands with his red-edged mats hanging over his back and chest, like a herald's coat; and the girl with her basket of walnuts lifts her brown-stained fingers to her mouth, as she screams, 'Fine warnuts! sixteen a penny, fine war-r-nuts.' A bootmaker, to 'ensure custom,' has illuminated his shop-front with a line of gas, and in its full glare stands a blind beggar, his eyes turned up so as to show only 'the whites,' and mumbling some begging rhymes, that are drowned in the shrill notes of the bamboo-flute-player next to him. The boy's sharp cry, the woman's cracked voice, the gruff, hoarse shout of the man, are all mingled together. Sometimes an Irishman is heard with his 'fine ating apples'; or else the jingling music of an unseen organ breaks out, as the trio of street singers rest between the verses.

Then the sights, as you elbow your way through the crowd, are equally multifarious. Here is a stall glittering with new tin saucepans; there another, bright with its blue and yellow crockery, and sparkling with white glass. Now you come to a row of old shoes arranged along the pavement; now to a stand of gaudy tea-trays; then to a shop with red handkerchiefs and blue checked shirts, fluttering backwards and forwards, and a counter built up outside on the kerb, behind which are boys beseeching custom. At the door of a tea-shop, with its hundred white globes of light, stands a man

THE LONDON COSTERMONGER

THE IRISH STREET-SELLER

delivering bills, thanking the public for past favours, and 'defying competition.' Here, alongside the road, are some half-dozen headless tailor's dummies, dressed in Chesterfields and fustian jackets, each labelled, 'Look at the prices,' or 'Observe the quality.' After this is a butcher's shop, crimson and white with meat piled up to the first-floor, in front of which the butcher himself, in his blue coat, walks up and down, sharpening his knife on the steel that hangs to his waist. A little further on stands the clean family, begging; the father with his head down as if in shame, and a box of lucifers held forth in his hand—the boys in newly-washed pinafores, and the tidily got-up mother with a child at her breast. This stall is green and white with bunches of turnips—that red with apples, the next yellow with onions, and another purple with pickling cabbages. One minute you pass a man with an umbrella turned inside up and full of prints; the next, you hear one with a peepshow of Mazeppa, and Paul Jones the pirate, describing the pictures to the boys looking in at the little round windows. Then is heard the sharp snap of the percussion-cap from the crowd of lads firing at the target for nuts; and the moment afterwards, you see either a black man halfclad in white, and shivering in the cold with tracts in his hand, or else you hear the sounds of music from 'Frazier's Circus,' on the other side of the road, and the man outside the door of the penny concert, beseeching you to 'Be in time—be in time!' as Mr. Somebody is just about to sing his favourite song of the 'Knife Grinder.' Such, indeed, is the riot, the struggle, and the scramble for a living, that the confusion and uproar of the New-cut on Saturday night have a bewildering and saddening effect upon the thoughtful mind.

Each salesman tries his utmost to sell his wares, tempting the passers-by with his bargains. The boy with his stock of herbs offers 'a double 'andful of fine parsley for a penny'; the man with the donkey-cart filled with turnips has three lads to shout for him to their utmost, with their 'Ho! ho! hi-i-i! What do you think of this here? A penny a bunch—hurrah for free trade! *Here's* your turnips!' Until it is seen and heard, we have no sense of the scramble that is going on throughout London for a living. The same scene takes place at the Brill—the same in Leather-lane—the same in Tottenham-court-road—the same in Whitecross-street; go to whatever corner of the metropolis you please, either on a Saturday night or a

Sunday morning, and there is the same shouting and the same struggling to get the penny profit out of the poor man's Sunday's dinner.

THE SUNDAY MORNING MARKETS

NEARLY every poor man's market does its Sunday trade. For a few hours on the Sabbath morning, the noise, bustle, and scramble of the Saturday night are repeated, and but for this opportunity many a poor family would pass a dinnerless Sunday. The system of paying the mechanic late on the Saturday night—and more particularly of paying a man his wages in a public-house—when he is tired with his day's work, lures him to the tavern, and there the hours fly quickly enough beside the warm taproom fire, so that by the time the wife comes for her husband's wages, she finds a large portion of them gone in drink, and the streets half cleared, so that the Sunday market is the only chance of getting the Sunday's dinner.

Of all these Sunday-morning markets, the Brill, perhaps, furnishes the busiest scene; so that it may be taken as a type of the whole.

The streets in the neighbourhood are quiet and empty. The shops are closed with their different-coloured shutters, and the people round about are dressed in the shiny cloth of the holiday suit. There are no 'cabs,' and but few omnibuses to disturb the rest, and men walk in the road as safely as on the footpath.

As you enter the Brill the market sounds are scarcely heard. But at each step the low hum grows gradually into the noisy shouting, until at last the different cries become distinct, and the hubbub, din, and confusion of a thousand voices bellowing at once again fill the air. The road and footpath are crowded, as on the overnight; the men are standing in groups, smoking and talking; whilst the women run to and fro, some with the white round turnips showing out of their filled aprons, others with cabbages under their arms, and a piece of red meat dangling from their hands. Only a few of the shops are closed; but the butcher's and the coal-shed are filled with customers, and from the door of the shut-up baker's, the women come streaming forth with bags of flour in their hands, while men sally from the halfpenny barber's smoothing their clean-shaven chins. Walnuts, blacking, apples, onions, braces, combs, turnips, herrings, pens, and corn-plaster, are all bellowed out at the same time. Labourers and mechanics, still unshorn and undressed, hang about with their hands in their pockets, some with their pet terriers under their arms. The pavement is green with the refuse leaves of vegetables, and round a cabbage-barrow the women stand turning over the bunches, as the man shouts, 'Where you like, only a penny.' Boys are running home with the breakfast herring held in a piece of paper, and the side-pocket of the appleman's stuff coat hangs down with the weight of the halfpence stored within it. Presently the tolling of the neighbouring church bells breaks forth. Then the bustle doubles itself, the cries grow louder, the confusion greater. Women run about and push their way through the throng, scolding the saunterers, for in half an hour the market will close. In a little time the butcher puts up his shutters, and leaves the door still open; the policemen in their clean gloves come round and drive the street-sellers before them, and as the clock strikes eleven the market finishes, and the Sunday's rest begins.

HABITS AND AMUSEMENTS
OF COSTERMONGERS

I find it impossible to separate these two headings; for the habits of the costermonger are not domestic. His busy life is passed in the markets or the streets, and as his leisure is devoted to the beer-shop, the dancing-room, or the theatre, we must look for his habits to his demeanour at those places. Home has few attractions to a man whose life is a street-life. Even those who are influenced by family ties and affections, prefer to 'home'—indeed that word is rarely mentioned among them—the conversation, warmth, and merriment of the beer-shop, where they can take their ease among their 'mates.' Excitement or amusement are indispensable to uneducated men. Of beer-shops resorted to by costermongers, and principally supported by them, it is computed that there are 400 in London.

Those who meet first in the beer-shop talk over the state of trade and of the markets, while the later comers enter at once into what may be styled the serious business of the evening—amusement. Business topics are discussed in a most peculiar style. One man takes the pipe from his mouth and says, 'Bill made a doogheno hit this morning.' 'Jem,' says another, to a man just entering, 'you'll stand a top o' reeb?' 'On,' answers Jem, 'I've had a trosseno tol,

and have been doing dab.' For an explanation of what may be
obscure in this dialogue, I must refer my readers to my remarks
concerning the language of the class. If any strangers are present,
the conversation is still further clothed in slang, so as to be unintel-
ligible even to the partially initiated. The evident puzzlement of
any listener is of course gratifying to the costermonger's vanity,
for he feels that he possesses a knowledge peculiarly his own.

Among the in-door amusements of the costermonger is card-
playing, at which many of them are adepts. The usual games are
all-fours, all-fives, cribbage, and put. Whist is known to a few, but
is never played, being considered dull and slow. Of short whist they
have not heard; 'but,' said one, whom I questioned on the subject,
'if it's come into fashion, it'll soon be among us.' The play is
usually for beer, but the game is rendered exciting by bets both
among the players and the lookers-on. 'I'll back Jem for a yane-
patine,' says one. 'Jack for a gen,' cries another. A penny is the
lowest sum laid, and five shillings generally the highest, but a
shilling is not often exceeded. 'We play fair among ourselves,'
said a costermonger to me—'aye, fairer than the aristocrats—but
we'll take in anybody else.' Where it is known that the landlord
will not supply cards, 'a sporting coster' carries a pack or two
with him. The cards played with have rarely been stamped; they
are generally dirty, and sometimes almost illegible, from long
handling and spilled beer. Some men will sit patiently for hours at
these games, and they watch the dealing round of the dingy cards
intently, and without the attempt—common among politer game-
sters—to appear indifferent, though they bear their losses well. In
a full room of card-players, the groups are all shrouded in tobacco-
smoke, and from them are heard constant sounds—according to
the games they are engaged in—of 'I'm low, and Ped's high.' 'Tip
and me's game.' 'Fifteen four and a flush of five.' I may remark
it is curious that costermongers, who can neither read nor write,
and who have no knowledge of the multiplication tables, are skilful
in all the intricacies and calculations of cribbage. There is not much
quarrelling over the cards, unless strangers play with them, and
then the costermongers all take part one with another, fairly or
unfairly.

It has been said that there is a close resemblance between many
of the characteristics of a very high class, socially, and a very low

class. Those who remember the disclosures on a trial a few years back, as to how men of rank and wealth passed their leisure in card-playing—many of their lives being one continued leisure— can judge how far the analogy holds when the card-passion of the costermongers is described.

'Shove-halfpenny' is another game played by them; so is 'Three up.' Three halfpennies are thrown up, and when they fall all 'heads' or all 'tails,' it is a mark; and the man who gets the greatest number of marks out of a given amount—three, or five, or more—wins. 'Three-up' is played fairly among the coster-mongers; but is most frequently resorted to when strangers are present to 'make a pitch,'—which is, in plain words, to cheat any stranger who is rash enough to bet upon them. 'This is the way, sir,' said an adept to me; 'bless you, I can make them fall as I please. If I'm playing with Jo, and a stranger bets with Jo, why, of course, I make Jo win.' This adept illustrated his skill to me by throwing up three halfpennies, and, five times out of six, they fell upon the floor, whether he threw them nearly to the ceiling or merely to his shoulder, all heads or all tails. The halfpence were the proper current coins—indeed, they were my own; and the result is gained by a peculiar position of the coins on the fingers, and a peculiar jerk in the throwing. There was an amusing manifestation of the pride of art in the way in which my obliging informant displayed his skill.

'Skittles' is another favourite amusement, and the coster-mongers class themselves among the best players in London. The game is always for beer, but betting goes on.

A fondness for 'sparring' and 'boxing' lingers among the rude members of some classes of the working men, such as the tanners. With the great majority of the costermongers this fondness is still as dominant as it was among the 'higher classes,' when boxers were the pets of princes and nobles. The sparring among the costers is not for money, but for beer and 'a lark'—a convenient word covering much mischief. Two out of every ten landlords, whose houses are patronised by these lovers of 'the art of self-defence,' supply gloves. Some charge 2d. a night for their use; others only 1d. The sparring seldom continues long, sometimes not above a quarter of an hour; for the costermongers, though excited for a while, weary of sports in which they cannot personally participate, and in the beer-shops only two spar at a time, though fifty or sixty may be present. The shortness of the duration of this pastime may be one reason why it seldom leads to quarrelling. The stake is usually a 'top of reeb,' and the winner is the man who gives the first 'noser'; a *bloody* nose however is required to show that the blow was veritably a noser. The costermongers boast of their skill in pugilism as well as at skittles. 'We are all handy with our fists,' said one man, 'and are matches, aye, and more than matches, for anybody but reg'lar boxers. We've stuck to the ring, too, and gone reg'lar to the fights, more than any other men.'

'Twopenny-hops' are much resorted to by the costermongers, men and women, boys and girls. At these dances decorum is sometimes, but not often, violated. 'The women,' I was told by one man, 'doesn't show their necks as I've seen the ladies do in them there pictures of high life in the shop-winders, or on the stage. Their Sunday gowns, which is their dancing gowns, ain't made that way.' At these 'hops' the clog-hornpipe is often danced, and sometimes a collection is made to ensure the performance of a first-rate professor of that dance; sometimes, and more frequently, it is volunteered gratuitously. The other dances are jigs, 'flash jigs'— hornpipes in fetters—a dance rendered popular by the success of the acted 'Jack Sheppard'—polkas, and country-dances, the last-mentioned being generally demanded by the women. Waltzes are as yet unknown to them. Sometimes they do the 'pipe-dance.' For this a number of tobacco-pipes, about a dozen, are laid close together on the floor, and the dancer places the toe of his boot between the different pipes, keeping time with the music. Two of the pipes are arranged as a cross, and the toe has to be inserted between each of the angles, without breaking them. The numbers present at these 'hops' vary from 30 to 100 of both sexes, their ages being from 14 to 45, and the female sex being slightly predominant as to the proportion of those in attendance. At these 'hops' there is nothing of the leisurely style of dancing—half a glide and half a skip—but vigorous, laborious capering. The hours are from half-past eight to twelve, sometimes to one or two in the morning, and never later than two, as the costermongers are early risers. There is sometimes a good deal of drinking; some of the young girls being often pressed to drink, and frequently yielding to the temptation. From 1*l.* to 7*l.* is spent in drink at a hop; the youngest men or lads present spend the most, especially in that act of costermonger politeness—'treating the gals.' The music is always a fiddle, sometimes with the addition of a harp and a cornopean. The band is provided by the costermongers, to whom the assembly is confined; but during the present and the last year, when the costers' earnings have been less than the average, the landlord has provided the harp, whenever that instrument has added to the charms of the fiddle. Of one use to which these 'hops' are put I have given an account, under the head of 'Marriage.'

The other amusements of this class of the community are the theatre and the penny concert, and their visits are almost entirely confined to the galleries of the theatres on the Surrey-side—the Surrey, the Victoria, the Bower Saloon, and (but less frequently) Astley's. Three times a week is an average attendance at theatres and dances by the more prosperous costermongers. The most intelligent man I met with among them gave me the following account. He classes himself with the many, but his tastes are really those of an educated man:—'Love and murder suits us best, sir; but within these few years I think there's a great deal more liking for deep tragedies among us. They set men a thinking; but then we all consider them too long. Of *Hamlet* we can make neither end nor side; and nine out of ten of us—ay, far more than that—would like it to be confined to the ghost scenes, and the funeral, and the killing off at the last. *Macbeth* would be better liked, if it was only the witches and the fighting. The high words in a tragedy we call jaw-breakers, and say we can't tumble to that barrikin. We always stay to the last, because we've paid for it all, or very few costers would see a tragedy out if any money was returned to those leaving after two or three acts. We are fond of music. Nigger music was very much liked among us, but it's stale now. Flash songs are liked, and sailor's songs, and patriotic songs. Most costers—indeed, I can't call to mind an exception—listen very quietly to songs that they don't in the least understand. We have among us translations of the patriotic French songs. "Mourir pour la patrie" is very popular, and so is the "Marseillaise." A song to take hold of us must have a good chorus.' 'They like something, sir, that is worth hearing,' said one of my informants, 'such as the "Soldier's Dream," "The Dream of Napoleon," or "I 'ad a dream—an'appy dream."'

The songs in ridicule of Marshal Haynau, and in laudation of

Barclay and Perkin's draymen, were and are very popular among the costers; but none are more popular than Paul Jones—'A noble commander, Paul Jones was his name.' Among them the chorus of 'Britons never shall be slaves,' is often rendered 'Britons always shall be slaves.' The most popular of all songs with the class, however, is 'Duck-legged Dick,' of which I give the first verse.

> 'Duck-legged Dick had a donkey,
>   And his lush loved much for to swill,
> One day he got rather lumpy,
>   And got sent seven days to the mill.
> His donkey was taken to the green-yard,
>   A fate which he never deserved.
> Oh! it was such a regular mean yard,
>   That alas! the poor moke got starved.
> Oh! bad luck can't be prevented,
>   Fortune she smiles or she frowns,
> He's best off that's contented,
>   To mix, sirs, the ups and the downs.'

Their sports are enjoyed the more, if they are dangerous and require both courage and dexterity to succeed in them. They prefer, if crossing a bridge, to climb over the parapet, and walk along on the stone coping. When a house is building, rows of coster lads will climb up the long ladders, leaning against the unslated roof, and then slide down again, each one resting on the other's shoulders. A peep show with a battle is sure of its coster audience, and a favourite pastime is fighting with cheap theatrical swords. They are, however, true to each other, and should a coster, who is the hero of his court, fall ill and go to a hospital, the whole of the inhabitants of his quarter will visit him on the Sunday, and take him presents of various articles so that 'he may live-well.'

Among the men, rat-killing is a favourite sport. They will enter an old stable, fasten the door and then turn out the rats. Or they will find out some unfrequented yard, and at night time build up a pit with apple-case boards, and lighting up their lamps, enjoy the sport. Nearly every coster is fond of dogs. Some fancy them greatly, and are proud of making them fight. If when out working, they see a handsome stray, whether he is a 'toy' or 'sporting' dog, they whip him up—many of the class not being *very* particular whether the animals are stray or not.

Their dog fights are both cruel and frequent. It is not uncommon to see a lad walking with the trembling legs of a dog shivering under a bloody handkerchief, that covers the bitten and wounded body of an animal that has been figuring at some 'match.' These fights take place on the sly—the tap-room or back-yard of a beer-shop, being generally chosen for the purpose. A few men are let into the secret, and they attend to bet upon the winner, the police being carefully kept from the spot.

Pigeons are 'fancied' to a large extent, and are kept in lath cages on the roofs of the houses. The lads look upon a visit to the Redhouse, Battersea, where the pigeon-shooting takes place, as a great treat. They stand without the hoarding that encloses the ground, and watch for the wounded pigeons to fall, when a violent scramble takes place among them, each bird being valued at 3*d*. or 4*d*. So popular has this sport become, that some boys take dogs with them trained to retrieve the birds, and two Lambeth costers attend regularly after their morning's work with their guns, to shoot those that escape the 'shots' within.

A good pugilist is looked up to with great admiration by the costers, and fighting is considered to be a necessary part of a boy's education. Among them cowardice in any shape is despised as being degrading and loathsome, indeed the man who would avoid a fight, is scouted by the whole of the court he lives in. Hence it is important for a lad and even a girl to know how to 'work their fists well'—as expert boxing is called among them. If a coster man or woman is struck they are obliged to fight. When a quarrel takes place between two boys, a ring is formed, and the men urge them on to have it out, for they hold that it is a wrong thing to stop a battle, as it causes bad blood for life; whereas, if the lads fight it out they shake hands and forget all about it. Everybody practises fighting, and the man who has the largest and hardest muscle is spoken of in terms of the highest commendation. It is often said in admiration of such a man that 'he could muzzle half a dozen bobbies before breakfast.'

To serve out a policeman is the bravest act by which a coster-monger can distinguish himself. Some lads have been imprisoned upwards of a dozen times for this offence; and are consequently looked upon by their companions as martyrs. When they leave prison for such an act, a subscription is often got up for their bene-fit. In their continual warfare with the force, they resemble many savage nations, from the cunning and treachery they use. The lads endeavour to take the unsuspecting 'crusher' by surprise, and often crouch at the entrance of a court until a policeman passes, when a stone or a brick is hurled at him, and the youngster immediately disappears. Their love of revenge too, is extreme—their hatred being in no way mitigated by time; they will wait for months, following a policeman who has offended or wronged them, anxiously looking out for an opportunity of paying back the injury. One boy, I was told, vowed vengeance against a member of the force, and for six months never allowed the man to escape his notice. At length, one night, he saw the policeman in a row outside a public-house, and running into the crowd kicked him savagely, shouting at the same time: 'Now, you b——, I've got you at last.' When the boy heard that his persecutor was injured for life, his joy was very great, and he declared the twelvemonth's imprisonment he was sentenced to for the offence to be 'dirt cheap.' The whole of the court where the lad resided sympathized with the boy, and vowed to a man, that had he escaped, they would have subscribed a pad or two of dry herrings, to send him into the country until the affair had blown over, for he had shown himself a 'plucky one.'

It is called 'plucky' to bear pain without complaining. To flinch from expected suffering is scorned, and he who does so is sneered at and told to wear a gown, as being more fit to be a woman. To show a disregard for pain, a lad, when without money, will say to his pal, 'Give us a penny, and you may have a punch at my nose.'

They also delight in tattooing their chests and arms with anchors, and figures of different kinds. During the whole of this painful operation, the boy will not flinch, but laugh and joke with his admiring companions, as if perfectly at ease.

GAMBLING OF COSTERMONGERS

It would be difficult to find in the whole of this numerous class, a youngster who is not—what may be safely called—a desperate gambler. At the age of fourteen this love of play first comes upon the lad, and from that time until he is thirty or so, not a Sunday passes but he is at his stand on the gambling ground. Even if he has no money to stake he will loll away the morning looking on, and so borrow excitement from the successes of others. Every attempt made by the police, to check this ruinous system, has been unavailing, and has rather given a gloss of daring courage to the sport, that tends to render it doubly attractive.

If a costermonger has an hour to spare, his first thought is to gamble away the time. He does not care what he plays for, so long as he can have a chance of winning something. Whilst waiting for a market to open, his delight is to find out some pieman and toss him for his stock, though, by doing so, he risks his market-money and only chance of living, to win that which he will give away to the first friend he meets. For the whole week the boy will work untiringly, spurred on by the thought of the money to be won on the Sunday. Nothing will damp his ardour for gambling, the most continued ill-fortune making him even more reckless than if he were the luckiest man alive.

Many a lad who has gone down to the gambling ground, with a good warm coat upon his back and his pocket well filled from the Saturday night's market, will leave it at evening penniless and coatless, having lost all his earnings, stock-money, and the better part of his clothing. Some of the boys, when desperate with 'bad luck,' borrow to the utmost limit of their credit; then they mortgage their 'king'sman' or neck-tie, and they will even change their cord trousers, if better than those of the winner, so as to have one more chance at the turn of fortune. The coldest winter's day will not stop the Sunday's gathering on the riverside, for the heat of play warms them in spite of the sharp wind blowing down the Thames. If the weather be wet, so that the half-pence stick to the ground, they find out some railway-arch or else a beer-shop, and having filled the tap-room with their numbers, they muffle the table with handkerchiefs, and play secretly. When the game is very exciting, they will even forget their hunger, and continue to gamble until it is too dark to see, before they think of eating. One man told me, that when he was working the races with lemonade, he had often, seen in the centre of a group, composed of costers, thimbleriggers and showmen, as much as 100*l.* on the ground at one time, in gold and silver. A friend of his, who had gone down in company with him, with a pony-truck of toys, lost in less than an hour his earnings, truck, stock of goods, and great-coat. Vowing to have his revenge next time, he took his boy on his back, and started off on the tramp to London, there to borrow sufficient money to bring down a fresh lot of goods on the morrow, and then gamble away his earnings as before.

It is perfectly immaterial to the coster with whom he plays, whether it be a lad from the Lambeth potteries, or a thief from the Westminster slums. Very often, too, the gamblers of one coster-monger district, will visit those of another, and work what is called 'a plant' in this way. One of the visitors will go before hand, and joining a group of gamblers, commence tossing. When sufficient time has elapsed to remove all suspicion of companionship, his mate will come up and commence betting on each of his pals' throws with those standing round. By a curious quickness of hand, a coster can make the toss tell favourably for his wagering friend, who meets him after the play is over in the evening, and shares the spoil.

The spots generally chosen for the Sunday's sport are in secret places, half-hidden from the eye of the passers, where a scout can give quick notice of the approach of the police: in the fields about King's-cross, or near any unfinished railway buildings. The Mint, St. George's-fields, Blackfriars'-road, Bethnal-green, and Maryle-bone, are all favourite resorts. Between Lambeth and Chelsea, the shingle on the left side of the Thames, is spotted with small rings of lads, half-hidden behind the barges. One boy (of the party) is always on the look out, and even if a stranger should advance, the cry is given of 'Namous' or 'Kool Eslop.' Instantly the money is whipped-up and pocketed, and the boys stand chattering and laughing together. It is never difficult for a coster to find out where the gambling parties are, for he has only to stop the first lad he meets, and ask him where the 'erth pu' or 'three up' is going on, to discover their whereabouts.

If during the game a cry of 'Police!' should be given by the looker-out, instantly a rush at the money is made by any one in the group, the costers preferring that a stranger should have the money rather than the policeman. There is also a custom among them, that the ruined player should be started again by a gift of 2*d.* in every shilling lost, or, if the loss is heavy, a present of four or five shillings is made; neither is it considered at all dishonourable for the party winning to leave with the full bloom of success upon him.

That the description of one of these Sunday scenes might be more truthful, a visit was paid to a gambling-ring close to——. Although

not twenty yards distant from the steam-boat pier, yet the little
party was so concealed among the coal-barges, that not a head
could be seen. The spot chosen was close to a narrow court, leading
from the street to the water-side, and here the lad on the look-out
was stationed. There were about thirty young fellows, some tall
strapping youths, in the costers' cable-cord costume,—others, mere
boys, in rags, from the potteries, with their clothes stained with
clay. The party was hidden from the river by the black dredger-
boats on the beach; and it was so arranged, that should the alarm
be given, they might leap into the coal-barges, and hide until the
intruder had retired. Seated on some oars stretched across two
craft, was a mortar-stained bricklayer, keeping a look-out towards
the river, and acting as a sort of umpire in all disputes. The two
that were tossing had been playing together since early morning;
and it was easy to tell which was the loser, by the anxious-looking
eye and compressed lip. He was quarrelsome too; and if the crowd
pressed upon him, he would jerk his elbow back savagely, saying,
'I wish to C——t you'd stand backer.' The winner, a short man,
in a mud-stained canvas jacket, and a week's yellow beard on his
chin, never spake a word beyond his 'heads,' or 'tails'; but his
cheeks were red, and the pipe in his mouth was unlit, though he
puffed at it.

In their hands they each held a long row of halfpence, extending
to the wrist, and topped by shillings and half-crowns. Nearly every
one round had coppers in his hands, and bets were made and taken
as rapidly as they could be spoken. 'I lost a sov. last night in less
than no time,' said one man, who, with his hands in his pockets,
was looking on; 'never mind—I mustn't have no wenson this week,
and try again next Sunday.'

The boy who was losing was adopting every means to 'bring
back his luck again.' Before crying, he would toss up a halfpenny
three times, to see what he should call. At last, with an oath, he
pushed aside the boys round him, and shifted his place, to see what
that would do; it had a good effect, for he won toss after toss in a
curiously fortunate way, and then it was strange to watch his
mouth gradually relax and his brows unknit. His opponent was
a little startled, and passing his fingers through his dusty hair, said,
with a stupid laugh, 'Well, I never see the likes.' The betting also
began to shift. 'Sixpence Ned wins!' cried three or four; 'Sixpence

he loses!' answered another; 'Done!' and up went the halfpence. 'Half-a-crown Joe loses!'—'Here you are,' answered Joe, but he lost again. 'I'll try you a "gen"' (shilling) said a coster; 'And a "rouf yenap"' (fourpence), added the other. 'Say a "exes"' (sixpence).—'Done!' and the betting continued, till the ground was spotted with silver and halfpence.

'That's ten bob he's won in five minutes,' said Joe (the loser), looking round with a forced smile; but Ned (the winner) never spake a word, even when he gave any change to his antagonist; and if he took a bet, he only nodded to the one that offered it, and threw down his money. Once, when he picked up more than a sovereign from the ground, that he had won in one throw, a washed sweep, with a black rim round his neck, said, 'There's a hog!' but there wasn't even a smile at the joke. At last Joe began to feel angry, and stamping his foot till the water squirted up from the beach, cried, 'It's no use; luck's set in him—he'd muck a thousand!' and so he shifted his ground, and betted all round on the chance of better fortune attending the movement. He lost again, and some one bantering said, 'You'll win the shine-rag, Joe,' meaning that he would be 'cracked up' or ruined, if he continued.

When one o'clock struck, a lad left, saying, he was 'going to get an inside lining' (dinner). The sweep asked him what he was going to have. 'A two-and-half plate, and a ha'p'orth of smash' (a plate of soup and a ha'p'orth of mashed potatoes), replied the lad, bounding into the court. Nobody else seemed to care for his dinner, for all stayed to watch the gamblers.

Every now and then some one would go up the court to see if the lad watching for the police was keeping a good look-out; but the boy never deserted his post, for fear of losing his threepence. If he had, such is the wish to protect the players felt by every lad, that even whilst at dinner, one of them, if he saw a policeman pass, would spring up and rush to the gambling ring to give notice.

When the tall youth, 'Ned,' had won nearly all the silver of the group, he suddenly jerked his gains into his coat-pocket, and saying, 'I've done,' walked off, and was out of sight in an instant. The surprise of the loser and all around was extreme. They looked at the court where he had disappeared, then at one another and at last burst out into one expression of disgust. 'There's a scurf!' said one; 'He's a regular scab,' cried another; and a coster declared that he was 'a trosseno, and no mistake.' For although it is held to be fair for the winner to go whenever he wishes, yet such conduct is never relished by the losers.

It was then determined that 'they would have him to rights' the next time he came to gamble; for every one would set at him, and win his money, and then 'turn up,' as he had done.

The party was then broken up, the players separating to wait for the new-comers that would be sure to pour in after dinner.

'VIC GALLERY'

On a good attractive night, the rush of costers to the threepenny gallery of the Coburg (better known as 'the Vic') is peculiar and almost awful.

The long zig-zag staircase that leads to the pay box is crowded to suffocation at least an hour before the theatre is opened; but, on the occasion of a piece with a good murder in it, the crowd will frequently collect as early as three o'clock in the afternoon. Lads stand upon the broad wooden bannisters about 50 feet from the ground, and jump on each others' backs, or adopt any expedient they can think of to obtain a good place.

The walls of the well-staircase having a remarkably fine echo, and the wooden floor of the steps serving as a sounding board, the shouting, whistling, and quarrelling of the impatient young costers is increased tenfold. If, as sometimes happens, a song with a chorus is started, the ears positively ache with the din, and when the chant has finished it seems as though a sudden silence had fallen on the people. To the centre of the road, and all round the door, the mob is in a ferment of excitement, and no sooner is the money-taker at his post than the most frightful rush takes place, every one heaving with his shoulder at the back of the person immediately in front of him. The girls shriek, men shout, and a nervous fear is felt lest the massive staircase should fall in with the weight of the throng, as it lately did with the most terrible results. If a hat tumbles from the top of the staircase, a hundred hands snatch at it as it descends. When it is caught a voice roars above the tumult, 'All right, Bill, I've got it'—for they all seem to know one another—'Keep us a pitch and I'll bring it.'

To any one unaccustomed to be pressed flat it would be impossible to enter with the mob. To see the sight in the gallery it is better to wait until the first piece is over. The hamsandwich men and pigtrotter women will give you notice when the time is come, for with the first clatter of the descending footsteps they commence their cries.

There are few grown-up men that go to the 'Vic' gallery. The generality of the visitors are lads from about twelve to three-and-twenty, and though a few black-faced sweeps or whitey-brown dustmen may be among the throng, the gallery audience consists mainly of costermongers. Young girls, too, are very plentiful, only one-third of whom now take their babies, owing to the new regulation of charging half-price for infants. At the foot of the staircase stands a group of boys begging for the return checks, which they sell again for 1½d. or 1d., according to the lateness of the hour.

At each step up the well-staircase the warmth and stench increase, until by the time one reaches the gallery doorway, a furnace-heat rushes out through the entrance that seems to force you backwards, whilst the odour positively prevents respiration. The mob on the landing, standing on tip-toe and closely wedged together, resists any civil attempt at gaining a glimpse of the stage, and yet a coster lad will rush up, elbow his way into the crowd, then jump up on to the shoulders of those before him, and suddenly disappear into the body of the gallery.

The gallery at 'the Vic' is one of the largest in London. It will hold from 1,500 to 2,000 people, and runs back to so great a distance, that the end of it is lost in shadow, excepting where the little gas-jets, against the wall, light up the two or three faces around them. When the gallery is well packed, it is usual to see piles of boys on each others shoulders at the back, while on the partition boards, dividing off the slips, lads will pitch themselves, despite the spikes.

As you look up the vast slanting mass of heads from the upper boxes, each one appears on the move. The huge black heap, dotted with faces, and spotted with white shirt sleeves, almost pains the eye to look at, and should a clapping of hands commence, the twinkling nearly blinds you. It is the fashion with the mob to take off their coats; and the cross-braces on the backs of some, and the bare shoulders peeping out of the ragged shirts of others, are the only variety to be found. The bonnets of the 'ladies' are hung over the iron railing in front, their numbers nearly hiding the panels, and one of the amusements of the lads in the back seats consists in pitching orange peel or nutshells into them, a good aim being rewarded with a shout of laughter.

When the orchestra begins playing, before 'the gods' have settled into their seats, it is impossible to hear a note of music. The puffed-out cheeks of the trumpeters, and the raised drumsticks tell you that the overture has commenced, but no tune is to be heard, an occasional burst of the full band being caught by gushes, as if a high wind were raging. Recognitions take place every moment, and 'Bill Smith' is called to in a loud voice from one side, and a shout in answer from the other asks 'What's up?' Or family secrets are revealed, and 'Bob Triller' is asked where 'Sal' is, and replies amid a roar of laughter, that she is 'a-larning the pynanney.'

By-and-by a youngster, who has come in late, jumps over the shoulders at the door, and doubling himself into a ball, rolls down over the heads in front, leaving a trail of commotion for each one as he passes aims a blow at the fellow. Presently a fight is sure to begin, and then every one rises from his seat whistling and shouting; three or four pairs of arms fall to, the audience waving their hands till the moving mass seems like microscopic eels in paste. But the commotion ceases suddenly on the rising of the curtain, and then the cries of 'Silence!' 'Ord-a-a-r!' 'Ord-a-a-r!' make more noise than ever.

The 'Vic' gallery is not to be m oved b touching sentiment. They prefer vigorous exercise to any emotional speech. 'The Child of the Storm's' declaration that she would share her father's 'death or imprisonment as her duty,' had no effect at all, compared with the split in the hornpipe. The shrill whistling and brayvos that followed the tar's performance showed how highly it was relished, and one 'god' went so far as to ask 'how it was done.' The comic actor kicking a dozen Polish peasants was encored, but the grand banquet of the Czar of all the Russians only produced merriment, and a request that he would 'give them a bit' was made directly the Emperor took the willow-patterned plate in his hand. All affecting situations were sure to be interrupted by cries of 'orda-a-r'; and the lady begging for her father's life was told to 'speak up old gal'; though when the heroine of the 'dummestic dreamer' (as they call it) told the general of all the Cossack forces 'not to be

a fool,' the uproar of approbation grew greater than ever,—and
when the lady turned up her swan's-down cuffs, and seizing four
Russian soldiers shook them successively by the collar, then the
enthusiasm knew no bounds, and the cries of 'Bray-vo Vincent!
Go it my tulip,' resounded from every throat.

Altogether the gallery audience do not seem to be of a gentle
nature. One poor little lad shouted out in a crying tone, 'that he
couldn't see,' and instantly a dozen voices demanded 'that he
should be thrown over.'

Whilst the pieces are going on, brown, flat bottles are frequently
raised to the mouth, and between the acts a man with a tin can,
glittering in the gas-light, goes round crying, 'Port-a-a-a-r! who's
for port-a-a-a-r.' As the heat increased the faces grew bright red,
every bonnet was taken off, and ladies could be seen wiping the
perspiration from their cheeks with the play-bills.

No delay between the pieces will be allowed, and should the
interval appear too long, some one will shout out—referring to the
curtain—'Pull up that there winder blind!' or they will call to the
orchestra, saying, 'Now then you catgut-scrapers! Let's have a
ha'purth of liveliness.' Neither will they suffer a play to proceed
until they have a good view of the stage, and 'Higher the blue,'
is constantly shouted, when the sky is too low, or 'Light up the
moon,' when the transparency is rather dim.

The dances and comic songs, between the pieces, are liked
better than anything else. A highland fling is certain to be repeated,
and a stamping of feet will accompany the tune, and a shrill
whistling, keep time through the entire performance.

But the grand hit of the evening is always when a song is sung
to which the entire gallery can join in the chorus. Then a deep
silence prevails all through the stanzas. Should any burst in before
his time, a shout of 'orda-a-r' is raised, and the intruder put down
by a thousand indignant cries. At the proper time, however, the
throats of the mob burst forth in all their strength. The most
deafening noise breaks out suddenly, while the cat-calls keep up
the tune, and an imitation of a dozen Mr. Punches squeak out the
words. Some actors at the minor theatres make a great point of
this, and in the bill upon the night of my visit, under the tite of
'There's a good time coming, boys,' there was printed, 'assisted by
the most numerous and effective chorus in the metropolis'—mean-

ing the whole of the gallery. The singer himself started the mob, saying, 'Now then, the Exeter Hall touch if you please gentlemen,' and beat time with his hand, parodying M. Jullien with his *baton*. An 'angcore' on such occasions is always demanded, and, despite a few murmurs of 'change it to "Duck-legged Dick,"' invariably insisted on.

THE POLITICS OF COSTERMONGERS— POLICEMEN

THE notion of the police is so intimately blended with what may be called the politics of the costermongers that I give them together.

The politics of these people are detailed in a few words—they are nearly all Chartists. 'You might say, sir,' remarked one of my informants, 'that they *all* were Chartists, but as it's better you should rather be under than over the mark, say *nearly* all.' Their ignorance, and their being impulsive, makes them a dangerous class. I am assured that in every district where the costermongers are congregated, one or two of the body, more intelligent than the others, have great influence over them; and these leading men are all Chartists, and being industrious and not unprosperous persons, their pecuniary and intellectual superiority cause them to be regarded as oracles. One of these men said to me: 'The costers think that working-men know best, and so they have confidence in us. I like to make men discontented, and I will make them discontented while the present system continues, because it's all for the middle and the moneyed classes, and nothing, in the way of rights, for the poor. People fancy when all's quiet that all's stagnating. Propagandism is going on for all that. It's when all's quiet that the seed's a growing. Republicans and Socialists are pressing their doctrines.'

The costermongers have very vague notions of an aristocracy; they call the more prosperous of their own body 'aristocrats.' Their notions of an aristocracy of birth or wealth seem to be formed on their opinion of the rich, or reputed rich salesmen with whom they deal; and the result is anything but favourable to the nobility.

Concerning free-trade, nothing, I am told, can check the costermonger's fervour for a cheap loaf. A Chartist costermonger told me that he knew numbers of costers who were keen Chartists without understanding anything about the six points.

The costermongers frequently attend political meetings, going there in bodies of from six to twelve. Some of them, I learned, could not understand why Chartist leaders exhorted them to peace and quietness, when they might as well fight it out with the police at once. The costers boast, moreover, that they stick more together in any 'row' than any other class. It is considered by them a reflection on the character of the thieves that they are seldom true to one another.

It is a matter of marvel to many of this class that people can live without working. The ignorant costers have no knowledge of 'property,' or 'income,' and conclude that the non-workers all live out of the taxes. Of the taxes generally they judge from their knowledge that tobacco, which they account a necessary of life, pays 3s. per lb. duty.

As regards the police, the hatred of a costermonger to a 'peeler' is intense, and with their opinion of police, all the more ignorant unite that of the governing power. 'Can you wonder at it, sir,' said a costermonger to me, 'that I hate the police? They drive us about, we must move on, we can't stand here, and we can't pitch there. But if we're cracked up, that is if we're forced to go into the Union (I've known it both at Clerkenwell and the City of London workhouses), why the parish gives us money to buy a barrow, or a shallow, or to hire them, and leave the house and start for ourselves; and what's the use of that, if the police won't let us sell our goods?—Which is right, the parish or the police?'

To thwart the police in any measure the costermongers readily aid one another. One very common procedure, if the policeman has seized a barrow, is to whip off a wheel, while the officers have gone for assistance; for a large and loaded barrow requires two men to convey it to the green-yard. This is done with great dexterity; and the next step is to dispose of the stock to any passing costers, or to any 'standing' in the neighbourhood, and it is honestly accounted for. The policemen, on their return, find an empty, and unwheelable barrow, which they must carry off by main strength, amid the jeers of the populace.

I am assured that in case of a political riot every 'coster' would seize his policeman.

MARRIAGE AND CONCUBINAGE
OF COSTERMONGERS

ONLY one-tenth—at the outside one-tenth—of the couples living together and carrying on the costermongering trade, are married. In Clerkenwell parish, however, where the number of married couples is about a fifth of the whole, this difference is easily accounted for, as in Advent and Easter the incumbent of that parish marries poor couples without a fee. Of the rights of 'legitimate' or 'illegitimate' children the costermongers understand nothing, and account it a mere waste of money and time to go through the ceremony of wedlock when a pair can live together, and be quite as well regarded by their fellows, without it. The married women associate with the unmarried mothers of· families without the slightest scruple. There is no honour attached to the marriage state, and no shame to concubinage. Neither are the unmarried women less faithful to their 'partners' than the married; but I understand that, of the two classes, the unmarried betray the most jealousy.

As regards the fidelity of those women I was assured that, 'in anything like good times,' they were rigidly faithful to their husbands or paramours; but that, in the worst pinch of poverty, a departure from this fidelity—if it provided a few meals or a fire— was not considered at all heinous. An old costermonger, who had been mixed up with other callings, and whose prejudices were certainly not in favour of his present trade, said to me, 'What I call the working girls, are as industrious and as faithful a set as can well be. I'm satisfied that they're more faithful to their mates than other poor working women. I never knew one of these working girls do wrong that way. They're strong, hearty, healthy girls, and keep clean rooms. Why, there's numbers of men leave their stockmoney with their women, just taking out two or three shillings to gamble with and get drunk upon. They sometimes take a little drop themselves, the women do, and get beaten by their husbands for it, and hardest beaten if the man's drunk himself. They're sometimes beaten for other things too, or for nothing at all. But they seem to like the men better for their beating them. I never could make that out.' Notwithstanding this fidelity, it appears that the 'larking and joking' of the young, and sometimes of the middle-aged people, among themselves is anything but delicate. The unmarried separate as seldom as the married. The fidelity characterizing the women does not belong to the men. The dancing-rooms are the places where matches are made up. There the boys go to look out for 'mates' and sometimes a match is struck up the first night of meeting, and the couple live together forthwith. The girls at these dances are all the daughters of coster-mongers, or of persons pursuing some other course of street life. Unions take place when the lad is but 14. Two or three out of 100 have their female helpmates at that early age; but the female is generally a couple of years older than her partner. Nearly all the costermongers form such alliances as I have described, when both parties are under twenty. One reason why these alliances are con-tracted at early ages is, that when a boy has assisted his father, or any one engaging him, in the business of a costermonger, he knows that he can borrow money, and hire a shallow or a barrow—or he may have saved 5s—'and then if the father vexes him or snubs him,' said one of my informants, 'he'll tell his father to go to h—l, and he and his gal will start on their own account.'

Most of the costermongers have numerous families, but not those who contract alliances very young. The women continue working down to the day of their confinement.

'Chance children,' as they are called, or children unrecognized by any father, are rare among the young women of the coster-mongers.

RELIGION OF COSTERMONGERS

AN intelligent and trustworthy man, until very recently actively engaged in costermongering, computed that not 3 in 100 coster-mongers had ever been in the interior of a church, or any place of worship, or knew what was meant by Christianity. The same person gave me the following account, which was confirmed by others:

'The costers have no religion at all, and very little notion, or none at all, of what religion or a future state is. Of all things they hate tracts. They hate them because the people leaving them never give them anything, and as they can't read the tract—not one in forty—they're vexed to be bothered with it. And really what is the use of giving people reading before you've taught them to read? Now, they respect the City Missionaries, because they read to them —and the costers will listen to reading when they don't understand it—and because they visit the sick, and sometimes give oranges and such like to them and the children. I've known a City Missionary buy a shilling's worth of oranges of a coster, and give them away to the sick and the children—most of them belonging to the costermongers—down the court, and that made him respected there. I think the City Missionaries have done good. But I'm satisfied that if the costers had to profess themselves of some religion to-morrow, they would all become Roman Catholics, every one of them. This is the reason:—London costers live very often in the same courts and streets as the poor Irish, and if the Irish are sick, be sure there comes to them the priest, the Sisters of Charity—they *are* good women—and some other ladies. Many a man that's not a Catholic, has rotted and died without any good person near him. Why, I lived a good while in Lambeth, and there wasn't one coster in 100, I'm satisfied, knew so much as the rector's name,—though Mr. Dalton's a very good man. But the reason I was telling you of, sir, is that the costers reckon *that* religion's the best that gives the most in charity, and they think the Catholics do this.'

OF THE UNEDUCATED STATE
OF COSTERMONGERS

I HAVE stated elsewhere, that only about one in ten of the regular costermongers is able to read. The want of education among both men and women is deplorable, and I tested it in several instances. The following statement, however, from one of the body, is no more to be taken as representing the ignorance of the class generally, than are the clear and discriminating accounts I received from intelligent costermongers to be taken as representing the intelligence of the body.

The man with whom I conversed, and from whom I received the following statement, seemed about thirty. He was certainly not ill-looking, but with a heavy cast of countenance, his light blue eyes having little expression. His statements, or opinions, I need hardly explain, were given both spontaneously in the course of conversation, and in answer to my questions. I give them almost verbatim, omitting oaths and slang:

'Well, times is bad, sir,' he said, 'but it's a deadish time. I don't do so well at present as in middlish times, I think. When I served the Prince of Naples, not far from here (I presume that he alluded to the Prince of Capua), I did better and times was better. That was five years ago, but I can't say to a year or two. He was a good customer, and was wery fond of peaches. I used to sell them to him, at 12*s.* the plasket when they was new. The plasket held a dozen, and cost me 6*s.* at Covent-garden—more sometimes; but I didn't charge him more when they did. His footman was a black man, and a ignorant man quite, and his housekeeper was a English-woman. He was the Prince o' Naples, was my customer; but I don't know what he was like, for I never saw him. I've heard that he was the brother of the king of Naples. I can't say where Naples is, but if you was to ask at Euston-square, they'll tell you the fare there and the time to go it in. It may be in France for anything I know may Naples, or in Ireland. Why don't you ask at the square? I went to Croydon once by rail, and slept all the way without stirring, and so you may to Naples for anything I know. I never heard of the Pope being a neighbour of the King of Naples. Do you mean living next door to him? But I don't know nothing of the King of Naples, only the prince. I don't know what the Pope is. Is he any trade? It's nothing to me, when he's no customer of mine. I have nothing to say about nobody that ain't no customers. My crabs is caught in the sea, in course. I gets them at Billingsgate. I never saw the sea, but it's salt-water, I know. I can't say where-abouts it lays. I believe it's in the hands of the Billingsgate sales-men—all of it. I've heard of shipwrecks at sea, caused by drownd-ing, in course. I never heard that the Prince of Naples was ever at sea. I like to talk about him, he was such a customer when he lived near here.' (Here he repeated his account of the supply of peaches to his Royal Highness). 'I never was in France, no, sir, never. I don't know the way. Do you think I could do better there? I never was in the Republic there. What's it like? Bonaparte? O, yes; I've heard of him. He was at Waterloo. I didn't know he'd been alive now and in France, as you ask me about him. I don't think you're larking, sir. Did I hear of the French taking possession of Naples, and Bonaparte making his brother-in-law king? Well, I didn't, but it may be true, because I served the Prince of Naples, what *was* the brother of the king. I never heard whether the Prince was the king's older brother or his younger. I wish he may turn out his older if there's any property coming to him, as the oldest has the first turn; at least so I've heard—first come, first served. I've worked the streets and the courts at all times. I've worked them by moonlight, but you couldn't see the moonlight where it was busy. I can't say how far the moon's off us. It's nothing to me, but I've seen it a good bit higher than St. Paul's. I don't know nothing about the sun. Why do you ask? It must be nearer than the moon for it's warmer, —and if they're both fire, that shows it. It's like the tap-room grate and that bit of a gas-light; to compare the two is. What was St. Paul's that the moon was above? A church, sir; so I've heard. I never was in a church. O, yes, I've heard of God; he made heaven and earth; I never heard of his making the sea; that's another thing, and you can best learn about that at Billingsgate. (He seemed to think that the sea was an appurtenance of Billingsgate). Jesus Christ? Yes. I've heard of him. Our Redeemer? Well, I only wish I could redeem my Sunday togs from my uncle's.'

LANGUAGE OF COSTERMONGERS

THE slang language of the costermongers is not very remarkable for originality of construction; it possesses no humour: but they boast that it is known only to themselves; it is far beyond the Irish, they say, and puzzles the Jews. The *root* of the costermonger tongue, so to speak, is to give the words spelt backward, or rather pronounced rudely backward. With this backward pronunciation, which is very arbitrary, are mixed words reducible to no rule and seldom referable to any origin; while any syllable is added to a proper slang word, at the discretion of the speaker.

Slang is acquired very rapidly, and some costermongers will converse in it by the hour. The women use it sparingly; the girls more than the women; the men more than the girls; and the boys most of all. The most ignorant of all these classes deal most in slang and boast of their cleverness and proficiency in it. In their conversations among themselves, the following are invariably the terms used in money matters:

Flatch	Halfpenny.
Yenep	Penny.
Owl-yenep	Twopence.
Erth-yenep	Threepence.
Rouf-yenep	Fourpence.
Ewif-yenep	Fivepence.
Exis-yenep	Sixpence.
Neves-yenep	Sevenpence.
Teaich-yenep	Eightpence.
Enine-yenep	Ninepence.
Net-yenep	Tenpence.
Leven	Elevenpence.
Gen	Twelvepence.
Yenep-flatch	Three-half-pence.

and so on through the penny-halfpennies.

It was explained to me by a costermonger, who had introduced some new words into the slang, that 'leven' was allowed so closely to resemble the proper word, because elevenpence was almost an unknown sum to costermongers, the transition—weights and measures notwithstanding—being immediate from 10*d*. to 1*s*.

'Gen' is a shilling and the numismatic sequence is pursued with the gens, as regards shillings, as with the 'yeneps' as regards pence. The blending of the two is also according to the same system as 'Owt-gen, teaich-yenep' two-and-eightpence. The exception to the uniformity of the 'gen' enumeration is in the sum of 8*s*., which instead of 'teaich-gen' is 'teaich-guy'; a deviation with ample precedents in all civilised tongues.

As regards the larger coins the translation into slang is not reducible into rule. The following are the costermonger coins of the higher value:

Couter	Sovereign.
Half-Couter, or *Net-gen*	Half-sovereign.
Ewif-gen	Crown.
Flatch-ynork	Half-crown.

The costermongers still further complicate their slang by a mode of multiplication. They thus say, 'Erth Ewif-gens' or 3 times 5*s*., which means of course 15*s*.

Speaking of this language, a costermonger said to me: 'The Irish can't tumble to it anyhow; the Jews can tumble better, but we're *their* masters. Some of the young salesmen at Billingsgate understand us,—but only at Billingsgate; and they think they're uncommon clever, but they're not quite up to the mark. The police don't understand us at all. It would be a pity if they did.' I give a few more phrases:

A doogheno or dabheno?	Is it a good or bad market?
A regular trosseno	A regular bad one
On	No.
Say	Yes.
Tumble to your barrikin	Understand you.
Top o' reeb	Pot of beer.
Doing dab	Doing badly.
Cool him	Look at him.

The latter phrase is used when one costermonger warns another of the approach of a policeman 'who might order him to move on, or be otherwise unpleasant.' 'Cool' (look) is exclaimed, or 'Cool him' (look at him). One costermonger told me as a great joke that a very stout policeman, who was then new to the duty, was when in a violent state of perspiration, much offended by a costermonger saying 'Cool him.'

Cool the esclop	Look at the police.
Cool the namesclop	Look at the policeman.
Cool ta the dillo nemo	Look at the old woman;

said of any woman, young or old, who, according to costermonger notions, is 'giving herself airs.'

This language seems confined, in its general use, to the immediate objects of the costermonger's care; but is, among the more acute members of the fraternity, greatly extended, and is capable of indefinite extension.

The costermonger's oaths, I may conclude, are all in the vernacular; nor are any of the common salutes, such as 'How d'you do?' or 'Good-night' known to their slang.

Kennetseeno	Stinking;
(applied principally to the quality of fish).	
Flatch kanurd	Half-drunk.

Flash it	. . . .	Show it;	
(in cases of bargains offered).			
On doog	. . . .	No good.	
Cross chap	. . . .	A thief.	
Showfulls	. . . .	Bad money;	
(seldom in the hands of costermongers).			
I'm on to the deb	. . .	I'm going to bed.	
Do the tightner	. . .	Go to dinner.	
Nommus	. . . .	Be off.	
Tol	. . . . .	Lot, Stock, or Share.	

Many costermongers, 'but principally—perhaps entirely,'— I was told, 'those who had not been regular born and bred to the trade, but had taken to it when cracked up in their own,' do not trouble themselves to acquire any knowledge of slang. It is not indispensable for the carrying on of their business; the grand object, however, seems to be, to shield their bargainings at market, or their conversation among themselves touching their day's work and profits, from the knowledge of any Irish or uninitiated fellow-traders.

ON THE NICKNAMES OF COSTERMONGERS

LIKE many rude, and almost all wandering communities, the costermongers, like the cabmen and pickpockets are hardly ever known by their real names; even the honest men among them are distinguished by some strange appellation. Indeed, they are all known one to another by nicknames, which they acquire either by some mode of dress, some remark that has ensured costermonger applause, some peculiarity in trading, or some defect or singularity in personal appearance. Men are known as 'Rotten Herrings,' 'Spuddy' (a seller of bad potatoes, until beaten by the Irish for his bad wares), 'Curly' (a man with a curly head), 'Foreigner' (a man who had been in the Spanish-Legion), 'Brassy' (a very saucy person), 'Gaffy' (once a performer), 'The One-eyed Buffer,' 'Jaw-breaker,' 'Pine-apple Jack,' 'Cast-iron Poll' (her head having been struck with a pot without injury to her), 'Whilky,' 'Blackwall Poll' (a woman generally having two black eyes), 'Lushy Bet,' 'Dirty Sall' (the costermongers generally objecting to dirty women), and 'Dancing Sue.'

OF THE EDUCATION OF COSTERMONGERS'
CHILDREN

I HAVE used the heading of 'Education' but perhaps to say 'non-education,' would be more suitable. Very few indeed of the coster-mongers' children are sent even to the Ragged Schools; and if they are, from all I could learn, it is done more that the mother may be saved the trouble of tending them at home, than from any desire that the children shall acquire useful knowledge. Both boys and girls are sent out by their parents in the evening to sell nuts, or-anges, &c., at the doors of the theatres, or in any public place, or 'round the houses' (a stated circuit from their place of abode). This trade they pursue eagerly for the sake of 'bunts,' though some carry home the money they take, very honestly. The costermongers are kind to their children, 'perhaps in a rough way, and the women make regular pets of them very often.' One experienced man told me, that he had seen a poor costermonger's wife—one of the few who could read—instructing her children in reading; but such instances were very rare.

THE LITERATURE OF THE COSTERMONGERS

IT may appear anomalous to speak of the literature of an unedu-cated body, but even the costermongers have their tastes for books. They are very fond of hearing any one read aloud to them, and listen very attentively. One man often reads the Sunday paper of the beer-shop to them, and on a fine summer's evening a coster-monger, or any neighbour who has the advantage of being 'a schol-lard,' reads aloud to them in the courts they inhabit. What they love best to listen to—and, indeed, what they are most eager for—are Reynolds's periodicals, especially the 'Mysteries of the Court.' 'They're got tired of Lloyd's blood-stained stories,' said one man, who was in the habit of reading to them, 'and I'm satisfied that, of all London, Reynolds is the most popular man among them. They stuck to him in Trafalgar-square, and would again. They all say he's "a trump," and Feargus O'Connor's another trump with them.'

One intelligent man considered that the spirit of curiosity mani-fested by the costermongers, as regards the information or excitement derived from hearing stories read, augured well for the improvability of the class.

Another intelligent costermonger, who had recently read some of the cheap periodicals to ten or twelve men, women, and boys, all costermongers, gave me an account of the comments made by his auditors. They had assembled, after their day's work or their rounds, for the purpose of hearing my informant read the last number of some of the penny publications.

'The costermongers,' said my informant, 'are very fond of illustrations. I have known a man, what couldn't read, buy a periodical what had an illustration, a little out of the common way perhaps, just that he might learn from some one, who *could* read, what it was all about. They have all heard of Cruikshank, and they think everything funny is by him—funny scenes in a play and all. His "Bottle" was very much admired. I heard one man say it was very prime, and showed what "lush" did, but I saw the same man,' added my informant, 'drunk three hours afterwards. Look you here, sir,' he continued, turning over a periodical, for he had the number with him, 'here's a portrait of "Catherine of Russia." "Tell us all about her, ' said one man to me last night; "read it; what was she? ' When I had read it,' my informant continued, 'another man, to whom I showed it, said, "Don't the cove as did that know a deal?" for they fancy—at least, a many do—that one man writes a whole periodical, or a whole newspaper. Now here,' proceeded my friend, 'you sees an engraving of a man hung up, burning over a fire, and some costers would go mad if they couldn't learn what he'd been doing, who he was, and all about him. "But about the picture?" they would say, and this is a very common question put by them whenever they see an engraving.

'Here's one of the passages that took their fancy wonderfully,' my informant observed:

"With glowing cheeks, flashing eyes, and palpitating bosom, Venetia Trelawney rushed back into the refreshment-room, where she threw herself into one of the arm-chairs already noticed. But scarcely had she thus sunk down upon the flocculent cushion, when a sharp click, as of some mechanism giving way, met her ears; and at the same instant her wrists were caught in manacles which sprang out of the arms of the treacherous chair, while two steel bands started from the richly-carved back and grasped her shoulders. A shriek burst from her lips—she struggled violently, but all to no purpose; for she was a captive—and powerless! We should observe that the manacles and the steel bands which had thus fastened upon her, were covered with velvet, so that they inflicted no positive injury upon her, nor even produced the slightest abrasion of her fair and polished skin.

'Here all my audience,' said the man to me, 'broke out with— "Aye! that's the way the harristocrats hooks it. There's nothing o' that sort among us; the rich has all that barrikin to themselves." "Yes, that's the b—— way the taxes goes in," shouted a woman.

'Anything about the police sets them a talking at once. This did when I read it:

"The Ebenezers still continued their fierce struggle, and, from the noise they made, seemed as if they were tearing each other to pieces, to the wild roar of a chorus of profane swearing. The alarm, as Bloomfield had predicted, was soon raised, and some two or three policemen, with their bull's-eyes, and still more effective truncheons, speedily restored order.

"The blessed crushers is everywhere," shouted one. "I wish I'd been there to have had a shy at the eslops," said another. And then a man sung out: "O, don't I like the Bobbys?

'If there's any foreign language which can't be explained, I've seen the costers,' my informant went on, 'annoyed at it—quite annoyed. Another time I read part of one of Lloyd's numbers to them—but they like something spicier. One article in them—here it is—finishes in this way:

"The social habits and costumes of the Magyar *noblesse* have almost all the characteristics of the corresponding class in Ireland. This word *noblesse* is one of wide significance in Hungary; and one may with great truth say of this strange nation, that '*qui n'est point noble n'est rien.*"

"I can't tumble to that barrikin," said a young fellow; "it's a jaw-breaker. But if this here—what d'ye call it, you talk about—was like the Irish, why they was a rum lot." "Noblesse," said a man that's considered a clever fellow, from having once learned his letters, though he can't read or write. "Noblesse! Blessed if I know what he's up to." Here there was a regular laugh.'

OF THE HONESTY OF COSTERMONGERS

I HEARD on all hands that the costers never steal from one another, and never wink at any one stealing from a neighbouring stall. Any stall-keeper will leave his stall untended to get his dinner, his neighbour acting for him; sometimes he will leave it to enjoy a game of skittles. It was computed for me, that property worth 10,000*l.* belonging to costers is daily left exposed in the streets or at the markets, almost entirely unwatched, the policeman or market-keeper only passing at intervals. And yet thefts are rarely heard of, and when heard of are not attributable to costermongers, but to regular thieves. The way in which the sum of 10,000*l.* was arrived at, is this: 'In Hooper-street, Lambeth,' said my informant, 'there are thirty barrows and carts exposed on an evening, left in the street, with nobody to see them; left there all night. That is only one street. Each barrow and board would be worth, on the average, 2*l.* 5*s.*, and that would be 75*l.* In the other bye-streets and courts off the New-cut are six times as many, Hooper-street having the most. This would give 525*l.* in all, left unwatched of a night. There are, throughout London, twelve more districts besides the New-cut—at least twelve districts—and, calculating the same amount in these, we have, altogether, 6,300*l.* worth of barrows. Taking in other bye-streets, we may safely reckon it at 4,000 barrows; for the numbers I have given in the thirteen places are 2,520, and 1,480 added is moderate. At least half those which are in use next day, are left unwatched; more, I have no doubt, but say half. The stock of these 2,000 will average 10*s.* each, or 1,000*l.*; and the barrows will be worth 4,500*l.*; in all 5,500*l.*, and the property exposed on the stalls and the markets will be double in amount, or 11,000*l.* in value, every day, but say 10,000*l.*

'Besides, sir,' I was told, 'the thieves won't rob the costers so often as they will the shopkeepers. It's easier to steal from a butcher's or bacon-seller's open window than from a costermonger's stall or barrow, because the shopkeeper's eye can't be always on his goods. But there's always some one to give an eye to a coster's property. At Billingsgate the thieves will rob the salesmen far readier than they will us. They know we'd take it out of them readier if they were caught. It's Lynch law with us. We never give them in charge.'

The costermongers' boys will, I am informed, cheat their employers, but they do not steal from them. The costers' donkey stables have seldom either lock or latch, and sometimes oysters, and other things which the donkey will not molest, are left there, but are never stolen.

THE BAKED POTATO MAN

THE LONDON COFFEE STALL

OF THE CONVEYANCES OF THE COSTER-MONGERS AND OTHER STREET-SELLERS

WE now come to consider the matters relating more particularly to the commercial life of the costermonger.

All who pass along the thoroughfares of the Metropolis, bestowing more than a cursory glance upon the many phases of its busy street life, must be struck with astonishment to observe the various modes of conveyance, used by those who resort to the public thoroughfares for a livelihood. From the more provident costermonger's pony and donkey cart, to the old rusty iron tray slung round the neck by the vendor of blacking, and down to the little grey-eyed Irish boy with his lucifer-matches, in the last remains of a willow handbasket—the shape and variety of the means resorted to by the costermongers and other street-sellers, for carrying about their goods, are almost as manifold as the articles they vend.

The pony—or donkey—carts (and the latter is by far the more usual beast of draught), of the prosperous costermongers are of three kinds:—the first is of an oblong shape, with a rail behind, upon which is placed a tray filled with bunches of greens, turnips, celery, &c., whilst other commodities are laid in the bed of the cart. Another kind is the common square cart without springs, which is so constructed that the sides, as well as the front and back, will let down and form shelves whereon the stock may be arranged to advantage. The third sort of pony-cart is one of home manufacture, consisting of the framework of a body without sides, or front, or hind part. Sometimes a coster's barrow is formed into a donkey cart merely by fastening, with cord, two rough poles to the handles. All these several kinds of carts are used for the conveyance of either fruit, vegetables, or fish; but besides those, there is the salt and mustard vendor's cart, with and without the tilt or covering, and a square piece of tin (stuck into a block of salt), on which is painted 'salt 3 lbs. a penny,' and 'mustard a penny an ounce.' Then there is the poultry cart, with the wild ducks, and rabbits dangling at its sides, and with two uprights and a cross-stick, upon which are suspended birds, &c., slung across in couples.

The above conveyances are all of small dimensions, the barrows being generally about five feet long and three wide, while the carts are mostly about four feet square.

Every kind of harness is used; some is well blacked and greased and glittering with brass, others are almost as grey with dust as the donkey itself. Some of the jackasses are gaudily caparisoned in an old carriage harness, which fits it like a man's coat on a boy's back, while the plated silver ornaments are pink, with the copper showing through; others have rope traces and belly-bands, and not a few indulge in old cotton handkerchiefs for pads.

The next conveyance (which, indeed, is the most general) is the costermonger's hand-barrow. These are very light in their make, with springs terminating at the axle. Some have rails behind for the arrangement of their goods; others have not. Some have side rails, whilst others have only the frame-work. The shape of these barrows is oblong, and sloped from the hind-part towards the front; the bottom of the bed is not boarded, but consists of narrow strips of wood nailed athwart and across. When the coster is hawking his fish, or vending his green stuff, he provides himself with a wooden tray, which is placed upon his barrow. Those who cannot afford a tray get some pieces of board and fasten them together, these answering their purpose as well. Pine-apple and pine-apple rock barrows are not unfrequently seen with small bright coloured flags at the four corners, fluttering in the wind.

OF THE 'SMITHFIELD RACES'

HAVING set forth the costermonger's usual mode of conveying his goods through the streets of London, I shall now give the reader a description of the place and scene where and when he purchases his donkeys.

When a costermonger wishes to see or buy a donkey, he goes to Smithfield-market on a Friday afternoon. On this day, between the hours of one and five, there is a kind of fair held, attended solely by costermongers, for whose convenience a long paved slip of ground, about eighty feet in length, has been set apart. The animals for sale are trotted up and down this—the 'racecourse,' as it is called—and on each side of it stand the spectators and purchasers, crowding among the stalls of peas-soup, hot eels, and other street delicacies.

Everything necessary for the starting of a costermonger's barrow can be had in Smithfield on a Friday,—from the barrow itself to the weights—from the donkey to the whip. The animals can be purchased at prices ranging from 5s. to 3l. On a brisk market-day as many as two hundred donkeys have been sold. The barrows for sale are kept apart from the steeds, but harness to any amount can be found everywhere, in all degrees of excellence, from the bright japanned cart saddle with its new red pads, to the old mouldy trace covered with buckle marks. Wheels of every size and colour, and springs in every stage of rust, are hawked about on all sides. To the usual noise and shouting of a Saturday night's market is added the shrill squealing of distant pigs, the lowing of the passing oxen, the bleating of sheep, and the braying of donkeys. The paved road all down the 'race-course' is level and soft, with the mud trodden down between the stones. The policeman on duty there wears huge fisherman's or flushermen's boots, reaching to their thighs; and the trouser ends of the costers' corduroys are black and sodden with wet dirt. Every variety of odour fills the air; you pass from the stable smell that hangs about the donkeys, into an atmosphere of apples and fried fish, near the eating-stalls, while a few paces further on you are nearly choked with the stench of goats. The crowd of black hats, thickly dotted with red and yellow plush caps, reels about; and the 'hi-hi-i-i' of the donkey-runners sounds on all sides. Sometimes a curly-headed bull, with a fierce red eye, on its way to or from the adjacent cattle-market, comes trotting down the road, making all the visitors rush suddenly to the railings, for fear—as a coster near me said—of 'being taught the hornpipe.'

The donkeys standing for sale are ranged in a long line on both sides of the 'race-course,' their white velvety noses resting on the wooden rail they are tied to. Many of them wear their blinkers and head harness, and others are ornamented with ribbons, fastened in their halters. The lookers-on lean against this railing, and chat with the boys at the donkey's heads, or with the men who stand behind them, and keep continually hitting and shouting at the poor still beasts to make them prance. Sometimes a party of two or three will be seen closely examining one of these 'Jerusalem ponys,' passing their hands down its legs, or looking quietly on, while the proprietor's ash stick descends on the patient brute's back, making a dull hollow sound. As you walk in front of the long line of donkeys, the lads seize the animals by their nostrils, and show their large teeth, asking if you 'want a hass, sir,' and all warranting the creature to be 'five years old next buff-day.' Dealers are quarrelling among themselves, downcrying each other's goods. 'A hearty man,' shouted one proprietor, pointing to his rival's stock, 'could eat three sich donkeys as yourn at a meal.'

One fellow, standing behind his steed, shouts as he strikes, 'Here's the real Britannia mettle'; whilst another asks. 'Who's for the Pride of the Market?' and then proceeds to flip 'the pride' with his whip, till she clears away the mob with her kickings. Here, standing by its mother, will be a shaggy little colt, with a group of ragged boys fondling it, and lifting it in their arms from the ground.

During all this the shouts of the drivers and runners fill the air, as they rush past each other on the race-course. Now a tall fellow, dragging a donkey after him, runs by crying, as he charges in amongst the mob, 'Hulloa! Hulloa! hi! hi!' his mate, with his long coat-tails flying in the wind, hurrying after and roaring, between his blows, 'Keem-up!'

On nearly every post are hung traces or bridles; and in one place, on the occasion of my visit, stood an old collar with a donkey nibbling at the straw that had burst out. Some of the lads, in smock-frocks, walk about with cart-saddles on their heads, and crowds gather round the trucks, piled up with a black heap of harness studded with brass. Those without trays have spread out old sacks on the ground, on which are laid axle-trees, bound-up springs, and battered carriage-lamps. There are plenty of rusty nails and iron bolts to be had, if a barrow should want mending; and if the handles are broken, an old cab-shaft can be bought cheap, to repair them.

In another 'race-course,' opposite to the donkeys,—the ponies are sold. These make a curious collection, each one showing what was his last master's whim. One has its legs and belly shorn of its hair, another has its mane and tail cut close, and some have switch tails, muddy at the end from their length. A big-hipped black nag, with red tinsel-like spots on its back, had its ears cut close, and another curly-haired brute that was wet and streaming with having been shown off, had two huge letters burnt into its hind-quarters. Here the clattering of the hoofs and the smacking of whips added to the din; and one poor brute, with red empty eye-holes, and carrying its head high up—as a blind man does—sent out showers of sparks from its hoofs as it spluttered over the stones, at each blow it received. Occasionally, in one part of the pony market, there may be seen a crowd gathered round a nag, that some one swears has been stolen from him.

Raised up over the heads of the mob are bundles of whips, and men push their way past, with their arms full of yellow-handled curry-combs; whilst, amongst other cries, is heard that of 'Sticks ½*d*. each! sticks—real smarters.' At one end of the market the barrows for sale are kept piled up one on another, or filled with old wheels, and some with white unpainted wood, showing where they have been repaired. Men are here seen thumping the wooden trays, and trying the strength of the springs by leaning on them; and here, too, stood, on the occasion of my visit, a ragged coster lad trying to sell his scales, now the cherry-season had passed.

On all sides the refreshment-barrows are surrounded by cus-tomers. The whelk-man peppers his lots, and shouts, 'A lumping penn'orth for a ha'penny'; and a lad in a smock-frock carries two full pails of milk, slopping it as he walks, and crying, 'Ha'penny a mug-full, new milk from the ke-ow!' The only quiet people to be seen are round the pea-soup stall, with their cups in their hands; and there is a huge crowd covering in the hot-eel stand, with the steam rising up in the centre. Baskets of sliced cake, apples, nuts, and pine-apple rock, block up the pathway; and long wicker baskets of live fowls hem you in, round which are grouped the costers, handling and blowing apart the feathers on the breast.

OF THE DONKEYS OF THE COSTERMONGERS

THE costermongers almost universally treat their donkeys with kindness. Many a costermonger will resent the ill-treatment of a donkey, as he would a personal indignity. These animals are often not only favourites, but pets, having their share of the coster-monger's dinner when bread forms a portion of it, or pudding, or anything suited to the palate of the brute. Those well-used, mani-fest fondness for their masters, and are easily manageable; it is, however, difficult to get an ass, whose master goes regular rounds, away from its stable for any second labour during the day, unless it has fed and slept in the interval. The usual fare of a donkey is a peck of chaff, which costs 1*d.*, a quart of oats and a quart of beans, each averaging 1½*d.*, and sometimes a pennyworth of hay, being an expenditure of 4*d.* or 5*d.* a day; but some give double this quantity in a prosperous time. Only one meal a day is given. Many coster-mongers told me, that their donkeys lived well when they themselves lived well.

It's all nonsense to call donkeys stupid,' said one costermonger to me; 'them's stupid that calls them so: they're sensible. Not long since I worked Guildford with my donkey-cart and a boy. Jack (the donkey) was slow and heavy in coming back, until we got in sight of the lights at Vauxhall-gate, and then he trotted on like one o'clock, he did indeed! just as if he smelt it was London besides seeing it, and knew he was at home. He had a famous appetite in the country, and the fresh grass did him good. I gave a country lad 2*d.* to mind him in a green lane there. I wanted my own boy to do so, but he said, 'I'll see you further first.'' A London boy hates being by himself in a lone country part. He's afraid of being burked; he is indeed. One can't quarrel with a lad when he's away with one in the country; he's very useful. I feed my donkey well. I sometimes give him a carrot for a luxury, but carrots are dear now. He's fond of mashed potatoes, and has many a good mash when I can buy them at 4 lb.a penny.'

OF THE COSTERMONGERS' CAPITAL

THE costermongers, though living by buying and selling, are seldom or never capitalists. It is estimated that not more than one-fourth of the entire body trade upon their own property. Some borrow their stock money, others borrow the stock itself, others again borrow the donkey-carts, barrows, or baskets, in which their stock is carried round, whilst others borrow even the weights and measures by which it is meted out.

The reader, however uninformed he may be as to the price the poor usually have to pay for any loans they may require, doubt-lessly need not be told that the remuneration exacted for the use of the above-named commodities is not merely confined to the legal 5*l.* per centum per annum; still many of even the most 'knowing' will hardly be able to credit the fact that the ordinary rate of interest in the costermongers' money-market amounts to 20 per cent. per week, or no less than 1,040*l*. a year, for every 100*l*. advanced.

But the iniquity of this usury in the present instance is felt, not so much by the costermongers themselves, as by the poor people whom they serve; for, of course, the enormous rate of interest must be paid out of the profits on the goods they sell, and consequently added to the price, so that coupling this overcharge with the customary short allowances—in either weight or measure, as the case may be—we can readily perceive how cruelly the poor are defrauded, and how they not only get often too little for what they do, but have as often to pay too much for what they buy.

OF THE 'SLANG' WEIGHTS AND MEASURES

ALL counterfeit weights and measures, the costermongers call by the appropriate name of 'slang.' 'There are not half so many slangs as there was eighteen months ago,' said a 'general dealer' to me. 'You see, sir, the letters in the *Morning Chronicle* set people a talking, and some altered their way of business. Some was very angry at what was said in the articles on the street-sellers, and swore that costers was gentlemen, and that they'd smash the men's noses that had told you, sir, if they knew who they were. There's plenty of costers wouldn't use slangs at all, if people would give a fair price; but you see the boys *will* try it on for their bunts, and how is a man to sell fine cherries at 4*d*. a pound that cost him 3½*d*., when there's a kid alongside of him a selling his "tol" at 2*d*. a pound, and singing it out as bold as brass? So the men slangs it, and cries "2*d*. a pound," and gives half-pound, as the boy does; which brings it to the same thing. We doesn't 'dulterate our goods like the tradesmen—that is, the regular hands doesn't. It wouldn't be easy, as you say, to 'dulterate cabbages or oysters; but we deals fair to all that's fair to us,—and that's more than many a tradesman does, for all their juries.'

The slang quart is a pint and a half. It is made precisely like the proper quart; and the maker, I was told, 'knows well enough what it's for, as it's charged, new, 6*d*. more than a true quart measure; but it's nothing to him, as he says, what it's for, so long as he gets his price.' The slang quart is let out at 2*d*. a day—1*d*. extra being charged 'for the risk.' The slang pint holds in some cases three-fourths of the just quantity, having a very thick bottom; others hold only half a pint, having a false bottom half-way up. These are used chiefly in measuring nuts, of which the proper quantity is hardly ever given to the purchaser; 'but, then,' it was often said, or implied to me, the 'price is all the lower, and people just brings it on themselves, by wanting things for next to nothing; so it's all right; it's people's own faults.' The hire of the slang pint is 2*d*. per day.

OF THE BOYS OF THE COSTERMONGERS, AND THEIR BUNTS

But there are still other 'agents' among the costermongers, and these are the 'boys' deputed to sell a man's goods for a certain sum, all over that amount being the boys' profit or 'bunts.' Almost every costermonger who trades through the streets with his barrow is accompanied by a boy. The ages of these lads vary from ten to sixteen, there are few above sixteen, for the lads think it is then high time for them to start on their own account. These boys are useful to the man in 'calling,' their shrill voices being often more audible than the loudest pitch of an adult's lungs. Many persons, moreover, I am assured, prefer buying off a boy, believing that if the lad did not succeed in selling his goods he would be knocked about when he got home; others think that they are safer in a boy's hands, and less likely to be cheated; these, however, are equally mistaken notions. The boys also are useful in pushing at the barrow, or in drawing it along by tugging at a rope in front. Some of them are the sons of costermongers; some go round to the costermongers' abodes and say: 'Will you want me to-morrow?' 'Shall I come and give you a lift?' The parents of the lads thus at large are, when they *have* parents, either unable to support them, or, if able, prefer putting their money to other uses (such as drinking); and so the lads have to look out for themselves, or, as they say, 'pick up a few halfpence and a bit of grub as we can.' Such lads, however, are the smallest class of costermongering youths; and are sometimes called 'cas'alty boys,' or 'nippers.'

The boys—and nearly the whole of them—soon become very

quick, and grow masters of slang, in from six weeks to two or three months. 'I suppose,' said one man familiar with their character, 'they'd learn French as soon, if they was thrown into the way of it. They must learn slang to live, and as they have to wait at markets every now and then, from one hour to six, they associate one with another and carry on conversations in slang about the 'penny gaffs' (theatres), criticising the actors; or may be they toss the pieman, if they've got any ha'pence, or else they chaff the passers by. The older ones may talk about their sweethearts; but they always speak of them by the name of "nammow" (girls).

'The boys are severe critics too (continued my informant) on dancing. I heard one say to another; "What do you think of Johnny Millicent's new step?" for they always recognise a new step, or they discuss the female dancer's legs, and not very decently. At other times the boys discuss the merits or demerits of their masters, as to who feeds them best. I have heard one say, "O, ain't Bob stingy? We have bread and cheese!" Another added, "*We* have steak and beer, and I've the use of Bill's (the master's) 'baccy box." '

Some of these lads are paid by the day, generally from 2*d*. or 3*d*. and their food, and as much fruit as they think fit to eat, as by that they soon get sick of it. They generally carry home fruit in their pockets for their playmates, or brothers, or sisters; the coster-mongers allow this, if they are satisfied that the pocketing is not for sale. Some lads are engaged by the week, having from 1*s*. to 1*s* 6*d*., and their food when out with their employer. Their lodging is found only in a few cases, and then they sleep in the same room with their master and mistress. Of master or mistress, however, they never speak, but of Jack and Bet. They behave respectfully to the women, who are generally kind to them. They soon desert a very surly or stingy master; though such a fellow could get fifty boys next day if he wanted them, but not lads used to the trade, for to these he's well known by their talk one with another, and they soon tell a man his character very plainly—'*very* plainly indeed, sir, and to his face too,' said one.

Some of these boys are well beaten by their employers; this they put up with readily enough, if they experience kindness at the hands of the man's wife; for, as I said before, parties that have never thought of marriage, if they live together, call one another husbands and wives.

In 'working the country' these lads are put on the same footing as their masters, with whom they eat, drink, and sleep; but they do not gamble with them. A few, however, go out and tempt country boys to gamble, and—as an almost inevitable consequence —to lose. 'Some of the boys,' said one who had seen it often, 'will keep a number of countrymen in a beer-shop in a roar for the hour, while the countrymen ply them with beer, and some of the street-lads can drink a good deal. I've known three bits of boys order a pot of beer each, one after the other, each paying his share, and a quartern of gin each after that—drunk neat; they don't understand water. Drink doesn't seem to affect them as it does men. I don't know why.' 'Some costermongers,' said another informant, 'have been known, when they've taken a fancy to a boy—I know of two—to dress him out like themselves, silk handkerchiefs and all; for if they didn't find them silk handkerchiefs, the boys would soon get them out of their "*bunts*". They like silk handkerchiefs, for if they lose all their money gambling, they can pledge their hand-kerchiefs.'

I have mentioned the term '*bunts.*' Bunts is the money made by the boys in this manner:—If a costermonger, after having sold a sufficiency, has 2*s.* or 3*s.* worth of goods left, and is anxious to get home, he says to the boy, 'Work these streets, and bring me 2*s.* 6*d.* for the tol' (lot), which the costermonger knows by his eye—for he seldoms measures or counts—is easily worth that money. The lad then proceeds to sell the things entrusted to him, and often shows great ingenuity in so doing. If, for instance, turnips be tied up in penny bunches, the lad will open some of them, so as to spread them out to nearly twice their previous size, and if anyone ask if that be a penn'orth, he will say, 'Here's a larger for $1\frac{1}{2}d$., marm,' and so palm off a penny bunch at $1\frac{1}{2}d$. Out of each bunch of onions he takes one or two, and makes an extra bunch. All that the lad can make in this way over the half-crown is his own, and called 'bunts.' Boys have made from 6*d.* to 1*s* 6*d.* 'bunts,' and this day after day. Many of them will, in the course of their traffic, beg old boots or shoes, if they meet with better sort of people, and so 'work it to rights,' as they call it among themselves; servants often give them cast-off clothes. It is seldom that a boy carries home less than the stipulated sum. The above is what is understood as 'fair bunts.' 'Unfair bunts' is what the lad may make unknown to his master; as, if a customer call from the area for goods cried at 2*d*., the lad may get 2½*d*., by pretending what he had carried was a superior sort to that called at 2*d*.,—or by any similar trick.

'I have known some civil and industrious boys,' said a coster-monger to me, 'get to save a few shillings, and in six months start with a shallow, and so rise to a donkey-cart. The greatest drawback to struggling boys is their sleeping in low lodging-houses, where they are frequently robbed, or trepanned to part with their money, or else they get corrupted.'

OF THE EDUCATION OF THE 'COSTER-LADS'

AMONG the costers the term education is (as I have already inti-mated) merely understood as meaning a complete knowledge of the art of 'buying in the cheapest market and selling in the dearest.' There are few lads whose training extends beyond this. The father is the tutor, who takes the boy to the different markets, instructs him in the art of buying, and when the youth is perfect on this point, the parent's duty is supposed to have been performed. Nearly all these boys are remarkable for their precocious sharpness. To use the words of one of the class, 'these young ones are as sharp as terriers, and learns every dodge of the business in less than no time. There's one I knows about three feet high, that's up to the business as clever as a man of thirty. Though he's only twelve years old he'll chaff down a peeler so uncommon severe, that the only way to stop him is to take him in charge!'

As soon as the boy is old enough to shout well and loudly, his father takes him into the streets. Some of these youths are not above seven years of age, and it is calculated that not more than one in a hundred has ever been to a school of any kind. The boy walks with the barrow, or guides the donkey, shouting by turns with the father, who, when the goods are sold, will as a reward, let him ride home on the tray. The lad attends all markets with his father, who teaches him his business and shows him his tricks of trade; 'for,' said a coster, 'a governor in our line leaves the knowledge of all his dodges to his son, jist as the rich coves do their tin.'

The life of a coster-boy is a very hard one. In summer he will have to be up by four o'clock in the morning, and in winter he is never in bed after six. When he has returned from market, it is generally his duty to wash the goods and help dress the barrow. About nine he begins his day's work, shouting whilst his father pushes; and as very often the man has lost his voice, this share of the labour is left entirely to him. When a coster has regular customers, the vegetables or fish are all sold by twelve o'clock, and in many coster families the lad is then packed off with fruit to hawk in the streets. When the work is over, the father will perhaps take the boy to a public-house with him, and give him part of his beer. Sometimes a child of four or five is taken to the tap-room, especially if he be pretty and the father proud of him. 'I have seen,' said a coster to me, 'a baby of five year old reeling drunk in a tap-room. His governor did it for the lark of the thing, to see him chuck hisself about—sillyfied like.'

The love of gambling soon seizes upon the coster boy. Youths of about twelve or so will as soon as they can get away from work go to a public-house and play cribbage for pints of beer, or for a pint a corner. They generally continue playing till about midnight, and rarely—except on a Sunday—keep it up all night.

It ordinarily happens that when a lad is about thirteen, he quarrels with his father, and gets turned away from home. Then he is forced to start for himself. He knows where he can borrow stock-money and get his barrow, for he is as well acquainted with the markets as the oldest hand at the business, and children may often be seen in the streets under-selling their parents. 'How's it possible,' said a woman, 'for people to live when there's their own son at the end of the court a-calling his goods as cheap again as we can afford to sell ourn?'

If a boy is lucky in trade, his next want is to get a girl to keep home for him. I was assured, that it is not at all uncommon for a lad of fifteen to be living with a girl of the same age, as man and wife. It creates no disgust among his class, but seems rather to give him a position among such people. Their courtship does not take long when once the mate has been fixed upon. The girl is invited to 'raffles,' and treated to 'twopenny hops' and half-pints of beer. Perhaps a silk neck handkerchief—a 'King's man'—is given as a present; though some of the lads will, when the arrangement has been made, take the gift back again and wear it themselves. The boys are very jealous, and if once made angry behave with great brutality to the offending girl. A young fellow of about sixteen told me, as he seemed to grow angry at the very thought, 'If I seed my gal talking to another chap I'd fetch her sich a punch of the nose as should plaguy quick stop the whole business.' Another lad informed me, with a knowing look, 'that the gals—it was a rum thing now he come to think on it—axully liked a feller for walloping them. As long as the bruises hurted, she was always thinking on the cove as gived 'em her.' After a time, if the girl continues faithful, the young coster may marry her; but this is rarely the case, and many live with their girls until they have grown to men, or perhaps they may quarrel the very first year, and have a fight and part.

These boys hate any continuous work. So strong is this objection to continuity that they cannot even remain selling the same article for more than a week together. Moreover none of them can be got to keep stalls. They must be perpetually on the move—or to use their own words 'they like a roving life.' They all of them delight in dressing 'flash' as they call it. If a 'governor' was to try and 'palm off' his old cord jacket upon the lad that worked with him, the boy wouldn't take it. 'It's too big and seedy for me,' he'd say, 'and I ain't going to have your leavings.' They try to dress like the men, with large pockets in their cord jackets and plenty of them. Their trousers too must fit tight at the knee, and their boots they like as good as possible. A good 'King's-man,' a plush skull cap, and a seam down the trousers are the great points of ambition with the coster boys.

A lad of about fourteen informed me that 'brass buttons, like a huntsman's, with foxes' heads on 'em, looked stunning flash, and the gals liked 'em.' As for the hair, they say it ought to be long in front, and done in 'figure-six' curls, or twisted back to the ear 'Newgate-knocker style.' 'But the worst of hair is,' they add, 'that it is always getting cut off in quod, all along of muzzling the bobbies.'

The whole of the coster-boys are fond of good living. I was told that when a lad started for himself, he would for the first week or so live almost entirely on cakes and nuts. When settled in business they always manage to have what they call 'a relish' for breakfast and tea, 'a couple of herrings, or a bit of bacon, or what not.' Many of them never dine excepting on the Sunday—the pony and donkey proprietors being the only costers whose incomes will permit them to indulge in a 'fourpenny plate of meat at a cook's shop.' The whole of the boys too are extremely fond of pudding, and should the 'plum duff' at an eating-house contain an unusual quantity of plums, the news soon spreads, and the boys then endeavour to work that way so as to obtain a slice. While waiting for a market, the lads will very often spend a shilling in the cakes and three-cornered puffs sold by the Jews. The owners toss for them, and so enable the young coster to indulge his two favourite passions at the same time—his love of pastry, and his love of gambling. The Jews' crisp butter biscuits also rank very high with the boys, who declare that they 'slip down like soapsuds down a gully hole.' In fact it is curious to notice how perfectly unrestrained are the passions and appetites of these youths. The only thoughts that trouble them are for their girls, their eating and their gambling—beyond the love of self they have no tie that binds them to existence.

THE LIFE OF A COSTER-LAD

ONE lad that I spoke to gave me as much of his history as he could remember. He was a tall stout boy, about sixteen years old, with a face utterly vacant. His two heavy lead-coloured eyes stared unmeaningly at me, and, beyond a constant anxiety to keep his front lock curled on his cheek, he did not exhibit the slightest trace of feeling. He sank into his seat heavily and of a heap, and when once settled down he remained motionless, with his mouth open and his hands on his knees—almost as if paralyzed. He was dressed in all the slang beauty of his class, with a bright red handkerchief and unexceptionable boots.

'My father,' he told me in a thick unimpassioned voice, 'was a waggoner, and worked the country roads. There was two on us at home with mother, and we used to play along with the boys of our court, in Golding-lane, at buttons and marbles. I recollects nothing more than this—only the big boys used to cheat like bricks and thump us if we grumbled—that's all I recollects of my infancy, as you calls it. Father I've heard tell died when I was three and brother only a year old. It was worse luck for us!—Mother was so easy with us. I once went to school for a couple of weeks, but the cove used

to fetch me a wipe over the knuckles with his stick, and as I wasn't
going to stand that there, why you see I ain't no great schollard.
We did as we liked with mother, she was so precious easy, and I
never learned anything but playing buttons and making leaden
"bonces," that's all,' (here the youth laughed slightly). 'Mother
used to be up and out very early washing in families—anything for
a living. She was a good mother to us. We was left at home with
the key of the room and some bread and butter for dinner. Afore
she got into work—and it was a goodish long time—we was shocking hard up, and she pawned nigh everything. Sometimes, when we
hadn't no grub at all, the other lads, perhaps, would give us some
of their bread and butter, but often our stomachs used to ache with
the hunger, and we would cry when we was werry far gone. She
used to be at work from six in the morning till ten o'clock at night,
which was a long time for a child's belly to hold out again, and
when it was dark we would go and lie down on the bed and try and
sleep until she came home with the food. I was eight year old then.
  'A man as know'd mother, said to her, "Your boy's got nothing
to do, let him come along with me and yarn a few ha'pence," and
so I became a coster. He gave me 4d. a morning and my breakfast.
I worked with him about three year, until I learnt the markets,
and then I and brother got baskets of our own, and used to keep
mother. One day with another, the two on us together could make
2s. 6d. by selling greens of a morning, and going round to the
publics with nuts of a evening, till about ten o'clock at night.
Mother used to have a bit of fried meat or a stew ready for us when
we got home, and by using up the stock as we couldn't sell, we
used to manage pretty tidy. When I was fourteen I took up with
a girl. She lived in the same house as we did, and I used to walk out
of a night with her and give her half-pints of beer at the publics.
She were about thirteen, and used to dress werry nice, though she
weren't above middling pretty. Now I'm working for another man
as gives me a shilling a week, victuals, washing, and lodging, just
as if I was one of the family.
  'On a Sunday I goes out selling, and all I yarns I keeps. As for
going to church, why, I can't afford it,—besides, to tell the truth, I
don't like it well enough. Plays, too, ain't in my line much; I'd
sooner go to a dance—it's more livelier. The "penny gaffs" is rather
more in my style; the songs are out and out, and makes our gals

laugh. The smuttier the better, I thinks; bless you! the gals likes it as much as we do. If we lads ever has a quarrel, why, we fights for it. If I was to let a cove off once, he'd do it again; but I never give a lad a chance, so long as I can get anigh him. I never heard about Christianity; but if a cove was to fetch me a lick of the head, I'd give it him again, whether he was a big 'un or a little 'un. I'd precious soon see a henemy of mine shot afore I'd forgive him,—where's the use? Do I understand what behaving to your neighbour is?—In coorse I do. If a feller as lives next me wanted a basket of mine as I wasn't using, why, he might have it; if I was working it though, I'd see him further! I can understand that all as lives in a court is neighbours; but as for policemen, they're nothing to me, and I should like to pay 'em all off well. No; I never heerd about this here creation you speaks about. In coorse God Almighty made the world, and the poor bricklayers' labourers built the houses arterwards—that's *my* opinion; but I can't say, for I've never been in no schools, only always hard at work, and knows nothing about it. I have heered a little about our Saviour,—they seem to say he were a goodish kind of man; but if he says as how a cove's to forgive a feller as hits you, I should say he know'd nothing about it. In coorse the gals and lads goes and lives with thinks our walloping 'em wery cruel of us, but we don't. Why don't we?—why, because we don't. Before father died, I used sometimes to say my prayers, but after that mother was too busy getting a living to mind about my praying. Yes, I knows!—in the Lord's prayer they says, "Forgive us our trespasses, as we forgive them as trespasses agin us." It's a very good thing, in coorse, but no costers can't do it.'

OF THE 'PENNY GAFF'

In many of the thoroughfares of London there are shops which have been turned into a kind of temporary theatre (admission one penny), where dancing and singing take place every night. Rude pictures of the performers are arranged outside, to give the front a gaudy and attractive look, and at night-time coloured lamps and transparencies are displayed to draw an audience. These places are called by the costers 'Penny Gaffs'; and on a Monday night as many as six performances will take place, each one having its two hundred visitors.

Not wishing to believe in the description which some of the more intelligent of the costermongers had given of these places, it was thought better to visit one of them, so that all exaggeration might be avoided. One of the least offensive of the exhibitions was fixed upon.

The 'penny gaff' chosen was situated in a broad street near Smithfield; and for a great distance off, the jingling sound of music was heard, and the gas-light streamed out into the thick night air as from a dark lantern, glittering on the windows of the houses opposite, and lighting up the faces of the mob in the road, as on an illumination night. The front of a large shop had been entirely removed, and the entrance was decorated with paintings of the 'comic singers,' in their most 'humourous' attitudes. On a table against the wall was perched the band, playing what the costers call 'dancing tunes' with great effect, for the hole at the money-taker's box was blocked up with hands tendering the penny. The crowd without was so numerous, that a policeman was in attendance to preserve order, and push the boys off the pavement—the music having the effect of drawing them insensibly towards the festooned green-baize curtain.

The shop itself had been turned into a waiting-room, and was crowded even to the top of the stairs leading to the gallery on the first floor. The ceiling of this 'lobby 'was painted blue, and spotted with whitewash clouds, to represent the heavens; the boards of the trap-door, and the laths that showed through the holes in the plaster, being all the same colour. A notice was here posted, over the canvas door leading into the theatre, to the effect that 'LADIES AND GENTLEMEN TO THE FRONT PLACES MUST PAY TWOPENCE.'

The visitors, with a few exceptions, were all boys and girls, whose ages seemed to vary from eight to twenty years. Some of the girls—though their figures showed them to be mere children—were dressed in showy cotton-velvet polkas, and wore dowdy feathers in their crushed bonnets. They stood laughing and joking with the lads, in an unconcerned, impudent manner, that was almost appalling. Some of them, when tired of waiting, chose their partners, and commenced dancing grotesquely, to the admiration of the lookers-on, who expressed their approbation in obscene terms, that, far from disgusting the poor little women, were received as compliments, and acknowledged with smiles and coarse repartees. The boys clustered together, smoking their pipes, and laughing at each other's anecdotes, or else jingling halfpence in time with the tune, while they whistled an accompaniment to it. Presently one of the performers, with a gilt crown on his well greased locks, descended from the staircase, his fleshings covered by a dingy dressing-gown, and mixed with the mob, shaking hands with old acquaintances. The 'comic singer' too, made his appearance among the throng—the huge bow to his cravat, which nearly covered his waistcoat, and the red end to his nose, exciting neither merriment nor surprise.

To discover the kind of entertainment, a lad near me and my companion was asked 'if there was any flash dancing.' With a knowing wink the boy answered, 'Lots! show their legs and all, prime!' and immediately the boy followed up his information by a request for a 'yenep' to get a 'tib of occabat.' After waiting in the lobby some considerable time, the performance inside was concluded, and the audience came pouring out through the canvas door. As they had to pass singly, I noticed them particularly. Above three-fourths of them were women and girls, the rest consisting chiefly of mere boys—for out of about two hundred persons I counted only eighteen men. Forward they came, bringing an overpowering stench with them, laughing and yelling as they pushed their way through the waiting-room. One woman carrying a sickly child with a bulging forehead, was reeling drunk, the saliva running down her mouth as she stared about her with a heavy fixed eye. Two boys were pushing her from side to side, while the poor infant slept, breathing heavily, as if stupefied, through the din. Lads jumping on girls' shoulders, and girls laughing hysterically from being tickled by the youth behind them, every one shouting and jumping, presented a mad scene of frightful enjoyment.

When these had left, a rush for places by those in waiting began, that set at defiance the blows and struggles of a lady in spangles who endeavoured to preserve order and take the checks. As time was a great object with the proprietor, the entertainment within began directly the first seat was taken, so that the lads without, rendered furious by the rattling of the piano within, made the canvas partition bulge in and out, with the strugglings of those seeking admission, like a sail in a flagging wind.

To form the theatre, the first floor had been removed; the white-washed beams however still stretched from wall to wall. The lower room had evidently been the warehouse, while the upper apartment had been the sitting-room, for the paper was still on the walls. A gallery, with a canvas front, had been hurriedly built up, and it was so fragile that the boards bent under the weight of those above. The bricks in the warehouse were smeared over with red paint, and had a few black curtains daubed upon them. The coster-youths require no very great scenic embellishment, and indeed the stage—which was about eight feet square—could admit of none. Two jets of gas, like those outside a butcher's shop, were placed on each side of the proscenium, and proved very handy for the gentlemen whose pipes required lighting. The band inside the 'theatre' could not compare with the band without. An old grand piano, whose canvas-covered top extended the entire length of the stage, sent forth its wiry notes under the be-ringed fingers of a 'professor Wilkinsini,' while another professional, with his head resting on his violin, played vigorously, as he stared unconcernedly at the noisy audience.

Singing and dancing formed the whole of the hour's performance, and, of the two, the singing was preferred. A young girl, of about fourteen years of age, danced with more energy than grace, and seemed to be well-known to the spectators, who cheered her on by her Christian name. When the dance was concluded, the proprietor of the establishment threw down a penny from the gallery, in the hopes that others might be moved to similar acts of generosity; but no one followed up the offering, so the young lady hunted after the money and departed. The 'comic singer' in a battered hat and the huge bow to his cravat, was received with deafening shouts. Several songs were named by the costers, but the 'funny gentleman' merely requested them 'to hold their jaws,' and putting on a knowing' look, sang a song, the whole point of which consisted in the mere utterance of some filthy word at the end of each stanza. Nothing, however, could have been more successful. The lads stamped their feet with delight; the girls screamed with enjoyment. Once or twice a young shrill laugh would anticipate the fun —as if the words were well known—or the boys would forestall the point by shouting it out before the proper time. When the song was ended the house was in a delirium of applause. The canvas front to the gallery was beaten with sticks, drum-like, and sent down showers of white powder on the heads in the pit. Another song followed, and the actor knowing on what his success depended, lost no opportunity of increasing his laurels. The most obscene thoughts, the most disgusting scenes were coolly described, making a poor child near me wipe away the tears that rolled down her eyes with the enjoyment of the poison. There were three or four of these songs sung in the course of the evening, each one being encored, and then changed. One written about 'Pine-apple rock,' was the grand treat of the night, and offered greater scope to the rhyming powers of the author than any of the others. In this, not a single chance had been missed; ingenuity had been exerted to its utmost lest an obscene thought should be passed by, and it was absolutely awful to behold the relish with which the young ones jumped to the hideous meaning of the verses.

There was one scene yet to come, that was perfect in its wickedness. A ballet began between a man dressed up as a woman, and a country clown. The most disgusting attitudes were struck, the most immoral acts represented, without one dissenting voice. If there had been any feat of agility, any grimacing, or, in fact, anything with which the laughter of the uneducated classes is usually associated, the applause might have been accounted for; but here were two ruffians degrading themselves each time they stirred a limb, and forcing into the brains of the childish audience before them thoughts that must embitter a lifetime, and descend from father to child like some bodily infirmity.

OF THE COSTER GIRLS

THE costermongers, taken as a body, entertain the most imperfect idea of the sanctity of marriage. To their undeveloped minds it merely consists in the fact of a man and woman living together, and sharing the gains they may each earn by selling in the street. The father and mother of the girl look upon it as a convenient means of shifting the support of their child over to another's exertions; and so thoroughly do they believe this to be the end and aim of matrimony, that the expense of a church ceremony is considered as a useless waste of money, and the new pair are received by their companions as cordially as if every form of law and religion had been complied with.

The story of one coster girl's life may be taken as a type of the many. When quite young she is placed out to nurse with some neighbour, the mother—if a fond one—visiting the child at certain periods of the day, for the purpose of feeding it, or sometimes, knowing the round she has to make, having the infant brought to her at certain places, to be 'suckled.' As soon as it is old enough to go alone, the court is its play-ground, the gutter its school-room, and under the care of an elder sister the little one passes the day, among children whose mothers like her own are too busy out in the streets helping to get the food, to be able to mind the family at home. When the girl is strong enough, she in her turn is made to assist the mother by keeping guard over the younger children, or, if there be none, she is lent out to carry about a baby, and so made to add to the family income by gaining her sixpence weekly. Her time is from the earliest years fully occupied; indeed, her parents cannot afford to keep her without doing and getting *something*. Very few of the children receive the least education. 'The parents,' I am told, 'never give their minds to learning, for they say, "What's the use of it? *that* won't yarn a gal a living." ' Everything is sacrificed— as, indeed, under the circumstances it must be—in the struggle to live—aye! and to live *merely*. Mind, heart, soul, are all absorbed in the belly. The rudest form of animal life, physiologists tell us, is simply a locomotive stomach. Verily, it would appear as if our social state had a tendency to make the highest animal sink to the lowest.

At about seven years of age the girls first go into the streets to sell. A shallow-basket is given to them, with about two shillings for stock-money, and they hawk, according to the time of year, either oranges, apples, or violets; some begin their street education with the sale of water-cresses. The money earned by this means is strictly given to the parents. Sometimes—though rarely—a girl who has been unfortunate during the day will not dare return home at night, and then she will sleep under some dry arch or about some market, until the morrow's gains shall ensure her a safe reception and shelter in her father's room.

The life of the coster-girls is as severe as that of the boys. Between four and five in the morning they have to leave home for the markets, and sell in the streets until about nine. Those that have more kindly parents, return then to breakfast, but many are obliged to earn the morning's meal for themselves. After breakfast, they generally remain in the streets until about ten o'clock at night; many having nothing during all that time but one meal of bread and butter and coffee, to enable them to support the fatigue of walking from street to street with the heavy basket on their heads. In the course of a day, some girls eat as much as a pound of bread, and very seldom get any meat, unless it be on a Sunday.

THE LIFE OF A COSTER GIRLS

I WISHED to have obtained a statement from the girl whose portrait is here given, but she was afraid to give the slightest information about the habits of her companions, lest they should recognize her by her engraving and persecute her for the revelations she might make. After disappointing me some dozen times, I was forced to seek out some other coster girl.

The one I fixed upon was a fine-grown young woman of eighteen. She had a habit of curtsying to every question that was put to her. Her plaid shawl was tied over the breast, and her cotton-velvet bonnet was crushed in with carrying her basket. She seemed dreadfully puzzled where to put her hands, at one time tucking them under her shawl, warming them at the fire, or measuring the length of her apron, and when she answered a question she invariably addressed the fireplace. Her voice was husky from shouting apples.

'My mother has been in the streets selling all her lifetime. Her uncle learnt her the markets and she learnt me. When business grew bad she said to me, "Now you shall take care on the stall, and I'll go and work out charing." The way she learnt me the markets was to judge the weight of the baskets of apples, and then saifl she, "Always bate 'em down, a'most a half." I always liked the street-life very well, that was if I was selling. I have mostly kept a stall myself, but I've known gals as walk about with apples, as have told me that the weight of the baskets is sich that the neck cricks, and when the load is took off, it's just as if you'd a stiff neck, and the head feels as light as a feather. The gals begins working very early at our work; the parents makes them go out when a'most babies. There's a little gal, I'm sure she ain't more than half-past seven, that stands selling water-cresses next my stall, and mother was saying, "Only look there, how that little one has to get her living afore she a'most knows what a penn'orth means."

'There's six on us in family, and father and mother makes eight. Father used to do odd jobs with the gas-pipes in the streets, and when work was slack we had very hard times of it. Mother always liked being with us at home, and used to manage to keep us employed out of mischief—she'd give us an old gown to make into pinafores for the children and such like! She's been very good to us, has mother, and so's father. She always liked to hear us read to her whilst she was washing or such like! and then we big ones had to learn the little ones. But when father's work got slack, if she had no employment charing, she'd say, "Now I'll go and buy a bushel of apples," and then she'd turn out and get a penny that way. I suppose by sitting at the stall from nine in the morning till the shops shut up—say ten o'clock at night, I can earn about 1s.6d. a day. I'ts all according to the apples—whether they're good or not—what we makes. If I'm unlucky, mother will say, "Well, I'll go out to-morrow and see what I can do"; and if I've done well, she'll say "Come, you're a good hand at it; you've done famous." Yes mother's very fair that way. Ah! there's many a gal I knows whose back has to suffer if she don't sell her stock well; but, thank God! I never get more than a blowing up. My parents is very fair to me.

'I dare say there ain't ten out of a hundred gals what's living with men, what's been married Church of England fashion. I know plenty myself, but I don't, indeed, think it right. It seems to me that the gals is fools to be 'ticed away, but, in coorse, they needn't go without they likes. This is why I don't think it's right. Perhaps a man will have a few words with his gal, and he'llsay, "Oh! I ain't obligated to keep her!" and he'll turn her out: and then where's that poor gal to go? Now, there's a gal I knows as came to me no later than this here week, and she had a dreadful swole face and a awful black eye; and I says, "Who's done that?" and she says, says she, "Why, Jack"—just in that way; and then she says, says she, "I'm going to take a warrant out to-morrow." Well, he gets the warrant that same night, but she never appears again him, for fear of getting more beating. That don't seem to me to be like married people ought to be. Besides, if parties is married, they ought to bend to each other; and they won't, for sartain, if they're only living together. A man as is married is obligated to keep his wife if they quarrels or not; and he says to himself, says he, "Well, I may as well live happy, like." But if he can turn a poor gal off, as soon as he tires of her, he begins to have noises with her, and then gets quit of her altogether. Again, the men takes the money of the gals, and in coorse ought to treat 'em well—which they don't. This is another reason: when the gal is in the family way, the lads mostly sends them to the workhouse to lay in, and only goes sometimes to take them a bit of tea and shuggar; but, in course, married men wouldn't behave in such likes to their poor wives. After a quarrel, too, a lad goes and takes up with another young gal, and that isn't pleasant for the first one. The first step to ruin is them places of "penny gaffs," for they hears things there as oughtn't to be said to young gals. Besides, the lads is very insinivating, and after leaving them places will give a gal a drop of beer, and make her half tipsy, and then they makes their arrangements. I've often heerd the boys boasting of having ruined gals, for all the world as if they was the first noblemen in the land.

'It would be a good thing if these sort of goings on could be stopped. It's half the parents' fault; for if a gal can't get a living, they turns her out into the streets, and then what's to become of her? I'm sure the gals, if they was married, would be happier, because they couldn't be beat worse. And if they was married, they'd get a nice home about 'em; whereas, if they's only living together, they takes a furnished room. I'm sure, too, that it's a bad plan; for I've heerd the gals themselves say, "Ah! I wish I'd never seed Jack" (or Tom, or whatever it is); "I'm sure I'd never be half so bad but for him."

OF THE DRESS OF THE COSTERMONGERS

We pass to a consideration of their dress.

The costermonger's ordinary costume partakes of the durability of the warehouseman's, with the quaintness of that of the stable-boy. A well-to-do 'coster,' when dressed for the day's work, usually wears a small cloth cap, a little on one side. A close-fitting worsted tie-up skull-cap, is very fashionable, just now, among the class, and ringlets at the temples are looked up to as the height of elegance. Hats they never wear—excepting on Sunday—on account of their baskets being frequently carried on their heads. Coats are seldom indulged in; their waistcoats, which are of a broad-ribbed corduroy, with fustian back and sleeves, being made as long as a groom's, and buttoned up nearly to the throat. If the corduroy be of a light sandy colour, then plain brass, or sporting buttons, with raised fox's or stag's heads upon them—or else black bone-buttons, with a flower-pattern—ornament the front; but if the cord be of a dark rat-skin hue, then mother-of-pearl buttons are preferred. Two large pockets—sometimes four—with huge flaps or lappels, like those in a shooting-coat, are commonly worn. If the coster-monger be driving a good trade and have his set of regular customers, he will sport a blue cloth jacket, similar in cut to the cord ones above described; but this is looked upon as an extravagance of the highest order, for the slime and scales of the fish stick to the sleeves and shoulders of the garment, so as to spoil the appearance of it in a short time. The fashionable stuff for trousers, at the present, is a dark-coloured 'cable-cord,' and they are made to fit tightly at the knee and swell gradually until they reach the boot, which they nearly cover. Velveteen is now seldom worn, and knee-breeches are quite out of date. Those who deal wholly in fish wear a blue serge apron, either hanging down or tucked up around their waist. The costermonger, however, prides himself most of all upon his neckerchief and boots. Men, women, boys and girls, all have a passion for these articles. The man who does not wear his silk neckerchief—his 'King's-man' as it is called—is known to be in desperate circumstances; the inference being that it has gone to supply the morning's stock-money. A yellow flower on a green ground, or a red and blue pattern, is at present greatly in vogue. The women wear their kerchiefs tucked-in under their gowns, and the men have theirs wrapped loosely round the neck, with the ends hanging over their waistcoats. Even if a costermonger has two or three silk handkerchiefs by him already, he seldom hesitates to buy another, when tempted with a bright showy pattern hanging from a Field-lane door-post.

The costermonger's love of a good strong boot is a singular prejudice that runs throughout the whole class. From the father to the youngest child, all will be found well shod. So strong is their predilection in this respect, that a costermonger may be immediately known by a glance at his feet. He will part with everything rather than his boots, and to wear a pair of second-hand ones, or 'translators' (as they are called), is felt as a bitter degradation by them all. Among the men, this pride has risen to such a pitch, that many will have their upper-leathers tastily ornamented, and it is not uncommon to see the younger men of this class with a heart or a thistle, surrounded by a wreath of roses, worked below the instep, on their boots. The general costume of the women or girls is a black velveteen or straw bonnet, with a few ribbons or flowers, and almost always a net cap fitting closely to the cheek. The silk 'King's-man' covering their shoulders, is sometimes tucked into the neck of the printed cotton-gown, and sometimes the ends are brought down outside to the apron-strings. Silk dresses are never worn by them— they rather despise such articles. The petticoats are worn short, ending at the ankles, just high enough to show the whole of the much-admired boots. Coloured, or 'illustrated shirts,' as they are called, are especially objected to by the men.

On the Sunday no costermonger will, if he can possibly avoid it, wheel a barrow. If a shilling be an especial object to him, he may, perhaps, take his hallow and head-basket as far as Chalk-farm, or some neighbouring resort; but even then he objects strongly to the Sunday-trading. They leave this to the Jews and Irish, who are always willing to earn a penny— as they say.

The prosperous coster *will* have his holiday on the Sunday, and, if possible, his Sunday suit as well—which usually consists of a rough beaver hat, brown Petersham, with velvet facings of the same colour, and cloth trousers, with stripes down the side. The women, generally, manage to keep by them a cotton gown of a bright showy pattern, and a new shawl. As one of the craft said to me—'Costers likes to see their gals and wives look lady-like when they takes them out.' Such of the costers as are not in a flourishing way of business, seldom make any alteration in their dress on the Sunday. There are but five tailors in London who make the garb proper to costermongers; one of these is considered somewhat 'slop,' or as a coster called him, a 'springer-up.'

This springer-up is blamed by some of the costermongers, who condemn him for employing women at reduced wages. A whole court of costermongers, I was assured, would withdraw their custom from a tradesman, if one of their body, who had influence among them, showed that the tradesman was unjust to his workpeople. The tailor in question issues bills after the following fashion. I give one verbatim, merely withholding the address for obvious reasons:

ONCE TRY YOU'LL COME AGAIN

Slap-up Tog and out-and-out Kicksies Builder.

Mr. —— nabs the chance of putting his customers awake, that he has just made his escape from Russia, not forgetting to clap his mawleys upon some of the right sort of Ducks, to make single and double backed Slops for gentlemen in black, when on his return home he was stunned to find one of the top manufacturers of Manchester had cut his lucky and stepped off to the Swan Stream, leaving behind him a valuable stock of Moleskins, Cords, Velveteens, Plushes, Swandowns, &c., and I having some ready in my kick, grabbed the chance, and stepped home with my swag, and am now safe landed at my crib. I can turn out toggery of every description very slap up, at the following low prices for

Ready Gilt—Tick being no go.

Upper Benjamins, built on a downey plan, a monarch to half a finnuff. Slap up Velveteen Togs, lined with the same, 1 pound 1 quarter and a peg. Moleskin ditto, any colour, lined with the same, 1 couter. A pair of Kerseymere Kicksies, any colour, built very slap up, with the artful dodge, a canary. Pair of stout Cord ditto, built in the "Melton Mowbray" style half a sov. Pair of very good broad Cord ditto, made very saucy, 9 bob and a kick. Pair of long sleeve Moleskin, all colours, built hanky-spanky, with a double fakement down the side and artful buttons at bottom, half a monarch. Pair of stout ditto, built very serious, 9 times. Pair of out-and-out fancy sleeve Kicksies, cut to drop down on the trotters, 2 bulls. Waist Togs, cut long, with moleskin back and sleeves, 10 peg. Blue Cloth ditto, cut slap, with pearl buttons, 14 peg. Mud Pipes, Knee Caps, and Trotter Cases, built very low.

'A decent allowance made to Seedy Swells, Tea Kettle Purgers, Head Robbers, and Flunkeys out of Collar.

'N. B. Gentlemen finding their own Broady can be accommodated.'

OF THE DIET AND DRINK OF COSTERMONGERS

IT is less easy to describe the diet of costermongers than it is to describe that of many other of the labouring classes, for their diet, so to speak, is an 'out-door diet.' They breakfast at a coffee-stall, and (if all their means have been expended in purchasing their stock, and none of it be yet sold) they expend on the meal only 1*d*., reserved for the purpose. For this sum they can procure a small cup of coffee, and two 'thin' (that is to say two thin slices of bread and butter). For dinner—which on a week-day is hardly ever eaten at the costermonger's abode—they buy 'block ornaments,' as they call the small, dark-coloured pieces of meat exposed on the cheap butchers' blocks or counters. These they cook in a tap-room; half a pound costing 2*d*. If time be an object, the coster buys a hot pie or two; preferring fruit-pies when in season, and next to them meat-pies. 'We never eat eel-pies,' said one man to me, 'because we know they're often made of large dead eels. *We*, of all people, are not to be had that way. But the haristocrats eats 'em and never knows the difference.' I did not hear that these men had any repugnance to meat-pies; but the use of the dead eel happens to come within the immediate knowledge of the costermongers, who are, indeed, its purveyors. Saveloys, with a pint of beer, or a glass of 'short' (neat gin) is with them another common week-day dinner. The costers make all possible purchases of street-dealers, and pride themselves in thus 'sticking to their own.' On Sunday, the costermonger, when not 'cracked up,' enjoys a good dinner at his own abode. This is always a joint—most frequently a shoulder or half-shoulder of mutton—and invariably with 'lots of good taturs baked along with it.' In the quality of their potatoes these people are generally particular.

The costermonger's usual beverage is beer, and many of them drink hard, having no other way of spending their leisure but in drinking and gambling. It is not unusual in 'a good time,' for a costermonger to spend 12*s*. out of every 20*s*. in beer and pleasure.

I ought to add, that the 'single fellows,' instead of living on 'block ornaments' and the like, live, when doing well, on the best fare, at the 'spiciest' cook-shops on their rounds, or in the neighbourhood of their residence.

There are some families of costermongers who have persevered in carrying out the principles of teetotalism. One man thought there might be 200 individuals, including men, women, and children, who practised total abstinence from intoxicating drinks. These parties are nearly all somewhat better off than their drinking companions. The number of teetotalers amongst the costers, however, was more numerous three or four years back.

OF THE CRIES AND ROUNDS
OF COSTERMONGERS

I SHALL now proceed to treat of the London costermongers' mode of doing business.

In the first place all the goods they sell are cried or 'hawked,' and the cries of the costermongers in the present day are as varied as the articles they sell. The principal ones, uttered in a sort of cadence, are now, 'Ni-ew mackerel, 6 a shilling.' ('I've got a good jacketing many a Sunday morning,' said one dealer, 'for waking people up with crying mackerel, but I've said, "I must live while you sleep."') 'Buy a pair of live soles, 3 pair for 6*d*.'—or, with a barrow, 'Soles, 1*d*. a pair, 1*d*. a pair;' 'Plaice alive, alive, cheap;' 'Buy a pound crab, cheap;' 'Pine-apples, ½*d*. a slice;' 'Mussels a penny a quart;' 'Oysters, a penny a lot;' 'Salmon alive, 6*d*. a pound;' 'Cod alive, 2*d*. a pound;' 'Real Yarmouth bloaters, 2 a penny;' 'New herrings alive, 16 a groat' (this is the loudest cry of any); 'Penny a bunch turnips' (the same with greens, cabbages, &c.); 'All new nuts, 1*d*. half-pint;' 'Oranges, 2 a penny;' 'All large and alive-O, new sprats, O, 1*d*. a plate;' 'Wi-ild Hampshire rabbits, 2 a shilling;' 'Cherry ripe, 2*d*. a pound;' 'Fine ripe plums, 1*d*. a pint;' 'Ing-uns, a penny a quart;' 'Eels, 3lbs. a shilling—large live eels 3lbs. a shilling.'

The continual calling in the streets is very distressing to the voice. One man told me that it had broken his, and that very often while out he had lost his voice altogether. 'They seem to have no breath,' the men say, 'after calling for a little while.' The repeated shouting brings on a hoarseness, which is one of the peculiar characteristics of hawkers in general. The costers mostly go out with a boy to cry their goods for them. If they have two or three hallooing together, it makes more noise than one, and the boys can shout better and louder than the men. The more noise they can make in a place the better they find their trade. Street-selling has been so bad lately that many have been obliged to have a drum for their bloaters, 'to drum the fish off,' as they call it.

In the second place, the costermongers, as I said before, have mostly their little bit of a 'round;' that is, they go only to certain places; and if they don't sell their goods they 'work back' the same way again. If they visit a respectable quarter, they confine themselves to the mews near the gentlemen's houses. They generally prefer the poorer neighbourhoods. They go down or through almost all the courts and alleys—and avoid the better kind of streets, unless with lobsters, rabbits, or onions. If they have anything inferior, they visit the low Irish districts—for the Irish people, they say, want only quantity, and care nothing about quality—*that* they don't study. But if they have anything they wish to make a price of, they seek out the mews, and try to get it off among the gentlemen's coachmen, for *they* will have what is good; or else they go among the residences of mechanics,—for their wives, they say, like good-living as well as the coachmen. Some costers, on the other hand, go chance rounds.

OF THE EARNINGS OF COSTERMONGERS

Some costers, I am told, make upwards of 30*s.* a week all the year round; but allowing for cessations in the street trade, through bad weather, neglect, ill-health, or casualty of any kind, and taking the more prosperous costers with the less successful—the English with the Irish—the men with the women—perhaps 10*s.* a week may be a fair average of the earnings of the entire body the year through.

These earnings, I am assured, were five years ago at least 25 per cent. higher; some said they made half as much again: 'I can't make it out how it is,' said one man, 'but I remember that I could go out and sell twelve bushel of fruit in a day, when sugar was dear, and now, when sugar's cheap, I can't sell three bushel on the same round. Perhaps we want thinning.'

Such is the state of the working-classes, say all the costers, they have little or no money to spend. 'Why, I can assure you,' declared one of the parties from whom I obtained much important information, 'there's my missus—she sits at the corner of the street with fruit. Eight years ago she would have taken 8*s.* out of that street on a Saturday, and last Saturday week she had one bushel of apples, which cost 1*s.* 6*d.* She was out from ten in the morning till ten at night, and all she took that day was 1*s.* 7½*d.* Go to whoever you will you will hear much upon the same thing.' Another told me, 'The costers are often obliged to sell the things for what they gave for them. The people haven't got money to lay out with them— they tell us so; and if they are poor we must be poor too. If we can't get a profit upon what goods we buy with our stock-money, let it be our own or anybody's else, we are compelled to live upon it, and, when that's broken into, we must either go to the workhouse or starve. If we go to the workhouse, they'll give us a piece of dry bread, and abuse us worse than dogs.' Indeed, the whole course of my narratives shows how the costers generally—though far from universally—complain of the depressed state of their trade.

OF THE TRICKS OF THE COSTERMONGERS

I shall now treat of the tricks of trade practised by the London costermongers. Of these the costers speak with as little reserve and as little shame as a fine gentleman of his peccadilloes. 'I've boiled lots of oranges,' chuckled one man, 'and sold them to Irish hawkers, as wasn't wide awake, for stunning big uns. The boiling swells the oranges and so makes 'em look finer ones, but it spoils them, for it takes out the juice. People can't find that out though until it's too late. I boiled the oranges only a few minutes, and three or four dozen at a time.' Oranges thus prepared will not keep, and any unfortunate Irishwoman, tricked as were my informant's customers, is astonished to find her stock of oranges turn dark-coloured and worthless in forty-eight hours. The fruit is 'cooked' in this way for Saturday night and Sunday sale—times at which the demand is the briskest. Some prick the oranges and express the juice, which they sell to the British wine-makers.

Apples cannot be dealt with like oranges, but they are mixed. A cheap red-skinned fruit, known to costers as 'gawfs,' is rubbed hard, to look bright and feel soft, and is mixed with apples of a superior description. 'Gawfs are sweet and sour at once,' I was told, 'and fit for nothing but mixing.' Some foreign apples, from Holland and Belgium, were bought very cheap last March, at no more than 16*d.* a bushel, and on a fine morning as many as fifty boys might be seen rubbing these apples, in Hooper-street, Lambeth. 'I've made a crown out of a bushel of 'em on a fine day,' said one sharp youth. The larger apples are rubbed sometimes with a piece of woollen cloth, or on the coat skirt, if that appendage forms part of the dress of the person applying the friction, but most frequently they are rolled in the palms of the hand. The smaller apples are thrown to and fro in a sack, a lad holding each end. 'I wish I knew how the shopkeepers manages *their* fruit,' said one youth to me; 'I should like to be up to some of their moves; they do manage their things so plummy.'

Cherries are capital for mixing, I was assured by practical men. They purchase three sieves of indifferent Dutch, and one sieve of good English cherries, spread the English fruit over the inferior and sell them as the best. Strawberry pottles are often half cabbage leaves, a few tempting strawberries being displayed on the top of the pottle. 'Topping up,' said a fruit dealer to me, 'is the principal thing, and we are perfectly justified in it. You ask any coster that knows the world, and he'll tell you that all the salesmen in the markets tops up. It's only making the best of it.' Filberts they bake to make them look brown and ripe. Prunes they boil to give them a plumper and finer appearance. The latter trick, however, is not unusual in the shops.

The more honest costermongers will throw away fish when it is unfit for consumption, less scrupulous dealers, however, only throw away what is utterly unsaleable; but none of them fling away the dead eels, though their prejudice against such dead fish prevents their indulging in eel-pies. The dead eels are mixed with the living often in the proportion of 20 lb. dead to 5 lb. alive, equal quantities of each being accounted very fair dealing. 'And after all,' said a street fish dealer to me, 'I don't know why dead eels should be objected to; the aristocrats don't object to them. Nearly all fish is dead before it's cooked, and why not eels? Why not eat them when they're sweet, if they're ever so dead, just as you eat fresh herrings? I believe it's only among the poor and among our chaps, that there's this prejudice. Eels die quickly if they're exposed to the sun.'

Herrings are made to look fresh and bright by candle-light, by the lights being so disposed 'as to give them,' I was told, 'a good reflection. Why, I can make them look splendid; quite a pictur. I can do the same with mackerel, but not so prime as herrings.'

OF THE STREET SELLERS OF FISH

BILLINGSGATE

To see this market in its busiest costermonger time, the visitor should be there about seven o'clock on a Friday morning. The market opens at four, but for the first two or three hours, it is attended solely by the regular fishmongers and 'bummarees' who have the pick of the best there. As soon as these are gone, the costers' sale begins.

Many of the costers that usually deal in vegetables, buy a little fish on the Friday. It is the fast day of the Irish, and the mechanics' wives run short of money at the end of the week, and so make up their dinners with fish; for this reason the attendance of costers' barrows at Billingsgate on a Friday morning is always very great. As soon as you reach the Monument you see a line of them, with one or two tall fishmonger's carts breaking the uniformity, and the din of the cries and commotion of the distant market, begins to break on the ear like the buzzing of a hornet's nest. The whole neighbourhood is covered with the hand-barrows, some laden with baskets, others with sacks. Yet as you walk along, a fresh line of costers' barrows are creeping in or being backed into almost impossible openings; until at every turning nothing but donkeys and rails are to be seen. The morning air is filled with a kind of seaweedy odour, reminding one of the sea-shore; and on entering the market, the smell of fish, of whelks, red herrings, sprats, and a hundred others, is almost overpowering.

The wooden barn-looking square where the fish is sold, is soon after six o'clock crowded with shiny cord jackets and greasy caps. Everybody comes to Billingsgate in his worst clothes, and no one knows the length of time a coat can be worn until they have been to a fish sale. Through the bright opening at the end are seen the tangled rigging of the oyster-boats and the red worsted caps of the sailors. Over the hum of voices is heard the shouts of the salesmen, who, with their white aprons, peering above the heads of the mob, stand on their tables, roaring out their prices.

All are bawling together—salesmen and hucksters of provisions, capes, hardware, and newspapers—till the place is a perfect Babel of competition. 'Ha-a-ansome cod! best in the market! All alive!

alive! alive O!' 'Ye-o-o! Ye-o-o! here's your fine Yarmouth bloaters!
Who's the buyer?' 'Here you are, governor, splendid whiting! some
of the right sort!' 'Turbot! turbot! all alive! turbot!' 'Glass of nice
peppermint! this cold morning a ha'penny a glass!' 'Here you are
at your own price! Fine soles, O!' 'Oy, oy! oy! Now's your time!
fine grizzling sprats! all large and no small!' 'Hullo! hullo here!
beautiful lobsters! good and cheap! fine cock crabs all alive O!'
'Five brill and one turbot—have that lot for a pound! Come and
look at 'em, governor; you won't see a better sample in the market.'
'Here, this way! this way for splendid skate! skate O! skate O!'
'Had-had-had-had-haddick! all fresh and good!' 'Currant and
meat puddings! a ha'penny each!' 'Now, you mussel-buyers, come
along! come along! come along! now's your time for fine fat
mussels!' 'Here's food for the belly, and clothes for the back,
but I sell food for the mind' (shouts the newsvender). 'Here's
smelt O!' 'Here ye are, fine Finney haddick!' 'Hot soup! nice
peas-soup! nice peas-soup! a-all hot! hot!' 'Ahoy! ahoy here! live
plaice! all alive O!' 'Now or never! whelk! whelk! whelk!' 'Who'll
buy brill O! brill O!' 'Capes! water-proof capes! sure to keep the
wet out! a shilling a piece!' 'Eels O! eels O! Alive! alive O!' 'Fine
flounders, a shilling a lot! Who'll have this prime lot of flounders?'
'Shrimps! shrimps! fine shrimps!' 'Wink! wink! wink!' 'Hi! hi-i!
here you are, just eight eels left, only eight!' 'O ho! O ho! this
way—this way—this way! Fish alive! alive! alive O!'

In the darkness of the shed, the white bellies of the turbots,
strung up bow-fashion, shine like mother-of-pearl, while the
lobsters, lying upon them, look intensely scarlet, from the contrast.
Brown baskets piled up on one another, and with the herring-scales
glittering like spangles all over them, block up the narrow paths.
Men in coarse canvas jackets, and bending under huge hampers,
push past, shouting 'Move on! move on, there!' and women, with
the long limp tails of cod-fish dangling from their aprons, elbow
their way through the crowd. Round the auction-tables stand
groups of men turning over the piles of soles, and throwing them
down till they slide about in their slime; some are smelling them,
while others are counting the lots. 'There, that lot of soles are
worth your money,' cries the salesman to one of the crowd as he
moves on leisurely; 'none better in the market. You shall have
'em for a pound and half-a-crown.' 'Oh!' shouts another salesman,

'it's no use to bother him—he's no go.' Presently a tall porter, with a black oyster-bag, staggers past, trembling under the weight of his load, his back and shoulders wet with the drippings from the sack. 'Shove on one side!' he mutters from between his clenched teeth, as he forces his way through the mob. Here is a tray of reddish-brown shrimps piled up high, and the owner busy sifting his little fish into another stand, while a doubtful customer stands in front, tasting the flavour of the stock and consulting with his companion in speculation. Little girls carrying matting-bags, that they have brought from Spitalfields, come up, and ask you in a begging voice to buy their baskets; and women with bundles of twigs for stringing herrings, cry out. 'Half-penny a bunch!' from all sides. Then there are blue-black piles of small live lobsters, moving about their bound-up claws and long 'feelers', one of them occasionally being taken up by a looker-on, and dashed down again, like a stone. Everywhere every one is asking, 'What's the price, master?' while shouts of laughter from round the stalls of the salesmen, bantering each other, burst out, occasionally, over the murmuring noise of the crowd. The transparent smelts on the marble-slabs, and the bright herrings, with the lump of transparent ice magnifying their eyes like a lens, are seldom looked at until the market is over, though the hampers and piles of huge maids, dropping slime from the counter, are eagerly examined and bartered for.

One side of the market is set aside for whelks. There they stand in sackfuls, with the yellow shells piled up at the mouth, and one or two of the fish, curling out like corkscrews, placed as a sample. The coster slips one of these from its shell, examines it, pushes it back again, and then passes away, to look well round the market. In one part the stones are covered with herring-barrels, packed closely with dried fish, and yellow heaps of stiff haddock rise up on all sides. Here a man walks up with his knot on his shoulder, waiting for a job to carry fish to the trucks. Boys in ragged clothes, who have slept during the night under a railway-arch, clamour for employment; while the heads of those returning from the oyster-boats, rise slowly up the stone sides of the wharf.

The costermongers have nicknamed the long row of oyster-boats moored close alongside the wharf 'Oyster-street.' On looking down the line of tangled ropes and masts, it seems as though the little boats would sink with the crowds of men and women thronged together on their decks. It is as busy a scene as one can well behold. Each boat has its black sign-board, and salesman in his white apron walking up and down 'his shop,' and on each deck is a bright pewter pot and tin-covered plate, the remains of the salesman's breakfast. 'Who's for Baker's?' 'Who's for Archer's?' 'Who'll have Alston's?' shout the oyster-merchants, and the red cap of the man in the hold bobs up and down as he rattles the shells about with his spade. These holds are filled with oysters—a gray mass of sand and shell—on which is a bushel measure well piled up in the centre, while some of them have a blue muddy heap of mussels divided off from the 'natives.' The sailors in their striped guernseys sit on the boat sides smoking their morning's pipe, allowing themselves to be tempted by the Jew boys with cloth caps, old shoes, and silk handkerchiefs. Lads with bundles of whips skip from one boat to another, and seedy-looking mechanics, with handfuls of tin fancy goods, hover about the salesmen, who are the principal supporters of this trade. The place has somewhat the appearance of a little Holywell-street; for the old clothes' trade is entirely in the hands of the Jew boys, and coats, caps, hats, umbrellas, and old shoes, are shouted out in a rich nasal twang on all sides.

At length nearly all the busy marketing has finished, and the costers hurry to breakfast. At one house, known as 'Rodway's Coffee-house,' a man can have a meal for 1*d*.—a mug of hot coffee and two slices of bread and butter, while for two-pence what is elegantly termed 'a tightener,' that is to say, a most plentiful repast, may be obtained. Here was a large room, with tables all round, and so extremely silent, that the smacking of lips and sipping of coffee were alone heard. Upwards of 1,500 men breakfast here in the course of the morning, many of them taking as many as three such meals. On the counter was a pile of white mugs, and the bright tin cans stood beside the blazing fire, whilst Rodway himself sat at a kind of dresser, cutting up and buttering the bread, with marvellous rapidity. It was a clean, orderly, and excellent establishment, kept by a man, I was told, who had risen from a saloop stall.

Everybody was soon busy laying out their stock. The wrinkled dull-eyed cod was freshened up, the red-headed gurnet placed in rows, the eels prevented from writhing over the basket sides by cabbage-leaves, and the soles paired off like gloves. Then the little trucks began to leave, crawling, as it were, between the legs of the horses in the vans crowding Thames-street, and plunging in between huge waggons, but still appearing safely on the other side; and the 4,000 costers who visit Billingsgate on the Friday morning were shortly scattered throughout the metropolis.

OF COVENT GARDEN MARKET

On a Saturday—the coster's business day—it is computed that as many as 2,000 donkey-barrows, and upwards of 3,000 women with shallows and head-baskets visit this market during the forenoon. About six o'clock in the morning is the best time for viewing the wonderful restlessness of the place, for then not only is the 'Garden' itself all bustle and activity, but the buyers and sellers stream to and from it in all directions, filling every street in the vicinity. From Long Acre to the Strand on the one side, and from Bow-street to Bedford-street on the other, the ground has been seized upon by the market-goers. As you glance down any one of the neighbouring streets, the long rows of carts and donkey-barrows seem interminable in the distance. They are of all kinds, from the greengrocer's taxed cart to the coster's barrow—from the showy excursion-van to the rude square donkey-cart and bricklayer's truck. In every street they are ranged down the middle and by the kerb-stones. Along each approach to the market, too, nothing is to be seen, on all sides, but vegetables; the pavement is covered with heaps of them waiting to be carted; the flag-stones are stained green with the leaves trodden under foot; sieves and sacks full of apples and potatoes, and bundles of broccoli and rhubarb, are left unwatched upon almost every door-step; the steps of Covent Garden Theatre are covered with fruit and vegetables; the road is blocked up with mountains of cabbages and turnips; and men and women push past with their arms bowed out by the cauliflowers under them, or the red tips of carrots pointing from their crammed aprons, or else their faces are red with the weight of the loaded head-basket.

The donkey-barrows, from their number and singularity, force you to stop and notice them. Every kind of ingenuity has been exercised to construct harness for the costers' steeds; where a buckle is wanting, tape or string make the fastening secure; traces are made of rope and old chain, and an old sack or cotton handkerchief is folded up as a saddle-pad. Some few of the barrows make a magnificent exception, and are gay with bright brass; while one of the donkeys may be seen dressed in a suit of old plated carriage-harness, decorated with coronets in all directions. At some of the coster conveyances stands the proprietor, arranging his goods, the dozing animal starting up from its sleep each time a heavy basket is hoisted on the tray. Others, with their green and white and red load neatly arranged, are ready for starting, but the coster is finishing his breakfast at the coffee-stall. On one barrow there may occasionally be seen a solitary sieve of apples, with the horse of some neighbouring cart helping himself to the pippins while the owner is away. The men that take charge of the trucks, whilst the costers visit the market, walk about, with their arms full of whips and sticks. At one corner a donkey has slipped down, and lies on the stones covered with the cabbages and apples that have fallen from the cart.

The market itself presents a beautiful scene. In the clear morning air of an autumn day the whole of the vast square is distinctly seen from one end to the other. The sky is red and golden with the newly-risen sun, and the rays falling on the fresh and vivid colours of the fruit and vegetables, brighten up the picture as with a coat of varnish. There is no shouting, as at other markets, but a low murmuring hum is heard, like the sound of the sea at a distance, and through each entrance to the market the crowd sweeps by. Under the dark Piazza little bright dots of gas-lights are seen burning in the shops; and in the paved square the people pass and cross each other in all directions, hampers clash together, and excepting the carters from the country, every one is on the move. Sometimes a huge column of baskets is seen in the air, and walks away in a marvellously steady manner, or a monster railway van, laden with sieves of fruit, and with the driver perched up on his high seat, jolts heavily over the stones. Cabbages are piled up into stacks as it were. Carts are heaped high with turnips, and bunches of carrots like huge red fingers, are seen in all directions. Flower-girls, with large bundles of violets under their arms, run past, leaving a trail of perfume behind them. Waggons, with their shafts sticking up in the air, are ranged before the salesmen's shops, the high green load railed in with hurdles, and every here and there bunches of turnips are seen flying in the air over the heads of the people. Groups of apple-women, with straw pads on their crushed bonnets, and coarse shawls crossing their bosoms, sit on their porter's knots, chatting in Irish, and smoking short pipes; every passer-by is hailed with the cry of, 'Want a baskit, yer honor?' The porter, trembling under the piled-up hamper, trots along the street, with his teeth clenched and shirt wet with the weight, and staggering at every step he takes.

Inside the market all is bustle and confusion. The people walk along with their eyes fixed on the goods, and frowning with thought. Men in all costumes, from the coster in his corduroy suit to the greengrocer in his blue apron, sweep past. A countryman, in an old straw hat and dusty boots, occasionally draws down the anger of a woman for walking about with his hands in the pockets of his smock-frock, and is asked, 'if that is the way to behave on a market-day?' Even the granite pillars cannot stop the crowd, for it separates and rushes past them, like the tide by a bridge pier. At every turn there is a fresh odour to sniff at; either the bitter aromatic perfume of the herbalists' shops breaks upon you, or the scent of oranges, then of apples, and then of onions is caught for an instant as you move along. The broccoli tied up in square packets, the white heads tinged slightly red, as it were, with the sunshine—the sieves of crimson love-apples, polished like china,—the bundles of white glossy leeks, their roots dangling like fringe,—the celery, with its pinky stalks and bright green tops,—the dark purple pickling-cabbages, the scarlet carrots,—the white knobs of turnips,—the bright yellow balls of oranges, and the rich brown coats of the chestnuts—attract the eye on every side. Then there are the apple-merchants, with their fruit of all colours, from the pale yellow green to the bright crimson, and the baskets ranged in rows on the pavement before the little shops. Round these the customers stand examining the stock, then whispering together over their bargain, and counting their money. 'Give you four shillings for this here lot, master,' says a coster, speaking for his three companions. 'Four and six is my price,' answers the salesman. 'Say four, and it's a bargain,' continues the man. 'I said my price,' returns the dealer; 'go and look round, and see if you can get 'em cheaper; if not,

come back. I only wants what's fair.' The man, taking the salesman's advice, moves on. The walnut merchant, with the group of
women before his shop, peeling the fruit, their fingers stained deep
brown, is busy with the Irish purchasers. The onion stores, too,
are surrounded by Hibernians, feeling and pressing the gold-
coloured roots, whose dry skins crackle as they are handled. Cases
of lemons in their white paper jackets, and blue grapes, just seen
above the sawdust are ranged about, and in some places the
ground is slippery as ice from the refuse leaves and walnut husks
scattered over the pavement.

Against the railings of St. Paul's Church are hung baskets and
slippers for sale, and near the public-house is a party of countrymen
preparing their bunches of pretty coloured grass—brown and
glittering, as if it had been bronzed. Between the spikes of the
railing are piled up square cakes of green turf for larks; and at the
pump, boys, who probably have passed the previous night in the
baskets about the market, are washing, and the water dripping
from their hair that hangs in points over the face. The kerb-stone
is blocked up by a crowd of admiring lads, gathered round the bird-
catcher's green stand, and gazing at the larks beating their breasts
against their cages. The owner, whose boots are red with the soil
of the brick-field, shouts, as he looks carelessly around, 'A cock
linnet for tuppence,' and then hits at the youths who are poking
through the bars at the fluttering birds.

Under the Piazza the costers purchase their flowers (in pots)
which they exchange in the streets for old clothes. Here is ranged
a small garden of flower-pots, the musk and mignonette smelling
sweetly, and the scarlet geraniums, with a perfect glow of coloured
air about the flowers, standing out in rich contrast with the dark
green leaves of the evergreens behind them. 'There's myrtles, and
larels, and boxes,' says one of the men selling them, 'and there's a
harbora witus, and lauristiners, and that bushy shrub with pink
spots is heath.' Men and women, selling different articles, walk
about under the cover of the colonnade. One has seed-cake, another
small-tooth and other combs, others old caps, or pig's feet, and one
hawker of knives, razors, and short hatchets, may occasionally be
seen driving a bargain with a countryman, who stands passing his
thumb over the blade to test its keenness. Between the pillars are
the coffee-stalls, with their large tin cans and piles of bread and

butter, and protected from the wind by paper screens and sheets thrown over clothes-horses; inside these little parlours, as it were, sit the coffee-drinkers on chairs and benches, some with a bunch of cabbages on their laps, blowing the steam from their saucers, others, with their mouths full, munching away at their slices, as if not a moment could be lost. One or two porters are there besides, seated on their baskets, breakfasting with their knots on their heads.

As you walk away from this busy scene, you meet in every street barrows and costers hurrying home. The pump in the market is now surrounded by a cluster of clattering wenches quarrelling over whose turn it is to water their drooping violets, and on the steps of Covent Garden Theatre are seated the shoeless girls, tying up the halfpenny and penny bundles.

OF THE ORANGE AND NUT MARKET

IN Houndsditch there is a market supported principally by coster-mongers, who there purchase their oranges, lemons, and nuts. This market is entirely in the hands of the Jews; and although a few tradesmen may attend it to buy grapes, still it derives its chief custom from the street-dealers who say they can make far better bargains with the Israelites, (as they never refuse an offer), than they can with the Covent-garden salesmen, who generally cling to their prices. This market is known by the name of 'Duke's-place,' although its proper title is St. James's-place. The nearest road to it is through Duke's-street, and the two titles have been so confound-ed that at length the mistake has grown into a custom.

Duke's-place—as the costers call it—is a large square yard, with the iron gates of a synagogue in one corner, a dead wall form-ing one entire side of the court, and a gas-lamp on a circular pave-ment in the centre. The place looks as if it were devoted to money-making—for it is quiet and dirty. Not a gilt letter is to be seen over a doorway; there is no display of gaudy colour, or sheets of plate-glass, such as we see in a crowded thoroughfare when a customer is to be caught by show. As if the merchants knew their trade was certain, they are content to let the London smoke do their painter's work. On looking at the shops in this quarter, the idea forces itself upon one that they are in the last stage of dilapidation. Never did property in Chancery look more ruinous. Each dwelling seems as though a fire had raged in it, for not a shop in the market has a window to it; and, beyond the few sacks of nuts exposed for sale, they are empty, the walls within being blackened with dirt, and the paint without blistered in the sun, while the door-posts are worn round with the shoulders of the customers, and black as if charred. A few sickly hens wander about, turning over the heaps of dried leaves that the oranges have been sent over in, or roost the time away on the shafts and wheels of the nearest truck. Excepting on certain days, there is little or no business stirring, so that many of the shops have one or two shutters up, as if a death had taken place, and the yard is quiet as an inn of court. At a little distance the warehouses, with their low ceilings, open fronts, and black sides, seem like dark holes or coal-stores; and, but for the mahogany backs of chairs showing at the first floors, you would scarcely believe the houses to be inhabited, much more to be elegantly furnished as they are. One of the drawing-rooms that I entered here was warm and red with morocco leather, Spanish mahogany, and curtains and Turkey carpets; while the ormolu chandelier and the gilt frames of the looking-glass and pictures twinkled at every point in the fire-light.

The householders in Duke's-place are all of the Jewish persuasion, and among the costers a saying has sprung up about it. When a man has been out of work some time, he is said to be 'Cursed, like a pig in Duke's-place.'

OF ORANGE AND LEMON SELLING IN THE STREETS

OF foreign fruits, the oranges and nuts supply by far the greater staple for the street trade, and, therefore, demand a brief, but still a fuller, notice than other articles.

STREET-SELLERS OF GREEN STUFF

OF WATERCRESS-SELLING IN FARRINGDON-MARKET

THE first coster-cry heard of a morning in the London streets is that of 'Fresh wo-orter-creases.' Those that sell them have to be on their rounds in time for the mechanics' breakfast, or the day's gains are lost. As the stock-money for this calling need only consist of a few halfpence, it is followed by the very poorest of the poor; such as young children, who have been deserted by their parents, and whose strength is not equal to any great labour, or by old men and women, crippled by disease or accident, who in their dread of a workhouse life, linger on with the few pence they earn by street-selling.

As winter draws near, the Farringdon cress-market begins long before daylight. On your way to the City to see this strange sight, the streets are deserted; in the squares the blinds are drawn down before the windows, and the shutters closed, so that the very houses seem asleep. All is so silent that you can hear the rattle of the milk-maids' cans in the neighbouring streets, or the noisy song of three or four drunken voices breaks suddenly upon you, as if the singers had turned a corner, and then dies away in the distance. On the cab-stands, but one or two crazy cabs are left, the horses dozing with their heads down to their knees, and the drawn-up windows covered with the breath of the driver sleeping inside. At the corners of the streets, the bright fires of the coffee-stalls sparkle in the darkness, and as you walk along, the policeman, leaning against some gas-lamp, turns his lantern full upon you, as if in suspicion that one who walks abroad so early could mean no good to house-holders. At one house there stands a man, with dirty boots and loose hair, as if he had just left some saloon, giving sharp single knocks, and then going into the road and looking up at the bed-rooms, to see if a light appeared in them. As you near the City, you meet, if it be a Monday or Friday morning, droves of sheep and bullocks, tramping quietly along to Smithfield, and carrying a fog of steam with them, while behind, with his hands in his pockets, and his dog panting at his heels, walks the sheep-drover.

At the principal entrance to Farringdon-market there is an open space, running the entire length of the railings in front, and extending from the iron gates at the entrance to the sheds down the centre of the large paved court before the shops. In this open space the cresses are sold, by the salesmen or saleswomen to whom they are consigned, in the hampers they are brought in from the country.

The shops in the market are shut, the gas-lights over the iron gates burn brightly, and every now and then you hear the half-smothered crowing of a cock, shut up in some shed or bird-fancier's shop. Presently a man comes hurrying along, with a can of hot coffee in each hand, and his stall on his head, and when he has arranged his stand by the gates, and placed his white mugs between the railings on the stone wall, he blows at his charcoal fire, making the bright sparks fly about at every puff he gives. By degrees the customers are creeping up, dressed in every style of rags; they shuffle up and down before the gates, stamping to warm their feet, and rubbing their hands together till they grate like sandpaper. Some of the boys have brought large hand-baskets, and carry them with the handles round their necks, covering the head entirely with the wicker-work as with a hood; others have their shallows fastened to their backs with a strap, and one little girl, with the bottom of her gown tattered into a fringe like a blacksmith's apron, stands shivering in a large pair of worn-out Vestris boots, holding in her blue hands a bent and rusty tea-tray. A few poor creatures have made friends with the coffee-man, and are allowed to warm their fingers at the fire under the cans, and as the heat strikes into them, they grow sleepy and yawn.

The market—by the time we reach it—has just begun; one dealer has taken his seat, and sits motionless with cold—for it wants but a month to Christmas—with his hands thrust deep into the pockets of his gray driving coat. Before him is an opened hamper, with a candle fixed in the centre of the bright green cresses, and as it shines through the wicker sides of the basket, it casts curious patterns on the ground—as a night shade does. Two or three customers, with their 'shallows' slung over their backs, and their hands poked into the bosoms of their gowns, are bending over the hamper, the light from which tinges their swarthy features, and they rattle their half-pence and speak coaxingly to the dealer, to hurry him in their bargains.

Just as the clocks are striking five, a stout saleswoman enters the gates, and instantly a country-looking fellow, in a waggoner's cap and smock-frock, arranges the baskets he has brought up to London. The other ladies are soon at their posts, well wrapped up in warm cloaks, over their thick shawls, and sit with their hands under their aprons, talking to the loungers, whom they call by their names. Now the business commences; the customers come in by twos and threes, and walk about, looking at the cresses, and listening to the prices asked. Every hamper is surrounded by a black crowd, bending over till their heads nearly meet, their foreheads and cheeks lighted up by the candle in the centre. The saleswomen's voices are heard above the noise of the mob, sharply answering all objections that may be made to the quality of their goods. 'They're rather spotty, mum,' says an Irishman, as he examines one of the leaves. 'No more spots than a new-born babe, Dennis,' answers the lady tartly, and then turns to a new comer. At one basket, a street-seller in an old green cloak, has spread out a rusty shawl to receive her bunches, and by her stands her daughter, in a thin cotton dress, patched like a quilt. 'Ah! Mrs. Dolland,' cried the saleswoman in a gracious tone, 'can you keep yourself warm? it bites the fingers like biling water, it do.' At another basket, an old man, with long gray hair streaming over a kind of policeman's cape, is bitterly complaining of the way he has been treated by another saleswoman. 'He bought a lot of her, the other morning, and by daylight they were quite white; for he only made threepence on his best day.' 'Well, Joe,' returns the lady, 'you should come to them as knows you, and allers treats you well.'

As the morning twilight came on, the paved court was crowded with purchasers. The sheds and shops at the end of the market grew every moment more distinct, and a railway-van, laden with carrots, came rumbling into the yard. The pigeons, too, began to fly on to the sheds, or walk about the paving-stones, and the gas-man came round with his ladder to turn out the lamps. Then every one was pushing about; the children crying, as their naked feet were trodden upon, and the women hurrying off, with their baskets or shawls filled with cresses, and the bunch of rushes in their hands. In one corner of the market, busily tying up their bunches, were three or four girls seated on the stones, with their legs curled up under them, and the ground near them was green with the leaves they had thrown away. A saleswoman, seeing me looking at the group, said to me, 'Ah! you should come here of a summer's morning, and then you'd see 'em, sitting tying up, young and old, upwards of a hundred poor things as thick as crows in a ploughed field.'

As it grew late, and the crowd had thinned, none but the very poorest of the cress-sellers were left. Many of these had come without money, others had their halfpence tied up carefully in their shawl-ends, as though they dreaded the loss. A sickly-looking boy, of about five, whose head just reached above the hampers, now crept forward, treading with his blue naked feet over the cold stones as a cat does over wet ground. At his elbows and knees, his skin showed in gashes through the rents in his clothes, and he looked so frozen, that the buxom saleswoman called to him, asking if his mother had gone home. The boy knew her well, for without answering her question, he went up to her, and, as he stood shivering on one foot, said, 'Give us a few old cresses, Jinney,' and in a few minutes was running off with a green bundle under his arm.

As you walk home—although the apprentice is knocking at the master's door—the little water-cress girls are crying their goods in every street. Some of them are gathered round the pumps, washing the leaves and piling up the bunches in their baskets, that are tattered and worn as their own clothing; in some of the shallows the holes at the bottom have been laced up or darned together with rope and string, or twigs and split laths have been fastened across; whilst others are lined with oilcloth, or old pieces of sheet-tin. Even by the time the cress-market is over, it is yet so early that the maids are beating the mats in the road, and mechanics, with their tool-baskets slung over their shoulders, are still hurrying to their work.

OF THE STREET-SELLERS OF EATABLES AND DRINKABLES

THESE dealers were more numerous, even when the metropolitan population was but half its present extent. I heard several causes assigned for this,—such as the higher rate of earnings of the labouring people at that time, as well as the smaller number of shopkeepers who deal in such cheap luxuries as penny pies, and the fewer places of cheap amusement, such as the 'penny gaffs.' These places, I was told, 'run away with the young people's pennies,' which were, at one period, expended in the streets.

Men and women, and most especially boys, purchase their meals day after day in the streets. The coffee-stall supplies a warm breakfast; shell-fish of many kinds tempt to a luncheon; hot-eels or pea-soup, flanked by a potato 'all hot,' serve for a dinner; and cakes and tarts, or nuts or oranges, with many varieties of pastry, confectionary, and fruit, woo to indulgence in a dessert; while for supper there is a sandwich, a meat pudding, or a 'trotter.'

The street provisions consist of cooked or prepared victuals, which may be divided into solids, pastry, confectionary, and drinkables. The solids, according to street estimation, consist of hot-eels, pickled whelks, oysters, sheep's-trotters, pea-soup, fried fish, ham-sandwiches, hot green peas, kidney puddings, boiled meat puddings, beef, mutton, kidney, and eel pies, and baked potatoes. In each of these provisions the street poor find a mid-day or midnight meal. The pastry and confectionary which tempt the street eaters are tarts of rhubarb, currant, gooseberry, cherry, apple, damson, cranberry, and (so called) mince pies; plum dough and plum-cake; lard, currant, almond and many other varieties of cakes, as well as of tarts; gingerbread-nuts and heart-cakes; Chelsea buns; muffins and crumpets; 'sweet stuff' includes the several kinds of rocks, sticks, lozenges, candies, and hard-bakes; the medicinal confectionary of cough-drops and horehound; and, lastly, the more novel and aristocratic luxury of street-ices; and strawberry cream, at 1*d.* a glass (in Greenwich Park).

The drinkables are tea, coffee, and cocoa; ginger-beer, lemonade, Persian sherbet, and some highly-coloured beverages which have no specific name, but are introduced to the public as 'cooling' drinks; hot elder cordial or wine; peppermint water; curds and whey; water (as at Hampstead); rice milk; and milk in the parks.

A gentleman, who has taken an artist's interest in all connected with the streets, and has been familiar with their daily and nightly aspect from the commencement of the present century, considers that the great change is not so much in what has ceased to be sold, but in the introduction of fresh articles into street-traffic—such as pine-apples and Brazil-nuts, rhubarb and cucumbers, ham-sand-wiches, ginger-beer, &c. The coffee-stall, he represents, has but superseded the saloop-stall (of which I have previously spoken); while the class of street customers who supported the saloop-dealer now support the purveyor of coffee.

Concerning the bygone street-cries, I had also the following account from the personal observation of an able correspondent:—

'First among the old "musical cries," may be cited the "Tiddy Doll!"—immortalised by Hogarth—then comes the last person, who, with a fine bass voice, coaxed his customers to buy *sweets* with, "Quack, quack, quack, quack! Browns, browns, browns! have you got any mouldy browns?" There was a man, too, who sold tripe, &c., in this way, and to some purpose; he was as fine a man as ever stepped, and his deep rich voice would ring through a whole street, "Dog's-meat! cat's-meat! nice tripe! neat's feet! Come buy my trotters!" The last part would not have disgraced Lablache. He discovered a new way of pickling tripe—got on—made contracts for supplying the Navy during the war, and acquired a large property. One of our most successful artists is his grandson. Then there was that delight of our childhood—the eight o'clock "Hot spiced gingerbread! hot spiced gingerbread! buy my spiced gingerbread! smo-o-o-king hot!"' Another informant remembered a very popular character (among the boys), whose daily cry was: 'Hot spiced gingerbread nuts, nuts, nuts! If *one*'ll warm you, *wha-at*'ll a pound do—? *Wha-a-a-at*'ll a pound do?' Gingerbread was formerly in much greater demand than it is now.

OF THE STREET-SELLERS
OF PEA-SOUP AND HOT EELS

Two of the condiments greatly relished by the chilled labourers and others who regale themselves on street luxuries, are 'pea-soup' and 'hot eels.' Of these tradesmen there may be 500 now in the streets on a Saturday. As the two trades are frequently carried on by the same party, I shall treat of them together. The greatest number of these stands is in Old-street, St. Luke's, about twenty. In warm weather these street-cooks deal only in 'hot eels' and whelks; as the whelk trade is sometimes an accompaniment of the others, for then the soup will not sell. These dealers are stationary, having stalls or stands in the street, and the savoury odour from them attracts more hungry-looking gazers and longers than does a cook-shop window. They seldom move about, but generally frequent the same place.

Near the Bricklayers' Arms, at the junction of the Old and New Kent-roads, a hot-eel man dispenses what a juvenile customer assured me was 'as spicy as any in London, as if there was gin in it'. But the dealer in Clare-market does the largest trade of all in the hot-eel line. He is 'the head man.' On one Saturday he was known to sell 100 lbs. of eels, and on most Saturdays he will get rid of his four 'draughts' of eels (a draught being 20 lbs.). He and his son are dressed in Jenny Lind hats, bound with blue velvet, and both dispense the provisions, while the daughter attends to wash the cups. 'On a Sunday, anybody,' said my informant, 'would think him the first nobleman or squire in the land, to see him dressed in his white hat, with black crape round it, and his drab paletot and mother-o'-pearl buttons, and black kid gloves, with the fingers too long for him.'

I may add, that even the very poorest, who have only a half-penny to spend, as well as those with better means, resort to the stylish stalls in preference to the others. The eels are all purchased at Billingsgate early in the morning. The parties themselves, or their sons or daughters, go to Billingsgate, and the watermen row them to the Dutch eel vessels moored off the market.

The price of the hot eels is a halfpenny for five or seven pieces of fish, and three-parts of a cupful of liquor. The charge for a half-pint of pea-soup is a halfpenny, and the whelks are sold, according to the size, from a halfpenny each to three or four for the same sum. These are put out in saucers.

There are now in the trade almost more than can get a living at it, and their earnings are less than they were formerly. One party attributed this to the opening of a couple of penny-pie shops in his neighbourhood. Before then he could get 2s. 6d. a day clear, take one day with another; but since the establishment of the business in the penny-pie line he cannot take above 1s. 6d. a day clear. On the day the first of these pie-shops opened, it made as much as 10 lbs., or half a draught of eels, difference to him. There was a band of music and an illumination at the pie-shop, and it was impossible to stand against *that*. The fashionable dress of the trade is the 'Jenny Lind' or 'wide-awake' hat, with a broad black ribbon tied round it, and a white apron and sleeves. The dealers usually go to Hampton-court or Greenwich on a fine Sunday. They are partial to the pit of Astley's. One of them told his waterman at Billingsgate the other morning that 'he and his good lady had been werry amused with the osses at Hashley's last night.'

OF THE STREET-SELLERS
OF PICKLED WHELKS

THE trade in whelks is one of which the costermongers have the undisputed monopoly. The wholesale business is all transacted in

Billingsgate, where this shell-fish is bought by the measure (a double peck or gallon), half-measure, or wash.

About one-half of the whelks are sold alive (wholesale) and the other half 'cooked (boiled), some of the salesmen having 'convenience for cooking' near the market; but they are all brought to London alive, 'or what should be alive.' When bought alive, which ensures a better quality, I was told—for, 'whelks'll boil after they're dead and gone, you see, sir, as if they was alive and hungry'— the costermonger boils them in the largest saucepan at his command for about ten minutes, and then leaves them until they cool. 'They never kicks as they boils, like lobsters or crabs,' said one whelk dealer, 'they takes it quiet. A missionary cove said to me, "Why don't you kill them first? it's murder." *They* doesn't suffer; *I've* suffered more with a toothache than the whole of a measure of whelks has in a boiling, that I'm clear upon.' The boiling is generally the work of the women. The next process is to place them in a tub, throw boiling water over them, and stir them up for ten or fifteen minutes with a broom-handle. If the quantity be a wash, two broom-handles, usually wielded by the man and his wife, are employed. This is both to clean them and 'to make them come out easier to be wormed.' The 'worming' is equivalent to the removing of the beard of an oyster or mussel. The whelks are wormed one by one. The operator cuts into the fish, rapidly draws out the 'worm,' and pushes the severed parts together, which closes.

The whelks are sold at the stalls at two, three, four, six, and eight a penny, according to size. Four is an average pennyworth for good whelks; the six a penny are small, and the eight a penny very small. The principal place for their sale is in Old-street, City-road. The other principal places are the street-markets, which I have before particularised. The whelks are sold in saucers, generally small and white, and of common ware, and are contained in jars, ready to be 'shelled' into any saucer that may have been emptied. Sometimes a small pyramid of shells, surmounted by a candle protected by a shade, attracts the regard of the passer-by.

For sale in the public-houses, the whelks are most frequently carried in jars, and transferred in a saucer to the consumer. 'There's often a good sale,' said a man familiar with the business, 'when a public room's filled. People drinking there always want to eat. They buy whelks, not to fill themselves, but for a relish. A man that's used to the trade will often get off inferior sorts to the lushing-tons; he'll have them to rights. Whelks is all the same, good, bad, or middling, when a man's drinking, if they're well seasoned with pepper and vinegar.'

OF THE STREET-SELLERS,
AND OF THE PREPARATION OF FRIED FISH

AMONG the cooked food which has for many years formed a portion of the street trade is fried fish.

In the public-houses, a slice of bread, 16 or 32 being cut from a quartern loaf—as they are whole or half slices—is sold or offered with the fish for a penny. The cry of the seller is, 'fish and bread, a penny.' Sometimes for an extra-sized piece, with bread, 2*d*. is obtained, but very seldom, and sometimes two pieces are given for 1½*d*. At the stalls bread is rarely sold with the edible in question.

For the itinerant trade, a neatly painted wooden tray, slung by a leathern strap from the neck, is used: the tray is papered over generally with clean newspapers; and on the paper is spread the shapeless brown lumps of fish. Parsley is often strewn over them, and a salt-box is placed at the discretion of the customer. The trays contain from two to five dozen pieces.

The itinerant fried fish-sellers, when pursuing their avocation, wear generally a jacket of cloth or fustian buttoned round them, but the rest of their attire is hidden by the white sleeves and apron some wear, or by the black calico sleeves and dark woollen aprons worn by others.

The capital required to start properly in the business is:—frying-pan 2*s*. (second-hand 9*d*.); tray 2*s*. 6*d*. (second-hand 8*d*); salt-box 6*d*. (second-hand 1*d*.); and stock-money 5*s*.—in all 10*s*. A man has gone into the trade, however, with 1*s*., which he expended in fish and oil, borrowed a frying-pan, borrowed an old tea-board, and so started on his venture.

OF THE EXPERIENCE OF A FRIED FISH-
SELLER AND OF THE CLASS OF CUSTOMER

THE man who gave me the following information was well-looking, and might be about 45 or 50. He was poorly dressed, but his old

brown surtout fitted him close and well, was jauntily buttoned up
to his black satin stock, worn, but of good quality; and, altogether,
he had what is understood among a class as 'a *betterly* appearance
about him.'

'I've been in the trade,' he said, 'seventeen years. Before that,
I was a gentleman's servant, and I married a servant maid, and
we had a family, and, on that account, couldn't, either of us, get
a situation, though we'd good characters.

'I've lived in good families, where there was first rate men cooks,
and I know what good cooking means. I bought a dozen plaice;
I forgot what I gave for them, but they were dearer then than now.
For all that, I took between 11s. and 12s. the first night—it was
Saturday—that I started; and I stuck to it, and took from 7s. to
10s. every night, with more, of course, on Saturday, and it was half
of it profit then. I cleared a good mechanic's earnings at that time
—30s. a week and more. Soon after, I was told, if agreeable, my
wife could have a stall with fried fish opposite a wine vaults just
opened, and she made nearly half as much as I did on my rounds.
I served the public-houses, and soon got known. With some landlords I had the privilege of the parlour, and tap-room, and bar,
when other tradesmen have been kept out. The landlords will say
to me still: "*You* can go in, Fishy." Somehow, I got the name of
"Fishy" then, and I've kept it ever since. There was hospitality in
those days. I've gone into a room in a public-house, used by
mechanics, and one of them has said: "I'll stand fish round, gentlemen"; and I've supplied fifteen penn'orths. Perhaps he was a stranger, such a sort of customer, that wanted to be agreeable. Now, it's
more likely I hear: "Jack, lend us a penny to buy a bit of fried";
and then Jack says: "You be d—d! here, lass, let's have another
pint." The insults and difficulties I've had in the public-house
trade is dreadful.

'I've had my tray kicked over for a lark in a public-house, and
a scramble for my fish, and all gone, and no help and no money for
me. The landlords always prevent such things, when they can,
and interfere for a poor man; but then it's done sudden, and over
in an instant. That sort of thing wasn't the worst. I once had some
powdery stuff flung over me at a parlour door. My fish fell off, for
I jumped, because I felt blinded, and what became of them I don't
know; but I aimed at once for home—it was very late—and had

to feel my way almost like a blind man. I can't tell what I suffered. I found it was something black, for I kept rubbing my face with my apron, and could just tell it came away black. I let myself in with my latch, and my wife was in bed, and I told her to get up and look at my face and get some water, and she thought I was joking, as she was half asleep; but when she got up and got a light, and a glass, she screamed, and said I looked such a shiny image; and so I did, as well as I could see, for it was blacklead—such as they use for grates—that was flung on me. I washed it off, but it wasn't easy, and my face was sore days after.'

OF THE PREPARATION AND QUANTITY OF SHEEP'S TROTTERS, AND OF THE STREET-SELLERS

THE sale of sheep's trotters, as a regular street-trade, is confined to London, Liverpool, Newcastle-on-Tyne, and a few more of our greater towns. The 'trotter,' as it is commonly called, is the boiled foot of the sheep.

From fifteen to twenty years ago glue and size, owing principally to improved modes of manufacture, became cheaper, so that it paid the fellmonger better to dispose of the trotters as an article 'cooked' for the poor, than to the glue-boiler.

The process of cookery is carried on rapidly at the fellmonger's in question. The feet are first scalded for about half an hour. After that from ten to fifteen boys are employed in scooping out the hoofs, which are sold for manure or to manufacturers of Prussian blue, which is extensively used by painters. Women are then employed, forty being an average number, 'to scrape the hair off,'— for hair it is called—quickly, but softly, so that the skin should not be injured, and after that the trotters are boiled for about four hours, and they are then ready for market.

OF THE STREET TRADE IN BAKED POTATOES

THE *baked potato trade*, in the way it is at present carried on, has not been known more than fifteen years in the streets. Before that, potatoes were sometimes roasted as chestnuts are now, but only on a small scale. The trade is more profitable than that in fruit, but continues for but six months of the year.

There are usually from 280 to 300 potatoes in the cwt.; these are cleaned by the huckster, and, when dried, taken in baskets, about a quarter cwt. at a time, to the baker's, to be cooked. They are baked in large tins, and require an hour and a half to do them well. The charge for baking is 9*d.* the cwt., the baker usually finding the tins. They are taken home from the bakehouse in a basket, with a yard and a half of green baize in which they are covered up, and so protected from the cold. The huckster then places them in his can, which consists of a tin with a half-lid; it stands on four legs, and has a large handle to it, while an iron fire-pot is suspended immediately beneath the vessel which is used for holding the potatoes. Directly over the fire-pot is a boiler for hot water. This is concealed within the vessel, and serves to keep the potatoes always hot. Outside the vessel where the potatoes are kept is, at one end, a small compartment for butter and salt, and at the other end another compartment for fresh charcoal. Above the boiler, and beside the lid, is a small pipe for carrying off the steam. These potato-cans are sometimes brightly polished, sometimes painted red, and occasionally brass-mounted. Some of the handsomest are all brass, and some are highly ornamented with brass-mountings. Great pride is taken in the cans. The baked-potato man usually devotes half an hour to polishing them up, and they are mostly kept as bright as silver. The handsomest potato-can is now in Shoreditch. It cost ten guineas, and is of brass mounted with German silver. There are three lamps attached to it, with coloured glass, and of a style to accord with that of the machine; each lamp cost 5*s.*

OF 'TROTTING' OR 'HAWKING' BUTCHERS

These two appellations are, or have been, used somewhat confusedly in the meat trade. Thirty, or forty, or fifty years ago—for each term was mentioned to me—the butcher in question was a man who went 'trotting' on his small horse to the more distant suburbs to sell meat. This was when the suburbs, in any direction, were 'not built up to' as they are now, and the appearance of the trotting butcher might be hailed as saving a walk of a mile, or a mile and a half, to a butcher's shop, for only tradesmen of a smaller capital then opened butcher's shops in the remoter suburbs.

Of 'trotting' butchers, keeping their own horses, there are now

none, but there are still, I am told, about six of the class who
contrive, by hiring, or more frequently borrowing, horses of some
friendly butcher, to live by trotting. These men are all known,
and all call upon known customers—often those whom they have
served in their prosperity, for the trotting butcher is a 'reduced'
man—and are not likely to be succeeded by any in the same line,
or—as I heard is called—'ride' of business.

The present class of street-traders in raw meat are known to the
trade as 'hawking' butchers, and they are as thoroughly street-
sellers as are the game and poultry 'hawkers.' Their number, I am
assured, is never less than 150, and sometimes 200 or even 250.
They have all been butchers, on journeymen butchers, and are
broken down in the one case, or unable to obtain work in the other.
They then 'watch the turn of the markets,' as small meat 'jobbers,'
and—as on the Stock Exchange—'invest,' when they account the
market at the lowest. The meat so purchased is hawked in a large
basket carried on the shoulders, if of a weight too great to be sustained in a basket on the arm. The sale is confined almost entirely
to public-houses, and those at no great distance from the great
meat markets of Newgate, Leadenhall, and Whitechapel. The hawkers do not go to the suburbs. Their principal trade is in pork and
veal,—for those joints weigh lighter, and present a larger surface in
comparison with to weight, than do beef or mutton. The same
may be said of lamb; but of that they do not buy one quarter so
much as of pork or veal.

OF THE STREET-SELLERS
OF HAM-SANDWICHES

THE ham-sandwich-seller carries his sandwiches on a tray or flat
basket, covered with a clean white cloth; he also wears a white
apron, and white sleeves. His usual stand is at the doors of the
theatres.

The trade was unknown until eleven years ago, when a man
who had been unsuccessful in keeping a coffee-shop in Westminster,
found it necessary to look out for some mode of living, and he hit
upon the plan of vending sandwiches, precisely in the present style,
at the theatre doors. The attempt was successful; the man soon
took 10s. a night, half of which was profit. He 'attended' both the

great theatres, and was 'doing well'; but at five or six weeks' end, competitors appeared in the field, and increased rapidly, and so his sale was affected, people being regardless of his urging that he 'was the original ham-sandwich.' The capital required to start in the trade was small; a few pounds of ham, a proportion of loaves, and a little mustard was all that was required, and for this 10s. was ample.

The persons carrying on this trade have been, for the most part, in some kind of service—errand-boys, pot-boys, foot-boys (or pages), or lads engaged about inns. Some few have been mechanics. Their average weekly earnings hardly exceed 5s., but some 'get odd jobs' at other things.

'There are now, sir, at the theatres this (the Strand) side the water, and at Ashley's, the Surrey, and the Vic., two dozen and nine sandwiches.' So said one of the trade, who counted up his brethren for me. This man calculated also that at the Standard, the saloons, the concert-rooms, and at Limehouse, Mile-end, Bethnal-green-road, and elsewhere, there might be more than as many again as those 'working' the theatres—or 70 in all. They are nearly all men, and no boys or girls are now in the trade. The number of these people, when the large theatres were open with the others, was about double what it is now.

The information collected shows that the expenditure in ham-sandwiches, supplied by street-sellers, is 1,820l. yearly, and a consumption of 436,800 sandwiches.

To start in the ham-sandwich street-trade requires 2s. for a basket, 2s. for kettle to boil ham in, 6d. for knife and fork, 2d. for mustard-pot and spoon, 7d. for ½ cwt. of coals, 5s. for ham, 1s. 3d. for bread, 4d. for mustard, 9d. for basket, cloth, and apron, 4d. for over-sleeves—or a capital of 12s. 11d.

OF THE STREET-SELLERS OF BREAD

THE street-trade in bread is not so extensive as might be expected, from the universality of the consumption. It is confined to Petticoat-lane and the poorer districts in that neighbourhood.

One of my elder informants remembered his father telling him that in 1800 and 1801, George III. had set the example of eating brown bread at his one o'clock dinner, but he was sometimes assailed as he passed in his carriage, with the reproachful epithet of

'*Brown* George.' This feeling continues, for the poor people, and even the more intelligent working-men, if cockneys, have still a notion that only 'white' bread is fit for consumption.

Some of these traders have baskets containing the bread offered for street-sale; others have barrows, and one has a barrow resembling a costermonger's, with a long basket made to fit upon it. The dress of these vendors is a light coat of cloth or fustian; corduroy, fustian, or cloth trousers, and a cloth cap or a hat, the whole attire being, what is best understood as 'dusty,' ingrained as it is with flour.

OF THE STREET-SELLERS
OF HOT GREEN PEAS

THE sale of hot green peas in the streets is of great antiquity, that is to say, if the cry of 'hot peas-cod,' recorded by Lydgate (and formerly alluded to), may be taken as having intimated the sale of the same article. In many parts of the country it is, or was, customary to have '*scaldings* of peas,' often held as a sort of rustic feast. The peas were not shelled, but boiled in the pod, and eaten by the pod being dipped in melted butter, with a little pepper, salt, and vinegar, and then drawn through the teeth to extract the peas, the pod being thrown away.

The sellers of green peas have no stands, but carry a round or oval tin pot or pan, with a swing handle; the pan being wrapped round with a thick cloth, to retain the heat. The peas are served out with a ladle, and eaten by the customers, if eaten in the street, out of basins, provided with spoons, by the pea-man. Salt, vinegar, and pepper are applied from the vendor's store, at the customer's discretion.

There are now four men carrying on this trade. They wear no particular dress, 'just what clothes we can get,' said one of them. One, who has been in the trade twenty-five years, was formerly an inn-porter; the other three are ladies' shoemakers in the day-time and pea-sellers in the evening, or at early morning, in any market

OF CATS' AND DOGS'-MEAT DEALERS

THE supply of food for cats and dogs is far greater than may be generally thought. 'Vy, sir,' said one of the dealers to me, 'can you tell me'ow many people's in London?' On my replying, upwards of two millions; 'I don't know nothing vatever,' said my informant, 'about millions, but I think there's a cat to every ten people, aye, and more than that; and so, sir, you can reckon.'

'I must know, for they all knows me, and I sarves about 200 cats and 70 dogs. Mine's a middling trade, but some does far better. Some cats has a hap'orth a day, some every other day; werry few can afford a penn'orth, but times is inferior. Dogs is better pay when you've a connection among 'em.'

The cat and dogs'-meat dealers, or 'carriers,' as they call themselves, generally purchase the meat at the knackers' (horse-slaughterers') yards.

The carriers then take the meat round town, wherever their 'walk' may lie. They sell it to the public at the rate of $2\frac{1}{2}d$. per 1b., and in small pieces, on skewers, at a farthing, a halfpenny, and a penny each. Some carriers will sell as much as a hundred-weight in a day, and about half a hundred-weight is the average quantity disposed of by the carriers in London. Some sell much cheaper than others.

But the trade is much worse now. There are so many at it, they say, that there is barely a living for any. A carrier assured me that he seldom went less than 30, and frequently 40 miles, through the streets every day. The best districts are among the houses of tradesmen, mechanics, and labourers. The coachmen in the mews at the back of the squares are very good customers. 'The work lays thicker there,' said my informant. Old maids are bad, though very plentiful, customers. They cheapen the carriers down so, that they can scarcely live at the business. 'They will pay one halfpenny and owe another, and forget that after a day or two.' The cats' meat dealers generally complain of their losses from bad debts.

One gentleman has as much as 4 lbs. of meat each morning for two Newfoundland dogs; and there was one woman—a black—who used to have as much as 16 pennyworth every day. This person used to get out on the roof of the house and throw it to the cats on the tiles. By this she brought so many stray cats round about the neighbourhood, that the parties in the vicinity complained; it was quite a nuisance. She *would* have the meat always brought to her before ten in the morning, or else she would send to a shop for it, and between ten and eleven in the morning the noise and cries of the hundreds of stray cats attracted to the spot was 'terrible to hear.' When the meat was thrown to the cats on the roof, the riot, and confusion, and fighting, was beyond description. 'A beer-shop man,' I was told, 'was obliged to keep five or six dogs to drive the cats from his walls.'

The generality of the dealers wear a shiny hat, black plush waistcoat and sleeves, a blue apron, corduroy trousers, and a blue and white spotted handkerchief round their necks. Some, indeed, will wear two and three hadkerchiefs around their necks, this being fashionable among them.

OF THE STREET SALE OF DRINKABLES

THE street-sellers of the drinkables, who have now to be considered, belong to the same class as I have described in treating of the sale of street-provisions generally. The buyers are not precisely of the same class, for the street-eatables often supply a meal, but with the exception of the coffee-stalls, and occasionally of the rice-milk, the drinkables are more of a luxury than a meal. Thus the buyers are chiefly those who have 'a penny to spare,' rather than those who have 'a penny to dine upon.'

OF COFFEE-STALL KEEPERS

THE vending of tea and coffee, in the streets, was little if at all known twenty years ago, saloop being then the beverage supplied from stalls to the late and early wayfarers. Nor was it until after 1842 that the stalls approached to anything like their present number, which is said to be upwards of 300—the majority of the proprietors being women.

The best 'pitch' in London is supposed to be at the corner of Duke-street, Oxford-street. The proprietor of that stall is said to take full 30s. of a morning, in halfpence. One stall-keeper, I was informed, when 'upon the drink' thinks nothing of spending his 10l. or 15l. in a week. A party assured me that once, when the stall-keeper above mentioned was away 'on the spree,' he took up his stand there, and got from 4s. to 5s. in the course of ten minutes, at the busy time of the morning.

Some of the stall-keepers make their appearance at twelve at night, and some not till three or four in the morning. Those that come out at midnight, are for the accommodation of the 'night-walkers'—'fast gentlemen' and loose girls; and those that come out in the morning, are for the accommodation of the working men.

It is, I may add, piteous enough to see a few young and good-looking girls, some without the indelible mark of habitual depravity on their countenances, clustering together for warmth round a coffee-stall, to which a penny expenditure, or the charity of the proprietor, has admitted them. The thieves do not resort to the coffee-stalls, which are so immediately under the eye of the policeman.

OF THE STREET SALE OF GINGER-BEER, SHERBET, LEMONADE, &c.

THE street-trade in ginger-beer—now a very considerable traffic—was not known to any extent until about thirty years ago.

About five years ago 'fountains' for the production of ginger-beer became common in the streets. The largest and handsomest ginger-beer fountain in London was—I speak of last summer—in use at the East-end, usually standing in Petticoat-lane, and is the property of a dancing-master. It is made of mahogany, and presents somewhat the form of an upright piano on wheels. It has two pumps, and the brass of the pump-handles and the glass receivers is always kept bright and clean, so that the whole glitters handsomely to the light. Two persons 'serve' at this fountain; and on a fine Sunday morning, from six to one; that being the best trading time, they take 7*l*. or 8*l*. in halfpennies—for 'the beer' is ½*d*. a glass—and 2*l*. each other day of the week. This machine, as it may be called, is drawn by two ponies, said to be worth 10*l*. a-piece; and the whole cost is pronounced—perhaps with a sufficient exaggeration—to have been 150*l*. There were, in the same neighbourhood, two more fountains on a similar scale, but commoner, each drawn by only one pony instead of the aristocratic 'pair.'

OF THE STREET-SELLERS OF HOT ELDER WINE

THE sale of hot elder wine in the streets is one of the trades which have been long established, but it is only within these eight or ten years that it has been carried on in its present form. It continues for about four months in the winter.

Elder wine is made from the berries of the elder-tree. Elder syrup—also made from the berries—was formerly famous in the north of England as a curative for colds, and was frequently taken, with a small admixture of rum, at bedtime. Some of the street-sellers make the wine themselves; the majority, however, buy it of the British wine makers.

The apparatus in which the wine is now kept for sale in the streets is of copper or brass, and is sometimes 'handsome.' It is generally an urn of an oblong form, erected on a sort of pedestal, with the lid or top ornamented with brass mouldings, &c. The interior of these urns holds theree or four quarts of elder wine, which is surrounded with boiling water, and the water and wine are kept up to boiling pitch by means of a charcoal fire at the foot of the vessel.

OF MILK SELLING IN ST. JAMES'S PARK

THE principal sale of milk from the cow is in St. James's Park. The once fashionable drink known as syllabubs—the milk being drawn warm from the cow's udder, upon a portion of wine, sugar, spice, &c.—is now unknown. As the sellers of milk in the park are merely the servants of cow-keepers, and attend to the sale as a part of their business, no lengthened notice is required.

The milk-sellers obtain leave from the Home Secretary, to ply their trade in the park. There are eight stands in the summer, and as many cows, but in the winter there are only four cows.

A somewhat sour-tempered old woman, speaking as if she had been crossed in love, but experienced in this trade, gave me the following acount:

'It's not at all a lively sort of life, selling milk from the cows, though some thinks it's a gay time in the Park! I've often been dull enough, and could see nothing to interest one, sitting alongside a cow. People drink new milk for their health, and I've served a good many such. They're mostly young women, I think, that's delicate, and makes the most of it. There's twenty women, and more, to one man what drinks new milk. If they was set to some good hard work, it would do them more good than new milk, or ass's milk either, I think. Let them go on a milk-walk to cure them—that's what I say. Some children come pretty regularly with their nurses to drink new milk. Some bring their own china mugs to drink it out of; nothing less was good enough for them. I've seen the nurse-girls frightened to death about the mugs. I've heard one young child say to another: "I shall tell mama that Caroline spoke to a mechanic, who came and shook hands with her." The girl was as red as fire, and said it was her brother. Oh, yes, there's a deal of brothers comes to look for their sisters in the Park.'

OF THE STREET SALE OF MILK

DURING the summer months milk is sold in Smithfield, Billingsgate, and other markets, and on Sundays in Battersea-fields, Clapham-common, Camberwell-green, Hampstead-heath, and similar places. About twenty men are engaged in this sale. They usually wear a smock frock, and have the cans and yoke used by the regular milk-sellers; they are not itinerant. The skim milk—for they sell none else—is purchased at the dairies at 1½d. a quart, and even the skim milk is also further watered by the street-sellers. Their cry is 'Half-penny half-pint! Milk!' The tin measure however in which the milk-and-water is served is generally a 'slang', and contains but half of the quantity proclaimed. The purchasers are chiefly boys and children; rarely men, and never costermongers, I was told, 'for they reckon milk sickly.'

OF THE STREET SALE OF CURDS
AND WHEY

THE preparations of milk which comprise the street-trade, are curds and whey and rice-milk, the oldest street-sellers stating that these were a portion of the trade in their childhood. The one is a summer, and the other a winter traffic, and both are exclusively in the hands of the same middle-aged and elderly women.

The street-sale is confined to stalls; the stall, which is the ordinary stand, being covered with a white cloth, or in some cases an oil-cloth, and on this the curds, in a bright tin kettle or pan, are deposited. There are six mugs on the board, and a spoon in each, but those who affect a more modern style have glasses. One of the neatest stalls, as regards the display of glass, and the bright cleanli-

THE COSTER BOY AND GIRL TOSSING THE PIEMAN

LONG-SONG SELLER

ness of the vessel containing the curds, is in Holborn; but the curd-seller there has only an average business.

OF THE STREET-SELLERS OF RICE-MILK

To make rice-milk, the street-seller usually boils four quarts, of the regular measure, of 'skim' with one pound of rice, which has been previously boiled in water. An hour suffices for the boiling of the milk; and the addition of the rice, swollen by the boiling water, increases the quantity to six quarts. No other process is observed, except that some sweeten their rice-milk before they offer it for sale; the majority, however, sweeten it to the customer's liking when he is 'served,' unless—to use the words of one informant—'he have a werry, werry sweet tooth indeed, sir; and that can't be stood.'

OF WATER-CARRIERS

It may surprise many to learn that there are still existing water-carriers in London, and some of them depending upon the trade for a livelihood; while others, the 'odd men' of the neighbourhood, carry pails of spring water to the publicans or eating-house keepers, who may not have servants to send to the nearest pump for it, and who require it fresh and cool for those who drink it at their meals. Of these men there are, as near as I can ascertain, from 100 to 150; their charge is 1*d.* per pail. Their earnings per day 6*d.* to 1*s.*

An old man who sells water on the summer Sunday mornings, generally leaving off his sale at church-time, told me that his best customers were ladies and gentlemen who loved an early walk, and bought of him 'as it looked like a bit of country life,' he supposed, more than from being thirsty. When such customers were not inhabitants of the neighbourhood, they came to him to ask their way, or to make inquiries concerning the localities. Sometimes he dispensed water to men who 'looked as if they had been on the loose all night. One gentleman,' he said, 'looks sharp about him, and puts a dark-coloured stuff—very likely it's brandy—into the two or three glasses of water which he drinks every Sunday, or which he used to drink rather, for I missed him all last summer, I think. His hand trembled like an aspen; he mostly gave me 6*d.*' The water-seller spoke with some indignation of boys, and sometimes men, going to the well on a Sunday morning and 'drinking out of their own tins that they'd taken with 'em.'

OF THE STREET-SELLERS OF PASTRY AND CONFECTIONARY

THE cooked provisions sold in the streets, it has been before stated, consist of three kinds—solids, liquids, and pastry and confectionary. The two first have now been fully described, but the last still remains to be set forth.

The street pastry may be best characterised as of a *strong* flavour. This, is for the most part, attributable to the use of old or rancid butter,—possessing the all-important recommendations of cheapness,—or to the substitution of lard, dripping, or some congenial substance. The 'strong' taste, however, appears to possess its value in the estimation of street pastry-buyers, especially among the boys.

The articles of pastry sold in the London streets are meat and fruit pies, boiled meat and kidney puddings, plum 'duff' or pudding, and an almost infinite variety of tarts, cakes, buns, and biscuits; while the confectionary consists of all the several preparations included under the wide denomination of 'sweet-stuff,' as well as the more 'medicinal' kind known as 'cough drops'; in addition to these there are the more 'aristocratic' delicacies recently introduced into street traffic, viz., penny raspberry creams and ices.

OF STREET PIEMEN

THE itinerant trade in pies is of the most ancient of the street callings of London. The meat pies are made of beef or mutton; the fish pies of eels; the fruit of apples, currants, gooseberries, plums, damsons, cherries, raspberries, or rhubarb, according to the season —and occasionally of mince-meat. A few years ago the street pie-trade was very profitable, but it has been almost destroyed by the 'pie-shops,' and further, the few remaining street-dealers say 'the people now haven't the pennies to spare.' Summer fairs and races are the best places for the piemen.

At the public-houses a few pies are sold, and the pieman makes a practice of 'looking in' at all the taverns on his way. Here his customers are found principally in the tap-room. 'Here's all 'ot!'

the pieman cries, as he walks in; 'toss or buy! up and win 'em!' This is the only way that the pies can be got rid of. 'If it wasn't for tossing we shouldn't sell one.'

To 'toss the pieman' is a favourite pastime with costermongers' boys and all that class; some of whom aspire to the repute of being gourmands, and are critical of the quality of the comestible. If the pieman win the toss, he receives 1*d.* without giving a pie; if he lose, he hands it over for nothing. The pieman himself never 'tosses,' but always calls head or tail to his customer. At the week's end it comes to the same thing, they say, whether they toss or not, or rather whether they win or lose the toss: 'I've taken as much as 2*s.* 6*d.* at tossing, which I shouldn't have had if I hadn't done so. Very few people buy without tossing, and the boys in particular. Gentlemen "out on the spree" at the late public-houses will frequently toss when they don't want the pies, and when they win they will amuse themselves by throwing the pies at one another, or at me.'

OF THE STREET-SELLERS OF BOILED PUDDINGS

THE sale of *boiled* puddings, meat and currant—which might perhaps be with greater correctness called dumplings—has not been known in London, I was informed by one in the trade, more than twelve or fourteen years. The ingredients for the meat puddings are not dissimilar to those I have described as required for the meat pies, but the puddings are boiled, in cotton bags, in coppers or large pans, and present the form of a round ball. The charge is a half-penny each.

OF THE STREET-SELLERS OF PLUM 'DUFF' OR DOUGH

PLUM dough is one of the street-eatables—though perhaps it is rather a violence to class it with the street-pastry—which is usually made by the vendors. It is simply a boiled plum, or currant, pudding, of the plainest description. It is sometimes made in the rounded form of the plum-pudding; but more frequently in the 'roly-poly' style. Hot pudding used to be of much more extensive sale in the streets. One informant told me that twenty or thirty years ago, batter, or Yorkshire, pudding, 'with plums in it,' was a popular street business. The 'plums,' as in the orthodox plum-puddings, are raisins. The street-vendors of plum 'duff' are now very few, only six as an average, and generally women, or if a man be the salesman he is the woman's husband.

OF THE STREET-SELLERS OF CAKES, TARTS, &c.

THESE men and boys—for there are very few women or girls in the trade—constitute a somewhat numerous class. They are computed (including Jews) at 150 at the least, all regular hands, with an addition, perhaps, of 15 or 20, who seek to earn a few pence on a Sunday, but have some other, though poorly remunerative, employment on the week-days. The cake and tart-sellers in the streets have been, for the most part, mechanics or servants; a fifth of the body, however, have been brought up to this or to some other street-calling.

The cake-men carry their goods on a tray slung round their shoulders when they are offering their delicacies for sale, and on their heads when not engaged in the effort to do business. They are to be found in the vicinity of all public places. Their goods are generally arranged in pairs on the trays; in bad weather they are covered with a green cloth.

None of the street-vendors make the articles they sell; indeed, the diversity of those articles renders that impossible. Among the regular articles of this street-sale are 'Coventrys,' or three-cornered puffs with jam inside; raspberry biscuits; cinnamon biscuits; 'chonkeys,' or a kind of mince-meat baked in crust; Dutch butter-cakes; Jews' butter-cakes; 'bowlas,' or round tarts made of sugar, apple, and bread; 'jumbles,' or thin crisp cakes made of treacle, butter, and flour; and jams, or open tarts with a little preserve in the centre. All these things are made for the street-sellers by about a dozen Jew pastry-cooks, the most of whom reside about Whitechapel.

OF THE STREET-SELLERS OF GINGERBREAD-NUTS, &c.

THE sale of gingerbread, as I have previously observed, was much more extensive in the streets than it is at present. Indeed, what was formerly known in the trade as 'toy' gingerbread is now unseen in the streets, except occasionally, and that only when the whole has not been sold at the neighbouring fairs, at which it is still offered. But, even at these fairs, the principal, and sometimes the only, toy gingerbread that is vended is the 'cock in breeches;' a formidable-looking bird, with his nether garments of gold. Twenty or thirty years ago, 'king George on horseback' was popular in gingerbread. His Majesty, wearing a gilt crown, gilt spurs, and a gilt sword, bestrode the gilt saddle of his steed, and was eaten with great relish by his juvenile subjects. There were also sheep, and dogs, and other animals, all adorned in a similar manner, and looking as if they had been formed in close and faithful imitation of children's first attempts at cattle drawing. These edible toys were then sold in 'white,' as well as in 'brown' gingerbread, the white being the same in all other respects as the brown, except that a portion of sugar was used in its composition instead of treacle.

There are now only two men in London who make their own gingerbread-nuts for sale in the streets.

OF THE STREET-SELLERS OF HOT-CROSS BUNS, AND OF CHELSEA BUNS

PERHAPS no cry—though it is only for one morning—is more familiar to the ears of a Londoner, than that of 'One-a-penny, two-a-penny, hot-cross buns,' on Good Friday. The sale is unknown in the Irish capital; for among Roman Catholics, Good Friday, I need hardly say, is a strict fast, and the eggs in the buns prevent their being used. One London gentleman, who spoke of fifty years ago, told me that the street-bun-sellers used to have a not unpleasing distich. On reflection, however, my informant could not be certain whether he had heard this distich cried, or had remembered hearing the elders of his family speak of it as having been cried, or how it was impressed upon his memory. It seems hardly in accordance with the usual style of street poetry:—

'One-a-penny, two-a-penny, hot-cross buns!
If your daughters will not eat them, give them to your sons.
But if you hav'n't any of those pretty little elves,
You cannot then do better than eat them all yourselves.'

A tradesman who had resided more than fifty years in the Borough had, in his boyhood, heard, but not often, this ridiculous cry:—

> 'One-a-penny, poker; two-a-penny tongs,
> One-a-penny; two-a-penny, hot-cross buns.'

OF MUFFIN AND CRUMPET-SELLING IN THE STREETS

THE street-sellers of muffins and crumpets rank among the old street-tradesmen. It is difficult to estimate their numbers, but they were computed for me at 500, during the winter months. They are for the most part boys, young men, or old men, and some of them infirm. There are a few girls in the trade, but very few women.

The ringing of the muffin-man's bell—attached to which the pleasant associations are not a few—was prohibited by a recent Act of Parliament, but the prohibition has been as inoperative as that which forbade the use of a drum to the costermonger, for the muffin bell still tinkles along the streets, and is rung vigorously in the suburbs.

I did not hear of any street-seller who made the muffins or crumpets he vended. Indeed, he could not make the small quantity required, so as to be remunerative. The muffins are bought of the bakers, and at prices to leave a profit of 4*d*. in 1*s*. Some bakers give thirteen to the dozen to the street-sellers whom they know. The muffin-man carries his delicacies in a basket, wherein they are well swatched in flannel, to retain the heat: 'People likes them warm, sir,' an old man told me, 'to satisfy them they're fresh, and they almost always *are* fresh; but it can't matter so much about their being warm, as they have to be toasted again. I only wish good butter was a sight cheaper, and that would make the muffins go. Butter's half the battle.'

A sharp London lad of fourteen, whose father had been a journeyman baker, and whose mother (a widow) kept a small chandler's shop, gave me the following account:—

'I turns out with muffins and crumpets, sir, in October, and continues until it gets well into the spring, according to the weather. I carries a fust-rate article; werry much so. If you was to taste 'em, sir, you'd say the same. If I sells three dozen muffins at ½*d*. each,

and twice that in crumpets, it's a werry fair day, werry fair; all
beyond that is a *good* day. The profit on the three dozen and the
others is 1*s*., but that's a great help, really a wonderful help, to
mother, for I should be only mindin' the shop at home. Perhaps
I clears 4*s*. a week, perhaps more, perhaps less; but that's about it,
sir. Some does far better than that, and some can't hold a candle
to it. If I has a hextra day's sale, mother'll give me 3*d*. to go to the
play, and that hencourages a young man, you know, sir. If there's
any unsold, a coffee-shop gets them cheap, and puts 'em off cheap
again next morning. My best customers is genteel houses, 'cause
I sells a genteel thing. I likes wet days best, 'cause there's werry
respectable ladies what don't keep a servant, and they buys to save
themselves going out. We're a great conwenience to the ladies, sir
—a great conwenience to them as likes a slap-up tea. I *have* made
1*s*. 8*d*. in a day; that was my best. I once took only 2½*d*.—I don't
know why—that was my worst. The shops don't love me—I puts
their noses out. Sunday is no better day than others, or werry little.
I can read, but wish I could read easier.'

OF THE STREET SALE OF SWEET-STUFF

IN this sale there are now engaged, as one of the most intelligent
of the class calculated, 200 individuals, exclusive of twenty or
thirty Jew boys. The majority of the sellers are also the manufacturers of the articles they vend.

Treacle and sugar are the ground-work of the manufacture of
all kinds of sweet-stuff. 'Hard-bake,' 'almond toffy,' 'halfpenny
lollipops,' 'black balls,' the cheaper 'bulls eyes,' and 'squibs' are
all made of treacle. One informant sold more of treacle rock than
of anything else, as it was dispensed in larger half-penny- worths,
and no one else made it in the same way. Of peppermint rock and
sticks he made a good quantity.

Brandy balls are made of sugar, water, peppermint, and a little
cinnamon. Rose acid, which is a 'transparent' sweet, is composed
of loaf sugar at 6½*d*. per lb., coloured with cochineal. The articles
sold in 'sticks' are pulled into form along a hook until they present
the whitish, or speckled colour desired. A quarter of a stone of
materials will for instance, be boiled for forty minutes, and then
pulled a quarter of an hour, until it is sufficiently crisp and will

'set' without waste. The flavouring—or 'scent' as I heard it called in the trade—now most in demand is peppermint. Gibraltar rock and Wellington pillars used to be flavoured with ginger, but these 'sweeties' are exploded.

OF THE STREET-SELLERS OF COUGH DROPS AND OF MEDICAL CONFECTIONARY

THE street-traders in cough drops and their accompaniments, however, do not now exceed six, and of them only two—who are near relatives—manufacture their own stock-in-trade. I here treat of the street trade in 'cough drops,' as a branch of the itinerant sweet-stuff trade.

The two principal vendors of cough drops wheel their stalls, which are fixed upon barrows, to different parts of town, but one principal stand is in Holbrrn. On their boards are displayed the cough cures, both in the form of 'sticks' and 'drops', and a model of a small distillery. The portion inclosing the still is painted to resemble brick-work, and a tin tube, or worm, appears to carry the distillation to a receiver. Horehound, colts-foot, and some other herbs lie in a dried state on the stall, but principally horehound, to which popular (street) opinion seems to attach the most and the greatest virtues. There are also on the stalls a few bottles, tied up in the way they are dispensed from a regular practitioner, while the cough drops are in the form of sticks ($\frac{1}{2}d$. each), also neatly wrapped in paper. The cry is both expressive and simply descriptive —'Long life candy! Candy from herbs!'

OF THE STREET-SELLERS OF ICES AND OF ICE CREAM

I HAVE already treated of the street luxury of pine-apples, and have now to deal with the greater street rarity of ice-creams.

A quick-witted street-seller—but not in the 'provision' line— conversing with me upon this subject, said: 'Ices in the streets! Aye, and there'll be jellies next, and then mock turtle, and then the real ticket, sir. I don't know nothing of the difference between the real thing and the mock, but I once had some cheap mock in an eating-house, and it tasted like stewed tripe with a little glue.

You'll keep your eyes open, sir, at the Great Exhibition; and you'll see a new move or two in the streets, take my word for it. Penny glasses of champagne, I shouldn't wonder.'

Notwithstanding the sanguine anticipation of my street friend, the sale of ices in the streets has not been such as to offer any great encouragement to a perseverance in the traffic.

OF THE STREET-SELLERS OF STATIONERY, LITERATURE, AND THE FINE ARTS

THE street-sellers of stationery, literature, and the fine arts differ from all before treated of in the *general*, though far from universal, education of the sect. They constitute principally the class of street-orators, known in these days as 'patterers,' and formerly termed 'mountebanks,'—people who, in the words of Strutt, strive to 'help off their wares by pompous speeches, in which little regard is paid either to truth or propriety.' To patter, is a slang term, meaning to speak. To indulge in this kind of oral puffery, of course, requires a certain exercise of the intellect, and it is the conscious-ness of their mental superiority which makes the patterers look down upon the costermongers as an inferior body, with whom they object either to be classed or to associate. The scorn of some of the 'patterers' for the mere costers is as profound as the contempt of the pickpocket for the pure beggar.

For the present we have only to deal with that portion of the 'pattering' body who are engaged in the street sale of literature— or the 'paper-workers' as they call themselves. The latter include the 'running patterers,' or 'death-hunters'; being men (no women) engaged in vending last dying speeches and confessions—in hawk-ing 'se-cond edi-tions' of newspapers—or else in 'working,' that is to say, in getting rid of what are technically termed 'cocks'; which, in polite language, means accounts of fabulous duels be-tween ladies of fashion—of apocryphal elopements, or fictitious love-letters of sporting noblemen and certain young milliners not a hundred miles from the spot—'cooked' assassinations and sudden deaths of eminent individuals—pretended jealous affrays between Her Majesty and the Prince Consort (but these papers are now never worked)—or awful tragedies, including mendacious murders, impossible robberies, and delusive suicides.

Occasionally, however, the running patterer (who is especially literary) transmigrates into a standing one, betaking himself to 'board work,' as it is termed in street technology, and stopping at ithe corners of thoroughfares with a large pictorial placard raised upon a pole, and glowing with a highly-coloured exaggeration of the interesting terrors of the pamphlet he has for sale. This is either 'The Life of Calcraft, the Hangman,' 'The Diabolical Practices of Dr. —— on his Patients when in a state of Mesmerism,' or 'The Secret Doings at the White House, Soho,' and other similar attractively-repulsive details. Akin to this 'board work' is the practice of what is called 'strawing,' or selling straws in the street, and giving away with them something that is either really or fictionally forbidden to be sold,—as indecent papers, political songs, and the like. This practice, however, is now seldom resorted to, while the sale of 'secret papers' is rarely carried on in public. It is true, there are three or four patterers who live chiefly by professing to dispose of 'sealed packets' of obscene drawings and cards for gentlemen; but this is generally a trick adopted to extort money from old debauchees, young libertines, and people of degraded or diseased tastes; for the packets, on being opened, seldom contain anything but an odd number of some defunct periodical. There is, however, a large traffic in such secret papers carried on in what is called 'the public-house trade,' that is to say, by itinerant 'paper-workers' (mostly women), who never make their appearance in the streets.

There is another species of patterer, who, though usually included among the standing patterers, belongs rather to an intermediate class, viz., those who neither stand nor '*run*,' as they descant upon what they sell; but those walk at so slow a rate that, though never stationary, they can hardly be said to move. These are the reciters of dialogues, litanies, and the various street 'squibs' upon passing events; they also include the public propounders of conundrums, and the 'hundred and fifty popular song' enumerators—such as are represented in the engraving here given. Closely connected with them are the 'chaunters,' or those who do not cry, but (if one may so far stretch the English language) *sing* the contents of the 'papers' they vend.

In addition to them there are many others vending 'papers' in the public thoroughfares, who are mere traders resorting to no other acts for the disposal of their goods than a simple cry or exposition of them; and many of these are but poor, humble, struggling, and inoffensive dealers. They do not puff or represent what they have to sell as what it is not—(allowing them a fair commercial latitude). They are not of the 'enterprising' class of street tradesmen. Among these are the street-sellers of stationery— such as note-paper, envelopes, pens, ink, pencils, sealing-wax, and wafers. Belonging to the same class, too, are the street-vendors of almanacs, pocket-books, memorandum and account-books. Then there are the sellers of odd numbers of periodicals and broadsheets, and those who vend either playing cards, conversation cards, stenographic cards, and (at Epsom, Ascot, &c.) racing cards. Besides these, again, there are the vendors of illustrated cards, such as those embellished with engravings of the Crystal Palace, Views of the Houses of Parliament, as well as the gelatine poetry cards—all of whom, with the exception of the racing-card sellers (who belong generally to the pattering tribe), partake of the usual characteristics of the street-selling class.

After these may be enumerated the vendors of old engravings out of inverted umbrellas, and the hawkers of coloured pictures in frames. Then there are the old book-stalls and barrows, and 'the pinners-up,' as they are termed, or sellers of old songs pinned against the wall, as well as the vendors of manuscript music. Moreover, appertaining to the same class, there are the vendors of playbills and 'books of the performance' outside the theatre; and lastly, the pretended sellers of tracts—such as the Lascars and others, who use this kind of street traffic as a cloak for the more profitable trade of begging.

OF THE FORMER AND PRESENT STREET-PATTERERS

OF the street-patterers the running (or flying) trader announces the contents of the paper he is offering for sale, as he proceeds on his mission. It is usually the detail of some 'barbarious and horrible murder,' or of some extraordinary occurrence—such as the attack on Marshal Haynau—which has roused public attention; or the paper announced as descriptive of a murder, or of some exciting event, may in reality be some odd number of a defunct periodical. 'It's astonishing,' said one patterer to me, 'how few people ever complain of having been took in. It hurts their feelings to lose a halfpenny, but it hurts their pride too much, when they're had, to grumble in public about it.'

OF THE HABITS, OPINIONS, MORALS, AND RELIGION OF PATTERERS GENERALLY

In order that I might omit nothing which will give the student of that curious phase of London life in London streets—the condition of the patterers—a clear understanding of the subject, I procured the following account from an educated gentleman: 'I had lived,' he said, 'more than a year among the tradesmen and tramps, who herd promiscuously together in low lodging-houses. One afternoon I was taking tea at the same table with a brace of patterers. They eyed me with suspicion; but, determined to know their proceedings, I launched out the only cant word I had then learned. They spoke of going to Chatham. Of course, I knew the place, and asked them, "Where do you stall to in the huey?" which, fairly translated, means, "Where do you lodge in the town?" Convinced that I was "fly," one of them said, "We drop the main toper (go off the main road) and slink into the crib (house) in the back drum (street)." After some altercation with the "mot" of the "ken" (mistress of the lodging-house) about the cleanliness of a knife or fork, my new acquaintance began to arrange "ground", &c., for the night's work. I got into their confidence by degrees; and I give below a vocabulary of their talk to each other:

Word.	Meaning.
Crabshells	Shoes.
Kite	Paper.
Nests	Varieties.
Sticky	Wax.
Toff	Gentleman.
Burerk	Lady.
Camister	Minister.
Crocus	Doctor.
Bluff	An excuse.
Balmy	Insane.
Mill Tag	A shirt.
Smeesh	A shift.

Word.					Meaning.
Hay-bag	.	.	.	.	A woman.
Doxy .	.	.	.	.	A wife.
Flam .	.	.	.	.	A lie.
Teviss	.	.	.	.	A shilling.
Bull .	.	.	.	.	A crown.
Flag .	.	.	.	.	An apron.

'The cant or slang of the patterer is not the cant of the coster-monger, but a system of their own. As in the case of costers, it is so interlarded with their general remarks, while their ordinary language is so smothered and subdued, that unless when they are professionally engaged and talking of their wares, they might almost pass for foreigners.'

It would be a mistake to suppose that the patterers, although a vagrant, are a disorganized class. There is a telegraphic dispatch between them, through the length and breadth of the land. If two patterers (previously unacquainted) meet in the provinces, the following, or something like it, will be their conversation:—'Can you "voker romeny" (can you speak cant)? What is your "mone-keer" (name)?'—Perhaps it turns out that one is 'White-headed Bob,' and the other 'Plymouth Ned.' They have a 'shant of gatter' (pot of beer) at the nearest 'boozing ken' (ale-house), and swear eternal friendship to each other. The old saying, that 'When the liquor is in, the wit is out,' is remarkably fulfilled on these occasions, for they betray to the 'flatties' (natives) all their profits and pro-ceedings.

If a patterer has been 'crabbed,' that is (offended) at any of the 'cribbs' (houses), he mostly chalks a signal on or near the door. I give one or two instances:

◇ 'Bone,' meaning good.

▽ 'Cooper'd,' spoiled by the imprudence of some other patterer.

□ 'Gammy,' likely to have you taken up.

☉ 'Flummut,' sure of a month in quod.

In most lodging-houses there is an old man who is the guide to every 'walk' in the vicinity, and who can tell every house, on every round, that is 'good for a cold 'tater.' In many cases there is over the kitchen mantelpiece a map of the district, dotted here and there with memorandums of failure or success.

Patterers are fond of carving their names and avocations about the houses they visit. The old jail at Dartford has been some years a 'padding-ken.' In one of the rooms appears the following autographs:

'Jemmy, the Rake, bound to Bristol; bad beds, but no bugs. Thank God for all things.'

'Razor George and his moll slept here the day afore Christmas; just out of "stir" (jail), for "muzzling a peeler." '

'Scotch Mary, with "driz" (lace), bound to Dover and back, please God.'

Sometimes these inscriptions are coarse and obscene; sometimes very well written and orderly. Nor do they want illustrations.

The patterer sometimes gets 'out of stock,' and is obliged, at no great sacrifice of conscience, to 'patter' in another strain. In every large town sham official documents, with crests, seals, and signatures, can be got for half-a-crown. Armed with these, the patterer becomes a 'lurker,'—that is, an impostor; his papers certify any and every 'ill that flesh is heir to.' Shipwreck is called a 'shake lurk;' loss by fire is a 'glim.' Sometimes the petitioner has had a horse, which has dropped dead with the mad staggers; or has a wife ill or dying, and six or seven children at once sickening of the small-pox. Children are borrowed to support the appearance; the case is certified by the minister and churchwardens of a parish which exists only in imagination; and as many people dislike the trouble of investigation, the patterer gets enough to raise a stock in trade, and divides the spoil between the swag-shop and the gin-palace. Sometimes they are detected, and get a 'drag' (three months in prison).

OF THE CHAUNTERS

In the old times, the jougeleurs and jestours were assisted by the chaunters. In the present day the running patterer is accompanied generally by a chaunter, so presenting a further point of resemblance between ancient and modern street-folk. The chaunter now not only sings, but fiddles, for within these few years the running patterers, to render their performances more attractive, are sometimes accompanied by musicians.

I am told, however, that there are only fifty running patterers who are regularly their own chaunters, fiddling to their songs, while the mob work as usual, or one man sings, or speaks and sings, with the chaunter. Two of these men are known as Brummagem Jack, and the Country Paganini. From twenty to thirty patterers, however, are chaunters also, when they think the occasion requires it.

'Next to murders, fires are tidy browns,' I was told by a patterer experienced both in 'murders' and 'fires.' The burning of the old Houses of Parliament was very popular among street-sellers, and for the reason which ensures popularity to a commercial people; it was a source of profit, and was certainly made the most of. It was the work of incendiaries,—of ministers, to get rid of perplexing papers,—of government officers with troublesome accounts to balance,—of a sporting lord, for a heavy wager,—of a conspiracy of builders,—and of 'a unsuspected party.' The older 'hands' with whom I conversed on the subject, all agreed in stating that they 'did well' on the fire.

OF POLITICAL LITANIES, DIALOGUES, ETC.

To 'work a litany' in the streets is considered one of the higher exercises of professional skill in the part of the patterer. In working this, a clever patterer—who will not scruple to introduce anything out of his head which may strike him as suitable to his audience— is very particular in his choice of a mate, frequently changing his ordinary partner, who may be good 'at a noise' or a ballad, but not have sufficient acuteness or intelligence to patter politics as if he understood what he was speaking about. I am told that there are not twelve patterers in London whom a critical professor of street elocution will admit to be capable of 'working a catechism' or a litany.

This branch of a street profession continued to be followed, half surreptitiously, until after the subsidence of the political ferment consequent on the establishment of a new franchise and the partial abolition of an old one. The calling, however, has never been popular among street purchasers, and I believe that it is sometimes followed by a street-patterer as much from the promptings of the pride of art as from the hope of gain.

OF 'COCKS', ETC.

IT is necessary to give a short account of a few of the best and
longest known of those stereotyped 'literary forgeries,' if so they
may be called; no new cocks, except for an occasion, have been
printed for some years.

One of the stereotyped cocks is, the 'Married Man Caught in a
Trap.' One man had known it sold 'for years and years,' and it
served, he said, when there was any police report in the papers
about sweethearts in coal-cellars, &c. The illustration embraces
two compartments. In one a severe-looking female is assaulting a
man, whose hat has been knocked off by the contents of a water-
jug, which a very stout woman is pouring on his head from a
window. In the other compartment, as if from an adjoining room,
two women look on encouragingly. The subject matter, however,
is in no accordance with the title or the embellishment. It is a love-
letter from John S—n to his most 'adorable Mary.' He expresses
the ardour of his passion, and then twits his adored with something
beyond a flirtation with Robert E—, a 'decoyer of female innoc-
ence.' Placably overlooking this, however, John S—n continues:—

'My dearest angel consent to my request, and keep me no longer
in suspense—nothing, on my part, shall ever be wanting to make you
happy and comfortable. My apprenticeship will expire in four months
from hence, when I intend to open a shop in the small ware line, and
with your abilities in dress-making and self-adjusting stay-maker, and
the assistance of a few female mechanics, we shall be able to realize an
independency.'

'Many a turn in seductions talked about in the papers and not
talked about nowhere,' said one man, 'has that slum served for,
besides other things, such as love-letters, and confessions of a certain lady in this neighbourhood.'

OF THE LOW LODGING-HOUSES OF LONDON

THE patterers, as a class, usually frequent the low lodging-houses.
I shall therefore now proceed to give some further information
touching the abodes of these people—reminding the reader that I
am treating of patterers in general, and not of any particular order,
as the 'paper workers.'

In applying the epithet 'low' to these places, I do but adopt the word commonly applied, either in consequence of the small charge for lodging, or from the character of their frequenters.

The proprietors of these lodging-houses mostly have been, I am assured, vagrants, or, to use the civiller and commoner word, 'travellers' themselves, and therefore sojourners, on all necessary occasions, in such places. In four cases out of five I believe this to be the case. The proprietors have raised capital sufficient to start with, sometimes by gambling at races, sometimes by what I have often, and very vaguely, heard described as a 'run of luck'; and sometimes, I am assured, by the proceeds of direct robbery. A few of the proprietors may be classed as capitalists. One of them, who has a country house in Hampstead, has six lodging-houses in or about Thrawl-street, Whitechapel. He looks in at each house every Saturday, and calls his deputies—for he has a deputy in each house—to account; he often institutes a stringent check. He gives a poor fellow money to go and lodge in one of his houses, and report the number present. Sometimes the person so sent meets with the laconic repulse—'Full'; and woe to the deputy if his return do not evince this fulness. Perhaps one in every fifteen of the low lodging-houses in town is also a beer-shop. Very commonly so in the country.

To 'start' a low lodging-house is not a very costly matter. Furniture which will not be saleable in the ordinary course of auction, or of any traffic, is bought by a lodging-house 'starter.' A man possessed of some money, who took an interest in a brick-layer, purchased for 20*l*., when the Small Pox Hospital, by King's-cross, was pulled down, a sufficiency of furniture for *four* lodging-houses, in which he 'started' the man in question. None others would buy the furniture, from a dread of infection.

Some of the lodging-houses present no appearance differing from that of ordinary houses; except, perhaps, that their exterior is dirtier. Some of the older house have long flat windows on the ground-floor, in which there is rather more paper, or other substitutes, than glass. 'The windows there, sir,' remarked one man, 'are not to let the light in, but to keep the cold out.'

In the abodes in question there seems to have become tacitly established an arrangement as to what character of lodgers shall resort thither; the thieves, the prostitutes, and the better class of street-sellers or traders, usually resorting to the houses where they will meet the same class of persons. The patterers reside chiefly in Westminster and Whitechapel.

Some of the lodging-houses are of the worst class of low brothels, and some may even be described as brothels for children.

The beds are of flock, and as regards the mere washing of the rug, sheet, and blanket, which constitute the bed-furniture, are in better order than they were a few years back; for the visitations of the cholera alarmed even the reckless class of vagrants, and those whose avocations relate to vagrants. In perhaps a tenth of the low lodging-houses of London, a family may have a room to themselves, with the use of the kitchen, at so much a week—generally 2*s*. 6*d*. for a couple without family, and 3*s*. 6*d*. where there are children. To let out 'beds' by the night is however the general rule.

OF THE FILTH, DISHONESTY, AND IMMORALITY OF LOW LODGING-HOUSES

In my former and my present inquiries, I received many statements on this subject. Some details, given by coarse men and boys in the grossest language, are too gross to be more than alluded to, but the full truth must be manifested, if not detailed.

And first, as to the want of cleanliness, comfort, and decency: 'Why, sir,' said one man, who had filled a commercial situation of no little importance, but had, through intemperance, been reduced to utter want, 'I myself have slept in the top room of a house not far from Drury-lane, and you could study the stars, if you were so minded, through the holes left by the slates having been blown off the roof.'

The same man told me (and I received abundant corroboration of his statement, besides that incidental mention of the subject occurs elsewhere), that he had scraped together a handful of bugs from the bed-clothes, and crushed them under a candlestick, and had done that many a time, when he could only resort to the lowest places. He had slept in rooms so crammed with sleepers—he believed there were 30 where 12 would have been a proper number —that their breaths in the dead of night and in the unventilated chamber, rose (I use his own words) 'in one foul, choking steam of stench.' This was the case most frequently a day or two prior to

Greenwich Fair or Epsom Races, when the congregation of the wandering classes, who are the supporters of the low lodging-houses, was the thickest. It was not only that two or even three persons jammed themselves into a bed not too large for one full-sized man; but between the beds—and their partition one from another admitted little more than the passage of a lodger—were placed shake-downs, or temporary accommodation for nightly slumber. In the better lodging-houses the shake-downs are small palliasses or mattresses; in the worst, they are bundles of rags of any kind; but loose straw is used only in the country for shake-downs.

At some of the busiest periods, numbers sleep on the kitchen floor, all huddled together, men and women (when indecencies are common enough), and without bedding or anything but their scanty clothes to soften the hardness of the stone or brick floor. A penny is saved to the lodger by this means. More than 200 have been accommodated in this way in a large house. The Irish, at harvest-time, very often resort to this mode of passing the night.

Another man who had moved in good society, said, when asked about his resorting to a low lodging-house: 'When a man's lost caste in society, he may as well go the whole hog, bristles and all, and a low lodging-house is the entire pig.'

Notwithstanding many abominations, I am assured that the lodgers, in even the worst of these habitations, for the most part sleep soundly. But they have, in all probability, been out in the open air the whole of the day, and all of them may go to their couches, after having walked, perhaps, many miles, exceedingly fatigued, and some of them half-drunk. 'Why, in course, sir,' said a 'traveller,' whom I spoke to on this subject, 'if you is in a country town or village, where there's only one lodging-house, perhaps, and that a bad one—an old hand can always suit his-self in London —you *must* get half-drunk, or your money for your bed is wasted. There's so much rest owing to you, after a hard day; and bugs and bad air'll prevent its being paid, if you don't lay in some stock of beer, or liquor of some sort, to sleep on. It's a duty you owes your-self; but, if you haven't the browns, why, then, in course, you can't pay it.'

I have now to speak of the habitual violation of all the injunc-tions of law, of all the obligations of morality, and of all the restraints of decency, seen continually in the vilest of the lodging-houses.

Some of the 'fences' board, lodge, and clothe, two or three boys or girls, and send them out regularly to thieve, the fence usually taking all the proceeds, and if it be the young thief has been success-ful, he is rewarded with a trifle of pocket-money, and is allowed plenty of beer and tobacco.

The licentiousness of the frequenters, and more especially of the juvenile frequenters, of the low lodging-houses, must be even more briefly alluded to. In some of these establishments, men and women, boys and girls,—but perhaps in no case, or in very rare cases, unless they are themselves consenting parties, herd together promis-cously. The information which I have been given from a reverend informant indicates the nature of the proceedings, when the sexes are herded indiscriminately, and it is impossible to present to the reader, in full particularity, the records of the vice practised.

Boys have boastfully carried on loud conversations, and from distant parts of the room, of their triumphs over the virtue of girls, and girls have laughed at and encouraged the recital. Three, four, five, six, and even more boys and girls have been packed, head and feet, into one small bed; some of them perhaps never met before. On such occasions any clothing seems often enough to be regarded as merely an incumbrance. Sometimes there are loud quarrels and revilings from the jealousy of boys and girls, and more especially of girls whose 'chaps' have deserted or been inveigled from them. At others, there is an amicable interchange of partners, and next day a resumption of their former companionship.

The younger lodgers in such places live by thieving and pocket-picking, or by prostitution. The charge for a night's lodging is generally 2*d*., but smaller children have often been admitted for 1*d*. If a boy or girl resort to one of these dens at night without the means of defraying the charge for accommodation, the 'mot of the ken' (mistress of the house) will pack them off, telling them plainly that it will be no use their returning until they have stolen something worth 2*d*.

The indiscriminate admixture of the sexes among adults, in many of these places, is another evil. Even in some houses considered of the better sort, men and women, husbands and wives, old and young, strangers and acquaintances, sleep in the same apartment, and if they choose, in the same bed. Any remonstrance at some act of gross depravity or impropriety, on the part of a woman not so utterly hardened as the others, is met with abuse and derision. One man who described these scenes to me, and had long witnessed them, said that almost the only women who ever hid their faces or manifested dislike of the proceedings they could not but notice (as far as he saw), were poor Irishwomen, generally those who live by begging: 'But for all that,' the man added, 'an Irishman or Irishwoman of that sort will sleep anywhere, in any mess, to save a halfpenny, though they may have often a few shillings, or a good many, hidden about them.'

There are now fewer of such filthy receptacles than there were. Some have been pulled down—especially for the building of Commercial-street, in Whitechapel, and of New Oxford-street—and some have fallen into fresh and improved management. Of those of the worst class, however, there may now be at least thirty in London; while the low lodgings of all descriptions, good or bad, are more frequented than they were a few years back.

OF THE 'SCREEVERS', OR WRITERS OF BEGGING-LETTERS AND PETITIONS

'SCREEVING'—that is to say, *writing* false or exaggerated accounts of afflictions and privations, is a necessary corollary to 'Pattering,' or making pompous *orations* in public.

Of professional beggars there are two kinds—those who 'do it on the *blob*' (by word of mouth), and those who do it by '*screeving*,' that is, by petitions and letters, setting forth imaginary cases of distress.

'Of these documents there are two sorts, "slums" (letters) and "fakements" (petitions). These are seldom written by the persons who present or send them, but are the production of a class of whom the public little imagine either the number or turpitude. I mean the "professional begging-letter writers."

'Persons who write begging-letters for others sometimes, though seldom, beg themselves. They are in many cases well supported by the fraternity for whom they write. A professional of this kind is called by the "cadgers," "their man of business." Their histories vary as much as their abilities; generally speaking they have been clerks, teachers, shopmen, reduced gentlemen, or the illegitimate sons of members of the aristocracy; while others, after having received a liberal education, have broken away from parental control, and commenced the "profession" in early life, and will probably pursue it to their graves.'

OF THE STREET-SELLERS OF MANUFACTURED ARTICLES

THE street-sellers of manufactured articles present, as a body, so many and often such varying characteristics, that I cannot offer to give a description of them as a whole, as I have been able to do with other and less diversified classes.

Among them are several distinct and peculiar street-characters, such as the pack-men, who carry their cotton or linen goods in packs on their backs, and are all itinerants. Then there are duffers, who vend pretended smuggled goods, handkerchiefs, silks, tobacco or cigars; also, the sellers of sham sovereigns and sham gold rings for wagers. The crockery-ware and glass-sellers (known in the street-trade as 'crocks'), are peculiar from their principle of *bartering*. They will sell to any one, but they *sell* very rarely, and always clamour in preference for an exchange of their wares for wearing-apparel of any kind. They state, if questioned, that their reason for doing this is—at least I heard the statement from some of the most intelligent among them—that they do so because, if they 'sold outright,' they required a hawker's licence, and could not sell or 'swop' so cheap.

Some of the street-sellers of manufactured articles are also patterers. Among these are the 'cheap Jacks,' or 'cheap Johns'; the grease and stain removers; the corn-salve and plate-ball vendors; the sellers of sovereigns and rings for wagers; a portion of the lot-sellers; and the men who vend poison for vermin and go about the streets with live rats clinging to, or running about, their persons.

OF THE STREET-SELLERS OF MANUFACTURED ARTICLES IN METAL

THE result of my inquiries leads me to the conclusion, that the street-vendors of any article which is the product of the skill of the handicraftsman, have been, almost always, in their first outset in a street life, connected in some capacity or other with the trade, the manufactures of which they vend.

The metal sold in the street may be divided into street-hardware, street-tinware, and street-jewellery. I shall begin with the former.

The street-sellers of hardware are, I am assured, in number about 100, including single men and families; for women 'take their share' in the business, and children sell smaller things.

All these street-sellers obtain their supplies at 'the swag-shops;' of which I shall speak hereafter. The main articles of their trade are tea-boards, waiters, snuffers, candlesticks, bread-baskets, cheese-trays, Britannia metal tea-pots and spoons, iron kettles, pans, and coffee-pots. The most saleable things, I am told by a man who has been fifteen years in this and similar street trades, are at present 18-in. tea-boards, bought at 'the swags' at from 10*s*. 6*d*. a doz., to 4*s*. each; 24-in. boards, from 20*s*. the doz. to 5*s*. each; bread-baskets, 4*s*. 6*d*. the doz.; and Britannia metal tea-pots, 10*s*. the doz. These tea-pots have generally what is called 'loaded bottoms;' the lower part of the vessel is 'filled with composition, so as to look as if there was great weight of metal, and as if the pot would melt for almost the 18*d*. which is asked for it, and very often got.'

OF THE CHEAP JOHNS, OR STREET HANSELLERS

THIS class of street-salesmen, who are perhaps the largest dealers of all in hardware, are not so numerous as they were some few years ago—the Excise Laws, as I have before remarked, having interfered with their business. The principal portion of those I have met are Irishmen, who, notwithstanding, generally 'hail' from Sheffield, and all their sales are effected in an attempt at the York-shire dialect, interspersed, however, with an unmistakeable brogue. The brogue is the more apparent when cheap John gets a little out of temper—if his sales are flat, for instance, he'll say, 'By J—s, I don't belaive you've any money with you, or that you've lift any at home, at all, at all. Bad cess to you!'

There are, however, many English cheap Johns, but few of them are natives of Sheffield or Birmingham, from which towns they invariably 'hail.' Their system of selling is to attract a crowd of persons by an harangue after the following fashion: 'Here I am, the original cheap John from Sheffield. I've not come here to get money; not I; I've come here merely for the good of the public, and to let you see how you've been imposed upon by a parcel of pompous shopkeepers, who are not content with less than 100 per cent. for rubbish. They got up a petition—which I haven't time to read to you just now—offering me a large sum of money to keep away from here. But no, I had too much friendship for you to consent, and here I am, cheap John, born without a shirt, one day while my mother was out, in a haystack; consequently I've no parish, for the cows eat up mine, and therefore I've never no fear of going to the workhouse.'

The cheap John always takes care to receive payment before he hazards his jokes, which I need scarcely remark are ready made, and mostly ancient and worn threadbare, the joint property of the whole fraternity of cheap Johns. After supplying his audience with one particular article, he introduces another: 'Here is a carving-knife and fork, none of your wasters, capital buck-horn handle, manufactured of the best steel, in a regular workmanlike manner; fit for carving in the best style, from a sparrow to a bullock. I don't ask 7*s.* 6*d.* for this—although go over to Mr. ——, the ironmonger, and he will have the impudence to ask you 15*s.* for a worse article.' (The cheap Johns always make comparisons as to their own prices and the shopkeepers, and sometimes mention their names.) 'I say 5*s.* for the carving-knife and fork. Why, it's an article that'll almost fill your children's bellies by looking at it, and will always make 1 lb. of beef go as far as 6 lb. carved by any other knife and fork. Well, 4*s.*, 3*s.*, 2*s.*, 1*s.* 11*d.*, 1*s.* 10*d.*, 1*s.* 9*d.*, 1*s.* 8*d.*, 1*s.* 7*d.*, 18*d.* I ask no more, nor I'll take no less.'

They never under-sell each other (unless they get in a real passion); this but seldom happens, but when it does they are exceedingly bitter against each other. I cannot state the language they use, further than that it reaches the very summit of black-guardism. They have, however, assumed quarrels, for the purpose of holding a crowd together, and chaff goes round, intended to amuse their expected customers.

THE CRIPPLED STREET-SELLER OF
NUTMEG-GRATERS

I NOW give an example of one of the classes *driven* to the streets by utter inability to labour. I have already spoken of the sterling independence of some of these men possessing the strongest claims to our sympathy and charity, and yet preferring to *sell* rather than *beg*. As I said before, many ingrained beggars certainly use the street *trade* as a cloak for alms-seeking, but as certainly many more, with every title to our assistance, use it as a means of redemption from beggary. That the nutmeg-grater seller is a noble example of the latter class, I have not the least doubt.

His struggles to earn his own living (notwithstanding his physical incapacity even to put the victuals to his mouth after he has earned them), are instances of a nobility of pride that are I believe without a parallel. The poor creature's legs and arms are completely withered; indeed he is scarcely more than head and trunk. His thigh is hardly thicker than a child's wrist. His hands are bent inward from contraction of the sinews, the fingers being curled up and almost as thin as the claws of a bird's foot. He is unable even to stand, and cannot move from place to place but on his knees, which are shod with leather caps, like the heels of a clog, strapped round the joint; the soles of his boots are on the *upper* leathers, that being the part always turned towards the ground while he is crawling along. His countenance is rather handsome than otherwise; the intelligence indicated by his ample forehead is fully borne out by the testimony as to his sagacity in his business, and the mild expression of his eye by the statements as to his feeling for all others in affliction.

'I sell nutmeg-graters and funnels,' said the cripple to me; 'I sell them at 1*d*. and 1½*d*. a piece. I get mine of the man in whose house I live. He is a tinman, and makes for the street-trade and shops and all. I pay 7*d*. a dozen for them, and I get 12*d*. or 18*d*. a dozen, if I can when I sell them, but I mostly get only a penny a piece—it's quite a chance if I have a customer at 1½*d*. Some days I sell only three—some days not one—though I'm out from ten o'clock till six.

'On a wet day when I can't get out, I often go without food.

I may have a bit of bread and butter give me, but that's all—then I lie a-bed. I feel miserable enough when I see the rain come down of a week day, I can tell you. Ah, it *is* very miserable indeed lying in bed all day, and in a lonely room, without perhaps a person to come near one—helpless as I am—and hear the rain beat against the windows, and all that without nothing to put in your lips. I've done *that* over and over again where I lived before; but where I am now I'm more comfortable like. My breakfast is mostly bread and butter and tea; and my supper, bread and butter and tea with a bit of fish, or a small bit of meat. What my landlord and landlady has I share with them. I never break my fast from the time I go out in the morning till I come home—unless it is a halfpenny orange I buy in the street; I do that when I feel faint. I have only been selling in the streets since this last winter. I was in the workhouse with a fever all the summer. I was destitute afterwards, and obliged to begin selling in the streets. The Guardians gave me 5*s*. to get stock. I had always dealt in tin ware, so I knew where to go to buy my things.

'Often after I've been walking, my limbs and back ache so badly that I can get no sleep. Across my limbs it feels as if I'd got some great weight, and my knees are in a heat, and throb, and feel as if a knife was running into them. When I go up-stairs I have to crawl upon the back of my hands and knees. I can't lift nothing to my mouth. The sinews of my hands is all contracted. I am obliged to have things held to my lips for me to drink, like a child. I *can* use a knife and fork by leaning my arm on the table and then stooping my head to it. I can't wash nor undress myself. Sometimes I think of my helplessness a great deal. The thoughts of it used to throw me into fits at one time—very bad. It's the Almighty's will that I am so, and I must abide by it.'

OF THE SWAG-SHOPS OF THE METROPOLIS

By those who are not connected with the street trade, the proprietors of the swag-shops are often called 'warehousemen' or 'general dealers,' and even 'slaughterers.' These descriptions apply but partially. 'Warehousemen' or 'general dealers' are vague terms, which I need not further notice. The wretchedly underpaid and over-worked shoe-makers, cabinet-makers and others call these places 'slaughterhouses,' when the establishment is in the hands of tradesmen who buy their goods of poor workmen without having given orders for them. On Saturday afternoons pale-looking men may be seen carrying a few chairs, or bending under the weight of a chiffonier or a chest of drawers, in Tottenham-court Road, and thoroughfares of a similar character in all parts. These are 'small masters,' who make or (as one man said to me, 'No, sir, I don't make these drawers, I put them together, it can't be called making; it's not workmanship') who 'put together' in the hastiest manner, and in any way not positively offensive to the eye, articles of household furniture. The 'slaughterers' who supply all the goods required for the furniture of a house, buy at 'starvation prices' (the common term), the artificer being often kept waiting for hours, and treated with every indignity. One East-end 'slaughterer' (as I ascertained in a former inquiry) used habitually to tell that he prayed for wet Saturday afternoons, because it put 20*l.* extra into his pocket! This was owing to the damage sustained in the appearance of any painted, varnished, or polished article, by exposure to the weather; or if it had been protected from the weather, by the unwillingness of the small master to carry it to another slaughterhouse in the rain. Under such circumstances—and under most of the circumstances of this unhappy trade—the poor workman is at the mercy of the slaughterer.

The slaughterer buys as a rule, with hardly an exception, the furniture, or whatever it may be, made for the express purpose of being offered to him on speculation of sale. The swag shop-keeper *orders* his goods as a rule, and buys, as an exception, in the manner in which the slaughterer buys ordinarily. The slaughterer sells by retail; the swag shop-keeper only by wholesale.

Most of the articles, of the class of which I now treat, are 'Brummagen made.' An experienced tradesman said to me: 'All these low-priced metal things, fancy goods and all, which you see about, are made in Birmingham; in nineteen cases out of twenty at the least. They may be marked London, or Sheffield, or Paris, or any place—you can have them marked North Pole if you will—but they're genuine Birmingham. The carriage is lower from Birmingham than from Sheffield—that's one thing.'

The majority of the swag-shop proprietors are Jews. The wares which they supply to the cheap shops, the cheap Johns, and the street-sellers, in town and country, consist of every variety of article, apart from what is eatable, drinkable, or wearable, in which the trade class I have specified can deal. As regards what is wearable, indeed, such things as braces, garters, &c., form a portion of the stock of the swag-shop.

The window of a swag-shop presented, in confusion, an array of brooches (some in coloured glass to imitate rubies, topazes, &c., some containing portraits, deeply coloured, in purple attire, and red cheeks, and some being very large cameos), time-pieces (with and without glasses), French toys with moveable figures, telescopes, American clocks, musical boxes, shirt-studs, backgammon-boards, tea-trays (one with a nondescript bird of most gorgeous green plumage forming a sort of centre-piece), razor-strops, writing-desks, sailors' knives, hair-brushes, and tobacco-boxes.

Another window presented even a more 'miscellaneous assortment'; dirks (apparently not very formidable weapons), a mess of steel pens, in brown-paper packages and cases, and of black-lead pencils, pipe-heads, cigar-cases, snuff-boxes, razors, shaving-brushes, letter-stamps, metal tea-pots, metal tea-spoons, glass globes with artificial flowers and leaves within the glass (an improvement one man thought on the old ornament of a reel in a bottle), Peel medals, Exhibition medals, roulette-boxes, scent bottles, quill pens with artificial flowers in the feathery part, fans, sidecombs, glass pen-holders, and pot figures (caricatures) of Louis Phillippe, carrying a very red umbrella, Marshal Haynau, with some instrument of torture in his hand, while over all loomed a huge English seaman, in yellow waistcoat and with a brick-coloured face.

THE STREET-SELLERS OF CUTLERY

THE cutlery sold in the streets of London consists of razors, pen-knives, pocket-knives, table and carving-knives and forks, scissors, shears, nail-filers, and occasionally (if ordered) lancets. The knives are of various kinds—such as sailors' knives (with a hole through the handle), butchers' knives, together with choppers and steels (sold principally at Newgate and Billingsgate Markets, and round about the docks), oyster and fish-knives (sold principally at Billingsgate and Hungerford Markets), bread-knives (hawked at the bakers' shops), ham and beef knives (hawked at the ham and beef shops), cheese-knives with tasters, and ham-triers, shoemakers' knives, and a variety of others. These articles are usually purchased at the 'swag-shops,' and the prices of them vary from 2½*d*. to 1*s*. 1½*d*. each.

'Things within the last two or three years,' to quote the words of one of my informants, 'have been getting much worse in the streets; 'specially in the cutlery line. I can't give no account for it, I'm sure, sir; the sellers have not been half as many as they were. What's become of them that's gone, I can't tell; they're in the workhouse, I dare say.' But, notwithstanding this decrease in the number of sellers, there is a greater difficulty to vend their goods now than formerly. 'It's all owing to the times, that's all I can say. People, shopkeepers, and all says to me, I can't tell why things is so bad, and has been so bad in trade; but so they is. We has to walk farther to sell our goods, and people beat us down so terrible hard, that we can't get a penny out of them when we do sell. Sometimes they offers me 9*d*., yes, and often 6*d*. for an 8½*d*. knife; and often enough 4*d*. for one that stands you in 3¾*d*.—a ¼*d*. profit, think of that, sir. Then they say, "Well, my man, will you take my money?" and so as to make you do so, they'll flash it before your eyes, as if they knew you was a starving, and would be sure to be took in by the sight of it. Yes, sir, it is a very hard life, and we has to put up with a good deal—a good deal—starvation and hard-dealing, and insults and knockings about, and all. And then you see the swag-shops is almost as hard on us as the buyers. The swag-men will say, if you merely makes a remark, that a knife they've sold you is cracked in the handle, "Oh, is it; let me see whereabouts;" and when you hands it to 'em to show it 'em, they'll put it back where they took it from, and tell you, "You're too particular by half, my man. You'd better go and get your goods somewhere else; here take your money, and go about your business, for we won't serve you at all." They'll do just the same with the scissors too, if you complains about their being a bit rusty. "Go somewhere else," they'll say, "We won't serve you." Ah, sir, that's what it is to be a poor man; to have your poverty flung in your teeth every minute. People says, "to be poor and seem poor is the devil"; but to be poor, and be treated like a dog merely because you *are* poor, surely is ten thousand times worse. A street-seller now-a-days is looked upon as a "cadger," and is treated as one. To try to get a living for one's self is to do something shameful in these times.'

OF THE BLIND STREET-SELLERS
OF TAILORS' NEEDLES, &c.

It is customary with many trades, for the journeymen to buy such articles as they require in their business of those members of their craft who have become incapacitated for work, either by old age, or by some affliction. The tailors—the shoe-makers—the carpenters—and many others do this. These sellers are, perhaps, the most exemplary instances of men *driven* to the streets, or to hawking for a means of living; and they, one and all, are distinguished by that horror of the workhouse which I have before spoken of as constituting a peculiar feature in the operative's character.

The tailor's needle-sellers confining themselves more particularly to London consist of, at present, one old man, three blind, one paralyzed, and one widow; besides these, there are now in the alms-houses, two decrepit and one paralyzed; and one widow in the workhouse, all of whom, till recently, were needle-sellers, and originally connected with the trade.

The tailors' hawkers buy their trimmings mostly at the retail shops. They have not stock-money sufficient, I am assured, to purchase at the wholesale houses, for 'such a thing as a paper of needles large tradesmen don't care about of selling us poor men.' They tell me that if they could buy wholesale they could get their goods one-fourth cheaper, and to be 'obligated' to purchase retail is a great drawback on their profits. They call at the principal tailors' workshops, and solicit custom of the journeymen; they are almost all known to the trade, both masters and men, and, having no other means of living, they are allowed to enter the masters' shops.

The blind needle-seller whom I saw was a respectable-looking man, with the same delicacy of hand as is peculiar to tailors, and which forms so marked a contrast to the horny palms of other workmen. He was tall and thin, and had that upward look remarkable in all blind men. His eyes gave no signs of blindness (the pupils being full and black), except that they appeared to be directed to no one object, and though fixed, were so without the least expres-

'The Kitchen', Fox-court, Gray's-Inn-lane

THE STREET-SELLER OF GREASE-REMOVING COMPOSITION

sion of observation. His long black surtout, though faded in colour, was far from ragged, having been patched and stitched in many places, while his cloth waistcoat and trousers were clean and neat—very different from the garments of street-sellers in general. In his hand he carried his stick, which, as he sat, he seemed afraid to part with, for he held it fast between his knees. He came to me accompanied by his son, a good-looking rough-headed lad, habited in a washed-out-blue French kind of pinafore, and whose duty it was to lead his blind father about on his rounds. Though the boy was decently clad, still his clothes, like those of his father, bore many traces of that respectable kind of poverty which seeks by continuous mending to hide its rags from the world. The face of the father, too, was pinched, while there was a plaintiveness about his voice that told of a wretched spirit-broken and afflicted man. Altogether he was one of the better kind of handicraftsmen—one of those fine specimens of the operatives of this country—independent even in their helplessness, scorning to beg, and proud to be able to give some little equivalent for the money bestowed on them.

'I am 45 years of age next June,' said the blind tailor. 'It is upward of 30 years since I first went to work at the tailoring trade in London. I learnt my business under one of the old hands at Mr. Cook's, in Poland-street, and after that went to work at Guthrie's, in Bond-street.

'About 15 years ago my eyes began to fail me without any pain at all; they got to have as it were a thick mist, like smoke, before them. I couldn't see anything clear. Working by gas-light at first weakened and at last destroyed the nerve altogether. I'm now in total darkness. I can only tell when the gas is lighted by the heat of it.

'It is not the black clothes that is trying to the sight—black is the steadiest of all colours to work at; white and all bright colours makes the eyes water after looking at 'em for any long time; but of all colours scarlet, such as is used for regimentals, is the most blinding, it seems to burn the eye-balls, and makes them ache dreadful. After working at red there's always flying colours before the eyes; there's no steady colour to be seen in anything for some time. Everything seems all of a twitter, and to keep changing its tint. There's more military tailors blind than any others. A great number of tailors go blind, but a great many more has lost their sight since gas-light has come up. Candle-light was not half so pernicious to the sight. Gas-light is so very heating, and there's such a glare with it that it makes the eyes throb, and shoot too, if you work long by it. I've often continued working past midnight with no other light than that, and then my eyes used to feel like two bits of burning coals in my head. And you see, sir, the worst of it was, as I found my sight going bad I was obliged to try it more, so as to keep up with my mates in the shop. At last my eyes got so weak that I was compelled to give up work, and go into the country, and there I stopped, living on my savings, and unable to do any work for fear of losing my sight altogether. I was away about three years, and then all my money was gone, and I was obligated, in spite of my eyes, to go back to work again. But then, with my sight defective as it was, I could get no employment at the honourable trade, and so I had to take a seat in a shop at one of the cheap houses in the city, and that was the ruin of me entirely; for working there, of course, I got "scratched" from the trade Society, and so lost all hope of being provided for by them in my helplessness. The workshops at this cheap house was both small and badly ventilated. It was about seven foot square, and so low, that as you sat on the floor you could touch the ceiling with the tip of your finger. In this place seven of us worked—three on each side and one in the middle. Two of my shop-mates were boys, or else I am sure it would not have held us all. There was no chimney, nor no window that could be opened to let the air in. It was lighted by a skylight, and this would neither open nor shut. The only means for letting out the foul air was one of them working ventilators—like cockades, you know, sir—fixed in one of the panes of glass; but this wouldn't work, so there we were, often from 5 in the morning till 10 at night, working in this dreadful place. There was no fire in the winter, though we never needed one, for the workshop was over-hot from the suffocation, and in the summer it was like an oven. This is what it was in the daytime, but mortal tongue can't tell what it was at night, with the two gas-lights burning away, and almost stifling us. Many a time some of the men has been carried out by the others fainting for air. They all fell ill, every one of them, and I lost my eyes and my living entirely by it. We spoke to the master repeatedly, telling him he was killing us, and though when he came up to the work-shop hisself, he was nearly blown back by the stench and heat, he would not let us have any other room to work in—and yet he'd plenty of convenience up stairs. He paid little more than half the regular wages, and employed such men as myself—only those who couldn't get anything better to do. What with illness and all, I don't think my wages there averaged above 12*s.* a week; sometimes I could make 1*l.* in the week, but then, the next week, maybe I'd be ill, and would get but a few shillings. It was impossible to save anything then—even to pay one's way was a difficulty, and, at last, I was seized with rheumatics on the brain, and obliged to go into St. Thomas's Hospital. I was there eleven months, and *came out stone blind.* I am convinced I lost my eyesight by working in that cheap shop.'

THE PUBLIC-HOUSE HAWKERS OF METAL SPOONS, ETC.

THE public-house hawkers are never so prosperous as those who confine their calling to private houses; they are often invited to partake of drink; are not the most industrious class of hawkers, and, to use their own language, are more frequently *hard up* than those who keep away from tap-room selling. The profits of the small hawkers in public-houses vary considerably. Some of them, when they have earned a shilling or two, are content to spend it before they leave the tap-room, and so they lose both their stock and profit.

The man who gave me the routine of small hawkers' business I found in a tap-room in Ratcliffe Highway. He was hawking tea-spoons, and all the stock he possessed was half-a-dozen. These he importuned me to purchase with great earnestness. He prayed of me to lay out a trifle with him. He had not taken a penny the whole day he said, and had nothing to eat. 'What's much worse for such as me,' he added, 'I'm dying for a glass of rum.' I might have his tea-spoons, he told me, at any price. If I would but pay for a glass of rum for him they should be mine. I assured him some bread and cheese would do him more good, as he had not eaten anything that day; but still he *would* have the rum. With a trembling hand he threw the liquor down his throat, smacked his lips, and said 'that there dram has saved my life.' A few minutes afterwards he sold his spoons to a customer for sixpence; and he had another glass of rum. '*Now,*' said he, 'I'm all right for business; if I'd twopence more I could buy a dozen tea-spoons, and I should earn a "bob" or two yet before I went to bed.' After this he grew communicative, and told me he was as good a hawker as there was in London, and he thought he could do more than any other man with a small stock. He had two or three times resolved to better himself, and had '*put in the pin,*' meaning he had made a vow to refrain from drinking; but he had broken out again and gone on in his old course until he had melted the whole of his stock, though twice it had, during his sobriety, amounted to 5*l.*, and was often worth between 2*l.* and 3*l.* It was almost maddening when he came to his senses, he said, to find he had acted so foolishly; indeed, it was so disheartening to discover all the result of his good resolutions dissipated in a moment, that he declared he never intended to try again. After having drunk out his stock, he would if possible commence with half-a-dozen Britannia metal tea-spoons; these cost him 6*d.*, and would sell for 9*d.* or 1*s.* When one half-dozen were disposed of he would procure another, adding a knife, or a comb or two. If entirely destitute, he would stick a needle in a cork, and request to know of 'the parties' assembled in some tap-room, if they wanted anything in the ironmongery line, though the needle was all the stock he had. This was done for the purpose of 'raising the wind'; and by it he would be sure to obtain a glass or two of ale if he introduced himself with his 'ironmongery establishment' among the sailors.

OF THE BEGGAR STREET-SELLERS

UNDER this head I include only such of the beggar street-sellers as are neither infirm nor suffering from any severe bodily affliction or privation. I am well aware that the aged—the blind—the lame and the half often *pretend* to sell small articles in the street—such as boot-laces, tracts, cabbage-nets, lucifer-matches, kettle-holders, and the like; and that such matters are carried by them partly to keep clear of the law, and partly to evince a disposition to the public that they are willing to do something for their livelihood.

Such, though beggars, are not 'lurkers'—a lurker being strictly one who loiters about for some dishonest purpose. Many modes of thieving as well as begging are termed 'lurking'—the 'dead lurk,' for instance, is the expressive slang phrase for the art of entering dwelling-houses during divine service. The term 'lurk,' however, is mostly applied to the several modes of plundering by representations of sham distress.

An inmate of one of the low lodging-houses has supplied me with the following statement:—'Within my recollection,' says my informant, 'the great branch of trade among these worthies, was the sale of sewing cotton, either in skeins or on reels. In the former case, the article cost the "lurkers" about 8*d.* per pound; one pound would produce thirty skeins, which, sold at one penny each, or two for three halfpence, produced a heavy profit. The lurkers could mostly dispose of three pounds per day; the article was, of course, damaged, rotten, and worthless.

'The mode of sale consisted in the "lurkers" calling at the several houses in a particular district, and representing themselves as Manchester cotton spinners out of employ. Long tales, of course, were told of the distresses of the operatives, and of the oppression of their employers; these tales had for the most part been taught them at the padding-ken, by some old and experienced dodger of "the school"; and if the spokesman could patter well, a much larger sum was frequently obtained in direct alms than was reaped by the sale.'

Cotton on reels was—except to the purchaser—a still better speculation; the reels were large, handsomely mounted, and displayed in bold relief such inscriptions as the following:—

PIKE'S

PATENT COTTON.

120 YARDS

The reader, however, must divide the '120 yards,' here mentioned, by 12, and then he will arrive at something like the true secret as to the quantity; for the surface only was covered by the thread.

'The "cotton Lurk" is now "cooper'd" (worn out); a more common dodge—and, of course, only an excuse for begging—is to envelope a packet of "warranted" needles, or a few inches of "real Honiton lace" in an envelope, with a few lines to the "Lady of the House", or a printed bill, setting forth the misery of the manufacturers, and the intention of the parties leaving the "fakement" to presume to call for an answer in a few hours.'

There are besides these, two other classes known as 'Duffers' and as 'Lumpers,' and sometimes the same man is both 'Duffer' and 'Lumper.' The two names are often confounded, but an intelligent street-seller, versed in all the arts and mysteries of this trade, told me that he understood by a 'Duffer,' a man who sold goods under false pretences, making out that they were smuggled, or even stolen, so as to enhance the idea of their cheapness; whereas a 'Lumper' would sell linens, cottons, or silks, which might be really the commodities represented; but which, by some management or other, were made to appear new when they were old, or solid when they were flimsy.

OF THE HABERDASHERY SWAG-SHOPS

By this name the street-sellers have long distinguished the warehouses, or rather shops, where they purchase their goods. The term *Swag*, or *Swack*, or *Sweg*, is a Scotch word, meaning a large collection, a 'lot.' The haberdashery, however, supplied by these establishments is of a very miscellaneous character; which, perhaps, can best be shown by describing a 'haberdashery swag,' to which a street-seller, who made his purchases there, conducted me, and which, he informed me, was one of the most frequented by his fraternity, if not *the* most frequented, in the metropolis.

The window was neither dingy, nor, as my companion expressed it, 'gay.' It was in size, as well as in 'dressing,' or 'show'—for I heard the arrangement of the window goods called by both those names by street people—half-way between the quiet plainness of a really wholesale warehouse, and the gorgeousness of a retail drapery concern, when a 'tremendous sacrifice' befools the public. Not a quarter of an inch of space was lost, and the announcements and prices were written many of them in a bungling school-boy-like hand, while others were the work of a professional 'ticket writer,' and show the eagerness of so many of this class of trade to obtain custom. In one corner was this announcement: 'To boot-makers. Boot fronts cut to any size or quantity.' There was neither boot nor shoe visible, but how a boot front *can be* cut 'to any quantity,' is beyond my trade knowledge. Half hidden, and read through laces, was another announcement, sufficiently odd, in a window decorated with a variety of combustible commodities: 'Hawkers supplied with fuzees cheaper than any house in London.' On the 'ledge,' or the part shelving from the bottom of the window, within the shop, were paper boxes of steel purses with the price marked so loosely as to leave it an open question whether 1s. 0¾d. or 10¾d. was the cost.

In the centre of the window ledge was a handsome wreath of artificial flowers, marked 2½d. 'If a young woman was to go in to buy it at 2½d, I've seen it myself, sir,' said the street-seller, 'she's told that the ticket has got out of its place, for it belonged to the lace beneath, but as he'd made a mistake without thinking of the value, the flowers was 1s. 6d. to her, though they was cheap at 2s. 6d.'

From this account it will be seen that the swag or wholesale haberdashers are now very general traders; and that they trade 'retail' as well as 'wholesale.' Twenty or twenty-five years ago, I am informed, the greater part of these establishments were really haberdashery swags; but so fierce became the competition in the trade, so keen the desire 'to do business,' that gradually, and more especially within these four or five years, they became 'all kinds of swags.'

A highly respectable draper told me that he never could thoroughly understand where hosiery, haberdashery, or drapery, began or ended; for hosiers now were always glovers, and often shirt-makers; haberdashers were always hosiers (at the least), and drapers were everything; so that the change in the character of the shops from which the street-sellers of textile fabrics procure their supplies, is but in accordance with the change in the general dra-pery trade.

STATEMENT OF A PACKMAN

OF the way of trading of a travelling-pedlar I had the following account from one of the body.

When I saw him, his pack, which he carried slung over one shoulder, contained a few gown-pieces of printed cotton, nearly all with pink grounds; a few shawls of different sizes; and three rolls firmly packed, each with a card-label on which was neatly written, 'French Merino. Full duty paid. A.B.—L.F.—18—33—1851. French Chocolate.' There were also six neat paper packages, two marked 'worked collars,' three, 'gauze handkerchiefs,' and the other 'beautiful child's gros de naples.' The latter consisted of 4½ yards of black silk, sufficient for a child's dress. He carried with him, moreover, 5 umbrellas, one inclosed in a bright glazed cover, while from its mother-of-pearl handle hung a card addressed—'The Lady's Maid, Victoria Lodge, 13s. 6d.'

'This is a very small stock,' he said, 'to what I generally carry, but I'm going on a country round to-morrow, and I want to get through it before I lay in a new one. I tell people that I want to sell off my goods cheap, as they're too good for country sale; and that's true, the better half of it.

'I sell to women of all sorts. Smart-dressing servant-maids, perhaps, are my best customers, especially if they live a good way from any grand ticketing shop. I sold one of my umbrellas to one of them just before you spoke to me. She was standing at the door, and I saw her give half a glance at the umbrellas, and so I offered them. She first agreed to buy a very nice one at 3s. 3d. (which should have been 4s.), but I persuaded her to take one at 3s. 9d. (which should have been 4s. 6d.). "Look here, ma'am," said I, "this umbrella is much bigger you see, and will carry double, so when you're coming from a church of a wet Sunday evening, a friend can have the share of it, and very grateful he'll be, as he's sure to have his best hat on. There's been many a question put under an umbrella that way that's made a young lady blush, and take good care of her umbrella when she was married, and had a house of her own. I look sharp after the young and pretty ladies, Miss, and shall as long as I'm a bachelor." "O," says she, "such ridiculous nonsense. But I'll have the bigger umbrella, because it's often so windy about here, and then one must have a good cover if it rains as well."

'Now, that piece of silk I shall, most likely, sell to the landlady of a public-house, where I see there's children. I shall offer it after I've got a bit of dinner there, or when I've said I want a bit. It's no use offering it there, though, if it isn't cheap; they're too good judges. Innkeepers aren't bad customers, I think, taking it altogether, to such as me, if you can get to talk to them, as you sometimes can at their bars. They're generally wanting something, that's one step. I always tell them that they ought to buy of men, in my way, who live among them, and not of fine shop-keepers, who never came a-near their houses. I've sold them both cottons and linens, after such talk as that. I live at public-houses in the country. I sleep nowhere else.

'My trade in town is nothing to what it was ten or a dozen years back. I don't know the reason exactly. I think so many threepenny-busses is one; for they'll take any servant, when she's got an afternoon, to a thoroughfare full of ticket-shops, and bring her back and her bundle of purchases too, for another 3*d*. I shall cut it altogether, I think, and stick to the country.'

OF THE TALLY PACKMAN

THE pedlar tallyman is a hawker who supplies his customers with goods, receiving payment by weekly instalments, and derives his name from the tally or score he keeps with his customers. Linen drapery—or at least the general routine of linen-draper's stock, as silk-mercery, hosiery, woollen cloth, &c.—is the most prevalent trade of the tallyman. There are a few shoemakers and some household furniture dealers who do business in the tally or 'score' system.

The system does not prevail to so great an extent as it did some years back. The pedlar or hawking tallyman travels for orders, and consequently is said not to require a hawker's licence.

Their mode of doing business is as follows:—they seldom knock at a door except they have a customer upon whom they call for the weekly instalment, but if a respectable-looking female happens to be standing at her door, she, in all probability, is accosted by the Scotchman, 'Do you require anything in my way to-day, ma'am?' This is often spoken in broad Scotch, the speaker trying to make it sound as much like English as possible. Without waiting for a reply, he then runs over a programme of the treasures he has to dispose of, emphasising all those articles which he considers likely to suit the taste of the person he addresses. She doesn't want perhaps any—she has no money to spare then. 'She may want something in his way another day, may-be,' says the tallyman. 'Will she grant him permission to exhibit some beautiful shawls—the last new fashion? or some new style of dress, just out, and an extra-ordinary bargain?' The man's importunities, and the curiosity of the lady, introduces him into the apartment,—an acquaintance is called in to pass her opinion upon the tallyman's stock. Should she still demur, he says, 'O, I'm sure your husband cannot object—he will not be so unreasonable; besides, consider the easy mode of payment, you'll only have to pay 1*s*. 6*d*. a week for every pound's worth of goods you take; why it's like nothing; you possess yourself of respectable clothing and pay for them in such an easy manner that you never miss it; well, I'll call next week. I shall leave you this paper.' The paper left is a blank form to be filled up by the husband, and runs thus:—'I agree on behalf of my wife to pay, by weekly instalments of 1*s*. 6*d*. upon every pound's worth of goods she may purchase.'

The Scotchman takes stock of the furniture, &c.; the value of what the room contains gives him a sufficiently correct estimate of the circumstances of his customers. His next visit is to the nearest chandler's shop, and there as blandly as possible he inquires into the credit, &c., of Mr.——. If he deals, however, with the chandler, the tallyman accounts it a bad omen, as people in easy circumstances seldom resort to such places. 'It is unpleasant to me,' he says to the chandler, 'making these inquiries; but Mrs. —— wishes to open an account with me, and I should like to oblige them if I thought my money was safe.' 'Do *you* trust them, and what sort of players are they?' According to the reply — the tallyman determines upon his course. But he rarely stops here; he makes inquiries also at the greengrocer's, the beer shop, &c.

However charitably inclined the tallyman may be at first, he soon becomes, I am told, inured to scenes of misery, while the sole feeling in his mind at length is, 'I will have my money;' for he is often tricked, and in some cases most impudently victimised. I am told by a tallyman that he once supplied goods to the amount of 2*l*., and when he called for the first instalment, the woman said she didn't intend to pay, the goods didn't suit her, and she would return them. The tallyman expressed his willingness to receive them back, whereupon she presented him a pawnbroker's duplicate. She had pledged them an hour after obtaining them.

OF THE STREET-SELLERS OF CORN-SALVE

THE street purveyors of corn-salve, or corn-plaster, for I heard both words used, are not more than a dozen in number; but, perhaps, none depend *entirely* upon the sale of corn-salve for a

living. As is the wont of the pattering class to which they belong,
these men make rounds into the country and into the suburbs, but
there are sometimes, on one day, a dozen 'working the main
drags' (chief thoroughfares) of London; there are no women in
the trade. The salve is most frequently carried on a small tray,
slung in front of the street professional; but sometimes it is sold
at a small stall or stand.

One of the men in question speaks to the following purport:—
'Here you are! here you are! all that has to complain of corns.
As fast as the shoemaker lames you, I'll cure you. If it wasn't for
me he dursn't sing at his work; bless you, but he knows I'll make
his pinching easy to you. Hard corn, soft corn, any corn—sold
again? Thank you, sir, you'll not have to take a 'bus home when
you've used my corn-salve, and you can wear your boots out then;
you can't when you've corns. Now, in this little box you see a
large corn which was drawn by this very salve from the honourable
foot of the late lamented Sir Robert Peel. It's been in my possession
three years and four months, and though I'm a poor man—hard
corn, soft corn, or any corn—though I'm a poor man, the more's
the pity, I wouldn't sell that corn for the newest sovereign coined.
I call it the free-trade corn, gen'l'men and leddis. No cutting and
paring, and sharpening penknives, and venturing on razors to level
your corns; this salve draws them out—only one penny—and without pain. But wonders can't be done in a moment. To draw out
such a corn as I've shown you, the foot, the whole foot, must be
soaked five minutes in warm soap and water. That makes the
salve penetrate, and draw the corn, which then falls out, in three
days, like a seed from a flower. Hard corn, soft corn, &c., &c.'

The corn from 'the honourable foot' of Sir Robert Peel, or from
the foot of any one likely to interest the audience, has been scraped
and trimmed from a cow's heel, and may safely be submitted to
the inspection and handling of the incredulous. 'There it is,' the
corn-seller will reiterate—'it speaks for itself.'

One practice—less common than it was, however,—of the corn-
salve street-seller, is to get a friend to post a letter—expressive of
delighted astonishment at the excellence and rapidity of the corn-
cure—at some post-office not very contiguous. If the salve-seller
be anxious to remove the corns of the citizens, he displays this
letter, with the genuine post-mark of Piccadilly, St. James's-street,

Pall-mall, or any such quarter, to show how the fashionable world avails itself of his wares, cheap as they are, and fastidious as are the fashionable!

OF THE STREET-SELLERS
OF CRACKERS AND DETONATING BALLS

THIS trade, I am informed by persons familiar with it, would be much more frequently carried on by street-folk, and in much greater numbers, were it not the one which of all street callings finds the least toleration from the police. 'You must keep your eyes on both corners of the street,' said one man, 'when you sell crackers; and what good is it the police stopping us? The boys have only to go to a shop, and then it's all right.'

The trade is only known in the streets at holiday seasons, and is principally carried on for a few days before and after the 5th of November, and again at Christmas-tide. 'Last November was good for crackers,' said one man; 'it was either Guy Faux day, or the day before, I'm not sure which now, that I took 15s., and nearly all of boys, for waterloo crackers and ball crackers (the common trade names), "waterloo" being the "pulling crackers." At least three parts was ball crackers. I sold them from a barrow wheeling it about as if it was hearthstone, and just saying quietly when I could, "Six a penny crackers." The boys soon tell one another. All sorts bought of me; doctors' boys, school boys, pages, boys as was dressed beautiful, and boys as hadn't neither shoes nor stockings. It's sport for them all.'

OF THE STREET-SELLERS OF CIGAR LIGHTS,
OR FUZEES

THIS is one of the employments to which boys, whom neglect, ill-treatment, destitution, or a vagrant disposition, have driven or lured to a street life, seem to resort to almost as readily as to the offers, ''Old your 'os, sir?' 'Shall I carry your passel, marm?'

The trifling capital required to enter into the business is one cause of its numbering many followers. The 'fuzees,' as I most frequently heard them called, are sold at the 'Congreve shops,' and are chiefly German made. At one time, indeed, they were announced as 'German tinder.' The wholesale charge is $4\frac{1}{2}d$. per 1,000 'lights.' The 1,000 lights are apportioned into fifty rows, each of twenty self-igniting matches; and these 'rows' are sold in the streets, one or two for $\frac{1}{2}d$., and two, three, or four $1d$. It is common enough for a juvenile fuzee-seller to buy only 500; so that $2\frac{1}{4}d$. supplies his stock in trade.

The boys (for the majority of the street-traders who sell *only* fuzees, are boys) frequent the approaches to the steam-boat piers, the omnibus stands, and whatever places are resorted to by persons who love to smoke in the open air. Some of these young traders have neither shoes nor stockings, more especially the Irish lads, who are at least half the number, and their apology for a cap fully displays the large red ears, and flat features, which seem to distinguish a class of the Irish children in the streets of London. Some Irish boys hold out their red-tipped fuzees with an appealing look, meant to be plaintive, and say, in a whining tone, 'Spend a halfpenny on a poor boy, your honour.' Others offer them, without any appealing look or tone, either in silence, or saying—'Buy a fuzee to light your pipe or cigar, sir; a row of lights for a $\frac{1}{2}d$.'

OF THE STREET-SELLERS OF GUTTA-PERCHA HEADS

THERE are many articles which, having become cheap in the shops, find their way to the street-traders, and after a brief, or comparatively brief, and prosperous trade has been carried on in them, gradually disappear. These are usually things which are grotesque or amusing, but of no utility, and they are supplanted by some more attractive novelty—a main attraction being that it is a novelty.

Among such matters of street-trade are the elastic toys called 'gutta-percha heads'; these, however, have no gutta-percha in their composition, but consist solely of a composition made of glue and treacle—the same as is used for printer's rollers. The heads are small coloured models of the human face, usually with projecting nose and chin, and wide or distorted mouth, which admit of being squeezed into a different form of features, their elasticity causing them to return to the original caste. The trade carried on in the streets in these toys was at one time extensive, but it seems now to be gradually disappearing.

OF THE STREET-SELLERS OF FLY-PAPERS AND BEETLE-WAFERS

Fly-papers came, generally, into street-traffic, I am informed, in the summer of 1848. The fly-papers are sold wholesale at many of the oil-shops, but the principal shop for the supply of the street-traders is in Whitechapel. The wholesale price is $2\frac{1}{4}d$. a dozen, and the (street) retail charge is $\frac{1}{2}d$. a paper, or three $1d$. A young man, to whom I was referred, and whom I found selling, or rather bartering, crockery, gave me the following account of his experience of the fly-paper trade. He was a rosy-cheeked, strong-built young fellow, and said he thought he was 'getting on' in his present trade. He spoke merrily of his troubles, as I have found common among his class, when they are over.

'I went into the fly-paper trade,—it's nearly two years ago, I think—because a boy I slept with did tidy in it. We bought the papers at the first shop as was open, and then got leave of the deputy of the lodging-house to catch all the flies we could, and we stuck them thick on the paper, and fastened the paper to our hats. I used to think, when I was in service, how a smart livery hat, with a cockade to it, would look, but instead of that I turned out, the first time in my life that ever I sold anything, with my hat stuck round with flies. I felt so ashamed I could have cried. I was miserable, I felt so awkerd. But I spent my last $2d$. in some gin and milk to give me courage, and that brightened me up a bit, and I set to work. I went Mile-end way, and got out of the main streets, and I suppose I'd gone into streets and places where there hadn't often been fly-papers before, and I soon had a lot of boys following me, and I felt, almost, as if I'd picked a pocket, or done something to be 'shamed of. I could hardly cry "Catch 'em alive, only a half-penny!". But I found I could sell my papers to public-houses and shopkeepers, such as grocers and confectioners, and that gave me pluck. The boys caught flies, and then came up to me, and threw them against my hat, and if they stuck the lads set up a shout.'

OF THE STREET-SELLERS OF WALKING-STICKS

The walking-sticks sold in the streets of London are principally purchased at wholesale houses in Mint-street and Union-street, Borough, and their neighbourhoods. 'There's no street-trade,' said an intelligent man, 'and I've tried most that's been, or promised to be, a living in the streets, that is so tiresome as the walking-stick trade. There is nothing in which people are so particular. The stick's sure to be either too short or too long, or too thick or too thin, or too limp or too stiff. You would think it was a simple thing for a man to choose a stick out of a lot, but if you were with me a selling on a fine Sunday at Battersea Fields, you'd see it wasn't. O, it 's a tiresome job.'

OF THE STREET-SELLERS OF WHIPS, &c.

These traders are a distinct class from the stick-sellers, and have a distinct class of customers. The sale is considerable; for to many the possession of a whip is a matter of importance. If one be lost or stolen, for instance, from a butcher's cart at Newgate-market, the need of a whip to proceed with the cart and horse to its destination, prompts the purchase in the quickest manner, and this is usually effected of the street-seller who offers his wares to the carters at every established resort.

The commonest of the whips sold to cart-drivers is sometimes represented as whalebone covered with gut; but the whalebone is a stick, and the flexible part is a piece of leather, while the gut is a sort of canvas, made to resemble the worked gut of the better sort of whips, and is pasted to the stock; the thong—which in the common sort is called 'four-strands,' or plaits—being attached to the flexible part. Some of these whips are old stocks recovered, and many are sad rubbish.

Of these traders very few are the ordinary street-sellers. Most of them have been in some way or other connected with the care of horses, and some were described to me as 'beaten-out countrymen', who had come up to town in the hope of obtaining employment, and had failed.

OF THE STREET-SELLERS OF PIPES, AND OF SNUFF AND TOBACCO BOXES

THE pipes now sold in the streets and public-houses are the 'china bowls' and the 'comic heads.' The 'china-bowl' pipe has a bowl of white stone china, which unscrews, from a flexible tube or 'stem,' as it is sometimes called, about a foot long, with an imitation-amber mouth-piece. They are retailed at 6*d*. each, and cost 4*s*. a dozen at the swag-shops. The 'comic heads' are of the clay ordinarily used in the making of pipes, and cost 16*d*. the dozen, or 15*s*. the gross. They are usually retailed at 2*d*. Some of the 'comic heads' may be considered as hardly well described by the name, as among them are death's-heads and faces of grinning devils. 'The best sale of the comic heads,' said one man, 'was when the Duke put the soldiers' pipes out at the barracks; wouldn't allow them to smoke there. It was a Wellington's head with his thumb to his nose, taking a sight, you know, sir. They went off capital. Lots of people that liked their pipe bought 'em, in the public-houses especial, 'cause, as I heerd one man—he was a boot-closer—say, "it made the old boy a-ridiculing of hisself." At that time—well, really, then, I can't say how long it's since—I sold little bone "tobacco-stoppers"— they're seldom asked for now, stoppers is quite out of fashion—and one of them was a figure of "old Nosey," the Duke you know—it was intended as a joke, you see, sir; a tobacco-*stopper*.'

There are now nine men selling pipes, which they frequently raffle at the public-houses; it is not unusual for four persons to raffle at ½*d*. each, for a 'comic head.' The most costly pipes are not now offered in the streets, but a few are sold on race-courses. I am informed that none of the pipe-sellers depend entirely upon their traffic in those wares, but occasionally sell (and raffle) such things as china ornaments or table-covers, or tobacco or snuff-boxes.

One branch of this trade, concerning which I heard many street-sellers very freely express their opinions, is the sale of 'indecent snuff-boxes.' Most of these traders insisted, with a not unnatural bitterness, that it would be as easy to stop the traffic as it was to stop Sunday selling in the park, but then 'gentlemen was accommodated by it,' they added. These boxes and cigar-cases are, for the most part, I am told, French, the lowest price being 2s. 6d. a box. One man, whose information was confirmed to me by others, gave me the following account of what had come within his own knowledge:—

'There's eight and sometimes nine persons carrying on the indecent trade in snuff-boxes and cigar-cases. They make a good bit of money, but they're drunken characters, and often hard up. They've neither shame nor decency; they'll tempt lads or anybody. They go to public-houses which they know is used by fast gents that has money to spare. And they watch old and very young gents in the streets, or any gents indeed, and when they see them loitering and looking after the girls, they take an opportunity to offer a "spicy snuff-box, very cheap." It's a trade only among rich people, for I believe the indecent sellers can't afford to sell at all under 2s. 6d., and they ask high prices when they get hold of a green 'un; perhaps one up on a spree from Oxford or Cambridge. Well, I can't say where they get their goods, nor at what price. That's their secret. They carry them in a box, with proper snuff-boxes to be seen when it's opened, and the others in a secret drawer beneath; or in their pockets. You may have seen a stylish shop in Oxford-street, and in the big window is large pipe heads of a fine quality, and on them is painted, quite beautiful, naked figures of women, and there's snuff-boxes and cigar-cases of much the same sort, but they're nothing to what these men sell.'

OF THE STREET-SELLERS OF CIGARS

CIGARS, I am informed, have constituted a portion of the street-trade for upwards of 20 years, having been introduced not long after the removal of the prohibition on their importation from Cuba. It was not, however, until five or six years later that they were at all extensively sold in the streets; but the street-trade in cigars is no longer extensive, and in some respects has ceased to exist altogether.

I am told by experienced persons that the cigars first vended in the streets and public-houses were really smuggled. I say 'really' smuggled, as many now vended under that pretence never came from the smuggler's hands. 'Well, now, sir,' said one man, 'the last time I sold Pickwicks and Cubers a penny apiece with lights for nothing, was at Greenwich Fair, on the sly rather, and them as I could make believe was buying a smuggled thing, bought far freer. Everybody likes a smuggled thing.'

OF THE STREET-SELLERS OF SPONGE

THIS is one of the street-trades which has been long in the hands of the Jews, and, unlike the traffic in pencils, sealing-wax, and other articles of which I have treated, it remains so principally still.

In perhaps no article which is a regular branch of the street-trade, is there a greater diversity in the price and quality than in sponge. The street-sellers buy it at 1s. (occasionally 6d.), and as high as 21s. the pound. At one time, I believe about 20 years back, when fine sponge in large pieces was scarce and dear, some street-sellers gave 28s. the pound, or, in buying a smaller quantity, 2s. an ounce.

'I have sold sponge of all sorts,' said an experienced street-seller, 'both "fine toilet," fit for any lady or gentleman, and coarse stuff not fit to groom a ass with. That very common sponge is mostly 1s. the 1b. wholesale, but it's no manner of use, it's so sandy and gritty. It weighs heavy, or there might be a better profit on it. It has to be trimmed up and damped for showing it, and then it always feels hask (harsh) to the hand. It rubs to bits in no time. There was an old gent what I served with sponges, and he was very perticler, and the best customer I ever had, for his housekeeper bought her leathers of me. Like a deal of old coves that has nothing to do and doesn't often stir out, but hidles away time in reading or pottering about a garden, he was fond of a talk, and he'd give me a glass of something short, as if to make me listen to him, for I used to get fidgety, and he'd talk away stunning. He's dead now. He's told me, and more nor once, that sponges was more of a animal than a wegetable,' continued the incredulous street-seller, 'I do believe people reads theirselves silly. Such ——nonsense! Does it look like an animal? Where's its head and it's nose? He'd better have said it was a fish. And it's not a wegetable neither. But I'll tell you what it is, sir, and from them as has seen it where it's got with their own eyes. I have some relations as is sea-farin'-men, and I went a woyage once myself when a lad—one of my relations has seen it gathered by divers, I forgot where, from the rocks at the bottom and shores of the sea, and he says it's just sea-moss—stuff as grows there, as moss does to old walls in England. That's what it is, sir.'

OF THE STREET-SELLERS
OF WASH-LEATHERS

THE wash-leathers, sometimes called 'shammys' (chamois), now sold extensively in the streets, are for the most part the half of a sheep-skin, or of a larger lamb-skin. The skin is 'split' by machinery, and to a perfect nicety, into two portions. That known as the 'grain' (the part to which the fleece of the animal is attached) is very thin, and is dressed into a 'skiver,' a kind of leather used in the commoner requirements of book-binding, and for such purposes as the lining of hats. The other portion, the 'flesh,' is dressed as wash-leather. These skins are bought at the leather-sellers and the leather-dressers, at from 2s. to 20s. the dozen. The higher priced, or those from 12s. are often entire, and not 'split' skins. The great majority of the street-sellers of wash-leathers are women, and principally Irishwomen.

OF THE STREET-SELLERS
OF SPECTACLES AND EYE-GLASSES

TWENTY-FIVE years ago the street-trade in spectacles was almost entirely in the hands of the Jews, who hawked them in their boxes of jewellery, and sold them in the streets and public-houses, carrying them in their hands, as is done still. The trade was then far more remunerative that it is at the present time to the street-folk carrying it on. 'People had more money then,' one old spectacle-seller, now vending sponges, said, 'and there wasn't so many forced to take to the streets, Irish particularly, and opticians' charges were higher than they are now, and those who wanted glasses thought they were a take-in if they wasn't charged a fair price. O, times was very different then.'

The spectacles in the street-trade are bought at swag-shops in Houndsditch.

The spectacles are sold principally to working men, and are rarely hawked in the suburbs. The chief sale is in public-houses, but they are offered in all the busier thoroughfares and wherever a crowd is assembled. 'The eye-glasses,' said a man who vended them, 'is sold to what I call counter-hoppers and black-legs. You'll see most of the young swells that's mixed up with gaming concerns at races—for there's gaming still, though the booths is put down in many places—sport their eye-glasses; and so did them as used to be concerned in getting up Derby and St. Leger "sweeps" at public-houses; least-ways I've sold to them, where sweeps was held, and they was busy about them, and offered me a chance, sometimes, for a handsome eye-glass. But they're going out of fashion, is eye-glasses, I think. The other day I stood and offered them for nearly five hours at the foot of London-bridge, which used to be a tidy pitch for them, and I couldn't sell one. All that day I didn't take a halfpenny.'

There are sometimes 100 men, the half of whom are Jews and Irishmen in equal proportions, now selling spectacles and eye-glasses. Some of these traders are feeble from age, accident, continued sickness, or constitution, and represent that they must carry on a 'light trade,' being incapable of hard work, even if they could get it. Two women sell spectacles along with Dutch drops.

OF THE STREET-SELLERS OF DOLLS

THE making of dolls, like that of many a thing required for a mere recreation, a toy, a pastime, is often carried on amidst squalor, wretchedness, or privation, or—to use the word I have frequently heard among the poor—'pinching.' Of this matter, however, I shall have to treat when I proceed to consider the manufacture of and trade in dolls generally, not merely as respects street-sale.

Dolls are now so cheap, and so generally sold by open-air traders whose wares are of a miscellaneous character, as among the 'swag-barrow' or 'penny-a-piece' men of whom I have treated separately, that the sale of what are among the most ancient of all toys, as a 'business of itself,' is far smaller, numerically, than it was.

The dolls are most usually carried in baskets by street-sellers (who are not makers) and generally by women who are very poor. Here and there in the streets most frequented by the patrons of the open-air trade may be seen a handsome stall of dolls of all sizes and fashions, but these are generally the property of makers, although those makers may buy a portion of their stock. There are also smaller stalls which may present the stock of the mere seller. The dolls for street traffic may be bought at the swag-shops or of the makers. For the little armless 1*d.* dolls the maker charges the street-seller 8*s.*, and to the swag-shop keeper who may buy largely, 7*s.* 6*d.* the dozen. Some little stalls are composed entirely of penny dolls; on others the prices run from 1*d.* to 6*d.* The chief trade, however, among the class I now describe, is carried on by the display of dolls in baskets. If the vendor can only attract the notice of children—and more especially in a private suburban residence, where children are not used to the sight of dolls on stalls or barrows, or in shops—and can shower a few blessings and compliments, 'God be wid your bhutiful faces thin—and yours too, my lady, ma'am (with a curtsey to mistress or maid). Buy one of these dolls of a poor woman: shure they're bhutiful dolls and shuted for them angels o' the worruld'; under such circumstances, I say, a sale is almost certain.

A vendor of dolls expresses an opinion that as long as ever there are children from two years old to ten, there will always be purchasers of dolls; 'but for all that,' said he, 'somehow or another 'tis nothing of a trade to what it used to be. Spoiled children are our best customers. Whenever we sees a likely customer approaching—we, that is, those who know their business—always throw ourselves in the way, and spread out our dolls to the best advantage. If we hears young miss say *she will* have one, and cries for it, we are almost sure of a customer, and if we see her kick and fight a bit with the nuss-maid we are sure of a good price. If a child *cries well* we never baits our price. Most of the doll-sellers are the manufacturers of the dolls—that is, I mean, they puts 'em together. The heads are made in Hamburgh; the principal places for buying them in London are at Alfred Davis's, in Houndsditch; White's, in Houndsditch; and Joseph's, in Leadenhall-street.'

OF THE STREET-SELLERS OF POISON FOR RATS

THE number of Vermin-Destroyers and Rat-Catchers who ply their avocation in London has of late years become greatly diminished. One cause which I heard assigned for this was that many ruinous old buildings and old streets had been removed, and whole colonies of rats had been thereby extirpated. Another was that the race of rat-catchers had become distrusted, and had either sought some other mode of subsistence, or had resorted to other fields for the exercise of their professional labours.

The rat-catcher's dress is usually a velveteen jacket, strong corduroy trousers, and laced boots. Round his shoulder he wears an oil-skin belt, on which are painted the figures of huge rats, with fierce-looking eyes and formidable whiskers. His hat is usually glazed and sometimes painted after the manner of his belt. Occasionally—and in the country far more than in town—he carries in his hand an iron cage in which are ferrets, while two or three crop-eared terriers dog his footsteps. Sometimes a tamed rat runs about his shoulders and arms, or nestles in his bosom or in the large pockets of his coat. When a rat-catcher is thus accompanied, there is generally a strong aromatic odour about him, far from agreeable; this is owing to his clothes being rubbed with oil of thyme and oil of aniseed, mixed together. This composition is said to be so attractive to the sense of the rats (when used by a man who understands its due apportionment and proper application) that the vermin have left their holes and crawled to the master of the powerful spell. I heard of one man (not a rat-catcher professionally) who had in this way tamed a rat so effectually that the animal would eat out of his mouth, crawl upon his shoulder to be fed, and then 'smuggle into his bosom' (the words of my informant) 'and sleep there for hours.' The rat-catchers have many wonderful stories of the sagacity of the rat, and though in reciting their own feats, these men may not be the most trustworthy of narrators, any work on natural history will avouch that rats *are* sagacious may be trained to be very docile, and are naturally animals of great resources in all straits and difficulties.

One great source of the rat-catcher's employment and emolument thirty years ago, or even to a later period, is now comparatively a nonentity. At that time the rat-catcher or killer sometimes received a yearly or quarterly stipend to keep a London granary clear of rats. I was told by a man who has for twenty-eight years been employed about London granaries, that he had never known a rat-catcher employed in one except about twenty or twenty-two years ago, and that was in a granary by the river-side. The professional

man, he told me, certainly poisoned many rats, 'which stunk so,'
continued my informant—but then all evil odours in old buildings
are attributed to dead rats—'that it was enough to infect the corn.
He poisoned two fine cats as well. But I believe he was a young
hand and a bungler.' The rats, after these measures had been taken,
seem to have deserted the place for three weeks or a month, when
they returned in as great numbers as ever; nor were their ravages
and annoyances checked until the drains were altered and rebuilt.
It is in the better disposition of the drains of a corn-magazine, I am
assured, that the great check upon the inroads of these 'varmint' is
attained—by strong mason work and by such a series and arrangement of grates, as defy even the perseverance of a rat. Otherwise
the hordes which prey upon the garbage in the common sewers,
are certain to find their way into the granary along the drains and
channels communicating with those sewers, and will increase
rapidly despite the measures of the rat-catcher.

The same man told me that he had been five or six times applied
to by rat-catchers, and with liberal offers of beer, to allow them to
try and capture the black rats in the granary. One of these traders
declared he wanted them 'for a gent as vas curous in them there
hinteresting warmint'; but from the representations of the other
applicants, my informant was convinced that they were wanted
for rat-hunts, the Dog Billy being backed for 100*l* to kill so many
rats in so many minutes. 'You see, sir,' the corn merchant's man
continued, 'ours is an old concern, and there's black rats in it,
great big fellows; some of 'em must be old, for they're as white
about the muzzle as is the Duke of Wellington, and they have the
character of being very strong and very fierce. One of the catchers
asked me if I knew what a stunning big black rat would weigh, as
if I weighed rats! I always told them that I cared nothing about
rat-hunts and that I knew our people wouldn't like to be bothered;
and they was gentlemen that didn't admire sporting characters.'

The rat-catchers are also rat-killers. They destroy the animals
sometimes by giving them what is called in the trade 'an alluring
poison.' Every professional destroyer, or capturer, of rats will
pretend that as to poison he has his own particular method—his
secret—his discovery. But there is no doubt that arsenic is the basis
of all their poisons.

If the rats have to be taken alive, they are either trapped, so as not to injure them for a rat-hunt (or the procedure in the pit would be accounted 'foul'), or if driven out of their holes by ferrets, they can only run into some cask, or other contrivance, where they can be secured for the 'sportman's' purposes.

The grand consumption of rats, is in Bunhill-row, at a public-house kept by a pugilist. A rat-seller told me that from 200 to 500 rats were killed there weekly, the weekly average being, however, only the former number; while at Easter and other holidays, it is not uncommon to see bills posted announcing the destruction of 500 rats on the same day and in a given time, admittance 6*d*. Dogs are matched at these and similar places, as to which kills the greatest number of these animals in the shortest time. I am told that there are forty such places in London, but in some only the holiday times are celebrated in this small imitation of the beast combats of the ancients.

To show the nature of the sport of rat-catching, I print the following bill, of which I procured two copies. The words and type are precisely the same in each, but one bill is printed on good and the other on very indifferent paper, as if for distribution among distinct classes. The concluding announcement, as to the precise moment at which killing will commence, reads supremely business-like:—

RATTING FOR THE MILLION!

A SPORTING GENTLEMAN, Who is a Staunch
Supporter of the destruction of these VERMIN

WILL GIVE A

GOLD REPEATER
WATCH,

TO BE KILLED FOR BY

DOGS Under 13¾*lbs. Wt.*
15 *RATS EACH!*

TO COME OFF AT JEMMY MASSEY'S,

KING'S HEAD

COMPTON ST., SOHO,
On Tuesday, May 20, 1851.

☞ To be killed in a Large Wire Pit. A chalk
Circle to be drawn in the centre for the Second.—

Any man touching Dog or Rats, or acting in any
way unfair his dog will be disqualified.

To go to Scale at Half past 7 Killing to
Commence At Half past 8 Precisely.

OF THE HAWKING OF TEA

The hawking of tea in London cannot be considered as immediately
a street-trade, but it is in some respects blended with street callings
and street traffic, so that a brief account is necessary.

The branch of the tea trade closely connected with the street
business is that in tea-leaves. The exhausted leaves of the tea-pot
are purchased of servants or of poor women, and they are made
into 'new' tea. One gentleman—to whose information, and to the
care he took to test the accuracy of his every statement, I am
bound to express my acknowledgments—told me that it would be
fair to reckon that in London 1,500 lbs. of tea-leaves were weekly
converted into new tea, or 78,000 lbs. in the year! One house is
known to be very extensively and profitably concerned in this
trade, or rather *manufacture*, and on my asking the gentleman who
gave me the information if the house in question (he told me the
name) was accounted respectable by their fellow-citizens, the
answer was at once, '*Highly* respectable.'

The *old* tea-leaves, to be converted into *new*, are placed by the
manufactures on hot plates, and are re-dried and *re-dyed*. To give
the 'green' hue, a preparation of copper is used. For the 'black'
no dye is necessary in the generality of cases. This tea-manufacture
is sold to 'cheap' or 'slop' shopkeepers, both in town and country,
and is almost always sold ready mixed.

OF THE STREET-SELLERS
OF SECOND-HAND METAL ARTICLES

The wares sold by the vendors of the second-hand articles of metal
manufacture, or (as they are called in the streets) the 'old metal'
men may never be all found at one time upon one stall. 'Aye,
sir,' said one old man whom I conversed with, 'and there's more
things every now and then comes to the stalls, and there used to

be still more when I were young, but I can't call them all to mind, for times is worse with me, and so my memory fails. But there used to be a good many bayonets, and iron tinder-boxes, and steels for striking lights; I can remember them.'

Some of the sellers have strong heavy barrows, which they wheel from street to street. As this requires a considerable exertion of strength, such part of the trade is carried on by strong men, generally of the costermongering class. The weight to be propelled is about 300 lbs. Of this class there are now a few, rarely more than half-a-dozen, who sell on commission in the way I have described concerning the swag-barrowmen.

These are the 'old metal swags' of street classification, but their remuneration is less fixed than that of the other swag-barrowmen. It is sometimes a quarter, sometimes a third, and sometimes even a half of the amount taken. The men carrying on this traffic are the servants of the marine-store dealers, or vendors of old metal articles, who keep shops. If one of these people be 'lumbered up,' that is, if he find his stock increase too rapidly, he furnishes a barrow, and sends a man into the streets with it, to sell what the shopkeeper may find to be excessive. Sometimes if the tradesman can gain only the merest trifle more than he could gain from the people who buy for the melting-pot, he is satisfied.

There is, or perhaps was, an opinion prevalent that the street 'old metals' in this way of business got rid of stolen goods in such a manner as the readiest mode of sale, some of which were purposely rusted, and sold at almost any price, so that they brought but a profit to the 'fence,' whose payment to the thief was little more than the price of old metal at the foundry. I understand, however, that this course is not now pursued, nor is it likely that it ever was pursued to any extent. The street-seller is directly under the eye of the police, and when there is a search for stolen goods, it is not very likely that they would be paraded, however battered or rusted for the purpose, before men who possessed descriptions of all goods stolen. Until the establishment of the present system of police, this might have been an occasional practice. One street-seller had even heard, and he 'had it from the man what did it,' that a last-maker's shop was some years back broken into in the expectation that money would be met with, but none was found; and as the thieves could not bring away such heavy lumbering things as lasts, they cursed their ill-lulk, and brought away such tools as they could stow about their persons, and cover with their loose great coats. These were large knives, fixed to swivels, and resembling a small scythe, used by the artisan to rough hew the block of beech-wood; and a variety of excellent rasps and files (for they must be of the best), necessary for the completion of the last. These very tools were, in ten days after the robbery, sold from a street-barrow.

The second-hand metal goods are sold from stalls as well as from barrows, and these stalls are often tended by women whose husbands may be in some other branch of street-commerce. One of these stalls I saw in the care of a stout elderly Jewess, who was fast asleep, nodding over her locks and keys. She was awakened by the passing policeman, lest her stock should be pilfered by the boys: 'Come, wake up, mother, and shake yourself,' he said, 'I shall catch a weazel asleep next.'

Some of these barrows and stalls are heaped with the goods, and some are very scantily supplied, but the barrows are by far the best stocked. Many of them (especially the swag) look like collections of the different stages of rust, from its incipient spots to its full possession of the entire metal. But amongst these seemingly useless things there is a gleam of brass or plated ware. On one barrow I saw an old brass door-plate, on which was engraven the name of a late learned judge, Baron B——; another had formerly announced the residence of a dignitary of the church, the Rev. Mr. ——.

The second-hand metal sellers are to be seen in all the street-markets, especially on the Saturday nights; also in Poplar, Limehouse, and the Commercial-road, in Golden-lane, and in Old-street and Old-street-road, St. Luke's, in Hoxton and Shoreditch, in the Westminster Broadway, and the Whitechapel-road, in Rosemary-lane, and in the district where perhaps every street calling is pursued, but where some special street-trades seem peculiar to the genius of the place, in Petticoat-lane. A person unacquainted with the last-named locality may have formed an opinion that Petticoat-lane is merely a lane or street. But Petticoat-lane gives its name to a little district. It embraces Sandys-row, Artillery-passage, Artillery-lane, Frying-pan-alley, Catherine Wheel-alley, Tripe-yard, Fisher's-alley, Wentworth-street, Harper's-alley, Marlboroughcourt, Broad-place, Providence-place, Ellison-street, Swan-court, Little Love-court, Hutchinson-street, Little Middlesex-street, Hebrew-place, Boar's-head-yard, Black-horse-yard, Middlesex-street, Stoney-lane, Meeting-house-yard, Gravel-lane, White-street, Cutler-street, and Borer's-lane, until the wayfarer emerges into what appears the repose and spaciousness of Devonshire-square, Bishopsgate-street, up Borer's-lane, or into what in the contrast really looks like the aristocratic thoroughfare of the Aldgate High-street, down Middlesex-street; or into Houndsditch through the halls of the Old Clothes Exchange.

All these narrow streets, lanes, rows, passages, alleys, yards, courts, and places, are the sites of the street-trade carried on in this quarter. The whole neighbourhood rings with street cries, many uttered in those strange east-end Jewish tones which do not sound like English. Mixed with the incessant invitations to buy Hebrew dainties, or the 'sheepest pargains,' is occasionally heard the guttural utterance of the Erse tongue, for the 'native Irish,' as they are sometimes called, are in possession of some portion of the street-traffic of Petticoat-lane, the original Rag Fair. The savour of the place is moreover peculiar. There is fresh fish, and dried fish, and fish being fried in a style peculiar to the Jews; there is the fustiness of old clothes; there is the odour from the pans on which (still in the Jewish fashion) frizzle and hiss pieces of meat and onions; puddings are boiling and enveloped in steam; cakes with strange names are hot from the oven; tubs of big pickled cucumbers or of onions give a sort of acidity to the atmosphere; lemons and oranges abound; and altogether the scene is not only such as can only be seen in London, but only such as can be seen in this one part of the metropolis.

When I treat of the street-Jews, I shall have information highly curious to communicate, and when I come to the fifth division of my present subject, I shall more particularly describe Petticoat-lane, as the head-quarters of the second-hand clothes business.

I have here alluded to the character of this quarter as being one much resorted to formerly, and still largely used by the sellers of second-hand metal goods. Here I was informed that a strong-built man, known as Jack, or (appropriately enough) as Iron Jack, had, until his death six or seven years ago, one of the best-stocked barrows in London. This, in spite of remonstrances, and by a powerful exercise of his strength, the man lifted, as it were, on to the narrow foot-path, and every passer-by had his attention directed almost perforce to the contents of the barrow, for he must make a *'detour'* to advance on his way. One of this man's favourite pitches was close to the lofty walls of what, before the change in their charter, was one of the East India Company's vast warehouses. The contrast to any one who indulged a thought on the subject—and there is great food for thought in Petticoat-lane— was striking enough. Here towered the store-house of costly teas, and silks, and spices, and indigo; while at its foot was carried on the most minute and apparently worthless of all street-trades, rusty screws and nails, such as only few would care to pick up in the street, being objects of earnest bargaining!

OF THE STREET-SELLERS
OF SECOND-HAND MUSICAL INSTRUMENTS

OF this trade there are two branches; the sale of instruments which are really second-hand, and the sale of those which are pretendedly so; in other words, an honest and a dishonest business. As in street estimation the whole is a second-hand calling, I shall so deal with it.

At this season of the year, when fairs are frequent and the river steamers with their bands of music run off and regularly, and outdoor music may be played until late, the calling of the street-musician is 'at its best.' In the winter he is not unfrequently starving, especially if he be what is called 'a chance hand,' and have not the privilege of playing in public-houses when the weather renders it impossible to collect a street audience. Such persons are often compelled to part with their instruments, which they offer in the streets or the public-houses, for the pawn-brokers have been so often 'stuck' (taken in) with inferior instruments, that it is difficult to pledge even a really good violin. With some of these musical men it goes hard to part with their instruments, as they have their full share of the pride of art. Some, however, sell them recklessly and at almost any price, to obtain the means of prolonging a drunken carouse.

From a man who is now a dealer in second-hand musical instruments, and is also a musician, I had the following account of his start in the second-hand trade, and of his feelings when he first had to part with his fiddle.

'I was a gentleman's footboy,' he said, 'when I was young, but I was always very fond of music, and so was my father before me. He was a tailor in a village in Suffolk and used to play the bass-fiddle at church. I hardly know how or when I learned to play, but I seemed to grow up to it. There was two neighbours used to call at my father's and practise, and one or other was always showing me something, and so I learned to play very well. Everybody said so. Before I was twelve, I've played nearly all night at a dance in a farm-house. I never played on anything but the violin. You must stick to one instrument, or you're not up to the mark on any if you keep changing. When I got a place as footboy it was in a gentleman's family in the country, and I never was so happy as when master and mistress was out dining, and I could play to the servants in the kitchen or the servant's hall. Sometimes they got up a bit of a dance to my violin. If there was a dance at Christmas at any of the tenants', they often got leave for me to go and play. It was very little money I got given, but too much drink. At last master said, he hired me to be his servant and not for a parish fiddler, so I must drop it. I left him not long after—he got so cross and snappish. In my next place—no, the next but one—I was on board wages, in London, a goodish bit, as the family were travelling, and I had time on my hands, and used to go and play at public-houses of a night, just for the amusement of the company at first, but I soon got to know other musicians and made a little money. Yes, indeed, I could have saved money easily then, but I didn't; I got too fond of a public-house life for that, and was never easy at home.'

OF THE MUSIC 'DUFFERS'

SECOND-HAND GUITARS are vended by the street-sellers. The price varies from 7s 6d. to 15s. *Harps* form no portion of the second-hand business of the streets. A *drum* is occasionally, and only occasionally, sold to a showman, but the chief second-hand traffic is in violins. *Accordions*, both new and old, used to sell readily in the streets, either from stalls or in hawking, 'but,' said a man who had formerly sold them, 'they have been regularly "duffed" out of the streets, so much cheap rubbish is made to sell.

There's next to nothing done in them now. If one's offered to a man that's no judge of it, he'll be sure you want to cheat him, and perhaps abuse you; if he be a judge, of course it's no go, unless with a really good article.'

What I have called the 'dishonest trade' is known among the street-folk as 'music-duffing.' Among the swag-shopkeepers, at one place in Houndsditch more especially, are dealers in 'duffing fiddles.' These are German-made instruments, and are sold to the street-folk at 2*s*. or 3*s*. each, bow and all. When purchased by the music-duffers, they are discoloured so as to be made to look old. A music-duffer, assuming the way of a man half-drunk, will enter a public-house or accost any party in the street, saying: 'Here, I must have money, for I won't go home 'til morning, 'til morning, 'til morning, I won't go home 'til morning, 'til daylight does appear. And so I may as well sell my old fiddle myself as take it to a rogue of a broker. Try it anybody, it's a fine old tone, equal to any Cremonar. It cost me two guineas and another fiddle, and a good 'un too, in exchange, but I may as well be my own broker, for I must have money any how, and I'll sell it for 10*s*.'

Possibly a bargain is struck for 5*s*.; for the duffing violin is perhaps purposely damaged in some slight way, so as to appear easily reparable, and any deficiency in tone may be attributed to that defect, which was of course occasioned by the drunkenness of the possessor. Or possibly the tone of the instrument may not be bad, but it may be made of such unsound materials, and in such a slopway, though looking well to a little-practised eye, that it will soon fall to pieces. One man told me that he had often done the music-duffing, and had sold trash violins for 10*s*, 15*s*, and even 20*s*., 'according,' he said, 'to the thickness of the buyer's head,' but that was ten or twelve years ago.

OF THE STREET-SELLERS OF SECOND-HAND WEAPONS

THE sale of second-hand pistols, for to that weapon the street-sellers' or hawkers' trade in arms seems confined, is larger than might be cursorily imagined.

There must be something seductive about the possession of a pistol, for I am assured by persons familiar with the trade, that they have sold them to men who were ignorant, when first invited to purchase, how the weapon was loaded or discharged, and seemed half afraid to handle it. Perhaps the possession imparts a sense of security.

The pistols which are sometimes seen on the street-stalls are almost always old, rusted, or battered, and are useless to any one except to those who can repair and clean them for sale.

There are three men now selling new or second-hand pistols, I am told, who have been gunmakers.

This trade is carried on almost entirely by hawking to public-houses. I heard of no one who depended solely upon it, 'but this is the way,' one intelligent man stated to me, 'if I am buying second-hand things at a broker's, or in Petticoat-lane, or anywhere, and there's a pistol that seems cheap, I'll buy it as readily as any-thing I know, and I'll soon sell it a public-house, or I'll get it raffled for. Second-hand pistols sell better than new by such as me. If I was to offer a new one I should be told it was some Brum-magem slop rubbish. If there's a little silver-plate let into the wood of the pistol, and a crest or initials engraved on it—I've got it done sometimes—there's a better chance of sale, for people think it's been made for somebody of consequence that wouldn't be fobbed off with an inferior thing. I don't think I've often sold pistols to working-men, but I've known them join in raffles for them, and the winner has often wanted to sell it back to me, and has sold it to somebody. It's tradesmen that buy, or gentlefolks, if you can get at them. A pistol's a sort of a plaything with them.'

OF THE STREET-SELLERS OF SECOND-HAND CURIOSITIES

SEVERAL of the things known in the street-trade as 'curiosities' can hardly be styled second-hand with any propriety, but they are so styled in the streets, and are usually vended by street-merchants who trade in second-hand wares.

Curiosities are displayed, I cannot say temptingly (except perhaps to a sanguine antiquarian), for there is a great dinginess in the display, on stalls. One man whom I met wheeling his barrow in High-street, Camden-town, gave me an account of his trade. He was dirtily rather than meanly clad, and had a very self-satis-

fied expression of face. The principal things on his barrow were
coins, *shells*, and *old buckles*, with a pair of the very high and
wooden-heeled *shoes*, worn in the earlier part of the last century.
The coins were all of copper, and certainly did not lack variety.
Among them were tokens, but none very old. There was the head
of 'Charles Marquis Cornwallis' looking fierce in a cocked hat,
while on the reverse was Fame with her trumpet and a wreath, and
banners at her feet, with the superscription: 'His fame resounds
from east to west.' There was a head of Wellington with the date
1811, and the legend of 'Vincit amor patriae.' Also 'The R. Hon.
W. Pitt, Lord Warden Cinque Ports,' looking courtly in a bag
wig, with his hair brushed from his brow into what the curiosity-
seller called a 'topping.' This was announced as a 'Cinque Ports
token payable at Dover,' and was dated 1794. 'Wellingtons,' said
the man, 'is cheap; that one's only a half-penny, but here's one
here, sir, as you seem to understand coins, as I hope to get 2*d*. for,
and will take no less. It's "J. Lackington, 1794," you see, and
on the back there's a Fame, and round her is written—and it's a
good speciment of a coin—"Halfpenny of Lackington, Allen & Co.,
cheapest booksellers in the world." That's scarcer and more vally-
baller than Wellingtons or Nelsons either.' Of the current coin of
the realm, I saw none older than Charles II., and but one of his
reign, and little legible. Indeed the reverse had been ground quite
smooth, and some one had engraved upon it 'Charles Dryland
Tunbridg.' A small 'e' over the 'g' of Tunbridg perfected the
orthography. This, the street-seller said, was a 'love-token' as
well as an old coin, and 'them love-tokens was getting scarce.'
Of foreign and colonial coins there were perhaps 60. The oldest
I saw was one of Louis XV. of France and Navarre, 1774. There
was one also of the 'République Française' when Napoleon was
First Consul. The colonial coins were more numerous than the
foreign. There was the 'One Penny token' of Lower Canada; the
'one quarter anna' of the East India Company; the 'half stiver of
the colonies of Essequibo and Demarara;' the 'halfpenny token
of the province of Nova Scotia,' &c. &c. There were also counterfeit halfcrowns and bank tokens worn from their simulated silver
to rank copper. The principle on which this man 'priced' his coins,
as he called it, was simple enough. What was the size of a halfpenny
he asked a penny for; the size of a penny coin was 2*d*. 'It's a difficult

trade is mine, sir,' he said, 'to carry on properly, for you may be so easily taken in, if you're not a judge of coins and other curiosities.'

The shells of this man's stock in trade he called 'conks' and 'king conks.' He had no 'clamps' then, he told me, but they sold pretty well; he described them as 'two shells together, one fitting inside the other.' He also had sold what he called 'African cowries,' which were as 'big as a pint pot,' and the smaller cowries, which were 'money in India, for his father was a soldier and had been there and saw it.' The shells are sold from 1*d*. to 2*s*. 6*d*.

The old buckles were such as used to be worn on shoes, but the plate was all worn off, and 'such like curiosities,' the man told me, 'got scarcer and scarcer.'

OF THE STREET-SELLERS OF SECOND-HAND TELESCOPES AND POCKET GLASSES

In the sale of second-hand telescopes only one man is now engaged in any extensive way, except on mere chance occasions. Fourteen or fifteen years ago, I was informed, there was a considerable street sale in small telescopes at 1*s*. each. They were made at Birmingham, my informant believed, but were sold as second-hand goods in London. Of this trade there are now no remains.

The principal seller of second-hand telescopes takes a stand on Tower Hill or by the Coal Exchange, and his customers, as he sells excellent 'glasses,' are mostly sea-faring men. He has sold, and still sells, telescopes from 2*l*. 10*s*. to 5*l*. each, the purchasers generally 'trying' them, with strict examination, from Tower Hill, or on the Custom-House Quay. There are, in addition to this street-seller, six and sometimes eight others, who offer telescopes to persons about the docks or wharfs, who may be going some voyage. These are as often new as second-hand, but the second-hand articles are preferred. This, however, is a Jewish trade which will be treated under another head.

An old opera-glass, or the smaller articles best known as 'pocket-glasses,' are occasionally hawked to public-houses and offered in the streets, but so little is done in them that I can obtain no statistics. A spectacle seller told me that he had once tried to sell two second-hand opera-glasses at 2*s*. 6*d*. each, in the street, and then in the public-houses, but was laughed at by the people who were usually his customers. 'Opera-glasses!' they said, 'why, what did they want with opera-glasses? wait until they had opera-boxes.' He sold the glasses at last to a shop-keeper.

OF THE STREET-SELLERS OF OTHER MISCELLANEOUS SECOND-HAND ARTICLES

THE other second-hand articles sold in the streets I will give under one head, specifying the different characteristics of the trade, when any striking peculiarities exist. To give a detail of the whole trade, or rather of the several kinds of articles in the whole trade, is impossible. I shall therefore select only such as are sold the more extensively, or present any novel or curious features of second-hand stree-commerce.

Writing-desks, tea-caddies, dressing-cases, and *knife-boxes* used to be a ready sale, I was informed, when 'good second-hand'; but they are 'got up' now so cheaply by the poor fancy cabinet-makers who work for the 'slaughterers,' or furniture warehouses, and for some of the general-dealing swag-shops, that the sale of anything second-hand is greatly diminished. In fact I was told that as regards second-hand writing-desks and dressing cases, it might be said there was 'no trade at all now.' A few, however, are still to be seen at miscellaneous stalls, and are occasionally, but very rarely, offered at a public-house 'used' by artisans who may be considered 'judges' of work. The tea-caddies are the things which are in best demand. 'Working people buy them,' I was informed, and 'working people's wives. When women are the customers they look closely at the lock and key, as they keep "my uncle's cards" there' (pawn-broker's duplicates).

One man had lately sold second-hand tea-caddies at 9*d.*, 1*s.*, and 1*s.* 3*d.* each, and cleared 2*s.* in a day when he had stock and devoted his time to this sale. He could not persevere in it if he wished, he told me, as he might lose a day in looking out for the caddies; he might go to fifty brokers and not find one caddy cheap enough for his purpose.

Brushes are sold second-hand in considerable quantities in the streets, and are usually vended at stalls. Shoe-brushes are in the best demand, and are generally sold, when in good condition, at

1*s.* the set, the cost to the street-seller being 8*d.* They are bought, I was told, by the people who clean their own shoes, or have to clean other people's. Clothes' brushes are not sold to any extent, as the 'hard brush' of the shoe set is used by working people for a clothes' brush. Of late, I am told, second-hand brushes have sold more freely than ever. They were hardly to be had just when wanted, in a sufficient quantity, for the demand by persons going to Epsom, and Ascot races, who carry a brush of little value with them, to brush the dust gathered on the road from their coats. The costergirls buy very hard brushes, indeed mere stumps, with which they brush radishes; these brushes are vended at the street-stalls at 1*d.* each.

In *Stuffed Birds* for the embellishment of the walls of a room, there is still a small second-hand street sale, but none now in images or chimney-piece ornaments. 'Why,' said one dealer, 'I can now buy new figures for 9*d.*, such as not many years ago cost 7*s.*, so what chance of a second-hand sale is there?' The stuffed birds which sell the best are starlings. They are all sold as second-hand, but are often 'made up' for street-traffic; an old bird or two, I was told, in a new case, or a new bird in an old case. Last Saturday evening one man told me he had sold two 'long cases' of starlings and small birds for 2*s.* 6*d.* each. There are no stuffed parrots or foreign birds in this sale, and no pheasants or other game, except sometimes wretched old things which are sold because they happen to be in a case.

The street-trade in second-hand *Lasts* is confined principally to Petticoat and Rosemary lanes, where they are bought by the 'garret-masters' in the shoemaking trade who supply the large wholesale warehouses; that is to say, by small masters who find their own materials and sell the boots and shoes by the dozen pairs. The lasts are bought also by mechanics, street-sellers, and other poor persons who cobble their own shoes. A shoemaker told me that he occasionally bought a last at a street stall, or rather from street hampers in Petticoat and Rosemary lanes, and it seemed to him that second-hand stores of street lasts got neither bigger nor smaller: 'I suppose it's this way,' he reasoned; 'the garret-master buys lasts to do the slop-snobbing cheap, mostly women's lasts, and he dies or is done up and goes to the "great house," and his lasts find their way back to the streets. You notice, sir, the first time you're in Rosemary-lane, how little a great many of the lasts have been used, and that shows what a terrible necessity there was to part with them. In some there's hardly any peg-marks at all.' The lasts are sold from 1*d.* to 3*d.* each, or twice that amount in pairs, 'rights and lefts,' according to the size and the condition. There are about 20 street last-sellers in the second-hand trade of London—'at least 20,' one man said, after he seemed to have been making a mental calculation on the subject.

Second-hand harness is sold largely, and when good is sold very readily. There is, I am told, far less slop-work in harness-making than in shoe-making or in the other trades, such as tailoring, and 'many a lady's pony harness,' it was said to me by a second-hand dealer, 'goes next to a tradesman, and next to a costermonger's donkey, and if it's been good leather to begin with—as it will if it was made for a lady—why the traces'll stand slouting, and patching, and piecing, and mending for a long time, and they 'll do to cobble old boots last of all, for old leather'll wear just in treading, when it might snap at a pull. Give me a good quality to begin with, sir, and it's serviceable to the end.' In my inquiries among the costermongers I ascertained that if one of that body started his donkey, or rose from that to his pony, he never bought new harness, unless it were a new collar if he had a regard for the comfort of his beast, but bought old harness, and 'did it up' himself, often using iron rivets, or clenched nails, to reunite the broken parts, where, of course, a harness-maker would apply a patch. Nor is it the costermongers alone who buy all their harness second-hand. The sweep, whose stock of soot is large enough to require the help of an ass and a cart in its transport; the collector of bones and offal from the butchers' slaughter-houses or shops; and the many who may be considered as co-traders with the costermonger class—the greengrocer, the street coal-seller by retail, the salt-sellers, the gravel and sand dealer (a few have small carts)—all, indeed, of that class of traders, buy their harness second-hand, and generally in the streets.

OF SECOND-HAND STORE SHOPS

PERHAPS it may add to the completeness of the information here given concerning the trading in old refuse articles, and especially those of a miscellaneous character, the manner in which, and the parties by whom the business is carried on, if I conclude this branch of the subject by an account of the shops of the second-hand dealers. The distance between the class of these shop-keepers and of the stall and barrow-keepers I have described is not great. It may be said to be merely from the street to within doors. Marine-store dealers have often in their start in life been street-sellers, not unfrequently costermongers, and street-sellers they again become if their ventures be unsuccessful. Some of them, however, make a good deal of money in what may be best understood as a 'hugger-mugger way.'

On this subject I cannot do better than quote Mr. Dickens, one of the most minute and truthful of observers:—

'The reader must often have perceived in some by-street, in a poor neighbourhood, a small dirty shop, exposing for sale the most extraordinary and confused jumble of old, worn-out, wretched articles, that can well be imagined. Our wonder at their ever having been bought, is only to be equalled by our astonishment at the idea of their ever being sold again. On a board, at the side of the door, are placed about twenty books—all odd volumes; and as many wine-glasses—all different patterns; several locks, an old earthenware pan, full of rusty keys; two or three gaudy chimney ornaments—cracked, of course; the remains of a lustre, without any drops; a round frame like a capital O, which has once held a mirror; a flute, complete with the exception of the middle joint; a pair of curling-irons; and a tinder-box. In front of the shop-window, are ranged some half-dozen high-backed chairs, with spinal complaints and wasted legs; a corner cupboard; two or three very dark mahogany tables with flaps like mathematical problems; some pickle-bottles, some surgeons' ditto, with gilt labels and without stoppers; an unframed portrait of some lady who flourished about the beginning of the thirteenth century, by an artist who never flourished at all; an incalculable host of mis-cellanies of every description, including armour and cabinets, rags and bones, fenders and street-door knockers, fire-irons, wearing-apparel and bedding, a hall-lamp, and a room-door. Imagine, in addition to this incongruous mass, a black doll in a white frock, with two faces—one looking up the street, and the other looking down, swinging over the door; a board with the squeezed-up inscription "Dealer in marine stores," in lanky white letters, whose height is strangely out of proportion to their width; and you have before you precisely the kind of shop to which we wish to direct your attention.

'Although the same heterogeneous mixture of things will be found at all these places, it is curious to observe how truly and accurately some of the minor articles are exposed for sale—articles of wearing-apparel, for instance—mark the character of the neighbourhood. Take Drury-lane and Covent-garden for example.

'This is essentially a theatrical neighbourhood. There is not a potboy in the vicinity who is not, to a greater or less extent, a dramatic character. The errand-boys and chandlers'-shop-keepers' sons, are all stage-struck: they "get up" plays in back kitchens hired for the purpose, and will stand before a shop-window for hours, contemplating a great staring portrait of Mr. somebody or other, of the Royal Coburg Theatre, "as he appeared in the character of Tongo the Denounced." The consequence is, that there is not a marine-store shop in the neighbourhood, which does not exhibit for sale some faded articles of dramatic finery, such as three or four pairs of soiled buff boots with turn-over red tops, heretofore worn by a "fourth robber," or "fifth mob;" a pair of rusty broad-swords, a few gauntlets, and certain resplendent ornaments, which, if they were yellow instead of white, might be taken for insurance plates of the Sun Fire-office. There are several of these shops in the narrow streets and dirty courts, of which there are so many near the national theatres, and they all have tempting goods of this description, with the addition, perhaps, of a lady's pink dress covered with spangles; white wreaths, stage shoes, and a tiara like a tin lamp reflector. They have been purchased of some wretched supernumeraries, or sixth-rate actors, and are now offered for the benefit of the rising generation, who, on condition of making certain weekly payments, amounting in the whole to about ten times their value, may avail themselves of such desirable bargains.

'Let us take a very different quarter, and apply it to the same test. Look at a marine-store dealer's, in that reservoir of dirt, drunkenness, and drabs: thieves, oysters, baked potatoes, and pickled salmon—Ratcliff-highway. Here, the wearing-apparel is all nautical. Rough blue jackets, with mother-of-pearl buttons, oil-skin hats, coarse checked shirts, and large canvas trousers that look as if they were made for a pair of bodies instead of a pair of legs, are the staple commodities. Then, there are large bunches of cotton pocket-handkerchiefs, in colour and pattern unlike any one ever saw before, with the exception of those on the backs of the three young ladies without bonnets who passed just now. The furniture is much the same as elsewhere, with the addition of one or two models of ships, and some old prints of naval engagements in still older frames. In the window are a few compasses, a small tray containing silver watches in clumsy thick cases; and tobacco-boxes, the lid of each ornamented with a ship, or an anchor, or some such trophy. A sailor generally pawns or sells all he has before he has been long ashore, and if he does not, some favoured companion kindly saves him the trouble. In either case, it is an even chance that he afterwards unconsciously repurchases the same things at a higher price than he gave for them at first.

'Again: pay a visit, with a similar object, to a part of London, as unlike both of these as they are to each other. Cross over to the Surrey side, and look at such shops of this description as are to be found near the King's Bench prison, and in "the Rules." How different, and how strikingly illustrative of the decay of some of the unfortunate residents in this part of the metropolis! Imprisonment and neglect have done their work. There is contamination in the profligate denizens of a debtors' prison; old friends have fallen off; the recollection of former prosperity has passed away; and with it all thoughts for the past, all care for the future. First, watches and rings, then clocks, coats, and all the more expensive articles of dress, have found their way to the pawnbroker's. That miserable resource has failed at last, and the sale of some trifling article at one of these shops, has been the only mode left of raising a shilling or two, to meet the urgent demands of the moment. Dressing-cases and writing-desks, too old to pawn but too good to keep; guns, fishing-rods, musical instruments, all in the same condition; have first been sold, and the sacrifice has been but slightly felt. But hunger must be allayed, and what has already become a habit, is easily resorted to, when an emergency arises. Light articles of clothing, first of the ruined man, then of his wife, at last of their children, even of the youngest, have been parted with, piecemeal. There they are, thrown carelessly together until a purchaser presents himself, old, patched, and repaired, it is true; but the make and materials tell of better days: and the older they are, the greater the misery and destitution of those whom they once adorned.'

OF THE STREET-SELLERS OF SECOND-HAND APPAREL

The multifariousness of the articles of this trade is limited only by what the uncertainty of the climate, the caprices of fashion, or the established styles of apparel in the kingdom, have caused to be worn, flung aside, and reworn as a revival of an obsolete style. It is to be remarked, however, that of the old-fashioned styles none that are costly have been revived. Laced coats, and embroidered and lappeted waistcoats, have long disappeared from second-hand traffic—the last stage of fashions—and indeed from all places but court or fancy balls and the theatre.

The great mart for second-hand apparel was, in the last century, in Monmouth-street; now, by one of those arbitrary, and almost always inappropriate, changes in the nomenclature of streets, termed Dudley-street, Seven Dials. 'Monmouth-street finery' was a common term to express tawdriness and pretence. Now Monmouth-street, for its new name is hardly legitimated, has no finery. Its second-hand wares are almost wholly confined to old boots and shoes, which are vamped up with a good deal of trickery; so much so that a shoemaker, himself in the poorer practice of the 'gentle craft,' told me that blacking and brown paper were the materials of Monmouth-street cobbling. Almost every master in Monmouth-street now is, I am told, an Irishman; and the great majority of the workmen are Irishmen also. There were a few Jews and a few cockneys in this well-known street a year or two back, but now this branch of the second-hand trade is really in the hands of what may be called a clan. A little business is carried on in second-hand apparel, as well as boots and shoes, but it is insignificant.

The head-quarters of this second-hand trade are now in Petticoat and Rosemary lanes, especially in Petticoat-lane, and the traffic there carried on may be called enormous. As in other departments of commerce, both in our own capital, in many of our older cities, and in the cities of the Continent, the locality appropriated to this traffic is one of narrow streets, dark alleys, and most oppresive crowding. The traders seem to judge of a Rag-fair garment, whether a cotton frock or a ducal coachman's great-coat, by the touch, more reliably than by sight; inspect, so to speak, with their fingers more than their eyes. But the business in Petticoat and Rosemary lanes is mostly of a retail character. The wholesale mart —for the trade in old clothes has both a wholesale and retail form— is in a place of especial curiosity, and one of which, as being little known, I shall first speak.

OF THE OLD CLOTHES EXCHANGE

THE trade in second-hand apparel is one of the most ancient of callings, and is known in almost every country, but anything like the Old Clothes Exchange of the Jewish quarter of London, in the extent and order of its business, is unequalled in the world. There is indeed no other such place, and it is rather remarkable that a business occupying so many persons, and requiring such facilities for examination and arrangement, should not until the year 1843 have had its regulated proceedings. The Old Clothes Exchange is the latest of the central marts, established in the metropolis.

Smithfield, or the Cattle Exchange, is the oldest of all the markets; it is mentioned as a place for the sale of horses in the time of Henry II. Billingsgate, or the Fish Exchange, is of ancient, but uncertain era. Covent Garden—the largest Fruit, Vegetable, and Flower Exchange—first became established as the centre of such commerce in the reign of Charles II.; the establishment of the Borough and Spitalfields markets, as other marts for the sale of fruits, vegetables, and flowers, being nearly as ancient. The Royal Exchange dates from the days of Queen Elizabeth, and the Bank of England and the Stock-Exchange from those of William III., while the present premises for the Corn and Coal Exchanges are modern.

Were it possible to obtain the statistics of the last quarter of a century, it would, perhaps, be found that in none of the important interests I have mentioned has there been a greater increase of business than in the trade in old clothes. Whether this purports a high degree of national prosperity or not, it is not my business at present to inquire, and be it as it may, it is certain that, until the last few years, the trade in old clothes used to be carried on entirely in the open air, and this in the localities which I have pointed out in my account of the trade in old metal (p. 193) as comprising the Petticoat-lane district. The old clothes trade was also pursued in Rosemary-lane, but then—and so indeed it is now—this was but a branch of the more centralized commerce of Petticoat-lane. The head-quarters of the traffic at that time were confined to a space not more than ten square yards, adjoining Cutler-street. The chief traffic elsewhere was originally in Cutler-street, White-street, Carter-street, and in Harrow-alley—the districts of the celebrated Rag-fair.

The confusion and clamour before the institution of the present arrangements were extreme. Great as was the extent of the business transacted, people wondered how it could be accomplished, for it always appeared to a stranger, that there could be no order whatever in all the disorder. The wrangling was incessant, nor were the trade-contests always confined to wrangling alone. The passions of the Irish often drove them to resort to cuffs, kicks, and blows, which the Jews, although with a better command over their tempers, were not slack in returning. The East India Company, some of whose warehouses adjoined the market, frequently complained to the city authorities of the nuisance. Complaints from other quarters were also frequent, and sometimes as many as 200 constables were necessary to restore or enforce order. The nuisance, however, like many a public nuisance, was left to remedy itself, or rather it was left to be remedied by individual enterprise. Mr. L. Isaac, the present proprietor, purchased the houses which then filled up the back of Phil's-buildings, and formed the present Old Clothes Exchange. This was eight years ago; now there are no more policemen in the locality than in other equally populous parts.

Of Old Clothes Exchanges there are now two, both adjacent, the first one opened by Mr. Isaac being the most important. This is 100 feet by 70, and is the mart to which the collectors of the cast-off apparel of the metropolis bring their goods for sale. The goods are sold wholesale and retail, for an old clothes merchant will buy either a single hat, or an entire wardrobe, or a sackful of shoes,— I need not say *pairs*, for odd shoes are not rejected. In one depart-

ment of 'Isaac's Exchange,' however, the goods are not sold to
parties who buy for their own wearing, but to the old clothes
merchant, who buys to sell again. In this portion of the mart are
90 stalls, averaging about six square feet each.

In another department, which communicates with the first, and
is two-thirds of the size, are assembled such traders as buy the old
garments to dispose of them, either after a process of cleaning,
or when they have been repaired and renovated. These buyers
are generally shopkeepers, residing in the old clothes districts of
Marylebone-lane, Holywell-street, Monmouth-street, Union-street
(Borough), Saffron-hill (Field-lane), Drury-lane, Shoreditch, the
Waterloo-road, and other places of which I shall have to speak
hereafter.

The difference between the first and second class of buyers above
mentioned, is really that of the merchant and the retail shopkeeper.
The one buys literally anything presented to him which is vendible,
and in any quantity, for the supply of the wholesale dealers from
distant parts, or for exportation, or for the general trade of London.
The other purchases what suits his individual trade, and is likely
to suit regular or promiscuous customers.

In another part of the same market is carried on the *retail* old
clothes trade to any one—shop-keeper, artisan, clerk, costermonger,
or gentlemen. This indeed, is partially the case in the other parts.
'Yesh, inteet,' said a Hebrew trader, whom I conversed with on
the subject, 'I shall be clad to shell you one coat, sir. Dish von is
shust your shize; it is verra sheep, and vosh made by one tip-top
shnip.' Indeed, the keenness and anxiety to trade—whenever trade
seems possible—causes many of the frequenters of these marts to
infringe the arrangements as to the manner of the traffic, though
the proprietors endeavour to cause the regulations to be strictly
adhered to.

The second Exchange, which is a few yards apart from the other
is known as Simmons and Levy's Clothes Exchange, and is unemployed, for its more especial business purposes, except in the
mornings. The commerce is then wholesale, for here are sold collections of unredeemed pledges in wearing apparel, consigned there
by the pawnbrokers, or the buyers at the auctions of unredeemed
goods; as well as draughts from the stocks of the wardrobe dealers;
a quantity of military or naval stores, and such like articles. In the

afternoon the stalls are occupied by retail dealers. The ground is about as large as the first-mentioned exchange, but is longer and narrower.

OF THE WHOLESALE BUSINESS AT THE OLD CLOTHES EXCHANGE

A CONSIDERABLE quantity of the old clothes disposed of at the Exchange are bought by merchants from Ireland. They are then packed in bales by porters, regularly employed for the purpose, and who literally *build* them up square and compact. These bales are each worth from 50*l.* to 300*l.*, though seldom 300*l.*, and it is curious to reflect from how many classes the pile of old garments has been collected—how many privations have been endured before some of these habiliments found their way into the possession of the old clothes-man—what besotted debauchery put others in his possession—with what cool calculation others were disposed of —how many were procured for money, and how many by the tempting offers of flowers, glass, crockery, spars, table-covers, lace, or millinery—what was the clothing which could first be spared when rent was to be defrayed or bread to be bought, and what was treasured until the last—in what scenes of gaiety or gravity, in the opera-house or the senate, had the perhaps departed wearers of some of that heap of old clothes figured—through how many possessors, and again through what new scenes of middle-class or artisan comfort had these dresses passed, or through what accidents of 'genteel' privation and destitution—and lastly through what necessities of squalid wretchedness and low debauchery.

Every kind of old attire, from the highest to the *very lowest*, I was emphatically told, was sent to Ireland.

Some of the bales are composed of garments originally made for the labouring classes. These are made up of every description of colour and material—cloth, corduroy, woollen cords, fustian, moleskin, flannel, velveteen, plaids, and the several varieties of those substances. In them are to be seen coats, great-coats, jackets, trousers, and breeches, but no other habiliments, such as boots, shirts, or stockings. I was told by a gentleman, who between 40 and 50 years ago was familiar with the liberty and poorer parts of Dublin, that the most coveted and the most saleable of all second-hand apparel was that of leather breeches, worn commonly in some of the country parts of England half a century back, and sent in considerable quantities at that time from London to Ireland. These nether habiliments were coveted because, as the Dublin sellers would say, they 'would wear for ever, and look illigant after that.' Buck-skin breeches are now never worn except by grooms in their liveries, and gentlemen when hunting, so that the trade in them in the Old Clothes Exchange, and their exportation to Ireland, are at an end. The next most saleable thing—I may mention, incidentally—vended cheap and second-hand in Dublin, to the poor Irishmen of the period I speak of, was a wig! And happy was the man who could wear two, one over the other.

Some of the Irish buyers who are regular frequenters of the London Old Clothes Exchange, take a small apartment, often a garret or a cellar, in Petticoat-lane or its vicinity, and to this room they convey their purchases until a sufficient stock has been collected. Among these old clothes the Irish possessors cook, or at any rate eat, their meals, and upon them they sleep. I did not hear that such dealers were more than ordinarily unhealthy; though it may, perhaps, be assumed that such habits are fatal to health. What may be the average duration of life among old clothes sellers who live in the midst of their wares, I do not know, and believe that no facts have been collected on the subject; but I certainly saw among them some very old men.

Other wholesale buyers from Ireland occupy decent lodgings in the neighbourhood—decent considering the locality. In Phil's-buildings, a kind of wide alley which forms one of the approaches to the Exchange, are eight respectable apartments, almost always let to the Irish old clothes merchants.

Tradesmen of the same class come also from the large towns of England and Scotland to buy for their customers some of the left-off clothes of London.

Nor is this the extent of the wholesale trade. Bales of old clothes are exported to Belgium and Holland, but principally to Holland. Of the quantity of goods thus exported to the Continent not above one-half, perhaps, can be called old *clothes*, while among these the old livery suits are in the best demand. The other goods of this foreign trade are old serges, duffles, carpeting, drugget, and heavy woollen goods generally, of all the descriptions which I have before enumerated as parcel of the second-hand trade of the streets. Old merion curtains, and any second-hand decorations of fringes, woollen lace, &c., are in demand for Holland.

Twelve bales, averaging somewhere about 100*l.* each in value, but not fully 100*l.*, are sent direct every week of the year from the Old Clothes Exchange to distant places, and this is not the whole of the traffic, apart from what is done retail. I am informed on the best authority, that the average trade may be stated at 1500*l.* a week all the year round. When I come to the conclusion of the subject, however, I shall be able to present statistics of the amount turned over in the respective branches of the old clothes trade, as well as of the number of the traffickers, only one-fourth of whom are now Jews.

The conversation which goes on in the Old Clothes Exchange during business hours, apart from the 'larking' of the young sweet-stuff and orange or cake-sellers, is all concerning business, but there is, even while business is being transacted, a frequent interchange of jokes, and even of practical jokes. The business talk— I was told by an old clothes collector, and I heard similar remarks— is often to the following effect:—

'How much is this here?' says the man who comes to buy. 'One pound five,' replies the Jew seller. 'I won't give you above half the money.' 'Half de money,' cries the salesman, 'I can't take dat. Vat above the 16*s.* dat you offer now vill you give for it? Vill you give me eighteen? Vell, come, give ush your money, I've got ma rent to pay.' But the man says, 'I only bid you 12*s.* 6*d.*, and I shan't give no more.' And then, if the seller finds he can get him to 'spring' or advance no further, he says, 'I shupposh I musht take your money even if I loosh by it. You ll be a better cushtomer anoder time. [This is still a common 'deal', I am assured by one who began the business at 13 years old, and is now upwards of 60 years of age. The Petticoat-laner will always ask at least twice as much as he means to take.]

OF THE STREET-SELLERS
OF PETTICOAT AND ROSEMARY-LANES

Immediately connected with the trade of the central mart for old clothes are the adjoining streets of Petticoat-lane, and those of the not very distant Rosemary-lane. In these localities is a second-hand garment-seller at almost every step, but the whole stock of these traders, decent, frowsy, half-rotten, or smart and good habilments, has first passed through the channel of the Exchange. The men who sell these goods have all bought them at the Exchange—the exceptions being insignificant—so that this street-sale is but an extension of the trade of the central mart, with the addition that the wares have been made ready for use.

A cursory observation might lead an inexperienced person to the conclusion, that these old clothes traders who are standing by bundles of gowns, or lines of coats, hanging from their door-posts, or in the place from which the window has been removed, or at the sides of their houses, or piled in the street before them, are drowsy people, for they seem to sit among their property, lost in thought, or caring only for the fumes of a pipe. But let any one indicate, even by an approving glance, the likelihood of his becoming a customer, and see if there be any lack of diligence in business. Some, indeed, pertinaciously invite attention to their wares; some (and often well-dressed women) leave their premises a few yards to accost a stranger pointing to a 'good dress-coat' or 'an excellent frock' (coat). I am told that this practice is less pursued than it was, and it seems that the solicitations are now addressed chiefly to strangers. These strangers, persons happening to be passing, or visitors from curiosity, are at once recognised; for as in all not very extended localities, where the inhabitants pursue a similar calling, they are, as regards their knowledge of one another, as the members of one family. Thus a stranger is as easily recognised as he would be in a little rustic hamlet where a strange face is not seen once a quarter. Indeed so narrow are some of the streets and alleys in this quarter, and so little is there of privacy, owing to the removal, in warm weather, even of the casements, that the room is commanded in all its domestic details; and as among these details there is generally a further display of goods similar to the articles outside, the jammed-up places really look like a great family house with merely a sort of channel, dignified by the name of a street, between the right and left suites of apartments.

In one off-street, where on a Sunday there is a considerable demand for Jewish sweet-meats by Christian boys, and a little sly, and perhaps not very successful gambling on the part of the ingenuous youth to possess themselves of these confectionaries at the easiest rate, there are some mounds of builders' rubbish upon which, if an inquisitive person ascended, he could command the details of the upper rooms, probably the bed chambers—if in their crowded apartments these traders can find spaces for beds.

It must not be supposed that old clothes are more than the great staple of the traffic of this district. Wherever persons are assembled there are certain to be purveyors of provisions and of cool or hot drinks for warm or cold weather. The interior of the Old Clothes Exchange has its oyster-stall, its fountain of ginger-beer, its coffee-house, and ale-house, and a troop of peripatetic traders, boys principally, carrying trays. Outside the walls of the Exchange this trade is still thicker. A Jew boy thrusts a tin of highly-glazed cakes and pastry under the people's noses here; and on the other side a basket of oranges regales the same sense by its proximity. At the next step the thoroughfare is interrupted by a gaudy-looking ginger-beer, lemonade, raspberryade, and nectar fountain; 'a halfpenny a glass, a halfpenny a glass, sparkling lemonade!' shouts the vendor as you pass. The fountain and the glasses glitter in the sun, the varnish of the wood-work shines, the lemonade really does sparkle, and all looks clean—except the owner. Close by is a brawny young Irishman, his red beard unshorn for perhaps ten days, and his neck, where it had been exposed to the weather, a far deeper red than his beard, and he is carrying a small basket of nuts, and selling them as gravely as if they were articles suited to his strength. A little lower is the cry, in a woman's voice, 'Fish, fried fish! Ha'penny; fish, fried fish!' and so monotonously and mechanically is it ejaculated that one might think the seller's life was passed in uttering these few words, even as a rook's is in crying 'Caw, caw.' Here I saw a poor Irishwoman who had a child on her back buy a piece of this fish (which may be had 'hot' or 'cold'), and tear out a piece with her teeth, and this with all the eagerness and relish of appetite or hunger; first eating the brown outside and then *sucking* the bone. I never saw fish look firmer or whiter. That fried fish is to be procured is manifest to more senses than one, for you can hear the sound of its being fried, and smell the fumes from the oil. In an open window opposite frizzle on an old tray, small pieces of thinly-cut-meat, with a mixture of onions, kept hot by being placed over an old pan containing charcoal. In another room a mess of batter is smoking over a grate. 'Penny a lot, oysters,' resounds from different parts. Some of the sellers command two streets by establishing their stalls or tubs at a corner. Lads pass, carrying sweet-stuff on trays. I observed one very dark-eyed Hebrew boy chewing the hard-bake he vended—if it were not a substitute—with an expression of great enjoyment. Heaped-up trays of fresh-looking sponge-cakes are carried in tempting pyramids. Youths have stocks of large hard-looking biscuits, and walk about crying, 'Ha'penny biscuits, ha'penny; three a penny, biscuits;' these, with a morsel of cheese, often supply a dinner or a luncheon. Dates and figs, as dry as they are cheap, constitute the stock in trade of other street-sellers. 'Coker-nuts' are sold in pieces and entire; the Jew boy, when he invites to the purchase of an entire nut, shaking it at the ear of the customer. I was told by a costermonger that these juveniles had a way of drumming with their fingers on the shell so as to satisfy a 'green' customer that the nut offered was a sound one.

Such are the summer eatables and drinkables which I have lately seen vended in the Petticoat-lane district. In winter there are, as long as daylight lasts—and in no other locality perhaps does it last so short a time—other street provisions, and, if possible, greater zeal in selling them, the hours of business being circumscribed. There is then the potato-can and the hot elder-wine apparatus, and smoking pies and puddings, and roasted apples and chestnuts, and walnuts, and the several fruits which ripen in the autumn—apples, pears, &c.

Hitherto I have spoken only of such eatables and drinkables as are ready for consumption, but to these the trade in the Petticoat-lane district is by no means confined. There is fresh fish, generally of the cheaper kinds, and smoked or dried fish (smoked salmon, moreover, is sold ready cooked), and costermongers' barrows, with their loads of green vegetables, looking almost out of place amidst the surrounding dinginess. The cries of 'Fine cauliflowers,' 'Large penny cabbages,' 'Eight a shilling, mackerel,' 'Eels, live eels,' mix strangely with the hubbub of the busier street.

Other street-sellers also abound. You meet one man who says mysteriously, and rather bluntly, 'Buy a good knife, governor.' His tone is remarkable, and if it attract attention, he may hint that he has smuggled goods which he *must* sell anyhow. Such men,

I am told, look out mostly for seamen, who often resort to Petti-coat-lane; for idle men like sailors on shore, and idle uncultivated men often love to lounge where there is bustle. Pocket and pen knives and scissors, 'Penny a piece, penny a pair,' rubbed over with oil, both to hide and prevent rust, are carried on trays, and spread on stalls, some stalls consisting of merely a tea-chest lid on a stool. Another man, carrying perhaps a sponge in his hand, and well-dressed, asks you, in a subdued voice, if you want a good razor, as if he almost suspected that you meditated suicide, and were looking out for the means! This is another ruse to introduce smuggled (or 'duffer's') goods. Account-books are hawked. 'Penny-a-quire,' shouts the itinerant street stationer (who, if questioned, always declares he said 'Penny half quire'). 'Stockings, stockings, two pence a pair.' 'Here's your chewl-ry; penny, a penny; pick 'em and choose 'em.' [I may remark that outside the window of one shop, or rather parlour, if there be any such distinction here, I saw the handsomest, as far as I am able to judge, and the best cheap jewellery I ever saw in the streets.] 'Pencils, sir, pencils; steel-pens, steel-pens; ha'penny, penny; pencils, steel-pens; sealing-wax, wax, wax, wax!' shouts one, 'Green peas, ha'penny a pint!' cries another.

These things, however, are but the accompaniments of the main traffic. But as such things accompany all traffic, not on a small scale, and may be found in almost every metropolitan thorough-fare, where the police are not required, by the householders, to interfere, I will point out, to show the distinctive character of the street-trade in this part, what is *not* sold and not encouraged. I saw no old books. There were no flowers; no music, which indeed could not be heard except at the outskirts of the din; and no beggars plying their vocation among the trading class.

Another peculiarity pertaining alike to this shop and street locality is, that everything is at the veriest minimum of price; though it may not be asked, it will assuredly be taken. The bottle of lemonade which is elsewhere a penny is here a halfpenny. The tarts, which among the street-sellers about the Royal Exchange are a halfpenny each, are here a farthing. When lemons are two a-penny in St. George's-market, Oxford-street, as the long line of street stalls towards the western extremity is called—they are three and four a-penny in Petticoat and Rosemary lanes. Certainly there is a difference in size between the dearer and the cheaper tarts and lemons, and perhaps there is a difference in quality also but the rule of a minimized cheapness has no exceptions in this cheap-trading quarter.

But Petticoat-lane is essentially the old clothes district. Embracing the streets and alleys adjacent to Petticoat-lane, and including the rows of old boots and shoes on the ground, there is perhaps between two and three miles of old clothes. Petticoat-lane proper is long and narrow, and to look down it is to look down a vista of many coloured garments, alike on the sides and on the ground. The effect sometimes is very striking, from the variety of hues, and the constant flitting, or gathering, of the crowd into little groups of bargainers. Gowns of every shade and every pattern are hanging up, but none, perhaps, look either bright or white; it is a vista of dinginess, but many coloured dinginess, as regards female attire. Dress coats, frock coats, great coats, livery and game-keepers' coats, paletots, tunics, trousers, knee-breeches, waistcoats, capes, pilot coats, working jackets, plaids, hats, dressing gowns, shirts, Guernsey frocks, are all displayed. The predominant colours are black and blue, but there is every colour; the light drab of some aristocratic livery; the dull brown-green of velveteen; the deep blue of a pilot jacket; the variegated figures of the shawl dressing-gown; the glossy black of the restored garments; the shine of newly turpentined black satin waistcoats; the scarlet and green of some flaming tartan; these things—mixed with the hues of the women's garments, spotted and striped— certainly present a scene which cannot be beheld in any other part of the greatest city of the world, nor in any other portion of the world itself.

The ground has also its array of colours. It is covered with lines of boots and shoes, their shining black relieved here and there by the admixture of females' boots, with drab, green, plum or lavender-coloured 'legs,' as the upper part of the boot is always called in the trade. There is, too, an admixture of men's 'button-boots' with drab cloth legs; and of a few red, yellow, and russet coloured slippers; and of children's coloured morocco boots and shoes. Handkerchiefs, sometimes of a gaudy orange pattern, are heaped on a chair. Lace and muslins occupy small stands or are spread on the ground. Black and drab and straw hats are hung up, or piled one upon another and kept from falling by means of strings; while, incessantly threading their way through all this intricacy, is a mass of people, some of whose dresses speak of a recent purchase in the lane.

ROSEMARY-LANE

ROSEMARY-LANE, which has in vain been rechristened Royal Mint-street, is from half to three-quarters of a mile long—that is, if we include only the portion which runs from the junction of Leman and Dock streets (near the London Docks) to Sparrow-corner, where it abuts on the Minories. Beyond the Leman-street termination of Rosemary-lane, and stretching on into Shadwell, are many streets of a similar character as regards the street and shop supply of articles to the poor; but as the old clothes trade is only occasionally carried on there, I shall here deal with Rosemary-lane proper.

This lane partakes of some of the characteristics of Petticoat-lane, but without its so strongly marked peculiarities. Rosemary-lane is wider and airier, the houses on each side are loftier (in several parts), and there is an approach to a gin palace, a thing unknown in Petticoat-lane: there is no room for such a structure there.

Rosemary-lane, like the quarter I have last described, has its off-streets, into which the traffic stretches. Some of these off-streets are narrower, dirtier, poorer in all respects than Rosemary-lane itself, which indeed can hardly be stigmatized as very dirty. These are Glasshouse-street, Russel-court, Hairbrine-court, Parson's-court, Blue Anchor-yard (one of the poorest places and with a half-built look), Darby-street, Cartwright-street, Peter's-court, Princes-street, Queen-street, and beyond these and in the direction of the Minories, Rosemary-lane becomes Sharp's-buildings and Sparrow-corner. There are other small non-thoroughfare courts, sometimes called blind alleys, to which no name is attached, but which are very well known to the neighbourhood as Union-court, &c.; but as these are not scenes of street-traffic, although they may be the abodes of street-traffickers, they require no especial notice.

The dwellers in the neighbourhood or the off-streets of Rosemary-lane, differ from those of Petticoat-lane by the proximity of the former place to the Thames. The lodgings here are occupied by dredgers, ballast-heavers, coal-whippers, watermen, lumpers, and others whose trade is connected with the river, as well as the slop-workers and sweaters working for the Minories. The poverty of these workers compels them to lodge wherever the rent of the rooms is the lowest. As a few of the wives of the ballast-heavers, &c., are street-sellers in or about Rosemary-lane, the locality is often sought by them. About Petticoat-lane the off-streets are mostly occupied by the old clothes merchants.

In Rosemary-lane is a greater *street*-trade, as regards things placed on the ground for retail sale, &c., than in Petticoat-lane; for though the traffic in the last-mentioned lane is by far the greatest, it is more connected with the shops, and fewer traders whose dealings are strictly those of the street alone resort to it. Rosemary-lane, too, is more Irish. There are some cheap lodging-houses in the courts, &c., to which the poor Irish flock; and as they are very frequently street-sellers, on busy days the quarter abounds with them. At every step you hear the Erse tongue, and meet with the Irish physiognomy; Jews and Jewesses are also seen in the street, and they abound in the shops. The street-traffic does not begin until about one o'clock, except as regards the vegetable, fish, and oysterstalls, &c., but the chief business of this lane, which is as inappropriately as that of Petticoat is suitably named, is in the vending of the articles which have often been thrown aside as refuse, but from which numbers in London wring an existence.

One side of the lane is covered with old boots and shoes; old clothes, both men's, and women's, and children's; new lace for edgings, and a variety of cheap prints and muslins (also new); hats and bonnets; pots, and often of the commonest kinds; tins; old knives and forks, old scissors, and old metal articles generally; here and there is a stall of cheap bread or American cheese, or what is announced as American; old glass; different descriptions of second-hand furniture of the smaller size, such as children's chairs, bellows, &c. Mixed with these, but only very scantily, are a few bright-looking swag-barrows, with china ornaments, toys, &c. Some of the wares are spread on the ground on wrappers, or pieces of matting or carpet; and some, as the pots, are occasionally placed on straw. The cotton prints are often heaped on the ground; where are also ranges or heaps of boots and shoes, and piles of old clothes, or hats, or umbrellas. Other traders place their goods on stalls or barrows, or over an old chair or clothes-horse. And amidst all this motley display the buyers and sellers smoke, and shout, and doze,

and bargain, and wrangle, and eat and drink tea and coffee, and
sometimes beer. Altogether Rosemary-lane is more of a *street*
market than is Petticoat-lane.

OF THE STREET-SELLERS
OF MEN'S SECOND-HAND CLOTHES

In the following accounts of street-selling, I shall not mix up any
account of the retailers' modes of buying, collecting, repairing, or
'restoring' the second-hand garments, otherwise than incidentally.
I have already sketched the systems pursued, and more will have
to be said concerning them under the head of STREET BUYERS.
Neither have I thought it necessary, in the further accounts I have
collected, to confine myself to the trade carried on in the Petticoat-
and Rosemary-lane districts. The greater portion relates to those
places, but my aim, of course, is to give an account which will show
the character of the second-hand trade of the metropolis generally.

'People should remember,' said an intelligent shoemaker (not
a street-seller) with whom I had some conversation about cobbling
for the streets, 'that such places as Rosemary-lane have their uses
this way. But for them a very poor industrious widow, say, with
only 2*d*. or 3*d*. to spare, couldn't get a pair of shoes for her child;
whereas now, for 2*d*. or 3*d*., she can get them there, of some sort
or other. There's a sort of decency, too, in wearing shoes. And
what's more, sir—for I've bought old coats and other clothes in
Rosemary-lane, both for my own wear and my family's, and know
something about it—how is a poor creature to get such a decency
as a petticoat for a poor little girl, if she'd only a penny, unless
there were such places?'

In the present state of the very poor, it may be that such places
as those described have, on the principle that half a loaf is better
than no bread, their benefits. But whether the state of things in
which an industrious widow, or a host of industrious persons, *can*
spare but 1*d*. for a child's clothing (and nothing, perhaps, for their
own), is one to be lauded in a Christian country, is another question
fraught with grave political and social considerations.

The man from whom I received the following account of the sale
of men's wearing apparel was apparently between 30 and 40 years
of age. His face presented something of the Jewish physiognomy,

but he was a Christian, he said, though he never had time to go to church or chapel, and Sunday was often a busy day; besides, a man must live as others in his way lived. He had been connected with the sale of old clothes all his life, as were his parents, so that his existence had been monotonous enough, for he had never been more than five miles, he thought, from Whitechapel, the neighbourhood where he was born. In winter he liked a concert, and was fond of a hand at cribbage, but he didn't care for the play. His goods he sometimes spread on the ground—at other times he had a stall or a 'horse' (clothes-horse).

'My customers,' he said, 'are nearly all working people, some of them very poor, and with large families. For anything I know, some of them works with their heads, though, as well, and not their hands, for I've noticed that their hands is smallish and seems smoothish, and suits a tight sleeve very well. I don't know what they are. How should I? I asks no questions, and they'll tell me no fibs. To such as them I sell coats mostly; indeed, very little else. They're often very perticler about the fit, and often asks, "Does it look as if it was made for me?" Sometimes they is seedy, very seedy, and comes to such as me, most likely, 'cause we're cheaper than the shops. They don't like to try things on in the street, and I can always take a decent customer, or one as looks such, in there, to try on (pointing to a coffee-shop). Bob-tailed coats (dress-coats) is far the cheapest. I've sold them as low as 1s., but not often; at 2s. and 3s. often enough; and sometimes as high as 5s. Perhaps a 3s. or 3s. 6d. coat goes off as well as any, but bob-tailed coats is little asked for. Now, I've never had a frock (surtout or frock coat), as well as I can remember, under 2s. 6d., except one that stuck by me a long time, and I sold it at last for 20d., which was 2d. less than what it cost. It was only a poor thing, in course, but it had such a rum-coloured velvet collar, that was faded, and had had a bit let in, and was all sorts of shades, and that hindered its selling, I fancy. Velvet collars isn't worn now, and I'm glad of it. Old coats goes better with their own collars (collars of the same cloth as the body of the coat). For frocks, I've got as much as 7s. 6d., and cheap at it too, sir. Well, perhaps (laughing) at an odd time they wasn't so very cheap, but that's all in the way of trade. About 4s. 6d. or 5s. is perhaps the ticket that a frock goes off best at. It's working people that buys frocks most, and often working people's wives or mothers—that is as far as I know. They're capital judges as to what'll fit their men; and if they satisfy me it's all right, I'm always ready to undertake to change it for another if it don't fit. O, no, I never agree to give back the money if it don't fit; in course not; that wouldn't be business.

'No, sir, we're very little troubled with people larking. I have had young fellows come, half drunk, even though it might be Sunday morning, and say, "Guv'ner, what'll you give me to wear that coat for you, and show off your cut?" We don't stand much of their nonsense. I don't known what such coves are. Perhaps "torneys" journeymen, or pot-boys out for a Sunday morning's spree.' [This was said with such a bitterness that surprised me in so quiet-speaking a man]. 'In greatcoats and cloaks I don't do much, but it's a very good sale when you can offer them well worth the money. I've got 10s. often for a greatcoat, and higher and lower, oftener lower in course; but 10s. is about the card for a good thing. It's the like with cloaks. Paletots don't sell well. They're mostly thinner and poorer cloth to begin with at the tailors—them new-fashioned named things often is so—and so they show when hard worn. Why no, sir, they can be done up, certainly; anything can be touched up; but they get thin, you see, and there's nothing to work upon as there is in a good cloth greatcoat. You'll excuse me, sir, but I saw you a little bit since take one of them there square books that a man gives away to people coming this way, as if to knock up the second-hand business, but he won't, though; I'll tell you how them slops, if they come more into wear, is sure to injure us. If people gets to wear them low-figured things, more and more, as they possibly may, why where's the second-hand things to come from? I'm not a tailor, but I understands about clothes, and I believe that no person ever saw anything green in my eye. And if you find a slop thing marked a guinea, I don't care what it is, but I'll undertake that you shall get one that'll wear longer, and look better to the very last, second-hand, at less than half the money, plenty less. It was good stuff and good make at first, and hasn't been abused, and that's the reason why it always bangs a slop, because it was good to begin with.

'Trousers sell pretty well. I sell them, cloth ones, from 6d. up to 4s. They're cheaper if they're not cloth, but very seldom less or so low as 6d. Yes, the cloth ones at that is poor worn things, and little things too. They're not men's, they're youth's or boy's size. Good strong cords goes off very well at 1*s*. and 1*s*. 6*d*., or higher. Irish bricklayers buys them, and paviours, and such like. It's easy to fit a man with a pair of second-hand trousers. I can tell by his build what'll fit him directly. Tweeds and summer trousers is middling, but washing things sells worse and worse. It's an expense, and expenses don't suit my customers—not a bit of it.

'Waistcoats isn't in no great call. They're often worn very hard under any sort of a tidy coat, for a tidy coat can be buttoned over anything that's "dicky," and so, you see, many of'em' s half-way to the rag-shop before they comes to us. Well, I'm sure I can hardly say what sort of people goes most for weskets' [so he pronounced it]. 'If they're light, or there's anything "fancy" about them, I thinks it's mothers as makes them up for their sons. What with the strings at the back and such like, it ain't hard to make a wesket fit. They're poor people as buys certainly, but genteel people buys such things as fancy weskets, or how do you suppose they'd all be got through? O, there's ladies comes here for a bargain, I can tell you, and gentlemen, too; and many on 'em would go through fire for one. Second-hand satins (waistcoats) is good still, but they don't fetch the tin they did. I' ve sold weskets from 1½*d*. to 4*s*. Well, it's hard to say what the three-ha'pennies is made of; all sorts of things; we calls them "serge." Three-pence is a common price for a little wesket. There's no under-weskets wanted now, and there 's no rolling collars. It was better for us when there was, as there was more stuff to work on. The double-breasted gets scarcer, too. Fashions grows to be cheap things now-a-days.'

OF THE SECOND-HAND SELLERS OF SMITHFIELD-MARKET

No small part of the second-hand trade of London is carried on in the market-place of Smithfield, on the Friday afternoons. Here is a mart for almost everything which is required for the harnessing of beasts of draught, or is required for any means of propulsion or locomotion, either as a whole vehicle, or in its several parts, needed by street-traders: also of the machines, vessels, scales, weights, measures, baskets, stands, and all other appliances of street-trade.

The scene is animated and peculiar. Apart from the horse, ass, and goat trade (of which I shall give an account hereafter), it is a grand Second-hand Costermongers' Exchange. The trade is not confined to that large body, though they are the principal merchants, but includes greengrocers (often the costermonger in a shop), carmen, and others. It is, moreover, a favourite resort of the purveyors of street-provisions and beverages, of street dainties and luxuries. Of this class some of the most prosperous are those who are 'well known in Smithfield.'

The space devoted to this second-hand commerce and its accompaniments, runs from St. Bartholomew's Hospital towards Long-lane, but isolated peripatetic traders are found in all parts of the space not devoted to the exhibition of cattle or of horses. The crowd on the day of my visit was considerable, but from several I heard the not-always-very-veracious remarks of 'Nothing doing' and 'There's nobody at all here to-day.' The weather was sultry, and at every few yards arose the cry from men and boys, 'Ginger-beer, ha'penny a glass! Ha'penny a glass,' or 'Iced lemonade here! Iced raspberryade, as cold as ice, ha'penny a glass, only a ha'-penny!' A boy was elevated on a board at the end of a splendid affair of this kind. It was a square built vehicle, the top being about 7 feet by 4, and flat and surmounted by the lemonade fountain; long, narrow, champagne glasses, holding a raspberry coloured liquid, frothed up exceedingly, were ranged round, and the beverage dispensed by a woman, the mother or employer of the boy who was bawling. The sides of the machine, which stood on wheels, were a bright, shiny blue, and on them sprawled the lion and unicorn in gorgeous heraldry, yellow and gold, the artist being, according to a prominent announcement, a 'herald painter.' The apparatus was handsome, but with that exaggeration of handsomeness which attracts the high and low vulgar, who cannot distinguish between gaudiness and beauty. The sale was brisk. The ginger-beer sold in the market was generally dispensed from carts, and here I noticed, what occurs yearly in street-commerce, an innovation on the established system of the trade. Several sellers disposed of their ginger-beer in clear glass bottles, somewhat larger and fuller-necked than those introduced by M. Soyer for the sale of his 'nectar,' and the liquid was drank out of the bottle the moment the cork was withdrawn, and so the necessity of a glass was obviated.

Near the herald-painter's work, of which I have just spoken, stood a very humble stall on which were loaves of bread, and round the loaves were pieces of fried fish and slices of bread on plates, all remarkably clean. 'Oysters! Penny-a-lot! Penny-a-lot, oysters!' was the cry, the most frequently heard after that of ginger-beer, &c. 'Cherries! Twopence-a-pound! Penny-a-pound, cherries!' 'Fruit-pies! Try my fruit-pies!' The most famous dealer in all kinds of penny pies is, however, not a pedestrian, but an equestrian hawker. He drives a very smart, handsome pie-cart, sitting behind after the manner of the Hansom cabmen, the lifting up of a lid below his knees displaying his large stock of pies. His 'drag' is whisked along rapidly by a brisk chestnut pony, well-harnessed. The 'whole set out,' I was informed, ponny included, cost 50*l.* when new. The proprietor is a keen Chartist and teetotaller, and loses no opportunity to inculcate to his customers the excellence of teetotalism, as well as of his pies. 'Milk! ha'penny a pint! ha'-penny a pint, good milk!' is another cry. 'Raspberry cream! Iced raspberry-cream, ha'penny a glass!' This street-seller had a capital trade. Street-ices, or rather ice-creams, were somewhat of a failure last year, more especially in Greenwich-park, but this year they seem likely to succeed. The Smithfield man sold them in very small glasses, which he merely dipped into a vessel at his feet, and so filled them with the cream. The consumers had to use their fingers instead of a spoon, and no few seemed puzzled how to eat their ice, and were grievously troubled by its getting among their teeth. I heard one drover mutter that he felt 'as if it had snowed in his belly!' Perhaps at Smithfield-market on the Friday afternoons every street-trade in eatables and drinkables has its representative, with the exception of such things as sweet-stuff, curds and whey, &c., which are bought chiefly by women and children. There were plum-dough, plum-cake, pastry, pea-soup, whelks, periwinkles, ham-sandwiches, hot-eels, oranges, &c., &c., &c.

These things are the usual accompaniment of street-markets, and I now come to the subject matter of the work, the sale of second-hand articles.

In this trade, since the introduction of a new arrangement two months ago, there has been a great change. The vendors are not allowed to vend barrows in the market, unless indeed with a pony or donkey harnessed to them, or unless they are wheeled about by the owner, and they are not allowed to spread their wares on the ground. When it is considered of what those wares are composed, the awkwardness of the arrangement, to the sales-people, may be understood. They consist of second-hand collars, pads, saddles, bridles, bits, traces, every description of worn harness, whole or in parts; the wheels, springs, axles, &c., of barrows, and carts; the beams, chains, and bodies of scales;—these, perhaps, are the chief things which are sold separately, as parts of a whole. The traders have now no other option but to carry them as they best can, and offer them for sale. You saw men who really appear clad in harness. Portions were fastened round their bodies, collars slung on their arms, pads or small cart-saddles, with their shaft-gear, were planted on their shoulders. Some carried merely a collar, or a harness bridle, or even a bit or a pair of spurs. It was the same with the springs, &c., of the barrows and small carts. They were carried under men's arms, or poised on their shoulders. The wheels and other things which are too heavy for such modes of transport had to be placed in some sort of vehicle, and in the vehicles might be seen trestles, &c.

The complaints on the part of the second-hand sellers were neither few nor mild: 'If it had been a fat ox that had to be accommodated,' said one, 'before he was roasted for an alderman, they'd have found some way to do it. But it don't matter for poor men; though why we shouldn't be suited with a market as well as richer people is not the ticket, that's the fact.'

These arrangements are already beginning to be infringed, and will be more and more infringed, for such is always the case. The reason why they were adopted was that the ground was so littered, that there was not room for the donkey traffic and other requirements of the market. The donkeys, when 'shown,' under the old arrangement, often trod on boards of old metal, &c., spread on the ground, and tripped, sometimes to their injury, in consequence. Prior to the change, about twenty persons used to come from Petticoat-lane, &c., and spread their old metal or other stores on the ground.

Of these there are now none. These Petticoat-laners, I was told by a Smithfield frequenter, were men 'who knew the price of old rags,'—a new phrase expressive of their knowingness and keenness in trade.

OF THE STREET-SELLERS OF LIVE ANIMALS

THE live animals sold in the streets include beasts, birds, fish, and reptiles, all sold in the streets of London.

The class of men carrying on this business—for they are nearly all men—is mixed; but the majority are of a half-sporting and half-vagrant kind. One informant told me that the bird-catchers, for instance, when young, as more than three-fourths of them are, were those who 'liked to be after a loose end,' first catching their birds, as a sort of sporting business, and then sometimes selling them in the streets, but far more frequently disposing of them in the birdshops. 'Some of these boys,' a bird-seller in a large way of business said to me, 'used to become rat-catchers or dog-sellers, but there's not such great openings in the rat and dog line now. As far as I know, they're the same lads, or just the same sort of lads, anyhow, as you may see "helping," holding horses, or things like that, at concerns like them small races at Peckham or Chalk Farm, or helping any way at the foot-races at Camberwell.' There is in this bird-catching a strong manifestation of the vagrant spirit. To rise long before daybreak; to walk some miles before daybreak; from the earliest dawn to wait in some field, or common, or wood, watching the capture of the birds; then a long trudge to town to dispose of the fluttering captives; all this is done cheerfully, because there are about it the irresistible charms, to this class, of excitement, variety, and free and open-air life. Nor do these charms appear one whit weakened when, as happens often enough, all this early morn business is carried on fasting.

The old men in the bird-catching business are not to be ranked as to their enjoyment of it with the juveniles, for these old men are sometimes infirm, and can but, as one of them said to me some time ago, 'hobble about it.' But they have the same spirit, or the sparks of it. And in this part of the trade is one of the curious characteristics of a street-life; or rather of an open-air pursuit for the requirements of a street-trade. A man, worn out for other purposes, incapable of anything but a passive, or sort of lazy labour—such as lying in a field and watching the action of his trap-cages—will yet in a summer's morning, decrepit as he may be, possess himself of a dozen or even a score of the very freest and most aspiring of all our English small birds, a creature of the air beyond other birds of his 'order'—to use an ornithological term—of sky-larks.

The dog-sellers are of a sporting, trading, idling class. Their sport is now the rat-hunt, or the ferret-match, or the dog-fight; as it was with the predecessors of their stamp, the cock-fight; the bull, bear, and badger bait; the shrove-tide cock-shy, or the duck hunt. Their trading spirit is akin to that of the higher-class sporting fraternity, the trading members of the turf. They love to sell and to bargain, always with a quiet exultation at the time—a matter of loud tavern boast afterwards, perhaps, as respects the street-folk —how they 'do' a customer, or 'do' one another. 'It's not cheating,' was the remark and apology of a very famous jockey of the old times, touching such measures; 'it's not cheating, it's outwitting.' Perhaps this expresses the code of honesty of such traders; not to cheat, but to outwit or over-reach. Mixed with such traders, however, are found a few quiet, plodding, fair-dealing men, whom it is difficult to classify, otherwise than that they are 'in the line, just because they likes it.' The idling of these street-sellers is a part of their business. To walk by the hour up and down a street, and with no manual labour except to clean their dogs' kennels, and to carry them in their arms, is but an idleness, although, as some of these men will tell you, 'they work hard at it.'

Under the respective heads of dog and bird-sellers, I shall give more detailed characteristics of the class, as well as of the varying qualities and inducements of the buyers.

The street-sellers of foreign birds, such as parrots, parroquets, and cockatoos; of gold and silver fish; of goats, tortoises, rabbits, leverets, hedge-hogs; and the collectors of snails, worms, frogs, and toads, are also a mixed body. Foreigners, Jews, seamen, country-men, costermongers, and boys form a part, and of them I shall give a description under the several heads. The prominently-characterized street-sellers are the traders in dogs and birds.

OF THE FORMER STREET-SELLERS, 'FINDERS,' STEALERS, AND RESTORERS OF DOGS

BEFORE I describe the present condition of the street-trade in dogs, which is principally in spaniels, or in the description well

known as lap-dogs, I will give an account of the former condition
of the trade, if trade it can properly be called, for the 'finders' and
'stealers' of dogs were the more especial subjects of a parliamentary
inquiry, from which I derive the official information on the matter.
The Report of the Committee was ordered by the House of Commons to be printed, July 26, 1844.

In their Report the Committee observe, concerning the value
of pet dogs:—'From the evidence of various witnesses it appears,
that in one case a spaniel was sold for 105*l.*, and in another, under
a sheriff's execution, for 95*l.* at the hammer; and 50*l.* or 60*l.* are
not unfrequently given for fancy dogs of first-rate breed and
beauty.' The hundred guineas' dog above alluded to was a 'black
and tan King Charles's spaniel;'—indeed, Mr. Dowling, the editor
of *Bell's Life in London*, said, in his evidence before the Committee,
'I have known as much as 150*l.* given for a dog.' He said afterwards: 'There are certain marks about the eyes and otherwise,
which are considered "properties;" and it depends entirely upon
the property which a dog possesses as to its value.'

I cannot better show the extent and lucrativeness of this trade,
than by citing a list which one of the witnesses before Parliament,
Mr. W. Bishop, a gunmaker, delivered in to the Committee, of
'cases in which money had recently been extorted from the owners
of dogs by dog-stealers and their confederates.' There is no explanation of the space of time included under the vague term 'recently';
but the return shows that 151 ladies and gentlemen had been the
victims of the dog-stealers or dog-finders, for in this business the
words were, and still are to a degree, synonyms, and of these 62
had been so victimized in 1843 and in the six months of 1844, from
January to July. The total amount shown by Mr. Bishop to have
been paid for the restoration of stolen dogs was 977*l.* 4*s.* 6*d.*, or an
average of 6*l.* 10*s.* per individual practised upon.

These dog appropriators, as they found that they could levy
contributions not only on royalty, foreign ambassadors, peers,
courtiers, and ladies of rank, but on public bodies, and on the
dignitaries of the state, the law, the army, and the church, became
bolder and more expert in their avocations—a boldness which was
encouraged by the existing law. Prior to the parliamentary inquiry,
dog-stealing was not an indictable offence. The only mode of
punishment for dog-stealing was by summary conviction, the

STREET-SELLER OF BIRDS'-NESTS

SCENE IN PETTICOAT-LANE

penalty being fine or imprisonment; but Mr. Commissioner Mayne did not known of any instance of a dog-stealer being sent to prison in default of payment. Although the law recognised no property in a dog, the animal was taxed; and it was complained at the time that an unhappy lady might have to pay tax for the full term upon her dog, perhaps a year and a half after he had been stolen from her. One old offender, who stole the Duke of Beaufort's dog, was transported, not for stealing the dog, but his collar.

The difficulty of proving the positive theft of a dog was extreme. In most cases, where the man was not seen actually to seize a dog which could be identified, he escaped when carried before a magistrate. 'The dog-stealers,' said Inspector Shackell, 'generally go two together; they have a piece of liver; they say it is merely bullock's liver, which will entice or tame the wildest or savagest dog which there can be in any yard; they give it to him, and take him from his chain. At other times,' continues Mr. Shackell, 'they will go in the street with a little dog, rubbed over with some sort of stuff, and will entice valuable dogs away.... If there is a dog lost or stolen, it is generally known within five or six hours where that dog is, and they know almost exactly what they can get for it, so that it is a regular system of plunder.' Mr. G. White, 'dealer in live stock, dogs, and other animals,' and at one time a 'dealer in lions, and tigers, and all sorts of things,' said of the dog-stealers: 'In turning the corners of streets there are two or three of them together; one will snatch up a dog and put into his apron, and the others will stop the lady and say, "What is the matter?" and direct the party who has lost the dog in a contrary direction to that taken.'

In this business were engaged from 50 to 60 men, half of them actual stealers of the animals. The others were the receivers, and the go-betweens or 'restorers.' The thief kept the dog perhaps for a day or two at some public-house, and he then took it to a dog-dealer with whom he was connected in the way of business. These dealers carried on a trade in 'honest dogs,' as one of the witnesses styled them (meaning dogs honestly acquired), but some of them dealt principally with the dog-stealers. Their depots could not be entered by the police, being private premises, without a search-warrant—and direct evidence was necessary to obtain a search-warrant—and of course a stranger in quest of a stolen dog would not be admitted. Some of the dog-dealers would not purchase or receive dogs known to have been stolen, but others bought and speculated in them. If an advertisement appeared offering a reward for the dog, a negotiation was entered into. If no reward was offered, the owner of the dog, who was always either known or made out, was waited upon by a restorer, who undertook 'to restore the dog if terms could be come to.' A dog belonging to Colonel Fox was once kept six weeks before the thieves would consent to the Colonel's terms. One of the most successful restorers was a shoe-maker, and mixed little with the actual stealers; the dog-dealers, however, acted as restorers frequently enough. If the person robbed paid a good round sum for the restoration of a dog, and paid it speedily, the animal was almost certain to be stolen a second time, and a higher sum was then demanded. Sometimes the thieves threatened that if they were any longer trifled with they would inflict torture on the dog, or cut its throat. One lady, Miss Brown of Bolton-street, was so worried by these threats, and by having twice to redeem her dog, 'that she has left England,' said Mr. Bishop, 'and I really do believe for the sake of keeping the dog.' It does not appear, as far as the evidence shows, that these threats of torture or death were ever carried into execution; some of the witnesses had merely heard of such things.

OF A DOG-'FINDER'—A 'LURKER'S' CAREER

CONCERNING a dog-finder, I received the following account from one who had received the education of a gentleman, but whom circumstances had driven to an association with the vagrant class, and who has written the dog-finder's biography from personal knowledge—a biography which shows the *variety* that often characterizes the career of the 'lurker,' or street-adventurer.

'If your readers,' writes my informant, 'have passed the Rubicon of "forty years in the wilderness," memory must bring back the time when the feet of their childish pilgrimage have trodden a beautiful grass-plot—now converted into Belgrave-square; when Pimlico was a "village out of town," and the "five fields" of Chelsea were fields indeed. To write the biography of a living character is always delicate, as to embrace all its particulars is difficult; but of the truthfulness of my account there is no question.

'Probably about the year of the great rost (1814), a French Protestant refugee, named La Roche, sought asylum in this country, not from persecution, but from difficulties of a commercial character. He built for himself, in Chelsea, a cottage of wood, nondescript in shape, but pleasant in locality, and with ample accommodations for himself and his son. Wife he had none. This little bazaar of mud and sticks was surrounded with a bench of rude construction, on which the Sunday visitors to Ranelagh used to sit and sip their curds and whey, while from the entrance—far removed in those days from competition—

> 'There stood uprear' d, as ensign of the place,
> Of blue and red and white, a checquer d' mace,
> On which the paper lantern hung to tell
> How cheap its owner shaved you, and how well.

Things went on smoothly for a dozen years, when the old Frenchman departed this life.

'His boy carried on the business for a few months, when frequent complaints of "Sunday gambling" on the premises' and loud whispers of suspicion relative to the concealment of stolen goods, induced "Chelsea George"—the name the youth had acquired—to sell the good-will of the house, fixtures, and all, and at the eastern extremity of London to embark in business as a "mush or mush-room-faker." Independently of his appropriation of umbrellas, proper to the mush-faker's calling, Chelsea George was by no means scrupulous concerning other little matters within his reach, and if the proprietors of the "swell cribs" within his "beat" had no "umbrellas to mend," or "old 'uns to sell," he would ease the pegs in the passage of the incumbrance of a greatcoat, and telegraph the same out of sight (by a colleague), while the servant went in to make the desired inquiries. At last he was "bowl'd out" in the very act of "nailing a yack" (stealing a watch). He "expiated," as it is called, this offence by three months' exercise on the "cockchafer" (tread-mill). Unaccustomed as yet to the novelty of the exercise, he fell through the wheel and broke one of his legs. He was, of course, permitted to finish his time in the infirmary of the prison, and on his liberation was presented with five pounds out of "the Sheriffs' Fund."

'Although, as I have before stated, he had never been out of England since his childhood, he had some little hereditary knowledge of the French language, and by the kind and voluntary recommendation of one of the police-magistrates of the metropolis, he was engaged by an Irish gentleman proceeding to the Continent, as a sort of supernumerary servant, to "make himself generally useful." As the gentleman was unmarried, and mostly stayed at hotels, George was to have permanent wages and "find himself," a condition he invariably fulfilled, if anything was left in his way. Frequent intemperance, neglect of duty, and unaccountable departures of property from the portmanteau of his master, led to his dismissal, and Chelsea George was left, without friends or character, to those resources which have supported him for some thirty years.

'During his "umbrella" enterprise he had lived in lodging-houses of the lowest kind, and of course mingled with the most depraved society, especially with the vast army of trading sturdy mendicants, male and female, young and old, who assume every guise of poverty, misfortune, and disease, which craft and ingenuity can devise or well-tutored hypocrisy can imitate. Thus initiated, Chelsea George could "go upon any lurk," could be in the last stage of consumption —actually in his dying hour—but now and then convalescent for years and years together. He could take fits and counterfeit blindness, be a respectable broken-down tradesman, or a soldier maimed in the service, and dismissed without a pension.

'Thus qualified, no vicissitudes could be either very new or very perplexing, and he commenced operations without delay, and pursued them long without desertion. The "first move" in his mendicant career was *taking them on the fly;* which means meeting the gentry on their walks, and beseeching or at times menacing them till something is given; something in general *was* given to get rid of the annoyance, and, till the "game got stale," an hour's work, morning and evening, produced a harvest of success, and ministered to an occasion of debauchery.

'His less popular, but more upright father, had once been a dog-fancier, and George, after many years' vicissitude, at length took a "fancy" to the same profession, but not on any principles recognised by commercial laws. With what success he has practised, the ladies and gentlemen about the West-end have known, to their loss and disappointment, for more than fifteen years past.

'Although the police have been and still are on the alert, George has, in every instance, hitherto escaped punishment, while numerous detections connected with escape have enabled the offender to hold these officials at defiance. The "modus operandi" upon which George proceeds is to varnish his hands with a sort of gelatine, composed of the coarsest pieces of liver, fried, pulverised, and mixed up with tincture of myrrh.' This is the composition of which Inspector Shackell spoke before the Select Committee, but he did not seem to know of what the lure was concocted. My correspondent continues: 'Chelsea George caresses every animal who seems "a likely spec," and when his fingers have been rubbed over the dogs' noses they become easy and perhaps willing captives. A bag carried for the purpose, receives the victim, and away goes George, bag and all, to his printer's in Seven Dials. Two bills and no less—two and no more, for such is George's style of work—are issued to describe the animal that has thus been *found*, and which will be "restored to its owner on payment of expenses." One of these George puts in his pocket, the other he pastes up at a public-house whose landlord is "fly" to its meaning, and poor "bow-wow" is sold to a "dealer in dogs," not very far from Sharp's alley. In course of time the dog is discovered; the possessor refers to the "establishment" where he bought it; the "dealer makes himself *square*," by giving the address of "the chap he bought 'un of," and Chelsea George shows a copy of the advertisement, calls in the publican as a witness, and leaves the place "without the slightest imputation on his character." Of this man's earnings I cannot speak with precision: it is probable that in a "good year" his clear income is 200*l.*; in a bad year but 100*l.*, but, as he is very adroit, I am inclined to believe that the "good" years somewhat predominate, and that the average income may therefore exceed 150*l.* yearly.'

OF THE PRESENT STREET-SELLERS OF DOGS

IT will have been noticed that in the accounts I have given of the former street-transactions in dogs, there is no mention of the *sellers*. The information I have adduced is a condensation of the evidence given before the Select Committee of the House of Commons, and the inquiry related only to the stealing, finding, and restoring of dogs, the selling being but an incidental part of the evidence. Then, however, as now, the street-sellers were not implicated in the thefts or restitution of dogs, 'just except,' one man told me, 'as there was a black sheep or two in every flock.' The black sheep, however, of this street-calling more frequently meddled with restoring, than with 'finding.'

Another street dog-seller, an intelligent man,—who, however, did not know so much as my first informant of the state of the trade in the olden time,—expressed a positive opinion, that no dog-stealer was now a street-hawker ('hawker' was the word I found these men use). His reasons for this opinion, in addition to his own judgment from personal knowledge, are cogent enough: 'It isn't possible, sir,' he said, 'and this is the reason why. We are not a large body of men. We stick pretty closely, when we are out, to the same places. We are as well-known to the police, as any men whom they must know, by sight at any rate, from meeting them every day. Now, if a lady or gentleman has lost a dog, or it's been stolen or strayed—and the most petted will sometimes stray un-accountably and follow some stranger or other—why, where does she, and he, and all the family, and all the servants, first look for the lost animal? Why, where, but at the dogs we are hawking? No, sir, it can't be done now, and it isn't done in my knowledge, and it oughtn't to be done. I'd rather make 5s. on an honest dog than 5l. on one that wasn't, if there was no risk about it either.' Other information convinces me that this statement is correct.

There is one peculiarity in the hawking of fancy dogs, which distinguishes it from all other branches of street-commerce. The purchasers are all of the wealthier class. This has had its influence on the manners of the dog-sellers. They will be found, in the majority of cases, quiet and deferential men, but without servility, and with little of the quality of speech; and I speak only of speech which among English people is known as 'gammon,' and among Irish people as 'blarney.' This manner is common to many; to the established trainer of race-horses for instance, who is in constant communication with persons in a very superior position in life to his own, and to whom he is exceedingly deferential. But the trainer feels that in all points connected with his not very easy business, as well, perhaps, as in general turf knowingness, his royal highness (as was the case once), or his grace, or my lord, or Sir John, was inferior to himself; and so with all his deference there mingles a strain of quiet contempt, or rather, perhaps, of conscious superiority, which is one ingredient in the formation of the manners I have hastily sketched.

OF THE STREET-SELLERS OF SPORTING DOGS

THE way in which the sale of sporting dogs is connected with street-traffic is in this wise: Occasionally a sporting-dog is offered for sale in the streets, and then, of course, the trade is direct. At other times, gentlemen buying or pricing the smaller dogs, ask the cost of a bull-dog, or a bull-terrier or rat-killer, and the street-seller at once offers to supply them, and either conducts them to a dog-dealer's, with whom he may be commercially connected, and where they can purchase those dogs, or he waits upon them at their residences with some 'likely animals.' A dog-dealer told me that he hardly knew what made many gentlemen so fond of bull-dogs, and they were 'the fonder on 'em the more blackguarder and varmint-looking the creatures was,' although now they were useless for sport, and the great praise of a bull-dog, 'never flew but at head in his life,' was no longer to be given to him, as there were no bulls at whose heads he could now fly.

Another dog-dealer informed me—with what truth as to the judgment concerning horses I do not know, but no doubt with accuracy as to the purchase of the dogs—that Ibrahim Pacha, when in London, thought little of the horses which he saw, but was delighted with the bull-dogs, 'and he weren't so werry unlike one in the face hisself,' was said at the time by some of the fancy. Ibrahim, it seems, bought two of the finest and largest bull-dogs in London, of Bill George, giving no less than 70*l.* for the twain. The bull-dogs now sold by the street-folk, or through their agency in the way I have described, are from 5*l.* to 25*l.* each. The bull-terriers, of the best blood, are about the same price, or perhaps 10 to 15 per cent. lower, and rarely attaining the tip-top price.

The bull-terriers, as I have stated, are now the chief fighting-dogs, but the patrons of those combats—of those small imitations of the savage tastes of the Roman Colosseum, may deplore the decay of the amusement. From the beginning, until well on to the termination of the last century, it was not uncommon to see announcements of 'twenty dogs to fight for a collar,' though such advertisements were far more common at the commencement than towards the close of the century. Until within these twelve years, indeed, dog-matches were not unfrequent in London, and the favourite time for the regalement was on Sunday mornings. There were dog-pits in Westminster, and elsewhere, to which the admission was not very easy, for only known persons were allowed to enter. The expense was considerable, the risk of punishment was not a trifle, and it is evident that this Sunday game was *not supported by the poor or working classes*. Now dog-fights are rare. 'There's not any public dog-fights,' I was told, 'and very seldom any in a pit at a public-house, but there's a good deal of it, I know, *at the private houses of the nobs*.' I may observe that 'the nobs' is a common designation for the rich among these sporting people.

There are, however, occasionally dog-fights in a sporting-house, and the order of the combat is thus described to me: 'We'll say now that it's a scratch fight; two dogs each have their corner of a pit, and they're set to fight. They'll fight on till they go down together, and then if one leave hold, he's sponged. Then they fight again. If a dog has the worst of it he mustn't be picked up, but if he gets into his corner, then he can stay for as long as may be agreed upon, minute or half-minute time, or more than a minute. If a dog won't go to the scratch out of his corner, he loses the fight. If they fight on, why to settle it, one must be killed—though that very seldom happens, for if a dog's very much punished, he creeps to his corner and don't come out to time, and so the fight's settled. Sometimes it's agreed beforehand, that the master of a dog may give in for him; sometimes that isn't to be allowed; but there's next to nothing of this now, unless it's in private among the nobs.'

OF THE STREET-SELLERS OF LIVE BIRDS

THE bird-*sellers* in the streets are also the bird-*catchers* in the fields, plains, heaths, and woods, which still surround the metropolis; and in compliance with established precedent it may be proper that I should give an account of the catching, before I proceed to any further statement of the procedures subsequent thereunto. The bird-catchers are precisely what I have described them in my introductory remarks. An intelligent man, versed in every part of the bird business, and well acquainted with the character of all engaged in it, said they might be represented as of 'the fancy,' in a small way, and always glad to run after, and full of admiration of, fighting men. The bird-catcher's life is one essentially vagrant; a few gipsies pursue it, and they mix little in street-trades, except as regards tinkering; and the mass, not gipsies, who become bird-catchers, rarely leave it for any other avocation. They 'catch' until old age. During last winter two men died in the parish of Clerken-well, both turned seventy, and both bird-catchers—a profession they had followed from the age of six.

The mode of catching I will briefly describe. It is principally effected by means of nets. A bird-net is about twelve yards square; it is spread flat upon the ground, to which it is secured by four 'stars.' These are iron pins, which are inserted in the field, and hold the net, but so that the two 'wings', or 'flaps,' which are indeed the sides of the nets, are not confined by the stars. In the middle of the net is a cage with a fine wire roof, widely worked, containing the 'call-bird.' This bird is trained to sing loudly and cheerily, great care being bestowed upon its tuition, and its song attracts the wild birds. Sometimes a few stuffed birds are spread about the cage as if a flock were already assembling there. The bird-catcher lies flat and motionless on the ground, 20 or 30 yards distant from the edge of the net. As soon as he considers that a sufficiency of birds have congregated around his decoy, he rapidly draws towards him a line, called the 'pull-line,' of which he has kept hold. This is so looped and run within the edges of the net, that on being smartly pulled, the two wings of the net collapse and fly together, the stars still keeping their hold, and the net encircles the cage of the call-bird, and incloses in its folds all the wild birds allured round it. In fact it then resembles a great cage of net-work. The captives are secured in cages—the call-bird continuing to sing as if in mockery of their struggles—or in hampers proper for the purpose, which are carried on the man's back to London.

The use of the call-bird as a means of decoy is very ancient. Sometimes—and more especially in the dark, as in the taking of nightingales—the bird-catcher imitates the notes of the birds to be captured. A small instrument has also been used for the purpose, and to this Chaucer, although figuratively, alludes: 'So, the birde is begyled with the merry voice of the foulers' whistel, when it is closed in your nette.'

Sometimes, in the pride of the season, a bird-catcher engages a costermonger's pony or donkey cart, and perhaps his boy, the better to convey the birds to town. The net and its apparatus cost 1*l.* The call-bird, if he have a good wild note—goldfinches and linnets being principally so used is worth 10*s.* at the least.

The bird-catcher's life has many, and to the constitution of some minds, irresistible charms. There is the excitement of 'sport'—not the headlong excitement of the chase, where the blood is stirred by motion and exercise—but still sport surpassing that of the angler, who plies his finest art to capture one fish at a time, while the bird-catcher despises an individual capture, but seeks to ensnare a flock at one twitch of a line. There is, moreover, the attraction of idleness, at least for intervals, and sometimes long intervals—perhaps the great charm of fishing—and basking in the lazy sunshine, to watch the progress of the snares. Birds, however, and more especially linnets, are caught in the winter, when it is not quite such holiday work. A bird-dealer (not a street-seller) told me that the greatest number of birds he had ever heard of as having been caught at one pull was nearly 200. My informant happened to be present on the occasion. 'Pulls' of 50, 100, and 150 are not very unfrequent when the young broods are all on the wing.

Of the bird-catchers, including all who reside in Woolwich, Greenwich, Hounslow, Isleworth, Barnet, Uxbridge, and places of similar distance, all working for the London market, there are about 200. The localities where these men 'catch,' are the neighbourhoods of the places I have mentioned as their residences, and at Holloway, Hampstead, Highgate, Finchley, Battersea, Blackheath, Putney, Mortlake, Chiswick, Richmond, Hampton, Kingston, Eltham, Carshalton, Streatham, the Tootings, Woodford, Epping, Snaresbrook, Walthamstow, Tottenham, Edmonton— wherever, in fine, are open fields, plains, or commons around the metropolis.

I will first enumerate the several birds sold in the streets, as well as the supply to the shops by the bird-catchers. I have had recourse to the best sources of information. Of the number of birds which I shall specify as 'supplied,' or 'caught,' it must be remembered that a not-very-small proportion die before they can be trained to

song, or inured to a cage life. I shall also give the street prices. All
the birds are caught by the nets with call-birds, excepting such as
I shall notice. I take the singing birds first.

The *Linnet* is the cheapest and among the most numerous of what
may be called the London-caught birds, for it is caught in the
nearer suburbs, such as Holloway. The linnet, however,—the
brown linnet being the species—is not easily reared, and for some
time ill brooks confinement. About one-half of those birds die after
having been caged a few days. The other evening a bird-catcher
supplied 26 fine linnets to a shopkeeper in Pentonville, and next
morning ten were dead. But in some of those bird shops, and bird
chambers connected with the shops, the heat at the time the new
broods are caught and caged, is excessive; and the atmosphere,
from the crowded and compulsory fellowship of pigeons, and all
descriptions of small birds, with white rats, hedgehogs, guinea-pigs,
and other creatures, is often very foul; so that the wonder is, not
that so many die, but that so many survive.

Some bird-connoisseurs prefer the note of the linnet to that of
the canary, but this is far from a general preference. The young
birds are sold in the streets at 3*d*. and 4*d*. each; the older birds,
which are accustomed to sing in their cages, from 1*s*. to 2*s*. 6*d*.
The 'catch' of linnets—none being imported—may be estimated,
for London alone, at 70,000 yearly. The mortality I have mentioned
is confined chiefly to that year's brood, One-tenth of the catch is
sold in the streets. Of the quality of the street-sold birds I shall
speak hereafter.

The *Bullfinch*, which is bold, familiar, docile, and easily attached,
is a favourite cage-bird among the Londoners; I speak of course as
regards the body of the people. It is as readily sold in the streets
as any other singing bird. Piping bullfinches are also a part of street-
trade, but only to a small extent, and with bird-sellers who can
carry them from their street pitches, or call on their rounds, at
places where they are known, to exhibit the powers of the bird.
The piping is taught to these finches when very young, and they
must be brought up by their tutor, and be familiar with him. When
little more than two months old, they begin to whistle, and then
their training as pipers must commence. This tuition, among
professional bullfinch-trainers, is systematic. They have schools of
birds, and teach in bird-classes of from four to seven members in

each, six being a frequent number. These classes, when their education commences, are kept unfed for a longer time than they have been accustomed to, and they are placed in a darkened room. The bird is wakeful and attentive from the want of his food, and the tune he is to learn is played several times on an instrument made for the purpose, and known as a bird-organ, its notes resembling those of the bullfinch. For an hour or two the young pupils mope silently, but they gradually begin to imitate the notes of the music played to them. When one commences—and he is looked upon as the most likely to make a good piper—the others soon follow his ecample. The light is then admitted and a portion of food, but not a full meal, is given to the birds. Thus, by degrees, by the playing on the bird-organ (a flute is sometimes used), by the admission of light, which is always agreeable to the finch, and by the reward of more and more, and sometimes more relishable food, the pupil 'practises' the notes he hears continuously. The birds are then given into the care of boys, who attend to them without intermission in a similar way, their original teacher still overlooking, praising, or rating his scholars, till they acquire a tune which they pipe as long as they live. It is said, however, that only five per cent. of the number taught pipe in *perfect* harmony. The bullfinch is often pettish in his piping, and will in many instances not pipe at all, unless in the presence of some one who feeds it, or to whom it has become attached.

The system of training I have described is that practised by the Germans, who have for many years supplied this country with the best piping bullfinches. Some of the dealers will undertake to procure English-taught bullfinches which will pipe as well as the foreigners, but I am told that this is a prejudice, if not a trick, of trade. The mode of teaching in this country, by barbers, weavers, and bird-fanciers generally, who seek for a profit from their painstaking, is somewhat similar to that which I have detailed, but with far less elaborateness. The price of a piping bullfinch is about three guineas. These pipers are also reared and taught in Leicestershire and Norfolk, and sent to London, as are the singing bullfinches which do not 'pipe.'

The bullfinches netted near London are caught more numerously about Hounslow than elsewhere. In hard winters they are abundant in the outskirts of the metropolis. The yearly supply, including those sent from Norfolk, &c., is about 30,000. The bullfinch is 'hearty compared to the linnet,' I was told, but of the amount which are the objects of trade, not more than two-thirds live many weeks. The price of a good young bullfinch is 2*s*. 6*d*. and 3*s*. They are often sold in the streets for 1*s*. The hawking or street trade comprises about a tenth of the whole.

The sale of piping bullfinches is, of course, small, as only the rich can afford to buy them. A dealer estimated it at about 400 yearly.

The *Goldfinch* is also in demand by street customers, and is a favourite from its liveliness, beauty, and sometimes sagacity. It is, moreover, the longest lived of our caged small birds, and will frequently live to the age of fifteen or sixteen years. A goldfinch has been known to exist twenty-three years in a cage. Small birds, generally, rarely live more than nine years. This finch is also in demand because it most readily of any bird pairs with the canary, the produce being known as a 'mule,' which, from its prettiness and powers of song, is often highly valued.

Goldfinches are sold in the streets at from 6*d*. to 1*s*. each, and when there is an extra catch, and they are nearly all caught about London, and the shops are fully stocked, at 3*d*. and 4*d*. each. The yearly catch is about the same as that of the linnet, or 70,000, the mortality being perhaps 30 per cent. If any one casts his eye over the stock of hopping, chirping little creatures in the window of a bird-shop, or in the close array of small cages hung outside, or at the stock of a street-seller, he will be struck by the preponderating number of goldfinches. No doubt the dealer, like any other shop-keeper, dresses his window to the best advantage, putting forward his smartest and prettiest birds. The demand for the goldfinch, especially among women, is steady and regular. The street-sale is a tenth of the whole.

The *Chaffinch* is in less request than either of its congeners, the bullfinch or the goldfinch, but the catch is about half that of the bullfinch, and with the same rate of mortality. The prices are also the same.

Greenfinches (called *green birds*, or sometimes *green linnets*, in the streets) are in still smaller request than are chaffinches, and that to about one-half. Even this smaller stock is little saleable, as the bird is regarded as 'only a middling singer.' They are sold in the open air, at 2*d*. and 3*d*. each, but a good 'green bird' is worth 2*s*. 6*d*.

Larks are of good sale and regular supply, being perhaps more readily caught than other birds, as in winter they congregate in large quantities. It may be thought, to witness the restless throwing up of the head of the caged sky-lark, as if he were longing for a soar in the air, that he was very impatient of restraint. This does not appear to be so much the fact, as the lark adapts himself to the poor confines of his prison—poor indeed for a bird who soars higher and longer than any of his class—more rapidly than other wild birds, like the linnet, &c. The mortality of larks, however, approaches one-third.

The yearly 'take' of larks is 60,000. This includes sky-larks, wood-larks, tit-larks, and mud-larks. The sky-lark is in far better demand than any of the others for his 'stoutness of song,' but some prefer the tit-lark, from the very absence of such stoutness. 'Fresh-catched' larks are vended in the streets at 6*d*. and 8*d*., but a seasoned bird is worth 2*s*. 6*d*. One-tenth is the street-sale.

The larks for the supply of fashionable tables are never provided by the London bird-catchers, who catch only 'singing larks,' for the shop and street-traffic. The edible larks used to be highly esteemed in pies, but they are now generally roasted for consumption. They are principally the produce of Cambridgeshire, with some from Bedfordshire, and are sent direct (killed) to Leadenhall-market, where about 215,000 are sold yearly, being nearly two-thirds of the gross London consumption.

It is only within these twelve or fifteen years that the London dealers have cared to trade to any extent in *Nightingales*, but they are now a part of the stock of every bird-shop of the more flourishing class. Before that they were merely exceptional as cage-birds. As it is, the 'domestication,' if the word be allowable with reference to the nightingale, is but partial. Like all migratory birds, when the season for migration approaches, the caged nightingale shows symptoms of great uneasiness, dashing himself against the wires of his cage or his aviary, and sometimes dying in a few days. Many of the nightingales, however, let the season pass away without showing any consciousness that it was, with the race of birds to which they belonged, one for a change of place. To induce the nightingale to sing in the daylight, a paper cover is often placed over the cage, which may be gradually and gradually withdrawn until it can be dispensed with. This is to induce the appearance of twilight or night.

I am inclined to believe that the mortality among nightingales, before they are reconciled to their new life, is higher than that of any other bird, and much exceeding one-half. The dealers may be unwilling to admit this; but such mortality is, I have been assured on good authority, the case; besides that, the habits of the nightingale unfit him for a cage existence.

The capture of the nightingale is among the most difficult achievements of the profession. None are caught nearer than Epping, and the catchers travel considerable distances before they have a chance of success. These birds are caught at night, and more often by their captor's imitation of the nightingale's note, than with the aid of the call-bird. Perhaps 1,000 nightingales are reared yearly in London, of which three-fourths may be, more or less, songsters. The inferior birds are sold at about 2*s*. each, the street-sale not reaching 100, but the birds, 'caged and singing,' are worth 1*l*. each, when of the best; and 10*s*., 12*s*. and 15*s*. each when approaching the best. The mortality I have estimated.

Redbreasts are a portion of the street-sold birds, but the catch is not large, not exceeding 3,000, with a mortality of about a third. Even this number, small as it is, when compared with the numbers of other singing birds sold, is got rid of with difficulty. There is a popular feeling repugnant to the imprisonment or coercion in any way, of 'a robin,' and this, no doubt has its influence in moderating the demand. The redbreast is sold, when young, both in the shops and streets for 1*s*., when caged and singing, sometimes for 1*l*. These birds are considered to sing best by candlelight. The street-sale is a fifth, or sometimes a quarter, all young birds, or with the rarest exceptions.

The *Thrush, Throstle*, or (in Scottish poetry) *Mavis*, is of good sale. It is reared by hand, for the London market, in many of the villages and small towns at no great distance, the nests being robbed of the young, wherever they can be found. The nestling food of the infant thrush is grubs, worms, and snails, with an occasional moth or butterfly. On this kind of diet the young thrushes are reared until they are old enough for sale to the shopkeeper, or to any private patron. Thrushes are also netted, but those reared by hand are much the best, as such a rearing disposes the bird the more to enjoy his cage life, as he has never experienced the delights of the free hedges and thickets. This process the catchers call 'rising' from the nest. A throstle thus 'rose' soon becomes familiar with his owner—always supposing that he be properly fed and his cage duly cleaned, for all birds detest dirt—and among the working-men of England no bird is a greater favourite than the thrush; indeed few other birds are held in such liking by the artisan class. About a fourth of the thrushes supplied to the metropolitan traders have been thus 'rose,' and as they must be sufficiently grown before they will be received by the dealers, the mortality among them, when once able to feed themselves, in their wicker-work cages, is but small. Perhaps somewhere about a fourth perish in this hand-rearing, and some men, the aristocrats of the trade, let a number go when they have ascertained that they are hens, as these men exert themselves to bring up thrushes to sing well, and then they command good prices. Often enough, however, the hens are sold cheap in the streets. Among the catch supplied by netting, there is a mortality of perhaps more than a third. The whole take is about 35,000. Of the sale the streets have a tenth proportion. The prices run from 2*s*. 6*d*. and 3*s*. for the 'fresh-caught,' and 10*s*., 1*l*., and as much as 2*l*. for a seasoned throstle in high song. Indeed I may observe that for any singing bird, which is considered greatly to excel its mates, a high price is obtained.

Blackbirds appear to be less prized in London than thrushes, for, though with a mellower note, the blackbird is not so free a singer in captivity. They are 'rose' and netted in the same manner as the thrush, but the supply is less by one-fifth. The prices, mortality, street-sale, &c., are in the same ration.

The street-sale of *Canaries* is not large; not so large, I am assured by men in the trade, as it was six or seven years ago, more especially as regarded the higher-priced birds of this open-air traffic.

The foregoing enumeration includes all the singing-birds of street-traffic and street-folk's supply. The trade I have thus sketched is certainly one highly curious. We find that there is round London a perfect belt of men, employed from the first blush of a summer's dawn, through the heats of noon, in many instances during the night, and in the chills of winter; and all labouring to give to city-pent men of humble means one of the peculiar pleasures of the country—the song of the birds. It must not be supposed that I would intimate that the bird-catcher's life, as regards his field and wood pursuits, is one of hardship. On the contrary, it seems to me to be the very one which, perhaps unsuspected by himself, is best suited to his tastes and inclinations. Nor can we think similar pursuits partake much of hardship when we find independent men follow them for mere sport, to be rid of lassitude.

OF THE BIRD-CATCHERS WHO ARE STREET-SELLERS

The street-sellers of birds are called by themselves 'hawkers,' and sometimes 'bird hawkers.'

Among the bird-catchers I did not hear of any very prominent characters at present, three of the best known and most prominent having died within these ten months. I found among all I saw the vagrant characteristics I have mentioned, and often united with a quietness of speech and manner which might surprise those who do not know that any pursuit which entails frequent silence, watchfulness, and solitude, forms such manners. Perhaps the man most talked of by his fellow-labourers, was Old Gilham, who died lately. Gilham was his real name, for among the bird-catchers there is not that prevalence of nicknames which I found among the costermongers and patterers. One reason no doubt is, that these bird-folk do not meet regularly in the markets. It is rarely, however, that they know each other's surnames, Old Gilham being an exception. It is Old Tom, or Young Mick, or Jack, or Dick, among them. I heard of no John or Richard.

For 60 years, almost without intermission, Old Gilham caught birds. I am assured that to state that his 'catch' during this long period averaged 100 a week, hens included, is within the mark, for he was a most indefatigable man; even at that computation, however, he would have been the captor, in his lifetime, of three hundred and twelve thousand birds! A bird-catcher who used sometimes to start in the morning with Old Gilham, and walk with him until their roads diverged, told me that of late years the old man's talk was a good deal of where he had captured his birds in the old times: "Why, Ned," he would say to me, 'proceeded his companion, "I've catched goldfinches in lots at Chalk Farm, and all where there's that railway smoke and noise just by the hill (Primrose Hill). I can't think where they'll drive all the birds to by and bye. I dare say the first time the birds saw a railway with its smoke, and noise to frighten them, and all the fire too, they just thought it was the devil was come." He wasn't a fool, wasn't old Gilham, sir. "Why," he'd go on for to say, "I've laid many a day at Ball's Pond there, where it's nothing but a lot of houses now, and catched hundreds of birds. And I've catched them where there's all them grand squares Pimlico way, and in Britannia Fields, and at White Condic. What with all these buildings, and them barbers, I don't know what the bird-trade'll come to. It's hard for a poor man to have to go to Finchley for birds that he could have catched at Holloway once, but people never thinks of that. When I were young I could make three times as much as I do now. I've got a pound for a good sound chaffinch as I brought up myself." Ah, poor old Gilham, sir; I wish you could have seen him, he'd have told you of some queer changes in his time.'

OF THE STREET-SELLERS OF BIRDS'-NESTS

THE' young gypsy-looking lad, who gave me the following account of the sale of birds'-nests in the streets, was peculiarly picturesque in his appearance. He wore a dirty-looking smock-frock with large pockets at the side; he had no shirt; and his long black hair hung in curls about him, contrasting strongly with his bare white neck and chest. The broad-brimmed brown Italian-looking hat, broken in and ragged at the top, threw a dark half-mask-like shadow over the upper part of his face. His feet were bare and black with mud: he carried in one hand his basket of nests, dotted with their many-coloured eggs; in the other he held a live snake, that writhed and twisted as its metallic-looking skin glistened in the sun; now over, and now round, the thick knotty bough of a tree that he used for a stick. I have never seen so picturesque a specimen of the English nomad. He said, in answer to my inquiries:—

'I am a seller of birds'-nesties, snakes, slow-worms, adders, "effets"—lizards is their common name—hedgehogs (for killing black beetles); frogs (for the French—they eats 'em); snails (for birds); that's all I sell in the summer-time. In the winter I get all kinds of wild flowers and roots, primroses, "butter-cups" and daisies, and snow-drops, and "backing" off of trees; "backing" it's called, because it's used to put at the back of nosegays, it's got off the yew trees, and is the green yew fern. I gather bulrushes in the summer-time, besides what I told you; some buys bulrushes for stuffing; they 're the fairy rushes the small ones, and the big ones is bulrushes. The small ones is used for "stuffing," that is, for showing off the birds as is stuffed, and make 'em seem as if they was alive in their cases, and among the rushes; I sell them to the bird-stuffers at 1*d*. a dozen. The big rushes the boys buys to play with and beat one another—on a Sunday evening mostly. The birds'-nesties I get from 1*d*. to 3*d*. a-piece for. I never have young birds, I can never sell 'em; you see the young things generally dies of the cramp before you can get rid of them. I sell the birds'-nesties in the streets; the three-penny ones has six eggs, a half-penny a egg. The linnets has mostly four eggs, they're 4*d*. the nest; they're for putting under canaries, and being hatched by them. The thrushes has from four to five—five is the most; they're 2*d*.; they're merely for cur'osity—glass cases or anything like that. Moor-hens, wot build on the moors, has from eight to nine eggs, and is 1*d*. a-piece; they 're for hatching underneath a bantam-fowl, the same as partridges. Chaffinches has five eggs; they're 3*d*., and is for cur'osity. Hedge-sparrows, five eggs; they're the same price as the other, and is for cur'osity. The Bottle-tit—the nest and the bough are always put in glass cases; it's a long hanging nest, like a bottle, with a hole about as big as a sixpence, and there's mostly as many as eighteen eggs; they 've been known to lay thirty-three. To the house-sparrow there is five eggs; they're 1*d*. The yellow-hammers, with five eggs, is 2*d*. The water-wagtails, with four eggs, 2*d*. Blackbirds, with five eggs, 2*d*. The golden-crest wren, with ten eggs—it has a very handsome nest—is 6*d*. Bullfinches, four eggs, 1*s*.; they're for hatching, and the bullfinch is a very dear bird. Crows, four eggs, 4*d*. Magpies, four eggs, 4*d*. Starlings, five eggs, 3*d*. The egg-chats, five eggs, 2*d*. Goldfinches, five eggs, 6*d*., for hatching. Martins, five eggs, 3*d*. The swallow, four eggs, 6*d*.; it's so dear because the nest is such a cur'osity, they build up again the house. The butcher-birds— hedge murderers some calls them, for the number of birds they kills—five eggs, 3*d*. The cuckoo—they never has a nest, but lays in the hedge-sparrow's; there's only one egg (it's very rare you see the two, they has been got, but that's seldom) that is 4*d*., the egg is such a cur'osity. The greenfinches has four or five eggs, and is 3*d*. The sparrer-hawk has four eggs, and they're 6*d*. The reed-sparrow—they builds in the reeds close where the bulrushes grow; they has four eggs, and is 2*d*. The wood-pigeon has two eggs, and they're 4*d*. The horned owl, four eggs; they're 6*d*. The wood-pecker—I never see no more nor two—they're 6*d*. the two; they're a great cur'osity, very seldom found. The kingfishers has four eggs, and is 6*d*. That's all I know of.

'I gets the eggs mostly from Witham and Chelmsford, in Essex Chelmsford is 20 mile from Whitechapel Church, and Witham, 8 mile further. I know more about them parts than anywhere else, being used to go after moss for Mr. Butler, of the herb-shop in Covent Garden. Sometimes I go to Shirley Common and Shirley Wood, that's three miles from Croydon, and Croydon is ten from Westminster-bridge. When I'm out bird-nesting I take all the cross country roads across fields and into the woods. I begin bird-nesting in May and leave off about August, and then comes the bulrushing, and they last till Christmas; and after that comes the roots and wild flowers, which serves me up to May again. I go out bird-nesting three times a week. I go away at night, and come up on the morning of the day after. I'm away a day and two nights. I start between one and two in the morning and walk all night—for the coolness—you see the weather's so hot you can't do it in the daytime. When I get down I go to sleep for a couple of hours. I "skipper it" — turn in under a hedge or anywhere. I get down about nine in the morning, at Chelmsford, and about one if I go to Witham. After I've had my sleep I start off to get my nests and things. I climb the trees, often I go up a dozen in the day, and many a time there's nothing in the nest when I get up. I only fell once; I got on the end of the bough and slipped off. I p'isoned my foot once with the stagnant water going after the bulrushes,—there was horseleeches, and effets, and all kinds of things in the water, and they stung me, I think. I couldn't use my foot hardly for six weeks afterwards, and was obliged to have a stick to walk with. I couldn't get about at all for four days, and should have starved if it hadn't been that a young man kept me. He was a print-er by trade, and almost a stranger to me, only he seed me and took pity on me. When I fell off the bough I wasn't much hurt, nothing to speak of. The house-sparrow is the worst nest of all to take; it's no value either when it *is* got, and is the most difficult of all to get at. You has to get up a sparapet (a parapet) of a house, and either to get permission, or run the risk of going after it without. Partridges' eggs (they has no nest) they gives you six months for, if they see you selling them, because it's game, and I haven't no licence; but while you're hawking, that is showing 'em, they can't touch you. The owl is a very difficult nest to get, they builds so high in the trees. The bottle-tit is a hard nest to find; you may go all the year round, and, perhaps, only get one. The nest I like best to get is the chaffinch, because they're in the hedge, and is no bother. Oh, you hasn't got the skylark down, sir; they builds on the ground, and has five eggs; I sell them for 4*d*. The robin-redbreast has five eggs, too, and is 3*d*. The ringdove has two eggs, and is 6*d*. The tit-lark—that's five blue eggs, and very rare—I get 4*d*. for them. The jay has five eggs, and a flat nest, very wiry, indeed; it's a ground bird; that's 1*s*.—the egg is just like a partridge egg. When I first took a kingfisher's nest, I didn't know the name of it, and I kept wondering what it was. I daresay I asked three dozen people, and none of them could tell me. At last a bird-fancier, the lame man at the Mile-end gate, told me what it was. I likes to get the nesties to sell, but I haven't no fancy for birds. Sometimes I get squirrels' nesties with the young in 'em—about four of 'em there mostly is, and they're the only young things I take—the young birds I leaves; they're no good to me. The four squirrels brings me from 6*s*. to 8*s*. After I takes a bird's nest, the old bird comes dancing over it, chirupping, and crying, and flying all about. When they lose their nest they wander about, and don't know where to go. Oftentimes I wouldn't take them if it wasn't for the want of the victuals, it seems such a pity to disturb 'em after they've made their little bits of places. Bats I never take myself—I can't get over 'em. If I has an order for 'em, I buys 'em of boys.

'I mostly start off into the country on Monday and come up on Wednesday. The most nesties as ever I took is twenty-two, and I generally get about twelve or thirteen. These, if I've an order, I sell directly, or else I may be two days, and sometimes longer, hawking them in the street. Directly I've sold them I go off again that night, if it's fine; though I often go in the wet, and then I borrow a tarpaulin of a man in the street where I live. If I've a quick sale I get down and back three times in a week, but then I don't go so far as Witham, sometimes only to Rumford; that is 12 miles from Whitechapel Church. I never got an order from a bird-fancier; they gets all the eggs they want of the countrymen who comes up to market.

'It's gentlemen I gets my orders of, and then mostly they tells me to bring 'em one nest of every kind I can get hold of, and that will often last me three months in the summer. There's one gentleman as I sells to is a wholesale dealer in window-glass—and he has a hobby for them. He puts 'em into glass cases, and makes presents of 'em to his friends. He has been one of my best customers. I've sold him a hundred nesties, I'm sure. There's a doctor at Dalston I sell a great number to—he's taking one of every kind of me now. The most of my customers is stray ones in the streets. They're generally boys. I sells a nest now and then to a lady with a child; but the boys of twelve to fifteen years of age is my best friends. They buy 'em only for cur'osity. I sold three partritges' eggs yesterday to a gentleman, and he said he would put them under a bantam he'd got, and hatch 'em.

'The snakes, and adders, and slow-worms I get from where there's moss or a deal of grass. Sunny weather's the best for them, they won't come out when it's cold; then I go to a dung-heap, and turn it over. Sometimes, I find five or six there, but never so large as the one I had to-day, that's a yard and five inches long, and three-quarters of a pound weight Snakes is 5*s*. a pound. I sell all I can get to Mr. Butler, of Covent-Garden. He keeps 'em alive, for they're no good dead. I think it's for the skin they're kept. Some buys 'em to dissect: a gentleman in Theobalds-road does so, and so he does hedgehogs. Some buys 'em for stuffing, and others for cur'osities. Adders is the same price as snakes, 5*s*. a pound after they first comes in, when they're 10*s*. Adders is wanted dead; it's only the fat and skin that's of any value; the fat is used for curing p'isoned wounds, and the skin is used for any one as has cut their heads. Farmers buys the fat, and rubs it into the wound when they gets bitten or stung by anything p'isonous. I kill the adders with a stick, or, when I has shoes, I jumps on 'em. Some fine days I get four or five snakes at a time; but then they're mostly small, and won't weigh above half a pound. I don't get many adders—they don't weigh many ounces, adders don't—and I mostly has 9*d*. a-piece for each I gets. I sells *them* to Mr. Butler as well.

'The hedgehogs is 1s. each; gets them mostly in Essex. I've took one hedgehog with three young ones, and sold the lot for 2s. 6d. People in the streets bought them of me—they're wanted to kill the black-beetles; they're fed on bread and milk, and they'll suck a cow quite dry in their wild state. They eat adders, and can't be p'soned, at least it says so in a book I've got about 'em at home.

'The effets I gets orders for in the streets. Gentlemen gives me their cards, and tells me to bring them one; they're 2d. apiece. I get them at Hampstead and Highgate, from the ponds. They're wanted for cur'osity.

'The snails and frogs I sell to Frenchmen. I don't know what part they eat of the frog, but I know they buy them, and the dandelion root. The frogs is 6d. and 1s. a dozen. They like the yellow-bellied ones, the others they're afraid is toads. They always pick out the yellow-bellied first; I don't know how to feed 'em, or else I might fatten them. Many people swallows young frogs, they're reckoned very good things to clear the inside. The frogs I catch in ponds and ditches up at Hampstead and Highgate, but I only get them when I've a order. I've had a order for as many as six dozen, but that was for the French hotel in Leicester-square; but I *have* sold three dozen a week to one man, a Frenchman, as keeps a cigar shop in R——r's-court.

'The snails I sell by the pailful—at 2s. 6d. the pail. There is some hundreds in a pail. The wet weather is the best times for catching 'em; the French people eats 'em. They boils 'em first to get 'em out of the shell and get rid of the green froth; then they boils them again, and after that in vinegar. They eats 'em hot, but some of the foreigners likes 'em cold. They say they're better, if possible, than whelks. I used to sell a great many to a lady and gentleman in Soho-square, and to many of the French I sell 1s.'s worth, that's about three or four quarts. Some persons buys snails for birds, and some to strengthen a sickly child's back; they rub the back all over with the snails, and a very good thing they tell me it is. I used to take 2s.'s worth a week to one woman; it's the green froth that does the greatest good. There are two more birds'-nest sellers besides myself, they don't do as many as me the two of 'em. They're very naked, their things is all to ribbins; they only go into the country once in a fortnight. They was never nothing, no trade—

they never was in place—from what I've heard—either of them. I reckon I sell about 20 nesties a week take one week with another, and that I do for four months in the year. (This altogether makes 320 nests.) Yes, I should say, I do sell about 300 birds'-nests every year, and the other two, I'm sure, don't sell half that. Indeed they don't want to sell; they does better by what they gets give to them. I can't say what they takes, they're Irish, and I never was in conversation with them. I get about 4*s.* to 5*s.* for the 20 nests, that's between 2*d.* and 3*d.* apiece. I sell about a couple of snakes every week, and for some of them I get 1*s.*, and for the big ones 2*s.* 6*d.*; but them I seldom find. I've only had three hedgehogs this season, and I've done a little in snails and frogs, perhaps about 1*s.* The many foreigners in London this season hasn't done me no good. I haven't been to Leicester-square lately, or perhaps I might have got a large order or two for frogs.'

OF THE STREET-SELLERS OF GOLD AND SILVER FISH

OF these dealers, residents in London, there are about 70; but during my inquiry (at the beginning of July) there were not 20 in town. One of their body knew of ten who were at work live-fish selling, and there might be as many more, he thought, 'working' the remoter suburbs of Blackheath, Croydon, Richmond, Twickenham, Isleworth, or wherever there are villa residences of the wealthy. This is the season when the gold and silver fish-sellers, who are altogether a distinct class from the bird-sellers of the streets, resort to the country, to vend their glass globes, with the glittering fish swimming ceaselessly round and round. The gold fish-hawkers are, for the most part, of the very best class of the street-sellers. One of the principal fish-sellers is in winter a street-vendor of cough drops, hore-hound candy, coltsfoot-sticks, and other medicinal confectionaries, which he himself manufactures. Another leading gold-fish seller is a costermonger now 'on pine-apples.' A third, with a good connection among the innkeepers, is in the autumn and winter a hawker of game and poultry.

There are in London three wholesale dealers in gold and silver fish; two of whom—one in the Kingsland-road and the other close by Billingsgate—supply more especially the street-sellers, and the street-traffic is considerable. Gold fish is one of the things which people buy when brought to their doors, but which they seldom care to 'order.' The importunity of children when a man unexpectedly tempts them with a display of such brilliant creatures as gold fish, is another great promotive of the street-trade; and the street-traders are the best customers of the wholesale purveyors, buying somewhere about three-fourths of their whole stock. The dealers keep their fish in tanks suited to the purpose, but gold fish are never bred in London. The English-reared gold fish are 'raised' for the most part, as respects the London market, in several places in Essex. In some parts they are bred in warm ponds, the water being heated by the steam from adjacent machinery, and in some places they are found to thrive well. Some are imported from France, Holland, and Belgium; some are brought from the Indies, and are usually sold to the dealers to improve their breed, which every now and then, I was told, 'required a foreign mixture, or they didn't keep up their colour.' The Indian and foreign fish, however, are also sold in the streets; the dealers, or rather the Essex breeders, who are often in London, have 'just the pick of them,' usually through the agency of their town customers. The English-reared gold fish are not much short of three-fourths of the whole supply, as the importation of these fishes is troublesome; and unless they are sent under the care of a competent person, or unless the master or steward of a vessel is made to incur a share in the venture, by being paid so much freight-money for as many gold and silver fishes as are landed in good health, and nothing for the dead or dying, it is very hazardous sending them on shipboard at all, as in case of neglect they may all die during the voyage.

The gold and silver fish are of the carp species, and are natives of China, but they were first introduced into this country from Portugal about 1690. Some are still brought from Portugal. They have been common in England for about 120 years.

These fish are known in the street-trade as 'globe' and 'pond' fish. The distinction is not one of species, nor even of the 'variety' of a species, but merely a distinction of size. The larger fish are 'pond;' the smaller, 'globe.' But the difference on which the street-sellers principally dwell is that the pond fish are far more troublesome to keep by them in a 'slack time,' as they must be fed and tended most sedulously. Their food is stale bread or biscuit.

The 'globe' fish are not fed at all by the street-dealer, as the animalcules and the minute insects in the water suffice for their food. Soft rain, or sometimes Thames water, is used for the filling of the globe containing a street-seller's gold fish, the water being changed twice a day, at a public-house or elsewhere, when the hawker is on a round. Spring-water is usually rejected, as the soft water contains 'more feed.' One man, however, told me he had recourse to the street-pumps for a renewal of water, twice, or occasionally thrice a day, when the weather was sultry; but spring or well water 'wouldn't do at all.' He was quite unconscious that he was using it from the pump.

The wholesale price of these fish ranges from 5s. to 18s. per dozen, with a higher charge for 'picked fish,' when high prices must be paid. The cost of 'large silvers,' for instance, which are scarcer than 'large golds,' so I heard them called, is sometimes 5s. apiece, even to a retailer, and rarely less than 3s. 6d. The most frequent price, retail from the hawker—for almost all the fish are hawked, but only there, I presume, for a temporary purpose—is 2s. the pair. The gold fish are now always hawked in glass globes, containing about a dozen occupants, within a diameter of twelve inches. These globes are sold by the hawker, or, if ordered, supplied by him on his next round that way, the price being about 2s. Glass globes, for the display of gold fish, are indeed manufactured at from 6d. to 1l. 10s. each, but 2s. or 2s 6d. is the usual limit to the price of those vended in the street. The fish are lifted out of the water in the globe to consign to a purchaser, by being caught in a neat net, of fine and different-coloured cordage, always carried by the hawker, and manufactured for the trade at 2s. the dozen. Neat handles for these nets, of stained or plain wood, are 1s. the dozen. The dealers avoid touching the fish with their hands. Both gold fish and glass globes are much cheaper than they were ten years ago; the globes are cheaper, of course, since the alteration in the tax on glass, and the street-sellers are, numerically, nearly double what they were.

From a well-looking and well-spoken youth of 21 or 22, I had the following account. He was the son, and grandson, of coster-mongers, but was—perhaps, in consequence of his gold fish selling lying among a class not usually the costermongers' customers—of more refined manners than the generality of the costers' children.

'I've been in the streets, sir,' he said, 'helping my father, until I was old enough to sell on my own account, since I was six years old. *Yes, I like a street life, I'll tell you the plain truth, for I was put by my father to a paperstainer, and found I couldn't bear to stay in doors. It would have killed me.* Gold fish are as good a thing to sell as anything else, perhaps, but I've been a costermonger as well, and have sold both fruit and good fish—salmon and fine soles. Gold fish are not good for eating. I tried one once, just out of curiosity, and it tasted very bitter indeed; I tasted it boiled. I've worked both town and country on gold fish. I've served both Brighton and Hastings. The fish were sent to me by rail, in vessels with air-holes, when I wanted more. I never stopped at lodging-houses, but at respectable public-houses, where I could be well suited in the care of my fish. It's an expense, but there's no help for it.' [A costermonger, when I questioned him on the subject, told me that he had sometimes sold gold fish in the country, and though he had often enough slept in common lodging-houses, he never could carry his fish there, for he felt satisfied, although he had never tested the fact, that in nine out of ten such places, the fish, in the summer season, would half of them die during the night from the foul air.] 'Gold fish sell better in the country than town,' the street-dealer continued; 'much better. They're more thought of in the country. My father's sold them all over the world, as the saying is. I've sold both foreign and English fish. I prefer English. They're the hardiest; Essex fish. The foreign—I don't just know what part—are bred in milk ponds; kept fresh and sweet, of course; and when they're brought here, and come to be put in cold water, they soon die. In Essex they're bred in cold water. They live about three years; that's their lifetime if they're properly seen to. I don't know what kind of fish gold fish are. I've heard that they first came from China. No, I can't read, and I'm very sorry for it. If I have time next winter I'll get taught. Gentlemen sometimes ask me to sit down, and talk to me about fish, and their history (natural history), and I'm often at a loss, which I mightn't be if I could read. If I have fish left after my day's work, I never let them stay in the globe I've hawked them in, but put them into a large pan, a tub sometimes, threeparts full of water, where they have room. My customers are ladies and gentlemen, but I have sold to shop-keepers, such as buttermen, that often show gold fish and flowers in their shops.

The fish don't live long in the very small globes, but they're put in them sometimes just to satisfy children. I've sold as many as two dozen at a time to stock a pond in a gentleman's garden. It's the best sale a little way out of town, in any direction. I sell six dozen a week, I think, one week with another; they'll run as to price at 1s. apiece. That six dozen includes what I sell both in town and country. Perhaps I sell them nearly three-parts of the year. Some hawk all the year but it's a poor winter trade. Yes, I make a very fair living; 2s. 6d. or 3s. or so, a day perhaps, on gold fish, when the weather suits.'

OF THE STREET-SELLERS OF MINERAL PRODUCTIONS AND NATURAL CURIOSITIES

THE class of which I have now to treat, including as it does the street-sellers of coal, coke, tan-turf, salt, and sand, seem to have been called into existence principally by the necessities of the poorer classes. As the earnings of thousands of men, in all the slop, 'slaughter-house,' or 'scamping' branches of tailoring, shoe-making, cabinet-making, joining, &c. have become lower and lower, they are compelled to purchase the indispensable articles of daily consumption in the smallest quantities, and at irregular times, just as the money is in their possession. This is more especially the case as regards chamber-masters and garret-masters (among the shoemakers) and cabinet-makers, who, as they are small masters, and working on their own account, have not even such a regularity of payment as the journeyman of the slop-tailor. Among these poor artisans, moreover, the wife must slave with the husband, and it is often an object with them to save the time lost in going out to the chandler's-shop or the coal-shed, to have such things as coal and coke brought to their very doors, and vended in the smallest quantities. It is the same with the women who work for the slop-shirt merchants, &c., or make cap-fronts, &c., on their own account, for the supply of the shop-keepers, or the wholesale swag-men, who sell low-priced millinery. The street-sellers of the class I have now to notice are, then, the principal purveyors of the very poor.

The men engaged in the street-sale of coal and coke—the chief articles of this branch of the street-sale—are of the costermonger class, as, indeed, is usually the case where an exercise of bodily strength is requisite. Costermongers, too, are better versed than any other street-folk in the management of barrows, carts, asses, ponies, or horses, so that when these vehicles and these animals are a necessary part of any open-air business, it will generally be found in the hands of the coster class.

Nor is this branch of the street-traffic confined solely to articles of necessity. Under my present enumeration will be found the street-sale of *shells*, an ornament of the mantel-piece above the firegrate to which coal is a necessity.

The present division will complete the subject of Street *Sale* in the metropolis.

OF THE STREET-SELLERS OF COALS

ACCORDING to the returns of the coal market for the last few years, there has been imported into London, on an average, 3,500,000 tons of sea-borne coal annually. Besides this immense supply, the various railways have lately poured in a continuous stream of the same commodity from the inland districts, which has found a ready sale without sensibly affecting the accustomed vend of the north country coals, long established on the Coal Exchange.

The modes in which the coals imported into London are distributed to the various classes of consumers are worthy of observation, as they unmistakably exhibit not only the wealth of the few, but the poverty of the many. The inhabitants of Belgravia, the wealthy shopkeepers, and many others periodically see at their doors the well-loaded waggon of the coal merchant, with two or three swarthy 'coal-porters' bending beneath the black heavy sacks, in the act of laying in the 10 or 20 tons for yearly or half-yearly consumption. But this class is supplied from a very different quarter from that of the artisans, labourers, and many others, who, being unable to spare money sufficient to lay in at once a ton or two of coals, must have recourse to other means. To meet their limited resources, there may be found in every part, always in back streets, persons known as coal-shed men, who get the coals from the merchant in 7, 14, or 20 tons at a time, and retail them from ¼ cwt. upwards. The coal-shed men are a very numerous class, for there is not a low neighbourhood in any part of the city which contains not two or three of them in every street.

There is yet another class of purchasers of coals, however, which I have called the 'very poor,'—the inhabitants of two pairs back—the dwellers in garrets, &c. It seems to have been for the purpose of meeting the wants of this class that the street-sellers of coals have sprung into existence. Those who know nothing of the decent pride which often lingers among the famishing poor, can scarcely be expected to comprehend the great boon that the street-sellers of coals, if they could only be made honest and conscientious dealers, are calculated to confer on these people. 'I have seen,' says a correspondent, 'the starveling child of misery, in the gloom of the evening, steal timidly into the shop of the coal-shed man, and in a tremulous voice ask, as if begging a great favour, for *seven pounds of coals*. The coal-shed man has set down his pint of beer, taken the pipe from his mouth, blowing after it a cloud of smoke, and in a gruff voice, at which the little wretch has shrunk up (if it were possible) into a les space than famine had already reduced her to, and demanded—"Who told you as how I sarves seven pound o' coal?—Go to Bill C—he may sarve you if he likes—I won't, and that's an end on't—I wonders what people wants with seven pound o' coal." The coal-shed man, after delivering himself of this enlightened observation, has placidly resumed his pipe, while the poor child, gliding out into the drizzling sleet, disappeared in the darkness.'

As to the habits of the street-sellers of coals, they are as various as their different circumstances will admit; but they closely resemble each other in one general characteristic—their provident and careful habits. Many of them have risen from struggling coster-mongers, to be men of substance, with carts, vans, and horses of their own. Some of the more wealthy of the class may be met with now and then in the parlours of respectable public houses, where they smoke their pipes, sip their brandy and water, and are remarkable for the shrewdness of their remarks. They mingle freely with the respectable tradesmen of their own localities, and may be seen, especially on the Sunday afternoons, with their wives and showily-dressed daughters in the gardens of the New Globe, or Green Dragon—the Cremorne and Vauxhall of the east. I visited the house of one of those who I was told had originally been a coster-monger. The front portion of the shop was almost filled with coals, he having added to his occupation of street-seller the business of

THE JEW OLD-CLOTHES MAN

The Mud-Lark

a coal-shed man; this his wife and little boy managed in his absence; while, true to his early training, the window-ledge and a bench before it were heaped up with cabbages, onions, and other vegetables. In an open space opposite his door, I observed a one-horse cart and two or three trucks with his name painted thereon. At his invitation, I passed through what may be termed the shop, and entered the parlour, a neat room nicely carpeted, with a round table in the centre, chairs ranged primly round the walls, and a long looking-glass reflecting the china shepherds and shepherdesses on the mantel-piece, while, framed and glazed, all around were highly-coloured prints, among which, Dick Turpin, in flash red coat, gallantly clearing the toll-gate in his celebrated ride to York, and Jack Sheppard lowering himself down from the window of the lock-up house, were most conspicuous. In the window lay a few books, and one or two old copies of *Bell's Life*. Among the well-thumbed books, I picked out the *Newgate Calendar*, and the '*Calendar of Orrers*,' as he called it, of which he expressed a very high opinion. 'Lor' bless you,' he exclaimed, 'them there stories is the vonderfullest in the vorld! I'd never ha' believed it, if I adn't seed it with my own two hies, but there's can't be no mistake ven I read it hout o' the book, can there, now—I jist asks yer that 'ere plain question.'

OF THE STREET-SELLERS OF COKE

AMONG the occupations that have sprung up of late years is that of the purchase and distribution of the refuse cinders or coke obtained from the different gas-works, which are supplied at a much cheaper rate than coal. Several of the larger gas companies burn as many as 100,000 tons of coals per annum, and some even more, and every ton thus burnt is stated to leave behind two chaldrons of coke, returning to such companies 50 per cent. of their outlay upon the coal. The distribution of coke is of the utmost importance to those whose poverty forces them to use it instead of coal.

It is supposed that the ten gas companies in and about the metropolis produce at least 1,400,000 chaldrons of coke, which are distributed to the poorer classes by vans, one-horse carts, donkey carts, trucks, and itinerant vendors who carry one, and in some cases two sacks lashed together on their backs, from house to house,

The van proprietors are those who, having capital, contract with the companies at a fixed rate per chaldron the year through, and supply the numerous retail shops at the current price, adding 3d. per chaldron for carriage; thus speculating upon the rise or fall of the article, and in most cases carrying on a very lucrative business. This class numbers about 100 persons, and are to be distinguished by the words 'coke contractor,' painted on a showy ground on the exterior of their handsome well-made vehicles; they add to their ordinary business the occupation of conveying to their destination the coke that the companies sell from time to time. These men have generally a capital, or a reputation for capital, to the extent of 400l. or 500l., and in some cases more, and they usually enter into their contracts with the companies in the summer, when but small quantities of fuel are required, and the gas-works are incommoded for want of space to contain the quantity made. They are consequently able, by their command of means, to make good bargains, and several instances are known of men starting with a wheelbarrow in this calling and who are now the owners of the dwellings in which they reside, and have goods, vans, and carts besides.

Another class, to whom may be applied much that has been said of the van proprietors, are the possessors of one-horse carts, who in many instances keep small shops for the sale of greens, coal, &c. These men are scattered over the whole metropolis, but as they do not exclusively obtain their living by vending this article, they do not properly belong to this portion of the inquiry.

A very numerous portion of the distributors of coke are the donkey-cart men, who are to be seen in all the poorer localities with a quantity shot in the bottom of their cart, and two or three sacks on the top or fastened underneath—for it is of a light nature—ready to meet the demand, crying 'Coke! coke! coke!' morning, noon and night. This they sell as low as 2d. per bushel, coke having, in consequence of the cheapness of coals, been sold at the gas-works by the single sack as low as 7d., and although there is here a seeming contradiction—that of a man selling and living by the loss—such is not in reality the case. It should be remembered that a bushel of good coke will weigh 40 lbs., and that the bushels of these men rarely exceed 25 lbs.; so that it will be seen by this unprincipled mode of dealing they can seemingly sell for less than they give and yet realize a good profit.

OF THE STREET-SELLERS OF SHELLS

THE street-trade in shells presents the characteristics I have before had to notice as regards the trade in what are not necessaries, or an approach to necessaries, in contradistinction of what men must have to eat or wear. Shells, such as the green snail, ear shell, and others of that class, though extensively used for inlaying in a variety of ornamental works, are comparatively of little value; for no matter how useful, if shells are only well known, they are considered of but little importance; while those which are rarely seen, no matter how insignificant in appearance, command extraordinary prices. As an instance I may mention that on the 23rd of June there was purchased by Mr. Sowerby, shell-dealer, at a public sale in King-street, Covent-garden, a small shell not two inches long, broken and damaged, and withal what is called a 'dead shell,' for the sum of 30 guineas. It was described as the *Conus Glory Mary*, and had it only been perfect would have fetched 100 guineas.

Shells, such as conches, cowries, green snails, and ear shells (the latter being so called from their resemblance to the human ear), are imported in large quantities, as parts of cargoes, and are sold to the large dealers by weight. Conch shells are sold at 8*s.* per cwt.; cowries and clams from 10*s.* to 12*s.* per cwt.; the green snail, used for inlaying, fetches from 1*l.* to 1*l.* 10*s.* per cwt.; and the ear shell, on account of its superior quality, and richer variety of colours, as much as 3*l.* and 5*l.* per cwt. The conches are found only among the West India Islands, and are used principally for garden ornaments and grotto-work. The others come principally from the Indian Ocean and the China seas, and are used as well for chimney ornaments, as for inlaying, for the tops of work-tables and other ornamental furniture.

The shells which are considered of the most value are almost invariably small, and of an endless variety of shape. They are called 'cabinet' shells, and are brought from all parts of the world— land as well as sea—lakes, rivers, and oceans furnishing specimens to the collection. The Australian forests are continually ransacked to bring to light new varieties. I have been informed that there is not a river in England but contains valuable shells; that even in the Thames there are shells worth from 10*s.* to 1*l.* each. I have been shown a shell of the snail kind, found in the woods of New Holland, and purchased by a dealer for 2*l.*, and on which he confidently reckoned to make a considerable profit.

Although 'cabinet' shells are collected from all parts, yet by far the greater number come from the Indian Ocean. They are generally collected by the natives, who sell them to captains and mates of vessels trading to these parts, and very often to sailors, all of whom frequently speculate to a considerable extent in these things, and have no difficulty in disposing of them as soon as they arrive in this country, for there is not a shell dealer in London who has not a regular staff of persons stationed at Gravesend to board the homeward-bound ships at the Nore, and sometimes as far off as the Downs, for the purpose of purchasing shells. It usually happens that when three or four of these persons meet on board one ship, an animated competition takes place, so that the shells on board are generally bought up long before the ship arrives at London.

OF THE RIVER BEER-SELLERS, OR PURL-MEN

THERE is yet another class of itinerant dealers who, if not traders in the streets, are traders in what was once termed the silent highway—the river beer-sellers, or purl-men, as they are more commonly called. These should strictly have been included among the sellers of eatables and drinkables; they have, however, been kept distinct, being a peculiar class, and having little in common with the other out-door sellers.

I will begin my account of the river-sellers by enumerating the numerous classes of labourers, amounting to many thousands, who get their living by plying their respective avocations on the river, and who constitute the customers of these men. There are first the sailors on board the corn, coal, and timber ships; then the 'lumpers,' or those engaged in discharging the timber ships; the 'stevedores,' or those engaged in stowing craft; and the 'riggers,' or those engaged in rigging them; ballast-heavers, ballast-getters, corn-porters, coal-whippers, watermen and lightermen, and coal-porters, who, although engaged in carrying sacks of coal from the barges or ships at the river's side to the shore, where there are public-houses, nevertheless, when hard worked and pressed for time, frequently avail themselves of the presence of the purl-man to quench their thirst, and to stimulate them to further exertion.

It would be a remarkable circumstance if the fact of so many persons continually employed in severe labour, and who, of course, are at times in want of refreshment, had not called into existence a class to supply that which was evidently required; under one form or the other, therefore, river-dealers boast of an antiquity as old as the naval commerce of the country.

It appears to have been the practice at some time or other in this country to infuse wormwood into beer or ale previous to drinking it, either to make it sufficiently bitter, or for some medicinal purpose. This mixture was called *purl*—why I know not, but Bailey, the philologist of the seventeenth century, so designates it. The drink originally sold on the river was purl, or this mixture, whence the title, purl-man. Now, however, the wormwood is unknown; and what is sold under the name of purl is beer warmed nearly to boiling heat, and flavoured with gin, sugar, and ginger. The river-sellers, however, still retain the name, of *purl*-men, though there is not one of them with whom I have conversed that has the remotest idea of the meaning of it.

To set up as a purl-man, some acquaintance of the river, and a certain degree of skill in the management of a boat, are absolutely necessary; as, from the frequently crowded state of the pool, and the rapidity with which the steamers pass and repass, twisting and wriggling their way through craft of every description, the unskilful adventurer would run in continual danger of having his boat crushed like a nutshell. The purl-men, however, through long practice, are scarcely inferior to the watermen themselves in the management of their boats; and they may be seen at all times easily working their way through every obstruction, now shooting athwart the bows of a Dutch galliot or sailing-barge, then dropping astern to allow a steam-boat to pass till they at length reach the less troubled waters between the tiers of shipping.

The first thing required to become a purl-man is to procure a licence from the Waterman's Hall, which costs 3*s* 6*d*. per annum. The next requisite is the possession of a boat. The boats used are all in the form of skiffs, rather short, but of a good breadth, and therefore less liable to capsize through the swell of the steamers, or through any other cause. Thus equipped he then goes to some of the small breweries, where he gets two 'pins,' or small casks of beer, each containing eighteen pots; after this he furnishes himself with a quart or two of gin from some publican, which he carries in a tin vessel with a long neck, like a bottle—an iron or tin vessel to hold the fire, with holes drilled all round to admit the air and keep the fuel burning, and a huge bell, by no means the least important portion of his fit out. Placing his two pins of beer on a frame in the stern of the boat, the spiles loosened and the brass cocks fitted in, and with his tin gin bottle close to his hand beneath the seat, two or three measures of various sizes, a black tin pot for heating the beer, and his fire pan secured on the bottom of the boat, and sending up a black smoke, he takes his seat early in the morning and pulls away from the shore, resting now and then on his oars, to ring the heavy bell that announces his approach. Those on board the vessels requiring refreshment, when they hear the bell, hail 'Purl ahoy'; in an instant the oars are resumed, and the purl-man is quickly alongside the ship.

The bell of the purl-man not unfrequently performs another very important office. During the winter, when dense fogs settle down on the river, even the regular watermen sometimes lose themselves, and flounder about bewildered perhaps for hours. The direction once lost, their shouting is unheeded or unheard. The purl-man's bell, however, reaches the ear through the surrounding gloom, and indicates his position; when near enough to hear the hail of his customers, he makes his way unerringly to the spot by now and then sounding his bell; this is immediately answered by another shout, so that in a short time the glare of his fire may be distinguished as he emerges from the darkness, and glides noiselessly alongside the ship where he is wanted.

The present race of purl-men, unlike the weather-beaten tars who in former times alone were licensed, are generally young men, who have been in the habit of following some river employment, and who, either from some accident having befallen them in the course of their work, or from their preferring the easier task of sitting in their boat and rowing leisurely about to continuous labour, have started in the line, and ultimately superseded the old river dealers. This is easily explained. No man labouring on the river would purchase from a stranger when he knew that his own fellow-workman was afloat, and was prepared to serve him with as good an article; besides he might not have money, and a stranger could not be expected to give trust, but his old acquaintance would make little scruple in doing so. In this way the customers of the purl-men are secured; and many of these people do so much more than the average amount of business above stated, that it is no unusual thing to see some of them, after four or five years on the river, take a public-house, spring up into the rank of licensed victuallers, and finally become men of substance.

Beside the regular purl-men, or, as they may be called, bumboat-men, there are two or three others who, perhaps unable to purchase a boat, and take out the licence, have nevertheless for a number of years contrived to carry on a traffic in spirits among the ships in the Thames. Their practice is to carry a flat tin bottle concealed about their person, with which they go on board the first ship in a tier, where they are well known by those who may be there employed. If the seamen wish for any spirit the river-vendor immediately supplies it, entering the name of the customers served, as none of the vendors ever receive, at the time of sale, any money for what they dispose of; they keep an account till their customers receive their wages, when they always contrive to be present, and in general succeed in getting what is owing to them. What their profits are it is impossible to tell, perhaps they may equal those of the regular purl-man, for they go on board of almost every ship in the course of the day. When their tin bottle is empty they go on shore to replenish it, doing so time after time if necessary.

It is remarkable that although these people are perfectly well known to every purl-man on the river, who have seen them day by day, for many years going on board the various ships, and are thoroughly cognizant of the purpose of their visits, there has never been any information laid against them, nor have they been in any way interrupted in their business.

There is one of these river spirit-sellers who has pursued the avocation for the greater part of his life; he is a native of the south of Ireland, now very old, and a little shrivelled-up man. He may still be seen every day, going from ship to ship by scrambling over the quarters where they are lashed together in tiers—a feat some-times attended with danger to the young and strong; yet he works his way with the agility of a man of 20, gets on board the ship he wants, and when there, were he not so well known, he might be thought to be some official sent to take an inventory of the contents of the ship, for he has at all times an ink-bottle hanging from one of his coat buttons, a pen stuck over his ear, spectacles on his nose, a book in his hand, and really has all the appearance of a man determined on doing business of some sort or other. He possesses a sort of ubiquity, for go where you will through any part of the pool you are sure to meet him. He seems to be expected everywhere; no one appears to be surprised at his presence. Captains and mates pass him by unnoticed and unquestioned. As suddenly as he comes does he disappear, to start up in some other place. His visits are so regular, that it would scarcely look like being on board ship if 'old D——, the whiskey man,' as he is called, did not make his appearance some time during the day, for he seems to be in some strange way identified with the river, and with every ship that frequents it.

OF THE STREET-BUYERS

THE persons who traverse the streets, or call periodically at certain places to purchase articles which are usually sold at the door or within the house, are—according to the division I laid down in the first number of this work—STREET-BUYERS. The largest, and, in every respect, the most remarkable body of these traders, are the buyers of old clothes, and of them I shall speak separately, devoting at the same time some space to the STREET-JEWS.

The principal things bought by the itinerant purchasers consist of waste-paper, hare and rabbit skins, old umbrellas and parasols, bottles and glass, broken metal, rags, dripping, grease, bones, tea-leaves, and old clothes.

With the exception of the buyers of waste-paper, among whom are many active, energetic, and intelligent men, the street-buyers are of the lower sort, both as to means and intelligence. The only further exception, perhaps, which I need notice here is, that among some umbrella-buyers, there is considerable smartness, and some-times, in the repair or renewal of the ribs, &c., a slight degree of skill. The other street-purchasers—such as the hare-skin and old metal and rag buyers, are often old and infirm people of both sexes, of whom—perhaps by reason of their infirmities—not a few have been in the trade from their childhood, and are as well known by sight in their respective rounds, as was the 'long-remembered beggar' in former times.

It is usually the lot of a poor person who has been driven to the streets, or has adopted such a life when an adult, to *sell* trifling things—such as are light to carry and require a small outlay—in advanced age. Old men and women totter about offering lucifer-matches, boot and stay-laces, penny memorandum books, and such like. But the elder portion of the street-folk I have now to speak of do not sell, but *buy*.

OF THE STREET-BUYERS OF RAGS, BROKEN METAL, BOTTLES, GLASS, AND BONES

I class all these articles under one head, for, on inquiry, I find no individual supporting himself by the trading in any one of them. I shall, therefore, describe the buyers of rags, broken metal, bottles, glass, and bones, as a body of street-traders, but take the articles in which they traffic seriatim, pointing out in what degree they are, or have been, wholly or partially, the staple of several distinct callings.

The street-buyers, who are only buyers, have barrows, sometimes even carts with donkeys, and, as they themselves describe it, they 'buy everything.' These men are little seen in London, for they 'work' the more secluded courts, streets, and alleys, when in town; but their most frequented rounds are the poorer parts of the populous suburbs. There are many in Croydon, Woolwich, Greenwich, and Deptford. 'It's no use,' a man who had been in the trade said to me, 'such as us calling at fine houses to know if they've any old keys to sell! No, we trades with the poor.' Often, however, they deal with the servants of the wealthy; and their usual mode of business in such cases is to leave a bill at the house a few hours previous to their visit. This document has frequently the royal arms at the head of it, and asserts that the 'firm' has been established since the year ——, which is seldom less than half a century. The hand-bill usually consists of a short preface as to the increased demand for rags on the part of the paper-makers, and this is followed by a liberal offer to give the very best prices for any old linen, or old metal, bottles, rope, stair-rods, locks, keys, dripping, carpeting, &c., 'in fact, no rubbish or lumber, however worthless, will be refused;' and generally concludes with a request that this 'bill' may be shown to the mistress of the house and preserved, as it will be called for in a couple of hours.

The papers are delivered by one of the 'firm,' who marks on the door a sign indicative of the houses at which the bill has been taken in, and the probable reception there of the gentleman who is to follow him. The road taken is also pointed by marks before explained. These men are residents in all quarters within 20 miles of London, being most numerous in the places at no great distance from the Thames. They work their way from their suburban residences to London, which, of course, is the mart, or 'exchange,' for their wares. The reason why the suburbs are preferred is that in those parts the possessors of such things as broken metal, &c., cannot so readily resort to a marine-store dealer's as they can in town. I am informed, however, that the shops of the marine-store men are on the increase in the more densely-peopled suburbs; still the dwellings of the poor are often widely scattered in those parts, and few will go a mile to sell any old thing. They wait in preference, unless very needy, for the *visit* of the street-buyer.

A good many years ago—perhaps until 30 years back—*rags*, and especially white and good linen rags, were among the things most zealously inquired for by street-buyers, and then 3*d*. a pound was a price readily paid. Subsequently the paper-manufacturers brought to great and economical perfection the process of boiling rags in lye and bleaching them with chlorine, so that colour became less a desideratum. A few years after the peace of 1815, moreover, the foreign trade in rags increased rapidly. At the present time, about 1,200 tons of woollen rags, and upwards of 10,000 tons of linen rags, are imported yearly.

The linen buying is still prosecuted extensively by itinerant 'gatherers' in the country, and in the further neighbourhoods of London, but the collection is not to the extent it was formerly. The price is lower, and, owing to the foreign trade, the demand is less urgent; so common, too, is now the wear of cotton, and so much smaller that of linen, that many people will not sell linen rags, but reserve them for use in case of cuts and wounds, or for giving to their poor neighbours on any such emergency.

A street-buyer of the class I have described, upon presenting himself at any house, offers to buy rags, broken metal, or glass, and for rags especially there is often a serious bargaining, and sometimes, I was told by an itinerant street-seller, who had been an ear-witness, a little joking not of the most delicate kind. For coloured rags these men give ½d. a pound, or 1d. for three pounds; for inferior white rags ½d. a pound, and up to 1½d., for the best, 2d. the pound. It is common, however, and even more common, I am assured, among masters of the old rag and bottle shops, than among street-buyers, to announce 2d. or 3d., or oven as much as 6d., for the *best* rags, but, somehow or other, the rags taken for sale to those buyers never are of the best. To offer 6d. a pound for rags is ridiculous, but such an offer may be seen at some rag-shops, the figure 6, perhaps, crowning a painting of a large plum-pudding, as a representation of what may be a Christmas result, merely from the thrifty preservation of rags, grease, and dripping. Some of the street-buyers, when working the suburbs or the country, attach a similar 'illustration' to their barrows or carts. I saw the winter placard of one of these men, which he was reserving for a country excursion as far as Rochester, 'when the plum-pudding time was a-coming.' In this pictorial advertisement a man and woman, very florid and full-faced, were on the point of enjoying a huge plum-pudding, the man flourishing a large knife, and looking very hospitable. On a scroll which issued from his mouth were the words: 'From our rags! The best prices given by —— ——, of London.' The woman in like manner exclaimed: 'From dripping and house fat! The best prices given by —— ——, of London.'

This man told me that at some times, both in town and country he did not buy a pound of rags in a week. He had heard the old hands in the trade say, that 20 or 30 years back they could 'gather' (the word generally used for buying) twice and three times as many rags as at present. My informant attributed this change to two causes, depending more upon what he had heard from experienced street-buyers than upon his own knowledge. At one time it was common for a mistress to allow her maid-servant to 'keep a rag-bag,' in which all refuse linen, &c., was collected for sale for the servant's behoof; a privilege now rarely accorded. The other cause was that working-people's wives had less money at their command now than they had formerly, so that instead of gathering a good heap for the man who called on them periodically, they ran to a marine store-shop and sold them by one, two, and three penny-worths at a time. This related to all the things in the street-buyer's trade, as well as to rags.

OF THE 'RAG-AND-BOTTLE' AND THE 'MARINE-STORE' SHOPS

THE principal purchasers of any refuse or worn-out articles are the proprietors of the rag-and-bottle-shops. Some of these men make a good deal of money, and not unfrequently unite with the business the letting out of vans for the conveyance of furniture, or for pleasure excursions, to such places as Hampton Court, The stench in these shops is positively sickening. Here in a small apartment may be a pile of rags, a sack-full of bones, the many varieties of grease and 'kitchen-stuff,' corrupting an atmosphere which, even without such accompaniments, would be too close. The windows are often crowded with bottles, which exclude the light; while the floor and shelves are thick with grease and dirt. The inmates seem unconscious of this foulness,—and one comparatively wealthy man, who showed me his horses, the stable being like a drawing-room compared to his shop, in speaking of the many deaths among his children, could not conjecture to what cause it could be owing. This indifference to dirt and stench is the more remarkable, as many of the shopkeepers have been gentlemen's servants, and were therefore once accustomed to cleanliness and order. The door-posts and windows of the rag-and-bottle-shops are often closely placarded, and the front of the house is sometimes one glaring colour, blue or red; so that the place may be at once recognised, even by the illiterate, as the 'red house,' or the 'blue house.' If these men are not exactly street-buyers, they are street-billers, continually distributing hand-bills, but more especially before Christmas. The more aristocratic, however, now send round cards, and to the following purport:—

No.—   THE ——HOUSE IS —'S   No.—
RAG, BOTTLE, AND KITCHEN STUFF
WAREHOUSE,
—— STREET, —— TOWN,

Where you can obtain Gold and Silver to any amount.

ESTABLISHED ——

THE HIGHEST PRICE GIVEN

For all the undermentioned articles, viz:—

Wax and Sperm Pieces	Bones, Phials, & Broken Flint Glass
Kitchen Stuff, &c.	Old Copper, Brass, Pewter, &c.
Wine & Beer Bottles	Lead, Iron, Zinc, Steel, &c., &c.
Eau de Cologne, Soda Water	Old Horse Hair, Mattresses, &c.
Doctors Bottles, &c.	Old Books, Waste Paper, &c.
White Linen Rags	All kinds of Coloured Rags

The utmost value given for all kinds of Wearing Apparel.
Furniture and Lumber of every description bought, and
full value given at his Miscellaneous Warehouse.
Articles sent for.

The *rag-and-bottle* and the *marine-store shops* are in many instances but different names for the same description of business. The chief distinction appears to be this: the marine-store shopkeepers (proper) do not meddle with what is a very principal object of traffic with the rag-and-bottle man, the purchase of dripping, as well as of every kind of refuse in the way of fat or grease. The marine-store man, too, is more miscellaneous in his wares than his contemporary of the rag-and-bottle-store, as the former will purchase any of the smaller articles of household furniture, old tea-caddies, knife-boxes, fire-irons, books, pictures, draughts and backgammon boards, bird-cages, Dutch clocks, cups and saucers, tools and brushes. The rag-and-bottle tradesman will readily purchase any of these things to be disposed of as old metal or waste-paper, but his brother tradesman buys them to be re-sold and re-used for the purposes for which they were originally manufactured. When furniture, however, is the staple of one of these second-hand storehouses, the proprietor is a furniture-broker, and not a marine-store dealer. If, again, the dealer in these stores confine his business to the purchase of old metals, for instance, he is classed as an old metal dealer, collecting it or buying it of collectors, for sale to iron founders, coppersmiths, brass-founders, and plumbers. In perhaps the majority of instances there is little or no distinction between the establishments I have spoken of. The *dolly* business is common to both, but most common to the marine-store dealer, and of it I shall speak afterwards.

These shops are exceedingly numerous. Perhaps in the poorer and smaller streets they are more numerous even than the chandlers' or the beer-sellers' places. At the corner of a small street, both in town and the nearer suburbs, will frequently be found the chandler's shop, for the sale of small quantities of cheese, bacon, groceries, &c., to the poor. Lower down may be seen the beer-sellers; and in the same street there is certain to be one rag-and-bottle or marine-store shop, very often two, and not unfrequently another in some adjacent court.

I was referred to the owner of a marine-store shop, as to a respectable man, keeping a store of the best class. Here the counter, or table, or whatever it is to be called, for it was somewhat nondescript, by an ingenious contrivance could be pushed out into the street, so that in bad weather the goods which were at other times exposed in the street could be drawn inside without trouble. The glass frames of the window were removable, and were placed on one side in the shop, for in the summer an open casement seemed to be preferred. This is one of the remaining old trade customs still seen in London; for previously to the great fire in 1666, and the subsequent rebuilding of the city, shops with open casements, and protected from the weather by overhanging eaves, or by a sloping wooden roof, were general.

The house I visited was an old one, and abounded in closets and recesses. The fire-place, which apparently had been large, was removed, and the space was occupied with a mass of old iron of every kind; all this was destined for the furnace of the iron-founder, wrought iron being preferred for several of the requirements of that trade. A chest or range of very old drawers, with defaced or worn-out labels—once a grocer's or a chemist's—was stuffed, in every drawer, with old horse-shoe nails (valuable for steel manufacturers), and horse and donkey shoes; brass knobs; glass stoppers; small bottles (among them a number of the cheap cast 'hartshorn bottles'); broken pieces of brass and copper; small tools (such as shoemakers' and harness-makers' awls), punches, gimlets, plane-irons, hammer heads, &c.; odd dominoes, dice, and backgammon-men; lock escutcheons, keys, and the smaller sort of locks, especially padlocks; in fine, any small thing which could be stowed away in such a place.

In one corner of the shop had been thrown, the evening before, a mass of old iron, then just bought. It consisted of a number of screws of different lengths and substance; of broken bars and rails; of the odds and ends of the cogged wheels of machinery, broken up or worn out; of odd-looking spikes, and rings, and links; all heaped together and scarcely distinguishable. These things had all to be assorted; some to be sold for re-use in their then form; the others to be sold that they might be melted and cast into other forms. The floor was intricate with hampers of bottles; heaps of old boots and shoes; old desks and work-boxes; pictures (all modern) with and without frames; waste-paper, the most of it of quarto, and some larger sized, soiled or torn, and strung closely together in weights of from 2 to 7 lbs.; and a fire-proof safe, stuffed with old fringes, tassels, and other upholstery goods, worn and discoloured. The miscellaneous wares were carried out into the street, and ranged by the door-posts as well as in front of the house. In some small out-houses in the yard were piles of old iron and tin pans, and of the broken or separate parts of harness.

From the proprietor of this establishment I had the following account:—

'I've been in the business more than a dozen years. Before that, I was an auctioneer's, and then a furniture broker's, porter. I wasn't brought up to any regular trade, but just to jobbing about, and a bad trade it is, as all trades is that ain't regular employ for a man. I had some money when my father died—he kept a chandler's shop—and I bought a marine.' [An elliptical form of speech among these traders.] 'I gave 10*l*. for the stock, and 5*l*. for entrance and good-will, and agreed to pay what rents and rates was due. It was a smallish stock then, for the business had been neglected, but I have no reason to be sorry for my bargain, though it might have been better. There's lots taken in about good-wills, but perhaps not so many in my way of business, because we're rather "fly to a dodge." It's confined sort of life, but there's no help for that. Why, as to my way of trade, you'd be surprised, what different sorts of people come to my shop. I don't mean the regular hands; but the chance comers. I've had men dressed like gentlemen —and no doubt they was respectable when they was sober—bring two or three books, or a nice cigar case, or anythink that don't show in their pockets, and say, when as drunk as blazes, "Give me what you can for this; I want it sold for a particular purpose." That particular purpose was more drink, I should say; and I've known the same men come back in less than a week, and buy what they'd sold me at a little extra, and be glad if I had it by me still. O, we sees a deal of things in this way of life. Yes, poor people run to such as me. I've known them come with such things as teapots, and old hair mattresses, and flock beds, and *then* I'm sure they're hard up—reduced for a meal. I don't like buying big things like mattresses, though I do purchase 'em sometimes. Some of these sellers are as keen as Jews at a bargain; others seem only anxious to get rid of things and have hold of some bit of money anyhow. Yes, sir, I've known their hands tremble to receive the money, and mostly the women's. They haven't been used to it, I know, when that's the case. Perhaps they comes to sell to me what the pawns won't take in, and what they wouldn't like to be seen selling to any of the men that goes about buying things in the street.

'Why, I've bought everythink; at sales by auction there's often "lots" made up of different things, and they goes for very little. I buy of people, too, that come to me, and of the regular hands that supply such shops as mine. I sell retail and I sell to hawkers. I sell to anybody, for gentlemen'll come into my shop to buy anythink that's took their fancy in passing. Yes, I've bought old oil paintings. I've heard of some being bought by people in my way as have turned out stunners, and was sold for a hundred pounds or more, and cost, perhaps, half-a-crown or only a shilling. I never experienced such a thing myself. There's a good deal of gammon about it. Well, it's hardly possible to say anything about a scale of prices. I give 2*d*. for an old tin or metal teapot, or an old saucepan, and sometimes, two days after I've bought such a thing, I've sold it for 3*d*. to the man or woman I've bought it of. I'll sell cheaper to them than to anybody else, because they come to me in two ways—both as sellers and buyers. For pictures I've given from 3*d*. to 1*s*. I fancy they're among the last things some sorts of poor people, which is a bit fanciful, parts with. I've bought them of hawkers, but often I refuse them, as they've given more than I could get. Pictures requires a judge. Some brought to me was published by newspapers and them sort of people. Waste-paper I buy as it comes. I can't read very much, and don't understand about books. I take the backs off and weighs them, and gives 1*d*., and 1¼*d*., and 2*d*. a pound, and there's an end. I sell them at about ¼*d*. a pound profit, or sometimes less, to men as we calls "waste" men. It's a poor part of our business, but the books and paper takes up little room, and then it's clean and can be stowed anywhere, and is a sure sale. Well, the people as sells "waste" to me is not such as can read, I think; I don't know what they is; perhaps they're such as obtains possession of the books and whatnot after the death of old folk, and gets them out of the way as quick as they can. I know nothink about what they are. Last week, a man in black—he didn't seem rich—came into my shop and looked at some old books, and said "Have you any black lead?" He didn't speak plain, and I could hardly catch him. I said, "No, sir, I don't sell black lead, but you'll get it at No. 27," but he answered, "No, black lead, but black letter," speaking very pointed. I said, "No," and I haven't a notion what he meant.'

OF THE BUYERS OF KITCHEN-STUFF, GREASE, AND DRIPPING

THIS body of traders cannot be classed as street-buyers, so that only a brief account is here necessary. The buyers are not now chance people, itinerant on any round, as at one period they were to a great extent, but they are the proprietors of the rag and bottle and marine-store shops, or those they employ.

In this business there has been a considerable change. Until of late years women, often wearing suspiciously large cloaks and carrying baskets, ventured into perhaps every area in London, and asked for the cook at every house where they thought a cook might be kept, and this often at early morning. If the well-cloaked woman was known, business could be transacted without delay: if she were a stranger, she recommended herself by offering very liberal terms for 'kitchen-stuff'. The cook's, or kitchen-maid's, or servant-of-all-work's 'perquisites', were then generally disposed of to these collectors, some of whom were charwomen in the houses they resorted to for the purchase of the kitchen-stuff. They were often satisfied to purchase the dripping, &c., by the lump, estimating the weight and the value by the eye. In this traffic was frequently mixed up a good deal of pilfering, directly or indirectly. Silver spoons were thus disposed of. Candles, purposely broken and crushed, were often part of the grease; in the dripping, butter occasionally added to the weight; in the 'stock' (the remains of meat boiled down for the making of soup) were sometimes portions of excellent meat fresh from the joints which had been carved at table; and among the broken bread, might be frequently seen small loaves, unbroken.

There is no doubt that this mode of traffic by itinerant char-women, &c., is still carried on, but to a much smaller extent than formerly. The cook's perquisites are in many cases sold under the inspection of the mistress, according to agreement; or taken to the shop by the cook or some fellow-servant; or else sent for by the shopkeeper. This is done to check the confidential, direct, and immediate trade-intercourse between merely two individuals, the buyer and seller, by making the transaction more open and regular. I did not hear of any persons who merely purchase the kitchen-stuff, as street-buyers, and sell it at once to the tallow-melter or the soap-boiler; it appears all to find its way to the shops I have described, even when bought by charwomen; while the shop-keepers send for it or receive it in the way I have stated, so that there is but little of street traffic in the matter.

One of these shopkeepers told me that in this trading, as far as his own opinion went, there was as much trickery as ever, and that many gentlefolk quietly made up their minds to submit to it, while others, he said, 'kept the house in hot water' by resisting it. I found, however, the general opinion to be, that when servants could only dispose of these things to known people, the responsi-bility of the buyer as well as the seller was increased, and acted as a preventive check.

The price of kitchen-stuff is $1d$. and $1\frac{1}{2}d$, the pound; for dripping —used by the poor as a substitute for butter—$3\frac{1}{2}d$. to $5d$.

OF THE STREET-BUYERS OF HARE AND RABBIT SKINS

These buyers are for the most part poor, old, or infirm people, and I am informed that the majority have been in some street business, and often as buyers, all their lives.

I received an account of hareskin-buying from a woman, upwards

of fifty, who had been in the trade, she told me, from childhood,
'as was her mother before her.' The husband, who was lame, and
older than his wife, had been all *his* life a field-catcher of birds,
and a street-seller of hearth-stones. They had been married 31
years, and resided in a garret of a house, in a street off Drury-lane—
a small room, with a close smell about it. The room was not unfurnished—it was, in fact, crowded. There were bird-cages, with
and without birds, over what *was* once a bed; for the bed, just prior
to my visit, had been sold to pay the rent, and a month's rent was
again in arrear; and there were bird-cages on the wall by the door,
and bird-cages over the mantelshelf. There was furniture, too, and
crockery; and a vile oil painting of 'still life'; but an eye used to
the furniture in the rooms of the poor could at once perceive that
there was not *one* article which could be sold to a broker or marine-
store dealer, or pledged at a pawn-shop. I was told the man and
woman both drank hard. The woman said:—

'I've sold hareskins all my life, sir, and was born in London;
but when the hareskins isn't in, I sells flowers. I goes about now
(in November) for my skins every day, wet or dry, and all day
long—that is, till it's dark. To-day I've not laid out a penny, but
then it's been such a day for rain. I reckon that if I gets hold of
eighteen hare and rabbit skins in a day, that is my greatest day's
work. I gives 2*d.* for good hares, what's not riddled much, and sells
them all for 2½*d.* I sells what I pick up, by the twelve or the twenty,
if I can afford to keep them by me till that number's gathered, to
a Jew. I don't know what is done with them. I can't tell you just
what use they're for—something about hats.' (The Jew was no
doubt a hat-furrier, or supplying a hat-furrier.) 'Jews gives us
better prices than Christians, and buys readier; so I find. Last
week I sold all I bought for 3*s.* 6*d.* I take some weeks as much as
8*s.* for what I pick up, and if I could get that every week I should
think myself a lady. The profit left me a clear half-crown. There's
no difference in any perticler year—only that things get worse.
The game laws, as far as I knows, hasn't made no difference in my
trade. Indeed, I can't say I knows anything about game laws at
all, or hears anything consarning 'em. I goes along the squares
and streets. I buys most at gentlemen's houses. We never calls at
hotels. The servants, and the women that chars, and washes, and
jobs, manages it there. Hareskins is in—leastways I c'lets them—

from September to the end of March, when hares, they says, goes mad. I can't say what I makes one week with another—perhaps 2*s*. 6*d*. may be cleared every week.'

These buyers go regular rounds, carrying the skins in their hands, and crying, 'Any hareskins, cook? Hareskins.' It is for the most part a winter trade; but some collect the skins all the year round, as the hares are now vended the year through; but by far the most are gathered in the winter.

OF THE STREET-JEWS

ALTHOUGH my present inquiry relates to London life in London streets, it is necessary that I should briefly treat of the Jews generally, as an integral, but distinct and peculiar part of street-life.

During the eighteenth century the popular feeling ran very high against the Jews, although to the masses they were almost strangers, except as men employed in the not-very-formidable occupation of collecting and vending second-hand clothes. The old feeling against them seems to have lingered among the English people, and their own greed in many instances engendered other and lawful causes of dislike, by their resorting to unlawful and debasing pursuits. They were considered—and with that exaggeration of belief dear to any ignorant community—as an entire people of misers, usurers, extortioners, receivers of stolen goods, cheats, brothel-keepers, sheriff's-officers, clippers and sweaters of the coin of the realm, gaming-house keepers; in fine, the charges, or rather the accusations, of carrying on every disreputable trade, and none else, were 'bundled at their doors.' That there was too much foundation for many of these accusations, and still *is*, no reasonable Jew can now deny; that the wholesale prejudice against them was absurd, is equally indisputable.

In what estimation the street, and, incidentally, all classes of Jews are held at the present time, will be seen in the course of my remarks; and in the narrative to be given. I may here observe, however, that among some the dominant feeling against the Jews on account of their faith still flourishes, as is shown by the following statement:—A gentleman of my acquaintance was one evening, about twilight, walking down Brydges-street, Covent-garden, when an elderly Jew was preceding him, apparently on his return from a day's work, as an old clothesman. His bag accidentally touched the bonnet of a dashing woman of the town, who was passing, and she turned round, abused the Jew, and spat at him, saying with an oath: 'You old rags humbug! *You* can't do that!' —an allusion to a vulgar notion that Jews have been unable to do more than *slobber*, since spitting on the Saviour.

The number of Jews now in England is computed at 35,000. This is the result at which the Chief Rabbi arrived a few years ago, after collecting all the statistical information at his command. Of these 35,000, more than one-half, or about 18,000, reside in London. I am informed that there may now be a small increase to this population, but only small, for many Jews have emigrated—some to California. A few years ago—a circumstance mentioned in my account of the Street-Sellers of Jewellery—there were a number of Jews known as 'hawkers,' or 'travellers,' who traversed every part of England selling watches, gold and silver pencil-cases, eye-glasses, and all the more portable descriptions of jewellery, as well as thermometers, barometers, telescopes, and microscopes. This trade is now little pursued, except by stationery dealers; and the Jews who carried it on, and who were chiefly foreign Jews, have emigrated to America. The foreign Jews, who, though a fluctuating body, are always numerous in London, are included in the computation of 18,000; of this population two-thirds reside in the city, or the streets adjacent to the eastern boundaries of the city.

OF THE TRADES AND LOCALITIES OF THE STREET-JEWS

THE trades which the Jews most affect, I was told by one of them-selves, are those in which, as they describe it, 'there's a chance'; that is, they prefer a trade in such commodity as is not subjected to a fixed price, so that there may be abundant scope for specula-tion, and something like a gambler's chance for profit or loss. In this way, Sir Walter Scott has said, trade has 'all the fascination of gambling, without the moral guilt'; but the absence of moral guilt in connection with such trading is certainly dubious.

The wholesale trades in foreign commodities which are now principally or solely in the hands of the Jews, often as importers and exporters, are, watches and jewels, sponges—fruits, especially green fruits, such as oranges, lemons, grapes, walnuts, cocoa-nuts, &c., and dates among dried fruits—shells, tortoises, parrots and foreign birds, curiosities, ostrich feathers, snuffs, cigars, and pipes; but cigars far more extensively at one time.

The localities in which these wholesale and retail traders reside are mostly at the East-end—indeed the Jews of London, as a congregated body, have been, from the times when their numbers were sufficient to institute a 'settlement' or 'colony,' peculiar to themselves, always resident in the eastern quarter of the metropolis.

Of course a wealthy Jew millionaire—merchant, stock-jobber, or stock-broker—resides where he pleases—in a villa near the Marquis of Hertford's in the Regent's-park, a mansion near the Duke of Wellington's in Piccadilly, a house and grounds at Clapham or Stamford-hill; but these are exceptions. The quarters of the Jews are not difficult to describe. The trading-class in the capacity of shopkeepers, warehousemen, or manufacturers, are the thickest in Houndsditch, Aldgate, and the Minories, more especially as regards the 'swag-shops' and the manufacture and sale of wearing apparel. The wholesale dealers in fruit are in Duke's-place and Pudding-lane (Thames-street), but the superior retail Jew fruiterers—some of whose shops are remarkable for the beauty of their fruit—are in Cheapside, Oxford-street, Piccadilly, and most of all in Covent-garden market. The inferior jewellers (some of whom deal with the first shops) are also at the East-end, about Whitechapel, Bevis-marks, and Houndsditch; the wealthier goldsmiths and watch-makers having, like other tradesmen of the class, their shops in the superior thoroughfares. The great congregation of working watchmakers is in Clerkenwell, but in that locality there are only a few Jews. The Hebrew dealers in second-hand garments, and second-hand wares generally, are located about Petticoat-lane. The manufacturers of such things as cigars, pencils, and sealing-wax; the wholesale importers of sponge, bristles and toys, the dealers in quills and in 'looking-glasses,' reside in large private-looking houses, when display is not needed for purposes of business, in such parts as Maunsell-street, Great Prescott-street, Great Ailie-street, Leman-street, and other parts of the eastern quarter known as Goodman's-fields. The wholesale dealers in foreign birds and shells, and in the many foreign things known as 'curiosities,' reside in East Smithfield, Ratcliffe-highway, High-street (Shadwell), or in some of the parts adjacent to the Thames. In the long range of river-side streets, stretching from the Tower to Poplar and Black-wall, are Jews, who fulfil the many capacities of slop-sellers, &c., called into exercise by the requirements of seafaring people on their return from or commencement of a voyage. A few Jews keep boarding-houses for sailors in Shadwell and Wapping. Of the localities and abodes of the poorest of the Jews I shall speak here-after.

Concerning the street-trades pursued by the Jews, I believe there is not at present a single one of which they can be said to have a monopoly: nor in any one branch of the street-traffic are there so many of the Jew traders as there were a few years back.

This remarkable change is thus to be accounted for. Strange as the fact may appear, the Jew has been undersold in the streets, and he has been beaten on what might be called his own ground —the buying of old clothes. The Jew boys, and the feebler and elder Jews, had, until some twelve or fifteen years back, almost the monopoly of orange and lemon street-selling, or street-hawking. The costermonger class had possession of the theatre doors and the approaches to the theatres; they had, too, occasionally their barrows full of oranges; but the Jews were the daily, assiduous, and itinerant street-sellers of this most popular of foreign, and perhaps of all, fruits. In their hopes of sale they followed any one a mile if encouraged, even by a few approving glances. The great theatre of this traffic was in the stagecoach yards in such inns as the Bull and Mouth (St. Martin's-le-Grand), the Belle Sauvage (Ludgate-hill), the Saracen's Head (Snow-hill), the Bull (Aldgate), the Swan-with-two-Necks (Lad-lane, City), the George and Blue Boar (Holborn), the White Horse (Fetter-lane), and other such places. They were seen too, 'with all their eyes about them,' as one informant expressed it, outside the inns where the coaches stopped to take up passengers—at the White Horse Cellar in Piccadilly, for instance, and the Angel and the (now defunct) Peacock in Islington. A commercial traveller told me that he could never leave town by any 'mail' or 'stage,' without being besieged by a small army of Jew boys, who most pertinaciously offered him oranges, lemons, sponges, combs, pocket-books, pencils, sealing-wax, paper, many-bladed pen-knives, razors, pocket-mirrors, and shaving-boxes—as if a man could not possibly quit the metropolis without requiring a stock of such commodities. In the whole of these trades, unless in some degree in sponges and blacklead-pencils, the Jew is now out-numbered or displaced.

I have before alluded to the underselling of the Jew boy by the Irish boy in the street-orange trade; but the characteristics of the change are so peculiar, that a further notice is necessary. It is curious to observe that the most assiduous, and hitherto the most successful of street-traders, were supplanted, not by a more persevering or more skilful body of street-sellers, but simply by a more *starving body*.

Some few years since poor Irish people, and chiefly those connected with the culture of the land, 'came over' to this country in great numbers, actuated either by vague hopes of 'bettering themselves' by emigration, or working on the railways, or else influenced by the restlessness common to an impoverished people. These men, when unable to obtain employment, without scruple became street-sellers. Not only did the adults resort to street-traffic, generally in its simplest forms, such as hawking fruit, but the children, by whom they were accompanied from Ireland, in great numbers, were put into the trade; and if two or three children earned 2*d.* a day each, and their parents 5*d.* or 6*d.* each, or even 4*d.*, the subsistence of the family was better than they could obtain in the midst of the miseries of the southern and western part of the Sister Isle. An Irish boy of fourteen, having to support himself by street-trade, as was often the case, owing to the death of parents and to divers casualties, would undersell the Jew boys similarly circumstanced.

The Irish boy could live *harder* than the Jew—often in his own country he subsisted on a stolen turnip a day; he could lodge harder —lodge for 1*d.* a night in any noisome den, or sleep in the open air, which is seldom done by the Jew boy; he could dispense with the use of shoes and stockings—a dispensation at which his rival in trade revolted; he drank only water, or if he took tea or coffee, it was as a meal, and not merely as a beverage; to crown the whole, the city-bred Jew boy required some evening recreation, the penny or twopenny concert, or a game at draughts or dominoes; but this the Irish boy, country bred, never thought of, for *his* sole luxury was a deep sleep, and, being regardless or ignorant of all such recreations, he worked longer hours, and so sold more oranges, than his Hebrew competitor. Thus, as the Munster or Connaught

lad could live on less than the young denizen of Petticoat-lane,
he could sell at a smaller profit, and did so sell, until gradually the
Hebrew youths were displaced by the Irish in the street orange
trade.

It is the same, or the same in a degree, with other street-trades,
which were at one time all but monopolised by the Jew adults.
Among these were the street-sale of spectacles and sponges. The
prevalence of slop-work and slop-wages, and the frequent difficulty
of obtaining properly-remunerated employment—the pinch of
want, in short—have driven many mechanics to street-traffic; so
that the numbers of street-traffickers have been augmented, while
no small portion of the new-comers have adopted the more knowing
street avocations, formerly pursued only by the Jews.

OF THE JEW OLD-CLOTHES MEN

FIFTY years ago the appearance of the street-Jews, engaged in the
purchase of second-hand clothes, was different from what it is at the
present time. The Jew then had far more of the distinctive garb
and aspect of a foreigner. He not unfrequently wore the gabardine,
which is never seen now in the streets, but some of the long loose
frock coats worn by the Jew clothes' buyers resemble it. At that
period, too, the Jew's long beard was far more distinctive than it
is in this hirsute generation.

In other respects the street-Jew is unchanged. Now, as during
the last century, he traverses every street, square, and road, with
the monotonous cry, sometimes like a bleat, of 'Clo'! Clo'!' On
this head, however, I have previously remarked, when describing
the street Jew of a hundred years ago.

In an inquiry into the condition of the old-clothes dealers a year
and a half ago, a Jew gave me the following account. He told me,
at the commencement of his statement, that he was of opinion that
his people were far more speculative than the Gentiles, and therefore the English liked better to deal with them. 'Our people,' he
said, 'will be out all day in the wet, and begrudge themselves a
bit of anything to eat till they go home, and then, may be, they'll
gamble away their crown, just for the love of speculation.' My
informant, who could write or speak several languages, and had
been 50 years in the business, then said, 'I am no bigot; indeed

I do not care where I buy my meat, so long as I can get it. I often go into the Minories and buy some, without looking to how it has been killed, or whether it has a seal on it or not.'

He then gave me some account of the Jewish children, and the number of men in the trade, which I have embodied under the proper heads. The itinerant Jew clothes man, he told me, was generally the son of a former old-clothes man, but some were cigar-makers, or pencil-makers, taking to the clothes business when those trades were slack; but that nineteen out of twenty had been born to it. If the parents of the Jew boy are poor, and the boy a sharp lad, he generally commences business at ten years of age, by selling lemons, or some trifle in the streets, and so, as he expressed it, the boy 'gets a round,' or street-connection, by becoming known to the neighbourhoods he visits. If he sees a servant, he will, when selling his lemons, ask if she have any old shoes or old clothes, and offer to be a purchaser. If the clothes should come to more than the Jew boy has in his pocket, he leaves what silver he has as 'an earnest upon them,' and then seeks some regular Jew clothes man, who will advance the purchase money. This the old Jew agrees to do upon the understanding that he is to have 'half Rybeck,' that is, a moiety of the profit, and then he will accompany the boy to the house, to pass his judgment on the goods, and satisfy himself that the stripling has not made a blind bargain, an error into which he very rarely falls. After this he goes with the lad to Petticoat-lane, and there they share whatever money the clothes may bring over and above what has been paid for them. By such means the Jew boy gets his knowledge of the old-clothes business; and so quick are these lads generally, that in the course of two months they will acquire sufficient experience in connection with the trade to begin dealing on their own account. There are some, he told me, as sharp at 15 as men of 50.

'It is very seldom,' my informant stated, 'very seldom indeed, that a Jew clothes man takes away any of the property of the house he may be called into. I expect there's a good many of 'em,' he continued, for he sometimes spoke of his co-traders, as if they were not of his own class, 'is fond of cheating—that is, they won't mind giving only 2*s*. for a thing that's worth 5*s*. They are fond of money, and will do almost anything to get it. Jews are perhaps the most money-loving people in all England. There are certainly some old clothes men who will buy articles at such a price that they must know them to have been stolen. Their rule, however, is to ask no questions, and to get as cheap an article as possible. A Jew clothes man is seldom or never seen in liquor. They gamble for money, either at their own homes or at public-houses. The favourite games are tossing, dominoes, and cards. I was informed, by one of the people, that he had seen as much as 30*l.* in silver and gold lying upon the ground when two parties had been playing at throwing three halfpence in the air. On a Saturday, some gamble away the morning and the greater part of the afternoon.' (Saturday, I need hardly say, is the Hebrew Sabbath.) 'They meet in some secret back place, about ten, and begin playing for "one a time"—that is, tossing up three halfpence, and staking 1*s.* on the result. Other Jews, and a few Christians, will gather round and bet. Sometimes the bets laid by the Jew bystanders are as high as 2*l.* each; and on more than one occasion the old-clothes men have wagered as much as 50*l.*, but only after great gains at gambling. Some, if they *can*, will cheat, by means of a halfpenny with a head or a tail on both sides, called a "gray." The play lasts till the Sabbath is nearly over, and then they go to business or the theatre. They seldom or never say a word while they are losing, but merely stamp on the ground; it is dangerous, though, to interfere when luck runs against them. The rule is, when a man is losing leave him alone. I have known them play for three hours together, and nothing be said all that time but "head" or "tail." They seldom go to synagogue, and on a Sunday evening have card parties at their own houses. They seldom eat anything on their rounds. The reason is, not because they object to eat meat killed by a Christian, but because they are afraid of losing a "deal," or the chance of buying a lot of old clothes by delay. They are generally too lazy to light their own fires before they start of a morning, and nineteen out of twenty obtain their breakfasts at the coffee-shops about Houndsditch.

'When they return from their day's work they have mostly some stew ready, prepared by their parents or wife. If they are not family men they go to an eating-house. This is sometimes a Jewish house, but if no one is looking they creep into a Christian "cook-shop," not being particular about eating "tryfer"—that is, meat which has been killed by a Christian. Those that are single generally go to a neighbour and agree with him to be boarded on the Sabbath; and for this the charge is generally about 2*s*. 6*d*. On a Saturday there's cold fish for breakfast and supper; indeed, a Jew would pawn the shirt off his back sooner than go without fish then; and in holiday-time he *will* have it, if he has to get it out of the stones. It is not reckoned a holiday unless there's fish.'

'Forty years ago I have made as much as 5*l*. in a week by the purchase of old clothes in the streets,' said a Jew informant. 'Upon an average then, I could earn weekly about 2*l*. But now things are different. People are more wide a wake. Every one knows the value of an old coat now-a-days. The women know more than the men. The general average, I think, take the good weeks with the bad throughout the year, is about 1*l*. a week; some weeks we get 2*l*., and some scarcely nothing.'

I am informed that of the Jew Old-Clothes Men there are now only from 500 to 600 in London; at one time there might have been 1,000. Their average earnings may be something short of 20*s*. a week in second-hand clothes alone; but the gains are difficult to estimate.

OF A JEW STREET-SELLER

An elderly man, who, at the time I saw him, was vending spectacles, or bartering them for old clothes, old books, or any second-hand articles, gave me an account of his street-life, but it presented little remarkable beyond the not unusual vicissitudes of the lives of those of his class.

He had been in every street-trade, and had on four occasions travelled all over England, selling quills, sealing-wax, pencils, sponges, braces, cheap or superior jewellery, thermometers, and pictures. He had sold barometers in the mountainous parts of Cumberland, sometimes walking for hours without seeing man or woman. '*I liked it then,*' he said, '*for I was young and strong, and didn't care to sleep twice in the same town.* I was afterwards in the old-clothes line. I buy a few odd hats and light things still, but I'm not able to carry heavy weights, as my breath is getting rather short.' [I find that Jews generally object to the more laborious kinds of street-traffic.] 'Yes, I've been twice to Ireland, and sold a good many quills in Dublin, for I crossed over from Liverpool. Quills and wax were a great trade with us once; now it's quite different. I've had as much as 60*l*. of my own, and that more than half-a-dozen times, but all of it went in speculations. Yes, some went in gambling. I had a share in a gaming-booth at the races, for three years. O, I dare say that's more than 20 years back; but we did very little good. There was such fees to pay for the tent on a race-ground, and often such delays between the races in the different towns, and bribes to be given to the town-officers—such as town-sergeants and chief constables, and I hardly know who—and so many expenses altogether, that the profits were mostly swamped. Once at Newcastle races there was a fight among the pitmen, and our tent was in their way, and was demolished almost to bits. A deal of the money was lost or stolen. I don't know how much, but not near so much as my partners wanted to make out. I wasn't on the spot just at the time. I got married after that, and took a shop in the second-hand clothes line in Bristol, but my wife died in childbed in less than a year, and the shop didn't answer; so I got sick of it and at last got rid of it. O, I work both the country and London still. I shall take a turn into Kent in a day or two. I suppose I clear between 10*s.* and 20*s.* a week in anything, and as I've only myself, I do middling, and am ready for another chance if any likely speculation offers. I lodge with a relation, and sometimes live with his family. No, I never touch any meat but "Coshar." I suppose my meat now costs me 6*d.* or 7*d.* a day, but it has cost me ten times that—and 2*d.* for beer in addition.'

I am informed that there are about 50 adult Jews (besides old-clothes men) in the streets selling fruit, cakes, pencils, spectacles, sponge, accordions, drugs, &c.

OF THE JEW-BOY STREET-SELLERS

I HAVE ascertained, and from sources where no ignorance on the subject could prevail, that there are now in the streets of London, rather more than 100 Jew-boys engaged principally in fruit and cake-selling in the streets. Very few Jewesses are itinerant street-sellers. Most of the older Jews thus engaged have been street-sellers from their boyhood. The young Jews who ply in the street-callings however, are all men in matters of traffic, almost before they cease, in years, to be children. In addition to the Jew-boy street-sellers above enumerated, there are from 50 to 100, but usually about 50, who are occasional, or 'casual' street-traders, vending for the most part cocoa-nuts and grapes, and confining their sales chiefly to the Sundays.

I received from a Jew boy the following account of his trading pursuits and individual aspirations. There was somewhat of a thickness in his utterance, otherwise his speech was but little distinguishable from that of an English street-boy. His physiognomy was decidedly Jewish, but not of the handsomer type. His hair was light coloured, but clean, and apparently well brushed, without being oiled, or, as I heard a street-boy style it, 'greased'; it was long, and he said his aunt told him it 'wanted cutting sadly'; but he 'liked it that way'; indeed, he kept dashing his curls from his eyes, and back from his temples, as he was conversing, as if he were somewhat vain of doing so. He was dressed in a corduroy suit, old but not ragged, and wore a tolerably clean, very coarse, and altogether buttonless shirt, which he said 'was made for one bigger than me, sir.' He had bought it for $9\frac{1}{2}d$. in Petticoat-lane, and accounted it a bargain, as its wear would be durable. He was selling sponges when I saw him, and of the commonest kind, offering a large piece for 3d., which (he admitted) would be rubbed to bits in no time. This sponge, I should mention, is frequently 'dressed' with sulphuric acid, and an eminent surgeon informed me that on his servant attempting to clean his black dress coat with a sponge that he had newly bought in the streets, the colour of the garment, to his horror, changed to a bright purple. The Jew boy said—

'I believe I'm twelve. I've been to school, but it's long since, and my mother was very ill then, and I was forced to go out in the streets to have a chance. I never was kept to school. I can't read; I forgot all about it. I'd rather now that I could read, but very likely I could soon learn if I could only spare time, but if I stay long in the house I feel sick; it's not healthy. O, no, sir, inside or out it would be all the same to me, just to make a living and keep my health. I can't say how long it is since I began to sell, it's a good long time; one must do something. I could keep myself now, and do sometimes, but my father—I live with him (my mother's dead)—is often laid up. Would you like to see him, sir? He knows a deal. No, he can't write, but he can read a little. Can I speak Hebrew? Well, I know what you mean. O, no, I can't. I don't go to synagogue; I haven't time. My father goes, but only sometimes; so he says, and he tells me to look out, for we must both go by-and-by. I buy what I eat about Petticoat-lane. No, I don't like fish, but the stews, and the onions with them, is beautiful for two-pence; you may get a pennor'th. The pickles—cowcumbers is best—are stunning. But they're plummiest with a bit of cheese or anything cold—that's my opinion, but you may think different. Pork! Ah! No, I never touched it; I'd as soon eat a cat; so would my father. No, sir, I don't think pork smells nice in a cook-shop, but some Jew boys, as I knows, thinks it does. I don't know why it shouldn't be eaten, only that it's wrong to eat it. No, I never touched a ham-sandwich, but other Jew boys have, and laughed at it, I know.

'I don't know what I make in a week. I think I make as much on one thing as on another. I've sold strawberries, and cherries, and gooseberries, and nuts and walnuts in the season. O, as to what I make, that's nothing to nobody. Sometimes 6*d.* a day, sometimes 1*s.*; sometimes a little more, and sometimes nothing. No, I never sells inferior things if I can help it, but if one hasn't stock-money one must do as one can, but it isn't so easy to try it on. There was a boy beaten by a woman not long since for selling a big pottle of strawberries that was rubbish all under the toppers. It was all strawberry leaves, and crushed strawberries, and such like. She wanted to take back from him the two-pence she'd paid for it, and got hold of his pockets and there was a regular fight, but she didn't get a farthing back though she tried her very hardest, 'cause he slipped from her and hooked it. So you see it's dangerous to try it on.' [This last remark was made gravely enough, but the lad told of the feat with such manifest glee, that I'm inclined to believe that he himself was the culprit in question.] 'Yes, it was a Jew boy it happened to, but other boys in the streets is just the same. Do I like the streets? I can't say I do, there's too little to be made in them. *No, I wouldn't like to go to school, nor to be in a shop, nor be anybody's servant but my own.* O, I don't know what I shall be when I'm grown up. I shall take my chance like others.'

OF THE PURSUITS, DWELLINGS, TRAFFIC, &c., OF THE JEW-BOY STREET-SELLERS

To speak of the street Jew-boys as regards their traffic, manners, haunts, and associations, is to speak of the same class of boys who may not be employed regularly in street-sale, but are the comrades of those who are; a class, who, on any cessation of their employment in cigar manufactories, or indeed any capacity, will apply themselves temporarily to street-selling, for it seems to these poor and uneducated lads a sort of natural vocation.

These youths, *uncontrolled* or *uncontrollable* by their parents (who are of the lowest class of the Jews, and who often, I am told, care little about the matter, so long as the child can earn his own maintenance), frequently in the evenings, after their day's work, resort to coffee-shops, in preference even to a cheap concert-room. In these places they amuse themselves as men might do in a tavern where the landlord leaves his guests to their own caprices. Sometimes one of them reads aloud from some exciting or degrading book, the lads who are unable to read listening with all the intentness with which many of the uneducated attend to anyone reading. The reading is, however, not unfrequently interrupted by rude comments from the listeners. If a newspaper be read, the 'police,' or 'crimes,' are mostly the parts preferred. But the most approved way of passing the evening, among the Jew boys, is to play at draughts, dominoes, or cribbage, and to bet on the play. Draughts and dominoes are unpractised among the costermonger boys, but some of the young Jews are adepts in these games.

The dwellings of boys such as these are among the worst in London, as regards ventilation, comfort, or cleanliness. They reside in the courts and recesses about Whitechapel and Petticoat-lane, and generally in a garret. If not orphans they usually dwell with their father. I am told that the care of a mother is almost indispensable to a poor Jew boy, and having that care he seldom becomes an outcast. The Jewesses and Jew girls are rarely itinerant street-sellers—not in the proportion of one to twelve, compared with the men and boys; in this respect therefore the street Jews differ widely from the English costermongers and the street Irish, nor are the Hebrew females even stall-keepers in the same proportion.

One Jew boy's lodging which I visited was in a back garret, low and small. The boy lived with his father (a street-seller of fruit), and the room was very bare. A few sacks were thrown over an old palliass, a blanket seemed to be used for a quilt; there were no fire-irons nor fender; no cooking utensils. Beside the bed was an old chest, serving for a chair, while a board resting on a trestle did duty for a table (this was once, I presume, a small street-stall). The one not very large window was thick with dirt and patched all over. Altogether I have seldom seen a more wretched apartment. The man, I was told, was addicted to drinking.

The callings of which the Jew boys have the monopoly are not connected with the sale of any especial article, but rather with such things as present a variety from those ordinarily offered in the streets, such as cakes, sweetmeats, fried fish, and (in the winter) alder wine. The cakes known as 'boolers'—a mixture of egg, flour, and candied orange or lemon peel, cut very thin, and with a slight colouring from saffron or something similar—are now sold principally, and used to be sold exclusively, by the Jew boys. Almond cakes (little round cakes of crushed almonds) are at present vended by the Jew boys, and their sponge biscuits are in demand. All these dainties are bought by the street-lads of the Jew pastry-cooks. The difference in these cakes, in their sweetmeats, and their elder wine, is that there is a dash of spice about them not ordinarily met with. It is the same with the fried fish, a little spice or pepper being blended with the oil. In the street-sale of pickles the Jews have also the monopoly; these, however, are seldom hawked, but generally sold from windows and door-steads. The pickles are cucumbers or gherkins, and onions—a large cucumber being 2*d.*, and the smaller 1*d.* and ½*d.*

OF THE STREET JEWESSES
AND STREET JEW-GIRLS

I HAVE mentioned that the Jewesses and the young Jew girls, compared with the adult Jews and Jew boys, are not street-traders in anything like the proportion which the females were found to bear to the males among the Irish street-folk and the English costermongers. There are, however, a few Jewish females who are itinerant street-sellers as well as stall keepers, in the proportion, perhaps, of one female to seven or eight males. The majority of the street Jew-girls whom I saw on a round were accompanied by boys who were represented to be their brothers, and I have little doubt such were the facts, for these young Jewesses, although often pert and ignorant, are not unchaste. Of this I was assured by a medical gentleman who could speak with sufficient positiveness on the subject.

Fruit is generally sold by these boys and girls together, the lad driving the barrow, and the girl inviting custom and handing the purchases to the buyers. In tending a little stall or a basket at a regular pitch, with such things as cherries or strawberries, the little Jewess differs only from her street-selling sisters in being a brisker trader. The stalls, with a few old knives or scissors, or odds and ends of laces, that are tended by the Jew girls in the streets in the Jewish quarters (I am told there are not above a dozen of them) are generally near the shops and within sight of their parents or friends. One little Jewess, with whom I had some conversation, had not even heard the name of the Chief Rabbi, the Rev. Dr. Adler, and knew nothing of any distinction between German and Portuguese Jews; she had, I am inclined to believe, never heard of either. I am told that the whole, or nearly the whole, of these young female traders reside with parents or friends, and that there is among them far less than the average number of runaways. One Jew told me he thought that the young female members of his tribe did not tramp with the juveniles of the other sex—no, not in the proportion of one to a hundred in comparison, he said with a laugh, with 'young women of the Christian persuasion.' My informant had means of knowing this fact, as although still a young man, he had traversed the greater part of England hawking perfumery, which he had abandoned as a bad trade. A wire-worker, long familiar with tramping and going into the country—a man upon whose word I have every reason to rely—told me that he could not remember a single instance of his having seen a young Jewess 'travelling' with a boy.

OF THE STREET-FINDERS OR COLLECTORS

THESE men, for by far the great majority are men, may be divided, according to the nature of their occupations, into three classes:—

1. The bone-grubbers and rag-gatherers, who are, indeed, the same individuals, the pure-finders, and the cigar-end and old wood collectors.

2. The dredgermen, the mud-larks, and the sewer-hunters.

3. The dustmen and nightmen, the sweeps and the scavengers.

The first class go abroad daily to *find* in the streets, and carry away with them such things as bones, rags, 'pure' (or dogs'-dung), which no one appropriates. These they sell, and on that sale support a wretched life. The second class of people are also as strictly *finders*; but their industry, or rather their labour, is confined to the river, or to that subterranean city of sewerage unto which the Thames supplies the great outlets. These persons may not be immediately connected with the *streets* of London, but their pursuits are carried on in the open air (if the sewer-air may be so included), and are all, at any rate, out-of-door avocations. The third class is distinct from either of these, as the labourers comprised in it are not finders, but *collectors* or *removers* of the dirt and filth of our streets and houses, and of the soot of our chimneys.

The bone-grubber and the mud-lark (the searcher for refuse on the banks of the river) differ little in their pursuits or in their characteristics, excepting that the mud-larks are generally boys, which is more an accidental than a definite distinction. The grubbers are with a few exceptions stupid, unconscious of their degradation, and with little anxiety to be relieved from it. They are usually taciturn, but this taciturn habit is common to men whose callings, if they cannot be called solitary, are pursued with little communication with others. I was informed by a man who once kept a little beer-shop near Friar-street, Southwark Bridge-road (where then and still, he thought, was a bone-grinding establishment), that the bone-grubbers who carried their sacks of bones thither sometimes had a pint of beer at his house when they had received their money. They usually sat, he told me, silently looking at the corners of the floor—for they rarely lifted their eyes up—as if they were expecting to see some bones or refuse there available for their bags. Of this inertion, perhaps fatigue and despair may be a part. I asked some questions of a man of this class whom I saw pick up in a road in the suburbs something that appeared to have been a coarse canvas apron, although it was wet after a night's rain and half covered with mud. I inquired what he thought about when he trudged along looking on the ground on every side. His answer was, 'Of nothing, sir.' I believe that no better description could be given of that vacuity of mind or mental inactivity which seems to form a part of the most degraded callings. The minds of such men, even without an approach to idiocy, appear to be a blank. One characteristic of these poor fellows, bone-grubbers and mud-larks, is that they are very poor, although I am told some of them, the older men, have among the poor the reputation of being misers. It is not unusual for the youths belonging to these callings to live with their parents and give them the amount of their earnings.

The sewer-hunters are again distinct, and a far more intelligent and adventurous class; but they work in gangs. They must be familiar with the course of the tides, or they might be drowned at high water. They must have quick eyes too, not merely to descry the objects of their search, but to mark the points and bearings of the subterraneous roads they traverse; in a word, 'to know their way underground.' There is, moreover, some spirit of daring in venturing into a dark, solitary sewer, the chart being only in the memory, and in braving the possibility of noxious vapours, and the by no means insignificant dangers of the rats infesting these places.

The dredgermen, the finders of the water, are again distinct as being watermen, and working in boats.

Every one of these men works on his own account, being a 'small master,' which is one of the great attractions of open-air pursuits. The dredgermen also depend for their maintenance upon the sale of what they find, or the rewards they receive.

It is otherwise, however, as was before observed, with the third class of the street-finders, or rather collectors. In all the capacities of dustmen, nightmen, scavengers, and sweeps, the employers of the men are *paid* to do the work, the proceeds of the street-collection forming only a portion of the employer's remuneration. The sweep has the soot in addition to his 6*d*. or 1*s*; the master scavenger has a payment from the parish funds to sweep the streets, though the clearance of the cesspools, &c., in private houses, may be an individual bargain. The whole refuse of the streets belongs to the contractor to make the best of, but it must be cleared away, and so must the contents of a dust-bin; for if a mass of dirt become offensive, the householder may be indicted for a nuisance, and municipal by-laws require its removal. It is thus made a matter of compulsion that the dust be removed from a private house; but it is otherwise with the soot. Why a man should be permitted to let soot accumulate in his chimney—perhaps exposing himself, his family, and his lodgers to the dangers of fire, it may not be easy to account for, especially when we bear in mind that the same man may not accumulate cabbage-leaves and fish-tails in his yard.

The dustmen are of the plodding class of labourers, mere labourers, who require only bodily power, and possess little or no mental development. Many of the agricultural labourers are of this order, and the dustman often seems to be the stolid ploughman, modified by a residence in a city, and engaged in a peculiar calling. They are generally uninformed, and no few of them are dustmen because their fathers were. The same may be said of nightmen and scavengers. At one time it was a popular, or rather a vulgar notion that many dustmen had become possessed of large sums, from the plate, coins, and valuables they found in clearing the dust-bins—a manifest absurdity; but I was told by a marine-store dealer that he had known a young woman, a dustman's daughter, sell silver spoons to a neighbouring marine-store man, who was 'not very particular.'

BONE-GRUBBERS AND RAG-GATHERERS

THE habits of the bone-grubbers and rag-gatherers, the 'pure,' or dogs'-dung collectors, and the cigar-end finders, are necessarily similar. All lead a wandering, unsettled sort of life, being compelled to be continually on foot, and to travel many miles every day in search of the articles in which they deal. They seldom have any fixed place of abode, and are mostly to be found at night in one or other of the low lodging-houses throughout London. The majority are, moreover, persons who have been brought up to other employments, but who for some failing or mishap have been reduced to such a state of distress that they were obliged to take to their present occupation, and have never after been able to get away from it.

Of the whole class it is considered that there are from 800 to 1,000 resident in London, one-half of whom, at the least, sleep in the cheap lodging-houses.

Moreover there are in London during the winter a number of persons called 'trampers,' who employ themselves at that season in street-finding. These people are in the summer country labourers of some sort, but as soon as the harvest and potato-getting and hop-picking are over, and they can find nothing else to do in the country, they come back to London to avail themselves of the shelter of the night asylums or refuges for the destitute (usually called 'straw-yards' by the poor). As soon as the 'straw-yards' close, which is generally about the beginning of April, the 'trampers' again start off to the country in small bands of two or three, and without any fixed residence keep wandering about all the summer, sometimes begging their way through the villages and sleeping in the casual wards of the unions, and sometimes, when hard driven, working at hay-making or any other light labour.

Those among the bone-grubbers who do not belong to the regular 'trampers' have been either navvies, or men who have not been able to obtain employment at their own business, and have been driven to it by necessity as a means of obtaining a little bread for the time being, and without any intention of pursuing the calling regularly; but, as I have said, when once in the business they cannot leave it, for at least they make certain of getting a few halfpence by it, and their present necessity does not allow them time to look after other employment.

The bone-picker and rag-gatherer may be known at once by the greasy bag which he carries on his back. Usually he has a stick in his hand, and this is armed with a spike or hook, for the purpose of more easily turning over the heaps of ashes or dirt that are thrown out of the houses, and discovering whether they contain anything that is saleable at the rag-and-bottle or marine-store shop. The bone-grubber generally seeks out the narrow back streets, where dust and refuse are cast, or where any dust-bins are accessible. The articles for which he chiefly searches are rags and bones— rags he prefers—but waste metal, such as bits of lead, pewter, copper, brass, or old iron, he prizes above all. Whatever he meets with that he knows to be in any way saleable he puts into the bag at his back. He often finds large lumps of bread which have been thrown out as waste by the servants, and occasionally the house-keepers will give him some bones on which there is a little meat remaining; these constitute the morning meal of most of the class. One of my informants had a large rump of beef given to him a few days previous to my seeing him, on which 'there was not less than a pound of meat.'

The bone-pickers and rag-gatherers are all early risers. They have all their separate beats or districts, and it is most important to them that they should reach their district before any one else of the same class can go over the ground. Some of the beats lie as far as Peckham, Clapham, Hammersmith, Hampstead, Bow, Stratford, and indeed all parts within about five miles of London. In summer time they rise at two in the morning, and sometimes earlier. It is not quite light at this hour—but bones and rags can be discovered before daybreak. The 'grubbers' scour all quarters of London, but abound more particularly in the suburbs. In the neighbourhood of Petticoat-lane and Ragfair, however, they are the most numerous on account of the greater quantity of rags which the Jews have to throw out. It usually takes the bone-picker from seven to nine hours to go over his rounds, during which time he travels from 20 to 30 miles with a quarter to a half hundredweight on his back. In the summer he usually reaches home about eleven of the day, and in the winter about one or two. On his return home he proceeds to sort the contents of his bag. He separates the rags from the bones, and these again from the old metal (if he be lucky enough to have found any). He divides the rags into various lots, according as they are white or coloured; and if he have picked up any pieces of canvas or sacking, he makes these also into a separate parcel. When he has finished the sorting he takes his several lots to the rag-shop or the marine-store dealer, and realizes upon them whatever they may be worth. For the white rags he gets from 2*d*. to 3*d*. per pound, according as they are cleaned 'or soiled. The white rags are very difficult to be found; they are mostly very dirty, and are therefore sold with the coloured ones at the rate of about 5 lbs. for 2*d*. The bones are usually sold with the coloured rags at one and the same price. For fragments of canvas or sacking the grubber gets about three-farthings a pound; and old brass, copper, and pewter about 4*d*. (the marine-store keepers say 5*d*.), and old iron one farthing per pound, or six pounds for 1*d*. The bone-grubber thinks he has done an excellent day's work if he can earn 8*d*.; and some of them, especially the very old and the very young, do not earn more than from 2*d*. to 3*d*. a day. To make 10*d*. a day, at the present price of rags and bones, a man must be remarkably active and strong,—'ay! and lucky, too,' adds my informant. The average amount of earnings, I am told, varies from about 6*d*. to 8*d*. per day, or from 3*s*. to 4*s*. a week; and the highest amount that a man, the most brisk and persevering at the business, can by any possibility earn in one week is about 5*s*., but this can only be accomplished by great good fortune and industry—the usual weekly gains are about half that sum. In bad weather the bone-grubber cannot do so well, because the rags are wet, and then they cannot sell them. The majority pick up bones only in wet weather; those who *do* gather rags during or after rain are obliged to wash and dry them before they can sell them. The state of the shoes of the rag and bone-picker is a very important matter to him; for if he be well shod he can get quickly over the ground; but he is frequently lamed, and unable to make any progress from the blisters and gashes on his feet, occasioned by the want of proper shoes.

Sometimes the bone-grubbers will pick up a stray sixpence or a shilling that has been dropped in the street. 'The handkerchief I have round my neck,' said one whom I saw, 'I picked up with 1*s*. in the corner. The greatest prize I ever found was the brass cap of the nave of a coach-wheel; and I *did* once find a quarter of a pound of tobacco in Sun-street, Bishopsgate. The best bit of luck of all that I ever had was finding a cheque for 12*l*. 15*s*. lying in the gateway of the mourning-coach yard in Titchborne-street, Hay-market. I was going to light my pipe with it, indeed I picked it up for that purpose, and then saw it was a cheque. It was on the London and County Bank, 21, Lombard-street. I took it there, and got 10*s*. for finding it. I went there in my rags, as I am now, and the cashier stared a bit at me. The cheque was drawn by a Mr. Knibb, and payable to a Mr. Cox. I *did* think I should have got the odd 15*s*. though.'

It has been stated that the average amount of the earnings of the bone-pickers is 6*d*. per day, or 3*s*. per week, being 7*l*. 16*s*. per annum for each person. It has also been shown that the number of persons engaged in the business may be estimated at about 800; hence the earnings of the entire number will amount to the sum of 20*l*. per day, or 120*l*. per week, which gives 6,240*l*. as the annual earnings of the bone-pickers and rag-gatherers of London. It may also be computed that each of the grubbers gathers on an average 20 lbs. weight of bone and rags; and reckoning the bones to con-stitute three-fourths of the entire weight, we thus find that the gross quantity of these articles gathered by the street-finders in the course of the year, amounts to 3,744,000 lbs. of bones, and 1,240,000 lbs. of rags.

Between the London and St. Katherine's Docks and Rosemary Lane, there is a large district interlaced with narrow lanes, courts, and alleys ramifying into each other in the most intricate and dis-orderly manner, insomuch that it would be no easy matter for a stranger to work his way through the interminable confusion without the aid of a guide, resident in and well conversant with the locality. The houses are of the poorest description, and seem as if they tumbled into their places at random. Foul channels, huge dust-heaps, and a variety of other unsightly objects, occupy every open space, and dabbling among these are crowds of ragged dirty children who grub and wallow, as if in their native element. None reside in these places but the poorest and most wretched of the population, and, as might almost be expected, this, the cheapest and filthiest locality of London, is the head-quarters of the bone-grubbers and other street-finders. I have ascertained on the best authority, that from the centre of this place, within a circle of a mile in diameter, there dwell not less than 200 persons of this class.

To show how bone-grubbers occasionally manage to obtain shelter during the night, the following incident may not be out of place. A few mornings past I accidentally encountered one of this class in a narrow back lane; his ragged coat—the colour of the rubbish among which he toiled—was greased over, probably with the fat of the bones he gathered, and being mixed with the dust it seemed as if the man were covered with bird-lime. His shoes—torn and tied on his feet with pieces of cord—had doubtlessly been picked out of some dust-bin, while his greasy bag and stick unmistakably announced his calling. Desirous of obtaining all the information possible on this subject, I asked him a few questions, took his address, which he gave without hesitation, and bade him call on me in the evening. At the time appointed, however, he did not appear; on the following day therefore I made my way to the address he had given, and on reaching the spot I was astonished to find the house in which he had said he lived was uninhabited. A padlock was on the door, the boards of which were parting with age. There was not a whole pane of glass in any of the windows, and the frames of many of them were shattered or demolished. Some persons in the neighbourhood, noticing me eyeing the place, asked whom I wanted. On my telling the man's name, which it appeared he had not dreamt of disguising, I was informed that he had left the day before, saying he had met the landlord in the morning (for such it turned out he had fancied me to be), and that the gentleman had wanted him to come to his house, but he was afraid to go lest he should be sent to prison for breaking into the place. I found, on inspection, that the premises, though locked up, could be entered by the rear, one of the window-frames having been removed, so that admission could be obtained through the aperture. Availing myself of the same mode of ingress, I proceeded to examine the premises. Nothing could well be more dismal or dreary than the interior. The floors were rotting with damp and mildew, especially near the windows, where the wet found easy entrance. The walls were even slimy and discoloured, and everything bore the appearance of desolation. In one corner was strewn a bundle of dirty straw, which doubtlessly had served the bonegrubber for a bed, while scattered about the floor were pieces of bones, and small fragments of dirty rags, sufficient to indicate the calling of the late inmate. He had had but little difficulty in removing his property, seeing that it consisted solely of his bag and his stick.

OF THE 'PURE'-FINDERS

Dogs'-dung is called 'Pure,' from its cleansing and purifying properties.

The name of 'Pure-finders,' however, has been applied to the men engaged in collecting dogs'-dung from the public streets only, within the last 20 or 30 years. Previous to this period there appears to have been no men engaged in the business, old women alone gathered the substance, and they were known by the name of 'bunters,' which signifies properly gatherers of rags; and thus plainly intimates that the rag-gatherers originally added the collecting of 'Pure' to their original and proper vocation. Hence it appears that the bone-grubbers, rag-gatherers, and pure-finders, constituted formerly but one class of people, and even now they have, as I have stated, kindred characteristics.

The pure-finders meet with a ready market for all the dogs'-dung they are able to collect, at the numerous tanyards in Bermondsey, where they sell it by the stable-bucket full, and get from 8d. to 10d. per bucket, and sometimes 1s. and 1s. 2d. for it, according to its quality. The 'dry limy-looking sort' fetches the highest price at some yards, as it is found to possess more of the alkaline, or purifying properties; but others are found to prefer the dark moist quality. Strange as it may appear, the preference for a particular kind has suggested to the finders of Pure the idea of adulterating it to a very considerable extent; this is effected by means of mortar broken away from old walls, and mixed up with the whole mass, which it closely resembles; in some cases, however, the mortar is rolled into small balls similar to those found. Hence it would appear, that there is no business or trade, however insignificant or contemptible, without its own peculiar and appropriate tricks.

The pure-finders are in their habits and mode of proceeding nearly similar to the bone-grubbers. Many of the pure-finders are, however, better in circumstances, the men especially, as they earn more money. They are also, to a certain extent, a better educated class. Some of the regular collectors of this substance have been mechanics, and others small tradesmen, who have been reduced. Those pure-finders who have 'a good connection,' and have been granted permission to cleanse some kennels, obtain a very fair living at the business, earning from 10*s*. to 15*s*. a week. These, however, are very few; the majority have to seek the article in the streets, and by such means they can obtain only from 6*s*. to 10*s*. a week. The average weekly earnings of this class are thought to be about 7*s*. 6*d*.

From all the inquiries I have made on this subject, I have found that there cannot be less than from 200 to 300 persons constantly engaged solely in this business. There are about 30 tanyards large and small in Bermondsey, and these all have their regular pure collectors from whom they obtain the article. Leomont and Roberts's, Bavingtons', Beech's, Murrell's, Cheeseman's, Powell's, Jones's, Jourdan's, Kent's, Moorcroft's, and Davis's, are among the largest establishments, and some idea of the amount of business done in some of these yards may be formed from the fact, that the proprietors severally employ from 300 to 500 tanners. At Leomont and Roberts's there are 23 regular street-finders, who supply them with pure, but this is a large establishment, and the number supplying them is considered far beyond the average quantity; moreover, Messrs. Leomont and Roberts do more business in the particular branch of tanning in which the article is principally used, viz., in dressing the leather for book-covers, kid-gloves, and a variety of other articles. Some of the other tanyards, especially the smaller ones, take the substance only as they happen to want it, and others again employ but a limited number of hands. If, therefore, we strike an average, and reduce the number supplying each of the several yards to eight, we shall have 240 persons regularly engaged in the business: besides these, it may be said that numbers of the starving and destitute Irish have taken to picking up the material, but not knowing where to sell it, or how to dispose of it, they part with it for 2*d*. or 3*d*. the pail-full to the regular purveyors of it to the tanyards, who of course make a considerable profit by the transaction. The children of the poor Irish are usually employed in this manner, but they also pick up rags and bones, and anything else which may fall in their way.

I have stated that some of the pure-finders, especially the men, earn a considerable sum of money per week; their gains are sometimes as much as 15*s*.; indeed I am assured that seven years ago, when they got from 3*s*. to 4*s*. per pail for the pure, that many of them would not exchange their position with that of the best paid mechanic in London. Now, however, the case is altered, for there are twenty now at the business for every one who followed it then; hence each collects so much the less in quantity, and, moreover, from the competition gets so much less for the article. Some of the collectors at present do not earn 3*s*. per week, but these are mostly old women who are feeble and unable to get over the ground quickly; others make 5*s*. and 6*s*. in the course of the week, while the most active and those who clean out the kennels of the dog fanciers may occasionally make 9*s*. and 10*s*. and even 15*s*. a week still, but this is of very rare occurrence. Allowing the finders, one with the other, to earn on an average 5*s*. per week, it would give the annual earnings of each to be 13*l*., while the income of the whole 200 would amount to 50*l*. a week, or 2,600*l*. per annum. The kennel 'pure' is not much valued, indeed many of the tanners will not even buy it, the reason is that the dogs of the 'fanciers' are fed on almost anything, to save expense; the kennel cleaners consequently take the precaution of mixing it with what is found in the street, previous to offering it for sale.

The pure-finder may at once be distinguished from the bone-grubber and rag-gatherer; the latter, as I have before mentioned, carries a bag, and usually a stick armed with a spike, while he is most frequently to be met with in back streets, narrow lanes, yards and other places, where dust and rubbish are likely to be thrown out from the adjacent houses. The pure-finder, on the contrary, is often found in the open streets, as dogs wander where they like. The pure-finders always carry a handle basket, generally with a cover, to hide the contents, and have their right hand covered with a black leather glove; many of them, however, dispense with the glove, as they say it is much easier to wash their hands than to keep the glove fit for use. The women generally have a large pocket for the reception of such rags as they may chance to fall in with, but they pick up those only of the very best quality, and will not go out of their way to search even for them. Thus equipped they may be seen pursuing their avocation in almost every street in and about London, excepting such streets as are now cleansed by the 'street orderlies,' of whom the pure-finders grievously complain, as being an unwarrantable interference with the privileges of their class.

The pure collected is used by leather-dressers and tanners, and more especially by those engaged in the manufacture of morocco and kid leather from the skins of old and young goats, of which skins great numbers are imported, and of the roans and lambskins which are the sham morocco and kids of the 'slop' leather trade, and are used by the better class of shoemakers, book-binders, and glovers, for the inferior requirements of their business. Pure is also used by the tanners, as is pigeon's dung, for the tanning of the thinner kinds of leather, such as calf-skins, for which purpose it is placed in pits with an admixture of lime and bark.

In the manufacture of moroccos and roans the pure is rubbed by the hands of the workman into the skin he is dressing. This is done to 'purify' the leather, I was told by an intelligent leather-dresser, and from that term the word 'pure' has originated. The dung has astringent as well as highly alkaline, or, to use the expression of my informant, 'scouring,' qualities. When the pure has been rubbed into the flesh and grain of the skin (the 'flesh' being originally the interior, and the 'grain' the exterior part of the cuticle), and the skin, thus purified, has been hung up to be dried, the dung removes, as it were, all such moisture as, if allowed to remain, would tend to make the leather unsound or imperfectly dressed. This imperfect dressing, moreover, gives a disagreeable smell to the leather—and leather-buyers often use both nose and tongue in making their purchases—and would consequently prevent that agreeable odour being imparted to the skin which is found in some kinds of morocco and kid. The peculiar odour of the Russia leather, so agreeable in the libraries of the rich, is derived from the bark of young birch trees. It is now manufactured in Bermondsey.

Among the morocco manufacturers, especially among the old operatives, there is often a scarcity of employment, and they then dress a few roans, which they hawk to the cheap warehouses, or sell to the wholesale shoemakers on their own account. These men usually reside in small garrets in the poorer parts of Bermondsey, and carry on their trade in their own rooms, using and keeping the pure there; hence the 'homes' of these poor men are peculiarly uncomfortable, if not unhealthy. Some of these poor fellows or their wives collect the pure themselves, often starting at daylight for the purpose; they more frequently, however, buy it of a regular finder.

The number of pure-finders I heard estimated, by a man well acquainted with the tanning and other departments of the leather trade, at from 200 to 250. The finders, I was informed by the same person, collected about a pail-full a day, clearing 6s. a week in the summer—1s. and 1s. 2d. being the charge for a pail-full; in the short days of winter, however, and in bad weather, they could not collect five pail-fulls in a week.

In the wretched locality already referred to as lying between the Docks and Rosemary-lane, redolent of filth and pregnant with pestilential diseases, and whither all the outcasts of the metropolitan population seem to be drawn, either in the hope of finding fitting associates and companions in their wretchedness (for there is doubtlessly something attractive and agreeable to them in such companionship), or else for the purpose of hiding themselves and their shifts and struggles for existence from the world,—in this dismal quarter, and branching from one of the many narrow lanes which interlace it, there is a little court with about half-a-dozen houses of the very smallest dimensions, consisting of merely two rooms, one over the other. Here in one of the upper rooms (the lower one of the same house being occupied by another family and apparently *filled* with little ragged children), I discerned, after considerable difficulty, an old woman, a pure-finder. When I opened the door the little light that struggled through the small window, the many broken panes of which were stuffed with old rags, was not sufficient to enable me to perceive who or what was in the room. After a short time, however, I began to make out an old chair standing near the fire-place, and then to discover a poor old woman resembling a bundle of rags and filth stretched on some dirty straw in the corner of the apartment. The place was bare and almost naked. There was nothing in it except a couple of old tin kettles and a basket, and some broken crockeryware in the recess of the window. To my astonishment I found this wretched creature to be, to a certain extent, a 'superior' woman; she could read and write well, spoke correctly, and appeared to have been a person of natural good sense, though broken up with age, want, and infirmity, so that she was characterized by all that dull and hardened stupidity of manner which I have noticed in the class. She made the following statement:—

'I am about 60 years of age. My father was a milkman, and very well off; he had a barn and a great many cows. I was kept at school till I was thirteen or fourteen years of age; about that time my father died, and then I was taken home to help my mother in the business. After a while things went wrong; the cows began to die, and mother, alleging she could not manage the business herself, married again. I soon found out the difference. Glad to get away, anywhere out of the house, I married a sailor, and was very comfortable with him for some years; as he made short voyages, and was often at home, and always left me half his pay. At last he was pressed, when at home with me, and sent away; I forget now where he was sent to, but I never saw him from that day to this. The only thing I know is that some sailors came to me four or five years after, and told me that he deserted from the ship in which he had gone out, and got on board the *Neptune*, East Indiaman, bound for Bombay, where he had acted as boatswain's mate; some little time afterwards, he had got intoxicated while the ship was lying in harbour, and, going down the side to get into a bumboat, and buy more drink, he had fallen overboard and was drowned. I got some money that was due to him from the India House, and, after that was all gone, I went into service, in the Mile-end Road. There I stayed for several years, till I met my second husband, who was bred to the water, too, but as a waterman on the river. We did very well together for a long time, till he lost his health. He became paralyzed like, and was deprived of the use of all one side, and nearly lost the sight of one of his eyes; this was not very conspicuous at first, but when we came to get pinched, and to be badly off, then any one might have seen that there was something the matter with his eye. Then we parted with everything we had in the world; and, at last, when we had no other means of living left, we were advised to take to gathering "pure." At first I couldn't endure the business; I couldn't bear to eat a morsel, and I was obliged to discontinue it for a long time. My husband kept at it though, for he could do *that* well enough, only he couldn't walk as fast as he ought. He couldn't lift his hands as high as his head, but he managed to work under him, and so put the Pure in the basket. When I saw that he, poor fellow, couldn't make enough to keep us both, I took heart and went out again, and used to gather more than he did; that's fifteen years ago now; the times were good then, and we used to do very well. If we only gathered a pail-full in the day, we could live very well; but we could do much more than that, for there wasn't near so many at the business then, and the pure was easier to be had. For my part I can't tell where all the poor creatures have come from of late years; the world seems growing worse and worse every day. They have pulled down the price of pure, that's certain; but the poor things must do something, they can't starve while there's anything to be got. Why, no later than six or seven years ago, it was as high as 3*s.* 6*d.* and 4*d.* a pail-full, and a ready sale for as much of it as you could get; but now you can only get 1*s.* and in some places 1*s.* 2*d.* a pail-full; and, as I said before, there are so many at it, that there is not much left for a poor old creature like me to find. The men that are strong and smart get the most, of course, and some of them do very well, at least they manage to live. Six years ago, my husband complained that he was ill, in the evening, and lay down in the bed—we lived in Whitechapel then—he took a fit of coughing, and was smothered in his own blood. O dear' (the poor old soul here ejaculated), 'what troubles I have gone through! I had eight children at one time, and there is not one of them alive now. My daughter lived to 30 years of age, and then she died in childbirth, and, since then, I have had nobody in the wide world to care for me—none but myself, all alone as I am. After my husband's death I couldn't do much, and all my things went away, one by one, until I've nothing but bare walls, and that's the reason why I was vexed at first at your coming in, sir. I was yesterday out all day, and went round Aldgate, Whitechapel, St. George's East, Stepney, Bow, and Bromley, and then came home; after that, I

went over to Bermondsey, and there I got only 6*d*. for my pains.
To-day I wasn't out at all; I wasn't well; I had a bad headache,
and I'm so much afraid of the fevers that are all about here—
though I don't know why I should be afraid of them—I was lying
down, when you came, to get rid of my pains. There's such a
dizziness in my head now, I feel as if it didn't belong to me. No,
I have earned no money to-day. I have had a piece of dried bread
that I steeped in water to eat. I haven't eat anything else to-day;
but, pray, sir, don't tell anybody of it. I could never bear the
thought of going into the "great house" [workhouse]; I'm so used
to the air, that I'd sooner die in the street, as many I know have
done. I've known several of our people, who have sat down in the
street with their basket alongside them, and died. I knew one not
long ago, who took ill just as she was stooping down to gather up
the Pure, and fell on her face; she was taken to the London Hospital, and died at three o'clock in the morning. I'd sooner die like
them than be deprived of my liberty, and be prevented from going
about where I liked. No, I'll never go into the workhouse; my
master is kind to me' [the tanner whom she supplies]. 'When I'm
ill, he sometimes gives me a sixpence; but there's one gentleman
has done us great harm, by forcing so many into the business. He's
a poor-law guardian, and when any poor person applies for relief,
he tells them to go and gather pure, and that he'll buy it of them
(for he's in the line), and so the parish, you see, don't have to give
anything, and that's one way that so many have come into the
trade of late, that the likes of me can do little or no good at it. Almost every one I've ever known engaged in pure-finding were
people who were better off once. I knew a man who went by the
name of Brown, who picked up pure for years before I went to it;
he was a very quiet man; he used to lodge in Blue Anchor-yard, and
seldom used to speak to anybody. We two used to talk together
sometimes, but never much. One morning he was found dead in his
bed; it was of a Tuesday morning, and he was 'buried about 12
o'clock on the Friday following. About 6 o'clock on that afternoon,
three or four gentlemen came searching all through this place, looking for a man named Brown, and offering a reward to any who
would find him out; there was a whole crowd about them when I
came up. One of the gentlemen said that the man they wanted had
lost the first finger of his right hand, and then I knew that it was the

man that had been buried, only that morning. Would you believe it, Mr. Brown was a real gentleman all the time, and had a large estate, of I don't know how many thousand pounds, just left him, and the lawyers had advertised and searched everywhere for him, but never found him, you may say, till he was dead. We discovered that his name was not Brown; he had only taken that name to hide his real one, which, of course, he did not want any one to know. I've often thought of him, poor man, and all the misery he might have been spared, if the good news had only come a year or two sooner.'

Another informant, a pure-collector, was originally in the Manchester cotton trade, and held a lucrative situation in a large country establishment. His salary one year exceeded 250*l*., and his regular income was 150*l*. 'This,' he says, 'I lost through drink and neglect. My master was exceedingly kind to me, and has even assisted me since I left his employ. He bore with me patiently for many years, but the love of drink was so strong upon me that it was impossible for him to keep me any longer.' He has often been drunk, he tells me, for three months together; and he is now so reduced that he is ashamed to be seen. When at his master's it was his duty to carve and help the other assistants belonging to the establishment, and his hand used to shake so violently that he has been ashamed to lift the gravy spoon.

At breakfast he has frequently waited till all the young men had left the table before he ventured to taste his tea; and immediately, when he was alone, he has bent his head down to his cup to drink, being utterly incapable of raising it to his lips. He says he is a living example of the degrading influence of drink. All his friends have deserted him. He has suffered enough, he tells me, to make him give it up. He earned the week before I saw him 5*s*. 2*d*.; and the week before that 6*s*.

OF THE CIGAR-END FINDERS

THERE are, strictly speaking, none who make a living by picking up the ends of cigars thrown away as useless by the smokers in the streets, but there are very many who employ themselves from time to time in collecting them. Almost all the street-finders when they meet with such things, pick them up, and keep them in a pocket set apart for that purpose. The men allow the ends to accumulate till they amount to two or three pounds weight, and then some dispose of them to a person residing in the neighbourhood of Rosemary-lane, who buys them all up at from 6*d*. to 10*d*. per pound, according to their length and quality. The long ends are considered the best, as I am told there is more sound tobacco in them, uninjured by the moisture of the mouth. The children of the poor Irish, in particular, scour Ratcliff-highway, the Commercial-road, Mile-end-road, and all the leading thoroughfares of the East, and every place where cigar smokers are likely to take an evening's promenade. The quantity that each of them collects is very trifling indeed—perhaps not more than a handful during a morning's search. I am informed, by an intelligent man living in the midst of them, that these children go out in the morning not only to gather cigar-ends, but to pick up out of dust bins, and from amongst rubbish in the streets, the smallest scraps and crusts of bread, no matter how hard or filthy they may be. These they put into a little bag which they carry for the purpose, and, after they have gone their rounds and collected whatever they can, they take the cigar-ends to the man who buys them—sometimes getting not more than a halfpenny or a penny for their morning's collection. With this they buy a halfpenny or a pennyworth of oatmeal, which they mix up with a large quantity of water, and after washing and steeping the hard and dirty crusts, they put them into the pot or kettle and boil all together. Of this mess the whole family partake, and it often constitutes all the food they taste in the course of the day. I have often seen the bone-grubbers eat the black and soddened crusts they have picked up out of the gutter.

It would, indeed, be a hopeless task to make any attempt to get at the number of persons who occasionally or otherwise pick up cigar-ends with the view of selling them again. For this purpose almost all who ransack the streets of London for a living may be computed as belonging to the class; and to these should be added the children of the thousands of destitute Irish who have inundated the metropolis within the last few years, and who are to be found huddled together in all the low neighbourhoods in every suburb of the City. What quantity is collected, or the amount of money obtained for the ends, there are no means of ascertaining.

Let us, however, make a conjecture. There are in round numbers

300,000 inhabited houses in the metropolis; and allowing the married people living in apartments to be equal in number to the unmarried 'housekeepers,' we may compute that the number of families in London is about the same as the inhabited houses. Assuming one young or old gentleman in every one of these families to smoke one cigar per diem in the public thoroughfares, we have 30,000 cigar-ends daily, or 210,000 weekly cast away in the London streets. Now, reckoning 150 cigars to go to the pound, we may assume that each end so cast away weighs about the thousandth part of a pound; consequently the gross weight of the ends flung into the gutter will, in the course of the week, amount to about 2 cwt.; and calculating that only a sixth part of these are picked up by the finders, it follows that there is very nearly a ton of refuse tobacco collected annually in the metropolitan thoroughfares.

The aristocratic quarters of the City and the vicinity of theatres and casinos are the best for the cigar-finders. In the Strand, Regent-street, and the more fashionable thoroughfares, I am told, there are many ends picked up; but even in these places they do not exclusively furnish a means of living to any of the finders. All the collectors sell them to some other person, who acts as middle-man in the business. How he disposes of the ends is unknown, but it is supposed they are resold to some of the large manufacturers of cigars, and go to form the component part of a new stock of the 'best Havannahs'; or, in other words, they are worked up again to be again cast away, and again collected by the finders, and so on perhaps, till the millennium comes. Some suppose them to be cut up and mixed with the common smoking tobacco, and others that they are used in making snuff. There are, I am assured, five persons residing in different parts of London, who are known to purchase the cigar-ends.

OF THE OLD WOOD GATHERERS

ALL that has been said of the cigar-end finders may, in a great measure, apply to the wood-gatherers. No one can make a living exclusively by the gathering of wood, and those who *do* gather it, gather as well rags, bones, and bits of metal. They gather it, indeed, as an adjunct to their other findings, on the principle that 'every little helps.' Those, however, who most frequently look

for wood are the very old and feeble, and the very young, who are
both unable to travel far, or to carry a heavy burden, and they may
occasionally by seen crawling about in the neighbourhood of any
new buildings in the course of construction, or old ones in the
course of demolition, and picking up small odds and ends of wood
and chips swept out amongst dirt and shavings; these they deposit
in a bag or basket which they carry for that purpose. Should there
happen to be what they call 'pulling-down work,' that is, taking
down old houses, or palings, the place is immediately beset by a
number of wood-gatherers, young and old, and in general all the
poor people of the locality join with them, to obtain their share
of the spoil. What the poor get they take home and burn, but the
wood-gatherers sell all they procure for some small trifle.

Some short time ago a portion of the wood-pavement in the
city was being removed; a large number of the old blacks, which
were much worn and of no further use, were thrown aside, and
became the perquisite of the wood-gatherers. During the repair of
the street, the spot was constantly besieged by a motley mob of
men, women, and children, who, in many instances, struggled and
fought for the wood rejected as worthless. This wood they either
sold for a trifle as they got it, or took home and split, and made
into bundles for sale as firewood.

OF THE DREDGERS, OR RIVER FINDERS

THE dredgermen of the Thames, or river finders, naturally occupy
the same place with reference to the street-finders, as the purlmen
or river beer-sellers do to those who get their living by selling
in the streets. It would be in itself a curious inquiry to trace the
origin of the manifold occupations in which men are found to be
engaged in the present day, and to note how promptly every
circumstance and occurrence was laid hold of, as it happened to
arise, which appeared to have any tendency to open up a new
occupation, and to mark the gradual progress, till it became a
regularly-established employment, followed by a separate class of
people, fenced round by rules and customs of their own, and who
at length grew to be both in their habits and peculiarities plainly
distinct from the other classes among whom they chanced to be
located.

There has been no historian among the dredgers of the Thames to record the commencement of the business, and the utmost that any of the river-finders can tell is that his father had been a dredger, and so had his father before him, and that *that's* the reason why they are dredgers also. But no such people as dredgers were known on the Thames in remote days; and before London had become an important trading port, where nothing was likely to be got for the searching, it is not probable that people would have been induced to search. In those days, the only things searched for in the river were the bodies of persons drowned, accidentally or otherwise. For this purpose, the Thames fishermen of all others, appeared to be the best adapted. They were on the spot at all times, and had various sorts of tackle, such as nets, lines, hooks, &c. The fishermen well understood everything connected with the river, such as the various sets of the tides, and the nature of the bottom, and they were therefore on such occasions invariably applied to for these purposes.

It is known to all who remember anything of Old London Bridge, that at certain time of the tide, in consequence of the velocity with which the water rushed through the narrow apertures which the arches then afforded for its passage, to bring a boat in safety through the bridge was a feat to be attempted only by the skilful and experienced. This feat was known as 'shooting' London Bridge; and it was no unusual thing for accidents to happen even to the most expert. In fact, numerous accidents occurred at this bridge, and at such times valuable articles were sometimes lost, for which high rewards were offered to the finder. Here again the fishermen came into requisition, the small drag-net, which they used while rowing, offering itself for the purpose; for, by fixing an iron frame round the mouth of the drag-net, this part of it, from its specific gravity, sunk first to the bottom, and consequently scraped along as they pulled forward, collecting into the net everything that came in its way; when it was nearly filled, which the rower always knew by the weight, it was hauled up to the surface, its contents examined, and the object lost generally recovered.

It is thus apparent that the fishermen of the Thames were the men originally employed as dredgermen; though casually, indeed, at first, and according as circumstances occurred requiring their services. By degrees, however, as the commerce of the river increased, and a greater number of articles fell overboard from the shipping, they came to be more frequently called into requisition, and so they were naturally led to adopt the dredging as part and parcel of their business. Thus it remains to the present day.

The fishermen all serve a regular apprenticeship, as they say themselves, 'duly and truly' for seven years. During the time of their apprenticeship they are (or rather, in former times they *were*) obliged to sleep in their master's boat at night to take care of his property, and were subject to many other curious regulations, which are foreign to this subject.

I have said that the fishermen of the Thames to the present day unite the dredging to their proper calling. By this I mean that they employ themselves in fishing during the summer and autumn, either from Barking Creek downwards, or from Chelsea Reach upwards, catching dabs, flounders, eels, and other sorts of fish for the London markets. But in winter when the days are short and cold, and the weather stormy, they prefer stopping at home, and dredging the bed of the river for anything they may chance to find. There are others, however, who have started wholly in the dredging line, there being no hindrance or impediment to any one doing so, nor any licence required for the purpose: these dredge the river winter and summer alike, and are, in fact, the only real dredgermen of the present day living solely by that occupation.

There are in all about 100 dredgermen at work on the river, and these are located as follows:—

From Putney to Vauxhall there are	20
From Vauxhall to London-bridge	40
From London-bridge to Deptford	20
And from Deptford to Gravesend	20
	100

All these reside, in general, on the south side of the Thames, the two places most frequented by them being Lambeth and Rotherhithe. They do not, however, confine themselves to the neighbourhoods wherein they reside, but extend their operations to all parts of the river, where it is likely that they may pick up anything; and it is perfectly marvellous with what rapidity the intelligence of any accident calculated to afford them employment is spread among them; for should a loaded coal barge be sunk over night, by daylight the next morning every dredgerman would be sure to be upon the spot, prepared to collect what he could from the wreck at the bottom of the river.

The boats of the dredgermen are of a peculiar shape. They have no stern, but are the same fore and aft. They are called Peter boats, but not one of the men with whom I spoke had the least idea as to the origin of the name. These boats are to be had at almost all prices, according to their condition and age—from 30s. to 20l. The boats used by the fishermen dredgermen are decidedly the most valuable. One with the other, perhaps the whole may average 10l. each; and this sum will give 1,000l. as the value of the entire number. A complete set of tackle, including drags, will cost 2l., which comes to 200l. for all hands; and thus we have the sum of 1,200l. as the amount of capital invested in the dredging of the Thames.

It is by no means an easy matter to form any estimate of the earnings of the dredgermen, as they are a matter of mere chance. In former years, when Indiamen and all the foreign shipping lay in the river, the river finders were in the habit of doing a good business, not only in their own line, through the greater quantities of rope, bones, and other things which were thrown or fell overboard, but they also contrived to smuggle ashore great quantities of tobacco, tea, spirits, and other contraband articles, and thought it a bad day's work when they did not earn a pound independent of their dredging. An old dredger told me he had often in those days made 5l. before breakfast time. After the evacuation of the various docks, and after the larger shipping had departed from the river, the finders were obliged to content themselves with the chances of mere dredging; and even then, I am informed, they were in the habit of earning one week with another throughout the year, about 25s. per week, each, or 6,500l. per annum among all. Latterly, however, the earnings of these men have greatly fallen off, especially in the summer, for then they cannot get so good a price for the coal they find as in the winter—6d. per bushel being the summer price; and, as they consider three bushels a good day's work, their earnings at this period of the year amount only to 1s. 6d. per day, excepting when they happen to pick up some bones or pieces of metal, or to find a dead body for which there is a reward. In the winter, however, the dredgermen can readily get 1s. per bushel for all the coals they find; and far more coals are to be found then than in summer, for there are more colliers in the river, and far more accidents at that season. Coal barges are often sunk in the winter, and on such occasions they make a good harvest. Moreover there is the finding of bodies, for which they not only get the reward, but 5s., which they call inquest money; together with many other chances, such as the finding of money and valuables among the rubbish they bring up from the bottom; but as the last-mentioned are accidents happening throughout the year, I am inclined to think that they have understated the amount which they are in the habit of realizing even in the summer.

The dredgers, as a class, may be said to be altogether uneducated, not half a dozen out of the whole number being able to read their own name, and only one or two to write it; this select few are considered by the rest as perfect prodigies. 'Lor' bless you!' said one, 'I on'y wish you'd 'ear Bill S——read; I on'y jist wish you'd 'ear him. Why that 'ere Bill can read faster nor a dog can trot. Anad, what's more, I seed him write an 'ole letter hisself, ev'ry word on it! What do you think o' that now?' The ignorance of the dredgermen may be accounted for by the men taking so early to the water, the bustle and excitement of the river being far more attractive to them than the routine of a school. Almost as soon as they are able to do anything, the dredgermen's boys are taken by their fathers afloat to assist in picking out the coals, bones, and other things of any use, from the midst of the rubbish brought up in their dragnets; or else the lads are sent on board as assistants to one or other of the fishermen during their fishing voyages. When once engaged in this way it has been found impossible afterwards to keep the youths from the water; and if they have learned anything previously they very soon forget it.

It might be expected that the dredgers, in a manner depending on chance for their livelihood, and leading a restless sort of life on the water, would closely resemble the costermongers in their habits; but it is far otherwise. There can be no two classes more dissimilar, except in their hatred of restraint. The dredgers are sober and steady; gambling is unknown amongst them; and they are, to an extraordinary degree, laborious, persevering, and patient. They are in general men of short stature, but square built, strong, and capable of enduring great fatigue, and have a silent and thoughtful look. Being almost always alone, and studying how they may best succeed in finding what they seek, marking the various sets of the tide, and the direction in which things falling into the water at a particular place must necessarily be carried, they become the very opposite to the other river people, especially to the watermen, who are brawling and clamorous, and delight in continually 'chaffing' each other. In consequence of the sober and industrious habits of the dredgermen their homes are, as they say, 'pretty fair' for working men, though there is nothing very luxurious to be found in them, nor indeed anything beyond what is absolutely necessary. After their day's work, especially if they have 'done well,' these men smoke a pipe over a pint or two of beer at the nearest public-house, get home early to bed, and if the tide answers may be found on the river patiently dredging away at two or three o'clock in the morning.

Whenever a loaded coal barge happens to sink, as I have already intimated, it is surprising how short a time elapses before that part of the river is alive with the dredgers. They flock thither from all parts. The river on such occasions presents a very animated appearance. At first they are all in a group, and apparently in confusion, crossing and re-crossing each other's course; some with their oars pulled in while they examine the contents of their nets, and empty the coals into the bottom of their boats; others rowing and tugging against the stream, to obtain an advantageous position for the next cast; and when they consider they have found this, down go the dredging-nets to the bottom, and away they row again with the stream, as if pulling for a wager, till they find by the weight of their net that it is full; then they at once stop, haul it to the surface, and commence another course. Others who have been successful in getting their boats loaded may be seen pushing a way from the main body, and making towards the shore. Here they busily employ themselves, with what help they can get, in emptying the boat of her cargo—carrying it ashore in old coal buckets, bushel measures, or anything else which will suit their purpose; and when this is completed they pull out again to join their comrades, and commence afresh. They continue working thus till the returning tide puts an end to their labours, but these are resumed after the tide has fallen to a certain depth; and so they go on, working night and day while there is anything to be got.

The dredgerman and his boat may be immediately distinguished from all others; there is nothing similar to them on the river. The sharp cutwater fore and aft, and short rounded appearance of the vessel, marks it out at once from the skiff or wherry of the waterman. There is, too, always the appearance of labour about the boat, like a ship returning after a long voyage, daubed and filthy, and looking sadly in need of a thorough cleansing. The grappling irons are over the bow, resting on a coil of rope; while the other end of the boat is filled with coals, bones, and old rope, mixed with the mud of the river. The ropes of the dredging-net hang over the side. A short stout figure, with a face soiled and blackened with perspiration, and surmounted by a tarred sou'-wester, the body habited in a soiled check shirt, with the sleeves turned up above the elbows, and exhibiting a pair of sunburnt brawny arms, is pulling at the sculls, not with the ease and lightness of the waterman, but toiling and tugging away like a galley slave, as he scours the bed of the river with his dredging-net in search of some hoped-for prize.

The dredgers, as was before stated, are the men who find almost all the bodies of persons drowned. If there be a reward offered for the recovery of a body, numbers of the dredgers will at once endeavour to obtain it, while if there be no reward, there is at least the inquest money to be had—beside other chances. What these chances are may be inferred from the well-known fact, that no body recovered by a dredgerman ever happens to have any money about it, when brought to shore. There may, indeed, be a watch in the fob or waistcoat pocket, for that article would be likely to be traced. There may, too, be a purse or pocket-book forthcoming, but somehow it is invariably empty. The dredgers cannot by any reasoning or argument be made to comprehend that there is anything like dishonesty in emptying the pockets of a dead man. They say that any one who finds a body does precisely the same, and that if they did not do so the police would.

One of the most industrious, and I believe one of the most skilful and successful of this peculiar class, gave me the following epitome of his history.

'Father was a dredger, and grandfather afore him; grandfather was a dredger and a fisherman too. A'most as soon as I was able to crawl, father took me with him in the boat to help him to pick the coals, and bones, and other things out of the net, and to use me to the water. When I got bigger and stronger, I was sent to the parish school, but I didn't like it half as well as the boat, and couldn't be got to stay two days together. At last I went above bridge, and went along with a fisherman, and used to sleep in the boat every night. I liked to sleep in the boat; I used to be as comfortable as could be. Lor'bless you! there's a tilt to them boats, and no rain can't git at you. I used to lie awake of a night in them times, and listen to the water slapping ag'in the boat, and think it fine fun. I might a got bound 'prentice, but I got aboard a smack, where I stayed three or four year, and if I'd a stayed there, I'd a liked it much better. But I heerd as how father was ill, so I com'd home, and took to the dredging, and am at it off and on ever since. I got no larnin', how could I? There's on'y one or two of us dredgers as knows anything of larnin', and they're no better off than the rest. Larnin's no use to a dredger, he hasn't got no time to read; and if he had, why it wouldn't tell him where the holes and furrows is at the bottom of the river, and where things is to be found. To be sure there's holes and furrows at the bottom. I know a good many. I know a furrow off Lime'us Point, no wider nor the dredge, and I can go there, and when others can't git anything but stones and mud, I can git four of five bushel o' coal. You see they lay there; they get in with the set of the tide, and can't git out so easy like. Dredgers don't do so well now as they used to do. You know Pelican Stairs? well, before the Docks was built, when the ships lay there, I could go under Pelican Pier and pick up four or five shilling of a morning. What was that tho' to father? I hear him say he often made 5*l.* afore breakfast, and nobody ever the wiser. Them were fine times! there was a good livin' to be picked up on the water them days. About ten year ago, the fishermen at Lambeth, them as sarves their time "duly and truly" thought to put us off the water, and went afore the Lord Mayor, but they couldn't do nothink after all. They do better nor us, as they go fishin' all the summer, when the dredgin' is bad, and come back in winter. Some on us down here' [Rother-hithe] 'go a deal-portering in the summer, or unloading 'tatoes, or anything else we can get; when we have nothin' else to do, we go on the river. Father don't dredge now, he's too old for that; it takes a man to be strong to dredge, so father goes to ship scrapin'. He on'y sits on a plank outside the ship, and scrapes off the old tar with a scraper. We does very well for all that—why he can make his half a bull a day [2s. 6d.] when he gits work, but that's not always; howsomever I helps the old man at times, when I'm able. I've found a good many bodies. I got a many rewards, and a tidy bit of inquest money. There's 5s. 6d. inquest money at Rother-hithe, and on'y a shillin' at Deptford; I can't make out how that is, but that's all they give, I know. I never finds anythink on the bodies. Lor' bless you! people don't have anythink in their pockets when they gits drowned, they are not such fools as all that. Do you see them two marks there on the back of my hand? Well, one day— I was on'y young then—I was grabblin' for old rope in Church Hole, when I brings up a body, and just as I was fixing the rope on his leg to tow him ashore, two swells comes down in a skiff, and lays hold of the painter of my boat, and tows me ashore. The hook of the drag went right thro' the trousers of the drowned man and my hand, and I couldn't let go no how, and tho' I roared out like mad, the swells didn't care, but dragged me into the stairs. When I got there, my arm, and the corpse's shoe and trousers, was all kivered with my blood. What do you think the gents said?—why, they told me as how they had done me good, in towin' the body in, and ran away up the stairs. Tho' times ain't near so good as they was, I manages purty tidy, and hasn't got no occasion to hollor much; but there's some of the dredgers as would hollor, if they was ever so well off.'

OF THE SEWER-HUNTERS

Some few years ago, the main sewers, having their outlets on the river side, were completely open, so that any person desirous of exploring their dark and uninviting recesses might enter at the river side, and wander away, provided he could withstand the combination of villainous stenches which met him at every step, for many miles, in any direction. At that time it was a thing of very frequent occurrence, especially at the spring tides, for the water to rush into the sewers, pouring through them like a torrent and then to burst up through the gratings into the streets, flooding all the low-lying districts in the vicinity of the river, till the streets of Shadwell and Wapping resembled a Dutch town, intersected by a series of muddy canals. Of late, however, to remedy this defect, the Commissioners have had a strong brick wall built within the entrance to the several sewers. In each of these brick walls there is an opening covered by a strong iron door, which hangs from the top and is so arranged that when the tide is low the rush of the water and other filth on the inner side, forces it back and allows the contents of the sewer to pass into the river, whilst when the tide rises the door is forced so close against the wall by the pressure of the water outside that none can by any possibility enter, and thus the river neighbourhoods are secured from the deluges which were heretofore of such frequent occurrence.

Were it not a notorious fact, it might perhaps be thought impossible, that men could be found who, for the chance of obtaining a living of some sort or other, would, day after day, and year after year, continue to travel through these underground channels for the offscouring of the city; but such is the case even at the present moment. In former times, however, this custom prevailed much more than now, for in those days the sewers were eniirely open and presented no obstacle to any one desirous of entering them. Many wondrous tales are still told among the people of men having lost their way in the sewers, and of having wandered among the filthy passages—their lights extinguished by the noisome vapours—till, faint and overpowered, they dropped down and died on the spot. Other stories are told of sewer-hunters beset by myriads of enormous rats, and slaying thousands of them in their struggle for life, till at length the swarms of the savage things overpowered them, and in a few days afterwards their skeletons were discovered picked to the very bones. Since the iron doors, however, have been placed on the main sewers a prohibition has been issued against entering them, and a reward of 5l. offered to any person giving information so as to lead to the conviction of any offender. Nevertheless many still travel through the foul labyrinths, in search of such valuables as may have found their way down the drains.

The persons who are in the habit of searching the sewers, call themselves 'shore-men' or 'shore-workers.' They belong, in a certain degree, to the same class as the 'mud-larks,' that is to say, they travel through the mud along shore in the neighbourhood of ship-building and ship-breaking yards, for the purpose of picking up copper nails, bolts, iron, and old rope. The shore-men, however, do not collect the lumps of coal and wood they meet with on their way, but leave them as the proper perquisites of the mud-larks.

The sewer-hunters were formerly, and indeed are still, called by the name of 'Toshers,' the articles which they pick up in the course of their wanderings along shore being known among themselves by the general term 'tosh,' a word more particularly applied by them to anything made of copper. These 'Toshers' may be seen, especially on the Surrey side of the Thames, habited in long greasy velveteen coats, furnished with pockets of vast capacity, and their nether limbs encased in dirty canvas trousers, and any old slops of shoes, that may be fit only for wading through the mud. They carry a bag on their back, and in their hand a pole seven or eight feet long, on one end of which there is a large iron hoe. The uses of this instrument are various; with it they try the ground wherever it appears unsafe, before venturing on it, and, when assured of its safety, walk forward steadying their footsteps with the staff. Should they, as often happens, even to the most experienced, sink in some quagmire, they immediately throw out the long pole armed with the hoe, which is always held uppermost for this purpose, and with it seizing hold of any object within their reach, are thereby enabled to draw themselves out; without the pole, however, their danger would be greater, for the more they struggled to extricate themselves from such places, the deeper they would sink; and even with it, they might perish, I am told, in some part, if there were nobody at hand to render them assistance. Finally, they make use of this pole to rake about the mud when searching for iron, copper, rope, and bones. They mostly exhibit great skill in discovering these things in unlikely places, and have a knowledge of the various sets of the tide, calculated to carry articles to particular points, almost equal to the dredgermen themselves. Although they cannot 'pick up' as much now as they formerly did, they are still able to make what they call a fair living, and can afford to look down with a species of aristocratic contempt on the puny efforts of their less fortunate brethren the 'mud-larks.'

To enter the sewers and explore them to any considerable distance is considered, even by those acquainted with what is termed 'working the shores,' an adventure of no small risk. There are a variety of perils to be encountered in such places. The brickwork in many parts—especially in the old sewers—has become rotten through the continual action of the putrefying matter and moisture and parts have fallen down and choked up the passage with heaps of rubbish; over these obstructions, nevertheless, the sewer-hunters have to scramble 'in the best way they can.' In such part they are careful not to touch the brickwork over head, for the slightest tap might bring down an avalanche of old bricks and earth, and severely injure them, if not bury them in the rubbish. Since the construction of the new sewers, the old ones are in general abandoned by the 'hunters;' but in many places the former channels cross and re-cross those recently constructed, and in the old sewers a person is very likely to lose his way. It is dangerous to venture far into any of the smaller sewers branching off from the main, for in this the 'hunters' have to stoop low down in order to proceed; and, from the confined space, there are often accumulated in such places, large quantities of foul air, which, as one of them stated, will 'cause instantious death.' Moreover, far from there being any romance in the tales told of the rats, these vermin are really numerous and formidable in the sewers, and have been known, I am assured, to attack men when alone, and even sometimes when accompanied by others, with such fury that the people have escaped from them with difficulty. They are particularly ferocious and dangerous, if driven into some corner whence they cannot escape, when they will immediately fly at any one that opposes their progress. I received a similar account to this from one of the London fishermen. There are moreover, in some quarters, ditches or trenches which are filled with water as the water rushes up the sewers with the tide; in these ditches the water is retained by a sluice, which is shut down at high tide, and lifted again at low tide, when it rushes down the sewers with all the violence of a mountain torrent, sweeping everything before it. If the sewer-hunter be not close to some branch sewer, so that he can run into it, whenever the opening of these sluices takes place, he must inevitably perish. The trenches or water reservoirs for the cleansing of the sewers are chiefly on the south side of the river, and, as a proof of the great danger to which the sewer-hunters are exposed in such cases, it may be stated, that not very long ago, a sewer on the south side of the Thames was opened to be repaired; a long ladder reached to the bottom of the sewer, down which the bricklayer's labourer was going with a hod of bricks, when the rush of water from the sluice, struck the bottom of the ladder, and instantly swept away ladder, labourer, and all. The bricklayer fortunately was enjoying his 'pint and pipe' at a neighbouring public-house. The labourer was found by my informant, a 'shore-worker,' near the mouth of the sewer quite dead, battered, and disfigured in a frightful manner. There was likewise great danger in former times from the rising of the tide in the sewers, so that it was necessary for the shore-men to have quitted them before the water had got any height within the entrance. At present, however, this is obviated in those sewers where the main is furnished with an iron door towards the river.

The shore-workers, when about to enter the sewers, provide themselves, in addition to the long hoe already described, with a canvas apron, which they tie round them, and a dark lantern similar to a policeman's; this they strap before them on their right breast, in such a manner that on removing the shade, the bull's-eye throws the light straight forward when they are in an erect position, and enables them to see everything in advance of them for some distance; but when they stoop, it throws the light directly under them, so that they can then distinctly see any object at their feet. The sewer-hunters usually go in gangs of three or four for the sake of company, and in order that they may be the better able to defend themselves from the rats. The old hands who have been often up (and every gang endeavours to include at least one experienced person), travel a long distance, not only through the main sewers, but also through many of the branches. Whenever the shore-men come near a street grating, they close their lanterns and watch their opportunity of gliding silently past unobserved, for otherwise a crowd might collect over head and intimate to the policeman on duty, that there were persons wandering in the sewers below. The shore-workers never take dogs with them, lest their barking when hunting the rats might excite attention. As the men go along they search the bottom of the sewer, raking away the mud with their hoe, and pick, from between the crevices of the brick-work, money, or anything else that may have lodged there. There are in many parts of the sewers holes where the brick-work has been worn away, and in these holes clusters of articles are found, which have been washed into them from time to time, and perhaps been collecting there for years; such as pieces of iron, nails, various scraps of metal, coins of every description, all rusted into a mass like a rock, and weighing from a half hundred to two hundred weight altogether. These 'conglomerates' of metal are too heavy for the men to take out of the sewers, so that if unable to break them up, they are compelled to leave them behind; and there are very many such masses, I am informed, lying in the sewers at this moment, of immense weight, and growing larger every day by continual additions. The shore-men find great quantities of money —of copper money especially; sometimes they dive their arm down to the elbow in the mud and filth and bring up shillings, sixpences, half-crowns, and occasionally half-sovereigns and sovereigns. They always find the coins standing edge uppermost between the bricks in the bottom, where the mortar has been worn away. The sewer-hunters occasionally find plate, such as spoons, ladles, silver-handled knives and forks, mugs and drinking cups, and now and then articles of jewellery; but even while thus 'in luck' as they call it, they do not omit to fill the bags on their backs with the more cumbrous articles they meet with—such as metals of every description, rope and bones. There is always a great quantity of these things to be met with in the sewers, they being continually washed down from the cesspools and drains of the houses. When the sewer-hunters consider they have searched long enough, or when they have found as much as they can conveniently take away, the gang leave the sewers and, adjourning to the nearest of their homes, count out the money they have picked up, and proceed to dispose of the old metal, bones, rope, &c.; this done, they then, as they term it, 'wack' the whole lot; that is, they divide it equally among all hands. At these divisions, I am assured, it frequently occurs that each member of the gang will realise from 30s. to 2l.— this at least was a frequent occurrence some few years ago. Of late, the shore-men are obliged to use far more caution, as the police, and especially those connected with the river, who are more on the alert, as well as many of the coal-merchants in the neighbour-hood of the sewers, would give information if they saw any suspicious persons approaching them.

The principal localities in which the shore-hunters reside are in Mint-square, Mint-street, and Kent-street, in the Borough—Snow's-fields, Bermondsey—and that never-failing locality be-tween the London Docks and Rosemary-lane which appears to be a concentration of all the misery of the kingdom. There were known to be a few years ago nearly 200 sewer-hunters, or 'toshers,' and, incredible as it may appear, I have satisfied myself that, taking one

THE LONDON DUSTMAN

THE LONDON SWEEP

week with another, they could not be said to make much short of 2*l.* per week. Their probable gains, I was told, were about 6*s.* per day all the year round. At this rate the property recovered from the sewers of London would have amounted to no less than 20,000*l.* per annum, which would make the amount of property lost down the drains of each house amount to 1*s.* 4*d.* a year. The shore-hunter of the present day greatly complain of the recent restrictions, and inveigh in no measured terms against the constituted authorities. 'They won't let us in to work the shores,' say they, 'cause there's a little danger. They fears as how we'll get suffocated, at least they tells us so; but they don't care if we get starved! no, they doesn't mind nothink about that.'

The sewer-hunters, strange as it may appear, are certainly smart fellows, and take decided precedence of all the other 'finders' of London, whether by land or water, both on account of the greater amount of their earnings, and the skill and courage they manifest in the pursuit of their dangerous employment. But like all who make a living as it were by a game of chance, plodding, carefulness, and saving habits cannot be reckoned among their virtues; they are improvident, even to a proverb. With their gains, superior even to those of the better-paid artisans, and far beyond the amount received by many clerks, who have to maintain a 'respectable appearance,' the shore-men might, with but ordinary prudence, live well, have comfortable homes, and even be able to save sufficient to provide for themselves in their old age. Their practice, however, is directly the reverse. They no sooner make a 'haul,' as they say, than they adjourn to some low public-house in the neighbourhood, and seldom leave till empty pockets and hungry stomachs drive them forth to procure the means for a fresh debauch. It is principally on this account that, despite their large gains, they are to be found located in the most wretched quarter of the metropolis.

It might be supposed that the sewer-hunters (passing much of their time in the midst of the noisome vapours generated by the sewers, the odour of which, escaping upwards from the gratings in the streets, is dreaded and shunned by all as something pestilential) would exhibit in their pallid faces the unmistakable evidence of their unhealthy employment. But this is far from the fact. Strange to say, the sewer-hunters are strong, robust, and healthy men, generally florid in their complexion, while many of them know illness only by name. Some of the elder men, who head the gangs when exploring the sewers, are between 60 and 80 years of age, and have followed the employment during their whole lives. The men appear to have a fixed belief that the odour of the sewers contributes in a variety of ways to their general health; nevertheless they admit that accidents occasionally occur from the air in some places being fully impregnated with mephitic gas.

I found one of these men, from whom I derived much information and who is really an active intelligent man, in a court off Rosemary-lane. Access is gained to this court through a dark narrow entrance, scarcely wider than a doorway, running beneath the first floor of one of the houses in the adjoining street. The court itself is about 50 yards long, and not more than three yards wide, surrounded by lofty wooden houses, with jutting abutments in many of the upper stories that almost exclude the light, and give them the appearance of being about to tumble down upon the heads of the intruders. This court is densely inhabited; every room has its own family, more or less in number; and in many of them, I am assured, there are two families residing, the better to enable the one to whom the room is let to pay the rent. At the time of my visit, which was in the evening, after the inmates had returned from their various employments, some quarrel had arisen among them. The court was so thronged with the friends of the contending individuals and spectators of the fight that I was obliged to stand at the entrance, unable to force my way through the dense multitude, while labourers and street-folk with shaggy heads, and women with dirty caps and fuzzy hair, thronged every window above, and peered down anxiously at the affray. There must have been some hundreds of people collected there, and yet all were inhabitants of this very court, for the noise of the quarrel had not yet reached the street. On wondering at the number, my informant, when the noise had ceased, explained the matter as follows: 'You see, sir, there's more than 30 houses in this here court, and there's not less than eight rooms in every house; now there's nine or ten people in some of the rooms, I knows, but just say four in every room, and calculate what that there comes to.' I did, and found it, to my surprise, to be 960. 'Well,' continued my informant, chuckling and rubbing his hands in evident delight at the result, 'you may as well just tack a couple a hundred on to the tail o' them for make-weight, as we're not werry pertikler about a hundred or two one way or the other in these here places.'

In this court, up three flights of narrow stairs that creaked and trembled at every footstep, and in an ill-furnished garret, dwelt the shore-worker—a man who, had he been careful, according to his own account, at least, might have money in the bank and be the proprietor of the house in which he lived. The sewer-hunters, like the street-people, are all known by some peculiar nickname, derived chiefly from some personal characteristic. It would be a waste of time to inquire for them by their right names, even if you were acquainted with them, for none else would know them, and no intelligence concerning them could be obtained; while under the title of Lanky Bill, Long Tom, One-eyed George, Short-armed Jack, they are known to every one.

My informant, who is also dignified with a title, or as he calls it, a 'handle to his name,' gave me the following account of himself: 'I was born in Birmingham, but afore I recollects anythink, we came to London. The first thing I remembers is being down on the shore at Cuckold's P'int, when the tide was out and up to my knees in mud, and a gitting down deeper and deeper every minute till I was picked up by one of the shore-workers. I used to git down there every day, to look at the ships and boats a sailing up and down; I'd niver be tired a looking at them at that time. As last father 'prenticed me to a blacksmith in Bermondsey, *and then I couldn't git down to the river when I liked so I got to hate the forge and the fire, and blowing the bellows, and couldn't stand the confinement no how,—at last I cuts and runs*. After some time they gits me back ag'in, but I cuts ag'in. I was determined not to stand it. I wouldn't go home for fear I'd be sent back, so I goes down to Cuckold's P'int and there I sits near half the day, when who should I see but the old un as had picked me up out ot the mud when I was a sinking. I tells him all about it, and he takes me home along with hisself, and gits me a bag and an o, and takes me out next day, and shows me what to do, and shows me the dangerous places, and the places what are safe, and how to rake in the mud for rope, and bones, and iron, and that's the way I comed to be a shore-worker. Lor' bless you, I've worked Cuckold's P'int for more nor twenty year. I know places where you'd go over head and ears in the mud, and jist alongside on 'em you may walk as safe as you can on this floor.

But it don't do for a stranger to try it, he'd wery soon git in, and it's not so easy to git out agin, I can tell you. I stay'd with the old un a long time, and we used to git lots o' tin, specially when we'd go to work the sewers. I liked that well enough. I could git into small places where the old un couldn't, and when I'd got near the grating in the street, I'd search about in the bottom of the sewer; I'd put down my arm to my shoulder in the mud and bring up shillings and half-crowns, and lots of coppers, and plenty other things. I once found a silver jug as big as a quart pot, and often found spoons and knives and forks and everything you can think of. Bless your heart, the smell's nothink; it's a roughish smell at first, but nothink near so bad as you thinks, 'cause, you see, there's sich lots o' water always a coming down the sewer, and the air gits in from the gratings, and that helps to sweeten it a bit. There's some places, 'specially in the old sewers, where they say there's foul air, and they tells me the foul air 'll cause instantious death, but I niver met with anythink of the kind, and I think if there was sich a thing, I should know somethink about it, for I've worked the sewers, off and on, for twenty year. When we comes to a narrow-place as we don't know, we takes the candle out of the lantern and fastens it on the head of the o, and then runs it up the sewer, and if the light stays in, we knows as there a'n't no danger.

'The rats is wery dangerous, that's sartin, but we always goes three or four on us together, and the varmint's too wide awake to tackle us then, for they know they'd git off second best. You can go a long way in the sewers it you like; I don't know how far. I niver was at the end on them myself, for a cove can't stop in longer than six or seven hour, 'cause of the tide; you must be out before that's up. There's a many branches on ivery side, but we don't go into all; we go where we know, and where we're always sure to find somethink. I know a place now where there's more than two or three hundred weight of metal all rusted together, and plenty of money among it too; but it's too heavy to carry it out, so it 'll stop there I s'pose till the world comes to an end. I often brought out a piece of metal half a hundred in weight, and took it under the harch of the bridge, and broke it up with a large stone to pick out the money.

'We shore-workers sometimes does very well other ways. When we hears of a fire anywheres, we goes and watches where they shoots the rubbish, and then we goes and sifts it over, and washes it afterwards, then all the metal sinks to the bottom. The way we does it is this here: we takes a barrel cut in half, and fills it with water, and then we shovels in the siftings, and stirs 'em round and round and round with a stick; then we throws out that water and puts in some fresh, and stirs that there round ag'in; arter some time the water gets clear, and every thing heavy's fell to the bottom, and then we sees what it is and picks it out. I've made from a pound to thirty shilling a day, at that there work on lead alone. The time the Parliament House was burnt, the rubbish was shot in Hyde Park, and Long J—— and I goes to work it, and while we were at it, we didn't make less nor three pounds apiece a day; we found sovereigns and half sovereigns, and lots of silver half melted away, and jewellery, such as rings, and stones, and brooches; but we never got half paid for them. We found so many things, that at last Long J—— and I got to quarrel about the "whacking"; there was cheatin' a goin' on; it wasn't all fair and above board as it ought to be, so we gits to fightin', and kicks up sich a jolly row, that they wouldn't let us work no more, and takes and buries the whole on the rubbish. There's plenty o' things under the ground along with it now, if anybody could git at them. There was jist two loads o' rubbish shot at one time in Bishop Bonner's-fields, which I worked by myself, and what do you think I made out of that there?—why I made 3*l.* 5*s.* The rubbish was got out of a cellar, what hadn't been stirred for fifty year or more, so I thinks there ought to be somethink in it, and I keeps my eye on it, and watches where it's shot; then I turns to work, and the first thing I gits hold on is a chain, which I takes to be copper; it was so dirty, but it turned out to be all solid goold, and I gets 1*l.* 5*s.* for it from the Jew; arter that I finds lots o' coppers, and silver money, and many things besides. *The reason I likes this sort of life is, 'cause I can sit down when I likes, and nobody can't order me about. When I'm hard up, I knows as how I must work, and then I goes at it like sticks a breaking;* and tho' the times isn't as they was, I can go now and pick up my four or five bob a day, where another wouldn't know how to get a brass farden.'

There is a strange tale in existence among the shore-workers, of a race of wild hogs inhabiting the sewers in the neighbourhood of Hampstead. The story runs, that a sow in young, by some accident got down the sewer through an opening, and, wandering away from the spot, littered and reared her offspring in the drain; feeding on the offal and garbage washed into it continually. Here, it is alleged, the breed multiplied exceedingly, and have become almost as ferocious as they are numerous. This story, apocryphal as it seems, has nevertheless its believers, and it is ingeniously argued, that the reason why none of the subterranean animals have been able to make their way to the light of day, is that they could only do so by reaching the mouth of the sewer at the river-side, while, in order to arrive at that point, they must necessarily encounter the Fleet ditch, which runs towards the river with great rapidity, and as it is the obstinate nature of a pig to swim *against* the stream, the wild hogs of the sewers invariably work their way back to their original quarters, and are thus never to be seen. What seems strange in the matter is, that the inhabitants of Hampstead never have been known to see any of these animals pass beneath the gratings, nor to have been disturbed by their gruntings. The reader of course can believe as much of the story as he pleases, and it is right to inform him that the sewer-hunters themselves have never yet encountered any of the fabulous monsters of the Hampstead sewers.

OF THE MUD-LARKS

THERE is another class who may be termed river-finders, although their occupation is connected only with the shore; they are commonly known by the name of 'mud-larks,' from being compelled, in order to obtain the articles they seek, to wade sometimes up to their middle through the mud left on the shore by the retiring tide. These poor creatures are certainly about the most deplorable in their appearance of any I have met with in the course of my inquiries. They may be seen of all ages, from mere childhood to positive decrepitude, crawling among the barges at the various wharfs along the river; it cannot be said that they are clad in rags, for they are scarcely half covered by the tattered indescribable things that serve them for clothing; their bodies are grimed with the foul soil of the river, and their torn garments stiffened up like boards with dirt of every possible description.

Among the mud-larks may be seen many old women, and it is indeed pitiable to behold them, especially during the winter, bent nearly double with age and infirmity, paddling and groping among the wet mud for small pieces of coal, chips of wood, or any sort of refuse washed up by the tide. These women always have with them an old basket or an old tin kettle, in which they put whatever they chance to find. It usually takes them a whole tide to fill this receptacle, but when filled, it is as much as the feeble old creatures are able to carry home.

The mud-larks generally live in some court or alley in the neighbourhood of the river, and, as the tide recedes, crowds of boys and little girls, some old men, and many old women, may be observed loitering about the various stairs, watching eagerly for the opportunity to commence their labours. When the tide is sufficiently low they scatter themselves along the shore, separating from each other, and soon disappear among the craft lying about in every direction. This is the case on both sides of the river, as high up as there is anything to be found, extending as far as Vauxhall-bridge, and as low down as Woolwich. The mud-larks themselves, however, know only those who reside near them, and whom they are accustomed to meet in their daily pursuits; indeed, with but few exceptions, these people are dull, and apparently stupid; this is observable particularly among the boys and girls, who, when engaged in searching the mud, hold but little converse one with another. The men and women may be passed and repassed, but they notice no one; they never speak, but with a stolid look of wretchedness they plash their way through the mire, their bodies bent down while they peer anxiously about, and occasionally stoop to pick up some paltry treasure that falls in their way.

The mud-larks collect whatever they happen to find, such as coals, bits of old-iron, rope, bones, and copper nails that drop from ships while lying or repairing along shore. Copper nails are the most valuable of all the articles they find, but these they seldom obtain, as they are always driven from the neighbourhood of a ship while being new-sheathed. Sometimes the younger and bolder mud-larks venture on sweeping some empty coal-barge, and one little fellow with whom I spoke, having been lately caught in the act of so doing, had to undergo for the offence seven days' imprisonment in the House of Correction: this, he says, he liked much better than mud-larking, for while he staid there he wore a coat and shoes and stockings, and though he had not over much to eat, he certainly was never afraid of going to bed without anything at all—as he often had to do when at liberty. He thought he would try it on again in the winter, he told me, saying, it would be so comfortable to have clothes and shoes and stockings then, and not be obliged to go into the cold wet mud of a morning.

The coals that the mud-larks find, they sell to the poor people of the neighbourhood at 1*d*. per pot, holding about 14 lbs. The iron and bones and rope and copper nails which they collect, they sell at the rag-shops. They dispose of the iron at 5 lbs. for 1*d*., the bones at 3 lbs. a 1*d*., rope a ½*d*. per lb. wet, and ¾*d*. per lb. dry, and copper nails at the rate of 4*d*. per lb. They occasionally pick up tools, such as saws and hammers; these they dispose of to the seamen for biscuit and meat, and sometimes sell them at the rag-shops for a few halfpence. In this manner they earn from 2½*d*. to 8*d*. per day, but rarely the latter sum; their average gains may be estimated at about 3*d*. per day. The boys, after leaving the river, sometimes scrape their trousers, and frequent the cab-stands, and try to earn a trifle by opening the cab-doors for those who enter them, or by holding gentlemen's horses. Some of them go, in the evening, to a ragged school in the neighbourhood of which they live; more, as they say, because other boys go there, than from any desire to learn.

At one of the stairs in the neighbourhood of the pool, I collected about a dozen of these unfortunate children; there was not one of them over twelve years of age, and many of them were but six. It would be almost impossible to describe the wretched group, so motley was their appearance, so extraordinary their dress, and so stolid and inexpressive their countenances. Some carried baskets, filled with the produce of their morning's work, and other old tin kettles with iron handles. Some, for want of these articles, had old hats filled with the bones and coals they had picked up; and others, more needy still, had actually taken the caps from their own heads, and filled them with what they had happened to find. The muddy slush was dripping from their clothes and utensils, and forming a puddle in which they stood. There did not appear to be among the whole group as many filthy cotton rags to their backs as, when stitched together, would have been sufficient to form the material of one shirt. There were the remnants of one or two jackets among them, but so begrimed and tattered that it

would have been difficult to have determined either the original
material or make of the garment. On questioning one, he said his
father was a coal-backer; he had been dead eight years; the boy
was nine years old. His mother was alive; she went out charing and
washing when she could get any such work to do. She had 1s. a day
when she could get employment, but that was not often; he remembered once to have had a pair of shoes, but it was a long time since.
'It is very cold in winter,' he said, 'to stand in the mud without
shoes,' but he did not mind it in the summer. He had been three
years mud-larking, and supposed he should remain a mud-lark all
his life. What else could he be? for there was nothing else that he
knew *how* to do. Some days he earned a 1d., and some days 4d.; he
never earned 8d. in one day, that would have been a 'jolly lot of
money.' He never found a saw or a hammer, he 'only wished' he
could, they would be glad to get hold of them at the dolly's. He
had been one month at school before he went mud-larking. Some
time ago he had gone to the ragged-school; but he no longer went
there, for he forgot it. He could neither read nor write, and did
not think he could learn if he tried 'ever so much.' He didn't know
what religion his father and mother were, nor did know what
religion meant. God was God, he said. He had heard he was good,
but didn't know what good he was to him. He thought he was a
Christian, but he didn't know what a Christian was. He had heard
of Jesus Christ once, when he went to a Catholic chapel, but he
never heard tell of who or what he was, and didn't 'particular
care' about knowing. His father and mother were born in Aberdeen,
but he didn't know where Aberdeen was. London was England,
and England, he said, was in London, but he couldn't tell in what
part. He could not tell where he would go to when he died, and
didn't believe any one could tell *that*. Prayers, he told me, were
what people said to themselves at night. *He* never said any, and
didn't know any; his mother sometimes used to speak to him about
them, but he could never learn any. His mother didn't go to church
or to chapel, because she had no clothes. All the money he got he
gave to his mother, and she bought bread with it, and when they
had no money they lived the best way they could.

Such was the amount of intelligence manifested by this unfortunate child.

Another was only seven years old. He stated that his father was

a sailor who had been hurt on board ship, and been unable to go to
sea for the last two years. He had two brothers and a sister, one
of them older than himself; and his elder brother was a mud-lark
like himself. The two had been mud-larking more than a year; they
went because they saw other boys go, and knew that they got
money for the things they found. They were often hungry, and
glad to do anything to get something to eat. Their father was not
able to earn anything, and their mother could get but little to do.
They gave all the money they earned to their mother. They didn't
gamble, and play at pitch and toss when they had got some money,
but some of the big boys did on the Sunday, when they didn't go
a mud-larking. He couldn't tell why they did nothing on a Sunday,
'only they didn't'; though sometimes they looked about to see
where the best place would be on the next day. He didn't go to
the ragged school; he should like to know how to read a book,
though he couldn't tell what good it would do him. He didn't like
mud-larking, would be glad of something else, but didn't know
anything else that he could do.

Another of the boys was the son of a dock labourer,—casually
employed. He was between seven and eight years of age, and his
sister, who was also a mud-lark, formed one of the group. The
mother of these two was dead, and there were three children
younger than themselves.

The rest of the histories may easily be imagined, for there was a
painful uniformity in the stories of all the children: they were
either the children of the very poor, who, by their own improvi-
dence or some overwhelming calamity, had been reduced to the
extremity of distress, or else they were orphans, and compelled
from utter destitution to seek for the means of appeasing their
hunger in the mud of the river. That the majority of this class are
ignorant, and without even the rudiments of education, and that
many of them from time to time are committed to prison for petty
thefts, cannot be wondered at. Nor can it even excite our astonishment that, once within the walls of a prison, and finding how much
more comfortable it is than their previous condition, they should
return to it repeatedly. As for the females growing up under such
circumstances, the worst may be anticipated of them; and in proof
of this I have found, upon inquiry, that very many of the unfortunate creatures who swell the tide of prostitution in Ratcliff-

highway, and other low neighbourhoods in the East of London, have originally been mud-larks; and only remained at that occupation till such time as they were capable of adopting the more easy and more lucrative life of the prostitute.

As to the numbers and earnings of the mud-larks, the following calculations fall short of, rather than exceed, the truth. From Execution Dock to the lower part of Limehouse Hole, there are 14 stairs or landing-places, by which the mud-larks descend to the shore in order to pursue their employment. There are about as many on the opposite side of the water similarly frequented.

At King James's Stairs, in Wapping Wall, which is nearly a central position, from 40 to 50 mud-larks go down daily to the river; the mud-larks 'using' the other stairs are not so numerous. If, therefore, we reckon the number of stairs on both sides of the river at 28, and the average number of mud-larks frequenting them at 10 each, we shall have a total of 280. Each mud-lark, it has been shown, earns on a average 3*d.* a day, or 1*s.* 6*d.* per week; so that the annual earnings of each will be 3*l.* 18*s.*, or say 4*l.* a year, and hence the gross earnings of the 280 will amount to rather more than 1,000*l.* per annum.

But there are, in addition to the mud-larks employed in the neighbourhood of what may be called the pool, many others who work down the river at various places as far as Blackwall, on the one side, and at Deptford, Greenwich, and Woolwich, on the other. These frequent the neighbourhoods of the various 'yards' long shore, where vessels are being built; and whence, at certain times, chips, small pieces of wood, bits of iron, and copper nails, are washed out into the river. There is but little doubt that this portion of the class earn much more than the mud-larks of the pool, seeing that they are especially convenient to the places where the iron vessels are constructed; so that the presumption is, that the number of mud-larks 'at work' on the banks of the Thames (especially if we include those above bridge), and the value of the property extracted by them from the mud of the river, may be fairly estimated at double that which is stated above, or say 550 gaining 2,000*l.* per annum.

As an illustration of the doctrines I have endeavoured to enforce throughout this publication, I cite the following history of one of the above class. It may serve to teach those who are still sceptical as to the degrading influence of circumstances upon the poor, that many of the humbler classes, if placed in the same easy position as ourselves, would become, perhaps, quite as 'respectable' members of society.

The lad of whom I speak was discovered by me now nearly two years ago 'mud-larking' on the banks of the river near the docks. He was a quick intelligent little fellow, and had been at the business, he told me, about three years. He had taken to mud-larking, he said, because his clothes were too bad for him to look for anything better. He worked every day, with 20 or 30 boys, who might all be seen at daybreak with their trousers tucked up, groping about, and picking out the pieces of coal from the mud on the banks of the Thames. He went into the river up to his knees, and in searching the mud he often ran pieces of glass and long nails into his feet. When this was the case, he went home and dressed the wounds, but returned to the river-side directly, 'for should the tide come up,' he added, 'without my having found something, why I must starve till next low tide.' In the very cold weather he and his other shoeless companions used to stand in the hot water that ran down the river side from some of the steam-factories, to warm their frozen feet.

At first he found it difficult to keep his footing in the mud, and he had known many beginners fall in. He came to my house, at my request, the morning after my first meeting with him. It was the depth of winter, and the poor little fellow was nearly destitute of clothing. His trousers were worn away up to his knees, he had no shirt, and his legs and feet (which were bare) were covered with chilblains. On being questioned by me he gave the following account of his life: —

He was fourteen years old. He had two sisters, one fifteen and the other twelve years of age. His father had been dead nine years. The man had been a coal-whipper, and, from getting his work from one of the publican employers in those days, had become a confirmed drunkard. When he married he held a situation in a warehouse, where his wife managed the first year to save 4*l*. 10*s*. out of her husband's earnings; but from the day he took to coal-whipping she had never saved one halfpenny, indeed she and her children were often left to starve. The man (whilst in a state of intoxication) had fallen between two barges, and the injuries he received had been so severe that he had lingered in a helpless state for three years before his death. After her husband's decease the poor woman's neighbours subscribed 1*l.* 5*s.* for her; with this sum she opened a greengrocer's shop, and got on very well for five years.

When the boy was nine years old his mother sent him to the Red Lion school at Green-bank, near Old Gravel-lane, Ratcliffe-highway; she paid 1*d.* a week for his learning. He remained there for a year; then the potato-rot came, and his mother lost upon all she bought. About the same time two of her customers died 30*s.* in her debt; this loss, together with the potato disease, completely ruined her, and the whole family had been in the greatest poverty from that period. Then she was obliged to take all her children from their school, that they might help to keep themselves as best they could. Her eldest girl sold fish in the streets, and the boy went to the river-side to 'pick up' his living. The change, however, was so great that shortly afterwards the little fellow lay ill eighteen weeks with the ague. As soon as the boy recovered his mother and his two sisters were 'taken bad' with a fever. The poor woman went into the 'Great House,' and the children were taken to the Fever Hospital. When the mother returned home she was too weak to work, and all she had to depend on was what her boy brought from the river. They had nothing to eat and no money until the little fellow had been down to the shore and picked up some coals, selling them for a trifle.

OF THE DUSTMEN OF LONDON

Dust and rubbish accumulate in houses from a variety of causes, but principally from the residuum of fires, the white ash and cinders, or small fragments of unconsumed coke, giving rise to by far the greater quantity. Some notion of the vast amount of this refuse annually produced in London may be formed from the fact that the consumption of coal in the metropolis is, according to the official returns, 3,500,000 tons per annum, which is at the rate of a little more than 11 tons per house; the poorer families, it is true, do not burn more than 2 tons in the course of the year, but then many such families reside in the same house, and hence the average will appear in no way excessive. Now the ashes and cinders arising from this enormous consumption of coal would, it is evident, if allowed to lie scattered about in such a place as London, render, ere long, not only the back streets, but even the important thoroughfares, filthy and impassable. Upon the Officers of the various parishes, therefore, has devolved the duty of seeing that the refuse of the fuel consumed throughout London is removed almost as fast as produced; this they do by entering into an agreement for the clearance of the 'dust-bins' of the parishioners as often as required, with some person who possesses all necessary appliances for the purpose—such as horses, carts, baskets, and shovels, together with a plot of waste ground whereon to deposit the refuse. The persons with whom this agreement is made are called 'dust-contractors,' and are generally men of considerable wealth.

Formerly the custom was otherwise; but then, as will be seen hereafter, the residuum of the London fuel was far more valuable. Not many years ago it was the practice for the various master dustmen to send in their tenders to the vestry, on a certain day appointed for the purpose, offering to pay a considerable sum yearly to the parish authorities for liberty to collect the dust from the several houses. The sum formerly paid to the parish of Shadwell, for instance, though not a very extensive one, amounted to between 400*l.* or 500*l.* per annum; but then there was an immense demand for the article, and the contractors were unable to furnish a sufficient supply from London; ships were frequently freighted with it from other parts, especially from Newcastle and the northern ports, and at that time it formed an article of considerable international commerce—the price being from 15*s.* to 1*l.* per chaldron. Of late years, however, the demand has fallen off greatly, while the supply has been progressively increasing, owing to the extension of the metropolis, so that the Contractors have not only declined paying anything for liberty to collect it, but now stipulate to receive a certain sum for the removal of it. It need hardly be stated that the parishes always employ the man who requires the least money for the performance of what has now become a matter of duty rather than an object of desire. Some idea may be formed of the change which has taken place in this business, from the fact, that the aforesaid parish of Shadwell, which formerly received the sum of 450*l.* per annum for liberty to collect the dust, now pays the Contractor the sum of 240*l.* per annum for its removal.

The Court of Sewers of the City of London, in 1846, through

the advice of Mr. Cochrane, the president of the National Philan-
tropic Association, were able to obtain from the contractors the
sum of 5,000*l.* for liberty to clear away the dirt from the streets and
the dust from the bins and houses in that district. The year following, however, the contractors entered into a combination, and
came to a resolution not to bid so high for the privilege; the result
was, that they obtained their contracts at an expense of 2,200*l.* By
acting on the same principle in the year after, they not only offered
no premium whatever for the contract, but the City Commissioners
of Sewers were obliged to pay them the sum of 300*l.* for removing
the refuse, and at present the amount paid by the City is as much
as 4,900*l.*! This is divided among four great contractors, and would,
if equally apportioned, give them 1,250*l.* each.

A dust-contractor, who has been in the business upwards of 20
years, stated that, from his knowledge of the trade, he should
suppose that at present their might be about 80 or 90 contractors
in the metropolis. Now, according to the returns before given,
there are within the limits of the Metropolitan Police District 176
parishes, and comparing this with my informant's statement, that
many persons contact for more than one parish (of which, indeed,
he himself is an instance), there remains but little reason to doubt
the correctness of his supposition—that there are, in all, between
80 or 90 dust-contractors, large and small, connected with the
metropolis. Assuming the aggregate number to be 88, there would
be one contractor to every two parishes.

These dust-contractors are likewise the contractors for the
cleansing of the streets, except where that duty is performed by
the Street-Orderlies; they are also the persons who undertake the
emptying of the cesspools in their neighbourhood; the latter operation, however, is effected by an arrangement between themselves
and the landlords of the premises, and forms no part of their
parochial contacts. At the office of the Street Orderlies in Leicester
Square, they have knowledge of only 30 contractors connected
with the metropolis; but this is evidently defective, and refers to
the 'large masters' alone; leaving out of all consideration, as it
does, the host of small contractors scattered up and down the
metropolis, who are able to employ only two or three carts and six
or seven men each; many of such small contractors being merely
master sweeps who have managed to 'get on a little in the world,'

and who are now able to contract, 'in a small way,' for the removal of dust, street sweepings, and night-soil.

Computing the London dust-contractors at 90, and the inhabited houses at 300,000, it follows that each contractor would have 3,333 houses to remove the refuse from. Now it has been calculated that the ashes and cinders alone from each house average about three loads per annum, so that each contractor would have, in round numbers, 10,000 loads of dust to remove in the course of the year. I find, from inquiries, that every two dustmen carry to the yard about five loads a day, or about 1,500 loads in the course of the year, so that at this rate, there must be between six and seven carts and twelve and fourteen collectors employed by each master. But this is exclusive of the men employed in the yards. In one yard that I visited there were fourteen people busily employed. Six of these were women, who were occupied in sifting, and they were attended by three men who shovelled the dust into their sieves, and the foreman, who was hard at work loosening and dragging down the dust from the heap, ready for the 'fillers-in.' Besides these there were two carts and four men engaged in conveying the sifted dust to the barges alongside the wharf. At a larger dust-yard, that formerly stood on the banks of the Regent's-canal, I am informed that there were sometimes as many as 127 people at work. It is but a small yard, which has not 30 or 40 labourers connected with it; and the lesser dust-yards have generally from four to eight sifters, and six or seven carts. There are, therefore, employed in a medium-sized yard twelve collectors or cartmen, six sifters, and three fillers-in, besides the foreman or forewoman, making altogether 22 persons; so that, computing the contractors at 90, and allowing 20 men to be employed by each, there would be 1,880 men thus occupied in the metropolis, which appears to be very near the truth.

The next part of the subject is—what becomes of this vast quantity of dust—to what use it is applied.

The dust thus collected is used for two purposes, (1) as a manure for land of a peculiar quality; and (2) for making bricks. The fine portion of the house-dust called 'soil,' and separated from the 'brieze,' or coarser portion, by sifting, is found to be peculiarly fitted for what is called breaking up a marshy healthy soil at its first cultivation, owing only to the dry nature of the dust, but

to its possessing in an eminent degree a highly separating quality,
almost, if not quite, equal to sand. In former years the demand
for this finer dust was very great, and barges were continually in
the river waiting their turn to be loaded with it for some distant
part of the country. At that time the contractors were unable to
supply the demand, and easily got 1*l.* per chaldron for as much as
they could furnish, and then, as I have stated, many ships were
in the habit of bringing cargoes of it from the North, and of realizing a good profit on the transaction. Of late years, however—and
particularly, I am told, since the repeal of the corn-laws—this
branch of the business has dwindled to nothing. The contractors
say that the farmers do not cultivate their land now as they used;
it will not pay them, and instead, therefore, of bringing fresh land
into tillage, and especially such as requires this sort of manure,
they are laying down that which they previously had in cultivation,
and turning it into pasture grounds. It is principally on this
account, say the contractors, that we cannot sell the dust we collect
so well or so readily as formerly. There are, however, some cargoes
of the dust still taken, particularly to the lowlands in the neighbourhood of Barking, and such other places in the vicinity of the
metropolis as are enabled to realize a greater profit, by growing
for the London markets. Nevertheless, the contractors are obliged
now to dispose of the dust at 2*s.* 6*d.* per chaldron, and sometimes
less. The finer dust is also used to mix with the clay for making
bricks, and bargeloads are continually shipped off for this purpose.

But during the operation of sifting the dust, many things are
found which are useless for either manure or brick-making, such
as oyster shells, old bricks, old boots and shoes, old tin kettles, old
rags and bones,&c. These are used for various purposes.

The bricks, &c., are sold sinking beneath foundations, where
a thick layer of concrete is spread over them. Many old bricks,
too, are used in making new roads, especially where the land is
low and marshy. The old tin goes to form the japanned fastenings
for the corners of trunks, as well as to other persons, who re-manu-
facture it into a variety of articles. The old shoes are sold to the
London shoemakers, who use them as stuffing between the i n-sole
and the outer one; but by far the greater quantity is sold to the
manufacturers of Prussian blue, that substance being formed out

of refuse animal matter. The rags and bones are of course disposed of at the usual places—the marine-store shops.

The dust-yards, or places where the dust is collected and sifted, are generally situated in the suburbs, and they may be found all round London, sometimes occupying open spaces adjoining back streets and lanes, and surrounded by the low mean houses of the poor; frequently, however, they cover a large extent of ground in the fields, and there the dust is piled up to a great height in a conical heap, and having much the appearance of a volcanic mountain.

A visit to any of the large metropolitan dust-yards is far from uninteresting. Near the centre of the yard rises the highest heap, composed of what is called the 'soil,' or finer portion of the dust used for manure. Around this heap are numerous lesser heaps, consisting of the mixed dust and rubbish carted in and shot down previous to sifting. Among these heaps are many women and old men with sieves made of iron, all busily engaged in separating the 'brieze' from the 'soil.' There is likewise another large heap in some other part of the yard, composed of the cinders or 'brieze' waiting to be shipped off to the brickfields. The whole yard seems alive, some sifting and others shovelling the sifted soil on to the heap, while every now and then the dust-carts return to discharge their loads, and proceed again on their rounds for a fresh supply. Cocks and hens keep up a continual scratching and cackling among the heaps, and numerous pigs seem to find great delight in rooting incessantly about after the garbage and offal collected from the houses and markets.

In a dust-yard lately visited the sifters formed a curious sight; they were almost up their middle in dust, ranged in a semi-circle in front of that part of the heap which was being 'worked;' each had before her a small mound of soil which had fallen through her sieve and formed a sort of embankment, behind which she stood. The appearance of the entire group at their work was most peculiar. Their coarse dirty cotton gowns were tucked up behind them, their arms were bared above their elbows, their black bonnets crushed and battered like those of fish-women; over their gowns they wore a strong leathern apron, extending from their necks to the extremities of their petticoats, while over this, again, was another leathern apron, shorter, thickly padded, and fastened by a stout string or strap round the waist. In the process of their work they pushed the sieve from them and drew it back again with apparent violence, striking it against the outer leathern apron with such force that it produced each time a hollow sound, like a blow on the tenor drum. All the women present were middle aged, with the exception of one who was very old—68 years of age she told me— and had been at the business from a girl. She was the daughter of a dustman, the wife or woman of a dustman, and the mother of several young dustmen—sons and grandsons—all at work at the dust-yards at the east end of the metropolis.

We now come to speak of the labourers engaged in collecting, sifting, or shipping off the dust of the metropolis.

The dustmen, scavengers, and nightmen are, to a certain extent, the same people. The contractors generally agree with the various parishes to remove both the dust from the houses and the mud from the streets; the men in their employ are indiscriminately engaged in these two diverse occupations, collecting the dust to-day, and often cleansing the streets on the morrow, and are designated either dustmen or scavengers, according to their particular avocation at the moment. The case is somewhat different, however, with respect to the nightmen. There is no such thing as a contract with the parish for removing the nightsoil. This is done by private agreement with the landlord of the premises whence the soil has to be removed. When a cesspool requires emptying, the occupying tenant communicates with the landlord, who makes an arrangement with a dust-contractor or sweep-nightman for this purpose. This operation is totally distinct from the regular or daily labour of the dust-contractor's men, who receive extra pay for it; sometimes one set go out at night and sometimes another, according either to the selection of the master or the inclination of the men. There are, however, some dutsmen who have never been at work as nightmen, and could not be induced to do so, from an invincible antipathy to the employment; still, such instances are few, for the men generally go whenever they can, and occasionally engage in night work for employers unconnected with their masters.

There are four different modes of payment prevalent among the several labourers employed at the metropolitan dust-yards:—(1) by the day; (2) by the piece or load; (3) by the lump; (4) by perquisites.

1st. The foreman of the yard, where the master does not perform this duty himself, is generally one of the regular dustmen picked out by the master, for this purpose. He is paid the sum of 2*s*. 6*d*. per day, or 15*s*. per week.

2nd. The gangers or collectors are generally paid 8*d*. per load for every load they bring into the yard. This is, of course, piece work, for the more hours the men work the more loads will they be enabled to bring, and the more pay will they receive.

3rd. The loaders of the carts for shipment are the same persons as those who collect the dust, but thus employed for the time being. The pay for this work is by the 'piece' also, 2*d*. per chaldron between four persons being the usual rate, or ½*d*. per man. The men so engaged have no perquisites.

4th. The carriers of cinders to the cinder heap. I have mentioned that, ranged round the sifters in the dust-yard, are a number of baskets, into which are put the various things found among the dust. The cinders and old bricks are the property of the master, and to remove them to their proper heaps boys are employed by him at 1*s*. per day. These boys are almost universally the children of dustmen and sifters at work in the yard, and thus not only help to increase the earnings of the family, but qualify themselves to become the dustmen of a future day.

5th. The hill-man or hill-woman. The hill-man enters into an agreement with the contractor to sift *all* the dust in the yard throughout the year at so much per load and perquisites. The usual sum per load is 6*d*. The perquisites of the hill-man or hill-woman, are rags, bones, pieces of old metal, old tin or iron vessels, old boots and shoes, and one-half of the money, jewellery, or other valuables that may be found by the sifters.

The hill-man or hill-woman employs the following persons, and pays them at the following rates.

1st. The sifters are paid 1*s*. per day when employed.

2nd. 'The fillers-in,' or shovellers of dust into the sieves of sifters, are in general any poor fellows who may be straggling about in search of employment. They are sometimes, however, the grown-up boys of dustmen, not yet permanently engaged by the contractor. These are paid 2*s*. per day for their labour.

3rd. The little fellows, the children of the dustmen, who follow their mothers to the yard, and help them to pick rags, bones, &c., out of the sieve and put them into the baskets, as soon as they are able to carry a basket between two of them to the separate heaps, are paid 3*d*. or 4*d* per day for this work by the hill-man.

The wages of the dustmen have been increased within the last seven years from 6*d*. per load to 8*d*. among the large contractors—the 'small masters,' however, still continue to pay 6*d*. per load. This increase in the rate of remuneration was owing to the men complaining to the commisioners that they were not able to live upon what they earned at 6*d*.; an enquiry was made into the truth of the men's assertion, and the result was that the commissioners decided upon letting the contracts to such parties only as would undertake to pay a fair price to their workmen.

The dustmen are, generally speaking, an hereditary race; when children, they are reared in the dust-yard, and are habituated to the work gradually as they grow up, after which, almost as a natural consequence, they follow the business for the remainder of their lives. These may be said to be born-and-bred dustmen. The numbers of the regular men are, however, from time to time recruited from the ranks of the many ill-paid labourers with which London abounds. When hands are wanted for any special occasion an employer has only to go to any of the dock-gates, to find at all times hundreds of starving wretches anxiously watching for the chance of getting something to do, even at the rate of 4*d*. per hour. As the operation of emptying a dust-bin requires only the ability to handle a shovel, which every labouring man can manage, all workmen, however unskilled, can at once engage in the occupation; and it often happens that the men thus casually employed remain at the calling for the remainder of their lives. There are no houses of call whence the men are taken on when wanting work. There are certainly public-houses, which are denominated houses of call, in the neighbourhood of every dust-yard, but these are merely the drinking shops of the men, whither they resort of an evening after the labour of the day is accomplished, and whence they are furnished in the course of the afternoon with beer; but such houses cannot be said to constitute the dustman's 'labour-market,' as in the tailoring and other trades, they being never resorted to as hiring-places, but rather used by the men only when hired. If a master have not enough 'hands' he usually inquires among his men, who mostly know some who—owing, perhaps, to the failure of their previous master in getting his usual contract—are only casually employed at other places. Such men are immediately engaged in preference to others; but if these cannot be found, the contractors at once have recourse to the system already stated.

The manner in which the dust is collected is very simple. The 'filler' and the 'carrier' perambulate the streets with a heavily-built high box cart, which is mostly coated with a thick crust of filth, and drawn by a clumsy-looking horse. These men used, before the passing of the late Street Act, to ring a dull-sounding bell so as to give notice to housekeepers of their approach, but now they merely cry, in a hoarse unmusical voice, 'Dust oy-eh!' Two men accompany the cart, which is furnished with a short ladder and two shovels and baskets. These baskets one of the men fills from the dust-bin, and then helps them alternately, as fast as they are filled, upon the shoulder of the other man, who carries them one by one to the cart, which is placed immediately alongside the pavement in front of the house where they are at work. The carrier mounts up the side of the cart by means of the ladder, discharges into it the contents of the basket on his shoulder, and then returns below for the other basket which his mate has filled for him in the interim. This process is pursued till all is cleared away, and repeated at different houses till the cart is fully loaded; then the men make the best of their way to the dust-yard, where they shoot the contents of the cart on to the heap, and again proceed on their regular rounds.

The dustmen, in their appearance, very much resemble the waggoners of the coal-merchants. They generally wear knee-breeches, with ankle boots or gaiters, short smockfrocks or coarse grey jackets, and fantail hats. In one particular, however, they are at first sight distinguishable from the coal-merchants' men, for the latter are invariably black from coal dust, while the dust-men, on the contrary, are grey with ashes.

In their personal appearance the dustmen are mostly tall stalwart fellows; there is nothing sickly-looking about them, and yet a considerable part of their lives is passed in the yards and in the midst of effluvia most offensive, and, if we believe 'zymotic theorists,' as unhealthy to those unaccustomed to them; nevertheless, the children, who may be said to be reared in the yard and to have inhaled the stench of the dust-heap with their first breath, are healthy and strong.

In London, the dustmen boast that, during both the recent visitations of the cholera, they were altogether exempt from the disease. 'Look at that fellow, sir!' said one of the dust-contractors to me, pointing to his son, who was a stout red-cheeked young man of about twenty. 'Do you see anything ailing about him? Well, he has been in the yard since he was born. There stands my house just at the gate, so you see he hadn't far to travel, and when quite a child he used to play and root away here among the dust all his time. I don't think he ever had a day's illness in his life. The people about the yard are all used to the smell and don't complain about it. It's all stuff and nonsense, all this talk about dust-yards being unhealthy. I've never done anything else all my days and I don't think I look very ill. I shouldn't wonder now but what I'd be set down as being fresh from the sea-side by those very fellows that write all this trash about a matter that they don't know just *that* about;' and he snapped his fingers contemptuously in the air, and, thrusting them into his breeches pockets, strutted about, apparently satisfied that he had the best of the argument. He was, in fact, a stout, jolly, red-faced man. Indeed, the dustmen, as a class, appear to be healthy, strong men, and extraordinary instances of longevity are common among them. I heard of one dustman who lived to be 115 years; another, named Wood, died at 100; and the well-known Richard Tyrrell died only a short time back at the advanced age of 97. The misfortune is, that we have no large series of facts on this subject, so that the longevity and health of the dustmen might be compared with those of other classes.

In almost all their habits the Dustmen are similar to the Costermongers, with the exception that they seem to want their cunning and natural quickness, and that they have little or no predilection for gaming. Costermongers, however, are essentially traders, and all trade is a species of gambling—the risking of a certain sum of money to obtain more; hence spring, perhaps, the gambling propensities of low traders, such as costers, and Jew clothes-men; and hence, too, that natural sharpness which characterizes the same classes. The dustmen, on the contrary, have regular employment and something like regular wages, and therefore rest content with what they can earn in their usual way of business.

Very few of them understand cards, and I could not learn that they ever play at 'pitch and toss.' I remarked, however, a number of parallel lines such as are used for playing 'shove halfpenny,' on a deal table in the tap-room frequented by them. The great amusement of their evenings seems to be, to smoke as many pipes of tobacco and drink as many pots of beer as possible.

One-half, at least, of the dustmen's earnings, is, I am assured, expended on drink, both man and woman assisting in squandering their money in this way. They usually live in rooms for which they pay from 1s. 6d. to 2s. per week rent, three or four dust-men and their wives frequently lodging in the same house. Those rooms are cheerless-looking, and almost unfurnished—and are always situated in some low street or lane not far from the dust-yard. The men have rarely any clothes but those in which they work. For their breakfast the dustmen on their rounds mostly go to some cheap coffee-house, where they get a pint or half-pint of coffee, taking their bread with them as a matter of economy. Their midday meal is taken in the public-house, and is almost always bread and cheese and beer, or else a saveloy or a piece of fat pork or bacon, and at night they mostly 'wind up' by deep potations at their favourite house of call.

There are many dustmen now advanced in years, born and reared at the East-end of London, who have never in the whole course of their lives been as far west as Temple-bar, who know nothing whatever of the affairs of the country, and who have never attended a place of worship. As an instance of the extreme ignorance of these people, I may mention that I was furnished by one of the contractors with the address of a dustman whom his master considered to be one of the most intelligent men in his employ. Being desirous of hearing his statement from his own lips I sent for the man, and after some conversation with him was proceeding to note down what he said, when the moment I opened my note-book and took the pencil in my hand, he started up, exclaiming,—'No, no! I'll have none of that there work—I'm not such a b—— fool as you takes me to be—I doesn't understand it, I tells you, and I'll not have it, now that's plain;'—and so saying he ran out of the room, and descended the entire flight of stairs in two jumps. I followed him to explain, but unfortunately the pencil was still in one hand and the book in the other, and immediately I made my appearance at the door he took to his heels again, with three others who seemed to be waiting for him there. One of the most

difficult points in my labours is to make such men as these comprehend the object or use of my investigations.

Among 20 men whom I met in one yard, there were only five
who could read, and only two out of that five could write, even
imperfectly. These two are looked up to by their companions as
prodigies of learning and are listened to as oracles, on all occasions,
being believed to understand every subject thoroughly. It need
hardly be added, however, that their acquirements are of the most
meagre character.

The dustmen are very partial to a song, and always prefer one
of the doggerel street ballads, with what they call a 'jolly chorus'
in which, during their festivities, they all join with stentorian
voices. At the conclusion there is usually a loud stamping of feet
and rattling of quart pots on the table, expressive of their approbation.

The dustmen never frequent the twopenny hops, but sometimes
make up a party for the 'theaytre.' They generally go in a body
with their wives, if married, and their 'gals,' if single. They are
always to be found in the gallery, and greatly enjoy the melo-
dramas performed at the second-class minor theatress, especially
if there be plenty of murdering scenes in them. The Garrick,
previous to its being burnt, was a favourite resort of the East-end
dustmen. Since that period they have patronized the Pavilion and
the City of London.

The politics of the dustman are on a par with their literary
attainments—they cannot be said to have any. I cannot say that
they are Chartists, for they have no very clear knowledge of what
'the charter' requires. They certainly have a confused notion that
it is something against the Government, and that the enactment
of it would make them all right; but as to the nature of the benefits
which it would confer upon them, or in what manner it would be
likely to operate upon their interest, they have not, as a body,
the slightest idea. They have a deep-rooted antipathy to the police,
the magistrates, and all connected with the administration of
justice, looking upon them as their natural enemies. They associate
with none but themselves; and in the public-houses where they
resort there is a room set apart for the special use of the 'dusties,'
as they are called, where no others are allowed to intrude, except
introduced by one of themselves, or at the special desire of the

majority of the party, and on such occasions the stranger is treated with great respect and consideration.

As to the morals of these people, it may easily be supposed that they are not of an over-strict character. One of the contractors said to me, 'I'd just trust one of them as far as I could fling a bull by the tail; *but then*,' he added, with a callousness that proved the laxity of discipline among the men was due more to his neglect of his duty to them than from any special perversity on their parts, *'that's none of my business; they do my work, and that's all I want with them, and all I care about.* You see they're not like other people, they're reared to it. Their fathers before them were dustmen, and when lads they go into the yard as sifters, and when they grow up they take to the shovel, and go out with the carts. They learn all they know in the dust-yards, and you may judge from that what their learning is likely to be. If they find anything among the dust you may be sure that neither you nor I will ever hear anything about it; ignorant as they are, they know a little too much for that. They know, as well as here and there one, where the dolly-shop is; *but as I said before, that's none of my business. Let every one look out for themselves, as I do, and then they need not care for any one.*

'As to their women,' continued the master, 'I don't trouble my head about such things. I believe the dustmen are as good to them as other men; and I'm sure their wives would be as good as other women, if they only had the chance of the best. But you see they're all such fellows for drink that they spend most of their money that way, and then starve the poor women, and knock them about at a shocking rate, so that they have the life of dogs, or worse. I don't wonder at anything they do. Yes, they're all married, as far as I know; that is, they live together as man and wife, though they're not very particular, certainly, about the ceremony. The fact is, a regular dustman don't understand much about such matters, and, I believe, don't care much, either.'

From all I could learn on this subject, it would appear that, for one dustman that is married, 20 live with women, but remain constant to them; indeed, both men and women abide faithfully by each other, and for this reason—the woman earns nearly half as much as the men. If the men and women were careful and prudent, they might, I am assured, live well and comfortable; but by far the greater portion of the earnings of both go to the publican, for I am informed, on competent authority, that a dustman will not think of sitting down for a spree without his woman. The children, as soon as they are able to go into the yard, help their mothers in picking out the rags, bones, &c., from the sieve, and in putting them in the basket. They are never sent to school, and as soon as they are sufficiently strong are mostly employed in some capity or other by the contractor, and in due time become dust-men themselves. Some of the children, in the neighbourhood of the river, are mud-larks, and others are bone-grubbers and rag-gatherers, on a small scale; neglected and thrown on their own resources at an early age, without any but the most depraved to guide them, it is no wonder to find that many of them turn thieves. To this state of the case there are, however, some few exceptions.

I visited a large dust-yard at the east end of London, for the purpose of getting a statement from one of the men. My informant was, at the time of my visit, shovelling the sifted soil from one of the lesser heaps, and, by a great effort of strength and activity, pitching each shovel-full to the top of a lofty mound, somewhat resembling a pyramid. Opposite to him stood a little woman, stoutly made, and with her arms bare above the elbow; she was his partner in the work, and was pitching shovel-full for shovel-full with him to the summit of the heap. She wore an old soiled cotton gown, open in front, and tucked up behind in the fashion of the last century. She had clouts of old rags tied round her ankles to prevent the dust from getting into her shoes, a sort of coarse towel fastened in front for an apron, and a red handkerchief bound tightly round her head. In this trim she worked away, and not only kept pace with the man, but often threw two shovels for his one, although he was a tall, powerful fellow. She smiled when she saw me noticing her, and seemed to continue her work with greater assiduity. I learned that she was deaf, and spoke so indistinctly that no stranger could understand her. She had also a defect in her sight, which latter circumstance had compelled her to abandon the sifting, as she could not well distinguish the various articles found in the dust-heap. The poor creature had therefore taken to the shovel, and now works with it every day, doing the labour of the strongest men.

OF THE LONDON SEWERAGE
AND SCAVENGERY

THE subject I have now to treat—principally as regards street-labour, but generally in its sanitary, social, and economical bearings—may really be termed vast. It is of the cleansing of a capital city, with its thousands of miles of streets and roads *on* the surface, and its thousands of miles of sewers and drains *under* the surface of the earth.

STATEMENT OF A 'REGULAR SCAVENGER'

THE following statement of his business, his sentiments, and, indeed, of the subjects which concerned him, or about which he was questioned, was given to me by a street-sweeper, so he called himself, for I have found some of these men not to relish the appellation of 'scavager.' He was a short, sturdy, somewhat red-faced man, without anything particular in his appearance to distinguish him from the mass of mere labourers, but with the sodden and sometimes dogged look of a man contented in his ignorance, and—for it is not a very uncommon case—rather proud of it.

'I don't know how old I am,' he said—I have observed, by the by, that there is not any excessive vulgarity in these men's tones or accent so much as grossness in some of their expressions—'and I can't see what that consarns any one, as I's old enough to have a jolly rough beard, and so can take care of myself. I should think so. My father was a sweeper, and I wanted to be a waterman, but father—he hasn't been dead long—didn't like the thoughts on it, as he said they was all drownded one time or 'nother; so I ran away and tried my hand as a Jack-in-the-water, but I was starved back in a week, and got a h——of a clouting. After that I sifted a bit in a dust-yard, and helped in any way; and I was sent to help at and larn honey-pot and other pot making, at Deptford; but honey-pots was a great thing in the business. Master's foreman married a relation of mine, some way or other. I never tasted honey, but I've heered it's like sugar and butter mixed. The pots was often wanted to look like foreign pots; I don't know nothing what was meant by it; some b——dodge or other. No, the trade didn't suit me at all, master, so I left. I don't know why it didn't suit me; cause it didn't. Just then, father had hurt his hand and arm, in a jam again' a cart, and so, as I was a big lad, I got to take his place, and gave every satisfaction to Mr.——. Yes, he was a contractor and a great man. I can't say as I knows how contracting's done; but it's a bargain atween man and man. So I got on. I'm now looked on as a stunning good workman, I can tell you.

Well, I can't say as I thinks sweeping the streets is hard work. I'd rather sweep two hours than shovel one. It tires one's arms and back so, to go on shovelling. You can't change, you see, sir, and the same parts keeps getting gripped more and more. Then you must mind your eye, if you're shovelling slop into a cart, perticler so; or some feller may run off with a complaint that he's been splashed o' purpose. *Is* a man eveer splashed o' purpose? No, sir, not as I knows on, in course not. [Laughing.] Why should he?

The streets *must* be done as they're done now. It always was so, and will always be so. Did I ever hear what London streets were like a thousand years ago? It's nothing to me, but they must have been like what they is now. Yes, there was always streets, or how was people that has tin to get their coals taken to them, and how was the public-houses to get their beer? It's talking nonsense, talking that way, a-asking sich questions.' [As the scavenger seemed likely to lose his temper, I changed the subject of conversation].

'Yes,' he continued, 'I have good health. I never had a doctor but twice; once was for a hurt, and the t'other I won't tell on. Well, I think nightwork's healthful enough, but I'll not say so much for it as you may hear some on 'em say. I don't like it, but I do it when I's obligated, under a necessity. It pays one as overwork; and werry like more one's in it, more one may be suited. I reckon no men works harder nor sich as me. O, as to poor journeymen tailors and sich like, I knows they'se stunning badly off, and many of their masters is the hardest of beggers. I have a nephew as works for a Jew slop, but I don't reckon that *work*; anybody might do it. You think not, sir? Werry well, it's all the same. No, I won't say as I could make a veskit, but I've sowed my own buttons on to one afore now.

'Yes, I've heered on the Board of Health. They've put down some night-yards, and if they goes on putting down more, what's to become of the night-soil? I can't think what they're up to;

but if they don't touch wages, it may be all right in the end on it. I don't know that them there consarns does touch wages, but one's naterally afeard on 'em. I could read a little when I was a child, but I can't now for want of practice, or I might know more about it. I yarns my money gallows hard, and requires support to do hard work, and if wages goes down, one's strength goes down. I'm a man as understands what things belongs. I was once out of work, through a mistake, for a good many weeks, perhaps five or six or more; I larned then what short grub meant. I got a drop of beer and a crust sometimes with men as I knowed, or I might have dropped in the street. What did I do to pass my time when I was out of work? Sartinly the days seemed very long; but I went about and called at dust-yards, till I didn't like to go too often; and I met men I 'd know'd at tap-rooms, and spent time that way, and axed if there was any openings for work. I've been out of collar odd weeks now and then, but when this happened, I'd been on slack work a goodish bit, and was bad for rent three weeks and more. My rent was 2s. a week then; its 1s. 9d. now, and my own traps.

'No, I can't say I was sorry when I was forced to be idle that way, that I hadn't kept up my reading, nor tried to keep it up, because I couldn't then have settled down my mind to read; I know I couldn't. I likes to hear the paper read well enough, if I's resting; but old Bill, as often wolunteers to read, has to spell the hard words so, that one can't tell what the devil he's reading about. I never heers anything about books; I never heered of Robinson Crusoe, if it wasn't once at the Wic. [Victoria Theatre]; I think there was some sich a name there. He lived on a deserted island, did he, sir, all by hisself? Well, I think, now you mentions it, I have heered on him. But one needn't believe all one hears, whether out of books or not. I don't know much good that ever anybody as I knows ever got out of books; they're fittest for idle people. Sartinly I've seen working people reading in coffee-shops; but they might as well be resting theirselves to keep up their strength. Do I think so? I'm sure on it, master. I sometimes spends a few browns a-going to the play; mostly about Christmas. It's werry fine and grand at the Wic., that's the place I goes to most; both the pantomimers and t'other things is werry stunning. I can't say how much I spends a year in plays; I keeps no account; perhaps

VIEW OF A DUST YARD

THE LONDON SCAVENGER

5*s*. or so in a year, including expenses, sich as beer, when one goes out after a stopper on the stage. I don't keep no accounts of what I gets, or what I spends, it would be no use; money comes and it goes, and it often goes a d——d sight faster than it comes; so it seems to me, though I ain't debt just at this time.

'I never goes to any church or chapel. Sometimes I hasn't clothes as is fit, and I s'pose I couldn't be admitted into sich fine places in my working dress. I was once in a church, but felt queer, as one does in them strange places, and never went again. They're fittest for rich people. Yes, I've heered about religion and about God Almighty. *What* religion have I heered on? Why, the regular religion. I'm satisfied with what I knows and feels about it' and that's enough about it. I came to tell you about trade and work, because Mr. —— told me it might do good; but religion hasn't nothing to do with it. Yes, Mr.——'s a good master, and a religious man; but I've known masters as didn't care a d—n for religion, as good as him; and so you see it comes to much the same thing. I cares nothing about politics neither; but I'm a chartist.

'I'm not a married man. I was a-going to be married to a young woman as lived with me a goodish bit as my housekeeper' [this he said very demurely]; 'but she went to the hopping to yarn a few shillings for herself, and never came back. I heered that she'd taken up with an Irish hawker, but I can't say as to the rights on it. Did I fret about her? Perhaps not; but I was wexed.

'I'm sure I can't say what I spends my wages in I sometimes makes 12*s*. 6*d*. a week, and sometimes better than 21*s*. with night-work. I suppose grub costs 1*s*. a day, and beer 6*d*.; but I keeps no accounts. I buy ready-cooked meat; often cold b'iled beef, and eats it at any tap-room. I have meat every day; mostly more than once a day. Wegetables I don't care about, only ingans and cabbage, if you can get it smoking hot, with plenty of pepper. The rest of my tin goes for rent and baccy and togs, and a little drop of gin now and then.'

There are yet accounts of habitations, statements of wages, &c., &c., to be given in connection with men working for the honourable, masters, before proceeding to the scurf-trades.

The working scavengers usually reside in the neighbourhood of the dust-yards, occupying 'second-floor backs,' kitchens (where the entire house is sublet, a system often fraught with great extortion), or garrets; they usually, and perhaps always, when married, or what they consider 'as good,' have their own furniture. The rent runs from 1*s*. 6*d*. to 2*s*. 3*d*. weekly, an average being 1*s*. 9*d*. or 1*s*. 10*d*. One room which I was in was but barely furnished,— a sort of dresser, serving also for a table; a chest; three chairs (one almost bottomless): an old turn-up bedstead, a Dutch clock, with the minute-hand broken, or as the scavenger very well called it when he saw me looking at it, 'a stump;' an old 'corner cupboard,' and some pots and domestic utensils in a closet without a door, but retaining a portion of the hinges on which a door had swung. The rent was 1*s*. 10*d* with a frequent intimation that it ought to be 2*s*. The place was clean enough, and the scavenger seemed proud of it, assuring me that his old woman (wife or concubine) was 'a good sort,' and kept things as nice as ever she could, washing everything herself, where 'other old women lushed.' The only ornaments in the room were three profiles of children, cut in black paper and pasted upon white card, tacked to the wall over the fire-place, for mantel-shelf there was none, while one of the three profiles, that of the eldest child (then dead), was 'framed,' with a glass, and a sort of bronze or 'cast' frame, costing, I was told, 15*d*. This was the apartment of a man in regular employ (with but a few exceptions).

The diet of the regular working scavenger (or nightman) seems generally to differ from that of mechanics, and perhaps of other working men, in the respect of his being fonder of salt and *strong-flavoured* food. I have before made the same remark concerning the diet of the poor generally. I do not mean, however, that the scavengers are fond of such animal food as is called 'high,' for I did not hear that nightmen or scavengers were more tolerant of what approached putridity than other labouring men, despite their calling, might sicken at the rankness of some haunches of venison; but they have a great relish for highly-salted cold boiled beef, bacon, or pork, with a saucer-full of red pickled cabbage, or dingy-looking pickled onions, or one or two big, strong, raw onions, of which most of them seem as fond as Spaniards of garlic. This sort of meat, sometimes profusely mustarded, is often eaten in the beer-shops with thick 'shives' of bread, cut into big mouthfuls with a clasp pocket-knife, while vegetables, unless indeed the beer-shop can supply a plate of smoking hot potatoes, are uncared for.

The drink is usually beer. The same style of eating and the same kind of food characterize the scavenger and nightman, when taking his meal at home with his wife and family; but so irregular, and often of necessity, are these men's hours, that they may be said to have no homes, merely places to sleep or doze in.

A working scavenger and nightman calculated for me his expenses in eating and drinking, and other necessaries, for the previous week. He had earned 15s., but 1s. of this went to pay off an advance of 5s. made to him by the keeper of a beer-shop, or, as he called it, a 'jerry.'

	Daily.	Weekly.	
	d.	*s.*	*d.*
Rent of an unfurnished room		1	9
Washing (average)			3
[The man himself washed the dress in which he worked, and generally washed his own stockings.]			
Shaving (when twice a week)			1
Tobacco	1		7
[Short pipes are given to these men at the beer-shops, or public-houses which they 'use.']			
Beer	4	2	4
[He usually spent more than 4d. a day in beer, he said, 'it was only a pot;' but this week more beer than usual had been given to him in nightwork.]			
Gin	2	1	2
[The same with gin.]			
Cocoa (pint at a coffee-shop)	1½		10½
Bread (quartern loaf) (sometimes 5½d.) . . .	6	3	6
Boiled salt beef (¾ lb. or ½ lb. daily, 'as happened,' for two meals, 6d. per pound, (average) .	4	2	4
Pickles or Onions	0¼		1¾
Butter			1
Soap			1
		13	2¼

Perhaps this informant was excessive in his drink. I believe he was so; the others not drinking so much regularly. The odd 9d., he told me, he paid to 'a snob,' because he said he was going to send his half-boots to be mended.

OF THE GENERAL CHARACTERISTICS OF THE WORKING CHIMNEY-SWEEPERS

THERE are many reasons why the chimney-sweepers have ever been a distinct and peculiar class. They have long been looked down upon as the lowest order of workers, and treated with contumely by those who were but little better than themselves. The peculiar nature of their work giving them not only a filthy appearance, but an offensive smell, of itself, in a manner, prohibited them from associating with other working men; and the natural effect of such proscription has been to compel them to herd together apart from others, and to acquire habits and peculiarities of their own widely differing from the characteristics of the rest of the labouring classes.

Sweepers, however, have not from this cause generally been an hereditary race—that is, they have not become sweepers from father to son for many generations. Their numbers were, in the days of the climbing boys, in most instances increased by parish apprentices, the parishes usually adopting that mode as the cheapest and easiest of freeing themselves from a part of the burden of juvenile pauperism. The climbing boys, but more especially the unfortunate parish apprentices, were almost always cruelly used, starved, beaten, and over-worked by their masters, and treated as outcasts by all with whom they came in contact: there can be no wonder, then, that, driven in this manner from all other society, they gladly availed themselves of the companionship of their fellow-sufferers; quickly imbibed all their habits and peculiarities; and, perhaps, ended by becoming themselves the most tyrannical masters to those who might happen to be placed under their charge.

Notwithstanding the disrepute in which sweepers have ever been held, there are many classes of workers beneath them in intelligence. All the tribe of finders and collectors (with the exception of the dredgermen, who are an observant race, and the sewer-hunters, who, from the danger of their employment, are compelled to exercise their intellects) are far inferior to them in this respect; and they are clever fellows compared to many of the dustmen and scavengers. The great mass of the agricultural labourers are known to be almost as ignorant as the beasts they drive; but the sweepers, from whatever cause it may arise, are known, in many instances, to be shrewd, intelligent, and active.

But there is much room for improvement among the operative chimney-sweepers. Speaking of the men generally, I am assured that there is scarcely one out of ten who can either read or write. One man in Chelsea informed me that some ladies, in connection with the Rev. Mr. Cadman's church, made an attempt to instruct the sweepers of the neighbourhood in reading and writing; but the master sweepers grew jealous, and became afraid lest their men should get too knowing for them. When the time came, therefore, for the men to prepare for the school, the masters always managed to find out some job which prevented them from attending at the appointed time, and the consequence was that the benevolent designs of the ladies were frustrated.

The sweepers, as a class, in almost all their habits, bear a strong resemblance to the costermongers. The habit of going about in search of their employment has, of itself, implanted in many of them the wandering propensity peculiar to street people. Many of the better-class costermongers have risen into coal-shed men and greengrocers, and become settled in life; in like manner the better-class sweepers have risen to be masters, and, becoming settled in a locality, have gradually obtained the trade of the neighbourhood; then, as their circumstances improved, they have been able to get horses and carts, and become nightmen; and there are many of them at this moment men of wealth, comparatively speaking. The great body of them, however, retain in all their force their original characteristics; the masters themselves, although shrewd and sensible men, often betray their want of education, and are in no way particular as to their expressions, their language being made up, in a great measure, of the terms peculiar to the costermongers, especially the denominations of the various sorts of money. I met with some sweepers, however, whose language was that in ordinary use, and their manners not vulgar. I might specify one, who although a workhouse orphan and apprentice, a harshly-treated climbing-boy, is now prospering as a sweeper and nightman, is a regular attendant at all meetings to promote the good of the poor, and a zealous ragged-school teacher, and teetotaller.

When such men are met with, perhaps the class cannot be looked upon as utterly cast away, although the need of reformation in the habits of the working sweepers is extreme, and especially in respect of drinking, gambling, and dirt. The journeymen (who have often a good deal of leisure) and the single-handed men are—in the great majority of cases at least—addicted to drinking, beer being their favourite beverage, either because it is the cheapest or that they fancy it the most suitable for washing away the sooty particles which find their way to their throats. These men gamble also, but with this proviso—they seldom play for money; but when they meet in their usual houses of resort—two famous ones are in Back C——lane and S—— street, Whitechapel—they spend their time and what money they may have in tossing for beer, till they are either drunk or penniless. Such men present the appearance of having just come out of a chimney. There seems never to have been any attempt made by them to wash the soot off their faces. I am informed that there is scarcely one of them who has a second shirt or any change of clothes, and that they wear their garments night and day till they literally rot, and drop in fragments from their backs. Those who are not employed as journeymen by the masters are frequently whole days without food, especially in summer, when the work is slack; and it usually happens that those who are what is called 'knocking about on their own account' seldom or never have a farthing in their pockets in the morning, and may, perhaps, have to travel till evening before they get a threepenny or sixpenny chimney to sweep. When night comes, and they meet their companions, the tossing and drinking again commences; they again get drunk; roll home to wherever it may be, to go through the same routine on the morrow; and this is the usual tenor of their lives, whether earning 5s. or 20s a week.

The chimney-sweepers generally are fond of drink; indeed their calling, like that of dustmen, is one of those which naturally lead to it. The men declare they are ordered to drink gin and smoke as much as they can, in order to rid the stomach of the soot they may have swallowed during their work.

Washing among chimney-sweepers seems to be much more frequent than it was. In the evidence before Parliament it was stated that some of the climbing-boys were washed once in six months, some once a week, some once in two or three months.

I do not find it anywhere stated that any of these children were never washed at all; but from the tenor of the evidence it may be reasonably concluded that such was the case.

A master sweeper, who was in the habit of bathing at the Marylebone baths once and sometimes twice a week, assured me that, although many now eat and drink and sleep sooty, washing is more common among his class than when he himself was a climbing-boy. He used then to be stripped, and compelled to step into a tub, and into water sometimes too hot and sometimes too cold, while his mistress, to use his own word, *scoured* him. Judging from what he had seen and heard, my informant was satisfied that, from 30 to 40 years ago, climbing-boys, with a very few exceptions, were but seldom washed; and then it was looked upon by them as a most disagreeable operation, often, indeed, as a species of punishment. Some of the climbing-boys used to be taken by their masters to bathe in the Serpentine many years ago: but one boy was unfortunately drowned, so that the children could hardly be coerced to go into the water afterwards.

There are some curious customs among the London sweepers which deserve notice. Their May-day festival is among the best known. The most intelligent of the masters tell me that they have taken this 'from the milkmen's garland.' Formerly, say they, on the first of May the milkmen of London went through the streets, performing a sort of dance, for which they received gratuities from their customers. The music to which they danced was simply brass plates mounted on poles, from the circumference of which plates depended numerous bells of different tones, according to size; these poles were adorned with leaves and flowers, indicative of the season, and may have been a relic of one of the ancient pageants or mummeries.

The sweepers, however, by adapting themselves more to the rude taste of the people, appear to have completely supplanted the milkmen, who are now never seen in pageantry.

With reference to the May-day festival of the sweepers Strutt writes in 'Sports and Pastimes of the People of England':—'The chimney-sweepers of London have also singled out the first of May for their festival, at which time they parade the streets in companies, disguised in various manners. Their dresses are usually decorated with gilt paper and other mock fineries; they have their shovels and brushes in their hands, which they rattle one upon the other; and to this rough music they jump about in imitation of dancing. Some of the larger companies have a fiddler with them, and a Jack in the Green, as well as a Lord and Lady of the May, who follow the minstrel with great stateliness, and dance as occasion requires. The Jack in the Green is a piece of pageantry consisting of a hollow frame of wood or wicker-work, made in the form of a sugar-loaf, but open at the bottom, and sufficiently large and high to recieve a man. The frame is covered with green leaves and bunches of flowers, interwoven with each other, so that the man within may be completely concealed, who dances with his companions; and the populace are mightily pleased with the oddity of the moving pyramid.'

Since the date of the above, the sweepers have greatly improved on their pageant, substituting for the fiddle the more noisy and appropriate music of the street-showman's drum and pipes, and adding to their party several diminutive imps, no doubt as representatives of the climbing-boys, clothed in caps, jackets, and trousers, thickly covered with party-coloured shreds. These still make a show of rattling their shovels and brushes, but the clatter is unheard alongside the thunders of the drum. In this manner they go through the various streets for three days, obtaining money at various places, and on the third night hold a feast at one of their favourite public-houses, where all the sooty tribes resort, and, in company with their wives or girls, keep up their festivity till the next morning. I find that this festival is beginning to disappear in many parts of London, but it still holds its ground, and is as highly enjoyed as ever, in all the eastern localities of the metropolis.

It is but seldom that any of the large masters go out on May-day; this custom is generally confined to the little masters and their men. The time usually spent on these occasions is four days, during which as much as from 2*l.* to 4*l.* a day is collected; the sums obtained on the three first days are divided according to the several kinds of work performed. But the proceeds of fourth day are devoted to a supper. The average gains of the several performers on these occasions are as follows:—

My lady, who acts as Columbine, and receives   2s. per day.
My lord, who is often the master himself, but
  usually one of the journeymen   .   .   .   .   3s.   ,,
Clown   .   .   .   .   3s.   ,,
Drummer   .   .   .   .   4s.   ,,
Jack in the green, who is often an individual
  acquaintance, and does not belong to the
  trade   .   .   .   .   3s.   ,,
And the boys, who have no term applied to
  them, receive from   .   .   .   .   .   1s. to 1s.6d.   ,,

The share accruing to the boys is often spent in purchasing some article of clothing for them, but the money got by the other individuals is mostly spent in drink.

The sweepers, however, not only go out on May-day, but likewise on the 5th of November. On the last Guy-Fawkes day, I am informed, some of them received not only pence from the public, but silver and gold. 'It was quite a harvest,' they say. One of this class, who got up a gigantic Guy Fawkes and figure of the Pope on the 5th of November, 1850, cleared, I am informed, 10l. over and above all expenses.

OF THE SUBTERRANEAN CHARACTER OF THE SEWERS

In my inquiries among that curious body of men, the 'Sewer Hunters,' I found them make light of any danger, their principal fear being from the attacks of rats in case they became isolated from the gang with whom they searched in common, while they represented the odour as a mere nothing in the way of unpleasantness. But these men pursued only known and (by them) beaten tracks at low water, avoiding any deviation, and so becoming but partially acquainted with the character and direction of the sewers. And had it been otherwise, they are not a class competent to describe what they saw, however keen-eyed after silver spoons.

The following account is derived chiefly from official sources. I may premise that where the deposit is found the greatest, the sewer is in the worst state. This deposit, I find it repeatedly stated, is of a most miscellaneous character. Some of the sewers, indeed, are represented as the dust-bins and dung-hills of the immediate neighbourhood. The deposit has been found to comprise all the ingredients from the breweries, the gas-works, and the several chemical and mineral manufactories; dead dogs, cats, kittens, and rats; offal from slaughter-houses, sometimes even including the entrails of the animals; street-pavement dirt of every variety; vegetable refuse; stable-dung; the refuse of pig-styes; night-soil; ashes; tin kettles and pans (panshreds); broken stoneware, as jars, pitchers, flower-pots, &c.; bricks; pieces of wood; rotten mortar and rubbish of different kinds; and even rags. Our criminal annals of the previous century show that often enough the bodies of murdered men were thrown into the Fleet and other ditches then the open sewers of the metropolis, and if found washed into the Thames, they were so stained and disfigured by the foulness of the contents of these ditches, that recognition was often impossible, so that there could be but one verdict returned—'Found drowned.' Clothes stripped from a murdered person have been, it was authenticated on several occasions in Old Bailey evidence, thrown into the open sewer ditches, when torn and defaced, so that they might not supply evidence of identity. So close is the connection between physical filthiness in public matters and moral wickedness.

The following particulars show the characteristics of the underground London of the sewers. The subterranean surveys were made after the commissions were consolidated.

'An old sewer, running between Great Smith-street and St. Ann-street (Westminster), is a curiosity among sewers, although it is probably only one instance out of many similar construction. that will be discovered in the course of the subterranean survey. The bottom is formed of planks laid upon transverse timbers, 6 inches by 6 inches, about 3 feet apart. The size of the sewer varies in width from 2 to 6 feet, and from 4 to 5 feet in height. The inclination of the bottom is very irregular: there are jumps up at two or three places, and it contains a deposit of filth averaging 9 inches in depth, the sickening smell from which escapes into the houses and yards that drain into it. In many places the side walls have given way for lengths of 10 and 15 feet. Across this sewer timbers have been laid, upon which the external wall of a workshop has been built; the timbers are in a decaying state, and should they give way, the wall will fall into the sewer.'

From the further accounts of this survey, I find that a sewer from the Westminster Workhouse, which was of all shapes and sizes, was in so wretched a condition that the leveller could scarcely work for the thick scum that covered the glasses of the spirit-level in a few minutes after being wiped. 'At the outfall into the Dean-street sewer, it is 3 feet 6 inches by 2 feet 8 inches for a short length. From the end of this, a wide sewer branches in each direction at right angles, 5 feet 8 inches by 5 feet 5 inches. Proceeding to the eastward about 30 feet, a chamber is reached about 30 feet in length, from the roof of which hangings of putrid matter *like stalactites* descend *three feet in length*. At the end of this chamber, the sewer passes under the public privies, the ceilings of which can be seen from it. Beyond this it is not possible to go.'

'In the Lucas-street sewer, where a portion of new work begins and the old terminates, a space of about 10 feet has been covered with boards, which, having broken, a dangerous chasm has been caused immediately under the road.'

'The West-street sewer had one foot of deposit. It was flushed while the levelling party was at work there, and the stream was so rapid that it nearly washed them away, instrument and all.'

There are further accounts of 'deposit,' or of 'stagnant filth,' in other sewers, varying from 6 to 14 inches, but that is insignificant compared to what follows.

The foregoing, then, is the pith of the first authentic account which has appeared in print of the actually surveyed condition of the subterranean ways, over which the super-terranean tides of traffc are daily flowing.

The account I have just given relates to the (former) Westminster and part of Middlesex district on the north bank of the Thames, as ascertained under the Metropolitan Commission. I now give some extracts concerning a similar survey on the south bank, in different and distant directions in the district, once the 'Surrey and Kent.' The Westminster, &c., survey took place in 1848; the Kent and Surrey in 1849. In the one case, 72 miles of sewers were surveyed; in the other, 69½ miles.

'The surveyors (in the Surrey and Kent sewers) find great difficulty in levelling the sewers of this district (I give the words of the Report); for, in the first place, the deposit is *usually* about two feet in depth, and in some cases it amounts to nearly *five feet* of putrid matter. The smell is usually of the most horrible description, the air being so foul that explosion and choke damp are very frequent. On the 12th January we were very nearly losing a whole party by choke damp, the last man being dragged out on his back (through two feet of black foetid deposits) in a state of insensibility. ...Two men of one party had also a narrow escape from drowning in the Alscot-road sewer, Rotherhithe.

'The sewers on the Surrey side are very irregular; even where they are inverted they frequently have a number of steps and inclinations the reverse way, causing the deposit to accumulate in *elongated cesspools*.

'It must be considered very fortunate that the subterranean parties did not first commence on the Surrey side, for if such had been the case, we should most undoubtedly have broken down. When compared with Westminster, the sewers are smaller and more full of deposit; and, bad as the smell is in the sewers in Westminster, it is infinitely worse on the Surrey side.'

Several details are then given, but they are only particulars of the general facts I have stated.

The following, however, are distinct facts concerning this branch of the subject.

In my inquiries among the working scavengers I often heard of their emptying street slop into sewers, and the following extract shows that I was not misinformed:—

'The detritus from the macadamized roads frequently forms a kind of grouting in the sewers so hard that it cannot be removed without hand labour.

'One of the sewers in Whitehall and another in Spring-gardens have from three to four feet of this sort of deposit; and another in Eaton-square was found filled up within a few inches of the "soffit," but it is supposed that the scavengers (scavagers) emptied the road-sweepings down the gully-grate in this instance;' and in other instances, too, there is no doubt—especially at Charing Cross, and the Regent Circus, Piccadilly.

Concerning the sewerage of the most aristocratic parts of the city of Westminster, and of the fashionable squares, &c., to the north of Oxford-street, I glean the following particulars (reported in 1849). They show, at any rate, that the patrician quarters have not been unduly favoured; that there has been no partiality in the construction of the sewerage. In the Belgrave and Eaton-square districts there are many faulty places in the sewers which abound with noxious matter, in many instances stopping up the house drains and 'smelling horribly.' It is much the same in the Grosvenor, Hanover, and Berkeley-square localities (the houses in the squares themselves included). Also in the neighbourhood of Covent-garden, Clare-market, Soho and Fitzroy-squares; while north of Oxford-street, in and about Cavendish, Bryanston, Manchester, and Portman-squares, there is so much rottenness and decay that there is no security for the sewers standing from day to day, and to flush them for the removal of their 'most loathsome deposit' might be 'to bring some of them down altogether.'

One of the accounts of a subterranean survey concludes with the following rather curious statement:—'Throughout the new Paddington district the neighbourhood of Hyde Park Gardens, and the costly squares and streets adjacent, the sewers abound with the foulest deposit, from which the most disgusting effluvium arises; indeed, amidst the whole of the Westminster District of Sewers the *only* little spot which can be mentioned as being in at all a satisfactory state is the Seven Dials.'

I may point out also that these very curious and authenticated accounts by no means bear out the zymotic doctrine of the Board of Health as to the cause of cholera; for where the zymotic influences from the sewers were the worst, in the patrician squares of what has been called Belgravia and Tyburnia, the cholera was the least destructive. This, however, is no reason whatever why the stench should not be stifled.

OF THE RATS IN THE SEWERS

I WILL now state what I have learned from long-experienced men, as to the characteristics of the rats in the sewers. To arrive even at a conjecture as to the numbers of these creatures—now, as it were, the population of the sewers—I found impossible, for no statistical observations have been made on the subject; but all my informants agreed that the number of the animals had been greatly diminished within these four or five years.

In the better-constructed sewers there are no rats. In the old sewers they abound. The sewer rat is the ordinary house or brown rat, excepting at the outlets near the river, and here the water-rat is seen.

The sewer-rat is the common brown or Hanovarian rat, said by the Jacobites to have come in with the first George, and established itself after the fashion of his royal family; and undoubtedly such was about the era of their appearance. One man, who had worked twelve years in the sewers before flushing was general, told me he had never seen but *two* black (or old English) rats; another man, of ten years, experience, had seen but one; others had noted no difference in the rats. I may observe that in my inquiries as to the sale of rats (as a part of the live animals dealt in by a class in the metropolis), I ascertained that in the older granaries, where there were series of floors, there were black as well as brown rats. Great black fellows,' said one man who managed a Bermondsey granary, 'as would frighten a lady into asterisks to see of a sudden.'

The rat is the only animal found in the sewers. I met with no flusherman or other sewer-worker who had ever seen a lizard, toad, or frog there, although the existence of these creatures, in such circumstances, has been presumed. A few live cats find their way into the subterranean channels when a house-drain is being built, or is opened for repairs, or for any purpose, and have been seen by the flushermen, &c., wandering about, looking lost, mewing as if in misery, and avoiding any contact with the sewage. The rats also—for they are not of the water-rat breed—are exceedingly averse to wetting their feet, and 'take to the sewage,' as it was worded to me, only in prospect of danger; that is, they then swim across or along the current to escape with their lives. It is said that when a luckless cat has ventured into the sewers, she is sometimes literally worried by the rats. I could not hear of such an attack having been witnessed by any one; but one intelligent and trustworthy man said, that a few years back (he believed about eight years) he had in one week found the skeletons of two cats in a particular part of an old sewer, 21 feet wide, and in the drains opening into it were perfect colonies of rats, raging with hunger, he had no doubt, because a system of trapping, newly resorted to, had prevented their usual ingress into the houses up the drains. A portion of their fur adhered to the two cats, but the flesh had been eaten from their bones. About that time a troop of rats flew at the feet of another of my informants and would no doubt have maimed him seriously, 'but my boots,' said he, 'stopped the devils.' 'The sewers generally swarms with rats,' said another man. 'I runs away from 'em; I don't like 'em. They in general gets away from us; but in case we comes to a stunt end where there's a wall and no place for' em to get away, and we goes to touch 'em, they fly at us. They've some of 'em as big as good-sized kittens. One of our men caught hold of one the other day by the tail, and he found it trying to release itself, and the tail slipping through his fingers; so he put up his left hand to stop it, and the rat caught hold of his finger, and the man's got an arm now as big as his thigh.' I heard from several that there had been occasionally battles among the rats, one with another.

'Why sir,' said one flusherman, 'as to the number of rats, it ain't possible to say. There hasn't been a census (laughing) taken of them. But I can tell you this—I was one of the first flushermen when flushing came in general—I think it was before Christmas, 1847, under Mr. Roe—and there was cart-loads and cart-loads of drowned rats carried into the Thames. It was in a West Strand *shore* that I saw the most. I don't exactly remember which, but I think Northumberland-street. By a block or a hitch of some sort, there was, I should say, just a bushel of drowned rats stopped at the corner of one of the gates, which I swept into the next stream. I see far fewer drowned rats now than before the *shores* was flushed. They're not so plenty, that's one thing. Perhaps, too, they may have got to understand about flushing, they're that 'cute and manage to keep out of the way. About Newgate-market was at one time the worst for rats. Men couldn't venture into the sewers then, on account of the varmint. It's bad enough still, I hear, but I haven't worked in the City for a few years.'

The rats, from the best information at my command, do not derive much of their sustenance from the matter in the sewers, or only in particular localities. These localities are the sewers neighbouring a connected series of slaughter-houses, as in Newgate-market, Whitechapel, Clare-market, parts adjoining Smithfield-market, &c. There, animal offal being (and having been to a much greater extent five or six years ago) swept into the drains and sewers, the rats find their food. In the sewers, generally, there is little food for them, and none at all in the best-constructed sewers, where there is a regular and sometimes rapid flow, and little or no deposit.

The sewers are these animals' breeding grounds. In them the broods are usually safe from the molestation of men, dogs, or cats. These 'breeding grounds' are sometimes in the holes (excavated by the industry of the rats into caves) which have been formed in the old sewers by a crumbled brick having fallen out. Their nests, however, are in some parts even more frequent in places where old rotting large house-drains or smaller sewers, empty themselves into a first-class sewer. Here, then, the rats breed, and, in spite of precautions, find their way up the drains or pipes, even through the openings into water-closets, into the houses for their food, and almost always at night. Of this fact, builders and those best informed, are confident, and it is proved indirectly by what I have stated as to the deficiency of food for a voracious creature in all the sewers except a few. One man, long in the service of the Commissioners of Sewers, and in different capacities, gave me the following account of what may be called a rat settlement. The statement I found confirmed by other working men, and by superior officers under the same employment.

'Why, sir, in the Milford-lane sewer, a goodish bit before you get to the river, or to the Strand—I can't say how far, a few hundred yards perhaps—I've seen, and reported, what was a regular chamber of rats. If a brick didn't fall out from being rotted, the rats would get it out, and send it among the other rubbish into the sewer, for this place was just the corner of a big drain. I couldn't get into the rat-hole, of course not, but I've brought my lamp to the opening, and—as well as others—have seen it plain. It was an open place like a lot of tunnels, one over another. Like a lot of rabbit burrows in the country—as I've known to be—or like the partitions in the pigeon-houses: one here and another there. The rat-holes, as far as I could tell, were worked one after another. I should say, in moderation, that it was the size of a small room; well, say about 6 yards by 4. I can't say about the height from the lowest tunnel to the highest. I don't see that any one could. Bless you, sir, I've sometimes heerd the rats fighting and squeaking there, like a parcel of drunken Irishmen—I have indeed. Some of them were rare big fellows. If you threw the light of your lamp on them sudden, they'd be off like a shot. Well, I should say, there was 100 pair of rats there—there might be more, besides all their young-uns. If a poor cat strayed into that sewer she dursn't tackle the rats, not she. There's lots of such places, sir, here, and there, and everywhere.'

CROSSING-SWEEPERS

THAT portion of the London street-folk who earn a scanty living by sweeping crossings constitute a large class of the Metropolitan poor. We can scarcely walk along a street of any extent, or pass through a square of the least pretensions to 'gentility,' without meeting one or more of these private scavengers. Crossing-sweeping seems to be one of those occupations which are resorted to as an excuse for begging; and, indeed, as many expressed it to me, 'it was the last chance left of obtaining an honest crust.'

The advantages of crossing-sweeping as a means of livelihood seem to be:

1st, the smallness of the capital required in order to commence the business;

2ndly, the excuse the apparent occupation affords for soliciting gratuities without being considered in the light of a street-beggar;

And 3rdly, the benefits arising from being constantly seen in the same place, and thus exciting the sympathy of the neighbouring householders, till small weekly allowances or 'pensions' are obtained.

The first curious point in connexion with this subject is what constitutes the '*property*,' so to speak, in a crossing, or the *right* to sweep a pathway across a certain thoroughfare. A nobleman, who has been one of Her Majesty's Ministers, whilst conversing with me on the subject of crossing-sweepers, expressed to me the curiosity he felt on the subject, saying that he had noticed some of the sweepers in the same place for years. 'What were the rights of property,' he asked, 'in such cases, and what constituted the title that such a man had to a particular crossing? Why did not the stronger sweeper supplant the weaker? Could a man bequeath a crossing to a son, or present it to a friend? How did he first obtain the spot?'

The answer is, that crossing-sweepers are, in a measure, under the protection of the police. If the accommodation afforded by a well-swept pathway is evident, the policeman on that district will protect the original sweeper of the crossing from the intrusion of a rival. I have, indeed, met with instances of men who, before taking to a crossing, have asked for and obtained permission of the police; and one sweeper, who gave me his statement, had even solicited the authority of the inhabitants before he applied to the inspector at the station-house.

If a crossing have been vacant for some time, another sweeper may take to it; but should the original proprietor again make his appearance, the officer on duty will generally re-establish him. One man to whom I spoke, had fixed himself on a crossing which for years another sweeper had kept clean on the Sunday morning only. A dispute ensued; the one claimant pleading his long Sabbath possession, and the other his continuous everyday service. The quarrel was referred to the police, who decided that he who was oftener on the ground was the rightful owner; and the option was given to the former possessor, that if he would sweep there every day the crossing should be his.

I believe there is only one crossing in London which is in the gift of a householder, and this proprietorship originated in a tradesman having, at his own expense, caused a paved footway to be laid down over the macadamized road in front of his shop, so that his customers might run less chance of dirtying their boots when they crossed over to give their orders.

Some bankers, however, keep a crossing-sweeper, not only to sweep a clean path for the 'clients' visiting house, but to open and shut the doors of the carriages calling at the house.

Concerning the *causes which lead or drive* people to this occupation, they are various. People take to crossing-sweeping either on account of their bodily afflictions, depriving them of the power of performing ruder work, or because the occupation is the last resource left open to them of earning a living, and they considered even the scanty subsistence it yields preferable to that of the workhouse. The greater proportion of crossing-sweepers are those who, from some bodily infirmity or injury, are prevented from a more laborious mode of obtaining their living. Among the bodily infirmities the chief old age, asthma, and rheumatism; and the injuries mostly consist of loss of limbs. Many of the rheumatic sweepers have been bricklayers' labourers.

The classification of crossing-sweepers is not very complex. They may be divided into the *casual* and the *regular*.

By the casual I mean such as pursue the occupation only on certain days in the week, as, for instance, those who make their appearance on the Sunday morning, as well as the boys who, broom in hand, travel about the streets, sweeping before the foot-passengers or stopping an hour at one place, and then, if not fortunate, moving on to another.

The regular crossing-sweepers are those who have taken up their posts at the corners of streets or squares; and I have met with some who have kept to the same spot for more than forty years.

The crossing-sweepers in the squares may be reckoned among the most fortunate of the class. With them the crossing is a kind of stand, where any one requiring their services knows they may be found. These sweepers are often employed by the butlers and servants in the neighbouring mansions for running errands, posting letters, and occasionally helping in the packing-up and removal of furniture or boxes when the family goes out of town. I have met with other sweepers who, from being known for years to the inhabitants, have at last got to be regularly employed at some of the houses to clean knives, boots, windows, &c.

It is not at all an unfrequent circumstance, however, for a sweeper to be in receipt of a weekly sum from some of the inhabitants in the district. The crossing itself is in these cases but of little value for chance customers, for were it not for the regular charity of the householders, it would be deserted. Broken victuals and old clothes also form part of a sweeper's means of living; nor are the clothes always old ones, for one or two of this class have for years been in the habit of having new suits presented to them by the neighbours at Christmas.

The irregular sweepers mostly consist of boys and girls who have formed themselves into a kind of company, and come to an agreement to work together on the same crossings. The principal resort of these is about Trafalgar-square, where they have seized upon some three or four crossings, which they visit from time to time in the course of the day.

One of these gangs I found had appointed its king and captain, though the titles were more honorary than privileged. They had framed their own laws respecting each one's right to the money he took, and the obedience to these laws was enforced by the strength of the little fraternity.

One or two girls whom I questioned, told me that they mixed up ballad-singing or lace-selling with crossing-sweeping, taking to the broom only when the streets were wet and muddy. These children are usually sent out by their parents, and have to carry home at night their earnings. A few of them are orphans with a lodging-house for a home.

Taken as a class, crossing-sweepers are among the most honest of the London poor. They all tell you that, without a good character and 'the respect of the neighbourhood,' there is not a living to be got out of the broom. Indeed, those whom I found best-to-do in the world were those who had been longest at their posts.

Among them are many who have been servants until sickness or accident deprived them of their situations, and nearly all of them have had their minds so subdued by affliction, that they have been tamed so as to be incapable of mischief.

The *earnings*, or rather '*takings*,' of crossing-sweepers are difficult to estimate—generally speaking—that is, to strike the average for the entire class. An erroneous idea prevails that crossing-sweeping is a lucrative employment. All whom I have spoken with agree in saying, that some thirty years back it was a good living; but they bewail piteously the spirit of the present generation. I have met with some who, in former days, took their 3*l.* weekly; and there are but few I have spoken to who would not, at one period, have considered fifteen shillings a bad week's work. But now 'the takings' are very much reduced. The man who was known to this class as having been the most prosperous of all— for from one nobleman alone he received an allowance of seven shillings and sixpence weekly—assured me that twelve shillings a-week was the average of his present gains, taking the year round; whilst the majority of the sweepers agree that a shilling is a good day's earnings.

A shilling a-day is the very limit of the average incomes of the London sweepers, and this is rather an over than an under calculation; for, although a few of the more fortunate, who are to be found in the squares or main thoroughfares or opposite the public buildings, may earn their twelve or fifteen shillings a-week, yet there are hundreds who are daily to be found in the by-streets of the metropolis who assert that eighteenpence a-day is their average taking;

and, indeed, in proof of their poverty, they refer you to the work-house authorities, who allow them certain quartern-loaves weekly. The old stories of delicate suppers and stockings full of money have in the present day no foundation of truth.

The black crossing-sweeper, who bequeathed 500*l.* to Miss Waithman, would almost seem to be the last of the class whose earnings were above his positive necessities.

Lastly, concerning the *numbers* belonging to this large class, we may add that it is difficult to reckon up the number of crossing-sweepers in London. There are few squares without a couple of these pathway scavengers; and in the more respectable squares, such as Cavendish or Portman, every corner has been seized upon. Again, in the principal thoroughfares, nearly every street has its crossing and attendant.

THE ABLE-BODIED
MALE CROSSING-SWEEPERS

THE 'ARISTOCRATIC' CROSSING-SWEEPER

'BILLY' is the popular name of the man who many years has swept the long crossing that cuts off one corner of Cavendish-square, making a 'short-cut' from Old Cavendish-street to the Duke of Portland's mansion.

Billy is a merry, good-tempered kind of man, with a face as red as a love-apple, and cheeks streaked with little veins.

His hair is white, and his eyes are as black and bright as a terrier's. He can hardly speak a sentence without finishing it off with a moist chuckle.

His clothes have that peculiar look which arises from being often wet through, but still they are decent, and far above what his class usually wear. The hat is limp in the brim, from being continually touched.

The day when I saw Billy was a wet one, and he had taken refuge from a shower under the Duke of Portland's stone gateway. His tweed coat, torn and darned, was black about the shoulders with the rain-drops, and his boots grey with mud, but, he told me, 'It was no good trying to keep clean shoes such a day as that, 'cause the blacking come off in the puddles.'

Billy is 'well up' in the *Court Guide*. He continually stopped in his statement to tell whom my Lord B. married, or where my Lady C. had gone to spend the summer, or what was the title of the Marquis So-and-So's eldest boy.

He was very grateful, moreover, to all who had assisted him, and *would* stop looking up at the ceiling, and God-blessing them all with a species of religious fervour.

His regret that the good old times had passed, when he made 'hats full of money,' was unmistakably sincere; and when he had occasion to allude to them, he always delivered his opinion upon the late war, calling it 'a cut-and-run affair,' and saying that it was 'nothing at all put alongside with the old war, when the half-pence and silver coin were twice as big and twenty times more plentiful' than during the late campaign.

Without the least hesitation he furnished me with the following particulars of his life and calling:—

'I was born in London, in Cavendish-square, and (he added, laughing) I ought to have a title, for I first came into the world at No. 3, which was Lord Bessborough's then. My mother went there to do her work, for she chared there, and she was took sudden and couldn't go no further. She couldn't have chosen a better place, could she? You see I was born in Cavendish-square, and I've *worked* in Cavendish-square—sweeping a crossing—for now near upon fifty year.

'Until I was nineteen— I'm sixty-nine now—I used to sell water-creases, but they felled off and then I dropped it. Both mother and myself sold water-creases after my Lord Bessborough died; for whilst he lived she wouldn't leave him not for nothing.

'We used to do uncommon well at one time; there wasn't nobody about then as there is now. I've sold flowers, too; they was very good then; they was mostly show carnations and moss roses, and such-like, but no common flowers—it wouldn't have done for me to sell common things at the houses I used to go to.

'The reason why I took to a crossing was, I had an old father and I didn't want him to go to the workus. I didn't wish too to do anything bad myself, and I never would—no, sir, for I've got as good a character as the first nobleman in the land, and that's a fine thing, ain't it? So as water-creases had fell off till they wasn't a living to me, I had to do summat else to help me to live.

'I saw the crossing-sweepers in Westminster making a deal of

money, so I thought to myself *I'll* do that, and I fixed upon Cavendish-square, because, I said to myself, I'm known there; it's
where I was born, and there I set to work.

'The very first day I was at work I took ten shillings. I never
asked nobody; I only bowed my head and put my hand to my hat,
and they knowed what it meant.

'By jingo, when I took that there I thought to myself, What a
fool I've been to stop at water-creases!

'For the first ten year I did uncommon well. Give me the old-
fashioned way; they were good times then; I like the old-fashioned
way. Give me the old penny pieces, and then the eighteen-penny
pieces, and the three-shilling pieces, and the seven-shilling pieces—
give me them, I says. The day the old half-pence and silver was
cried down, that is, the old coin was called in to change the cur-
rency, my hat wouldn't hold the old silver and halfpence I was given
that afternoon. I had *such* a lot, upon my word, they broke my
pocket. I didn't know the money was altered, but a fish-monger
says to me, "Have you got any old silver?" I said "Yes, I've got
a hat full;" and then says he, "Take 'em down to Couttseses and
change 'em." I went, and I was nearly squeeged to death.

'That was the first time I was like to be killed, but I was nigh
killed again when Queen Caroline passed through Cavendish-
square after her trial. They took the horses out of her carriage and
pulled her along. She kept a chucking money out of the carriage,
and I went and scrambled for it, and I got five-and-twenty shillin,
but my hand was nigh smashed through it; and, says a friend of
mine, before I went, "Billy," says he, "don't you go"; and I was
sorry after I did. She was a good woman, *she* was. The Yallers,
that is, the king's party, was agin her, and pulled up the paving-
stones when her funeral passed; but the Blues was for her.

'I can remember, too, the mob at the time of the Lord Castle-
reagh riots. They went to Portman-square and broke all the winders in the house. They pulled up all the rails to purtect theirselves
with I went to the Bishop of Durham's, and hid myself in the
coal-cellar then. My mother chared there, too. The Bishop of
Durham and Lord Harcourt opened their gates and hurrah'd
the mob, so they had nothing of theirs touched; but whether
they did it through fear or not I can't say. The mob was carrying
a quartern loaf dipped in bullock's blood, and when I saw it

I thought it was a man's head; so that frightened me, and I run off.

'I remember, too, when Lady Pembroke's house was burnt to the ground. That's about eighteen years ago. It was very lucky the family wasn't in town. The housekeeper was a nigh killed, and they had to get her out over the stables; and when her ladyship heard she was all right, she said she didn't care for the fire since the old dame was saved, for she had lived along with the family for many years. No, bless you, sir! I didn't help at the fire; I'm too much of a coward to do that.

'All the time the Duke of Portland was alive he used to allow me 7*s*. 6*d*. a-week, which was 1*s*. a-day and 1*s*. 6*d*. for Sundays. He was a little short man, and a very good man he was too, for it warn't only me as he gave money to, but to plenty others. He was the best man in England for that.

'Lord George Bentinck, too, was a good friend to me. He was a great racer, he was, and then he turned to be member of parliament, and then he made a good man they tell me; but he never comed over my crossing without giving me something. He was at the corner of Holly Street, he was, and he never put foot on my crossing without giving me a sovereign. Perhaps he wouldn't cross more than once or twice a month, but when he comed my way *that* was his money. Ah! he was a nice feller, he was. When he give it he always put it in my hand and never let nobody see it, and that's the way I like to have *my* fee give me.

'There's Mrs. D——, too, as lived at No. 6; she was a good friend of mine, and always allowed me a suit of clothes a-year; but she's dead, good lady, now.

'Dr. C—— and his lady, they, likewise, was very kind friends of mine, and gave me every year clothes, and new shoes, and blankets, aye, and a bed, too, if I had wanted it; but now they are all dead, down to the coachman. The doctor's old butler, Mr.——, he gave me twenty-five shillings the day of the funeral, and, says he, "Bill, I'm afraid this will be the last." Poor good friends they was all of them, and I did feel cut up when I see the hearse going off.

'There was another gentleman, Mr. W. T——, who lives in Harley-street; he never come by me without giving me half-a-crown. He was a real good gentleman; but I haven't seen him for a long time now, and perhaps he's dead too.

'All my friends is dropping off. I'm fifty-five, and they was men when I was a boy. All the good gentlemen's gone, only the bad ones stop.

'Another friend of mine is Lord B——. He always drops me a shilling when he comes by; and, says he, "You don't know me, but I knows you, Billy." But I *do* know him, for my mother worked for the family many a year, and, considering I was born in the house, I think to myself, "If I don't know you, why I ought." He's a handsome, stout young chap, and as nice a gentleman as any in the land.

'One of the best friends I had was Prince E——, as lived there in Chandos-street, the bottom house yonder. I had five sovereigns give me the day as he was married to his beautiful wife. Don't you remember what a talk there was about her diamonds, sir? They say she was kivered in 'em. He used to put his hand in his pocket and give me two or three shillings every time he crossed. He was a gentleman as was uncommon fond of the gals, sir. He'd go and talk to all the maid-servants round about, if they was only good-looking. I used to go and ring the hairy bells for him, and tell the gals to go and meet him in Chapel-street. God bless him! I says, he was a pleasant gentleman, and a regular good 'un for a bit of fun, and always looking lively and smiling. I see he's got his old coachman yet, though the Prince don't live in England at present, but his son does, and he always gives me a half-crown when he comes by too.

'I gets a pretty fine lot of Christmas boxes, but nothing like what I had in the old times. Prince E—— always gives me half a crown, and I goes to the butler for it. Pretty near all my friends gives me a box, them as knows me, and they say, "Here's a Christmas box, Billy."

'Last Christmas-day I took 36*s*., and that was pretty fair; but, bless you, in the old times I've had my hat full of money. I tells you again I've have had as much as 5*l*. in old times, all in old silver and halfpence; that was in the old war, and not this run-away shabby affair.

'My crossing has been a good living to me and mine. It's kept the whole of us. Ah! in the old time I dare say I've made as much as 3*l*. a week reg'lar by it. Besides, I used to have lots of broken vittals, and I can tell you I know'd where to take 'em to. Ah! I've had as much food as I could carry away, and reg'lar good stuff—chicken, and some things I couldn't guess the name of, they was so Frenchified. When the fam'lies is in town I gets a good lot of food given me, but you know when the nobility and gentlemen are away the servants is on board wages, and cuss them board wages, I says.

'I buried my father and mother as a son ought to. Mother was seventy-three and father was sixty-five,—good round ages, ain't they, sir? I shall never live to be that. They are lying in St. John's Wood cemetery along with many of my brothers and sisters, which I have buried as well. I've only two brothers living now; and, poor fellows, they're not very well to do. It cost me a good bit of money. I pay 2*s*. 6*d*. a-year for keeping up the graves of each of my parents, and 1*s*. 2*d*. for my brothers.

'There was the Earl of Gainsborough as I should like you to mention as well, please sir. He lived in Chandos-street, and was a particular nice man and very religious. He always gave me a shilling and a tract. Well, you see, I *did* often read the tract; they was all religious, and about where your souls was to go to—very good, you know, what there was, very good; and he used to buy 'em wholesale at a little shop, corner of High-street, Marrabum. He was a very good, kind gentleman, and gave away such a deal of money that he got reg'lar known, and the little beggar girls follered him at such a rate that he was at last forced to ride about in a cab to get away from 'em. He's many a time said to me, when he's stopped to give me my shilling. "Billy, is any of 'em follering me?" He was safe to give to every body as asked him, but you see it worried his soul out—and it was a kind soul, too—to be follered about by a mob.

'I don't take 4*s*. a-week on the crossing. Ah! I wish you'd give me 4*s*. for what I take. No, I make up by going of errands. I runs for the fam'lies, and the servants, and any of 'em. Sometimes they sends me to a bankers with a cheque. Bless you! they'd trust me with anythink, if it was a hat full. I've had a lot of money trusted to me at times. At one time I had as much as 83*l*. to carry for the Duke of Portland.

'Aye, that was a go—*that* was! You see the hall-porter had had it give to him to carry to the bank, and he gets me to do it for him; but the vallet heerd of it, so he wanted to have a bit of fun, and he wanted to put the hall-porter in a funk. I met the vallet in Holborn, and says he, "Bill, I want to have a lark," so he kept me back, and I did not get back till one o'clock. The hall-porter offered 5*l.* reward for me, and sends the police: but Mr. Freebrother, Lord George's vallet, he says, "I'll make it all right, Billy." They sent up to my poor old people, and says father. "Billy wouldn't rob anybody of a nightcap, much more 80*l.*" I met the policeman in Holborn, and says he, "I want you, Billy," and says I, "All right, here I am." When I got home the hall-porter, says he, "Oh, I am a dead man; where's the money?" and says I, "It's lost." "Oh! it's the Duke's not mine." says he. Then I pulls it out; and says the porter, "It's a lark of Freebrother's." So he gave me 2*l.* to make it all right. That *was* a game, and the hall-porter, says he, "I really thought you was gone, Billy;" but, says I, "If everybody carried as good a face as I do, everybody would be as honest as any in Cavendish-square'."

THE BEARDED CROSSING-SWEEPER AT THE EXCHANGE

SINCE the destruction by fire of the Royal Exchanges in 1838, there has been added to the curiosities of Cornhill a thickset, sturdy, and hirsute crossing-sweeper—a man who is as civil by habit as he is independent by nature. He has a long flowing beard, grey as wood smoke, and a pair of fierce moustaches, giving a patriarchal air of importance to a marked and observant face, which often serves as a painter's model. After half-an-hour's conversation, you are forced to admit that his looks do not all belie him, and that the old mariner (for such was his profession formerly) is worthy in some measure of his beard.

He wears an old felt hat—very battered and discoloured; around his neck, which is bared in accordance with sailor custom, he has a thick blue cotton neckerchief tied in a sailor's knot; his long iron-grey beard is accompanied by a healthy and almost ruddy face. He stands against the post all day, saying nothing, and taking what he can get without solicitation.

THE SWEEPER IN PORTLAND-SQUARE

A WILD-LOOKING man, with long straggling grey hair, which stood out from his head as if he brushed it the wrong way, and whiskers so thick and curling that they reminded one of the wool round a sheep's face. He seemed a kind-hearted, innocent creature, half scared by want and old age.

'I'm blest if I can tell which is the best crossing in London; but mine ain't no great shakes, for I don't take three shillings a-week, not with persons going across, take one week with another; but I thought I could get a honest currust (crust) at it, for I've got a crippled hand, which comed of its own accord, and I was in St. George's Hospital seven weeks. When I comed out it was a cripple with me, and I thought the crossing was better than my going into the workhouse—for I likes my liberty.

'I've been on this crossing since last Christmas was a twelve-month. Before that I was a bricklayer and plasterer. I've been thirty-two years in London. I can get as good a character as any one anywhere, please God.'

A REGENT-STREET CROSSING-SWEEPER

A MAN who had stationed himself at the end of Regent-street, near the County Fire Office, was far superior to the ordinary run of sweepers, and had formerly been a gentleman's servant. His costume was of that peculiar miscellaneous description which showed that it had from time to time been given to him in charity. A dress-coat so marvellously tight that the stitches were stretching open, a waistcoat with a remnant of embroidery, and a pair of trousers which wrinkled like a groom's top-boot, had all evidently been part of the wardrobe of the gentlemen whose errands he had run. His boots were the most curious portion of his toilette, for they were large enough for a fisherman, and the portion unoccupied by the foot had gone flat and turned up like a Turkish slipper.

He spoke with a tone and manner which showed some education. Once or twice whilst I was listening to his statement he insisted upon removing some dirt from my shoulder, and, on leaving, he by force seized my hat and brushed it—all which habits of attention he had contracted whilst in service. I was surprised to see stuck in the wristband of his coat-sleeve a row of pins, arranged as neatly as in the papers sold at the mercers'.

A TRADESMAN'S CROSSING-SWEEPER

HE was an old man, with a forehead so wrinkled that the dark, waved lines reminded me of the grain of oak. His thick hair was, despite his great age—which was nearly seventy—still dark; and as he conversed with me, he was continually taking off his hat, and wiping his face with what appeared to be a piece of flannel, about a foot sqare.

His costume was of what might be called 'the all-sorts' kind, and, from constant wear, it had lost its original colour, and had turned into a sort of dirty green-grey hue. It consisted of a waist-coat of tweed, fastened together with buttons of glass, metal, and bone; a tail-coat, turned brown with weather, a pair of trousers repaired here and there with big stitches, like the teeth of a comb, and these formed the extent of his wardrobe. Around the collar of the coat and waistcoat, and on the thighs of the pantaloons, the layers of grease were so thick that the fibre of the cloth was choked up, and it looked as if it had been pieced with bits of leather.

THE ABLE-BODIED FEMALE CROSSING-SWEEPERS

AN OLD WOMAN

SHE is the widow of a sweep—'as respectable and 'dustrious a man,' I was told, 'as any in the neighbourhood of the "Borough;" he was a short man, sir,—very short,' said my informant, 'and had a weakness for top-boots, white hats, and leather breeches,' and in that unsweeplike costume he would parade himself up and down the Dover and New Kent-roads. He had a capital connexion (or, as his widow terms it, 'seat of business'), and left behind him a good name and reputation that would have kept the 'seat of business' together, if it had not been for the misconduct of the children; two of them (sons) have been transported, while a daughter 'went wrong,' though she, wretched creature, paid a fearful penalty, I learnt, for her frailties, having been burnt to death in the middle of the night, through a careless habit of smoking in bed.

The old sweeper herself, eighty years of age, and almost beyond labour, very deaf, and rather feeble to all appearance, yet manages to get out every morning between four and five, so as to catch the workmen and 'time-keepers' on their way to the factories. She has the true obsequious curtsey, but is said to be very strong in her 'likes and dislikes.'

She bears a good character, though sometimes inclining, I was informed, towards 'the other half-pint,' but never guilty of any excess. She is somewhat profuse in her scriptural ejaculations and professions of gratitude.

THE CROSSING-SWEEPER WHO HAD BEEN A SERVANT-MAID

SHE is to be found any day between eight in the morning and seven in the evening, sweeping away in a convulsive, jerky sort of manner, close to —— square, near the Foundling. She may be known by her pinched-up straw bonnet, with a broad, faded, almost colourless ribbon. She has weak eyes, and wears over them a brownish shade. Her face is tied up, because of a gathering which she has on her head. She wears a small, old plaid cloak, a clean checked apron, and a tidy printed gown.

She is rather shy at first, but willing and obliging enough withal; and she lives down Little —— Yard, in Great —— street. The 'yard' that is made like a mousetrap—small at the entrance, but amazingly large inside, and dilapidated though extensive.

Here are stables and a couple of blind alleys, nameless, or bearing the same name as the yard itself, and wherein are huddled more people than one could count in a quarter of an hour, and more children than one likes to remember,—dirty children, listlessly trailing an old tin baking-dish, or a worn-out shoe, tied to a piece of string; sullen children, who turn a way in a fit of sleepy anger if spoken to; screaming children, setting all the parents in the 'yard' at defiance; and quiet children, who are arranging banquets of dirt in the reeking gutters.

The 'yard' is devoted principally to costermongers.

The crossing-sweeper lives in the top-room of a two-storied house, in the very depth of the blind alley at the end of the yard. She has not even a room to herself, but pays one shilling a week for the privilege of sleeping with a woman who gets her living by selling tapes in the streets

THE OCCASIONAL CROSSING-SWEEPERS

THE SUNDAY CROSSING-SWEEPER

'I'M a Sunday crossing-sweeper,' said an oyster-stall keeper, in answer to my inquiries. 'I mean by that, I only sweep a crossing

on a Sunday. I pitch in the Lorrimore-road, Newington, with a
few oysters on week-days, and I does jobs for the people about
there, sich as cleaning a few knives and forks, or shoes and boots,
and windows. I've been in the habit of sweeping a crossing about
four of five years.

'I never knowed my father, he died when I was a baby. He
was a 'terpreter, and spoke seven different languages. My father
used to go with Bonaparte's army, and used to 'terpret for him.
He died in the South of France. I had a brother, but he died quite
a child, and my mother supported me and a sister by being cook in
a gentleman's family; we was put out to nurse. My mother couldn't
afford to put me to school, and so I can't read nor write. I'm forty-
one years old.

'The best places is in front of chapels and churches, 'cause you
can take more money in front of a church or a chapel than wot
you can in a private road, 'cos they look at it more, and a good
many thinks when you sweeps in front of a public-house that you
go and spend your money inside in waste.

'The first Sunday I went at it, I took eighteenpence. I began
at nine o'clock in the morning and stopped till four in the afternoon.
The publican give fourpence, and the baker sixpence, and the
butcher threepence, so that altogether I got above a half-crown.
I stopped at this crossing a year, and I always knocked up about
two shillings of a half-crown on the Sunday. I very seldom got
anythink from the ladies; it was most all give by the gentlemen.
Little children used sometimes to give me ha'pence, but it was
when their father give it to 'em; the little children like to do that
sort of thing.'

THE AFFLICTED CROSSING-SWEEPERS

ONE-LEGGED SWEEPER AT CHANCERY-LANE

'I DON'T know what induced me to take that crossing, except it
was that no one was there, and the traffic was so good—fact
is, the traffic is too good, and people won't stop as they cross
over, they're very glad to get out of the way of the cabs and
the omnibuses.

'Tradespeople never give me anything—not even a bit of bread.
The only thing I get is a few cuttings, such as crusts of sandwiches

and remains of cheese, from the public-house at the corner of the court. The tradespeople are as distant to me now as they were when I came, but if I should pitch up a tale I should soon get acquainted with them.

'We have lived in this lodging two years and a half, and we pay one-and-ninepence a-week, as you may see from the rent-book, and that I manage to earn on Sundays. We owe four weeks now, and, thank God, it's no more.

'I was born, sir, in ——street, Berkeley-square, at Lord ——'s house, when my mother was minding the house. I have been used to London all my life, but not to this part; I have always been at the west-end, which is what I call the best end.

'I did not like the idea of crossing-sweeping at first, till I reasoned with myself, Why should I mind? I'm not doing any hurt to anybody. I don't care at all now—I know I'm doing what I ought to do.'

THE MOST SEVERELY AFFLICTED OF ALL THE CROSSING-SWEEPERS

PASSING the dreary portico of the Queen's Theatre, and turning to the right down Tottenham Mews, we came upon a flight of steps leading up to what is called 'The Gallery,' where an old man, gasping from the effects of a lung disease, and feebly polishing some old harness, proclaimed himself the father of the sweeper I was in search of, and ushered me into the room where he lay a-bed, having had a 'very bad night.'

The room itself was large and of a low pitch, stretching over some stables; it was very old and creaky (the sweeper called it 'an old wilderness'), and contained, in addition to two turn-up bedsteads, that curious medley of articles which, in the course of years, an old and poor couple always manage to gather up. There was a large lithograph of a horse, dear to the remembrance of the old man from an indication of a dog in the corner. 'The very spit of the one I had years; it's a real portrait, sir, for Mr. Hanbart, the printer, met me one day and sketched him.' There was an etching of Hogarth's in a black frame; a stuffed bird in a wooden case, with a glass before it; a piece of painted glass, hanging in a place of honour, but for which no name could be remembered, excepting that it was 'of the old-fashioned sort.' There were the odd remnants, too, of old china ornaments, but very little furniture; and, finally, a kitten.

The father, worn out and consumptive, had been groom to Lord Combermere. 'I was with him, sir, when he took Bonyparte's house at Malmasong. I could have had a pension then if I'd a liked, but I was young and foolish, and had plenty of money, and we never know what we may come to.'

The sweeper, although a middle-aged man, had all the appearance of a boy—his raw-looking eyes, which he was always wiping with a piece of linen rag, gave him a forbidding expression, which his shapeless, short, bridgeless nose tended to increase. But his manners and habits were as simple in their character as those of a child; and he spoke of his father's being angry with him for not getting up before, as if he were a little boy talking of his nurse.

He walks, with great difficulty, by the help of a crutch; and the sight of his weak eyes, his withered limb, and his broken shoulder (his old helpless mother, and his gasping, almost inaudible father), form a most painful subject for compassion.

The crossing-sweeper gave me, with no little meekness and some slight intelligence, the following statement:—

'I very seldom go out on a crossin' o' Sundays. I didn't do much good at it. I used to go to church of a Sunday—in fact, I do now when I'm well enough.

'It's fifteen year next January since I left Regent-street. I was there three years, and then I went on Sundays occasionally. Sometimes I used to get a shilling, but I have given it up now—it didn't answer; besides, a lady who was kind to me found me out, and said she wouldn't do any more for me if I went out on Sundays. She's been dead these three or four years now.

'When I was at Regent-street I might have made twelve shillings a-week, or something thereabout.

'I am seven-and-thirty the 26th day of last month, and I have been lame six-twenty years. My eyes have been bad ever since my birth.

'I went on the crossing first because my parents couldn't keep me, not being able to keep theirselves. I thought it was the best thing I could do, but it's like all other things, it's got very bad now. I used to manage to rub along at first—the streets have got shockin' bad of late.

'I am dreadful tired when I comes home of a night. Thank God my other leg's all right! I wish the t'other was as strong, but it never will be now.

'The police never try to turn me away; they're very friendly, they'll pass the time of day with me, or that, from knowing me so long in Oxford-street.

'My broom sometimes serves me a month; of course, they don't last long now it's showery weather. I give twopence-halfpenny a piece for'em, or threepence.

'I don't know who gives me the most; my eyes are so bad I can't see. I think, though, upon an average, the gentlemen give most.

'Often I hear the children, as they are going by, ask their mothers for something to give to me; but they only say, "Come along—come along!" It's very rare that they lets the children have a ha'-penny to give me.'

THE NEGRO CROSSING-SWEEPER WHO HAD LOST BOTH HIS LEGS

THIS man sweeps a crossing in a principal and central thoroughfare when the weather is cold enough to let him walk; the colder the better, he says, as it 'numbs his stumps like.' He is unable to follow this occupation in warm weather, as his legs feel 'just like corns,' and he cannot walk more than a mile a-day. Under these circumstances he takes to begging, which he thinks he has a perfect right to do, as he has been left destitute in what is to him almost a strange country, and has been denied what he terms 'his rights.' He generally sits while begging, dressed in a sailor shirt and trousers, with a black neckerchief round his neck, tied in the usual nautical knot. He places before him a placard and never moves a muscle for the purpose of soliciting charity. He always appears scrupulously clean.

I went to see him at his house early one morning—in fact, at half-past eight, but he was not then up. I went again at nine, and found him prepared for my visit in a little parlour, in a dirty and rather disreputable alley running out of a court in a street near Brunswick-square. The negro's parlour was scantily furnished with two chairs, a turn-up bedstead, and a sea-chest. A few odds and ends of crockery stood on the sideboard, and a kettle was singing over a cheerful bit of fire. The little man was seated on a chair, with his stumps of legs sticking straight out. He showed some amount of intelligence in answering my questions. We were quite alone, for he sent his wife and child—the former a pleasant-looking 'half-caste,' and the latter the cheeriest little crowing, smiling 'piccaninny' I have ever seen—he sent them out into the alley, while I conversed with himself.

His life is embittered by the idea that he has never yet had 'his rights'—that the owners of the ship in which his legs were burnt off have not paid him his wages (of which, indeed, he says, he never received any but the five pounds which he had in advance before starting), and that he has been robbed of 42*l.* by a grocer in Glasgow. How true these statements may be it is almost impossible to say, but from what he says, some injustice seems to have been done him by the canny Scotchman, who refuses him his 'pay,' without which he is determined 'never to leave the country.'

JUVENILE CROSSING-SWEEPERS

BOY CROSSING-SWEEPERS AND TUMBLERS

A REMARKABLY intelligent lad, who, on being spoken to, at once consented to give all the information in his power, told me the following story of his life.

It will be seen from this boy's account, and the one or two following that a kind of partnership exists among some of these young sweepers. They have associated themselves together, appropriated several crossings to their use, and appointed a captain over them. They have their forms of trial, and 'jury-house' for the settlement of disputes; laws have been framed, which govern their commercial proceedings, and a kind of language adopted by the society for its better protection from the arch-enemy, the policeman.

I found the lad who first gave me an insight into the proceedings of the associated crossing- sweepers crouched on the stone steps of a door in Adelaide-street, Strand; and when I spoke to him he was preparing to settle down in a corner and go to sleep—his legs and body being curled round almost as closely as those of a cat on a hearth. The moment he heard my voice he was upon his feet, asking me to 'give a halfpenny to poor little Jack.'

He was a good-looking lad, with a pair of large mild eyes, which he took good care to turn up with an expression of supplication as he moaned for a halfpenny.

A cap, or more properly a stuff bag, covered a crop of hair which had matted itself into the form of so many paint-brushes, while his face, from its roundness of feature and the complexion of dirt, had an almost Indian look about it; the colour of his hands, too, was such that you could imagine he had been shelling walnuts.

He ran before me, treading cautiously with his naked feet, until I reached a convenient spot to take down his statement, which was as follows:—

'I've got no mother or father; mother has been dead for two years, and father's been gone for more than that—more nigh five years—he died at Ipswich, in Suffolk. He was a perfumer by trade, and used to make hair-dye, and scent, and pomatum, and all kinds of scents. He didn't keep a shop himself, but he used to serve them as did; he didn't hawk his goods about, neether, but had regular customers, what used to send him a letter, and then he'd take them what they wanted. Yes, he used to serve some good shops: there was H——'s, of London Bridge, what's a large chemist's. He used to make a good deal of money, but he lost it betting; and so his brother, my uncle, did all his. He used to go up to High Park, and then go round by the Hospital, and then turn up a yard, where all the men are who play for money [Tattersall's]; and there he'd lose his money, or sometimes win,—but that wasn't often. I remember he used to come home tipsy, and say he'd lost on this or that horse, naming wot one he'd laid on; and then mother would coax him to bed, and afterwards sit down and begin to cry.

'Ah! she was a very good, kind mother, and very fond of both of us; though father wasn't, for he'd always have a noise with mother when he come home, only he was seldom with us when he was making his goods.

'After mother died, sister still kept on making nets, and I lived with her for some time. But she was keeping company with a young man, and one day they went out, and came back and said they'd been and got married. It was him as got rid of me.

'He was kind to me for the first two or three months, while he was keeping her company; but before he was married he got a little cross, and after he was married he begun to get more cross, and used to send me to play in the streets, and tell me not to come home again till night. One day he hit me, and I said I wouldn't be hit about by him, and then at tea that night sister gave me three shillings, and told me I must go and get my own living. So I bought a box and brushes (they cost me just the money) and went cleaning boots, and I done pretty well with them, till my box was stole from me by a boy where I was lodging. He's in prison now—got six calendar for picking pockets.

'I was fifteen the 24th of last May, sir, and I've been sweeping crossings now near upon two years. There's party of six of us, and we have the crossings from St. Martin's Church as far as Pall Mall. I always go along with them as lodges in the same place as I do. In the daytime, if it's dry, we do anythink what we can—open cabs, or anythink; but if it's wet, we separate, and I an' another gets a crossing—those who gets on it first, keeps it,—and we stand on each side and take our chance.

'We do it this way:—if I was to see two gentlemen coming, I should cry out, "Two toffs!" and then they are mine; and whether they give me anythink or not they are mine, and my mate is bound not to follow them; for if he did he would get a hiding from the whole lot of us. If we both cry out together, then we share. If it's a lady and a gentleman, then we cries, "A toff and a doll!" Sometimes we are caught out in this way. Perhaps it is a lady and gentleman and a child; and if I was to see them, and only say, "A toff and a doll," and leave out the child, then my mate can add the child; and as he is right and I wrong, then it's his party.

'When we see the rain we say together, "Oh! there's a jolly good rain! we'll have a good day to-morrow." If a shower comes on, and we are at our room, which we general are about three o'clock, to get somethink to eat—besides, we general go there to see how much each other's taken in the day—why, out we run with our brooms.

'At night-time we tumbles—that is, if the policeman ain't nigh. We goes general to Waterloo-place when the Opera's on. We sends on one of us ahead, as a looker-out, to look for the policeman, and then we follows. It's no good tumbling to gentlemen *going* to the Opera; it's when they're coming back they gives us money. When they've got a young lady on their arm they laugh at us tumbling; some will give us a penny, others threepence, sometimes a sixpence or a shilling, and sometimes a halfpenny. We either do the cat'unwhell, or else we keep before the gentleman and lady, turning head-over-heels, putting our broom on the ground and then turning over it.

'After the Opera we go into the Haymarket, where all the women are who walk the streets all night. They don't give us no money, but they tell the gentlemen to. Sometimes, when they are talking to the gentlemen, they say, "Go away, you young rascal!" and if they are saucy, then we say to them, "We're not talking to you, my doxy, we're talking to the gentleman,"—but that's only if they're rude, for if they speak civil we always goes. They knows what "doxy" means. What is it? Why that they are no better than us! If we are on the crossing, and we says to them as they go by, "Good luck to you!" they always give us somethink either that night or the next. There are two with bloomer bonnets, who always give us somethink if we says "Good luck."

'When we are talking together we always talk in a kind of slang. Each policeman we gives a regular name—there's "Bull's Head," "Bandy Shanks," and "Old Cherry Legs," and "Dot-and-carry-one;" they all knows their names as well as us. We never talks of crossings, but "fakes." We don't make no slang of our own, but uses the regular one.

'A broom doesn't last us more than a week in wet weather, and they costs us twopence halfpenny each; but in dry weather they are good a fortnight.'

YOUNG MIKE'S STATEMENT

THE next lad I examined was called Mike. He was a short, stout-set youth, with a face like an old man's, for the features were hard and defined, and the hollows had got filled up with dirt till his countenance was brown as an old wood carving. I have seldom seen so dirty a face, for the boy had been in a perspiration, and then wiped his cheeks, with his muddy hands, until they were marbled, like the covering to a copy-book.

The old lady of the house in which the boy lived seemed to be hurt by the unwashed appearance of her lodger. 'You ought to be ashamed of yourself—and that's God's truth—not to go and sluice yourself afore spaking to the jintlemin,' she cried, looking alternately at me and the lad, as if asking me to witness her indignation.

Mike wore no shoes, but his feet were as black as if cased in gloves with short fingers. His coat had been a man's, and the tails reached to his ankles; one of the sleeves was wanting, and a dirty rag had been wound round the arm in its stead. His hair spread about like a tuft of grass where a rabbit has been squatting.

GANDER—THE 'CAPTAIN' OF THE BOY CROSSING-SWEEPERS

GANDER, the captain of the gang of boy crossing-sweepers, was a big lad of sixteen, with a face devoid of all expression, until he laughed, when the cheeks, mouth, and forehead instantly became crumpled up with a wonderful quantity of lines and dimples. His hair was cut short, and stood up in all directions, like the bristles of a hearth-broom, and was a light dust tint, matching with the hue of his complexion, which also, from an absence of washing, had turned to a decided drab, or what house-painters term a stone-colour.

He spoke with a lisp, occasioned by the loss of two of his large front teeth, which allowed the tongue as he talked to appear through the opening in a round nob like a raspberry.

The boy's clothing was in a shocking condition. He had no coat, and his blue-striped shirt was as dirty as a French-polisher's rags, and so tattered, that the shoulder was completely bare, while the sleeve hung down over the hand like a big bag.

From the fish-scales on the sleeves of his coat, it had evidently once belonged to some coster in the herring line. The nap was all worn off, so that the lines of the web were showing a coarse carpet; and instead of buttons, string had been passed through holes pierced at the side.

Of course he had no shoes on, and his black trousers, which, with the grease on them, were gradually assuming a tarpaulin look, were fastened over one shoulder by means of a brace and bits of string.

During his statement, he illustrated his account of the tumbling backwards—the 'catenwheeling'—with different specimens of the art, throwing himself about on the floor with an ease and almost grace, and taking up so small a space of the ground for the performance, that his limbs seemed to bend as though his bones were flexible like cane.

'To tell you the blessed truth, I can't say the last shilling I handled.'

'Don't you go a-believing on him,' whispered another lad in my ear, whilst Gander's head was turned: 'he took thirteenpence last night, he did.'

THE 'KING' OF THE TUMBLING-BOY CROSSING-SWEEPERS

THE young sweeper who had been styled by his companions the 'King' was a pretty-looking boy, only tall enough to rest his chin comfortably on the mantel-piece as he talked to me, and with a pair of grey eyes that were as bright and clear as drops of sea-water. He was clad in a style in no way agreeing with his royal title; for he had on a kind of dirt-coloured shooting-coat of tweed, which was fraying into a kind of cobweb at the edges and elbows. His trousers, too, were rather faulty, for there was a pink-wrinkled dot of flesh at one of the knees; while their length was too great for his majesty's short legs, so that they had to be rolled up at the end like a washer-woman's sleeves.

His royal highness was of a restless disposition, and, whilst talking, lifted up, one after another, the different ornaments on the mantel-piece, frowning and looking at them sideways, as he pondered over the replies he should make to my questions.

When I arrived at the grandmother's apartment the 'king' was absent, his majesty having been sent with a pitcher to fetch some spring-water.

The 'king' also was kind enough to favour me with samples of his wondrous tumbling powers. He could bend his little legs round till they curved like the long German sausages we see in the ham-and-beef shops; and when he turned head over heels, he curled up his tiny body as closely as a wood-louse, and then rolled along, wabbling like an egg.

'The boys call me Johnny,' he said; 'and I'm getting on for eleven, and I goes with the Goose and Harry, a-sweeping at St. Martin's Church, and about there. I used, too, to go to the crossing where the statute is, sir, at the bottom of the Haymarket. I went along with the others; sometimes there were three or four of us, or sometimes one, sir. I never used to sweep unless it was wet. I don't go out not before twelve or one in the day; it ain't no use going before that; and beside, I couldn't get up before that, I'm too sleepy. I don't stop out so late as the other boys; they sometimes stop all night, but I don't like that. The Goose was out all night along with Martin; they went all along up Piccirilly, and there they climbed over the Park railings and went a birding all by themselves, and then they went to sleep for an hour on the grass—so they says. I likes better to come home to my bed. It kills me for the next day when I do stop out all night. The Goose is always out all night; he likes it.'

THE STREET WHERE THE BOY-SWEEPERS LODGED

I WAS anxious to see the room in which the gang of boy crossing-sweepers lived, so that I might judge of their peculiar style of house-keeping, and form some notion of their principles of domestic economy.

I asked young Harry and 'the Goose' to conduct me to their lodgings, and they at once sonsented, 'the Goose' prefacing his compliance with the remark, that 'it wern't such as genilmen had been accustomed to, but then I must take 'em as they was.'

The boys led me in the direction of Drury-lane; and before entering one of the narrow streets which branch off like the side-bones of a fish's spine from that long thoroughfare, they thought fit to caution me that I was not to be frightened, as nobody would touch me, for all was very civil.

The locality consisted of one of those narrow streets which, were it not for the paved cartway in the centre, would be called a court. Seated on the pavement at each side of the entrance was a costerwoman with her basket before her, and her legs tucked up mysteriously under her gown into a round ball, so that her figure resembled in shape the plaster tumblers sold by the Italians. These women remained as inanimate as if they had been carved images, and it was only when a passenger went by they gave signs of life, by calling out in a low voice, like talking to themselves, 'Two for three haarpence—herrens,'—'Fine hinguns.'

The street itself is like the description given of thoroughfares in the East. Opposite neighbours could not exactly shake hands out of window, but they could talk together very comfortably; and indeed, as I passed along, I observed several women with their arms folded like a cat's paws on the sill, and chatting with their friends over the way.

Nearly all the inhabitants were costermongers, and, indeed,

the narrow cartway seemed to have been made just wide enough for a truck to wheel down it. A beershop and a general store, together with a couple of sweeps,—whose residences were distinguished by a broom over the door,—formed the only exceptions to the street-selling class of inhabitants.

As I entered the place, it gave me the notion that it belonged to a district coster colony, and formed one large hawkers' home; for everybody seemed to be doing just as he liked, and I was stared at as if considered an intruder. Women were seated on the pavement, knitting, and repairing their linen; the doorways were filled up with bonnetless girls, who wore their shawls over their head, as the Spanish women do their mantillas; and the youths in corduroy and brass buttons, who were chatting with them, leant against the walls as they smoked their pipes, and blocked up the pavement, as if they were the proprietors of the place. Little children formed a convenient bench out of the kerbstone; and a party of four men were seated on the footway, playing with cards which had turned to the colour of brown paper from long usage, and marking the points with chalk upon the flags.

The parlour-windows of the houses had all of them wooden shutters, as thick and clumsy-looking as a kitchen flap-table, the paint of which had turned to the dull dirt-colour of an old slate. Some of these shutters were evidently never used as a security for the dwelling, but served only as tables on which to chalk the accounts of the day's sales.

Before most of the doors were costermongers' trucks—some standing ready to be wheeled off, and others stained and muddy with the day's work. A few of the costers were dressing up their barrows, arranging the sieves of waxy-looking potatoes—and others taking the stiff herrings, browned like a meerschaum with the smoke they had been dried in, from the barrels beside them, and spacing them out in pennyworths on their trays.

You might guess what each costermonger had taken out that day by the heap of refuse swept into the street before the doors. One house had a blue mound of mussel-shells in front of it— another, a pile of the outside leaves of broccoli and cabbages, turning yellow and slimy with bruises and moisture.

Hanging up beside some of the doors were bundles of old strawberry pottles, stained red with the fruit. Over the trap-doors to the cellars were piles of market-gardeners' sieves, ruddled like a sheep's back with big red letters. In fact, everything that met the eye seemed to be in some way connected with the coster's trade.

From the windows poles stretched out, on which blankets, petticoats, and linen were drying; and so numerous were they, that they reminded me of the flags hung out at a Paris fête. Some of the sheets had patches as big as trap-doors let into their centres; and the blankets were—many of them—as full of holes as a pigeon-house.

As I entered the court, a 'row' was going on; and from a first-floor window a lady, whose hair sadly wanted brushing, was haranguing a crowd beneath, throwing her arms about like a drowning man, and in her excitement thrusting her body half out of her temporary rostrum as energetically as I have seen Punch lean over his theatre.

'The willin dragged her,' she shouted, 'by the hair of her head, at least three yards into the court—the willin! and then he kicked her, and the blood was on his boot.'

It was a sweep who had been behaving in this cowardly manner; but still he had his defenders in the women around him. One with very shiny hair, and an Indian kerchief round her neck, answered the lady in the window, by calling her a 'd——d old cat;' whilst the sweep's wife rushed about clapping her hands together as quickly as if she was applauding at a theatre, and styled somebody or other 'an old wagabones as she wouldn't dirty her hands to fight with.'

This 'row' had the effect of drawing all the lodgers to the windows—their heads popping out as suddenly as dogs from their kennels in a fancier's yard.

THE BOY-SWEEPERS' ROOM

THE room where the boys lodged was scarcely bigger than a coach-house; and so low was the ceiling, that a fly-paper suspended from a clothes-line was on a level with my head, and had to be carefully avoided when I moved about.

One corner of the apartment was completely filled up by a big four-post bedstead, which fitted into a kind of recess as perfectly as if it had been built to order.

The old woman who kept this lodging had endeavoured to give

it a homely look of comfort, by hanging little black-framed pictures scarcely bigger than pocket-books, on the walls. Most of these were sacred subjects, with large yellow glories round the heads; though between the drawing representing the bleeding heart of Christ, and the Saviour bearing the Cross, was an illustration of a red-waistcoated sailor smoking his pipe. The Adoration of the Shepherds, again, was matched on the other side of the fireplace by a portrait of Daniel O'Connell.

A chest of drawers was covered over with a green baize cloth, on which books, shelves, and clean glasses were tidily set out.

Where so many persons (for there were about eight of them, including the landlady, her daughter, and grandson) could all sleep, puzzled me extremely.

The landlady wore a frilled nightcap, which fitted so closely to the skull, that it was evident she had lost her hair. One of her eyes was slowly recovering from a blow, which, to use her own words, 'a blackgeyard gave her.' Her lip, too, had suffered in the encounter, for it was swollen and cut.

'I've a nice flock-bid for the boys,' she said, when I inquired into the accommodation of her lodging-house, 'where three of them can slape aisy and comfortable.'

'It's a large bed, sir,' said one of the boys, 'and a warm covering over us; and you see it's better than a regular lodging-house; for, if you want a knife or a cup, you don't have to leave something on it till it's returned.'

The old woman spoke up for her lodgers, telling me that they were good boys, and very honest; 'for,' she added, 'they pays me rig-lar ivery night, which is threepence.'

The only youth as to whose morals she seemed to be at all doubtful was 'the Goose,' 'for he kept late hours, and sometimes came home without a penny in his pocket.'

THE GIRL CROSSING-SWEEPER SENT OUT BY HER FATHER

A LITTLE girl, who worked by herself at her own crossing, gave me some curious information on the subject.

This child had a peculiarly flat face, with a button of a nose, while her mouth was scarcely larger than a button-hole. When she spoke, there was not the slightest expression visible in her features;

indeed, one might have fancied she wore a mask and was talking behind it; but her eyes were shining the while as brightly as those of a person in a fever, and kept moving about, restless with her timidity. The green frock she wore was fastened close to the neck, and was turning into a kind of mouldy tint; she also wore a black stuff apron, stained with big patches of gruel, 'from feeding baby at home,' as she said. Her hair was tidily dressed, being drawn tightly back from the forehead, like the buy-a-broom girls; and as she stood with her hands thrust up her sleeves, she curtseyed each time before answering, bobbing down like a float, as though the floor under her had suddenly given way.

'I'm twelve years old, please, sir, and my name is Margaret R——, and I sweep a crossing in New Oxford-street, by Dunn's passage, just facing Moses and Sons', sir; by the Catholic school, sir. Mother's been dead these two year, sir, and father's a working cutler, sir; and I lives with him, but he don't get much to do, and so I'm obligated to help him, doing what I can, sir. Since mother's been dead, I've had to mind my little brother and sister, so that I haven't been to school; but when I goes a crossing-sweeping I takes them along with me, and they sits on the steps close by, sir. If it's wet I has to stop at home and take care of them, for father depends upon me for looking after them. Sister's three and a-half year old, and brother's five year, so he's just beginning to help me, sir. I hope he'll get something better than a crossing when he grows up.

'First of all I used to go singing songs in the streets, sir. It was when father had no work, so he stopped at home and looked after the children. I used to sing the "Red, White, and Blue," and "Mother, is the Battle over?" and "The Gipsy Girl," and sometimes I'd get fourpence or fivepence, and sometimes I'd have a chance of making ninepence, sir. Sometimes, though, I'd take a shilling of a Saturday night in the markets.

'At last the songs grew so stale people wouldn't listen to them, ans, as I carn't read, I couldn't learn any more, sir. My big brother and father used to learn me some, but I never could get enough out of them for the streets; besides, father was out of work still and we couldn't get money enough to buy ballads with, and it's no good singing without having them to sell. We live over there, sir, (pointing to a window on the other side of the narrow street).

'The notion come into my head all of itself to sweep crossings, sir. As I used to go up Regent-street I used to see men and women, and girls and boys, sweeping, and the people giving them money, so I thought I'd do the same thing. That's how it come about. Just now the weather is so dry, I don't go to my crossing, but goes out singing. I've learnt some new songs, such as "The Queen of the Navy for ever," and "The Widow's Last Prayer," which is about the wars. I only go sweeping in wet weather, because then's the best time. When I am there, there's some ladies and gentlemen as gives to me regular. I knows them by sight; and there's a beer-shop where they give me some bread and cheese whenever I go.

'I generally takes about sixpence, or sevenpence, or eightpence on the crossing, from about nine o'clock in the morning till four in the evening, when I come home. I don't stop out at nights because father won't let me, and I'm got to be home to see to baby.

'My broom costs me twopence ha'penny, and in wet weather it lasts a week, but in dry weather we seldom uses it.

'When I sees the buses and carriages coming I stands on the side, for I'm afeard of being runned over. In winter I goes out and cleans ladies' doors, general about Lincoln's-inn, for the house-keepers. I gets twopence a door, but it takes a long time when the ice is hardened, so that I carn't do only about two or three.

"I carn't tell whether I shall always stop at sweeping, but I've no clothes, and so I carn't get a situation; for, though I'm small and young, yet I could do housework, such as cleaning.

'No, sir, there's no gang on my crossing—I'm all alone. If another girl or boy was to come and take it when I'm not there, I should stop on it as well as him or her, and go shares with 'em.'

GIRL CROSSING-SWEEPER

I WAS told that a little girl formed one of the association of young sweepers, and at my request one of the boys went to fetch her.

She was a clean-washed little thing, with a pretty, expressive countenance, and each time she was asked a question she frowned, like a baby in its sleep, while thinking of the answer. In her ears she wore instead of rings loops of string, 'which the doctor had put there because her sight was wrong.' A cotton velvet bonnet, scarcely larger than the sun-shades worn at the sea-side, hung on

her shoulders, leaving exposed her head, with the hair as rough as
tow. Her green stuff gown was hanging in tatters, with long three-
cornered rents as large as penny kites, showing the grey lining
underneath; and her mantle was separated into so many pieces,
that it was only held together by the braiding at the edge.

As she conversed with me, she played with the strings of her
bonnet, rolling them up as if curling them, on her singularly small
and also singularly dirty fingers.

'I'll be fourteen, sir, a fortnight before next Christmas. I was
born in Liquorpond-street, Gray's Inn-lane. Father come over
from Ireland, and was a bricklayer. He had pains in his limbs and
wasn't strong enough, so he give it over. He's dead now,—been
dead a long time, sir. I was a littler girl then than I am now, for
I wasn't above eleven at that time. I lived with mother after father
died. She used to sell things in the streets—yes, sir, she was a coster.
About a twelvemonth after father's death, mother was taken bad
with the cholera, and died. I then went along with both grandmother and grandfather, who was a porter in Newgate Market;
I stopped there until I got a place as servant of all-work. I was
only turned, just turned, eleven then. I worked along with a French
lady and gentleman in Hatton Garden, who used to give me a
shilling a-week and my tea. I used to go home to grandmother's
to dinner every day. I hadn't to do any work, only just to clean the
room and nuss the child. It was a nice little thing. I couldn't
understand what the French people used to say, but there was
a boy working there, and he used to explain to me what they
meant.

'I left them because they was going to a place called Italy—
perhaps you may have heard tell of it, sir. Well, I suppose they
must have been Italians, but we calls everybody, whose talk we
don't understand, French. I went back to grandmother's, but,
after grandfather died, she couldn't keep me, and so I went out
begging—she sent me. I carried lucifer-matches and stay-laces fust.
I used to carry about a dozen laces, and perhaps I'd sell six out
of them. I suppose I used to make about sixpence a-day, and I
used to take it home to grandmother, who kept and fed me.

'At last, finding I didn't get much at begging, I thought I'd
go crossing-sweeping. I saw other children doing it. I says to myself,
"I'll go and buy a broom," and I spoke to another little girl, who

was sweeping up Holborn, who told me what I was to do. "But," says she, "don't come and cut up me."

'I went fust to Holborn, near to home, at the end of Red Lion-street. Then I was frightened of the cabs and carriages, but I'd get there early, about eight o'clock, and sweep the crossing clean and I'd stand at the side on the pavement, and speak to the gentle-men and ladies before they crossed.

'There was a couple of boys, sweepers at the same crossing before I went there. I went to them and asked if I might come and sweep there too, and they said Yes, if I would give them some of the halfpence I got. These was boys about as old as I was, and they said, if I earned sixpence, I was to give them twopence a-piece; but they never give me nothink of theirs. I never took more than sixpence, and out of that I had to give fourpence, so that I did not do so well as with the laces.

'The crossings made my hands sore with the sweeping, and, as I got so little, I thought I'd try somewhere else. Then I got right down to the Fountings in Trafalgar-square, by the crossing at the statey on 'orseback. There were a good many boys and girls on that crossing at the time—five of them; so I went along with them.

'When I fust went they said, "Here's another fresh 'un." They come up to me and says, "Are you going to sweep here?" and I says "Yes;" and they says, "You mustn't come here, there's too many;" and I says, "They're different ones every day,"—for they're not regular there, but shift about, sometimes one lot of boys and girls, and the next day another. They didn't say another word to me, and so I stopped.

'It's a capital crossing, but there's so many of us, it spiles it. I seldom gets more than sevenpence a-day, which I always takes home to grandmother.

'I've been on that crossing about three months. They always calls me Ellen, my regular name, and behaves very well to me. If I see anybody coming, I call them out as the boys does, and then they are mine.

'There's a boy and myself, and another strange girl, works on our side of the statey, and another lot of boys and girls on the other.

'I like Saturdays the best day of the week, because that's the time as gentlemen as has been at work has their money, and then they are more generous. I gets more then, perhaps ninepence, but not quite a shilling, on the Saturday.

'I've had a threepenny-bit give to me, but never sixpence. It was a gentleman, and I should know him again. Ladies gives me less than gentlemen. I foller 'em, saying, "If you please, sir, give a poor girl a halfpenny;" but if the police are looking, I stop still.

'I never goes out on Sunday, but stops at home with grandmother. I don't stop out at nights like the boys, but I gets home by ten at latest.'

THE RAT-KILLER

In 'the Brill,' or rather in Brill-place, Somers'-town, there is a variety of courts branching out into Chapel-street, and in one of the most angular and obscure of these is to be found a perfect nest of rat-catchers—not altogether professional rat-catchers, but for the most part sporting mechanics and costermongers. The court is not easily to be found, being inhabited by men not so well known in the immediate neighbourhood as perhaps a mile or two away, and only to be discovered by the aid and direction of the little girl at the neighbouring cat's-meat shop.

My first experience of this court was the usual disturbance at the entrance. I found one end or branch of it filled with a mob of eager listeners, principally women, all attracted to a particular house by the sounds of quarrelling. One man gave it as his opinion that the disturbers must have earned too much money yesterday; and a woman, speaking to another who had just come out, lifting up both her hands and laughing, said, 'Here they are—*at it* again!'

The rat-killer whom we were in search of was out at his stall in Chapel-street when we called, but his wife soon fetched him. He was a strong, sturdy-looking man, rather above the middle height, with light hair, ending in sandy whiskers, reaching under his chin, sharp deep-set eyes, a tight-skinned nose that looked as if the cuticle had been stretched to its utmost on its bridge. He was dressed in the ordinary corduroy costermonger habit, having, in addition, a dark blue Guernsey drawn over his waistcoat.

The man's first anxiety was to show us that rats were not his only diversion; and in consequence he took us into the yard of the house, where in a shed lay a bull-dog, a bull-bitch, and a litter of pups just a week old. They did not belong to him, but he said he did a good deal in the way of curing dogs when he could get 'em.

After I had satisfied him that I was not a collector of dog-tax, trying to find out how many animals he kept, he gave me what he evidently thought was 'a treat'—a peep at his bull-dog, which he fetched from upstairs, and let it jump about the room with a most unpleasant liberty, informing me the while how he had given five pounds for him, and that one of the first pups he got by a bull he had got five pounds for, and that cleared him. 'That Punch' (the bull-dog's name), he said, 'is as quiet as a lamb—wouldn't hurt nobody; I frequently takes him through the streets without a lead. Sartainly he killed a cat the t'other afternoon, but he couldn't help that, 'cause the cat flew at him; though he took it as quietly as a man would a woman in a passion, and only went at her just to save his eyes. But you couldn't-easy get him off, master, when he once got a holt. He was a good one for rats, and, he believed, the stanchest and trickiest dog in London.'

When he had taken the brute upstairs, for which I was not a little thankful, the man made the following statement:—

'I a'n't a Londoner. I've travelled all about the country. I'm a native of Iver, in Buckinghamshire. I've been three year here in London altogether up to last September.

'Before I come to London I was nothink, sir—a labouring man, an eshkewator. I come to London the same as the rest, to do anythink I could. I was at work at the eshkewations at King's Cross Station. I work as hard as any man in London, I think.

'When the station was finished, I, having a large family, thought I'd do the best I could, so I went to the foreman at the Caledonian Sawmills. I stopped there a twelve-month; but one day I went for a load and a-half of lime, and where you fetches a load and a-half of lime they always gives you fourpence. So as I was having a pint of beer out of it, my master come by and saw me drinking, and give me the sack. Then he wanted me to ax his pardon, and I might stop; but I told him I wouldn't beg no one's pardon for drinking a pint of beer as was give me. So I left there.

'Ever since the Great Western was begun, my family has been distributed all over the country, wherever there was a railway making. My brothers were contractors for Peto, and I generally worked for my brothers; but they've gone to America, and taken a contract for a railway at St. John's, New Brunswick, British North America. I can do anything in the eshkewating way—I don't care what it is.

'After I left the Caledonian Sawmills I went to Billingsgate, and bought anythink I could see a chance of gettin' a shilling out on, or to'ards keeping my family.

'All my lifetime I've been a-dealing a little in rats; but it was not till I come to London that I turned my mind fully to that sort of thing. My father always had a great notion of the same. We all like the sport. When any of us was in the country, and the farmers wanted us to, we'd do it. If anybody heerd tell of my being an activish chap like, in that sort of way, they'd get me to come for a day or so.

'If anybody has a place that's eaten up with rats, I goes and gets some ferruts, and takes a dog, if I've got one, and manages to kill em. Sometimes I keep my own ferruts, but mostly I borrows them. This young man that's with me, he'll sometimes have an order to go fifty or sixty mile into the country, and then he buys his ferruts, or gets them the best way he can. They charges a good sum for the loan of 'em—sometimes as much as you get for the job.

'You can buy ferruts at Leadenhall-market for 5*s* or 7*s*.—it all depends; you can't get them all at one price, some of 'em is real cowards to what others is; some won't even kill a rat. The way we tries 'em is, we puts 'em down anywhere, in a room maybe, with a rat, and if they smell about and won't go up to it, why they won't do; 'cause you see, sometimes the ferrut has to go up a hole, and at the end there may be a dozen or sixteen rats, and if he hasn't got the heart to tackle one on 'em, why he ain't worth a farden.

'I have kept ferruts for four or five months at a time, but they're nasty stinking things. I've had them get loose; but, bless you, they do no harm, they're as hinnocent as cats; they won't hurt nothink; you can play with them like a kitten. Some puts things down to ketch rats—sorts of pison, which is their secret—but I don't. I relies upon my dogs and ferruts, and nothink else.

'I went to destroy a few rats up at Russell-square; there was a shore come right along, and a few holes—they was swarmed with 'em there—and didn't know how it was; but the cleverest men in the world couldn't ketch many there, 'cause you see, master, they run down the hole into the shore, and no dog could get through a rat-hole.

'I coldn't get my living, though, at that business. If any gentle-man comes to me and says he wants a dog cured, or a few rats destroyed, I does it.

'In the country they give you fourpence a rat, and you can kill sometimes as many in a farmyard as you can in London. The most I ever got for destroying rats was four bob, and then I filled up the brickwork and made the holes good, and there was no more come.

'I calls myself a coster; some calls theirselves general dealers, but I doesn't. I goes to market, and if one thing don't suit, why I buys another.

'I don't know whether you've heerd of it, master, or not, but I'm the man as they say kills rats—that's to say, I kills 'em like a dog. I'm almost ashamed to mention it, and I shall never do it any more, but I've killed rats for a wager often. You see it's only been done like for a lark; we've bin all together daring one another, and trying to do something nobody else could. I remember the first time I did it for a wager, it was up at ——, where they've got a pit. There was a bull-dog a killing rats, so I says.

' "Oh, that's a duffin' dog; any dog could kill quicker than him. I'd kill again him myself."

'Well, then they chaffed me, and I warn't goin' to be done; so I says.

' "I'll kill again that dog for a sov'rin."

'The sov'rin was staked. I went down to kill eight rats again the dog, and I beat him. I killed 'em like a dog, with my teeth. I went down hands and knees and bit 'em. I've done it three times for a sov'rin, and I've won each time. I feels very much ashamed of it, though.

'On the hind part of my neck, as you may see, sir, there's a scar; that's where I was bit by one; the rat twisted himself round and held on like a vice. It was very bad, sir, for a long time; it festered, and broke out once or twice, but it's all right now.'

A NIGHT AT RAT-KILLING

CONSIDERING the immense number of rats which form an article of commerce with many of the lower orders, whose business it is to keep them for the purpose of rat matches, I thought it necessary, for the full elucidation of my subject, to visit the well-known public-house in London, where, on a certain night in the week, a pit is built up, and regular rat-killing matches take place, and where those who have sporting dogs, and are anxious to test their qualities, can, after such matches are finished, purchase half a dozen or a dozen rats for them to practise upon, and judge for themselves of their dogs' 'performances.'

To quote the words printed on the proprietor's card, 'he is always at his old house at home, as usual, to discuss the FANCY generally.'

I arrived at about eight o'clock at the tavern where the performances were to take place. I was too early, but there was plenty to occupy my leisure in looking at the curious scene around me, and making notes of the habits and conversation of the customers who were flocking in.

The front of the long bar was crowded with men of every grade of society, all smoking, drinking, and talking about dogs. Many of them had brought with them their 'fancy' animals, so that a kind of 'canine exhibition' was going on; some carried under their arm small bull-dogs, whose flat pink noses rubbed against my arm as I passed; others had Skye-terriers, curled up like balls of hair, and sleeping like children, as they were nursed by their owners. The only animals that seemed awake, and under continual excitement, were the little brown English terriers, who, despite the neat black leathern collars by which they were held, struggled to get loose, as if they smelt the rats in the room above, and were impatient to begin the fray.

There is a business-like look about this tavern which at once lets you into the character of the person who owns it. The drinking seems to have been a secondary notion in its formation, for it is a low-roofed room without any of those adornments which are now generally considered so necessary to tender a public-house attractive. The tubs where the spirits are kept are blistered with the heat of the gas, and so dirty that the once brilliant gilt hoops are now quite black.

Sleeping on an old hall-chair lay an enormous white bulldog, 'a great beauty,' as I was informed, with a head as round and smooth as a clenched boxing-glove, and seemingly too large for

the body. Its forehead appeared to protrude in a manner significant
of water on the brain, and almost overhung the short nose, through
which the animal breathed heavily. When this dog, which was
the admiration of all beholders, rose up, its legs were as bowed as
a tailor's, leaving a peculiar pear-shaped opening between them,
which, I was informed, was one of its points of beauty. It was a
white dog, with a sore look, from its being peculiarly pink round
the eyes, nose, and indeed at all the edges of its body.

On the other side of the fire-place was a white bull-terrier dog,
with a black patch over the eye, which gave him rather a disreputable look. This animal was watching the movements of the
customers in front, and occasionally, when the entrance-door was
swung back, would give a growl of inquiry as to what the fresh-
comer wanted. The proprietor was kind enough to inform me, as
he patted this animal's ribs, which showed like the hoops on a
butter-firkin, that he considered there had been a 'little of the
greyhound in some of his back generations.'

About the walls there hung clusters of black leather collars
adorned with brass rings and clasps, and pre-eminent was a silver
dog-collar, which, from the conversation of those about me, I
learnt was to be the prize in a rat-match to be 'killed for' in a
fortnight's time.

As the visitors poured in, they, at the request of the proprietor
'not to block up the bar,' took their seats in the parlour, and,
accompanied by a waiter, who kept shouting. 'Give your orders,
gentlemen,' I entered the room.

I found that, like the bar, no pains had been taken to render the
room attractive to the customers, for, with the exception of the
sporting pictures hung, against the dingy paper, it was devoid of
all adornment. Over the fire-place were square glazed boxes, in
which were the stuffed forms of dogs famous in their day. Pre-
eminent among the prints was that representing the 'Wonder
Tiny, five pounds and a half in weight,' as he appeared killing
200 rats. This engraving had a singular look, from its having been
printed upon a silk handkerchief. Tiny had been a great favourite
with the proprietor, and used to wear a lady's bracelet as a collar.

Among the stuffed heads was one of a white bull-dog, with
tremendous glass eyes sticking out, as if it had died in strangul-
ation. The proprietor's son was kind enough to explain to me the

qualities that had once belonged to this favourite. 'They've spoilt her in stuffing, sir,' he said; 'made her so short on the head; but she was the wonder of her day. There wasn't a dog in England as would come nigh her. There's her daughter,' he added, pointing to another head, something like that of a seal, 'but she wasn't reckoned half as handsome as her mother, though she was very much admired in her time.

'That there *is* a dog,' he continued, pointing to one represented with a rat in its mouth, 'it was as good as any in England, though it's so small. I've seen her kill a dozen rats almost as big as herself, though they killed *her* at last; for sewer-rats are dreadful for giving dogs canker in the mouth, and she wore herself out with continually killing them, though we always rinsed her mouth out well with peppermint and water while she were at work. When rats bite they are poisonous, and an ulcer is formed, which we are obleeged to lance; that's what killed her.'

The company assembled in 'the parlour' consisted of sporting men, or those who, from curiosity, had come to witness what a rat-match was like. Seated at the same table, talking together, were those dressed in the costermonger's suit of corduroy, soldiers with their uniforms carelessly unbuttoned, coachmen in their livery, and tradesmen who had slipped on their evening frock-coats, and run out from the shop to see the sport.

The dogs belonging to the company were standing on the different tables, or tied to the legs of the forms, or sleeping in their owners' arms, and were in turn minutely criticised—their limbs being stretched out as if they were being felt for fractures, and their mouths looked into, as if a dentist were examining their teeth.

Nearly all the little animals were marked with scars from bites. 'Pity to bring him up to rat-killing,' said one, who had been admiring a fierce-looking bull-terrier, although he did not mention at the same time what line in life the little animal ought to pursue.

At another table one man was declaring that his pet animal was the exact image of the celebrated rat-killing dog 'Billy,' at the same time pointing to the picture against the wall of that famous animal, 'as he performed his wonderful feat of killing 500 rats in five minutes and a half.'

There were amongst the visitors some French gentlemen, who had evidently witnessed nothing of the kind before; and whilst they endeavoured to drink their hot gin and water, they made their interpreter translate to them the contents of a large placard hung upon a hatpeg, and headed—

'EVERY MAN HAS HIS FANCY.
RATTING SPORTS IN REALITY.'

About nine o'clock the proprietor took the chair in the parlour, at the same time giving the order to 'shut up the shutters in the room above, and light up the pit.' This announcement seemed to rouse the spirits of the impatient assembly, and even the dogs tied to the legs of the tables ran out to the length of their leathern thongs, and their tails curled like eels, as if they understood the meaning of the words.

'Why, that's the little champion,' said the proprietor, patting a dog with thighs like a grasshopper, and whose mouth opened back to its ears. 'Well, it *is* a beauty! I wish I could gammon you to take a "fiver" for it.' Then looking round the room, he added, 'Well, gents, I'm glad to see you look so comfortable.'

The performances of the evening were hurried on by the entering of a young gentleman, whom the waiters called 'Cap'an.'

'Now, Jem, when is this match coming off?' the Captain asked impatiently; and despite the assurance that they were getting ready, he threatened to leave the place if kept waiting much longer. This young officer seemed to be a great 'fancier' of dogs, for he made the round of the room, handling each animal in its turn, feeling and squeezing its feet, and scrutinising its eyes and limbs with such minuteness, that the French gentlemen were forced to inquire who he was.

There was no announcement that the room above was ready, though everybody seemed to understand it; for all rose at once, and mounting the broad wooden staircase, which led to what was once the 'drawing-room,' dropped their shillings into the hand of the proprietor, and entered the rat-killing apartment.

'The pit,' as it is called, consists of a small circus, some six feet in diameter. It is about as large as a centre flower-bed, and is fitted with a high wooden rim that reaches to elbow height. Over it the branches of a gas lamp are arranged, which light up the white painted floor, and every part of the little arena. On one side of the room is a recess, which the proprietor calls his 'private box,' and this apartment the Captain and his friend soon took possession of, whilst the audience generally clambered upon the tables and forms, or hung over the side of the pit itself.

All the little dogs which the visitors had brought up with them were now squalling and barking, and struggling in their masters' arms, as if they were thoroughly acquainted with the uses of the pit; and when a rusty wire cage of rats, filled with the dark moving mass, was brought forward, the noise of the dogs was so great that the proprietor was obliged to shout out—'Now, you that have dogs *do* make 'em shut up.'

The Captain was the first to jump into the pit. A man wanted to sell him a bull-terrier, spotted like a fancy rabbit, and a dozen of rats the consequent order.

The Captain preferred pulling the rats out of the cage himself, laying hold of them by their tails and jerking them into the arena. He was cautioned by one of the men not to let them bite him, for 'believe me,' were the words, 'you'll never forget, Cap'an; these 'ere are none of the cleanest.'

Whilst the rats were being counted out, some of those that had been taken from the cage ran about the painted floor and climbed up the young officer's legs, making him shake them off and exclaim, 'Get out, you varmint!' whilst others of the ugly little animals sat upon their hind legs, cleaning their faces with their paws.

When the dog in question was brought forth and shown the dozen rats, he grew excited, and stretched himself in his owner's arms, whilst all the other animals joined in a full chorus of whining.

'Chuck him in,' said the Captain, and over went the dog; and in a second the rats were running round the circus, or trying to hide themselves between the small openings in the boards round the pit.

Although the proprietor of the dog endeavoured to speak up for it, by declaring 'it was a good 'un, and a very pretty performer,' still it was evidently not worth much in a rat-killing sense; and if it had not been for his 'second,' who beat the sides of the pit with his hand, and shouted 'Hi! hi! at'em!' in a most bewildering manner, we doubt if the terrier would not have preferred leaving the rats to themselves, to enjoy their lives. Some of the rats, when the dog advanced towards them, sprang up into his face, making him draw back with astonishment. Others, as he bit them, curled round in his mouth and fastened on his nose, so that he had to carry them as a cat does its kittens. It also required many shouts of 'Drop it—dead 'un,' before he would leave those he had killed.

We cannot say whether the dog was eventually bought; but from its owner's exclaiming, in a kind of apologetic tone, 'Why, he never saw a rat before in all his life,' we fancy no dealings took place.

The Captain seemed anxious to see as much sport as he could, for he frequently asked those who carried dogs in their arms whether 'his little 'un would kill,' and appeared sorry when such answers were given as—'My dog's mouth's a little out of order, Cap'an,' or 'I've only tried him at very small 'uns.'

One little dog was put in to amuse himself with the dead bodies. He seized hold of one almost as big as himself, shook it furiously till the head thumped the floor like a drumstick, making those around shout with laughter, and causing one man to exclaim, 'He's a good 'un at shaking heads and tails, ain't he?'

Preparations now began for the grand match of the evening, in which fifty rats were to be killed. The 'dead 'uns' were gathered up by their tails and flung into the corner. The floor was swept, and a big flat basket produced, like those in which chickens are brought to market, and under whose iron wire top could be seen small mounds of closely packed rats.

This match seemed to be between the proprietor and his son, and the stake to be gained was only a bottle of lemonade, of which the father stipulated he should have first drink.

It was strange to observe the daring manner in which the lad introduced his hand into the rat cage, sometimes keeping it there for more than a minute at a time, as he fumbled about and stirred up with his fingers the living mass, picking out, as he had been requested, 'only the big 'uns.'

When the fifty animals had been flung into the pit, they gathered themselves together into a mound which reached one-third up the sides, and which reminded one of the heap of hair-sweepings in a barber's shop after a heavy day's cutting. These were all sewer and water-ditch rats, and the smell that rose from them was like that from a hot drain.

The Captain amused himself by flicking at them with his pocket handkerchief, and offering them the lighted end of his cigar, which the little creatures tamely snuffed at, and drew back from, as they singed their noses.

It was also a favourite amusement to blow on the mound of rats, for they seemed to dislike the cold wind which sent them fluttering about like so many feathers; indeed, whilst the match was going on, whenever the little animals collected together, and formed a barricade as it were to the dog, the cry of 'Blow on 'em! blow on 'em!' was given by the spectators, and the dog's second puffed at them as if extinguishing a fire, when they would dart off like so many sparks.

The company was kept waiting so long for the match to begin that the impatient Captain again threatened to leave the house, and was only quieted by the proprietor's reply of 'My dear friend, be easy, the boy's on the stairs with the dog;' and true enough we shortly heard a wheezing and a screaming in the passage without, as if some strong-winded animal were being strangled, and presently a boy entered, carrying in his arms a bull-terrier in a perfect fit of excitement, foaming at the mouth and stretching its neck forward, so that the collar which held it back seemed to be cutting its throat in two.

The animal was nearly mad with rage—scratching and struggling to get loose. 'Lay hold a little closer up to the head or he'll turn round and nip yer,' said the proprietor to his son.

Whilst the gasping dog was fastened up in a corner to writhe its impatience away, the landlord made inquiries for a stop-watch, and also for an umpire to decide, as he added, 'whether the rats were dead or alive when they're "killed," as Paddy says.'

When all the arrangements had been made the 'second' and the dog jumped into the pit, and after 'letting him see 'em a bit,' the terrier was let loose.

The moment the dog was 'free,' he became quiet in a most business-like manner, and rushed at the rats, burying his nose in the mound till he brought out one in his mouth. In a short time a dozen rats with wetted necks were lying bleeding on the floor, and the white paint of the pit became grained with blood.

In a little time the terrier had a rat hanging to his nose, which, despite his tossing, still held on. He dashed up against the sides, leaving a patch of blood as if a strawberry had been smashed there.

'He doesn't squeal, that's one good thing,' said one of the lookers-on.

As the rats fell on their sides after a bite they were collected together in the centre, where they lay quivering in their death-gasps!

'Hi, Butcher! hi, Butcher!' shouted the second, 'good dog! bur-r-r-r-r-h!' and he beat the sides of the pit like a drum til the dog flew about with new life.

'Dead 'un! drop it!' he cried, when the terrier 'nosed' a rat kicking on its side, as it slowly expired of its broken neck.

'Time!' said the proprietor, when four of the eight minutes had expired, and the dog was caught up and held panting, his neck stretched out like a serpent's, staring intently at the rats which still kept crawling about.

The poor little wretches in this brief interval, as if forgetting their danger, again commenced cleaning themselves, some nibbling the ends of their tails, others hopping about, going now to the legs of the lad in the pit, and sniffing at his trousers, or, strange to say, advancing, smelling, to within a few paces of their enemy the dog.

The dog lost the match, and the proprietor, we presume, honour-ably paid the bottle of lemonade to his son. But he was evidently displeased with the dog's behaviour, for he said, 'He won't do for me—he's not one of my sort! Here, Jim, tell Mr. G. he may have him if he likes; I won't give him house room.'

A plentiful shower of halfpence was thrown into the pit as a reward for the second who had backed the dog.

A slight pause now took place in the proceedings, during which the landlord requested that the gentlemen 'would give their minds up to drinking; you know the love I have for you,' he added jocularly, 'and that I don't care for any of you;' whilst the waiter accompanied the invitation with a cry of 'Give your orders, gentle-men,' and the lad with the rats asked if 'any other gentleman would like any rats.'

Several other dogs were tried, and amongst them one who, from the size of his stomach, had evidently been accustomed to large dinners, and looked upon rat-killing as a sport and not as a business. The appearance of this fat animal was greeted with remarks such as 'Why don't you feed your dog?' and 'You shouldn't give him more than five meals a day.'

Another impatient bull-terrier was thrown into the midst of a dozen rats. He did his duty so well, that the admiration of the spectators was focussed upon him.

'Ah,' said one, '*he'd* do better at a hundred than twelve;' whilst another observed, 'Rat-killing's *his* game, I can see;' while the landlord himself said, 'He's a very pretty creetur,' and I'd back him to kill against anybody's dog at eight and a half or nine.'

The Captain was so startled with this terrier's 'cleverness,' that he vowed that if she could kill fifteen in a minute 'he'd give a hundred guineas for her.'

It was nearly twelve o'clock before the evening's performance concluded. Several of the spectators tried their dogs upon two or three rats, either the biggest or the smallest that could be found: and many offers as to what 'he wanted for the dog,' and many inquiries as to 'who was its father,' were made before the company broke up.

At last the landlord, finding that no 'gentleman would like a few rats,' and that his exhortations to 'give their minds up to drinking' produced no further effect upon the company, spoke the epilogue of the rat tragedies in these words:—

'Gentlemen, I give a very handsome solid silver collar to be killed for next Tuesday. Open to all the world, only they must be novice dogs, or at least such as is not considered *phee*nomenons. We shall have plenty of sport, gentlemen, and there will be loads of rat-killing. I hope to see all my kind friends, not forgetting your dogs, likewise; and may they be like the Irishman all over, who had good trouble to catch and kill 'em, and took good care they didn't come to life again. Gentlemen, there is a good parlour down-stairs, where we meets for harmony and entertainment.'

JACK BLACK

As I wished to obtain the best information about rat and vermin destroying, I thought I could not do better now than apply to that eminent authority 'the Queen's ratcatcher,' and accordingly I sought an interview with Mr. 'Jack' Black, whose hand-bills are headed—'V. R. Rat and mole destroyer to Her Majesty.'

I had already had a statement from the royal bug-destroyer relative to the habits and means of exterminating those offensive vermin, and I was desirous of pairing it with an account of the personal experience of the Queen of England's ratcatcher.

I was soon at home with Mr. Black. He was a very different man from what I had expected to meet, for there was an expression of kindliness in his countenance, a quality which does not exactly agree with one's preconceived notions of ratcatchers. His face had a strange appearance, from his rough, uncombed hair being nearly grey, and his eyebrows and whiskers black, so that he looked as if he wore powder.

Mr. Black informed me that the big iron-wire cage, in which the sparrows were fluttering about, had been constructed by him for rats, and that it held over a thousand when full—for rats are packed like cups, he said, one over the other. 'But,' he added, 'business is bad for rats, and it makes a splendid havery; besides, sparrers is the rats of birds, sir, for if you look at 'em in a cage they always huddles up in a corner like rats in a pit, and they are a'most vermin in colour and habits, and eats anything.'

Mr. Black stuffs animals and bird, and also catches fish for vivaria. Against the walls were the furred and feathered remains of departed favourites, each in its glazed box and appropriate attitude. There was a famous polecat—'a first-rater at rats' we were informed. Here a ferret 'that never was equalled.' This canary 'had earned pounds'. That linnet 'was the wonder of its day.' The enormous pot-bellied carp, with the miniature rushes painted at the back of its case, was caught in the Regent's Park waters.

In another part of the room hung fishing-lines, and a badger's skin, and lead-bobs and curious eel-hooks—the latter as big as the curls on the temples of a Spanish dancer, and from here Mr. Black took down a transparent-looking fish, like a slip of parchment, and told me that it was a fresh-water smelt, and that he caught it in the Thames—'the first he ever heard of.' Then he showed me a beetle suspended to a piece of thread, like a big spider to its web, and this he informed me was the Thames beetle, 'which either live by land or water.'

'You ketch 'em,' continued Mr. Black, 'when they are swimming on their backs, which is their nature, and when they turns over you finds 'em beautifully crossed and marked.'

Round the room were hung paper bags, like those in which

housewives keep their sweet herbs. 'All of them there, sir, contain cured fish for eating,' Mr. Black explained to me.

'I'm called down here the Battersea otter,' he went on, 'for I can go out at four in the morning, and come home by eight with a barrowful of freshwater fish. Nobody knows how I do it, because I never takes no nets or lines with me. I assure them I ketch 'em with my hands, which I do, but they only laughs increderlous like. I knows the fishes' harnts, and watches the tides. I sells fresh fish—perch, roach, dace, gudgeon, and such-like, and even small jack, at threepence a pound, or what they'll fetch; and I've caught near the Wandsworth "Black Sea," as we calls it, half a hundred weight sometimes, and I never took less than my handkerchey full.'

I was inclined—like the inhabitants of Battersea—to be incredulous of the rat-catcher's hand-fishing, until, under a promise of secrecy, he confided his process to me, and then not only was I perfectly convinced of its truth, but startled that so simple a method had never before been taken advantage of.

Later in the day Mr. Black became very communicative. We sat chatting together in his sanded bird shop, and he told me all his misfortunes, and how bad luck had pressed upon him, and driven him out of London.

'I was fool enough to take a public-house in Regent-street, sir,' he said. 'My daughter used to dress as the "Ratketcher's Daughter," and serve behind the bar, and that did pretty well for a time; but it was a brewer's house, and they ruined me.'

The costume of the 'ratketcher's daughter' was shown to me by her mother. It was a red velvet bodice, embroidered with silver lace.

'With a muslin shirt, and her hair down her back, she looked wery genteel,' added the parent.

Mr. Black's chief complaint was that he could not 'make an appearance,' for his 'uniform'—a beautiful green coat and red waistcoat—were pledged.

Whilst giving me his statement, Mr. Black, in proof of his assertions of the biting powers of rats, drew my attention to the leathern breeches he wore, 'as were given him twelve years ago by Captain B——.'

These were pierced in some places with the teeth of the animals, and in others were scratched and fringed like the washleather of a street knife-seller.

His hands, too, and even his face, had scars upon them from bites.

Mr. Black informed me that he had given up tobacco 'since a haccident he met with from a pipe. I was smoking a pipe,' he said 'and a friend of mine by chance jobbed it into my mouth, and it went right through to the back of my palate, and I nearly died.'

Here his wife added, 'There's a hole there to this day you could put your thumb into; you never saw such a mouth.'

Mr. Black informed me in secret that he had often, 'unbeknown to his wife,' tasted what cooked rats were like, and he asserted that they were as moist as rabbits, and quite as nice.

'If they are shewer-rats,' he continued, 'just chase them for two or three days before you kill them, and they are as good as barn-rats, I give you my word, sir.'

Mr. Black's statement was as follows:—

'I should think I've been at ratting a'most for five-and-thirty year; indeed, I may say from my childhood, for I've kept at it a'most all my life. I've been dead near three times from bites—as near as a toucher. I once had the teeth of a rat break in my finger, which was dreadful bad, and swole, and putrified, so that I had to have the broken bits pulled out with tweezers. When the bite is a bad one, if festers and forms a hard core in the ulcer, which is very painful, and throbs very much indeed; and after that core comes away, unless you cleans 'em out well, the sores, even after they seemed to be healed, break out over and over again, and never cure perfectly. This core is as big as a boiled fish's eye, and as hard as stone. I generally cuts the bite out clean with a lancet, and squeege the humour well from it, and that's the only way to cure it thorough—as you see my hands is all covered with scars from bites.

'I've been bitten nearly everywhere, even where I can't name to you, sir, and right through my thumb nail too, which, as you see, always has a split in it, though it's years since I was wounded. I suffered as much from that bite on my thumb as anything. It went right up to my ear. I felt the pain in both places at once— a regular twinge, like touching the nerve of a tooth. The thumb went black, and I was told I ought to have it off; but I knew a

THE RATCATCHERS OF THE SEWERS

THE BOY CROSSING-SWEEPERS

young chap at Middlesex Hospital who wasn't out of his time, and he said, "No, I wouldn't, Jack"; and no more I did; and he used to strap it up for me. But the worst of it was, I had a job at Camden town one afternoon after he had dressed the wound, and I got another bite lower down on the same thumb, and that flung me down on my bed, and there I stopped, I should think, six weeks.

'When a rat's bite touches the bone, it makes you faint in a minute, and it bleeds dreadful—ah, most terrible—just as if you had been stuck with a penknife. You couldn't believe the quantity of blood that come away, sir.

'The first rats I caught was when I was about nine years of age. I ketched them at Mr. Strickland's, a large cow-keeper, in Little Albany-street, Regent's-park. At that time it was all fields and meaders in them parts, and I recollect there was a big orchard on one side of the sheds. I was only doing it for a game, and there was lots of ladies and gents looking on, and wondering at seeing me taking the rats out from under a heap of old bricks and wood, where they had collected theirselves. I had a little dog—a little red 'un it was, who was well known through the fancy—and I wanted the rats for to test my dog with, I being a lad what was fond of the sport.

'I wasn't afraid to handle rats even then; it seemed to come nat'ral to me. I very soon had some in my pocket, and some in my hands, carrying them away as fast as I could, and putting them into my wire cage. You see, the rats began to run as soon as we shifted them bricks, and I had to scramble for them. Many of them bit me, and, to tell you the truth, I didn't know the bites were so many, or I dare say I shouldn't have been so venturesome as I was.

'After that I bought some ferruts—four of them—of a man of the name of Butler, what was in the rat-ketching line, and afterwards went out to Jamaicer, to kill rats there. I was getting on to ten years of age then, and I was, I think, the first that regularly began hunting rats to sterminate them; for all those before me used to do it with drugs, and perhaps never handled rats in their lives.

'With my ferruts I at first used to go out hunting rats round by the ponds in Regent's-park, and the ditches, and in the cow-sheds roundabout. People never paid me for ketching, though, maybe, if they was very much infested, they might give me a trifle;

but I used to make my money by selling the rats to gents as was of sport, and wanted them for their little dogs.

'I kept to this till I was thirteen or fourteen year of age, always using the ferruts; and I bred from them too,—indeed, I've still got the "strain" (breed) of them same ferruts by me now. I've sold them ferruts about everywhere; to Jim Burn I've sold some of the strain; and to Mr. Anderson, the provision-merchant; and to a man that went to Ireland. Indeed, that strain of ferruts has gone nearly all over the world.

'I never lost a ferrut out ratting. I always let them loose, and put a bell on mine—arranged in a peculiar manner, which is a secret—and I then puts him into the main run of the rats, and lets him go to work. But they must be ferruts that's well trained for working dwellings, or you'll lose them as safe as death. I've had 'em go away two houses off, and come back to me. My ferruts is very tame, and so well trained, that I'd put them into a house and guarantee that they'd come back to me. In Grosvenor-street I was clearing once, and the ferruts went next door, and nearly cleared the house—which is the Honourable Mrs. F——'s— before they came back to me.

'Ferruts are very dangerous to handle if not well trained. They are very savage, and will attack a man or a child as well as a rat. It was well known at Mr. Hamilton's at Hampstead—it's years ago this is—there was a ferrut got loose what killed a child, and was found sucking it. The bite of 'em is very dangerous—not so pisonous as a rat's—but very painful; and when the little things is hungry they'll attack anythink. I've seen two of them kill a cat, and then they'll suck the blood till they fills theirselves, after which they'll fall off like leeches.

'The weasel and the stoat are, I think, more dangerous than the ferrut in their bite. I had a stoat once, which I caught when out ratting at Hampstead for Mr. Cunningham, the butcher, and it bit one of my dogs—Black Bess by name, the truest bitch in the world, sir—in the mouth, and she died three days arterwards at the Ball at Kilburn. I was along with Captain K——, who'd come out to see the sport, and whilst we were at dinner, and the poor bitch lying under my chair, my boy says, says he, "Father, Black Bess is dying"; and had scarce spoke the speech when she was dead. It was all through the bite of that stoat, for I opened the wound in the lip, and it was all swole, and dreadful ulcerated, and all down the throat it was inflamed most shocking, and so was the lungs quite red and fiery. She was hot with work when she got the bite, and perhaps that made her take the pison quicker.

'When I was about fifteen, sir, I turned to bird-fancying. I was very fond of the sombre linnet. I was very successful in raising them and sold them for a deal of money. I've got the strain of them by me now. I've ris them from some I purchased from a person in the Coal-yard, Drury-lane. I give him 2*l.* for one of the periwinkle strain, but afterwards I heard of a person with, as I thought, a better strain—Lawson of Holloway—and I went and give him 30*s.* for a bird. I then ris them. I used to go and ketch the nestlings off the common, and ris them under the old trained birds.

'Originally linnets was taught to sing by a bird-organ—principally among the weavers, years ago,—but I used to make the old birds teach the young ones. I used to molt them off in the dark, by kivering the cages up, and then they'd learn from hearing the old ones singing, and would take the song. If any did not sing perfectly I used to sell 'em as cast-offs.

'The linnet's is a beautiful song. There are four-and-twenty changes in a linnet's song. It's one of the beautifullest song-birds we've got. It sings "toys," as we call them; that is, it makes sounds which we distinguish in the fancy as the "tollock eeke eeke quake le wheet; single eke eke quake wheets, or eek eek quake chowls; eege pipe chowl: laugh; eege poy chowls; rattle; pipe; fear; pugh and poy."

'This seems like Greek to you, sir, but it's the tunes we use in the fancy. What we terms "fear" is a sound like fear, as if they was frightened; "laugh" is a kind of shake, nearly the same as the "rattle."

'I know the sounds of all the English birds, and what they say. I could tell you about the nightingale, the black cap, hedge warbler, garden warbler, petty chat, red start—a beautiful song-bird—the willow wren—little warblers they are—linnets, or any of them, for I have got their sounds in my ear and my mouth.'

As if to prove this, he drew from a side-pocket a couple of tin bird-whistles, which were attached by a string to a button-hole. He instantly began to imitate the different birds, commencing with their call, and then explaining how, when answered to in such a way, they gave another note, and how, if still responded to, they uttered a different sound.

In fact, he gave me the whole of the conversation he usually carried on with the different kinds of birds, each one being as it were in a different language. He also showed me how he allured them to him, when they were in the air singing in the distance, and he did this by giving their entire song. His cheeks and throat seemed to be in constant motion as he filled the room with his loud imitations of the lark, and so closely did he resemble the notes of the bird, that it was no longer any wonder how the little things could be deceived.

In the same manner he illustrated the songs of the nightingale, and so many birds, that I did not recognise the names of some of them. He knew all their habits as well as notes, and repeated to me the peculiar chirp they make on rising from the ground, as well as the sound by which he distinguishes that it is 'uneasy with curiosity,' or that it has settled on a tree. Indeed, he appeared to be acquainted with all the chirps which distinguished any action in the bird up to the point when, as he told me, it 'circles about, and then falls like a stone to the ground with its pitch.'

'The nightingale,' he continued, 'is a beautiful song-bird. They're plucky birds, too, and they hear a call and answer to anybody; and when taken in April they're plucked enough to sing as soon as put in a cage. I can ketch a nightingale in less than five minutes; as soon as he calls, I calls to him with my mouth, and he'll answer me (both by night or day), either from a spinney (a little copse), a dell, or a wood, wherever he may be. I make my scrapes, (that is, clear away the dirt), set my traps, and catch 'em almost before I've tried my luck. I've ketched sometimes thirty in a day, for although people have got a notion that nightingales is scarce, still those who can distinguish their song in the daytime know that they are plentiful enough—almost like the lark. You see persons fancy that them nightingales as sings at night is the only ones living, but it's wrong, for many on them only sings in the day.

'You see it was when I was about eighteen, I was beginning to get such a judge about birds, sir. I sold to a butcher, of the name of Jackson, the first young 'un that I made money out of—for two pounds it was—and I've sold loads of 'em since for thirty shillings or two pounds each, and I've got the strain by me now. I've also

got by me now the bird that won the match at Mr. Lockwood's
in Drury-lane, and won the return match at my own place in
High-street, Marabun. It was in the presence of all the fancy.
He's moulted pied (pie-bald) since, and gone a little white on the
head and the back. We only sang for two pounds a side—it wasn't
a great deal of money. In our matches we sing by both gas and
daylight. He was a master-baker I sang against, but I forgot his
name. They do call him "Holy Face," but that's a nick-name,
because he's very much pock-marked. I wouldn't sell that bird
at all for anythink; I've been offered ten pounds for it. Captain
K—— put ten sovereigns down on the counter for him, and I
wouldn't pick 'em up, for I've sold lots of his strain for a pound
each.

'When I found I was master of the birds, then I turned to my
rat business again. I had a little rat dog—a black tan terrier of
the name of Billy—which was the greatest stock dog in London of
that day. He is the father of the greatest portion of small black tan
dogs in London now, which Mr. Isaac, the bird-fancier in Princess
street, purchased one of the strain for six or seven pounds; which
Jimmy Massey afterwards purchased another of the strain for a
monkey, a bottle of wine, and three pounds. That was the rummest
bargain I ever made.

'I've ris and trained monkeys by shoals. Some of mine is about
now in shows exhibiting; one in particular—Jimmy.

'One of the strain of this little black tan dog would draw a
badger twelve or fourteen lbs. to his six lbs., which was done for a
wager, 'cos it was thought the badger had his teeth drawn, but he
hadn't, as was proved by his bitting Mr. P——from Birmingham,
for he took a piece clean out of his trousers, which was pretty good
proof, and astonished them all in the room.

'I've been offered a sovereign a-pound for some of my little
terriers, but it wouldn't pay me at that price, for they weren't
heavier than two or three pounds. I once sold one of the dogs, of
this same strain, for fourteen pounds, to the Austrian Ambassador.
Mrs. H—— the baker's lady, wished to get my strain of terriers,
and she gave me five pounds for the use of him; in fact, my terrier
dog was known to all the London fancy. As rat-killing dogs, there's
no equal to that strain of black tan terriers.

'It's fifteen year ago since I first worked for Government. I found that the parks was much infested with rats, which had underminded the bridges and gnawed the drains, and I made application to Mr. Westley, who was superintendent of the park and he spoke of it, and then it was wrote to me that I was to fulfil the siterwation, and I was to have six pounds a-year. But after that it was altered, and I was to have so much a-head, which is threepence. After that, Newton, what was a warmint destroyer to her Majesty, dying, I wrote in to the Board of Hordnance, when they appointed me to each station in London—that was, to Regentsey-park-barracks, to the Knightsbridge and Portland-barracks, and to all the other barracks in the metropolis. I've got the letter now by me, in which they says "they is proud to appint me."

'I've taken thirty-two rats out of one hole in the islands in Regentsey-park, and found in it fish, birds, and loads of eggs—duck-eggs, and every kind.

'It must be fourteen year since I first went about the streets exhibiting with rats. I began with a cart and a'most a donkey; for it was a pony scarce bigger; but I've had three or four big horses since that, and ask anybody, and they'll tell you I'm noted for my cattle. I thought that by having a kind of costume, and the rats painted on the cart, and going, round the country, I should get my name about, and get myself knowed; and so I did, for folks 'ud come to me, so that sometimes I've had four jobs a-day, from people seeing my cart. I found I was quite the master of the rat, and could do pretty well what I liked with him; so I used to go round Finchley, Highgate, and all the suburbs, and show myself, and how I handled the warmint.

'I used to wear a costume of white leather breeches, and a green coat and scarlet waistkit, and a goold band round my hat, and a belt across my shoulder, I used to make a first-rate appearance, such as was becoming the uniform of the Queen's rat-catcher.

'Lor' bless you! I've travell'd all over London, an I'll kill rats again anybody. I'm open to all the world for any sum, from one pound to fifty. I used to have my belts painted at first by Mr. Bailey, the animal painter—with four white rats; but the idea come into my head that I'd cast the rats in metal, just to make more appearance for the belt, to come out in the world. I was nights and days at it, and it give me a deal of bother. I could manage it nohow; but by my own ingenuity and persewerance I succeeded. A man axed me a pound a-piece for casting the rats—that would ha' been four pound. I was very certain that my belt, being a handsome one, would help my business tremenjous in the sale of my composition. So I took a mould from a dead rat in plaster, and then I got some of my wife's sarsepans, and, by G—, I casted 'em with some of my own pewter-pots.'

The wife, who was standing by, here exclaimed—

'Oh, my poor sarsepans! I remember 'em. There was scarce one left to cook our wittels with.'

'Thousands of moulders,' continued Jack Black, 'used to come to see me do the casting of the rats, and they kept saying, "You 'll never do it, Jack." The great difficulty, you see, was casting the heye—which is a black bead—into the metal.

'When the belt was done, I had a great success; for, bless you, I couldn't go a yard without a crowd after me.

'When I was out with the cart selling my composition, my usual method was this. I used to put a board across the top, and form a kind of counter. I always took with me a iron-wire cage—so big a one, that Mr. Barnet, a Jew, laid a wager that he could get into it, and he did. I used to form this cage at one end of the cart, and sell my compositions at the other. There were rats painted round the cart—that was the only show I had about the wehicle. I used to take out the rats, and put them outside the cage; and used to begin the show by putting rats inside my shirt next my buzzum, or in my coat and breeches pockets, or on my shoulder—in fact, all about me, anywhere. The people would stand to see me take up rats without being bit. I never said much, but I used to handle the rats in every possible manner, letting 'em run up my arm, and stroking their backs and playing with 'em. Most of the people used to fancy they had been tamed on purpose, until they'd see me take fresh ones from the cage, and play with them in the same manner. I all this time kept on selling my composition, which my man Joe used to offer about; and whenever a packet was sold, I always tested its wirtues by killing a rat with it afore the people's own eyes.

'I once went to Tottenham to sell my composition, and to exhibit with my rats afore the country people. Some countrymen, which said they were rat-ketchers, came up to me whilst I was playing with some rats, and said—"Ugh, you're not a rat-ketcher; that's not the way to do it." They were startled at seeing me selling the pison at such a rate, for the shilling packets was going uncommon well, sir. I said, "No, I ain't a rat-ketcher, and don't know nothink about it. You come up and show me how to do it." One of them come up on the cart, and put his hand in the cage, and curous enough he got three bites directly, and afore he could take his hands out they was nearly bit to ribands. My man Joe, says he, "I tell you, if we ain't rat-ketchers, who is? We are the regular rat-ketchers; my master kills 'em, and then I eats 'em"—and he takes up a live one and puts its head into his mouth, and I puts my hand in the cage and pulls out six or seven in a cluster, and holds 'em up in the air, without even a bite. The countrymen bust out laughing; and they said, "Well, you're the best we ever see." I sold near 4*l*. worth of composition that day.

'Another day, when I'd been out flying pigeons as well—carriers, which I fancies to—I drove the cart, after selling the composition, to the King's Arms, Hanwell, and there was a feller there—a tailor by trade—what had turned rat-ketcher. He had got with him some fifty or sixty rats-the miserablest mangey brutes you ever seed in a tub—taking 'em up to London to sell. I, hearing of it, was determined to have a lark, so I goes up and takes out ten of them rats, and puts them inside my shirt, next my buzzum, and then I walks into the parlour nad sits down, and begins drinking my ale as right as if nothing had happened. I scarce had seated myself, when the landlord—who was in the lay—says, "I know a man who'll ketch rats quicker than anybody in the world." This put the tailor chap up, so he offers to bet half-a-gallon of ale he would, and I takes him. He goes to the tub and brings out a veery large rat, and walks with it into the room to show to the company. "Well," says I to the man, "why I, who ain't a rat-ketcher, I've got a bigger one here," and I pulls one out from my buzzum. "And here's another, and another," says I, till I had placed the whole ten on the table. "That's the way I ketch 'em," says I,—"they comes of their own accord to me." He tried to handle the warmints, but the poor fellow was bit, and his hands was soon bleeding fur'ously, and I without a mark. A gentleman as knowed me said, "This must be the Queen's rat-ketcher," and that spilt the fun. The poor fellow seemed regular done up, and said, "I shall give up rat-ketching, you've beat me! Here I've been travelling with rats all my life, and I never see such a thing afore."

'When I've been in a mind for travelling I've never sold less than ten shillings' worth of my composition, and I've many a time sold five pounds' worth. Ten shillings' worth was the least I ever sold. During my younger career, if I'd had a backer, I might, one week with another, have made my clear three pounds a-week, after paying all my expenses and feeding my horse and all.

'I also destroy black beedles with a composition which I always keep with me again it's wanted. I often have to destroy the beedles in wine-cellars, which gnaw the paper off the bottles, such as is round the champagne and French wine bottles. I've killed lots of beedles too for bakers. I've also sterminated some thousands of beedles for linen-drapers and pork sassage shops. There's two kinds of beedles, the hard-shell and the soft-shell beedle. The hard-shell one is the worst, and that will gnaw cork, paper, and anythink woollen. The soft-shell'd one will gnaw bread or food, and it also lays its eggs in the food, which is dreadful nasty.

'There's the house ant too, which there is some thousands of people as never saw—I sterminate them as well. There's a Mrs. B. at the William the Fourth public-house, Hampstead; she couldn't lay her child's clothes down without gettin' 'em full of ants. They've got a sting something in feel like a horse-fly's, and is more annoying than dangerous. It's cockroaches that are found in houses. They're dreadful nasty things, and will bite, and they are equal to the Spanish flies for blistering. I've tried all insects on my flesh to see how they bite me. Cockroaches will undermine similar to the ant, and loosen the bricks the same as the cricket. It's astonishing how so small an insect as them will scrape away such a quantity of mortar as they do—which thing infests grates, floorings, and suchlike.

'The beedle is a most 'stordinary thing, which will puzzle most people to sterminate, for they lays such a lot of eggs as I would never guarantee to do away with beedles—only to keep them clear; for if you kills the old ones the eggs will rewive, and young ones come out of the wainskitting and sitch-like, and then your employers will say, "Why, you were paid for sterminating, and yet here they are."

'One night in August—the night of a very heavy storm, which, maybe, you may remember, sir—I was sent for by a medical gent as lived opposite the Load of Hay, Hampstead, whose two children had been attacked by rats while they was sleeping in their little cots. I traced the blood, which had left lines from their tails, through the openings in the lath and plaster, which I follered to where my ferruts come out of, and they must have come up from the bottom of the house to the attics. The rats gnawed the hands and feet of the little children. The lady heard them crying, and got out of her bed and called to the servant to know what the child was making such a noise for, when they struck a light, and then they see the rats running away to the holes; their little night-gownds was kivered with blood, as if their throats had been cut. I asked the lady to give me one of the night-gownds to keep as a cur'osity, for I considered it a *phee*nomenon, and she give it to me, but I never was so vexed in all my life as when I was told the next day that a maid had washed it. I went down the next morning and sterminated them rats. I found they were of the specie of rat which we term the blood-rat, which is a dreadful spiteful feller—a snake-headed rat, and infests the dwellings. There may have been some dozens of 'em altogether, but it's so long ago I a'most forget how many I took in that house. The gent behaved uncommon handsome, and said, "Mr. Black, I can never pay you for this"; and ever afterwards, when I used to pass by that there house, the little dears when they see me used to call out to their mamma, "O, here's Mr. Ratty, ma!' They were very pretty little fine children—uncommon handsome, to be sure.

'I also sterminate moles for her Majesty, and the Woods and Forests, and I've sterminated some hundreds for different farmers in the country. It's a cur'ous thing, but a mole will kill a rat and eat it afterwards, and two moles will fight wonderful. They've got a mouth exactly like a shark, and teeth like saws; ah, a wonderful saw mouth. They're a very sharp-biting little animal, and very painful. A rat is frightened of one, and don't like fighting them at all.

'I've bred the finest collection of pied rats which has ever been knowed in the world. I had about eleven hundred of them—all wariegated rats, and of a different specie and colour, and all of them in the first instance breed from the Norwegian and the white rat, and afterwards crossed with other specie.

'I have ris some of the largest tailed rats ever seen. I've sent them to all parts of the globe, and near every town in England. When I sold 'em off, three hundred of them went to France. I ketched the first white rat I had at Hampstead, and the black ones at Messrs. Hodges and Lowman's, in Regent-street, and them I bred in. I have 'em fawn and white, black and white, brown and white, red and white, blue-black and white, black-white and red.

'People come from all parts of London to see them rats, and I supplied near all the "happy families" with them. Burke, who had the "happy family" showing about London, has had hundreds from me. They got very tame, and you could do anythink with them. I've sold many to ladies for keeping in squirrel cages. Years ago I sold 'em for five and ten shillings a-piece, but towards the end of my breeding them, I let 'em go for two-and-six. At a shop in Leicester-square, where Cantello's hatching-eggs machine was, I sold a sow and six young ones for ten shillings, which formerly I have had five pounds for, being so docile, like a sow sucking her pigs.'

HER MAJESTY'S BUG-DESTROYER

THE vending of a bug-poison in the London streets is seldom followed as a regular source of living. We have met with persons who remember to have seen men selling penny packets of vermin poison, but to find out the vendors themselves was next to an impossibility. The men seem merely to take to the business as a living when all other sources have failed. All, however, agree in acknowledging that there is such a street trade, but that the living it affords is so precarious that few men stop at it longer than two or three weeks.

Perhaps the most eminent of the bug-destroyers in London is that of Messrs. Tiffin and Son; but they have pursued their calling in the streets, and rejoice in the title of 'Bug-Destroyers to Her Majesty and the Royal Family.'

Mr. Tiffin, the senior partner in this house, most kindly obliged me with the following statement. It may be as well to say that Mr. Tiffin appears to have paid much attention to the subject of bugs, and has studied with much earnestness the natural history of this vermin.

'We can trace our business back,' he said, 'as far as 1695, when one of our ancestors first turned his attention to the destruction of bugs. He was a lady's stay-maker—men used to make them in those days, though, as far as that is concerned, it was a man that made my mother's dresses. This ancestor found some bugs in his house—a young colony of them, that had introduced themselves without his permission, and he didn't like their company, so he tried to turn them out of doors again, I have heard it said, in various ways. It is in history, and it has been handed down in my own family as well, that bugs were first introduced into England after the fire of London, in the timber that was brought for re-building the city, thirty years after the fire, and it was about that time that my ancestor first discovered the colony of bugs in his house. I can't say whether he studied the subject of bug-destroying, or whether he found out his stuff by accident; but he certainly *did* invent a compound which completely destroyed the bugs, and, having been so successful in his own house, he named it to some of his customers who were similarly plagued, and that was the com-mencement of the present connexion, which has continued up to this time.

'At the time of the illumination for the Peace, I thought I must have something over my shop, that would be both suitable for the event and to my business; so I had a transparency done, and stretched on a big frame, and lit up by gas, on which was written—

MAY THE

DESTROYERS OF PEACE

BE DESTROYED BY US.

TIFFIN & SON,
BUG-DESTROYERS TO HER MAJESTY.

'I mostly find the bugs in the bedsteads. But, if they are left unmolested, they get numerous and climb to the tops of the rooms, and about the corners of the ceilings. They colonize anywhere they can, though they're very high-minded and prefer lofty places. Where iron bedsteads are used the bugs are more in the *rooms*, and that's why such things are bad. They don't keep a bug away from the person sleeping. Bugs'll come, if they're thirty yards off.

'I knew a case of a bug who used to come every night about thirty or forty feet—it was an immense large room—from a corner

of the room to visit an old lady. There was only one bug, and he'd
been there for a long time. I was sent for to find him out. It took
me a long time to catch him. In that instance I had to examine
every part of the room, and when I got him I gave him an extra
nip to serve him out. The reason why I was so bothered was, the
bug had hidden itself near the window, the last place I should have
thought of looking for him, for a bug never by choice faces the light;
but when I came to inquire about it, I found that this old lady
never rose till three o'clock in the day, and the window-curtains
were always drawn, so that there was no light like.

'Lord! yes, I am often sent for to catch a single bug. I've had
to go many, many miles—even 100 or 200—into the country,
and perhaps catch only half-a-dozen bugs after all; but then that's
all that are there, so it answers our employer's purpose as well as
if they were swarming.

'I work for the upper classes only; that is, for carriage company
and such-like approaching it, you know. I have noblemen's names,
the first in England, on my books.

'My work is more method; and I may call it a scientific treating
of the bugs rather than wholesale murder. We don't care about
the thousands, it's the last bug we look for, whilst your carpenters
and upholsterers leave as many behind them, perhaps, as they
manage to catch.

'The bite of the bug is very curious. They bite all persons the
same (?) but the difference of effect lays in the constitution of the
parties. I've never noticed that a different kind of skin makes any
difference in being bitten. Whether the skin is moist or dry, it
don't matter. Wherever bugs are, the person sleeping in the bed
is sure to be fed on, whether they are marked or not; and as a
proof, when nodoby has slept in the bed for some time, the bugs
become quite flat; and, on the contrary, when the bed is always
occupied, they are round as a "lady-bird."

'The flat bug is more ravenous, though even he will allow you
time to go to sleep before he begins with you; or at least until he
thinks you ought to be asleep. When they find all quiet, not even
a light in the room will prevent their biting; but they are seldom
or ever found under the bed-clothes. They like a clear ground to
get off, and generally bite round the edges of the nightcap or the
nightdress. When they are found *in* the bed, it's because the parties

have been tossing about, and have curled the sheets round the bugs.

'The finest and fattest bugs I ever saw were those I found in a black man's bed. He was the favourite servant of an Indian general. He didn't want his bed done by me; he didn't want it touched. His bed was full of 'em, no beehive was ever fuller. The walls and all were the same, there wasn't a patch that wasn't crammed with them. He must have taken them all over the house wherever he went.

'I've known persons to be laid up for month through bug-bites. There was a very handsome fair young lady I knew once, and she was much bitten about the arms, and neck, and face, so that her eyes were so swelled up she couldn't see. The spots rose up like blisters, the same as if stung with a nettle, only on a very large scale. The bites were very much inflamed, and after a time they had the appearance of boils.

'Some people fancy, and it is historically recorded, that the bug smells because it has no vent; but this is fabulous, for they *have* a vent. It is not the human blood neither that makes them smell, because a young bug who has never touched a drop will smell. They breathe, I believe, through their sides; but I can't answer for that, though it's not through the head. They haven't got a mouth, but they insert into the skin the point of a tube, which is quite as fine as a hair, through which they draw up the blood. I have many a time put a bug on the back of my hand, to see how they bite; though I never felt the bite but once, and then I suppose the bug had pitched upon a very tender part, for it was a sharp prick, something like that of a leech-bite.

'I was once at work on the Princess Charlotte's own bedstead. I was in the room, and she asked me if I had found anything, and I told her no; but just at that minute I *did* happen to catch one, and upon that she sprang up on the bed, and put her hand on my shoulder, to look at it. She had been tormented by the creature, because I was ordered to come directly, and that was the only one I found. When the Princess saw it, she said, "Oh, the nasty thing! That's what tormented me last night; don't let him escape." I think he looked all the better for having tasted royal blood.'

PUNCH

THE performer of Punch that I saw was a short, dark, pleasant-looking man, dressed in a very greasy and very shiny green shooting-jacket. This was fastened together by one button in front, all the other button-holes having been burst through. Protruding from his bosom, a corner of the pandean pipes was just visible, and as he told me the story of his adventures, he kept playing with the band of his very limp and very rusty old beaver hat. He had formerly been a gentleman's servant, and was especially civil in his manners. He came to me with his hair tidily brushed for the occasion, but apologised for his appearance on entering the room. He was very communicative, and took great delight in talking like Punch, with his call in his mouth, while some young children were in the room, and who, hearing the well-known sound of Punch's voice, looked all about for the figure. Not seeing the show, they fancied the man had the figure in his pocket, and that the sounds came from it. The change from Punch's voice to the man's natural tone was managed without an effort, and instantaneously. It had a very peculiar effect.

'Punch, you know, sir, is a dramatic performance in two hacts. It's a play, you may say. I don't think it can be called a tragedy hexactly; a drama is what we names it. There is tragic parts, and comic and sentimental parts, too. Some families where I performs will have it most sentimental——in the original style; them families is generally sentimental theirselves. Others is all for the comic, and then I has to kick up all the games I can. To the sentimental folk I am obliged to perform werry steady and werry slow, and leave out all comic words and business. They won't have no ghost, no coffin, and no devil; and that's what I call spiling the performance entirely. It's the march of hintellect wot's a doing all this—it is, sir.

'I bought the show of old Porsini, the man as first brought Punch into the streets of England. To be sure, there was a woman over with it before then. Her name was——I can't think of it just now, but she never performed in the streets, so we consider Porsini as our real forefather. It isn't much more nor seventy years since Porsini (he was a werry old man when he died, and blind) showed the hexhibition in the streets of London. I've heerd tell that old

Porsini used to take very often as much as ten pounds a day, and he used to sit down to his fowls and wine, and the very best of everything, like the first gennelman in the land; indeed, he made enough money at the business to be quite a tip-top gennelman, that he did. But he never took care of a halfpenny he got. He was that independent, that if he was wanted to perform, sir, he'd come at his time, not your'n. At last, he reduced himself to want, and died in St. Giles's workhouse. Ah, poor fellow! he oughtn't to have been allowed to die where he did, after amusing the public for so many years. Every one in London knowed him. Lords, dukes, princes, squires, and wagabonds—all used to stop to laugh at his performance, and a funny clever old fellow he was. He was past performing when I bought my show of him, and werry poor. He was living in the Coal-yard, Drury-lane, and had scarcely a bit of food to eat. He had spent all he had got in drink, and in treating friends,—aye, any one, no matter who. He didn't study the world, nor himself neither. As fast as the money came it went, and when it was gone, why he'd go to work and get more. His show was a very inferior one, though it were the fust—nothing at all like them about now—nothing near so good. If you only had four sticks then, it was quite enough to make plenty of money out, of so long as it was Punch. I gave him thirty-five shillings for the stand, figures and all. I bought it cheap, you see, for it was thrown on one side, and was of no use to any one but such as myself. There was twelve figures and the other happaratus, such as the gallows, ladder, horse, bell, and stuffed dog. The characters was Punch, Judy, Child, Beadle, Scaramouch, Nobody, Jack Ketch, the Grand Senoor, the Doctor, the Devil (there was no Ghost used then), Merry Andrew, and the Blind Man. These last two kerrackters are quite done with now. The heads of the kerrackters was all carved in wood, and dressed in the proper costume of the country. There was at that time, and is now, a real carver for the Punch business. He was dear, but werry good and hexcellent. His Punch's head was the best as I ever seed. The nose and chin used to meet quite close together. A set of new figures, dressed and all, would come to about fifteen pounds. Each head cost five shillings for the bare carving alone, and every figure that we has takes at least a yard of cloth to dress him, besides ornaments and things that comes werry expensive. A good show at the present time will cost three pounds odd for the stand alone—that's including baize, the frontispiece, the back scene, the cottage, and the letter cloth, or what is called the drop-scene at the theatres. In the old ancient style, the back scene used to pull up and change into a gaol scene, but that's all altered now.

'We've got more upon the comic business now, and tries to do more with Toby than with the prison scene. The prison is what we calls the sentimental style. Formerly Toby was only a stuffed figure. It was Pike who first hit upon hintroducing a live dog, and a great hit it were—it made a grand alteration in the hexibition, for now the performance is called Punch and Toby *as well*. There is one Punch about the streets at present that tries it on with three dogs, but that ain't much of a go—too much of a good thing I calls it. Punch, as I said before, is a drama in two hacts. We don't drop the scene at the end of the first—the drum and pipes strikes up instead. The first act we consider to end with Punch being taken to prison for the murder of his wife and child. The great difficulty in performing Punch consists in the speaking. which is done by a call, or whistle in the mouth, such as this here.' He then produced the call from his waistcoat pocket. It was a small flat instrument, made of two curved pieces of metal about the size of a knee-buckle, bound together with black thread. Between these was a plate of some substance (apparently silk), which he said was a secret. The call, he told me, was tuned to a musical instrument, and took a considerable time to learn. He afterwards took from his pocket two of the small metallic plates unbound. He said the composition they were made of was also one of the 'secrets of the purfession.' They were not tin, nor zinc, because 'both of them metals were poisons in the mouth, and hinjurious to the constitution.' 'These calls,' he continued, 'we often sell to genelmen for a sovereign a-piece, and for that we give 'em a receipt how to use them. They ain't whistles, but calls, or unknown tongues, as we sometimes names 'em, because with them in the mouth we can pronounce each word as plain as any parson. We have two or three kinds—one for out-of-doors, one for in-doors, one for speaking and for singing, and another for selling. I've sold many a one to gennelmen going along, so I generally keeps a hextra one with me. Porsini brought the calls into this country with him from Italy, and we who are now in the purfession have all learnt how to make and use them, either from him or those as he had taght' em to. I larnt the use of mine from Porsini himself. My master whom I went out with at first would never teach me, and was werry partickler in keeping it all secret from me. Porsini taught me the call at the time I bought his show of him. I was six months in perfecting myself in the use of it. I kept practising away night and morning with it, until I got it quite perfect. It was no use trying at home 'cause it sounds quite different in the hopen hair. Often when I've made 'em at home, I'm obliged to take the calls to pieces after trying 'em out in the streets, they've been made upon too weak a scale. When I was practising, I used to go into the parks, and fields, and out-of-the-way places, so as to get to know how to use it in the hopen air. Now I'm reckoned one of the best speakers in the whole pur-fession.

'The best pitch of all in London is Leicester-square; there's all sorts of classes, you see, passing there. Then comes Regent-street (the corner of Burlington-street is uncommon good, and there's a good publican there besides). Bond-street ain't no good now. Oxford-street, up by Old Cavendish-street, or Oxford-market, or Wells-street, are all favourite pitches for Punch. We don't do much in the City. People has their heads all full of business there, and them as is greedy arter the money ain't no friend of Punch's. Tottenham-court-road, the New-road, and all the hen-virons of London, is pretty good. Hampstead, tho', ain't no good; they've got too poor there. I'd sooner not go out at all than to Hampstead. Belgrave-square, and all about that part, is uncommon good; but where there's many chapels Punch won't do at all. I did once, though, strike up hopposition to a street preacher wot was a holding forth in the New-road, and did uncommon well. All his flock, as he called 'em, left him, and come over to look at me. Punch and preaching is two different creeds—hopposition parties, I may say. We in generally walks from twelve to twenty mile every day, and carries the show, which weighs a good half-hundred, at the least. Arter great exertion, our woice werry often fails us; for speaking all day through the "call" is werry trying, 'specially when we are chirruping up so as to bring the children to the vinders. The boys is the greatest nuisances we has to contend with. Wherever we goes we are sure of plenty of boys for a hind-rance; but they've got no money, bother 'em! and they'll follow us for miles, so that we're often compelled to go miles to a avoid 'em. Many parts is swarming with boys, such as Vitechapel. Spitalfields, that's the worst place for boys I ever come a-near; they're like flies in summer there, only much more thicker. I never shows my face within miles of them parts. Chelsea, again, has an uncommon lot of boys; and wherever we know the children swarm, there's the spots we makes a point of avoiding. Why, the boys is such a hobstruction to our performance, that often we are obliged to drop the curtain for 'em. They'll throw one another's caps into the frame while I'm inside on it, and do what we will, we can't keep 'em from poking their fingers through the baize and making holes to peep through. Then they *will* keep tapping the drum; but the worst of all is, the most of 'em ain't got a farthing to bless themselves with, and they *will* shove into the best places. Soldiers, again, we don't like; they've got no money—no, not even so much as pockets, sir. Nusses ain't no good. Even if the mothers of the dear children has given 'em a penny to spend, why the nusses takes it from 'em, and keeps it for ribbins. Sometimes we can coax a penny out of the children, but the nusses knows too much to be gammoned by us. Indeed, servants in generally don't do the thing what's right to us—some is good to us, but the most of 'em will have poundage out of what we gets. About sixpence out of every half-crown is what the footman takes from us. We in generally goes into the country in the summer time for two or three months. Watering-places is werry good in July and August. Punch mostly goes down to the sea-side with the quality. Brighton, though, ain't no account; the Pavilion's done up with, and therefore Punch has discontinued his visits.'

Punch Talk

' "Bona parlare" means language; name of patter. "Yeute munjare"—no food. "Yeute lente"—no bed. "Yeute bivare"—no drink. I've "yeute munjare," and "yeute bivare," and, what's worse, "yeute lente." This is better than the costers' talk, because that ain't no slang at all, and this is a broken Italian, and much higher than the costers' lingo. We know what o'clock it is, besides.'

Scene with two Punchmen

' "How are you getting on?" I might say to another Punchman. "Ultra cateva," he'd say. If I was doing a little, I'd say, "Bonar."

Let us have a "shant a bivare"—pot o' beer.' If we has a good pitch
we never tell one another, for business is business. If they know
we've a "bonar" pitch, they'll oppose, which makes it bad.

'　"Co. and Co." is our term for partner, or "questa, questa," as
well. "Ultray cativa,"—no bona. "Slumareys"—figures, frame,
scenes, properties. "Slum"—call, or unknown tongue. "Ultray
cativa slum"—not a good call. "Tambora"—drum; that's Italian.
"Pipares"—pipes. "Questra homa a vardring the slum, scapar it,
Orderly"—there's someone a looking at the slum. Be off quickly.
"Fielia" is a child; "Homa" is a man; "Dona", a female; "Char-
fering-homa"—talking-man, policeman. Policeman can't interfere
with us, we're sanctioned. Punch is exempt out of the Police
Act. Some's very good men, and some on 'em are tyrants; but
generally speaking they're all werry kind to us, and allows us every
privilege. That's a flattery, you know, because you'd better not
meddle with them. Civility always gains its esteem.'

The man here took a large clasp-knife out of his breeches pocket.

The Punchman at the Theatre

'I used often when a youth to be very fond of plays and romances,
and frequently went to theatres to learn knowledge, of which I
think there is a deal of knowledge to be learnt from those places
(that gives the theatres a touch—helps them on a bit). I was very
partial and fond of seeing Romeau and Juliet; Otheller; and the
Knights of St. John, and the Pretty Gal of Peerlesspool; Macbeth
and the Three Dancing Witches. Don Goovarney pleased me best
of all though. What took me uncommon were the funeral purcession
of Juliet—it affects the heart, and brings us to our nat'ral feelings.
I took my ghost from Romeau and Juliet; the ghost comes from the
grave, and it's beautiful. I used to like Kean, the principal performer. Oh, admirable! most admirable he were, and especially in
Otheller, for then he was like my Jim Crow here, and was always
a great friend and supporter of his old friend Punch. Otheller
murders his wife, ye know, like Punch does. Otheller kills her,
'cause the green-eyed monster has got into his 'art, and he being so
extremely fond of her; but Punch kills his'n by accident, though
he did not intend to do it, for the Act of Parliament against husbands beating wives was not known in his time. A most excellent
law that there, for it causes husbands and wives to be kind and

natural one with the other, all through the society of life. Judy irritates her husband, Punch, for to strike the fatal blow, vich at the same time, vith no intention to commit it, not knowing at the same time, being rather out of his mind, vot he vas about. I hope this here will be a good example both to men and wives, always to be kind and obleeging to each other, and that will help them through the mainder with peace and happiness, and will rest in peace with all mankind (that's moral). It must be well worded, ye know, that's my beauty.'

Mr. Punch's Refreshment

'Always Mr. Punch, when he performs to any nobleman's juvenile parties, he requires a little refreshment and sperrits before commencing, because the performance will go far superior. But where teetotalers is he plays very mournful, and they don't have the best parts of the dramatical performance. Cos pump-vater gives a person no heart to exhibit his performance, where if any sperrits is given to him he woold be sure to give the best of satisfaction. I likes where I goes to perform for the gentleman to ring the bell, and say to the butler to bring this here party up whatever he chooses. But Punch is always moderate; he likes one eye wetted, then the tother after; but he likes the best: not particular to brandy, for fear of his nose of fading, and afeerd of his losing the colour. All theatrical people, and even the great Edmund Kean, used to take a drop before commencing performance, and Punch must do the same, for it enlivens his sperrits, cheers his heart up, and enables him to give the best of satisfaction imaginable.'

Description of Frame and Proscenium

' "Ladies and gents," the man says outside the show, afore striking up, "I'm now going to exhibit a performance worthy of your notice, and far superior to anythink you hever had a hopportunity of witnessing of before." (I am a doing it now, sir, as if I was addressing a company of ladies and gentleman, he added, by way of parenthesis.) "This is the original performance of Punch, ladies and gents; and it will always gain esteem. I am going to hintroduce a performance worthy of your notice, which is the dramatical performance of the original and old-established performance of Punch, experienced many year. I merely call your attention, ladies and gents, to the novel attraction, which I'm now about to hintroduce to you.

' "I only merely place this happaratus up to inform you what I am about to perform to you. The performance will continue for upwards of one hour—*provising as we meets with sufficient encouragement*. (That's business, ye know, master; just to give 'em to understand that we wants a little assistance afore we begins.) It will surpass anythink you've had the hopportunity of witnessing of before in all the hannuals of history. I hope, ladies and gents, I am not talking too grammatical for some of you."

'That there is the address, sir,' he continued, 'what I always gives to the audience outside before I begins to perform—just to let the respectable company know that I am a working for to get my living by honest industry.

' "Those ladies and gents," he then went on, as if addressing an imaginary crowd, "what are a-standing around, a-looking at the performance, will, I hope, be as willing to give as they is to see. There's many a lady and gent now at the present moment standing around me, perhaps, whose hearts might be good though not in their power." (This is Punch's patter, yer know, outside; and when you has to say all that yourself, you wants the affluency of a methodist parson to do the talk, I can tell ye.) "Now boys, look up yer ha'pence! Who's got a farden or a ha'penny? and I'll be the first brown towards it. I ain't particular if it's a half-crown. Now, my lads, feel in your pockets and see if you've got an odd copper. Here's one, and who'll be the next to make it even? We means to show it all through, *provising we meets with sufficient encouragement*." (I always sticks to them words, "sufficient encouragement.") "You'll have the pleasure of seeing Spring-heeled Jack, or the Roossian Bear, and the comical scene with Joey the clown, and the frying-pan of sassages!" (That's a kind of gaggery.)

'I'll now just explain to you, sir, the different parts of the frame. This here's the letter-cloth, which shows you all what we performs. Sometimes we has wrote on it—

THE DOMINION OF FANCY,

or,

PUNCH'S OPERA:

that fills up a letter-cloth; and Punch is a fancy for every person, you know, whoever may fancy it. I stands inside here on this footboard; and if there's any one up at the winders in the street, I puts my foot longways, so as to keep my nob out of sight. This here is the stage front, or *proceedings* (proscenium), and is painted over with flags and banners, or any different things. Sometimes there's George and the Dragging, and the Rile Queen's Arms, (we can have them up when we like, cos we are sanctioned, and I've played afore the rile princes). But anything for freshness. People's tired of looking at the Rile Arms, and wants something new to cause attraction, and so on.

'This here's the playboard, where sits Punch. The scenes behind are representing a garding scene, and the side scenes is a house and a cottage—they're for the exaunts, you know, just for convenience. The back scene draws up, and shows the prison, with the winders all cut out, and the bars showing, the same as there is to a gaol; though I never was in one in my life, and I'll take good care I never shall be.

'Our speaking instrument is an unknown secret, cos it's an "unknown tongue," that's known to one except those in our own purfession. It's a hinstrument like this which I has in my hand, and it's tuned to music. We has two or three kinds, one for outdoors, one for in-doors, one for speaking, one for singing, and one that's good for nothing, except selling on the cheap. They ain't whistles, but "calls," or "unknown tongues"; and with them in the mouth we can pronounce each word as plain a parson, and with as much affluency.

'The great difficulty in preforming Punch consists in speaking with this call in the mouth—cos it's produced from the lungs; it's all done from there, and is a great strain, and acquires suction—and that's brandy-and-water, or summat to moisten the whistle with.

'We're bound not to drink water by our purfession, when we can get anything stronger. It weaknes the nerves, but we always like to keep in the bounds of propriety, respectability, and decency. I drinks my beer with my call in my mouth, and never takes it out, cos it exposes it, and the boys (hang 'em!) is so inquisitive. They runs after us, and looks up in our face to see how we speaks; but we drives 'em away with civility.

'Punch is a dramatical preformance, sir, in two acts, patronised by the nobility and gentry at large. We don't drop the scene at the end of the first act, the drum and pipes strikes up instead. The first act we consider to end with Punch being took to prison for the murder of his wife and baby. You can pick out a good many Punch preformers, without getting one so well versed as I am in it; they in general makes such a muffing concern of it. A drama, or dramatical preformance, we calls it, of the original preformance of Punch. It ain't a tragedy; it's both comic and sentimental, in which way we think proper to preform it. There's comic parts, as with the Clown and Jim Crow, and cetera—that's including a deal more, yer know.

'It's pretty play Punch is, when preformed well, and one of the greatest novelties in the world; and most ancient; handed down, too, for many hundred years.

'The prison scene and the baby is what we calls the sentimental touches. Some folks where I preforms will have it most sentimental. in the original style. Them families is generally sentimental their-selves. To these sentimental folks I'm obliged to preform werry steady and werry slow; they won't have no ghost, no coffin, and no devil; and that's what I call spiling the preformance entirely. Ha, ha!' he added, with a deep sigh, 'it's the march of intellect that's doing all this: it is, sir.

'Other folks is all for the comic, specially the street people; and then we has to dwell on the bell scene, and the nursing the baby, and the frying-pan, and the sassages, and Jim Crow.

'A few years ago Toby was all the go. Formerly the dog was only a stuffed figure, and it was Mr. Pike what first hit upon introducing a live animal; and a great hit it war. It made a surprising alteration in the exhibition, for till lately the preformance was called Punch and Toby as well. We used to go about the streets with three dogs, and that was admirable, and it did uncommon well as a new novelty at first, but we can't get three dogs to do it now. The mother of them dogs, ye see, was a singer, and had two pups what was singers too. Toby was wanted to sing and smoke a pipe as well, shake hands as well as seize Punch by the nose. When Toby was quiet, ye see, sir, it was the timidation of Punch's stick, for directly he put it down he flew at him, knowing at the same time that Punch was not his master.

'Punch commences with a song. He does roo-too-rooey, and sings the "Lass of Gowrie" down below, and then comes up, saying, "Ooy-ey; Oh, yes, I'm a coming. How do you do, ladies and gents?" —ladies always first; and then he bows many times. "I'm so happy to see you," he says. "Your most obedient, most humble, and dutiful servant, Mr. Punch." (Ye see I can talk as affluent as can be with the call in my mouth.) "Ooy-ey, I wishes you all well and happy." Then Punch says to the drum-and-pipes-man, as he puts his hand out, "How do you do, master?—play up; play up a horn-pipe: I'm a most hexcellent dancer"; and then Punch dances. Then ye see him a-dancing the hornpipe; and after that Punch says to the pipes, "Master, I shall call my wife up, and have a dance"; so he sing out, "Judy, Judy! my pratty creetur! come up stairs, my darling! I want to speak to you—and he knocks on the play-board.— "Judy! Here she comes, bless her little heart!"

Enter Judy

Punch. What a sweet creatur! what a handsome nose and chin! *(He pats her on the face very gently.)*

Judy. (Slapping him.) Keep quiet, do!

Punch. Don't be cross, my dear, but give me a kiss.

Judy. Oh, to be sure, my love.   [*They kiss.*

Punch. Bless your sweet lips! *(Hugging her.)* This is melting moments. I'm very fond of my wife; we must have a dance.

Judy. Agreed.   [*They both dance.*

Punch. Get out of the way! you don't dance well enough for me. *(He hits her on the nose.)* Go and fetch the baby, and mind and take care of it, and not hurt it.   [*Judy exaunts.*

Judy. (Returning back with baby.) Take care of the baby, while I go and cook the dumplings.

Punch. (Striking Judy with his right hand.) Get out of the way! I'll take care of the baby.   [*Judy exaunts.*

Punch (sits down and sings to the baby)—

> 'Hush-a-by, baby, upon the tree-top,
> When the wind blows the cradle will rock,
> When the bough breaks the cradle will fall,
> Down comes the baby and cradle and all.'

[*Baby cries.*

Punch. (Shaking it.) What a cross boy] *(He lays it down on the playboard, and rolls it backwards and forwards, to rock it to sleep, and sings again.)*

> 'Oh, slumber, my, darling, thy sire is a knight,
> Thy mother's a lady so lovely and bright;
> The hills and the dales, and the tow'rs which you see,
> They all shall belong, my dear creature, to thee.

(Punch continues rocking the child. It still cries, and he takes it up in his arms, saying, What a cross child! I can't a-bear cross children. *Then he vehemently shakes it, and knocks its head up against the side of the proceedings several times, representing to kill it, and he then throws it out of the winder.)*

Enter JUDY

Judy. Where's the baby?

Punch. (In a meloncholy tone.) I have had a misfortune; the child was so terrible cross, I throwed it out of the winder. *(Lemontation of Judy for the loss of her dear child. She goes into asterisks, and then excites and fetches a cudgel, and commences beating Punch over the head.)*

Punch. Don't be cross, my dear: I didn't go to do it.

Judy. I'll pay yer for throwing the child out of the winder. *(She keeps on giving him knocks of the head, but Punch snatches the stick away and commences an attack upon his wife, and beats her severely.)*

Judy. I'll go to the constable, and have you locked up.

Punch. Go to the devil. I don't care where you go. Get out of the way! *(Judy exaunts, and Punch then sings, 'Cherry ripe,' or 'Cheer, boys, cheer.' All before is sentimental, now this here's comic. Punch goes through his roo-too-to-rooey, and then the Beadle comes up.)*

Beadle. Hi! hallo, my boy!

Punch. Hello, my boy. *(He gives him a wipe over the head with his stick, which knocks him down, but he gets up again.)*

Beadle. Do you know, sir, that I've a special order in my pocket to take you up?

Punch. And I've a special order to knock you down. *(He knocks him down with simplicity, but not with brutality, for the juvenial branches don't like to see severity practised.)*

Beadle. (Coming up again.) D'ye know, my boy, that I've an order to take you up?

Punch. And I've an order I tell ye to knock you down. *(He sticks him. Punch is a tyrant to the Beadle, ye know, and if he was took up he wouldn't go through his rambles, so in course he isn't.)*

Beadle. I've a warrant for you, my boy.

Punch. (Striking him.) And that's a warrant for you, my boy. *(The Beadle's a determined man, ye know, and resolved to go to the ends of justice as far as possible in his power by special authority, so a quarrel enshoos between them.)*

Beadle. You are a blackguard.

Punch. So are you.

(The Beadle hits Punch on the nose, and takes the law in his own hands. Punch takes it up momentary; strikes the Beadle, and a fight enshoos. The Beadle, faint and exhausted, gets up once more; then he strikes Punch over the nose, which is returned pro and con.

Beadle. That's a good 'un.

Punch. That's a better.

Beadle. That's a topper. *(He hits him jolly hard.)*

Punch. (With his cudgel.) That's a wopper. *(He knocks him out of his senses, and the Beadle exaunts.)*

Enter MERRY CLOWN

Punch sings 'Getting up Stairs,' in quick time, while the Clown is coming up. Clown dances round Punch in all directions, and Punch with his cudgel is determined to catch him if possible.

Clown. No bono, allez tooti sweet, Mounseer. Look out sharp! Make haste! catch 'em alive! Here we are! how are you? good morning! don't you wish you may get it? Ah! coward, strike a white man! *(Clown keeps bobbing up and down, and Punch trying to hit all the time till Punch is exhausted nearly.)*

(The Clown, ye see, sir, is the best friend to Punch, he carries him through all his tricks, and he's a great favorite of Punch's. He's too cunning for him though, and knows too much for him, so they both shake hands and make it up.)

Clown. Now it's all fair; ain't it, Punch?

Punch. Yes.

Clown. Now I can begin again.

(You see, sir, the Clown gets over Punch altogether by his artful ways, and then he begins the same tricks over again; that is, if we wants a long performance; if not, we cuts it off at the other pint. But I'm telling you the real original style, sir.)

Clown. Good! you can't catch me.

(Punch gives him one whack of the head, and Clown exaunts, or goes off.)

Enter JIM CROW

Jim sings 'Buffalo Gals,' while coming up, and on entering Punch hits him a whack of the nose backhanded, and almost breaks it.

Jim. What for you do that? Me nigger! me like de white man. Him did break my nose.

Punch. Humbly beg your pardon, I did not go to help it.

(For as it had been done, you know, it wasn't likely he could help it after he'd done it—he couldn't take it away from him again, could he?)

Jim. Me beg you de pardon. (For ye see, sir, he thinks he's offended Punch.) Nebber mind, Punch, come and sit down, and we'll hab a song.

JIM CROW *prepares to sing*

Punch. Bravo, Jimmy! sing away, my boy—give us a stunner while you're at it.

JIM *sings*

'I'm a roarer on the fiddle,
    Down in the ole Virginny;
And I plays it scientific.
    Like Master Paganinni'

Punch. *(Tapping him on the head.)* Bravo! well done, Jimmy! give us another bit of a song.

Jim. Yes, me will.   [*Sings again.*

'Oh, lubly Rosa, Sambo come;
    Don't you hear the banjo?
    Tum, tum, tum!

Jim hits Punch with his head over the nose, as if butting at him, while he repeats tum-tum-tum. Punch offended, beats him with the stick, and sings—

'Lubly Rosa, Sambo come;
    Don't you hear the banjo?
    Tum, tum, tum!

Jim. (Rising.) Oh mi! what for you strike a nigger? *(Holding up his leg.)* Me will poke your eye out. Ready—shoot—bang—fire. *(Shoves his leg into Punch's eye.)*

Punch. He's poked my eye out! I'll look out for him for the future.

Jim Crow excites, or exaunts. Exaunt we calls it in our purfession, sir,—that's going away, you know. He's done his part, you know, and ain't to appear again.

Judy has died through Punch's ill usage after going for the Beadle, for if she'd done so before she couldn't ha' fetched the constable, you know,—certainly not. The beholders only believe her to be dead though, for she comes to life again afterwards; if she was dead, it would do away with Punch's wife altogether—for Punch is doatingly fond of her, though it's only his fun after all's said and done.

The Ghost, you see, is only a representation, as a timidation to soften his bad morals, so that he shouldn't do the like again. The Ghost, to be sure, shows that she's really dead for a time, but it's not in the imitation; for if it was, Judy's ghost (the figure) would be made like her.

The babby's lost altogether. It's killed. It is supposed to be destroyed entirely, but taken care of for the next time when called upon to perform—as if it were in the next world, you know,—that's moral.

Enter Ghost. Punch sings meanwhile 'Home, sweet Home.' (This is original). The Ghost represents the ghost of Judy, because he's killed his wife, don't you see, the Ghost making her appearance; but Punch don't know it at the moment. Still he sits down tired, and sings in the corner of the frame the song of 'Home, sweet Home,' while the Sperrit appears to him.

Punch turns round and sees the Ghost, and is most terribly timidated. He begins to shiver and shake in great fear, bringing his guilty conscience to his mind of what he's been guilty of doing, and at last he falls down in a fit of frenzy. Kicking, screeching, hollaring, and shouting 'Fifty thousand pounds for a doctor!' Then he turns on his side, and draws hisself double with the screwmatics in his gills. [*Ghost excites*

Enter DOCTOR

Punch is represented to be dead. This is the dying speech of Punch.

Doctor. Dear me! bless my heart! here have I been running as fast as ever I could walk, and very near tumbled over a straw. I heard somebody call most lustily for a doctor. Dear me *(looking at Punch in all directions, and examining his body)*, this is my pertickler friend Mr. Punch; poor man! how pale he looks! I'll feel his pulse *(counts his pulse)*—1, 2, 14, 9, 11. Hi! Punch, are you dead? are you dead? are you dead?

Punch. (Hitting him with his right hand over the nose, and knocking him back.) Yes.

Doctor. (Rubbing his nose with his hand.) I never heard a dead man speak before. Punch, you are not dead!

Punch. Oh, yes I am.

Doctor. How long have you been dead?

Punch. About six weeks.

Doctor. Oh, you're not dead, you're only poorly; I must fetch you a little reviving medicine, such as some stick-lickerish and balsam, and extract of shillalagh.

Punch. (Rising.) Make haste—*(he gives the Doctor a wipe on the nose)*—make haste and fetch it.   [*Doctor exaunts.*

Punch. The Doctor going to get me some physic! I'm very fond of brandy-and-water, and rum-punch. I want my physic; the Doctor never brought me no physic at all. I wasn't ill; it was only my fun. *(Doctor reappears with the physic-stick, and he whacks Punch over the head no harder than he is able, and cries)*—'There's physic! physic! physic! physic! physic! pills! balsam! sticklickerish!'

Punch. (Rising and rubbing his head against the wing.) Yes; it is sticklickerish.

(Ah! it's a pretty play, sir, when it's showed well—that it is—it's delightful to read the morals; I am wery fond of reading the morals, I am.)

Punch. (Taking the stick from the Doctor.) Now, I'll give you physic! physic! physic! *(He strikes at the Doctor, but misses him every time.)* The Doctor don't like his own stuff.

Punch. (Presenting his stick, gun-fashion, at Doctor's head.) I'll shoot ye—one, two, three.

Doctor. (Closing with Punch.) Come to gaol along with me.

(He saves his own life by closing with Punch. He's a desperate character is Punch, though he means no harm, ye know.) A struggle enshoos, and the Doctor calls for help, Punch being too powerful for him.

Doctor. Come to gaol! You shall repent for all your past misdeeds. Help! assistance! help, in the Queen's name!

(He's acting as a constable, the Doctor is, though he's no business to do it; but he's acting in self-defence. He didn't know Punch, but he'd heard of his transactions, and when he came to examine him, he found it was the man. The Doctor is a very sedate kind of a person, and wishes to do good to all classes of the community at large, especially with his physic, which he gives gratis for nothink at all. The physic is called "Head-e-cologne, or a sure cure for the head-ache.")

Re-enter BEADLE. *(Punch and the Doctor still struggling together.)*

Beadle. (Closing with them.) Hi, hi! this is him; behold the head of a traitor! Come along! come to gaol!

Punch. (A-kicking.) I will not go.

Beadle. (Shouting.) More help! more help! more help! more help! Come along to gaol! come along! come along! More help! more help!

(Oh! it's a good lark just here, sir, but tremendous hard work, for there's so many figures to work—and all struggling, too,—and you have to work them all at once. This is comic, this is.)

Beadle. More help! be quick! be quick!

Re-enter JIM CROW

Jim Crow. Come de long! come de long; come de long! me nigger, and you beata me.

[*Exaunts all, Punch still singing out,* 'I'll not go.']

END OF FIRST ACT

Change of Scene for Second Act

Scene draws up, and discovers the exterior of a prison, with Punch peeping through the bars, and singing a merry song of the merry bells of England, all of the olden time, (That's an olden song, you know; it's old ancient, and it's a moral—a moral song, you know, to show that Punch is repenting, but pleased, and yet don't care nothink at all about it, for he's frolicsome, and on the height of his frolic and amusement to all the juveniles, old and young, rich and poor. We must put all classes together.)

Enter Hangman Jack Ketch, or MR. GRABALL

That's Jack Ketch's name, you know; he takes all, when they gets in his clutches. We mustn't blame him for he must do his duty, for the sheriffs is so close to him.)

[*Preparations commences for the execution of Punch. Punch is still looking through the bars of Newgate.*

The last scene as I had was Temple-bar Scene; it was a prison once, ye know; that's the old ancient, ye know, but I never let the others see it, cos it shouldn't become too public. But I think Newgate is better, in the new edition, though the prison is suspended, it being rather too terrific for the beholder. It was the old ancient style; the sentence is passed upon him, but by whom not known; he's not tried by one person, cos nobody can't.

Jack Ketch. Now, Mr. Punch, you are going to be executed by the British and Foreign laws of this and other countries, and you are to be hung up by the neck until you are dead—dead—dead.

Punch. What, am I to die three times?

Jack. No, no; you're only to die once.

Punch. How is that? you said I was to be hung up by the neck till I was dead—dead—dead? You can't die three times.

Jack. Oh, no; only once.

Punch. Why, you said dead—dead—dead.

Jack. Yes: and when you are dead—dead—dead—you will be quite dead.

Punch. Oh! I never knowed that before.

Jack. Now, prepare yourself for execution.

Punch. What for?

Jack. For killing your wife, throwing your dear little innocent baby out of the window, and striking the Beadle unmercifully over the head with a mop-stick. Come on.

[*Exaunt Hangman behind Scene, and re-enter, leading Punch slowly forth to the foot of the gallows. Punch comes most willingly, having no sense.*

Jack. Now, my boy, here is the corfin, here is the gibbet, and here is the pall.

Punch. There's the corfee-shop, there's giblets, and there's St. Paul's.

Jack. Get out, young foolish! Now then, place your head in here.

RATTING—'THE GRAHAM ARMS', GRAHAM STREET

JACK BLACK, HER MAJESTY'S RATCATCHER

Punch. What, up here?

Jack. No; a little lower down.

(There's quick business in this, you know; this is comic—a little comic business, this is.)

Punch. (Dodging the noose.) What, here?

Jack. No, no; in there *(showing the noose again.)*

Punch. This way?

Jack. No, a little more this way; in there.

[*Punch falls down, and pretends he's dead.*

Jack. Get up, you're not dead.

Punch. Oh, yes I am.

Jack. But I say, no.

Punch. Please, sir, *(bowing to the hangman)*—(Here he's an hypo-crite; he wants to exempt himself,)—do show me the way, for I never was hung before, and I don't know the way. Please, sir, do show me the way, and I'll feel extremely obliged to you, and return you my most sincere thanks.

(Now, that's well worded, sir; it's well put together; that's my beauty, that is; I am obliged to study my language, and not have anything vulgar whatsoever. All in simplicity, so that the young children may not be taught anything wrong. There aren't nothing to be learnt from it, because of its simplicity.)

Jack. Very well; as you're so kind and condescending, I will certainly oblige you by showing you the way. Here, my boy! now, place your head in here, like this *(hangman putting his head in the noose)*; this is the right and the proper way; now, you see the rope is placed under my chin; I'll take my head out, and I will place yours in (that's a rhyme) and when your head is in the rope, you must turn round to the ladies and gentlemen, and say—Good-by; fare you well.

(Very slowly then—a stop between each of the words; for that's not driving the people out of the world in quick haste without giving 'em time for repentance. That's another moral, yer see. Oh, I like all the morals to it.)

Punch (quickly pulling the rope). Good-by; fare you well. *(Hangs the hangman.)* (What a hypocrite he is again, yer see, for directly he's done it he says: "Now, I'm free again for frolic and fun"; calls Joey, the clown, his old friend, because they're both full of tricks and antics: "Joey, here's a man hung hisself";—that's his hypocrisy again, yer see, for he tries to get exempt after he's done it hisself.)

Enter CLOWN, *in quick haste, bobbing up against the gallows.*

Clown. Dear me, I've run against a milk-post! Why, dear Mr. Punch, you've hung a man! do take him down! How came you to do it?

Punch. He got wet through, and I hung him up to dry.

Clown. Dear me! why you've hung him up till he's dried quite dead!

Punch. Poor fellow! then he won't catch cold with the wet. Let's put him in this snuff-box.   [*Pointing to coffin.*

[*Joe takes the figure down and gives it to Punch to hold, so as the body do not tun away, and then proceeds to remove the gallows. In doing so he by accident hits Punch on the nose.*

Punch. Mind what you are about! (for Punch is game, yer know, right through to the back-bone.)

Clown. Make haste, Punch, here's somebody a-coming! (They hustle his legs and feet in; but they can't get his head in, the undertaker not having made the coffin large enough.)

Punch. We'd better double him up, place the pall on, and take the man to the brave,—not the grave, but the brave: cos he's been a brave man in his time maybe.—Sings the song of "Bobbing around," while with the coffin he bobs Joey on the head, and exaunt.

Re-enter PUNCH

Punch. That was a jolly lark, wasn't it?
Sings,—

> 'I'd be a butterfly in a bower,
> Making apple-dumplings without any flour.'

All this wit must have been born in me, or nearly so; but I got a good lot of it from Porsini and Pike—and gleanings, you know.

[*Punch disappears and re-enters with bell.*

Punch. This is my pianner-sixty: it plays fifty tunes all at one time.

[*Goes to the landlord of the public-house painted on the side-scene, or cottage, represented as a tavern or hotel. The children of the publican are all a-bed. Punch plays up a tune and solicits for money.*

Landlord wakes up in a passion through the terrible noise; pokes his head out of window and tells him to go away.

(There's a little window, and a little door to this side-scene.) If they was to play it all through, as you're a writing, it 'ud open Drury-lane Theatre.

*Punch.*Go away? Yes, play away! Oh, you means, O'er the hills and far away. (He misunderstands him, wilfully, the hypocrite.) [*Punch keeps on ringing his bell violently. Publican, in a violent passion, opens the door, and pushes him away, saying, 'Be off with you'*].

Punch. I will not. (*Hits him over the head with the bell.*) You're no judge of music. (*Plays away.*)

Publican exaunts to fetch cudgel to pay him out. Punch no sooner sees cudgel than he exaunts, taking his musical instrument with him. It's far superior to anything of the kind you did ever see, except "seldom." You know it's silver, and that's what we says "seldom"; silver, you know, is "seldom," because it's seldom you sees it.

Publican comes out of his house with his cudgel to catch old Punch on the grand hop. Must have a little comic.

Punch returns again with his bell, while publican is hiding secretly for to catch him. Publican pretends, as he stands in a corner, to be fast asleep, but keeps his eyes wide awake all the while, and says, "If he comes up here, I'll be one upon his tibby."

Punch comes out from behind the opposite side, and rings his bell violently. Publican makes a blow at him with his cudgel, and misses, saying, 'How dare you intrude upon my premises with that nasty, noisy bell?'

Punch, while publican is watching at this side-scene, appears over at the other, with a hartful dodge, and again rings his bell loudly, and again the publican misses him; and while publican is watching at this side-scene, Punch re-enters, and draws up to him very slowly, and rests his pianner-sixty on the board, while he slowly advances to him, and gives him a whack on the head with his fist. Punch then disappears, leaving his bell behind, and the landlord in pursession of his music.

Landlord (collaring the bell). Smuggings! prusession is nine points of the law! So this bell is mine, (*guarding over it with a stick*). Smuggings! this is mine, and when he comes up to take this bell away, I shall have him. Smuggings! it's mine.

Punch re-enters very slowly behind the publican as he is watching the bell, and snatching up the bell, cries out, 'That's mine,' and exaunts with it.

Publican. Dear me! never mind; I look after him; I shall catch him some day or other. *(Hits his nose up against the post as he is going away.)* (That's comic.) Oh, my nose! never mind, I'll have him again some time. [*Exaunt* PUBLICAN.

CLOWN *re-enters* with PUNCH

Clown. Oh, Punch, how are you?

Punch. I'm very glad to see you. Oh, Joey, my friend, how do you do?

Clown. Here, Punch, are you a mind for a lark? *(Peeping in at the cottage window, represented as a public house.)* Are you hungry, Punch? would you like something to eat?

Punch. Yes.

Clown. What would you like?

Punch. Not peculiar.

(Not particular, he means, you know; that's a slip word.)

Clown. I'll go up to the landlord, and see if he's got anything to eat. *(Exaunt into cottage, and poking his head of the window.)* Here, Punch; here's the landlord fast asleep in the kitchen cellar; here's a lot of sausages hanging up here.

(Joey's a-thieving; don't you see, he's a robbing the landlord now?)

Would you like some for supper, eh, Punch?

Punch. Yes, to be sure.

Clown. Don't make a noise; you'll wake the landlord.

Punch (whispering as loud as he can bawl through the window). Hand' em out here. *(Punch pulls them out of the window.)*

Clown. What are we to fry them in? I'll go and see if I can find a frying-pan.

[*Exaunt from window, and re-appears with frying-pan, which he hands out of window for Punch to cook sausages in and then disappears for a moment; after which he returns, and says, with his head out of window, "Would you like something hot, Punch?"*

Punch. Yes, to be sure.

(Punch is up to everything. He's a helping him to rob the publican. One's as much in the mud as the other is in the mire.)

Clown. (Thrusting red-hot poker out of window.) Here, lay hold— Here's a lark—Make haste—Here's the landlord a coming. *(Rubs Punch with it over the nose.)*

Punch. Oh my nose!—that is a hot 'un.   [*Takes poker.*

Clown. (Re-enters, and calls in at window.) Landlord, here's a fellow stole your sausages and frying-pan. *(Wakes up Landlord and exaunts.)*

Landlord. (Appears at window.) Here's somebody been in my house and axually stole my sausages frying-pan, and red-hot poker!

(Clown exhaunts when he has blamed it all to Punch. Joey stole 'em, and Punch took 'em, and the receiver is always worse than the thief, for if they was never no receivers there wouldn't never be no thieves.)

Landlord. (Seizing the sausages in Punch's hand.) How did you get these here?

Punch. Joey stole 'em, and I took 'em.

Landlord. Then you're both jolly thieves, and I must have my property. (A scuffle ensues. Punch hollars out, Joey! Joey! Here's the landlord a stealing the sausages!)

(So you see Punch wants to make the landlord a thief so as to exempt himself. He's a hypocrite there again, you see again—all through the piece he's the master-piece. Oh a most clever man is Punch, and such a hypocrite.)

(Punch, seizing the frying-pan, which has been on the playboard, knocks it on the publican's head; when, there being a false bottom to it, the head goes through it, and the sausages gets about the Publican's neck, and Punch pulls at the pan and the sausages with veheminence, till the landlord is exhausted, and exaunts with his own property back again; so there is no harm done, only merely for the lark to return to those people what belongs to 'em—What you take away from a person always give to them again.)

Re-enter CLOWN

Clown. Well, Mr. Punch, I shall wish you a pleasant good morning.

Punch. [*Hits him with his cudgel.*] Good morning to you, Joey.

Exaunt JOEY

Punch sits down by the side of the poker, and Scaramouch appears without a head.

Punch looks, and beholds, and he's frightened, and exaunts with the poker.

Scaramouch does a comic dance, with his long neck shooting up and down with the actions of his body, after which he exaunts.

Punch re-enters again with the poker, and places it beside of him, and takes his cudgel in his hand for protection, while he is singing the National Anthem of 'God save the Queen and all the Royal Family.'

Satan then appears as a dream (and it is all a dream after all), and dressed up as the Roossian Bear (leave Politics alone as much as you can, for Punch belongs to nobody).

Punch has a dreadful struggle with Satan, who seizes the red-hot poker and wants to take Punch away, for all his past mis-deeds, and frolic and fun, to the bottomless pit.

By struggling with Satan, Punch overpowers him, and he drops the poker, and Punch, kills him with his cudgel, and shouts 'Bravo! Hooray! Satan is dead,' he cries (we must have a good conclusion): 'we can now all do as we like!'—(That's the moral, you see.) 'Good-by, Ladies and Gentlemen: this is the whole of the original performance of Mr. Punch; and I remain still your most obedient and most humble servant to command. Good-by, good-by, good-by. God bless you all. I return you my most sincere thanks for your patronage and support, and I hope you'll come out handsome with your gold and silver.'

THE FANTOCCINI MAN

EVERY one who has resided for any time in London must have noticed in the streets a large roomy show upon wheels, about four times as capacious as those used for the performance of Punch and Judy.

The proprietor of one of these perambulating exhibitions was a person of some 56 years of age, with a sprightly half-military manner; but he is seldom seen by the public, on account of his habit of passing the greater part of the day concealed within his theatre, for the purpose of managing the figures. When he paid me a visit, his peculiar erect bearing struck me as he entered. He walked without bending his knees, stamped with his heels, and often rubbed his hands together as if washing them with an invisible soap. He wore his hair with the curls arranged in a Brutus, à la George the Fourth, and his chin was forced up into the air by a high black stock, as though he wished to increase his stature. He wore a frock coat buttoned at waist, and open on his expanded chest, so as to show off the entire length of his shirt-front.

He gave me the following interesting statement:—

'The Fantoccini,' he said, 'is the proper title of the exhibition of dancing dolls, though it has lately been changed to that of the "Marionettes," owing to the exhibition under that name at the Adelaide Gallery.

'That exhibition at the Adelaide Gallery was very good in its way, but it was nothing to be compared to the exhibition that was once given at the Argyll Rooms in Regent-street, (that's the old place that was burned down). It was called *"Le petit Théatre Matthieu,"* and in my opinion it was the best one that ever come into London, because they was well managed. They did little pieces—heavy and light. They did Shakespeare's tragedies and farces, and singing as well; indeed, it was the real stage, only with dolls for actors and parties to speak for 'em and work their arms and legs behind the scenes. I've known one of these parties take three parts—look at that for clever work—first he did an old man, then an old woman, and afterwards the young man. I assisted at that performance, and I should say it was full twenty years ago, to the best of my recollection. After the Marionettes removed to the Western Institution, Leicester-square, I assisted at them also. It was a passable exhibition, but nothing out of the way. The figures were only modelled, not carved, as they ought to be. I was only engaged to exhibit one figure, a sailor of my own making. It was a capital one, and stood as high as a table. They wanted it for the piece called the "Manager in Distress," where one of the performes is a sailor. Mine would dance a hornpipe, and whip its hat off in a minute; when I had finished performing it, I took good care to whip it into a bag, so they should not see how I arranged the strings, for they were very backwards in their knowledge. When we worked the figures it was very difficult, because you had to be up so high—like on the top of the ceiling, and to keep looking down all the time to manage the strings. There was a platform arranged, with a place to rest against.

'We used to do a great business with evening parties. At Christmas we have had to go three and four times in the same evening to different parties. We never had less than a guinea, and I have had as much as five pounds, but the usual price was two pounds ten shillings, and all refreshments found you. I had the honour of performing before the Queen when she was Princess Victoria. It was at Gloucester-house, Park-lane, and we was engaged by the royal household. A nice berth I had of it, for it was in May, and they put us on the landing of the drawing-room, where the folding-doors opened, and there was some place close by where hot air was admitted to warm the apartments; and what with the heat of the weather and this 'ere ventilation, with the heat coming up the grating-places and my anxiety performing before a princess, I was near baked, and the perspiration quite run off me; for I was packed up above, standing up and hidden, to manage the figures. There was the maids of honour coming down the stairs like so many nuns, dressed all in white, and the princess was standing on a sofa, with the Duke of Kent behind her. She was apparently very much amused, like others who had seen them. I can't recollect what we was paid, but it was very handsome and so forth.

'I've also performed before the Baroness Rothschild's, next the Duke of Wellington's, and likewise the Baron himself, in Grosvenor-place, and Sir Watkyn W. Wynne, and half the nobility in England. We've been in the very first of drawing-rooms.

'When we perform in the streets, we generally go through this programme. We begins with a female hornpipe dancer; then there is a set of quadrilles by some marionette figures, four females and no gentlemen. If we did the men we should want assistance, for four is as much as I can hold at once. It would require two men, and the street won't pay for it. After this we introduces a representation of Mr. Grimaldi the clown, who does tumbling and posturing, and a comic dance, and so forth, such as trying to catch a butterfly. Then comes the enchanted Turk. He comes on in the costume of a Turk, and he throws off his right and left arm, and then his legs, and they each change into different figures, the arms and legs into two boys and girls, a clergyman the head, and an old lady the body. That figure was my own invention, and I could if I like turn him into a dozen; indeed, I've got one at home, which turns into a parson in the pulpit, and a clerk under him, and a lot of little charity children, with a form to sit down upon. They are all carved figures, every one of them, and my own make. The next performance is the old lady, and her arms drop off and turn into two figures, and the body becomes a complete balloon and car in a minute, and not a flat thing, but round—and the figures get into the car and up they go. Then there's the tight-rope dancer, and next the Indian juggler—Ramo Samee, a representation—who chucks the balls about under his feet and under his arms, and catches them on the back of his head, the same as Ramo Samee did. Then there's the sailor's hornpipe—Italian Scaramouch (he's the old style). This one has a long neck and it shoots up to the top of the theatre. This is the original trick, and a very good one. Then comes the Polander, who balances a pole and two chairs, and stands on his head and jumps over his pole; he dresses like a Spaniard, and in the old style. It takes a quarter of an hour to do that figure well and make him do all his tricks. Then comes the Skeletons. They're regular first class, of course. This one also was my invention and I was the first to make them, and I'm the only one that can make them. Then there's Judy Callaghan, and that 'livens up after the skeletons. Then six figures jump out of her pockets, and she knocks them about. It's a sort of comic business. Then the next is a countryman who can't get his donkey to go, and it kicks at him and throws him off and all manner of comic antics, ofter Billy Button's style. Then I do the skeleton that falls to pieces, and then becomes whole again. Then there's another out of-the-way comic figure that falls to pieces similar to the skeleton. He catches hold of his head and chucks it from one hand to the other. We call him the Nondescript. We wind up with a scene in Tom and Jerry. The curtain winds up, and there's a watchman rowling the streets, and some of those larking gentlemen comes on and pitch into him. He looks round and he can't see anybody. Presently another comes in and gives him another knock, and then there's a scuffle, and off they go over the watch-box, and down comes the scene. That makes the juveniles laugh, and finishes up the whole performance merry like.

'I've forgot one figure now. I know'd there was another, and that's the Scotchman who dances the Highland fling. He's before the watchman. He's in the regular national costume, everything correct, and everything, and the music plays according to the performance. It's a beautiful figure when well handled, and the dresses cost something, I can tell you; all the joints are counter-sunk—them figures that shows above the knee. There's no joints to be seen, all works hidden like, something like Madame Vestris in Don Juan. All my figures have got shoes and stockings on. They have, indeed. If it wasn't my work, they'd cost a deal of money. One of them is more expensive than all those in Punch and Judy put together. Talk of Punch knocking the Fantoccini down! Mine's all show; Punch is nothing, and cheap as dirt.

'I've also forgot the flower-girl that comes in and dances with a garland. That's a very pretty figure in a fairy's dress, in a nice white skirt with naked carved arms, nice modelled, and the legs just the same; and the trunks come above the knee, the same as them ballet girls. She shows all the opera attitudes.

'The performance, to go through the whole of it, takes an hour and a half; and then you mustn't stand looking at it, but as soon as one thing goes off the music changes and another comes on. That ain't one third, nor a quarter of what I can do.

'When I'm performing I'm standing behind, looking down upon the stage. All the figures is hanging round on hooks, with all their strings ready for use. It makes your arms ache to work them, and especially across the loins. All the strength you have you must do, and chuck it out too; for those four figures which I uses at evening parties, which dance the polka, weighs six pounds, and that's to be kept dangling for twenty minutes together. They are two feet high, and their skirts take three quarters of a yard, and are covered with spangles, which gives 'em great weight.'

GUY FAWKESES

UNTIL within the last ten or twelve years, the exhibition of guys in the public thoroughfares every 5th of November, was a privilege enjoyed exclusively by boys of from 10 to15 years of age, and the money arising therefrom was supposed to be invested at night in a small pyrotechnic display of squibs, crackers, and catherine-wheels.

At schools, and at many young gentlemen's houses, for at least a week before the 5th arrived, the bonfires were prepared and guys built up.

At night one might see rockets ascending in the air from many of the suburbs of London, and the little back-gardens in such places as the Hampstead-road and Kennington, and, after dusk, suddenly illuminated with the blaze of the tar-barrel, and one might hear in the streets even banging of crackers mingled with the laughter and shouts of boys enjoying the sport.

In those days the street guys were of a very humble character, the grandest of them generally consisting of old clothes stuffed up with straw, and carried in state upon a kitchen-chair. The arrival of the guy before a window was announced by a juvenile chorus of 'Please to remember the 5th of November.' So diminutive, too, were some of these guys, that I have even seen dolls carried about as the representatives of the late Mr. Fawkes. In fact, none of these effigies were hardly ever made of larger proportions than Tom Thumb, or than would admit of being carried through the garden-gates of any suburban villa.

Of late years, however, the character of Guy Fawkes-day has entirely changed. It seems now to partake rather of the nature of a London May-day. The figures have grown to be of gigantic stature, and whilst clowns, musicians, and dancers have got to accompany them in their travels through the streets, the traitor Fawkes seems to have been almost laid aside, and the festive occasion taken advantage of for the expression of any political feeling, the guy being made to represent any celebrity of the day who has for the moment offended against the opinions of the people. The kitchen-chair has been changed to the costermongers' donkey-truck, or even vans drawn by pairs of horses. The bonfires and fireworks are seldom indulged in; the money given to the exhibitors being shared among the projectors at night, the same as if the day's work had been occupied with acrobating or nigger singing.

EXHIBITOR OF MECHANICAL FIGURES

'I AM the only man in London—and in England, I think—who is exhibiting the figuer of méchanique; that is to say, leetle figuers, that move their limbs by wheels and springs, as if they was de living creatures. I am a native of Parma in Italy, where I was born; that is, you understand, I was born in the Duchy of Parma, not in the town of Parma—in the campagne, where my father is a farmer;

not a large farmer, but a little farmer, with just enough land for living. I used to work for my father in his fields. I was married when I have 20 years of age, and I have a child aged 10 years. I have only 30 years of age, though I have the air of 40. Pardon, Monsieur! all my friends say I have the air of 40, and you say that to make me pleasure.

'When I am with my father, I save up all the money that I can, for there is very leetle business to be done in the campagne of Parma, and I determine myself to come to Londres, where there is affair to be done. I like Londres much better than the campagne of Parma, because there is so much affairs to be done. I save up all my money. I become very économique. I live of very leetle, and when I have a leetle money, I say adieu to my father and I commence my voyages.

'At Paris I buy a box of music. They are made at Genève these box of music. When I come to Londres, I go to the public-house—the palais de gin, you understand—and there I show my box of music—yes, musical box you call it—and when I get some money I live very économique, and then when it become more money I buy another machine, which I buy in Paris. It was a box of music, and on the top it had leetle figuers, which do move their eyes and their limbs when I mounts the spring with the key. And then there is music inside the box at the same time. I have three leetle figuers to this box; one was Judith cutting the head of the infidel chief—what you call him?—Holeferones. She lift her arm with the sword, and she roll her eyes, and then the other hand is on his head, which it lifts. It does this all the time the music play, until I put on another figuer of the soldat which mounts the guard—yes, which is on duty. The soldat goes to sleep, and his head falls on his bosom. Then he wake up again and lift his lance and roll his eyes. Then he goes to sleep again, so long until I put on the other figuer of the lady with the plate in her hand, and she make salutation to the company for to ask some money. and she continue to do this so long as any body give her money. All the time the music in the box continues to play.

'I take a great quantity of money with these figuers, 3s. a-day, and I live very économique until I put aside a sum large enough to buy the figuers which I exhibit now.

'My most aged child is at Parma, with my father in the cam-

pagne, but my wife and my other child, which has only 18 months
of age, are with me in Londres.

'It is two months since I have my new figuers. I did have them
sent from Germany to me. They have cost a great deal of money
to me; as much as 35*l*. without duty. They have been made in
Germany, and are very clever figuers. I will show them to you.
They perform on the round table, which must be level or they will
not turn round. This is the Impératrice of the French—Eugénie—
at least I call her so, for it is not like her, because her chevelure is
not arranged in the style of the Impératrice. The infants like better
to see the Impératrice than a common lady, that is why I call her
the Impératrice. She holds one arm in the air, and you will see she
turns round like a person waltzing. The noise you hear is from the
wheels of the méchanique, which is under her petticoats. You shall
notice her eyes do move as she waltz. The next figure is the carriage
of the Emperor of the French, with the Queen and Prince Albert
and the King de Sardaigne inside. It will run round the table, and
the horses will move as if they gallop. It is a very clever méchanique. I attache this wire from the front wheel to the centre of the
table, or it would not make the round of the table, but it would
run off the side and break itself. My most clever méchanique is the
elephant. It does move its trunk, and its tail, and its legs, as if
walking, and all the time it roll its eyes from side to side like a real
elephant. It is the cleverest elephant of méchanique in the world.
The leetle Indian on the neck, who is the driver, lift his arm, and
in the pavilion on the back the chieftain of the Indians lift his bow
and arrow to take aim, and put it down again. That méchanique
cost me very much money. The elephant is worth much more than
the Impératrice of the French. I could buy two—three—Impératrice for my elephant. I would like sooner lose the Impératrice than
any malheur arrive to my elephant. There are plenty more Impératrice, but the elephant is very rare. I have also a figuer of
Tyrolese peasant. She go round the table a short distance and then
turn, like a dancer. I must get her repaired. She is so weak in her
wheels and springs, which wind up under her petticoats, like the
Impératrice. She has been cleaned twice, and yet her méchanique
is very bad. Oh, I have oiled her; but it is no good, she must be
taken to pieces.

'When I sent to Germany to get these méchanique made for

me, I told the mechanician what I desired, and he made them for me. I invented the figuers out of my own head, and he did the méchanique. I have voyaged in Holland, and there I see some méchanique, and I noticed them, and then I gave the order to do so and so. My elephant is the best of my leetle figuers; there is more complication.

'I first come to England eighteen years ago, before I was married, and I stop here seven years; then I go back again to Parma, and then I come back again to England four years ago, and here I stop ever since.

'I exhibit my leetle figuers in the street. The leetle children like to see my figuers méchanique dance round the table, and the carriage, with the horses which gallop; but over all they like my elephant, with the trunk which curls up in front, like those in the Jardin des Plantes, or what you call it Zoological Gardens.'

THE TELESCOPE EXHIBITOR

'IT must be about eight years since I first exhibited the telescope, I have three telescopes now, and their powers vary from about 36 to 300. The instruments of the higher power are seldom used in the streets, because the velocity of the planets is so great that they almost escape the eye before it can fix it. The opening is so very small, that though I can pass my eye on a star in a minute, an ordinary observer would have the orb pass away before he could accustom his eye to the instrument. High power is all very well for separating stars, and so forth; but I'm like Dr. Kitchener, I prefer a low power for street purposes. A street-passer likes to see plenty of margin round a star. If it fills up the opening he don't like it.

'I've worked about five years with this last one that I've now. It weighs, with the stand, about 1cwt., and I have to get somebody to help me along with it. One of my boys in general goes along with me.

'It depends greatly upon the weather as to what business I do. I've known the moon for a month not to be visible for twenty days out of the lunation. I've known that for three moons together, the atmosphere is so bad in London. When I do get a good night I have taken 35*s*.; but then I've taken out two instruments, and my boy has minded one. I only charge a penny a peep. Saturdays, and Mondays, and Sundays, are the best nights in my neighbour-hood, and then I can mostly reckon on taking 20*s.* The other nights it may be 7*s.* or 8*s.* or even only 2*s.* 6*d.* Sometimes I put up the instrument when it's very fine, and then it'll come cloudy, and I have to take it down again and go home. Taking the year round, I should think I make 125*l.* a-year by the telescope. You see my business, as a tailor, keeps me in of a day, or I might go out in the day and show the sun. Now to-day the sun was very fine, and the spots showed remarkably well, and if I'd been out I might have done well. I sold an instrument of mine once to a fireman who had nothing to do in the day, and thought he could make some money exhibiting the telescope. He made 8*s.* or 10*s.* of an afternoon on Blackfriar's-bridge, showing the dome of St. Paul's at the time they were repairing it.'

PEEP-SHOWS

CONCERNING these, I received the subjoined narrative from a man of considerable experience in the 'profession':—

'The carawans comes to London about October, after the fairs is over. The scenes of them carawan shows is mostly upon recent battles and murders. Anything in that way, of late occurrence, suits them. Theatrical plays ain't no good for country towns, 'cause they don't understand such things there. People is werry fond of the battles in the country, but a murder wot is well known is worth more than all the fights. There was no more took with Rush's murder than there has been even by the Battle of Waterloo itself. Some of the carawan-shows does werry well. Their average taking is 30*s.* a-week for the summer months. It's a regular starving life now. We has to put up with the hinsults of people so. The back-shows generally exhibits plays of different kinds wot's been per-formed at the theayters lately. I've got many different plays to my show. I only exhibit one at a time. There's "Halonzer the Brave and the Fair Himogen;" "The Dog of Montargis and the Forest of Bondy," "Hyder Halley, or the Lions of Mysore;" "The Forty Thieves" (that never done no good to me); "The Devil and Dr. Faustus;" and at Christmas time we exhibit pantomimes. I has some other scenes as well. I've "Napoleon's Return from Helba," "Napoleon at Waterloo," "The Death of Lord Nelson," and also

"The Queen embarking to start for Scotland, from the Dockyard at Voolich." We takes more from children than grown people in London, and more from grown people than children in the country. You see, grown people has such remarks made upon them when they're a-peeping through in London, as to make it bad for us here. Lately I have been hardly able to get a living, you may say.

'There are from six to eight scenes in each of the plays that I shows; and if the scenes are a bit short, why I buts in a couple of battle-scenes; or I makes up a pannerammer for 'em. The children *will* have so much for their money now. I charge a halfpenny for a hactive performance. There is characters and all—and I explains what they are supposed to be a-talking about. There's about six back-shows in London. I don't think there's more. It don't pay now to get up a new play. We works the old ones over and over again, and sometimes we buys a fresh one of another showman, if we can rise the money—the price is 2*s*. and 2*s*. 6*d*. I've been obligated to get rid of about twelve of my plays, to get a bit of victuals at home. Formerly we used to give a hartist 1*s*. to go in the pit and sketch off the scenes and figures of any new play that was a-doing well, and we thought 'ud take, and arter that we used to give him from 1*s*. 6*d*. to 2*s*. for drawing and painting each scene and 1*d*. and 1½*d*. each for the figures, according to the size.

'The street-markets is the best of a Saturday night. I'm often obliged to take bottles instead of money, and they don't fetch more than threepence a dozen. Sometimes I take four dozen of bottles in a day. I lets 'em see a play for a bottle, and often two wants to see for one large bottle. The children is dreadful for cheapening things down. In the summer I goes out of London for a month at a stretch. In the country I works my battle-pieces. They're most pleased there with my Lord Nelson's death at the battle of Trafalgar. "That there is," I tell 'em, "a fine painting, representing Lord Nelson at the battle of Trafalgar." In the centre is Lord Nelson in his last dying moments, supported by Capt. Hardy and the chaplain. On the left is the hexplosion of one of the enemy's ships by ours. That represents a fine painting, representing the death of Lord Nelson at the battle of Trafalgar, wot was fought on the 12th of October, 1805.'

ACROBAT, OR STREET-POSTURER

A MAN who, as he said, 'had all his life been engaged in the profession of Acrobat,' volunteered to give me some details of the life
led and the earnings made by this class of street-performers.

He at the present moment belongs to a 'school' of five, who are
dressed up in fanciful and tight-fitting costumes of white calico,
with blue or red trimmings; and who are often seen in the quiet
by-streets going through their gymnastics performances, mounted
on each other's shoulders, or throwing somersaults in the air.

'There's five in our gang now. There's three high for "pyramids,"
and "the Arabs hang down;" that is, one a-top of his shoulders, and
one hanging down from his neck; and "the spread," that's one on
the shoulders, and one hanging from each hand; and "the Hercules," that is, one on the ground, supporting himself on his hands
and feet; whilst one stands on his knees, another on his shoulders,
and the other one a-top of them two, on their shoulders. There's
loads of tricks like them that we do, that would a'most fill up your
paper to put down. There's one of our gang dances, an Englishman,
whilst the fifth plays the drum and pipes. The dances are mostly
comic dances; or, as we call them, "comic hops." He throws his
legs about and makes faces, and he dresses as a clown.

'When it's not too windy, we do the perch. We carry a long
fir pole about with us, twenty-four feet long, and Jim the strong
man, as they calls me, that is I, holds the pole up at the bottom.
The one that runs up is called the sprite. It's the bottom man
that holds the pole that has the dangerous work in la perche.
He's got all to look to. Anybody, who has got any courage, can
run up the pole; but I have to guide and balance it; and the pole
weighs some 20 lbs., and the man about 8 stone. When it's windy
it's very awkward, and I have to walk about to keep him steady
and balance him; but I'm never frightened, I know it so well.
The man who runs up it does such feats as these; for instance,
"the bottle position", that is only holding by his feet, with his two
arms extended; and then "the hanging down by one toe," with only
one foot on the top of the pole, and hanging down with his arms
out, swimming on the top on his belly; and "the horizontal," as it
is called, or supporting the body out sideways by the strength

of the arms, and such-like, winding up with coming down head fust.

"The pole is fixed very tightly in a socket in my waistband, and it takes two men to pull it out, for it gets jammed in with his force on a top of it. The danger is more with the bottom one than the one a top, though few people would think so. You see, if he falls off, he is sure to light on his feet like a cat; for we're taught to do this trick; and a man can jump off a place thirty feet high, without hurting himself, easy. Now if the people was to go frontwards, it would be all up with me, because with the leverage and its being fixed so tight to my stomach, there's no help for it, for it would be sure to rip me up and tear out my entrails. I have to keep my eyes about me, for if it goes too fur, I could never regain the balance again. But it's easy enough when you're accustomed to it.

'The one that goes up the pole can always see into the drawing-rooms, and he'll tell us where it's good to go and get any money, for he can see the people peeping behind the curtains; and they generally give when they find they are discovered. It's part of his work to glance his eyes about him, and then he calls out whilst he is up, "to the right," or "the left," as it may be; and although the crowd don't understand him, we do.

'Our gang generally prefer performing in the West end, because there's more "calls" there. Gentlemen looking out of the window see us, and call to us to stop and perform; but we don't trust to them, even, but make a collection when the performance is half over; and if it's good we continue, and make two or three collections during the exhibition. And yet we like the poor people better than the rich, for it's the halfpence that tells up best. Perhaps we might take a half sovereign, but it's very rare, and since 1853 I don't remember taking more than twenty of them. There was a Princess—I'm sure I've forgotten her name, but she was German, and she used to live in Grosvenor-square—she used to give us half-a-sovereign every Monday during three months she was in London. The servants was ordered to tell us to come every Monday at three o'clock, and we always did; and even though there was nobody looking, we used to play all the same; and as soon as the drum ceased playing, there was the money brought out to us. We continued playing to her till we was told she had gone away. We have also had sovereign calls. When my gang was in the Isle of Wight, Lord Y——has often give us a sovereign, and plenty to eat and drink as well.

'Posturing as it is called (some people call it contortionists, that's a new name; a Chinese nondescript—that's the first name it came out as, although what we calls posturing is a man as can sit upon nothing; as, for instance, when he's on the back of two chairs and does a split with his legs stretched out and sitting on nothing like) —posturing is reckoned the healthiest life there is, because we never get the rheumatics; and another thing, we always eat hearty. We often put on wet dresses, such as at a fair, when they've been washed out clean, and we put them on before they're dry, and that's what give the rheumatism; but we are always in such a perspiration that it never affects us. It's very violent exercise, and at night we feels it in our thighs more than anywhere, so that if it's damp or cold weather it hurts us to sit down. If it's wet weather, or showery, we usually get up stiff in the morning, and then we have to "crick" each other before we go out, and practise in our bedrooms. On the Sunday we also go out and practise, either in a field, or at the "Tan" in Bermondsey. We used to go to the "Hops" in Maiden-lane, but that's done away with now.

'My father's very near seventy-six, and he has been a tumbler for fifty years; my children are staying with him, and he's angry that I won't bring them up to it: but I want them to be some trade or another, because I don't like the life for them. There's so much suffering before they begin tumbling, and then there's great temptation to drink, and such-like. I'd sooner send them to school, than let them get their living out of the streets. I've one boy and two girls. They're always at it at home, indeed; father and my sister-in-law can't keep them from it. The boy's very nimble.

'In the winter time we generally goes to the theatres. We are a'most always engaged for the pantomimes, to do the sprites. We always reckon it a good thirteen-weeks' job, but in the country it's only a month. If we don't apply for the job they come after us. The sprites in a pantomime is quite a new style, and we are the only chaps that can do it—the posturers and tumblers. In some theatres they find the dresses. Last winter I was at Liverpool, and wore a green dress, spangled all over, which belonged to Mr. Copeland, the manager. We never speak in the play, but just merely rush on, and throw somersualts, and frogs, and such-like, and then rush off again. Little Wheeler, the greatest tumbler of the day, was a posturer in the streets, and now he's in France doing his 10*l.* a-week, engaged for three years.'

THE STRONG MAN

'I HAVE been in the profession for about thirteen years, and I am thirty-two next birthday. Excepting four years that I was at sea, I've been solely by the profession. I'm what is termed a strong man, and perform feats of strength and posturing. What is meant by posturing is the distortion of the limbs, such as doing the splits, and putting your leg over your head and pulling it down your back, a skipping over your leg, and such-like business. Tumbling is different from posturing, and means throwing summersets and walking on your hands; and acrobating means the two together, with mounting three stories high, and balancing each other. These are the definitions I make.

'I was nineteen before I did anything of any note all, and got what I call a living salary. Long before that I had been trying the business, going in and out of these free concerts, and trying my hand at it, fancying I was very clever, but disgusting the audience, for they are mostly duffers at these free concerts; which is clearly the case, for they only do it for a pint every now and then, and depend upon passing the hat round after their performance. I never got much at collections, so I must have been a duffer.

'The first thing I did was at a little beer-shop, corner of South-wark-bridge-road and Union-street. I had seen Herbert do the Grecian statues at the Vic., in "Hercules, King of Clubs," and it struck me I could do 'em. So I knew this beer-shop, and I bought half-a-crown's worth of tickets to be allowed to do these statues. It was on a boxing-night, I remember, I did them, but they were dreadful bad. The people did certainly applaud, but what for, I don't know, for I kept shaking and wabbling so, that my marble statue was rather ricketty; and there was a strong man in the room, who had been performing them, and he came up to me and said that I was a complete duffer, and that I knew nothing about it at all. So I replied, that he knew nothing about his feats of strength, and that I'd go and beat him. So I set to work at it; for I was determined to lick him. I got five quarter-of-hundred weights an used to practise throwing them at a friend's back-yard in the Waterloo-road. I used to make myself all over mud at it, besides having a knock of the head sometimes. At last I got perfect chucking the quarter hundred, and then I tied a fourteen pound weight on to them, and at last I got up half-hundreds, I learnt to hold up one of them at arm's length, and even then I was obliged to push it up with the other hand. I also threw them over my head, as well as catching them by the ring.

'I went to this beer-shop as soon as I could do, and came out. I wasn't so good as he was at lifting, but that was all he could do; and I did posturing with the weights as well, and that licked him. He was awfully jealous, and I had been revenged. I had learnt to do a split, holding a half-hundred in my teeth, and rising with it, without touching the ground with my hands. Now I can lift five, for I've had more practice, I had tremendous success at this beer-shop.

'It hurt me awfully when I learnt to do the split with the weight on my teeth. It strained me all to pieces. I couldn't put my heels to the ground not nicely, for it physicked my thighs dreadful. When I was hot I didn't feel it; but as I cooled, I was cramped all to bits. It took me nine months before I could do it without feeling any pain.

'Another thing I learnt to do at this beer-shop was, to break the stone on the chest. This man used to do it as well, only in a very slight way—with thin bits and a cobbler's hammer. Now mine is regular flagstones. I've seen as many as twenty women faint seeing me do it. At this beer-shop, when I first did it, the stone weighed about three quarters of a hundred, and was an inch thick. I laid down on the ground, and the stone was put on my chest, and a man with a sledge hammer, twenty-eight pounds in weight, struck it and smashed it. The way it is done is this. You rest on your heels and hands and throw your chest up. There you are, like a stool, with the weight on you. When you see the blow coming, you have to give, or it would knock you all to bits.

'When I was learning to do this, I practised for nine months. I got a friend of mine to hit the stone. One day I cut my chest open doing it. I wasn't paying attention to the stone, and never noticed that it was hollow; so then when the blow came down, the sharp edges of the stone, from my having nothing but a fleshing suit on, cut right into the flesh, and made two deep incisions. I had to leave it off for about a month. Strange to say, this stone-breaking never hurt my chest or my breathing; I rather think it has done me good, for I'm strong and hearty, and never have illness of any sort.

'The first time I done it I was dreadful frightened. I knew if I didn't stop still I should have my brains knocked out, pretty well. When I saw the blow coming I trembled a good bit, but I kept still as I was able. It was a hard blow, for it broke the bit of Yorkshire paving, about an inch thick, into about sixty pieces.

'When I'm engaged for a full performance I do this. All the weights, and the stone and the hammer, are ranged in front of the stage. Then I come on dressed in silk tights with a spangled trunk. Then I enter at the back of the stage, and first do several feats of posturing, such as skipping through my leg or passing it down my back, or splits. Then I take a ladder and mount to the top, and stand up on it, and hold one leg in my hand, shouldering it; and then I give a spring with the other leg, and shoot off to the other side of the stage and squash down with both legs open, doing a split. It's very good trick, and always gets a round. Then I do a trick with a chair standing on the seat, and I take one foot in my hand and make a hoop of the leg, and then hop with one leg through the hoop of the other, and spring over the back and come down in a split on the other side. I never miss this trick, though, if the chair happens to be ricketty, I may catch the toe, but it doesn't matter much.

'Then I begin my weight business. I take one half-hundred weight and hold it up at arm's-length; and I also hold it out perpendicularly, and bring it up again and swing it two or three times round the head, and then throw it up in the air and catch it four or five times running; not by the ring, as others do, but in the open hand.

'The next trick is doing the same thing with both hands instead of one, that is with two weights at the same time; and then, after that, I take up a half-hundred by the teeth, and shouldering the leg at the same, and in that style I fall down into the splits. Then I raise myself up gradually, till I'm upright again. After I'm upright I place the weight on my forehead, and lay down flat on my back with it, without touching with the hands. I take it off when I'm down and place it in my mouth, and walk round the stage like a

Greenwich-pensioner, with my feet tucked up like crossing the arms, and only using my knees. Then I tie three together, and hold them in the mouth, and I put one in each hand. Then I stand up with them and support them. It's an awful weight, and you can't do much exhibiting with them.

'When I was at Vauxhall, Yarmouth, last year, I hurt my neck very badly in lifting those weights in the mouth. It pulled out the back of my neck, and I was obliged to give over work for months. It forced my head over one shoulder, and then it sunk, as if I'd got a stiff neck. I did nothing to it, and only went to a doctor-chap, who made me bathe the neck in hot water. That's all.

'One of my most curious tricks is what I call the braces trick. It's a thing just like a pair of braces, only, instead of a button, there's a half-hundred weight at each end, so that there are two behind and two in front. Then I mount on two swinging ropes with a noose at the end, and I stretch out my legs into a split, and put a half-hundred on each thigh, and take up another in my mouth. You may imagine how heavy the weight is, when I tell you that I pulled the roof of a place in once at Chelsea. It was a exhibition then. The tiles and all come down, and near smothered me. You must understand, that in these tricks I have to put the weights on myself, and raise them from the ground, and that makes it so difficult.

'I always wind up with breaking the stone, and I don't mind how thick it is, so long as it isn't heavy enough to crush me. A common curb-stone, or a Yorkshire-flag, is nothing to me, and I've got so accustomed to this trick, that once it took thirty blows with a twenty-eight pound sledge-hammer to break the stone, and I asked for a cigar and smoked it all the while.

'I'll tell you another trick I've done, and that's walking on the ceiling. Of course I darn't do it in the Professor Sands' style, for mine was a dodge. Professor Sands used an air-exhausting boot, on the model of a fly's foot, and it was a legitimate performance indeed; he and another man, to whom he gave the secret of his boots, are the only two who ever did it. The chap that came over here wasn't the real Sands. The fact is well known to the profession, that Sands killed himself on his benefit night in America. After walking on the marble slab in the Circus, somebody bet him he couldn't do it on any ceiling, and he for a wager went to a Town-hall, and done it, and the ceiling gave way, and he fell and broke his neck. The chap that came over here was Sands' attendant, and he took the name and the boots, and came over as Professor Sands.

'The first who ever walked on the ceiling, by a dodge, was a man of the name of Herman, a wizard, who wound up his entertainment at the City of London by walking on some planks suspended in the air. I was there, and at once saw his trick. I knew it was a sleight-of-hand thing. I paid great attention and found him out.

'I then went to work in this way. I bought two planks about thirteen feet long, and an inch thick. In these planks I had small traps, about two inches long by one inch wide, let into the wood, and very nicely fitted, so that the cracks could not be seen. The better to hide the cracks, I had the wood painted marble, and the blue veins arranged on the cracks. These traps were bound on the upper side with iron hooping to strengthen them. Then I made my boots. They were something like Chinese boots, with a very thick sole, made on the principle of the bellows of an accordion. These bellows were round, about the size of a cheese-plate, and six inches deep. To the sole of the boot I had an iron plate and a square tenter-hook riveted in.

'Then came the performance. There was no net under me, and the planks was suspended about twenty feet from the stage. I went up on the ladder and inserted the hook on one boot into the first trap. The sucker to the boot hid the hook, and made it appear as if I held by suction. The traps were about six inches apart, and that gave me a very small step. The hooks being square ones—tenter-hooks—I could slip them out easily. It had just the same appearance as Sands, and nobody ever taught me how to do it. I did this feat at the Albion Concert-rooms, just opposite the Effingham Saloon. I had eighteen shillings a-week there for doing it. I never did it anywhere else, for it was a bother to carry the planks about with me. I did it for a month, every night three times. One night I fell down. You see you can never make sure, for if you swung a little, it worked the hook off. I always had a chap walking along under me to catch me, and he broke my fall, so that I didn't hurt myself. I ran up again, and did it a second time without an accident. There was tremendous applause. I think I should have fallen on my hands if the chap hadn't been here.

'If the Secretary of State hadn't put down the balloon business,

I should a made a deal of money. There is danger of course, but so there is if you're twenty or thirty feet. They do it now fifty feet high, and that's as bad as if you were two hundred or a mile in the air. The only danger is getting giddy from the height, but those who go up are accustomed to it.

'I sold the ceiling-walking trick to another fellow for two pounds, after I had done with it, but he couldn't manage it. He thought he was going to do wonders. He took a half-hundred weight along with him, but he swung like a pendulum, and down he come.'

THE STREET JUGGLER

THE juggler from whom I received the following account, was spoken of by his companions and friends as 'one of the cleverest that ever came out.' He was at this time performing in the evening at one of the chief saloons on the other side of the water.

He certainly appears to have been successful enough when he first appeared in the streets, and the way in which he squandered the amount of money he then made is a constant source of misery to him, for he kept exclaiming in the midst of his narrative, 'Ah! I might have been a gentleman now, if I hadn't been the fool I was then.'

As a proof of his talents and success he assured me, that when Ramo Samee first came out, he not only learned how to do all the Indian's tricks, but also did them so dexterously, that when travelling 'Samee has often paid him ten shillings not to perform in the same town with him.'

'I'm a juggler,' he said, 'but I don't know if that's the right term, for some people call conjurers jugglers; but it's wrong. When I was in Ireland they called me a "manulist," and it was a gentleman wrote the bill out for me. The difference I makes between conjuring and juggling is, one's deceiving to the eye and the other's pleasing to the eye—yes, that's it—it's dexterity.

'I dare say I've been at juggling 40 years, for I was between 14 and 15 when I begun, and I'm 56 now. I remember Ramo Samee and all the first process of the art. He was the first as ever I knew, and very good indeed; there was no other to oppose him, and he must have been good then. I suppose I'm the oldest juggler alive.

'I'm too old now to go out regularly in the streets. It tires me too much, if I have to appear at a penny theatre in the evening. When I do go out in the streets, I carry a mahogany box with me, to put my things out in. I've got three sets of things now, knives, balls, and cups. In fact, I never was so well off in apparatus as now; and many of them have been given to me as presents, by friends as have gi'n over performing. Knives, and balls, and all, are very handsome. The balls, some a pound, and some 2 lbs. weight, and the knives about 1½ lbs.

'When I'm out performing, I get into all the open places as I can. I goes up the Commercial-road and pitches at the Mile-end-gate, or about Tower-hill, or such-like. I'm well known in London, and the police knows me so well they very seldom interfere with me. Sometimes they say, "That's not allowed, you know, old man!' and I say, "I shan't be above two or three minutes," and they say, "Make haste, then!' and then I go on with the performance.

'I think I'm the cleverest juggler out. I can do the pagoda, or the canopy as some calls it; that is a thing like a parasol balanced by the handle on my nose, and the sides held up by other sticks, and then with a pea-shooter I blow away the supports. I also do what is called "the birds and bush," which is something of the same, only you knock off the birds with a pea-shooter. The birds is only made of cork, but it's very difficult, because you have to take your balance agin every bird as falls; besides, you must be careful the birds don't fall in your eyes, or it would take away your sight and spoil the balance. The birds at back are hardest to knock off, because you have to bend back, and at the same time mind you don't topple the tree off.

'These are the only feats we perform in balancing, and the juggling is the same now as ever it was, for there ain't been no improvements on the old style as I ever heerd on; and I suppose balls and knives and rings will last for a hundred years to come yet.

'I and my wife are now engaged at the "Temple of Mystery" in Old Street-road, and it says on the bills that they are "at present exhibiting the following new and interesting talent," and then they calls me "The Renowned Indian Juggler, performing his extraordinary Feats with Cups, Balls, Daggers, Plates, Knives, Rings, Balancing, &c. &c."

'After the juggling I generally has to do conjuring. I does what they call "the pile of mags," that is, putting four halfpence on a boy's cap, and making them disappear when I say "Presto, fly!" Then there's the empty cups, and making 'taters come under 'em, or there's bringing a cabbage into a empty hat. There's also making a shilling pass from a gentleman's hand into a nest of boxes, and such-like tricks: but it ain't half so hard as juggling, nor anything like the work.

'I and my missis have 5s. 6d. a-night between us, besides a collection among the company, which I reckon, on the average, to be as good as another pound a-week, for we made that the last week we performed.

'I should say there ain't above twenty jugglers in all England—indeed, I'm sure there ain't—such as goes about pitching in the streets and towns. I know there's only four others besides myself in London, unless some new one has sprung up very lately. You may safely reckon their earnings for the year round at a pound a-week, that is, of they stick to juggling; but most of us joins some other calling along with juggling, such as the wizard's business, and that helps out the gains.

'Before this year, I used to go down to the sea-side in the summer, and perform at the watering-places. A chap by the name of Gordon is at Ramsgate now. It pays well on the sands, for in two or three hours, according to the tides, we picks up enough for the day.'

THE STREET CONJURER

'I CALL myself a wizard as well; but that's only the polite term for conjurer; in fact, I should think that wizard meant an astrologer, and more of a fortune-teller. I was fifteen years of age when I first began my professional life; the first pitch we made was near Bond-street. I did card tricks, such as the sautez-le-coup with the little finger. It's dividing the pack in half, and then bringing the bottom half to the top; and then, if there's a doubt, you can convey the top card to the bottom again; or if there's any doubt, you can bring the pack to its original position. It was Lord de Roos's trick. He won heaps of money at it. He had pricked cards. You see, if you prick a card at the corner, card-players skin their finger at the end, so as to make it sensitive, and they can tell a pricked card in a moment. Besides sautez-le-coup I used to do innumerable others, such as telling a named card by throwing a pack in the air and catching the card on a sword point. Then there was telling people's thoughts by the cards. All card tricks are feats of great dexterity and quickness of hand. I never used a false pack of cards. There are some made for amateurs, but professionals never use trick cards. The greatest art is what is termed forcing, that is, making a party take the card you wish him to; and let him try ever so well, he will have it, though he's not conscious of it. Another feat of dexterity is slipping the card, that is, slipping it from top bottom, or centre, or placing one or two cards from the top. If you're playing a game at all-fours and you know the ace of clubs is at the bottom, you can slip it one from the top, so that you know your partner opposite has it. These are the only two principal things in card tricks, and if you can do them dexterously you can do a great part of a wizard's art. Suatez-le-coup is the principal thing, and it's done by placing the middle finger in the centre of the pack, and then with the right hand working the change. I can do it with one hand.

'We did well with pitching in the streets. We'd take ten shillings of a morning, and then go out in the afternoon again and take perhaps fifteen shillings of nobbings. The footmen were our best customers in the morning, for they had leisure then. We usually went to the squares and such parts at the West-end. This was twenty years ago, and it isn't anything like so good now, in consequence of my partner dying of consumption; brought on, I think, by fire eating, for he was a very steady young fellow and not at all given to drink, I was for two years in the streets with the fire-eating, and we made I should say such a thing as fifty shillings a-week each. Then you must remember, we could have made more if we had liked; for some mornings, if we had had a good day before, we wouldn't go out if it were raining, or we had been up late. I next got a situation, and went to a wax-works to do conjuring. It was a penny exhibition in the New Cut, Lambeth. I had four shillings a day and nobbings—a collection, and what with selling my books, it came to ten shillings a-day, for we had never less than ten and often twenty performance a-day. They had the first dissecting figure there—a Samson—and they took off the cranium and showed the brains, and also the stomach, and showed the intestines. It was the first ever shown in this country, and the maker of it had (so they say) a pension of one hundred pounds a year for having composed it. He was an Italian.

'We were burnt down at Birmingham, and I lost all my rattle-traps. However, the inhabitants made up a subscription which amply repaid me for my loss, and I then came to London, hearing that the Epsom races was on at the time, which I wouldn't have missed Epsom races, not at that time, not for any amount of money, for it was always good to one as three pounds, and I have had as much as seven pounds from one carriage alone. It was Lord Chester-field's, and each gentleman in it gave us a sov. I went down with three acrobats to Epsom, but they were dealing unfair with me, and there was something that I didn't like going on; so I quarrelled with them and joined with another conjurer, and it was on this very occasion we got the seven pounds from one carriage. We both varied in our entertainments; because, when I had done my performance, he made a collection; and when he had done I got the nobbings. We went to Lord Chesterfield's carriage on the hill, and there I did the sovereign trick. "My Lord, will you oblige me with the temporary loan of a sovereign?" "Yes, old fellow: what are you going to do with it?" I then did passing the sovereign, he hav-ing marked it first; and then, though he held it tightly, I changed it for a farthing. I did this for Lord Waterford and Lord Waldegrave, and the whole of them in the carriage. I always said, "Now, my Lord, are you sure you hold it?" "Yes, old fellow." "Now, my Lord, if I was to take the sovereign away from you without you knowing it, wouldn't you say I was perfectly welcome to it?" He'd say, "Yes, old fellow; go on." Then, when he opened the handker-chief he had a farthing, and all of them made me a present of the sovereign I had performed with.

'Then we went to the Grand Stand, and then after our perform-ance they'd throw us halfpence from above. We had our table nicely fitted up. We wouldn't take halfpence. We would collect up the coppers, perhaps five or six shillings' worth, and then we'd throw the great handful among the boys. "A bit of silver, your honours, if you please"; then sixpence would come, and then a shilling, and in ten minutes we would have a sovereign. We must have earned our six pounds each that Epsom Day; but then our expenses were heavy, for we paid three shillings a-night for our lodging alone.'

THE SNAKE, SWORD, AND KNIFE
SWALLOWER

HE was quite a young man, and, judging from his countenance, there was nothing that could account for his having taken up so strange a method of gaining his livelihood as that of swallowing snakes.

He was very simple in his talk and manner. He readily confessed that the idea did not originate with him, and prided himself only on being the second to take it up. There is no doubt that it was from his being startled by the strangeness and daringness of the act that he was induced to make the essay. He said he saw nothing disgusting in it; that people liked it; that it served him well in his 'professional' engagements; and spoke of the snake in general as a reptile capable of affection, not unpleasant to the eye, and very cleanly in his habits.

'I swallow snakes, swords,and knives; but, of course, when I'm engaged at a penny theater I'm expected to do more than this, for it would only take a quarter of an hour, and that isn't long enough for them. They call me in the profession a "Sallementro," and that is what I term myself; though p'raps it's easier to say I'm a 'swallower."

'It was a mate of mine that I was with that first put me up to sword-and-snake swallowing. I copied off him, and it took me about three months to learn it. I began with a sword first—of course not a sharp sword, but one blunt-pointed—and didn't exactly know how to do it, for there's a trick in it. I see him, and I said, "Oh, I shall set up master for myself, and practise until I can do it."

'At first it turned me, putting it down my throat past my swallow, right down—about eighteen inches. It made my swallow sore—very sore, and I used lemon and sugar to cure it. It was tight at first, and I kept pushing it down further and further. There's one thing, you mustn't cough, and until you're used to it you want to very bad, and then you must pull it up again. My sword was about three-quarters of an inch wide.

'At first I didn't know the trick of doing it, but I found it out this way. You see the trick is, you must oil the sword—the best sweet oil, worth fourteen pence a pint—and you put it on with a sponge. Then, you understand, if the sword scratches the swallow it don't make it sore, 'cos the oil heals it up again. When first I put the sword down, before I oiled it, it used to come up quite slimy, but after the oil it slips down quite easy, is as clean when it comes up as before it went down.

'As I told you, we are called at concert-rooms where I perform the "Sallementro." I think it's French, but I don't know what it is exactly; but that's what I'm called amongst us.

'The knives are easier to do than the sword because they are shorter. We puts them right down till the handle rests on the mouth. The sword is about eighteen inches long, and the knives about eight inches in the blade. People run away with the idea that you slip the blades down your breast, but I always hold mine right up with the neck bare, and they see it go into the mouth atween the teeth. They also fancy it hurts you; but it don't, or what a fool I should be to do it. I don't mean to say it don't hurt you at first, 'cos it do, for my swallow was very bad, and I couldn't eat anything but liquids for two months whilst I was learning. I cured my swallow whilst I was stretching it with lemon and sugar.

'I was the second one that ever swallowed a snake. I was about seventeen or eighteen years old when I learnt it. The first was Clarke as did it. He done very well with it, but he wasn't out no more than two years before me, so he wasn't known much. In the country there is some places where, when you do it, they swear you are the devil, and won't have it nohow.

'The snakes I use are about eighteen inches long, and you must first cut the stingers out, 'cos it might hurt you. I always keep two or three by me for my performances. I keep them warm, but the winter kills 'em. I give them nothing to eat but worms or gentles. I generally keep them in flannel, or hay, in a box. I've three at home now.

'When first I began swallowing snakes they tasted queer like. They draw's the roof of the mouth a bit. It's a roughish taste. The scales rough you a bit when you draw them up. You see, a snake will go into ever such a little hole, and they are smooth one way.

'The head of the snake goes about an inch and a half down the throat, and the rest of it continues in the mouth, curled round like.

I hold him by the tail, and when I pinch it he goes right in. You must cut the stinger out or he'll injure you. The tail is slippery, but you nip it with the nails like pinchers. If you was to let him go, he'd go right down; but most snakes will stop at two inches down the swallow, and then they bind like a ball in the mouth.'

STREET CLOWN

HE was a melancholy-looking man, with the sunken eyes and other characteristics of semi-starvation, whilst his face was scored with lines and wrinkles, telling of paint and premature age.

I saw him performing in the streets with a school of acrobats soon after I had been questioning him, and the readiness and business-like way with which he resumed his professional buffoonery was not a little remarkable. His story was more pathetic than comic, and proved that the life of a street clown is, perhaps, the most wretched of all existence. Jest as he may in the street, his life is literally no joke at home.

'I have been a clown for sixteen years,' he said, 'having lived totally by it for that time. I was left motherless at two years of age, and my father died when I was nine. He was a carman, and his master took me as a stable-boy, and I stayed with him until he failed in business. I was then left destitute again, and got employed as a supernumerary at Astley's, at one shilling a-night. I was a "super" some time, and got an insight into theatrical life. I got acquainted, too, with singing people, and could sing a good song, and came out at last on my own account in the streets, in the Jim Crow line. My necessities forced me into a public line, which I am far from liking. I'd pull trucks at one shilling a-day, rather than get twelve shillings a-week at my business. I've tried to get out of the line. I've got a friend to advertise for me for any situation as groom. I've tried to get into the police, and I've tried other things, but somehow there seems an impossibility to get quit of the street business. Many times I have to play the clown, and indulge in all kinds of buffoonery, with a terrible heavy heart. I have travelled very much, too, but I never did over-well in the profession. At races I may have made ten shillings for two or three days, but that was only occasional; and what is ten shillings to keep a wife and family on, for a month maybe? I have three children, one now only eight weeks old. You can't imagine, sir, what a curse the street business often becomes, with its insults and starvations. The day before my wife was confined, I jumped and labor'd doing Jim Crow for twelve hours—in the wet, too—and earned one shilling and threepence; with this I returned to a home without a bit of coal, and with only half-a-quartern loaf in it. I knew it was one shilling and threepence; for I keep a sort of log of my earnings and my expenses; you'll see on it what I've earned as a clown, or the funnyman, with a party of acrobats, since the beginning of this year.'

'I dare say,' continued the man, 'that no persons think more of their dignity than such as are in my way of life. I would rather starve than ask for parochial relief. Many a time I have gone to my labour without breaking my fast, and played clown until I could raise dinner. I have to make jokes as clown, and could fill a volume with all I knows.'

He told me several of his jests; they were all of the most venerable kind, as for instance:—'A horse has ten legs: he has two fore legs and two hind ones. Two fores are eight, and two others are ten.' The other jokes were equally puerile, as, 'Why is the City of Rome,' (he would have it Rome), 'like a candle wick? Because it's in the midst of Greece.' 'Old and young are both of one age: your son at twenty is young, and your horse at twenty is old: and so old and young are the same.' 'The dress,' he continued, 'that I wear in the streets consists of red striped cotton stockings, with full trunks, dotted red and black. The body, which is dotted like the trunks, fits tight like a woman's gown, and has full sleeves and frills. The wig or scalp is made of horse-hair, which is sewn on to a white cap, and is in the shape of a cock's comb. My face is painted with dry white lead. I grease my skin first and then dab the white paint on (flake-white is too dear for us street clowns); after that I colour my cheeks and mouth with vermilion. I never dress at home; we all dress at public-houses. In the street where I lodge, only a very few know what I do for a living. I and my wife both strive to keep business a secret from our neighbours. My wife does a little washing when able, and often works eight hours for sixpence. I go out at eight in the morning and return at dark. My children hardly know what I do. They see my dresses lying about, but that is all. My eldest is a girl of thirteen. She has seen me dressed at Stapney fair, where she brought me my tea (I live near there); she laughs when she sees me in my clown's dress, and wants to stay with me: but I would rather see her lay dead before me (and I had two dead in my place at one time, last Whitsun Monday was a twelvemonth) than she should ever belong to my profession.'

I could see the tears start from the man's eyes as he said this. 'Frequently when I am playing the fool in the streets, I feel very sad at heart. I can't help thinking of the bare cupboards at home; but what's that to the world? I've often and often been at home all day when it has been wet, with no food at all, either to give my children or take myself, and have gone out at night to the public-houses to sing a comic song or play the funnyman for a meal—you may imagine with what feelings for the part—and when I've come home I've call'd my children up from their beds to share the loaf I had brought back with me. I know three or more clowns as miserable and bad off as myself. The way in which our profession is ruined is by the stragglers or outsiders, who are often men who are good tradesmen. They take to the clown's business only at holiday or fair time, when there is a little money to be picked up at it, and after that they go back to their own trades; so that, you see, we, who are obliged to continue at it the year through, are deprived of even the little bit of luck we should otherwise have. I know only of another regular street clown in London besides myself. Some schools of acrobats, to be sure, will have a comic character of some kind or other, to keep the pitch up; that is, to amuse the people while the money is being collected: but these, in general, are not regular clowns. They are mostly dressed and got up for the occasion. They certainly don't do anything else but the street comic business, but they are not pantomimists by profession. The street clowns generally go out with dancers and tumblers. There are some street clowns to be seen with the Jacks-in-the-greens; but they are mostly sweeps, who have hired their dress for the two or three days, as the case may be.'

THE PENNY-GAFF CLOWN

The 'professional' from whom I elicited my knowledge of penny-gaff clowning is known among his companions as 'Funny Billy.' He appeared not a little anxious to uphold the dignity of the penny theatre, frequently assuring me that 'they brought things out there

in a style that would astonish some of the big houses.' His whole
being seemed wrapped up in these cheap dramatic saloons, and he
told me wonderful stories of first-class actors at 'The Effingham,'
or of astonishing performers at 'The Bower,' or 'Rotunda.' He
was surprised, too, that the names of several of the artistes there
were not familiar to me, and frequently pressed me to go and see
so-and-so's 'Beadle,' or hear so-and-so sing his 'Oh! don't I like
my Father!'

Besides being a clown, my informant was also 'an author,' and
several of the most successful ballets, pantomimes, and dramas,
that of late years have been brought out at the City gaffs, have,
I was assured, proceeded from 'his pen.'

In build, even in his every-day clothes, he greatly resembles a
clown—perhaps from the broadness of his chest and high-buttoned
waistcoat, or from the shortness and crookedness of his legs; but
he was the first I had seen whose form gave any indication of his
calling.

Since the beginning of this year (1856) he has given up clowning,
and taken to pantalooning instead, for 'on last boxing-day', he
informed me, 'he met with an accident which dislocated his jaw,
and caused a swelling in his cheek as if he had an apple inside his
mouth.' This he said he could conceal in his make-up as a pantaloon, but it had ruined him for a clown.

His statement was as follows:—

'I'm a clown at penny gaffs and the cheap theatres, for some of
the gaffs are twopence and threepence—that's as high as they run.
The Rotunda in the Blackfriars'-road is the largest in London,
and that will hold one thousand comfortably seated, and they give
two in one evening, at one penny, twopence, and threepence, and
a first-class entertainment it is, consisting of a variety of singing
and dancing, and ballets, from one hour and a-half to two hours.
There are no penny theatres where speaking is legally allowed,
though they do it to a great extent, and at all of 'em at Christmas
a pantomime is played, at which Clown and Pantaloon speaks.

'The difference between a penny-gaff clown and a fair, or, as
we call it, a canvas clown, is this,—at the fairs the principal business
is outside on the parade, and there's very little done (seldom more
than two scenes) inside. Now at the penny gaffs they go through a
regular pantomime, consisting of from six to eight scenes, with

jumps and all complete, as at a regular theatre; so that to do clown to one of them, you must be equal to those that come out at the regular theatres; and what's more, you must strain every nerve; and what's more still, you may often please at a regular theatre when you won't go down at all at a penny gaff. The circus clown is as different from a penny-gaff clown as a coster is from a tradesman.

'What made me turn clown was this. I was singing comic songs at the Albion Saloon, Whitechapel, and playing in ballets, and doing the scene-painting. Business was none of the best. Mr. Paul Herring, the celebrated clown, was introduced into the company as a draw, to play ballets. The ballet which he selected was "The Barber and the Beadle"; and me being the only one who played the old men on the establishment, he selected me to play the Beadle to his Barber. He complimented me for what I had done, when the performance was over, for I done my uttermost to gain his applause, knowing him to be such a star, and what he said was—I think—deserved. We played together ballets for upwards of nine months, as well as pantomimes, in which I done the Pantaloon; and we had two clear benefits between us, in which we realised three pounds each, on both occasions. Then Mr. Paul Herring was engaged by Mr. Jem Douglass, of the Standard, to perform with the great clown, Mr. Tom Matthews, for it was intended to have two clowns in the piece. He having to go to the Standard for the Christmas, left about September, and we was without a clown, and it was proposed that I should play the clown. I accepted the offer, at a salary of thirty-five shillings a-week, under Hector Simpson, the great pantomimist—who was proprietor. This gentleman was well known as the great dog-and-beat man of Covent Garden, and various other theatres, where he played Valentine and Orson with a living bear. He showed me various things that I were deficient in, and with what I knew myself we went on admiringly well; and I continued at it as clown for upwards of a year, and became a great favourite.

'I remember clowning last Christmas (1856) particularly, for it was a sad year for me, and one of the busiest times I have ever known. I met with an accident then. I was worked to death. First of all, I had to do my rehearsals; then I had the scene-painting to go on with, which occupied me night and day, and what it brought

me in was three shillings a-day and three shillings a-night. The
last scene, equal to a pair of flats, was only given to me to do on
Christmas-eve, to accomplish by the boxing-day. I got them done
by five o'clock at Christmas morning, and then I had to go home
and complete my dress, likewise my little boys', who was
engaged to sing and play in ballets at two shillings a-night;
and he was only five years old, but very clever at singing,
combating, and ballet performing, as also the illustrations of
the Grecian statues, which he first done when he was two and a
half years old.

'The pantomime was the original Statue Blanche, as performed
by Joe Grimaldi, as Mr. Hector Simpson had produced it—for it
was under his superintendence—at Covent Garden Theatre. Its
title was, "The Statue Blanche, or Harlequin and the Magic Cross."
I was very successful on the boxing-night, but on the second
occasion of my acting in it I received an accident, which laid me up
for three months, and I was not off my bed for ten weeks.'

THE PENNY CIRCUS JESTER

A MAN who had passed many years of his life as jester at the cheap
circuses, or penny equestrian shows frequenting the fairs in the
neighbourhood of London, obliged me with the following details:—

'There are only two kinds of clowns, the stage and the circus
clown, only there is different denominations: for instance, the
clown at the fair and the clown at the regular theatre, as well as
the penny gaff (when they give pantomimes there), are one and the
same kind of clown, only better or worse, according to the pay
and kind of performance; but it's the same sort of business. Now
the circus clown is of the same kind as those that go about with
schools of acrobats and negro serenaders. He is expected to be
witty and say clever things, and invent anything he can for the
evening's performance; but the theatre clown is expected to do
nothing but what enters into the business of the piece. Them two
are the main distinctions we make in the perfession.

'I've travelled along with only two circuses; but then it's the
time you stop with them, for I was eighteen months along with a
man of the name of Johnson, who performed at the Albion, Whitechapel and in Museum-street, opposite Drury-lane (he had a

penny exhibition then), and for above two years and a half along
with Veale, who had a circus at the Birdcage, Hackney-road, and
at Walworth.

'At Museum-street we only had one "prad," which is slang for
pony, although we used to introduce all the circus business. We had
jugglers, and globe-runners, and tight-rope dancers also. We never
had no wing built, but only sawdust on the stage, and all the wings
taken out. They used to begin with a chant and a hop (singing and
dancing), after which there was tight-rope hopping. As soon as
ever the rope was drawn up, Johnson, who had a whip in his hand,
the same as if it was a regular circus, used to say, "Now, Mr. Merry-
man." Then I'd run on and answer, "Here I am, sir, all of a lump,
as the old man said what found the sixpence. I'm up and dressed,
like a watchbox. What shall I have the pleasure for to come for to
go, for to go for to fetch, for to fetch for to carry, to oblige you?"
I usually wore a ring dress, with red rings round my trunks, and a
fly to correspond. The tights had straight red lines. My wig was a
white one with a red comb. Then Johnson would say, "Have the
pleasure to announce Madame Leone." Then I give it: "Ladies and
gentlemen, this is Madame Leone, a young lady that threw her
clothes into bed and hung herself upon the door-nail." Then she
just gets up on the rope, and I go and sit down as if I was going to
sleep. Mr. Johnson then says, "Come, sir, you're going to sleep;
you've got your eyes shut." I answer, "I beg you pardon, sir, I
was not asleep." And then he says I was, and I contradict him, and
add, "If I had my eyes shut, I am the first of the family that went
to sleep so." Then he asks how that is? and I reply, "Because they
were afraid of having their pockets picked"; and he says, "Nonsense! all your family was very poor, there was nothing in their
pockets to pick"; and I add, "Yes, but there was the stitches
though." All these puns and catches goes immense. "Now, sir," he
continues, "chalk the rope." I say, "Whose place is it?" and he
replies, "The fool's." "Then do it yourself," I answer. And then we
go on in this style. He cries, "What did you say, sir?" "I said I'd
do it myself." "Now, Madame Leone, are you ready?" and she
nods; and then I tell the music to toodelloo and blow us up. She
then does a step or two—a little of the polka—and retires, and
I am told to chalk the rope again, and this is our talk: "Oh dear,
oh dear! there's no rest for the wicked. Sir, would you be so kind,

so obliging, as to inform me why I chalk the top of the rope?"
"To prevent the young lady from slipping down, sir." "Oh, indeed!
then I'll chalk underneath the rope." He then asks, "What are
you doing of, sir?" "Why, didn't you tell me when I chalked the
top it's to prevent the young lady from slipping down?" "Yes,
sir." "Then I chalked underneath, to prevent her from slipping
up again. Would you oblige me with your hand?" Then I look at it
and say, "Plenty of corns in it; you've done some hard work in
your time." "I have, sir." "Beautiful nails, too;" and then I run
the chalk on his hand, and when he asks what I'm doing of, I say,
"Chalking it." "What for, sir?" "Why, sir, to keep it from slipping
into other people's pockets." Then he gives me a click of whip and
says, "Out of the way, sir! Now, Madame Leone, proceed."

SILLY BILLY

THE character of 'Silly Billy' is a kind of clown, or rather a clown's
butt; but not after the style of Pantaloon, for the part is comparatively juvenile. Silly Billy is supposed to be a schoolboy, although
not dressed in a charity-boy's attire. He is very popular with the
audience at the fairs; indeed, they cannot do without him. 'The
people like to see Silly Billy,' I was told, 'much more than they
do Pantaloon, for he gets knocked about more though, but he gives
it back again. A good Silly,' said my informant, 'has to imitate
all the ways of a little boy,. When I have been going to a fair, I
have many a time stopped for hours watching boys at play, learning
their various games, and getting their sayings. For instance, some
will go about the streets singing:

> 'Eh, higgety, eh ho!
> Billy let the water go!

which is some song about a boy pulling a tap from a water-butt,
and letting the water run. There's another:

> 'Nicky nickey nite,
> I'll strike a light!'

I got these both from watching children whilst playing. Again,
boys will swear "By the liver and lights of a cobbler's lapstone!"
and their most desperate oath is,

> 'Ain't this wet? ain't it dry?
> Cut my throat I tells a lie',

They'll say, too, "S'elp my greens!" and "Upon my word and say so!" All these sayings I used to work up into my Silly Billy, and they had their success.

'I do such things as these, too, which is regularly boyish, such as "Give me a bit of your bread and butter, and I'll give you a bit of my bread and treacle." Again, I was watching a lot of boys playing at pitch-button, and one says, "Ah, you're up to the rigs of this hole; come to my hole—you can't play there!" I've noticed them, too, playing at ring-taw, and one of their exclamations is "Knuckle down fair, and no funking." All these sayings are very useful to make the character of Silly Billy perfect. Bless you, sir, I was two years studying boys before I came out as Silly Billy. But then I persevere when I take a thing in hand; and I stick so close to nature, that I can't go far wrong in that line. Now this is a regular boy's answer: when somebody says "Does your mother know you're out?" he replies, "Yes, she do; but I didn't know the organ-man had lost his monkey!' that always went immense.

'It's impossible to say when Silly Billy first come out at fairs, or who first supported the character. It's been popular ever since a fair can be remembered. The best I ever saw was Teddy Walters. He's been at all the fairs round the universe—England, Ireland, Scotland, Wales, and France. He belonged to a circus when he went abroad. He's done Silly Billy these forty year, and he's a great comic singer beside. I was reckoned very clever at it. I used to look at it by making up so young for it. It tires you very much, for there's so much exertion attached to it by the dancing and capering about. I've done it at the fairs, and also with tumblers in the street; only, when you do it in the street, you don't do one-half the business.

'The make-up for a Silly Billy is this: Short white trousers and shoes, with a strap round the ankle, long white pinafore with a frill round the neck, and red sleeves, and a boy's cap. We dress the head with the hair behind the ears, and a dab of red on the nose and two patches of black over the eyebrows. When I went to the fair I always took three pairs of white trousers with me. The girls used to get up playing larks with me, and smearing my white trousers with gingerbread. It's a very favourite character with the women—they stick pins into you, as if you were a pin-cushion. I've had my thighs bleeding sometimes. One time, during Greenwich, a ugly old woman come on the parade and kissed me, and made me a present of a silver sixpence, which, I needn't say, was soon spent in porter. Why, I've brought home with me sometimes toys enough to last a child a fortnight, if it was to break one every day, such as carts and horses, cock and breeches, whistles, &c. You see, Silly Billy is supposed to be a thievish sort of a character, and I used to take the toys away from the girls as they were going into the theatre, and then I'd show it to the Clown and say, "Oh, look what that nice lady's give me! I shall take it home to my mother." '

BALLET PERFORMERS

'THE BALLET,' said a street-dancer to me, 'is a very favourite amusement with the people who go to cheap penny theatres. They are all comic, like pantomimes; indeed, they come under that term, only there's no comic scenes or transformations. They're like the story of a pantomime, and nothing else. Nearly all the popular clowns are famous for their ballet performances; they take the comic parts mostly, and the pantallons take the old men's parts. Ballets have been favourites in this country for forty or fifty year. There is always a comic part in every ballet. I have known ballets to be very popular for ever since I can remember,—and that's thirty years. At all the gaffs, where they are afraid to speak their parts, they always have a ballet. Every one in London, and there are plenty of them, have one every night, for it's very seldom they venture upon a talking play.

'In all ballets the costume is fanciful. The young ladies come on in short petticoats, like them at the opera. Some of the girls we have are the same as have been in the opera corps-de-ballet. Mr. Flexmore, the celebrated clown, is a ballet performer, and there's not a greater man going for the ballet that he appears in, called "The Dancing Scotchman." There's Paul Herring, too; he's very famous. He's the only man I know of that can play Punch, for he works the speaker in his mouth; and he's been a great Punch-and-Judy man in his time. He's very clever in "The Sprite of the Vineyard, or the Merry Devil of Como." They've been playing it at Cremorne lately, and a very successful affair it was.

'When a professional goes to a gaff to get an engagement, they in general inquires whether he is a good ballet performer. Everything depends upon that. They also acts ballets at some of the concert-rooms. At the Rising Sun, Knightsbridge, as well as the Brown Bear, Knightsbridge, they play them for a week at a time, and then drop them for a fortnight for a change, and perhaps have tumblers instead; then they have them again for a week, and so on. In Ratcliffe Highway, at Ward's Hoop and Grapes, and also the Albion, and the Prince Regent, they always play ballets at stated intervals. Also the Effingham Saloon, Whitechapel, is a celebrated ballet-house. The admission to all these houses is 2*d*., I believe. At the Highway, when the ships are up and the sailors ashore, business is very brisk, and they are admitted to the rooms gratuitously; and a fine thing they make of them, for they are good-hearted fellows and don't mind what money they spend. I've known one who was a little way gone to chuck half-a-crown on the stage to some actor, and I've known others to spend a pound at one bit,—standing to all round! One night, when I was performing at the Rising Sun, Knightsbridge, Mr. Hill, the Queen's coachman, threw me two half-crowns on to the stage. We had been supposed to have been fighting,—I and my mate,—and to have got so exhausted we fell down, and Mr. Hill came and poured three glasses of port-wine negus down our throats as we laid. I've repeatedly had 1*s*. and 5*s*. thrown to me by the grooms of the different people of nobility, such as the Russells and various other families.

'A good ballet performer will get averaging from a pound to 35*s*. a-week. They call Paul Herring a star, and he is one, for he always draws wherever he goes. I generally get my 25*s*., that's my running price, though I try for my 30*s*, but 25 *s*. is about my mark. I have always made Paul Herring my study, and I try to get to perform with him, for he's the best clown of the day, and a credit to work with.

'It's impossible to say how many ballet performers there are. There are such a host of them it's impossible to state that, for they change so. Then a great many are out of employment until Christmas, for that generally fills vacancies up. My wife does a little in ballets, though she is principally a poses plastiques girl. I married my wife off the table.

'One of the most successful ballets is the Statue Blanche. It has been performed at every theatre in London, both the cheap and the regular. The Surrey is an enormous place for it. It came out, I believe, in Grimaldi's time. It was played a fortnight ago at the Bower, and I took the part of the old man, and I was very successful; so far so that I got a situation for Christmas. It's an excellent plot, and runs an hour and a quarter to play.'

THE TIGHT-ROPE DANCERS AND STILT-VAULTERS

'I AM the father of two little girls who perform on the tight-rope and on stilts. My wife also performs, so that the family by itself can give an entertainment that lasts an hour and a half altogether. I don't perform myself, but I go about making the arrangements and engagements for them. Managers write to me from the country to get up entertainments for them, and to undertake the speculation, at so much. Indeed I am a manager. I hire a place of amusement, and hire it at so much; or if they won't let it, then I take an engagement for the family. I never fancied any professional work myself except, perhaps, a bit of sculpture. I am rather partial to the poses plastiques, but that's all.

'Both my little girls are under eight years of age, and they do the stilt-waltzing, and the eldest does the tight-rope business as well. Their mother is a tight-rope dancer, and does the same business as Madame Sayin used to appear in, such as the ascension on the rope in the midst of fireworks. We had men in England who had done the ascension before Madame Sayin came out at Vauxhall, but I think she was the first woman that ever did it in this country. I remember her well. She lodged at a relation of mine during her engagement at the Gardens. She was a ugly little woman, very diminutive, and tremendously pitted with the small-pox. She was what may be called a horny woman, very tough and bony. I've heard my father and mother say she had 20*l.* a-night at Vauxhall, and she did it three times a-week; but I can't vouch for this, as it was only hearsay.

'My eldest little girl first began doing the stilts in public when she was three-and-a-half years old. I don't suppose she was much more than two-and-a-half years old when I first put her on the stilts. They were particularly short, was about four foot from the ground, so that she came to about as high as my arms. It was the funniest thing in the world to see her. She hadn't got sufficient strength in her knees to keep her legs stiff, and she used to wabble about just like a fellow drunk, and lost the use of his limbs. The object of beginning so soon was to accustom it, and she was only on for a few minutes once or twice a-day. She liked this very much, in fact so much, that the other little ones used to cry like blazes because I wouldn't let them have a turn at them. I used to make my girl do it just like a bit of fun. She'd be laughing fit to crack her sides, and we'd be laughing to see her little legs bending about. I had a new dress made for her, with a spangled bodice and gauze skirt, and she always put that on when she was practising, and that used to induce her to the exercise. She was pleased as Punch when she had her fine clothes on. When she wasn't good, I'd say to her, "Very well, miss, since you're so naughty, you shan't go out with us to perform; we'll teach your little sister, and take her with us, and leave you at home." That used to settle her in a moment ,for she didn't like the idea of having the other one take her place.

'Some people, when they teach their children for any entertainment, torture the little things most dreadful. There is a great deal of barbarity practised in teaching children for the various lines. It's very silly, because it only frightens the little things, and some children often will do much more by kindness than ill-usage. Now there are several children that I know of that have been severely injured whilst being trained for the Risley business. Why, bless your soul, a little thing coming down on its head, is done for the remainder of its life. I've seen them crying on the stage, publicly, from being sworn at and bullied, where they would have gone to it laughing, if they had only been coaxed and persuaded.

'Now my little things took to it almost naturally. It was bred and born in them, for my father was in the profession before me, and my wife's parents were also performers. We had both my little girls on the stilts before they were three years old. It's astonishing how soon the leg gets accustomed to the stilts, for in less than three months they can walk alone. Of course, for the first six weeks that they were put on we never leave go of their hands. The knees, which at first is weak and wabbly, gets strong, and when once that is used to the pad and stump (for the stilts are fastened on to just where the garter would come), then the child is all right. It does not enlarge the knee at all, and instead of crooking the leg, it acts in a similar way to what we see in a child born with the cricks, with irons on. I should say, that if any of my children had been born knock-kneed, or bow-legged, the stilts have been the means of making their legs straight. It does not fatigue their ankles at all, but the principal strain is on the hollow in the palm of the foot, where it fits into the tread of the stilt, for that's the thing that bears the whole weight. If you keep a child on too long, it will complain of pain there; but mine were never on for more than twenty minutes at a time, and that's not long enough to tire the foot. But one gets over this feeling.

'I've had my young ones on the stilts amusing themselves in my back-yard for a whole afternoon. They'll have them on and off three or four times in an hour, for it don't take a minute or two to put them on. They would put them on for play. I've often had them asking me to let them stop away from school, so as to have them on.

'My wife is very clever on the stilts. She does the routine of military exercise with them on. It's the gun exercise. She takes one stilt off herself, and remains on the other, and then shoulders the stilt she has taken off, and shows the gun practice. She's the only female stilt-dancer in England now. Those that were with her when she was a girl are all old women now. All of my family waltz and polka on stilts, and play tambourines whilst they dance. The little girls dance with their mother.

'It took longer to teach the children to do the tight-rope. They were five years old before I first began to teach them. The first thing I taught them to walk upon was on a pole passed through the rails at the back of two chairs. When you're teaching a child, you have got no time to go driving stakes into the ground to fix a rope upon. My pole was a bit of one of my wife's broken balance-poles. It was as thick as a broom handle, and not much longer. I had to lay hold of the little things' hands at first. They had no balance-pole to hold, not for some months afterwards. My young ones liked it very much; I don't know how other persons may. It was bred in them. They couldn't stand even upright when first they tried it, but after three months they could just walk across it by themselves. I exercised them once every day, for I had other business to attend to, and I'd give them a lesson for just, perhaps, half an hour at dinner time, or of an evening a bit after I came home. My wife never would teach them herself. I taught my wife rope-dancing, and yet I could not do it; but I understood it by theory, though not by experience. I never chalked my young ones' feet, but I put them on a little pair of canvas pumps, to get the feet properly formed to grasp the rope, and to bend round. My wife's feet, when she is on the rope, bend round from continual use, so they form a hollow in the palm of the foot, or the waist of the foot as some call it. My girls' feet soon took the form. The foot is a little bit tender at first, not to the pole, because that is round and smooth but the strands of the rope would, until the person has had some practice, blister the foot if kept too long on it. I never kept my young ones on the pole more than twenty minutes at a time, for it tired me more than them, and my arms used to ache with supporting them. Just when they got into the knack and habit of walking on the pole, then I shifted them to a rope, which I fixed up in my back-yard. The rope has to be a good cable size, about one-and-a-half inches in diameter. I always chalked the rope; chalk is of a very rough nature, and prevents slipping. The sole of the pump is always more or less hard and greasy. We don't rough the soles of the pumps, for the rope itself will soon make them rough, no matter how bright they may have been. My rope was three feet six inches from the ground, which was a comfortable height for me to go alongside of the children. I didn't give them the balance-pole till they were pretty perfect without it. It is a great help, is the pole. The one my wife takes on the rope with her is eighteen feet long. Some of the poles are weighted at both ends, but ours are not. My young ones were able to dance on the rope in a twelve-month's time. They weren't a bit nervous when I highered the rope in my yard. I was underneath to catch them. They seemed to like it.

'They appeared in public on the tight-rope in less than a twelve-month from their first lesson on the broom-stick on the backs of the chairs. My girl had done the stilts in public when she was only three years and six months old, so she was accustomed to an audience. It was in a gardens she made her first performance on the rope, and I was under her in case she fell. I always do that to this day.'

STREET RECITER

STREET reciters are somewhat scarce now-a-days, and I was a long time before meeting with one; for though I could always trace them through their wanderings about the streets, and learn where they had been seen the night before, still I could never find one myself. I believe there are not more than ten lads in London,—for they seem to be all lads,—who are earning a livelihood by street-reciting.

At length I heard that some street actors, as they call themselves, lived in court in the City. There were two of them—one a lad, who was dressed in a man's ragged coat and burst boots, and tucked-up trousers, and seemingly in a state of great want; and the other decently enough attired in a black paletot with a flash white-and-red handkerchief, or 'fogle,' as the costermongers call it, jauntily arranged so as to bulge over the closely-buttoned collar of his coat. There was a priggish look about the latter lad, while his manner was 'cute,' and smacked of Petticoat-lane; and though the other one seemed to slink back, *he* pushed himself saucily forward, and at once informed me that he belonged 'to the pro-fession' of street declaimer. 'I and this other boy goes out together,' he said, as he took a short pipe from his mouth; and in proof of his assertion, he volunteered that they should on the spot give me a specimen of their histrionic powers.

I preferred listening to the modest boy. He was an extremely good-looking lad, and spoke in a soft voice, almost like a girl's. He had a bright, cheerful face, and a skin so transparent and healthy, and altogether appeared so different from the generality of street lads, that I felt convinced that he had not long led a wandering life, and that there was some mystery connected with his present pursuits. He blushed when spoken to, and his answers were nervously civil.

When I had the better-natured boy alone with me, I found that he had been well educated. At first he seemed to be nervous, and little inclined to talk; but as we became better acquainted, he chatted on even faster than my pen could follow. He had picked up several of the set phrases of theatrical parlance, such as, 'But my dream has vanished in air;' or, 'I felt that a blight was on my hap-piness;' and delivered his words in a romantic tone, as though he fancied he was acting on a stage. He volunteered to show me his declamatory powers, and selected 'Othello's Apology.' He went to the back of the room, and after throwing his arms about him for a few seconds, and looking at the ceiling as if to inspire himself, he started off.

Whilst he had been chatting to us his voice was—as I said before —like a girl's; but no sooner did he deliver his, 'Most potent, grave, and reverend Signiors,' than I was surprised to hear him assume a deep stomachic voice— style evidently founded upon the melo-dramatic models at minor theatres. His good-looking face, however, became flushed and excited during the delivery of the speech, his eyes rolled about, and he passed his hands through his hair, comb-ing it with his fingers till it fell wildly about his neck like a mane.

When he had finished the speech he again relapsed into his quiet ways, and resuming his former tone of voice, seemed to think that an apology was requisite for the wildness of his acting, for he said, 'When I act Shakespeare I cannot restrain myself,—it seems to master my very soul.

'When I go out to recite, I generally go with another boy, and we take parts. The pieces that draw best with the public are, "The Gipsy's Revenge," "The Gold Digger's Revenge," "The Miser," "The Robber," "The Felon," and "The Highwayman." We take parts in these, and he always performs the villain, and I take the noble characters. He always dies, because he can do a splendid back-fall, and he looks so wicked when he's got the moustaches on. I generally draws the company by giving two or three recitations, and then we perform a piece; and whilst he goes round with the hat, I recite again. My favourite recitations are, "Othello's Apo-logy," beginning with "Most potent, grave, and reverend Signiors," and those from Hamlet, Richard III., and Macbeth. Of the rec-itations I think the people prefer that from Othello, for the ladies have often asked me to give them that from Othello (they like to hear about Desdemona), but the gentlemen ask for that from Hamlet. "To be, or not to be?"

'My principal place for giving performances is the Commercial-road, near Limehouse, but the most theatrically inclined neighbour-hood is the Walworth-road. The most money I ever took at one time in the streets was 4*s.* in the Walworth-road.

'The best receipts I ever had was got in a public-house near Brick-lane, for I took 12*s.*, and I was alone. There was a "lead" up there for a friend, and I knew of it, and I had my hair curled and got myself decently habited, I was there for about three or four hours, and in the intervals between the dances I used to recite. There were girls there, and they took my part, though they made me drink so much I was nearly tipsy.

'The only theatrical costume I put on is moustachios, and I

take a stick to use as a sword. I put myself into attitudes, and look as fierce as I can. When first the people came to hear me they laughed, and then they became quiet; and sometimes you could hear a pin drop.

'When I am at work regularly—that's when I am in voice and will—I make about 10s. a-week, if there's not much rain. If it's wet, people don't go to the public houses, and they are my best paying audiences. The least I have ever taken in a week is about 6s.

'There isn't many going about London reciting. It is a very rare class to be found; I only know about four who live that way, and I have heard of the others from hearsay—not that I have seen them myself.'

STREET MUSICIANS

CONCERNING street musicians they are of multifarious classes. As a general rule, they may almost be divided into the tolerable and the intolerable performers, some of them trusting to their skill in music for the reward for their exertions, others only making a *noise*, so that whatever money they obtain is given them merely as an inducement for them to depart. The well-known engraving by Hogarth, of 'the enraged musician,' is an illustration of the persecutions inflicted in olden times by this class of street performers; and in the illustrations by modern caricaturists we have had numerous proofs, that up to the present time the nuisance has not abated. Indeed, many of these people carry with them musical instruments, merely as a means of avoiding the officers of the Mendicity Society, or in some few cases as a signal of their coming to the persons in the neighbourhood, who are in the habit of giving them a small weekly pension.

These are a more numerous class than any other of the street performers I have yet dealt with. The musicians are estimated at 1,000, and the ballad singers at 250.

The street musicians are of two kinds, the skilful and the blind. The former obtain their money by the agreeableness of their performance, and the latter, in pity for their affliction rather than admiration of their harmony. The blind street musicians, it must be confessed, belong generally to the rudest class of performers. Music is not used by them as a means of pleasing, but rather as a mode of soliciting attention. Such individuals are known in the 'profession' by the name of 'pensioners'; they have their regular rounds to make, and particular houses at which to call on certain days of the week, and from which they generally obtain a 'small trifle.' They form, however, a most peculiar class of individuals. They are mostly well-known characters, and many of them have been performing in the streets of London for many years. They are also remarkable for the religious cast of their thoughts, and the comparative refinement of their tastes and feelings.

'OLD SARAH'

ONE of the most deserving and peculiar of the street musicians was an old lady who played upon the hurdy-gurdy. She had been about the streets of London for upwards of forty years, and being blind, had had during that period four guides, and worn out three instruments. Her cheerfulness, considering her privation and precarious mode of life, was extraordinary. Her love of truth, and the extreme simplicity of her nature, were almost childlike. Like the generality of blind people, she had a deep sense of religion, and her charity for a woman in her station of life was something marvellous; for though living on alms, she herself had, I was told, two or three little pensioners. When questioned on this subject, she laughed the matter off as a jest, though I was assured of the truth of the fact. Her attention to her guide was most marked. If a cup of tea was given to her after her day's rounds, she would be sure to turn to the poor creature who led her about, and ask, 'You comfortable, Liza?' or 'Is your tea to your liking, Liza?'

When conveyed to Mr. Beard's establishment to have her daguerreotype taken, she for the first time in her life rode in a cab; and then her fear at being pulled 'back'ards' as she termed it (for she sat with her back to the horse), was almost painful. She felt about for something to lay hold of, and did not appear comfortable until she had a firm grasp of the pocket. After her alarm had in a measure subsided, she turned to her guide and said, 'We must put up with those trials, Liza.' In a short time, however, she began to find the ride pleasant enough. 'Very nice, ain't it, Liza?' she said; 'but I shouldn't like to ride on them steamboats; they say they're shocking dangerous; and as for them railways, I've heard tell they're dreadful; but these cabs, Liza, is very nice.' On the road she was continually asking 'Liza' where they were, and wondering at the rapidity at which they travelled. 'Ah!' she said, laughing, 'if I had one of these here cabs, my "rounds" would soon be over.' Whilst ascending the high flight of stairs that led to the portrait-rooms, she laughed at every proposal made to her to rest. 'There's twice as many stairs as these to our church, ain't there, Liza?' she replied when pressed. When the portrait was finished she expressed a wish to feel it.

The following is the history of her life, as she herself related it, answering to the variety of questions put to her on the subject:—

'I was born the 4th April, 1786 (it was Good Friday that year), at a small chandler's shop, facing the White Horse, Stuart's-rents, Drury-lane. Father was a hatter, and mother an artificial-flower maker and feather finisher. When I was but a day old, the nurse took me out of the warm bed and carried me to the window, to show some people how like I was to father. The cold flew to my eyes and I caught inflammation in them. Owing to mother being forced to be from home all day at her work, I was put out to dry-nurse when I was three weeks old. My eyes were then very bad, by all accounts, and some neighbours told the woman I was with, that Turner's cerate would do them good. She got some and put it on my eyes, and when poor mother came to suckle me at her dinner-hour, my eyes was all "a gore of blood." From that time I never see afterwards. She did it, poor woman, for the best; it was no fault of her'n, and I'm sure I bears her no malice for it. I stayed at home with mother until I was thirteen, when I was put to the Blind-school, but I only kept there nine months; they turned me out because I was not clever with my hands, and I could not learn to spin or make sash-lines; my hands was ocker'd like. I had not been used at home to do anything for myself—not even to dress myself. Mother was always out at her work, so she could not learn me, and no one else would, so that's how I was turned out. I then went back to my mother, and kept with her till her death. I well remember that; I heard her last. When she died I was just sixteen year old. I way sent to the Union—"Pancridge" Union it was—and father with me (for he was ill at the time). He died too, and left me, in seven weeks after mother. When they was both gone, I felt I had lost my only friends, and that I was all alone in the world and blind. But, take it altogether, the world has been very good to me, and I have much to thank God for and the good woman I am with. I missed mother the most, she was so kind to me; there was no one like her; no, not even father. I was kept in the Union until I was twenty; the parish paid for my learning the "cymbal"; God bless them for it, I say. A poor woman in the workhouse first asked me to learn music; she said it would always be a bit of bread for me; I did as she told me, and I thank her to this day for it. It took me just five months to learn the—cymbal, if you please—the hurdy-gurdy ain't its right name. The first tune I ever played was "God save the King," the Queen as is now; then "Harlequin Hamlet," that took me a long time to get off; it was three weeks before they put me on a new one. I then learnt "Moll Brook"; then I did the "Turnpike-gate" and "Patrick's day in the morning": all of them I learnt in the Union. I got a poor man to teach me the "New-rigged ship." I soon learnt it, because it was an easy tune. Two-and-forty years ago I played "The Gal I left behind me." A woman learnt it me; she played my cymbal and I listened, and so got it. "Oh, Susannah!" I learnt myself by hearing it on the horgan. I always try and listen to a new tune when I am in the street, and get it off if I can: it's my bread. I waited to hear one to-day, quite a new one, but I didn't like it, so I went on. "Hasten to the Wedding" is my favourite; I played it years ago, and play it still. I like "Where have you been all night?" It's a Scotch tune. The woman as persuaded me to learn the cymbal took me out of the Union with her; I lived with her, and she led me about the streets. When she died I took her daughter for my guide. She walked with me for more then five-and-twenty year, and she might have been with me to this day, but she took to drinking and killed herself with it. She behaved very bad to me at last, for as soon as we got a few half-pence she used to go into the public and spend it all; and many a time I'm sure she's been too tipsy to take me home. One night I remember she rolled into the road at Kensington, and as near pulled me with her. We was both locked up in the station-house, for she couldn't stand for liquor, and I was obligated to wait till she could lead me home. It was very cruel of her to treat me so, but, poor creature, she's gone, and I forgive her, I'm sure. I'd many guides after her, but none of them was honest like Liza is; I don't think she'd rob me of a farden. Would you, Liza? Yes, I've my reg'lar rounds, and I've kept to 'em for near upon fifty year. All the children like to hear me coming along, for I always plays my cymbal as I goes. At Kentish-town they calls me Mrs. Tuesday, and at Kensington I'm Mrs. Friday, and so on. At some places they likes polkas, but at one house I plays at in Kensington they always ask me for "Haste to the Wedding." No, the cymbal isn't very hard to play; the only thing is, you must be very particular that the works is covered up, or the half-pence is apt to drop in. King David, they say, played on one of those here instruments. We're very tired by night-time; ain't we, Liza? but when I gets home the good woman I lodges with has always a bit of something for me to eat with my cup of tea. She's a good soul, and keeps me tidy and clean. I helps her all I can; when I comes in, I carries her a pail of water up-stairs, and such-like. Many ladies as has known me since they was children allows me a trifle. One maiden lady near Brunswick-square has given me sixpence a week for many a year, and another allows me eighteenpence a fortnight; so that, one way and another, I am very comfortable, and I've much to be thankful for.'

It was during one of old Sarah's journeys that an accident occurrred, which ultimately deprived London of the well-known old hurdy-gurdy woman. In crossing Seymour-street, she and her guide Liza were knocked down by a cab, as it suddenly turned a corner. They were picked up and placed in the vehicle (the poor guide dead, and Sarah with her limbs broken), and carried to the University Hospital. Old Sarah's description of that ride is more terrible and tragic than I can hope to make out to you. The poor blind creature was ignorant of the fate of her guide, she afterwards told us, and kept begging and praying to Liza to speak to her as the vehicle conveyed them to the asylum. She shook her, she said, and intreated her to say if she was hurt, but not a word was spoken in answer, and then she felt how terrible a privation was her blindness; and it was not until they reached the hospital, and they were lifted from the cab, that she knew, as she heard the people whisper to one another, that her faithful attendant was dead. In telling us this, the good old soul forgot her own sufferings for the time, as she lay with both her legs broken beneath hooped bed-clothes of the hospital bed; and when, after many long weeks, she left the medical asylum, she was unable to continue her playing on the hurdy-gurdy, her hand being now needed for the crutch that was requisite to bear her on her rounds.

The shock, however, had been too much for the poor old creature's feeble nature to rally against, and though she continued to hobble round to the houses of the kind people who had for years allowed her a few pence per week, and went limping along musicless through the streets for some months after she left the hospital, yet her little remaining strength at length failed her, and she took to her bed in a room in Bell-court, Gray's-inn-lane, never to rise from it again.

'FARM-YARD' PLAYER

A QUIET-LOOKING man, half-blind, and wrapped in a large, old, faded black-cotton great-coat, made the following statement, having first given me some specimens of his art:—

'I imitate all the animals of the farm-yard on my fiddle: I imitate the bull, the calf, the dog, the cock, the hen when she's laid an egg, the peacock, and the ass. I have done this in the streets for nearly twelve years. I was brought up as a musician at my own desire. When a young man (I am now 53) I used to go out to play at parties, doing middling until my sight failed me; I then did the farm-yard on the fiddle for a living. Though I had never heard of such a thing before, by constant practice I made myself perfect. I studied from nature. I never was in a farmyard in my life, but I went and listened to the poultry, anywhere in town that I could meet with them, and then I imitated them on my instrument. The Smithfield cattle gave me the study for the bull and the calf. My peacock I got at the Belvidere-gardens in Islington. The ass is common, and so is the dog; and them I studied anywhere. It took me a month, not more, if so much, to acquire what I thought a sufficient skill in my undertaking, and then I started it in the streets. It was liked the very first time I tried it. I never say what animal I am going to give; I leave that to the judgment of the listeners. They could always tell what it was. I could make 12s. a-week the year through. I play it in public-houses as well as in the streets. My pitches are all over London, and I don't know that one is better than another. Working-people are my best friends. Thursday and Friday are my worst days; Monday and Saturday my best, when I reckon 2s. 6d. a handsome taking. I am the only man who does the farm-yard.'

BLIND SCOTCH VIOLONCELLO PLAYER

A STOUT, hale-looking blind man, dressed very decently in coloured clothes, and scrupulously clean, gave me the following details:—

'I am one of the three blind Scotchmen who go about the streets in company, playing the violoncello, clarionet, and flute. We are really Highlanders, and can all speak Gaelic; but a good many London Highlanders are Irish. I have been thirty years in the streets of London; one of my mates has been forty years,—he's sixty-nine;—the other has been thirty years. I became partially blind, through an inflammation, when I was fourteen, and was stone-blind when I was twenty-two. Before I was totally blind I came to London, travelling up with the help of my bagpipes, guided by a little boy. I settled in London, finding it a big place, where a man could do well at that time, and I took a turn every now and then into the country. I could make 14s. a-week, winter and summer through, thirty years ago, by playing in the streets; now I can't make 6s. a-week, take winter and summer. I met my two mates, who are both blind men,—both came to England for the same reason as I did,—in my journeyings in London; and at last we agreed to go together,—that's twenty years ago. We've been together, on and off, ever since. Sometimes, one of us will take a turn round the coast of Kent, and another round the coast of Devon; and then join again in London, or meet by accident. We have always agreed very well, and never fought. We,—I mean the street-blind,—tried to maintain a burying and sick-club of our own; but we were always too poor. We live in rooms. I don't know one blind musician who lives in a lodging-house. I myself know a dozen blind men, now performing in the streets of London; these are not all exactly blind, but about as bad; the most are stone-blind. The blind musicians are chiefly married men. I don't know one who lives with a woman unmarried. The loss of sight changes a man. He doesn't think of women, and women don't think of him. We are of a religious turn, too, generally. I am a Roman Catholic; but the other Scotch blind men here are Presbyterians. The Scotch in London are our good friends, because they give us a little sum altogether, perhaps; but the English working-people are our main support: it is by them we live, and I always found them kind and liberal,—the most liberal in the world as I know. Through Marylebone is our best round, and Saturday night our best time. We play all three together. "Johnny Cope" is our best-liked tune. I think the blind Scotchmen don't come to play in London now. I can remember many blind Scotch musicians, or pipers, in London: they are all dead now! The trade's dead too,—it is so! When we thought of forming the blind club, there was never more than a dozen members. These were two basket-makers, one mat-maker, four violin-players, myself, and my two mates; which was the number when it dropped for want of funds; that's now fifteen years ago. We were to pay 1s. a month; and sick members were to have 5s. a week, when they'd paid two years. Our other rules were the same as other clubs, I believe.'

THE ENGLISH STREET BANDS

CONCERNING these, a respectable man gave me the following details:—

'I was brought up to the musical profession, and have been a street-performer 22 years, and I'm now only 26. I sang and played the guitar in the streets with my mother when I was four years old. We were greatly patronised by the nobility at that time. It was a good business when I was a child. A younger brother and I would go out into the streets for a few hours of an evening, from five to eight, and make 7s. or 8s. the two of us. Ours was, and is, the highest class of street music. For the last ten years I have been a member of a street band. Our band is now four in number. I have been in bands of eight, and in some composed of as many as 25; but a small band answers best for regularity. With eight in the band it's not easy to get 3s. a-piece on a fine day, and play all day, too. I consider that there are 1,000 musicians now performing in the streets of London; and as very few play singly, 1,000 performers, not reckoning persons who play with niggers or such-like, will give not quite 250 street bands. Four in number is a fair average for a street band; but I think the greater number of bands have more than four in them. All the better sorts of these bands play at concerts, balls, parties, processions, and water excursions, as well as in the streets. The class of men in the street bands is, very generally, those who can't read music, but play by ear; and their being unable to read music prevents their obtaining employment in theatres, or places where a musical education is necessary; and yet numbers of street musicians (playing by ear) are better instrumentalists than many educated musicians in the theatres. I only know a few who have left other businesses to become musicians. The great majority —19-20ths of us, I should say—have been brought regularly up to be street-performers. Children now are taught very early, and seldom leave the profession for any other business. Every year the street musicians increase. The better sort are, I think, prudent men, and struggle hard for a decent living. All the street-performers of wind-instruments are short-lived. Wind performers drink more, too, than the others. They must have their mouths wet, and they need some stimulant or restorative after blowing an hour in the streets. There are now twice as many wind as stringed instruments played in the streets; fifteen or sixteen years ago there used to be more stringed instruments. Within that time new wind instruments have been used in the streets. Cornopeans, or cornet-a-pistons, came into vogue about fourteen years ago; opheicleides about ten years ago (I'm speaking of the streets); and saxhorns about two years since. The cornopean has now quite superseded the bugle. The worst part of the street performers, in point of character, are those who play before or in public-houses. They drink a great deal, but I never heard of them being charged with dishonesty. In fact, I believe there's no honester set of men breathing than street musicians.'

THE GERMAN STREET BANDS

NEXT come the German Bands. I had the following statement from a young flaxen-haired and fresh-coloured German, who spoke English very fairly:—

'I am German, and have been six year in zis country. I was nearly fourteen when I come. I come from Oberfeld, eighteen miles from Hanover. I come because I would like to see how it was here. I heard zat London was a goot place for foreign music. London is as goot a place as I expect fo find him. There was other six come over with me, boys and men. We come to Hull, and play in ze country about half a year; we do middling. And zen we come to London. I didn't make money at first when I come, I had much to learn; but ze band, oh! it did well. We was seven. I play ze clarionet, and so did two others; two play French horns, one ze trambone, and one ze saxhorn. Sometime we make 7s. or 8s. a-piece in a-day now, but the business is not goot. I reckon 6*s*. a-day is goot now. We never play at fairs, nor for caravans. We play at private parties or public ball-rooms, and are paid so much a dance—sixpence a dance for the seven of us. If zare is many dances, it is goot; if not, it is bad. We play sheaper zan ze English, and we don't spent so much. Ze English players insult us, but we don't care about that. Zey abuse us for playing sheap. I don't know what zair terms for dances are. I have saved money in zis country, but very little of it. I want to save enough to take me back to Hanover. We all live together, ze seven of us. We have three rooms to sleep in, and one to eat in. We are all single men, but one; and his wife, a German woman, lives wis us, and cooks for us. She and her husband have a bedroom to themselves. Anysing does for us to eat. We all join in housekeeping and lodging, and pay alike. Our lodging costs 2*s*. a-week each, our board costs us about 15*s*. a-week each; sometime rather less. But zat include beer; and ze London beer is very goot, and sometime we drink a goot deal of it. We drink very little gin, but we live very well, and have goot meals every day. We play in ze streets, and I zink most places are alike to us. Ladies and gentlemen are our best friends; ze working people give us very little. We don't associate with any Englishmen. Zare are three public-houses kept by Germans, where we Germans meet. Sugar-bakers and other trades are of ze number. There are now five German brass-bands, with thirty-seven performers in zem, reckoning our own, in London. Our band lives near Whitechapel. I sink zare is one or two more German bands in ze country. I sink my country-men, some of them save money; but I have not saved much yet.'

SCOTCH PIPER AND DANCING GIRL

'I was full corporal in the 93rd Southern Highlanders, and I can get the best of characters from my commanding officers. If I couldn't get a good character I wouldn't be orderly to the colonel; and wherever he and the lady went, I was sure to be with them. Although I used to wear the colonel's livery, yet I had the full corporal's stripes on my coat. I was first orderly to Colonel Sparkes of the 93rd. He belonged to Dublin, and he was the best colonel that ever belonged to a regiment. After he died I was orderly to Colonel Aynsley. This shows I must have been a good man, and

have a good character. Colonel Aynsley was a good friend to me.
and he always gave me my clothes, like his other private servants.
The orderly's post is a good one, and much sought after, for it
exempts you from regimental duty. Colonel Aynsley was a severe
man on duty, but he was a good colonel after all. If he wasn't to
be a severe man he wouldn't be able to discharge the post he had
to discharge. Off duty he was as kind as anybody could be. There
was no man he hated more than a dirty soldier. He wouldn't muddle
a man for being drunk, not a quarter so much as for dirty clothing.
I was reckoned the cleanest soldier in the regiment; for if I was out
in a shower of rain, I'd polish up my brass and pipeclay my belt
to make it look clean again. Besides, I was very supple and active,
and many's the time Colonel Aynsley has sent me on a message,
and I have been there and back, and when I've met him he's
scolded me for not having gone, for I was back so quick he thought
I hadn't started.

'Whilst I was in the regiment I was attacked with blindness;
brought on, I think, by cold.

'I've served in India, and I was at the battles of Punjaub, 1848,
and Moultan, 1849. Sir Colin Campbell commanded us at both,
and says he, "Now, my brave 93rd, none of your nonsense here,
for it must be death and glory here to-day", and then Serjeant
Cameron says, "The men are all right, Sir Colin, but they're
afraid you won't be in the midst of them"; and says he, "Not in the
midst of them! I'll be here in ten minutes." Sir Colin will go in
anywhere; he's as brave an officer as any in the service. He's the
first into the fight and the last out of it.

'Although I had served ten years, and been in two battles, yet
I was not entitled to a pension. You must serve twenty-one years
to be entitled to 1s. 0½d. I left the 93rd in 1852, and since that time
I've been wandering about the different parts of England and
Scotland, playing on the bagpipes. I take my daughter Maria about
with me, and she dances whilst I play to her. I leave my wife and
family in town. I've been in London three weeks this last time
I visited it. I've been here plenty of times before. I've done duty
in Hyde-Park before the 46th came here.

'I left the army just two years before the war broke out, and
I'd rather than twenty thousand pounds I'd been in my health
to have gone to the Crimea, for I'd have had more glory after

that war than ever any England was in. Directly I found the 93rd
was going out, I went twice to try and get back to my old regiment;
but the doctor inspected me, and said I wouldn't be fit for service
again. I was too old at the time, and my health wasn't good, although I could stand the cold far better than many hundreds of
them that were out there, for I never wear no drawers, only my
kilt, and that very thin, for it's near worn. Nothing at all gives me
cold but the rain.

'The last time I was in London was in May. My daughter dances
the Highland fling and the sword dance called "Killim Callum."
That's the right Highland air to the dance—with two swords
laid across each other. I was a good hand at it before I got stiff.
I've done it before all the regiment. We'd take two swords from
the officers and lay them down when they've been newly ground.
I've gone within the eighth of an inch of them, and never cut my
shoe. Can you cut your shoes? aye, and your toes too if you're
not lithe. My brother was the best dancer in the army: so the Duke
of Argyle and his lady said. At one of the prize meetings at Blair
Athol one Tom Duff who is as good a dancer as from this to
where he is, says he, "There's ne'er a man of the Macgregor clan
can dance against me to-day!" and I, knowing my brother Tom
—he was killed at Inkerman in the 93rd—was coming, says I,
"Don't be sure of that, Tom Duff, for there's one come every inch
of the road here to-day to try it with you." He began, and he took
an inch off his shoes, and my brother never cut himself at all; and
he won the prize.

'My little girl dances that dance. She does it pretty, but I'd be
rather doubtful about letting her come near the swords, for fear
she'd be cutting herself, though I know she could do it at a pinch,
for she can be dancing across two baccy-pipes without breaking
them. When I'm in the streets, she always does it with two baccy-
pipes. She can dance reels, too, such as the Highland fling and the
reel Hoolow. They're the most celebrated.

'The chanter of the pipes I play on has been in my family very
near 450 years. It's the oldest in Scotland, and is a heir-loom in
our family, and they wouldn't part with it for any money. Many's
a time the Museum in Edinburgh has wanted me to give it to them,
but I won't give it to any one till I find myself near death, and then
I'll obligate them to keep it. Most likely my youngest son will

have it, for he's as steady as a man. You see, the holes for the fingers is worn as big round as sixpences, and they're quite sharp at the edges. The ivory at the end is the same original piece as when the pipe was made. It's breaking and splitting with age, and so is the stick. I'll have my name and the age of the stick engraved on the side of the ivory, and then, if my boy seems neglectful of the chanter, I'll give it to the Museum at Edinburgh. I'll have German silver rings put round the stick, to keep it together and then, with nice waxed thread bound round it, it will last for centuries yet.

'About my best friends in London are the French people,—they are the best I can meet, they come next to the Highlanders. When I meet a Highlander he will, if he's only just a labouring man, give me a few coppers. A Highlander will never close his eye upon me. It's the Lowlander that is the worst to me. They never takes no notice of me when I'm passing: they'll smile and cast an eye as I pass by. Many a time I'll say to them when they pass, "Well, old chap, you don't like the half-naked men, I know you don't!" and many will say, "No, I don't!" I never play the pipes when I go through the Lowlands,—I'd as soon play poison to them. They never give anything. It's the Lowlanders that get the Scotch a bad name for being miserable, and keeping their money, and using small provision. They're a disgrace to their country.

'The Highlander spends his money as free as a duke. If a man in the 93rd had a shilling in his pocket, it was gone before he could turn it twice. All the Lowlanders would like to be Highlander if they could, and they learn Gaelic, and then marry Highland lassies, so as to become Highlanders. They have some clever regiments composed out of the Lowlanders, but they have only three regiments and the Highlanders have seven; yet there's nearly three to one more inhabitants in the Lowlands. It's a strange thing, they'd sooner take an Irishman into a Highland regiment than a Lowlander. They owe them such a spleen, they don't like them. Bruce was a Lowlander, and he betrayed Wallace; and the Duke of Buccleuch, who was a Lowlander, betrayed Stuart.'

FRENCH HURDY-GURDY PLAYER WITH DANCING CHILDREN

'I PLAY on the same instrument as the Savoyards play, only, you understand, you can have good and bad instruments; and to have a good one you must put the price. The one I play on cost me 60 francs in Paris. There are many more handsome, but none better. This is all that there is of the best. The man who made it has been dead sixty years. It is the time that makes the value of it.

'My wife plays on the violin. She is a very good player. I am her second husband. She is an Italian by birth. She played on the violin when she was with her first husband. He used to accompany her on the organ, and that produced a very fine effect.

'My age is twenty-five, and I have voyaged for seventeen years. There are three months since I came in England. I was at Calais and at Boulogne, and it is there that I had the idea to come to England. Many persons who counselled us, told us that in England we should gain a great deal of money. That is why I came. It took three weeks before I could get permission to be married, and during that time I worked at the different towns. I did pretty well at Dover; and after that I went to Ramsgate, and I did very well there. Yes, I took a great deal of money on the sands of a morning. I have been married a month now—for I left Ramsgate to go to be married. At Ramsgate they understand my playing. Unless I have educated people to play to, I do not make much success with my instrument. I play before a public-house, or before a cottage, and they say, "That's all very well"; but they do not know that to make a hurdy-gurdy sound like a violin requires great art and patience. Besides, I play airs from operas, and they do not know the Italian music. Now if I was alone with my hurdy-gurdy, I should only gain a few pence; but it is by my children that I do pretty well.

'We came to London when the season was over in the country, and now we go everywhere in the town. I cannot speak English; but I have my address in my pocket, if I lose myself. *Je m'élance dans la ville.* To-day I went by a big park, where there is a château of the Queen. If I lose my way, I show my written address, and they go on speaking English, and show me the way to go. I don't understand the English, but I do the pointed finger; and when I get near home, then I recognise the quarter.

'When I am in the streets with good houses in them, and see anybody looking at the windows, then if I see them listening, I play pieces from the opera on my hurdy-gurdy. I do this between the dances. Those who go to the opera and frequent the theatres, like to hear distinguished music.'

POOR HARP PLAYER

A POOR, feeble, half-witted looking man, with the appearance of far greater age than he represented himself, (a common case with the very poor), told me of his sufferings in the streets. He was wretchedly clad, his clothes being old, patched, and greasy. He is well-known in London, being frequently seen with a crowd of boys at his heels, who amuse themselves in playing all kinds of tricks upon him.

'I play the harp in the streets,' he said, 'and have done so for the last two years, and should be very glad to give it up. My brother lives with me; we're both bachelors, and he's so dreadful lame, he can do nothing. He is a coach-body maker by business. I was born blind, and was brought up to music; but my sight was restored by Dr. Ware, the old gentleman in Bridge-street, Blackfriars, when I was nine years old, but it's a near sight now. I'm forty-nine in August. When I was young I taught the harp and the pianoforte, but that very soon fell off, and I have been teaching on or off these many years—I don't know how many. I had three guineas a quarter for teaching the harp at one time, and two guineas for the piano. My brother and I have 1s. and a loaf a-piece from the parish, and the 2s. pays the rent. Mine's not a bad trade now, but it's bad in the streets. I've been torn to pieces; I'm torn to pieces every day I go out in the streets, and I would be glad to get rid of the streets for 5s. a-week. The streets are full of ruffians. The boys are ruffians. The men in the streets too are ruffians, and encourage the boys. The police protect me as much as they can. I should be killed every week but for them; they're very good people. I've known poor women of the town drive the boys away from me, or try to drive them. It's terrible persecution I suffer— terrible persecution. The boys push me down and hurt me badly, and my harp too. They yell and make noises so that I can't be heard, nor my harp. The boys have cut off my harp-strings, three of them, the other day, which cost me 6½d. or 7d. I tell them it's a shame, but I might as well speak to stones. I never go out that they miss me. I don't make more than 3s. a-week in the streets, if I make that.'

ORGAN MAN, WITH FLUTE HARMONICON ORGAN

'WHEN I am come in this country I had nine or ten year old, so I know the English language better than mine. At that time there was no organ about but the old-fashioned one made in Bristol, with gold-organ-pipe in front. Then come the one with figure-dolls in front; and then next come the piano one, made at Bristol too; and now the flute one, which come from Paris, where they make them. He is an Italian man that make them, and he is the only man dat can make them, because he paid for them to the government (patented them), and now he is the only one.

'I belong to Parma,—to the small village in the duchy. My father keep a farm, but I had three year old, I think, when he died. There was ten of us altogeder; but one of us he was died, and one he drown in the water. I was very poor, and I was go out begging there; and my uncle said I should go to Paris to get my living. I was so poor I was afraid to die, for I get nothing to eat. My uncle say, I will take one of them to try to keep him. So I go along with him. Mother was crying when I went away. She was very poor. I went with my uncle to Paris, and we walk all the way. I had some white mice there, and he had a organ. I did middling. The French people is more kind to the charity than the English. There are not so many beggar there as in England. The first time the Italian come over here we was took a good bit of money, but now——!

'My organ plays eight tunes. Two are from opera, one is a song, one a waltz, one is hornpipe, one is a polka, and the other two is dancing tunes. One is from "I Lombardi," of Verdi. All the organs play that piece. I have sold that music to gentlemens. They say to me, "What is that you play?" and I say, "From I Lombardi." Then they ask me if I have the music; and I say "Yes;" and I sell it to them for 4s. I did not do this with my little organ; but when I went out with a big organ on two wheels. My little flute organ play the same piece. The other opera pieces is "I Trovatore." I have heard "Il Lombardi" in Italy. It is very nice music; but never hear "Il Trovatore." It is very nice music, too. It go very low. My gentlemens like it very much. I don't understand music at all. The other piece is English piece, which we call the "Liverpool Hornpipe." There is two Liverpool Hornpipe. I know one these twenty years. Then come "The Ratcatcher's Daughter"; he is a English song. It's get a little old: but when it's first come out the poor people do like it, but the gentlemens they like more the opera, you know. After that is what you call "Minnie," another English song. He is middling popular. He is not one of the new tune, but they do like

CAB DRIVER

PHOTOGRAPHIC SALOON, EAST END OF LONDON

it. The next one is a Scotch contry-dance. It is good tunes, but I
don't know the name of it. The next one is, I think, a polka; but
I think he's made from part of "Scotische." There is two or three
tunes belongs to the "Scotische." The next one is, I think, a valtz
of Vienna. I don't know which one, but I say to the organ-man, "I
want a valtz of Vienna"; and he say, "Which one? because there is
plenty of valtz of Vienna." Of course, there is nine of them. After the
opera music, the valtz and the polka is the best music in the organ.'

THE DANCING DOGS

I RECEIVED the following narrative from the old man who has been
so long known about the streets of London with a troop of performing dogs. He was especially picturesque in his appearance.
His hair, which was grizzled rather than grey, was parted down
the middle, and hung long and straight over his shoulders. He
was dressed in a coachman's blue greatcoat with many capes.
His left hand was in a sling made out of a dirty pocket-handkerchief
and in his other he held a stick, by means of which he could just
manage to hobble along. He was very ill, and very poor, not having
been out with his dogs for nearly two months. He appeared to
speak in great pain. The civility, if not politeness of his manner,
threw an air of refinement about him, that struck me more forcibly
from its contrast with the manners of the English belonging to the
same class. He began;—

'I have de dancing dogs for de street—now I have nothing else.
I have tree dogs—One is called Finette, anoder von Favorite,
that is her nomme, an de oder von Ozor. Ah!' he said, with a shrug
of the shoulders, in answer to my inquiry as to what the dogs did,
'un danse, un valse, un jomp a de stick and troo do hoop—non,
noting else. Sometimes I had de four dogs—I did lose de von. Ah!
she had beacoup d'esprit—plenty of vit, you say—she did jomp
a de hoop better dan all. Her nomme was Taborine!—she is dead
dare is long time. All ma dogs have des habillements—the dress
and de leetle hat. Dey have a leetle jackette in divers colours en
étoffe—some de red, and some de green, and some de bleu. Deir
hats is de rouge et noir—red and black, with a leetle plume-fedder,
you say. Dere is some 10 or 11 year I have been in dis country.
I come from Italie—Italie—Oui, Monsieur, oui. I did live in a
leetle vile, trento miglia, dirty mile, de Parma. Je travaille dans le

campagne, I vork out in de countrie—je ne sais comment vous appellez la campagne. There is no commerce in de montagne. I am come in dis country here. I have leetle business to come. I thought to gagner ma vie—to gain my life wid my leetel dogs in dis countrie. I have dem déja when I have come here from Parma— j'en avait dix. I did have de ten dogs—je les apporte. I have carried all de ten from Italie. I did learn—yes—yes—de dogs to dance in ma own countrie. It did make de cold in de montagne in winter, and I had not no vork dere, and I must look for to gain my life some oder place. Après ça, I have instruct my dogs to danse. Yes, ils learn to danse; I play de music, and dey do jomp. Non, non— pas du tout! I did not never beat ma dogs; dare is a way to learn de dogs without no vip. Premièrement, ven I am come here I have gained a leetel monnaie—plus que now—beaucoup d'avantage— plenty more. I am left ma logement—my lodging, you say, at 9 hours in de morning, and am stay away vid ma dogs till 7 or 8 hours in de evening. Oh! I cannot count how many times de leetel dogs have danse in de day—twenty—dirty—forty peut-être—all depends: sometimes I would gain de tree shilling—sometime de couple—sometime not nothing—all depend.'

PERFORMER ON DRUM AND PIPES

A STOUT, reddish-faced man, who was familiar with all kinds of exhibitions, and had the coaxing, deferential manner of many persons who ply for money in the streets, gave me an account of what he called 'his experience' as the '*drum and pipes*':—

'I have played the pandean pipes and the drum for thirty years to street exhibitions of all kinds. I was a smith when a boy, serving seven years' apprenticeship; but after that I married a young woman that I fell in love with, in the music line. She played a hurdy-gurdy in the streets, so I bought pandean pipes, as I was always fond of practising music, and I joined her. Times for street-musicianers were good then, but I was foolish. I'm aware of that now; but I wasn't particularly partial to hard work; besides, I could make more as a street-musicianer. When I first started, my wife and I joined a fantoccini. It did well. My wife and I made from 9s. to 10s. a-day. We had half the profits. At that time the public exhibitions were different to what they are now. Gentlemen's houses were good then, but now the profession's sunk to street corners. Bear-dancing was in vogue then, and clock-work on the round board, and Jack-i'-the-green was in all his glory every May, thirty years ago. Things is now very dead indeed. In the old times, only sweeps were allowed to take part with the Jack; they were particular at that time; all were sweeps but the musicianers. Now it's everybody's money, when there's any money. Every sweep showed his plate then when performing. "My lady" was anybody at all likely that they could get hold of; she was generally a watercress-seller, or something in the public way. "My lady" had 2*s*. 6*d*. a -day and her keep for three days—that was the general hire. The boys, who were climbing-boys, had 1*s*. or 6*d*., or what the master gave them; and they generally went to the play of a night, after washing themselves, in course. I had 6*s*. a-day and a good dinner—shoulder of mutton, or something prime—and enough to drink. "My lord" and the other characters shared and shared alike. They have taken, to my knowledge, 5*l*. on the 1st of May. This year, one set, with two "My ladies," took 3*l*. the first day. The master of the lot was a teetotaler, but the others drank as they liked. He turned teetotaler because drink always led him into trouble. The dress of the Jack is real ivy tied round hoops. The sweeps gather the ivy in the country, and make the dresses at their homes. My lord's and the other dresses are generally kept by the sweeps. My lord's dress costs a mere trifle at the second-hand clothes-shop, but it's gold papered and ornamented up to the mark required. What I may call war tunes, such as "The White Cockade," the "Downfall of Paris," (I've been asked for that five or six times a-day—I don't remember the composer), "Bonaparte's March," and the "Duke of York's March," were in vogue in the old times. So was "Scots wha hae" (very much), and "Off she goes!" Now new tunes come up every day. I play waltzes and pokers now chiefly. They're not to compare to the old tunes; it's like playing at musicianers, lots of the tunes now-a-days. I've played with Michael, the Italy Bear, I've played the fife and tabor with him. The tabor was a little drum about the size of my cap, and it was tapped with a little stick. There are no tabors about now. I made my 7*s*. or 8*s*. a-day with Michael. He spoke broken English. A dromedary was about then, but I knew nothing of that or the people; they was all foreigners together. Swinging monkeys were in vogue at that time as well. I was with them, with Antonio of

Saffron Hill. He was the original of the swinging monkeys, twenty years ago. They swing from a rope, just like slack-wire dancers. Antonio made money and went back to his own country. He sold his monkeys,—there was three of them,—small animals they were, for 70*l.* to another foreigner; but I don't know what became of them. Coarse jokes pleased people long ago, but don't now; people get more enlightened, and think more of chapel and church instead of amusements. My trade is a bad one now. Take the year through, I may make 12*s.* a-week, or not so much; say 10*s.* I go out sometimes playing single,—that's by myself,—on the drum and pipes; but it's thought nothing of, for I'm not a German. It's the same at Brighton as in London; brass bands is all the go when they've Germans to play them. The Germans will work at 2*s.* a-day at any fair, when an Englishman will expect 6*s.* The foreigners ruin this country, for they have more privileges than the English. The Germans pull the bells and knock at the doors for money, which an Englishman has hardly face for. I'm now with a fantoccini figures from Canton, brought over by a seaman. I can't form an exact notion of how many men there are in town who are musicianers to the street exhibitions; besides the exhibitions' own people, I should say about one hundred. I don't think that they are more drunken than other people, but they're liable to get top-heavy at times. None that I know live with women of the town. They live in lodgings, and not in lodging-houses. Oh! no, no, we've not come to that yet. Some of them succeeded their fathers as street-musicianers; others took it up casalty-like, by having learned different instruments; none that I know were ever theatrical performers. All the men I know in my line would object, I am sure, to hard work, if it was with confinement along with it. We can never stand being confined to hard work, after being used to the freedom of the streets. None of us save money; it goes either in a lump, if we get a lump, or in dribs and drabs, which is the way it mostly comes to us. I've known several in my way who have died in St. Giles's workhouse. In old age or sickness we've nothing but the parish to look to. The newest thing I know of is the singing dogs. I was with that as musician, and it answers pretty well amongst the quality. The dogs is three Tobies to a Punch-and-Judy show, and they sing,—that is, they make a noise,—it's really a howl,— but they keep time with Mr. Punch as he sings.'

STREET VOCALISTS

THE Street Vocalists are almost as large a body as the street musicians. It will be seen that there are 50 Ethiopian serenaders, and above 250 who live by ballad-singing alone.

STREET NEGRO SERENADERS

AT present I shall deal with the Ethiopian serenaders, and the better class of ballad-singers. Two young men who are of the former class gave the following account. Both were dressed like decent mechanics, with perfectly clean faces, excepting a little of the professional black at the root of the hair on the forehead:

'We are niggers,' said one man, 'as it's commonly called; that is, negro melodists. Nigger bands vary from four to seven, and have numbered as many as nine; our band is now six. We all share alike. I (said the same man) was the first who started the niggers in the streets, about four years ago.

'Last year was the best year I've known. We start generally about ten, and play till it's dark in fine weather. We averaged 1*l.* a-week last year. The evenings are the best time. Regent-street, and Oxford-street, and the greater part of St. James's, are our best places. The gentry are our best customers, but we get more from gentlemen than from ladies. The City is good, I fancy, but they won't let us work it; it's only the lower parts, Whitechapel and Smithfield ways, that we have a chance in. Business and nigger-songs don't go well together. The first four days of the week are pretty much alike for our business. Friday is bad, and so is Saturday, until night comes, and we then get money from the working people. The markets, such as Cleveland-street, Fitzroy-square (Tottenham-court-road's no good at any time). Carnaby-market, Newport-market, Great Marylebone-street, and the Edgeware-road, are good Saturday nights. Oxford-street is middling. The New-cut is as bad a place as can be. When we started, the songs we knew was "Old Mr. Coon," "Buffalo Gals," "Going ober de Mountain," "Dandy Jim of Carolina," "Rowly Body O," and "Old Johnny Booker." We stuck to them a twelvemonth. The "Buffalo Gals" was best liked. The "bones"—we've real bones, rib-of-beef bones, but some have ebony bones, which sound better than rib-bones—

they tell best in "Going ober de Mountain," for there's a symphony between every line. It's rather difficult to play the bones well; it requires hard practice, and it brings the skin off; and some men have tried it, but with so little success that they broke their bones and flung them away. The banjo is the hardest to learn of the lot. We have kept changing our songs all along; but some of the old ones are still sung. The other favourites are, or were, "Lucy Neale," "O, Susannah," "Uncle Ned," "Stop dat Knocking," "Ginger Blue," and "Black-eyed Susannah." Things are not so good as they were. We can average 1*l.* a-piece now in the week, but it's summer-time, and we can't make that in bad weather.'

STREET BALLAD-SINGERS, OR CHAUNTERS

THE street classes that are still undescribed are the lower class of street singers, the Street Artists, the Writers without Hands, and the Street Exhibition-keepers. I shall begin with the Street Singers.

Concerning the ordinary street ballad-singers, I received the following account from one of the class:—

'I am what may be termed a regular street ballad-singer — either sentimental or comic, sir, for I can take both branches. I have been, as near as I can guess, about five-and-twenty years at the business. My mother died when I was thirteen years old, and in consequence of a step-mother home became too hot to hold me, and I turned into the streets in consequence of the harsh treatment I met with. My father had given me no education, and all I know now I have picked up in the streets. Well, at thirteen years, I turned into the streets, houseless, friendless. My father was a picture-frame gilder. I was never taught any business by him— neither his own nor any other. I never received any benefit from him that I know. Well then, sir, there was I, a boy of thirteen, friend-less, houseless, untaught, and without any means of getting a living —loose in the streets of London. At first I slept anywhere: some-times I passed the night in the old Covent-garden-market; at others, in shutter-boxes; and at others, on door-steps near my father's house. I lived at this time upon the refuse that I picked up in the streets—cabbage-stumps out of the market, orange-peel, and the like. Well, sir, I was green then, and one of the Stamp-office spies got me to sell some of the *Poor Man's Guardians*, (an unstamped paper of that time), so that his fellow-spy might take me up. This he did, and I had a month at Coldbath-fields for the business. After I had been in prison, I got in a measure hardened to the frowns of the world, and didn't care what company I kept or what I did for a living. I wouldn't have you to fancy, though, that I did anything dishonest. I mean, I wasn't particular as to what I turned my hand to for a living, or where I lodged. I went to live in Church-lane, St. Giles's, at a threepenny house; and having a tidy voice of my own, I was there taught to go out ballad-singing, and I have stuck to the business ever since. I was going on for fifteen when I first took to it. The first thing I did was to lead at glee-singing; I took the air, and two others, old hands, did the second and the bass. We used to sing the "Red Cross Knight," "Hail, smiling Morn," and harmonize "The Wolf," and other popular songs. Excepting when we needed money, we rarely went out till the evening. Then our pitches were in quiet streets or squares, where we saw, by the light at the windows, that some party was going on. Wedding-parties was very good, in general quite a harvest. Public-houses we did little at, and then it was always with the parlour company; the tap-room people have no taste for glee-singing. At times we took from 9*s.* to 10*s.* of an evening, the three of us. I am speaking of the business as it was about two or three-twenty years ago. Now, glee-singing is seldom practised in the streets of London: it is chiefly confined to the provinces, at present. In London, concerts are so cheap now-a-days, that no one will stop to listen to the street glee-singers; so most of the "schools," or sets, have gone to sing at the cheap concerts held at the public-houses. Many of the glee-singers have given up the business, and taken to the street Ethiopians instead.

'When any popular song came up, that was our harvest. "Alice Gray," "The Sea," "Bridal Ring," "We met," "The Tartar Drum," (in which I was well known) "The Banks of the Blue Moselle," and such-like, not forgetting "The Mistletoe Bough"; these were all great things to the ballad-singers. We looked at the bill of fare for the different concert-rooms, and then went round the neighbourhood where these songs were being sung, because the airs being well known, you see it eased the way for us. The very best sentimental song that ever I had in my life, and which lasted me off and on for two years, was Byron's "Isle of Beauty." I could get a meal quicker with that than with any other.'

STREET ARTISTS

I NOW come to the Street Artists. These include the artists in coloured chalks on the pavements, the black profile-cutters, and others.

STREET PHOTOGRAPHY

WITHIN the last few years photographic portraits have gradually been diminishing in price, until at the present time they have become a regular article of street commerce. Those living at the west-end of London have but little idea of the number of persons who gain a livelihood by street photography.

There maybe one or two 'galleries' in the New-road, or in Tottenham-court-road, but these supply mostly shilling portraits. In the eastern and southern districts of London, however, such as in Bermondsey, the New-cut, and the Whitechapel-road, one cannot walk fifty yards without passing some photographic establishment, where for sixpence persons can have their portrait taken, and framed and glazed as well.

It was in Bermondsey that I met with the first instance of what may be called pure street photography. Here a Mr. F——l was taking sixpenny portraits in a booth built up out of old canvas, and erected on a piece of spare ground in a furniture-broker's yard.

Mr. F——l had been a travelling showman, but finding that photography was attracting more attention than giants and dwarfs, he relinquished the wonders of Nature for those of Science.

Into this yard he had driven his yellow caravan, where it stood like an enormous Noah's ark, and in front of the caravan (by means of clothes-horses and posts, over which were spread out the large sail-like paintings (show-cloths), which were used at fairs to decorate the fronts of booths), he had erected his operating-room, which is about as long and as broad as a knife-house, and only just tall enough to allow a not particularly tall customer to stand up with his hat off: whilst by means of two window-sashes a glazed roof had been arranged for letting light into this little tent.

On the day of my visit Mr. F——l was, despite the cloudy state of the atmosphere, doing a large business. A crowd in front of his tent was admiring the photographic specimens, which, of all sizes and in all kinds of frames, were stuck up against the canvas-wall, as irregularly as if a bill-sticker had placed them there. Others were gazing up at the chalky-looking paintings over the door-way, and on which a lady was represented photographing an officer, in the full costume of the 11th Hussars.

Inside the operating-room we found a crowd of women and children was assembled, all of them waiting their turn. Mr. F——l remarked, as I entered, that 'It was wonderful the sight of children that had been took'; and he added, 'when *one* girl comes for her portrait, there's a *dozen* comes along with her to see it took.'

The portraits I discovered were taken by Mrs. F——l, who, with the sleeves of her dress tucked up to the elbows, was engaged at the moment of my visit in pointing the camera at a lady and her little boy, who, from his wild nervous expression, seemed to have an idea that the operatress was taking her aim previous to shooting him. Mr. F——l explained to me the reason why his wife officiated. 'You see,' said he, 'people prefers more to be took by a woman than by a man. Many's a time a lady tells us to send that man away, and let the missus come. It's quite natural,' he continued; 'for a lady don't mind taking her bonnet off and tucking up her hair, or sticking a pin in here and there before one of her own sect, which before a man proves objectionable.'

After the portrait had been taken I found that the little square piece of glass on which it was impressed was scarcely larger than a visiting card, and this being handed over to a youth, was carried into the caravan at the back, where the process was completed. I was invited to follow the lad to the dwelling on wheels.

'So you've took him at last,' said the proprietor, who accompanied us as he snatched the portrait from the boy's hand. 'Well, the eyes ain't no great things, but as it's the third attempt it must do.'

On inspecting the portrait I found it to be one of those drab-looking portraits with a light back-ground, where the figure rises from the bottom of the plate as straight as a post, and is in the cramped, nervous attitude of a patient in a dentist's chair.

After a time I left Mr. F—— l's, and went to another establishment close by, which had originally formed part of a shop in the penny-ice-and-bull's-eye line—for the name-board over 'Photographic Depôt' was still the property of the confectioner—so that the portraits displayed in the window were surmounted by an announcement of 'Ginger beer 1*d*. and 2*d*.'

A touter at the door was crying out 'Hi! hi!—walk inside! walk inside! and have your c'rect likeness took, frame and glass complete, and only 6*d*.!—time of sitting only four seconds!'

A rough-looking, red-faced tanner, who had been staring at some coloured French lithographs which decorated the upper panes, and who, no doubt, imagined that they had been taken by the photographic process, entered, saying. 'Let me have my likeness took.'

The touter instantly called out, 'Here, a shilling likeness for this here gent.'

The tanner observed that he wanted only a sixpenny.

'Ah, very good, sir!' and raising his voice, the touter shouted louder than before—' A sixpenny one first, and a shilling one afterwards.'

'I tell yer I don't want only sixpennorth,' angrily returned the customer, as he entered.

At this establishment the portraits were taken in a little alley adjoining the premises, where the light was so insufficient, that even the blanket hung up at the end of it looked black from the deep shadows cast by the walls.

When the tanner's portrait was completed it was nearly black; and, indeed the only thing visible was a slight light on one side of the face, and which, doubtlessly, accounted for the short speech which the operator thought fit to make as he presented the likeness to his customer.

'There,' he said, 'there is your likeness, if you like! look at it yourself; and only eightpence'—'Only sixpence,' observed the man.—'Ah!' continued the proprietor, 'but you've got a patent American preserver, and that's twopence more.'

Then followed a discussion, in which the artist insisted that he lost by every sixpenny portrait he took, and the tanner as strongly protesting that he couldn't believe that, for they must get *some* profit any how. 'You don't tumble to the rig,' said the artist; 'it's the half-guinea ones, you see, that pays us.'

The touter, finding that this discussion was likely to continue, entered and joined the argument. 'Why, it's cheap as dirt,' he exclaimed indignantly; 'the fact is, our governor's a friend of the people, and don't mind losing a little money. He's determined that everybody shall have a portrait, from the highest to the lowest. Indeed, next Sunday, he *do* talk of taking them for threepence-ha'penny, and if that ain't philandery, what is?'

After the tout's oration the tanner seemed somewhat contented, and paying his eightpence left the shop, looking at his picture in all lights, and repeatedly polishing it up with the cuff of his coat-sleeve, as if he were trying to brighten it into something like distinctness.

THE PENNY PROFILE-CUTTER

THE young man from whom the annexed statement was gathered, is one of a class of street-artists now fast disappearing from view, but which some six or seven years ago occupied a very prominent position.

At the period to which I allude, the steamboat excursionist, or visitor to the pit of a London theatre, whom Nature had favoured with very prominent features, oftentimes found displayed to public view, most unexpectedly, a tolerably correct profile of himself in black paper, mounted upon a white card. As soon as attention was attracted, the exhibitor generally stepped forward, offering, in a respectful manner, to 'cut out any lady's or gentleman's like-ness for the small sum of one penny'; an offer which, judging from the account below given as to the artist's takings, seems to have been rather favourably responded to.

The appearance presented by the profile-cutter from whom I derived my information bordered on the 'respectable.' He was a tall thin man, with a narrow face and long features. His eyes were large and animated. He was dressed in black, and the absence of shirt collar round his bare neck gave him a dingy appearance. He spoke as follows:—

'I'm a penny profile-cutter, or, as we in the profession call ourselves, a profilist. I commenced cutting profiles when I was 14 years of age, always acquiring a taste for cutting out ornaments &c. One day I went to a fair at the Tenter-ground, Whitechapel. While I was walking about the fair, I see a young man I knew standing as "doorsman" at a profile-cutter's, and he told me that another profile-cutter in the fair wanted an assistant, and thought I should do for it. So I went to this man and engaged. I had to talk at the door, or "tout," as we call it, and put or mount the likenesses on cards. I was rather backward at touting at first, but I got over that in the course of the day, and could patter like anything before the day was over. I had to shout out, "Step inside, ladies and gentlemen, and have a correct likeness taken for one penny. We did a very good business the two days of the fair that I attended, for I was not there till the second day. We took about 4*l.*, but not all for penny likenesses, because, if we put the likeness on card we charged 2*d.*, and if they was bronzed we charged 6*d.*, and if they were framed complete, 1*s.* My pay was 4*s.* per day, and I was found in my keep.

'I always attend Greenwich-park regularly at holiday times, but never have a booth at the fair, because I can do better moving about. I have a frame of specimens tied round a tree, and get a boy to hold the paper and cards. At this I've taken as much as 35*s.* in one day, and though there was lots of cheap photographic booths down there last Easter Monday, in spite of 'em all I took above 8*s.* 6*d.* in the afternoon. Battersea-fields and Chalkfarm used to be out-and-out spots on a Sunday, at one time. I've often taken such a thing as 30*s.* on a Sunday afternoon and evening in the summer. After I left the steam-boats I built myself a small booth, and travelled the country to fairs, "statties," and feasts, and got a very comfortable living; but now the cheap photographs have completely done up profiles, so I'm compelled to turn to that. But I think I shall learn a trade, for that'll be better than either of them.

'The best work I've had of late years has been at the teetotal festivals. I was at Aylesbury with them, at St. Alban's, Luton, and Gore House. At Gore House last August, when the "Bands of Hope" were there, I took about a pound.'

WRITER WITHOUT HANDS

THE next in order are the Writers without Hands and the Chalkers on Flag-stones.

A man of 61, born in the crippled state he described, tall, and with an intelligent look and good manners, gave me this account:—

'I was born without hands—merely the elbow of the right arm and the joint of the wrist of the left. I have rounded stumps. I was born without feet also, merely the ankle and heel, just as if my feet were cut off close within the instep. My father was a farmer in

Cavan county, Ireland, and gave me a fair education. He had me taught to write. I'll show you how, sir.' (Here he put on a pair of spectacles, using his stumps, and then holding the pen on one stump, by means of the other he moved the two together, and so wrote his name in an old-fashioned hand.) 'I was taught by an ordinary schoolmaster. I served an apprenticeship of seven years to a turner, near Cavan, and could work well at the turning, but couldn't chop the wood very well. I handled my tools as I've shown you I do my pen. I came to London in 1814, having a prospect of getting a situation in the India-house; but I didn't get it, and waited for eighteen months, until my funds and my father's help were exhausted, and then I took to making fancy screens, flower-vases, and hand-racks in the streets. I did very well at them, making 15s. to 20s. a-week in the summer, and not half that, perhaps not much more than a third, in the winter. I continue this work still, when my health permits, and I now make handsome ornaments, flower-vases, &c. for the quality, and have to work before them frequently, to satisfy them. I could do very well but for ill-health. I charge from 5s. to 8s. for hand-screens, and from 7s. 6d. to 15s. for flower-vases. Some of the quality pay me handsomely— some are very near. I have done little work in the streets this way, except in very fine weather. Sometimes I write tickets in the street at a halfpenny each. The police never interfere unless the thorough-fare is obstructed badly. My most frequent writing is, "Naked came I into the world, and naked shall I return." "The Lord giveth, and the Lord taketh away; blessed be the name of the Lord." '

CHALKER ON FLAG-STONES

A SPARE, sad-looking man, very poorly dressed, gave me the following statement. He is well-known by his coloured drawings upon the flagstones:—

'I was usher in a school for three years, and had a paralytic stroke, which lost me my employment, and was soon the cause of great poverty. I was fond of drawing, and colouring drawings, when a child, using sixpenny boxes of colours, or the best my parents could procure me, but I never had lessons. I am a self-taught man. When I was reduced to distress, and indeed to starvation, I thought of trying some mode of living, and remembering having seen a man draw mackerel on the flags in the streets of

Bristol 20 years ago, I thought I would try what I could do that way. I first tried my hand in the New Kent-road, attempting a likeness of Napoleon, and it was passable, though I can do much better now; I made half-a-crown the first day. I saw a statement in one of your letters that I was making 1*l.* a-day, and was giving 14*d.* for a shilling. I never did: on the contrary, I've had a pint of beer given to me by publicans for supplying them with copper. It doesn't hurt me, so that you need not contradict it unless you like. The Morning Chronicle letters about us are frequently talked over in the lodging-houses. It's 14 or 15 years since I started in the New Kent-road, and I've followed up "screeving," as it's sometimes called, or drawing in coloured chalks on the flag-stones, until now.'

EXHIBITORS OF TRAINED ANIMALS

THE HAPPY FAMILY EXHIBITOR

'Happy Families,' or assemblages of animals of diverse habits and propensities living amicably, or at least quietly, in one cage, are so well known as to need no further description here. Concerning them I received the following account:—

'I have been three years connected with happy families, living by such connexion. These exhibitions were first started at Coventry, sixteen years ago, by a man who was my teacher. He was a stocking-weaver, and a fancier of animals and birds, having a good many in his place—hawks, owls, pigeons, starlings, cats, dogs, rats, mice, guinea-pigs, jackdaws, fowls, ravens, and monkeys. He used to keep them separate and for his own amusement, or would train them for sale, teaching the dogs tricks, and such-like. He found his animals agree so well together, that he had a notion—and a snake-charmer, an old Indian, used to advise him on the subject-that he could show in public animals and birds, supposed to be one another's enemies and victims, living in quiet together. He did show them in public, beginning with cats, rats, and pigeons in one cage; and then kept adding by degrees all the other creatures I have mentioned. He did very well at Coventry, but I don't know what he took. His way of training the animals is a secret, which he has taught to me. It's principally done, however, I may tell you, by continued kindness and petting, and studying the nature of the creatures. Hundreds have tried their hands at happy families, and have failed. The cat has killed the mice, the hawks have killed the birds, the dogs the rats, and even the cats, the rats, the birds, and even one another; indeed, it was anything but a happy family. By our system we never have a mishap; and have had animals eight or nine years in the cage—until they've died of age, indeed. In our present cage we have 54 birds and animals, and of 17 different kinds; 3 cats, 2 dogs (a terrier and a spaniel), 2 monkeys, 2 magpies, 2 jackdaws, 2 jays, 10 starlings (some of them talk), 6 pigeons, 2 hawks, 2 barn fowls, 1 screech owl, 5 common-sewer rats, 5 white rats (a novelty), 8 guinea-pigs, 2 rabbits (1 wild and 1 tame), 1 hedgehog, and 1 tortoise. Of all these, the rat is the most difficult to make a member of a happy family; among birds, the hawk. The easiest trained animal is a monkey, and the easiest trained bird a pigeon. They live together in their cages all night, and sleep in a stable, unattended by any one. They were once thirty-six hours, as a trial, without food—that was in Cambridge; and no creature was injured; but they were very peckish, especially the birds of prey.'

EXHIBITOR OF BIRDS AND MICE

A STOUT, acute-looking man, whom I found in a decently-furnished room with his wife, gave me an account of this kind of street exhibition:—

'I perform,' said he, 'with birds and mice, in the open air, if needful. I was brought up to juggling by my family and friends, but colds and heats brought on rheumatism, and I left juggling for another branch of the profession; but I juggle a little still. My birds are nearly all canaries—a score of them sometimes, sometimes less. I have names for them all. I have Mr. and Mrs. Caudle, dressed quite in character: they quarrel at times, and that's self-taught with them. Mrs. Caudle is not noisy, and is quite amusing. They ride out in a chariot drawn by another bird, a goldfinch mule. I give him any name that comes into my head. The goldfinch harnesses himself to a little wire harness. Mr. and Mrs. Caudle and the mule is very much admired by people of taste. Then I have Marshal Ney in full uniform, and he fires a cannon, to keep up the character. I can't say that he's bolder than others. I have a little canary called the Trumpeter, who jumps on to a trumpet when I sound it, and remains there until I've done sounding. Another canary goes up a pole, as if climbing for a leg of mutton, or any prize at the top, as they do at fairs, and when he gets to the top he answers me. He climbs fair, toe and heel—no props to help him along. These are the principal birds, and they all play by the word of command, and with the greatest satisfaction and ease to themselves. I use two things to train them—kindness and patience, and neither of these two things must be stinted.'

SKILLED AND UNSKILLED LABOUR

'GARRET-MASTERS'

The Cabinet-makers, socially as well as commercially considered, consist, like all other operatives, of two distinct classes, that is to say, of society and non-society men, or, in the language of political economy, of those whose wages are regulated by custom and those whose earnings are determined by competition. The former class numbers between 600 and 700 of the trade, and the latter between 4,000 and 5,000. As a general rule I may remark, that I find the society-men of every trade comprise about one-tenth of the whole.

I have already portrayed to the reader the difference between the homes of the two classes—the comfort and well-furnished abodes of the one, and the squalor and bare walls of the other. But those who wish to be impressed with the social advantages of a fairly-paid class of mechanics should attend a meeting of the Woodcarvers' Society. On the first floor of a small private house in Tottenham-street, Tottenham-court-road, is, so to speak, the museum of the working-men belonging to this branch of the cabinet-makers. The walls of the back-room are hung round with plaster casts of some of the choicest specimens of the arts, and in the front room the table is strewn with volumes of valuable prints and drawings in connexion with the craft. Round this table are ranged the members of the society—some forty or fifty were there on the night of my attendance—discussing the affairs of the trade. Among the collection of books may be found, 'The Architectural Ornaments and Decorations of Cottingham,' 'The Gothic Ornaments' of Pugin, Tatham's 'Greek Relics,' Raphael's 'Pilaster Ornaments of the Vatican,' Le Pautre's 'Designs,' and Baptiste's 'Collection of Flowers,' large size; while among the casts are articles of the same choice description. The objects of this society are, in the words of the preface to the printed catalogue, 'to enable wood-carvers to co-operate for the advancement of their art, and by forming a collection of books, prints, and drawings, to afford them facilities for self-improvement; also, by the diffusion of information among its members, to assist them in the exercise of their art, as well as to enable them to obtain employment.' The society does not interfere in the regulation of wages in any other way than, by the diffusion of information among its members, to assist them in the exercise of their art, as well as to enable them to obtain employment; so that both employers and employed may, by becoming members, promote their own and each other's interests.

In the whole course of my investigations I have never experienced more gratification than I did on the evening on my visit to this society. The members all gave evidence, both in manner and appearance, of the refining character of their craft; and it was indeed a hearty relief from the scenes of squalor, misery, dirt, vice, ignorance, and discontent, with which these inquiries too frequently bring one into connexion, to find one's self surrounded with an atmosphere of beauty, refinement, comfort, intelligence, and ease.

The public, generally, are deplorably misinformed as to the character and purpose of trade societies. The common impression is that they are combinations of working-men, instituted and maintained solely with the view of exacting an exorbitant rate of wages from their employers, and that they are necessarily connected with strikes, and with sundry other savage and silly means of attaining this object. It is my duty, however, to make known that the rate of wages which such societies are instituted to uphold has, with but few exceptions, been agreed upon at a conference of both masters and men, and that in almost every case I find the members as strongly opposed to strikes, as a means of upholding them, as the public themselves. But at all events the maintenance of the standard rate of wages is not the sole object of such societies —the majority of them being organised as much for the support of the sick and aged as for the regulation of the price of labour; and even in those societies whose efforts are confined to the latter purpose alone, a considerable sum is devoted annually for the subsistence of their members when out of work. The general cabinet-makers, I have already shown, have contributed towards this object as much as 1,000*l.* per annum for many years past. It is not generally known how largely the community is indebted to the trade and friendly societies of the working classes dispersed throughout the kingdom, or how much expense the public is saved by such means in the matter of poor-rates alone.

It is the slop-workers of the different trades—the cheap men or non-society hands—who constitute the great mass of paupers in this country. And here lies the main social distinction between the workmen who belong to societies and those who do not—the one maintain their own poor, the others are left to the mercy of the parish. The wages of the competitive men are cut down to a bare subsistence, so that, being unable to save anything from their earnings, a few days' incapacity from labour drives them to the workhouse for relief. In the matter of machinery, not only is the cost of working the engine, but the wear and tear of the machine, considered as a necessary part of the expense of production. With the human machine, however, it is different, slop-wages being sufficient to defray only the cost of keeping it at work, but not to compensate for the wear and tear of it. Under the allowance system of the old poor-law, wages, it is well known, were reduced far below subsistence-point, and the workmen were left to seek parish relief for the remainder; and so in the slop part of every trade, the underpaid workmen when sick or aged are handed over to the state to support.

The number of houses built in the metropolis has of late been considerably on the increase. Since 1839 there have been 200 miles of new streets formed in London, no less than 6,405 new dwellings having been erected annually since that time: and as it is but fair to assume that the majority of these new houses must have required new furniture, it is clear that it is impossible to account for the decline in the wages of the trade in question upon the assumption of an equal decline in the quantity of work. How, then, are we to explain the fact that, while the hands have decreased 33 per cent., and work increased at a considerable rate, wages a few years ago were 300 per cent. better than they are at present? The solution of the problem will be found in the extraordinary increase that has taken place within the last 20 years of what are called 'garret-masters' in the cabinet trade. These garret-masters are a class of small 'trade-working masters,' supplying both capital and labour.

They are in manufacture what the peasant-proprietors are in agriculture, their own employers and their own workmen. There is, however, this one marked distinction between the two classes,— the garret-master cannot, like the peasant-proprietor, eat what he produces: the consequence is, that he is obliged to convert each article into food immediately he manufactures it, no matter what the state of the market may be. The capital of the garret-master being generally sufficient to find him in the materials for the manufacture of only one article at a time, and his savings being barely enough for his subsistence while he is engaged in putting those materials together, he is compelled the moment the work is completed to part with it for whatever he can get. He cannot afford to keep it even a day, for to do so is generally to remain a day unfed. Hence, if the market be at all slack, he has to force a sale by offering his goods at the lowest possible price. What wonder, then, that the necessities of such a class of individuals should have created a special race of employers, known by the significant name of 'slaughter-house men?'—or that these, being aware of the inability of the garret-masters to hold out against any offer, no matter how slight a remuneration it affords for their labour, should continually lower and lower their prices until the entire body of the competitive portion of the cabinet trade is sunk in utter destitution and misery?

Another cause of the necessity of the garret-master to part with his goods as soon as made is the large size of the articles he manufactures, and the consequent cost of conveying them from slaughter-house to slaughter-house till a purchaser be found. For this purpose a van is frequently hired; and the consequence is, that he cannot hold out against the slaughterer's offer, even for an hour, without increasing the expense of carriage, and so virtually decreasing his gains. This is so well known at the slaughter-houses, that if a man, after seeking in vain for a fair remuneration for his work, is goaded by his necessities to call at a shop a second time to accept a price which he had previously refused, he seldom obtains what was first offered him. Sometimes when he has been ground down to the lowest possible sum, he is paid late on a Saturday night with a cheque, and forced to give the firm a liberal discount for cashing it.

These men work in their own rooms, in Spitalfields and Bethnal-green; and sometimes two or three men in different branches occupy one apartment, and work together there. They are a sober class of men, but seem so perfectly subdued by circumstances, that they cannot or do not struggle against the system which several of them told me they knew was undoing them

Concerning the hours of labour I had the following minute particulars from a garret-master who was a chairmaker.

'I work from 6 every morning to 9 at night—some work till 10— I breakfast at 8, which stops me for 10 minutes. I can breakfast in less time, but it's a rest; my dinner takes me say 20 minutes at the outside, and my tea 8 minutes. All the rest of the time I'm slaving at my bench. How many minutes' rest is that, sir? 38. Well, say three-quarters of an hour, and that allows a few sucks at a pipe when I rest; but I can smoke and work too. I have only one room to work and eat in, or I should lose more time. Altogether I labour 14½ hours every day, and I must work on Sundays at least 40 Sundays in the year. One may as well work as sit fretting. But on Sundays I only work till it's dusk, or till five or six in summer. When it's dusk I take a walk; I'm not well-dressed enough for a Sunday walk when its light, and I can't wear my apron very well on that day to hide patches. But there's eight hours that I reckon I take up every week in dancing about to the slaughterers'. I'm satisfied that I work very nearly 100 hours a-week the year through, deducting the time taken up by the slaughterers and buying stuff —say eight hours a-week, it gives more than 90 hours a-week for my work, and there's hundreds labour as hard as I do just for a crust.'

THE DOLL'S-EYE MAKER

A CURIOUS part of the street toy business is the sale of dolls and especially that odd branch of it, doll's-eye making. There are only two persons following this business in London, and by the most intelligent of these I was furnished with the following curious information:—

'I make all kinds of eyes,' the eye-manufacturer said, 'both dolls' and human eyes; birds' eyes are mostly manufactured in Birmingham. Of dolls' eyes there are two sorts, the common and the natural, as we call it. The common are simply small hollow glass spheres, made of white enamel, and coloured either black or blue, for only two colours of these are made. The bettermost dolls'

eyes, or the natural ones, are made in a superior manner, but after
a similar fashion to the commoner sort.

'I also make human eyes. These are two cases; in the one I have
black and hazel, and in the other blue and grey. Here you see are
the ladies' eyes,' he continued, taking one from the blue-eye tray.
'You see there's more sparkle and brilliance about them than the
gentlemen's. Here's two different ladies' eyes; they belong to fine-
looking young women, both of them. When a lady or gentleman
comes to us for an eye, we are obliged to have a sitting just like a
portrait-painter. We take no sketch, but study the tints of the
perfect eye. There are a number of eyes come over from France,
but these are generally what we call misfits; they are sold cheap,
and seldom match the other eye. Again, from not fitting tight over
the ball like those that are made expressly for the person, they
seldom move "consentaneously," as it is termed, with the natural
eye, and have therefore a very unpleasant and fixed stare, worse
almost than the defective eye itself. Now, the eyes we make move
so freely, and have such a natural appearance, that I can assure
you a gentleman who had one of his from me passed nine doctors
without the deception being detected.

'There is a lady customer of mine who has been married three
years to her husband, and I believe he doesn't know that she has
a false eye to this day.

'The generality of persons whom we serve take out their eyes
when they go to bed, and sleep with them either under their pillow,
or else in a tumbler of water on the toilet-table at their side. Most
married ladies, however, never take their eyes out at all.

'Some people wear out a false eye in half the time of others.
This doesn't arise from the greater use of them, or rolling them
about, but from the increased secretion of the tears, which act on
the false eye like acid on metal, and so corrodes and roughens the
surface. This roughness produces inflammation, and then a new
eye becomes necessary. The Scotch lose a great many eyes, why
I cannot say; and the men in this country lose more eyes, nearly
two to one. We generally make only one eye, but I did once make
two false eyes for a widow lady. She lost one first, and we repaired
the loss so well, that on her losing the other eye she got us to make
her a second.

'False eyes are a great charity to servants. If they lose an eye no one will engage them. In Paris there is a charitable institution for the supply of false eyes to the poor; and I really think, if there was a similar establishment in this country for furnishing artificial eyes to those whosebread depends on their looks, like servants, it would do a great deal of good. We always supplies eyes to such people at half-price. My usual price is 2*l.* 2*s.* for one of my best eyes. That eye is a couple of guineas, and as fine an eye as you would wish to see in any young woman's head.'

THE COAL-HEAVERS

THE transition from the artisan to the labourer is curious in many respects. In passing from the skilled operative of the west-end to the unskilled workman of the eastern quarter of London, the moral and intellectual change is so great, that it seems as if we were in a new land, and among another race. The artisans are almost to a man red-hot politicians. They are sufficiently educated and thoughtful to have a sense of their importance in the State. It is true they may entertain exaggerated notions of their natural rank and position in the social scale, but at least they have read, and reflected, and argued upon the subject, and their opinions are entitled to consideration. The political character and sentiments of the working classes appear to me to be a distinctive feature of the age, and they are a necessary consequence of the dawning intelligence of the mass. As their minds expand, they are naturally led to take a more enlarged view of their calling, and to contemplate their labours in relation to the whole framework of society. They begin to view their class, not as a mere isolated body of workmen, but as an integral portion of the nation, contributing their quota to the general welfare. If property has its duties as well as its rights; labour, on the other hand, they say, has its rights as well as its duties. The artisans of London seem to be generally well-informed upon these subjects. That they express their opinions violently, and often savagely, it is my duty to acknowledge; but that they are the unlightened and unthinking body of people that they are generally considered by those who never go among them, and who see them only as 'the dangerous classes,' it is my duty also to deny. So far as my experience has gone, I am bound to confess, that I have found the skilled labourers of the metropolis the very reverse, both morally and intellectually, of what the popular prejudice imagines them.

The unskilled labourers are a different class of people. As yet they are as unpolitical as footmen, and instead of entertaining violent democratic opinions, they appear to have no political opinions whatever; or, if they do possess any, they rather lead towards the maintenance of 'things as they are,' than towards the ascendancy of the working people. I have lately been investigating the state of the coalwhippers, and these reflections are forced upon me by the marked difference in the character and sentiments of these people from those of the operative tailors. Among the latter class there appeared to be a general bias towards the six points of the Charter; but the former were extremely proud of their having turned out to a man on the 10th of April, 1848, and become special constables for the maintenance of law and order on the day of the great Chartist demonstration. As to which of these classes are the better members of the state, it is not for me to offer an opinion; I merely assert a social fact. The artisans of the metropolis are intelligent, and dissatisfied with their political position: the labourers of London appear to be the reverse; and in passing from one class to the other, the change is so curious and striking, that the phenomenon deserves at least to be recorded in this place.

According to the Criminal Returns of the metropolis, the labourers occupy a most unenviable pre-eminence in police history. One in every twenty-eight labourers, according to these returns, has a predisposition for simple larceny: the average for the whole population of London is one in every 266 individuals; so that the labourers may be said to be more than nine times as dishonest as the generality of people resident in the metropolis. In drunkenness they occupy the same prominent position. One in every twenty-two individuals of the labouring class was charged with being intoxicated in the year 1848; whereas the average number of drunkards in the whole population of London is one in every 113 individuals. Nor are they less pugnaciously inclined; one in every twenty-six having been charged with a common assault, of a more or less aggravated form. The labourers of London are, therefore, nine times as dishonest, five times as drunken, and nine times as savage as the rest of the community.

As soon as a collier arrives at Gravesend, the captain sends the ship's papers up to the factor at the Coal Exchange, informing him of the quality and quantity of coal in the ship. The captain then falls into some tier near Gravesend, and remains there until he is ordered nearer London by the harbour-master. When the coal is sold and the ship supplied with the coal-meter, the captain receives orders from the harbour-master to come up into the Pool, and take his berth in a particular tier. The captain, when he has moored his ship into the Pool as directed, applies at the Coalwhippers' Office, and 'the gang' next in rotation is sent to him.

There are upwards of 200 gangs of coalwhippers. The class, supernumeraries included, numbers about 2,000 individuals. The number of meters is 150; the consequence is, that more than one-fourth of the gangs are unprovided with meters to work with them. Hence there are upwards of fifty gangs (of nine men each) of coal-whippers, or altogether 450 men more than there is any real occasion for. The consequence is, that each coalwhipper is neces-sarily thrown out of employment one-quarter of his time by the excess of hands. The cause of this extra number of hands being kept on the books is, that when there is a glut of vessels in the river, the coal merchants may not be delayed in having their cargoes deliv-ered from want of whippers. When such a glut occurs, the mer-chant has it in his power to employ a private meter; so that the 450 to 500 men are kept on the year through, merely to meet the particular exigency, and to promote the merchant's convenience. Did any good arise from this system to the public, the evil might be overlooked; but since, owing to the combination of the coal-factors, no more coals can come into the market than are sufficient to meet the demand *without lowering the price*, it is clear that the extra 450 or 500 men are kept on and allowed to deprive their fellow-labourers of one quarter of their regular work as whippers, without any advantage to the public.

The coalwhippers, previous to the passing of the Act of Parlia-ment in 1843, were employed and paid by the publicans in the neighbourhood of the river, from Tower-hill to Limehouse. Under this system, none but the most dissolute and intemperate obtained employment; in fact, the more intemperate they were the more readily they found work. The publicans were the relatives of the northern ship-owners; they mostly had come to London penniless, and being placed in a tavern by their relatives, soon became ship-owners themselves. There were at that time seventy taverns on the north side of the Thames, below bridge, employing coalwhippers, and all of the landlords making fortunes out of the earnings of the people. When a ship came to be 'made up,' that is, for the hands to be hired, the men assembled round the bar in crowds and began calling for drink, and out-bidding each other in the extent of their orders, so as to induce the landlord to give them employment. If one called for beer, the next would be sure to give an order for rum; for he who spent most at the public-house had the greatest chance of employment. After being 'taken on,' their first care was to put up a score at the public-house, so as to please their employer, the publican. In the morning before going to their work, they would invariably call at the house for a quartern of gin or rum; and they were obliged to take off with them to the ship 'a bottle,' holding nine pots of beer, and that of the worst description, for it was the invariable practice among the publicans to supply the coalwhippers with the very worst articles at the highest prices. When the men returned from their work they went back to the public-house, and there remained drinking the greater part of the night. He must have been a very steady man indeed, I am told, who could manage to return home sober to his wife and family. The consequence of this was, the men used to pass their days, and chief part of their nights, drinking in the public-house; and I am credibly informed that frequently, on the publican settling with them after leaving ship, instead of having anything to receive they were brought in several shillings in debt; this remained as a score for the next ship: in fact, it was only those who were in debt to the publican who were sure of employment on the next occasion. One publican had as many as fifteen ships; another had even more; and there was scarcely one of them without his two or three colliers. The children of the coalwhippers were almost reared in the tap-room, and a person who has had great experience in the trade, tells me he knew as many as 500 youths who were transported, and as many more who met with an untimely death. At one house there were forty young robust men employed, about seventeen years ago, and of these there are only two living at present.

The coal whippers all present the same aspect—they are all black. In summer, when the men strip more to their work, perspiration causes the coal-dust to adhere to the skin, and blackness is more than ever the rule. All about the ship partakes of the grimness of the prevailing hue. The sails are black; the gilding on the figurehead of the vessel becomes blackened, and the very visitor feels his complexion soon grow sable. The dress of the whippers is of every description; some have fustian jackets, some have sailors' jackets, some loose great coats, some Guernsey frocks. Many of them work in strong shirts, which once were white with a blue stripe; loose cotton neckerchiefs are generally worn by the whippers. All have black hair and black whiskers—no matter what the original hue; to the more stubby beards and moustachios the coaldust adheres freely between the bristles, and may even be seen, now and then, to glitter in the light amidst the hair. The barber, one of these men told me, charged nothing extra for shaving him, although the coal-dust must be a formidable thing to the best-tempered razor. In approaching a coal-ship in the river, the side has to be gained over barges lying alongside—the coal crackling under the visitor's feet. He must cross them to reach a ladder of very primitive construction, up which the deck is to be reached. It is a jest among the Yorkshire seamen that every thing is black in a collier, especially the soup. When the men are at work in whipping or filling, the only spot of white discernible on their hands is a portion of the nails.

THE COAL-BACKERS

I CONCLUDE with the statement of a coal-backer, or coalporter—a class to which the term coalheaver is usually given by those who are unversed in the mysteries of the calling. The man wore the approved fantail, and well-tarred short smock-frock, black velveteen knee breeches, dirty white stockings, and lace-up boots.

'I am a coalbacker,' he said. 'I have been so these twenty-two years. By a coalbacker, I mean a man who is engaged in carrying coals on his back from ships and craft to the waggons. The labour is very hard—there are few men who can continue at *it*.' My informant said it was too much for him; he had been obliged to give it up eight months back; he had overstrained himself at it, and been obliged to lay up for many months. 'I am forty-five years of age,' he continued, 'and have as many as eight children. None of them bring me in a sixpence. My eldest boy did, a little while back, but his master failed, and he lost his situation. My wife made slop-shirts at a penny each, and could not do more than three a-day. How we have lived through all my illness, I cannot say.'

Such accidents as overstraining are very common among the coalbackers. The labour of carrying such a heavy weight from the ship's hold is so excessive, that after a man turns forty he is considered to be past his work, and to be very liable to such accidents. It is usually reckoned that the strongest men cannot last more than twenty years at the business. Many of the heartiest of the men are knocked up through the bursting of blood-vessels and other casualties, and even the strongest cannot continue at the labour three days together. After the second day's work, they are obliged to hire some unemployed mate to do the work for them.

The coalbackers are generally at work at five o'clock in the morning, winter and summer. In the winter time, they have to work by the light of large fires and hanging caldrons, which they call bells.

Many of the backers are paid at the public-house; the wharfinger gives them a note to receive their daily earnings of the publican, who has the money from the merchant. Often the backers are kept waiting an hour at the public-house for their money, and they have credit through the day for any drink they may choose to call for. While waiting, they mostly have two or three pots of beer before they are paid; and the drinking once commenced, many of them return home drunk, with only half their earnings in their pockets. There is scarcely a man among the whole class of backers, but heartily wishes the system of payment at the public-house may be entirely abolished. The coalbackers are mostly an intemperate class of men. This arises chiefly from the extreme labour and the over-exertion of then men, the violent perspiration and the intense thirst produced thereby. Immediately a pause occurs in their work, they fly to the public-house for beer. One coalbacker made a regular habit of drinking sixteen half-pints of beer, with a pennyworth of gin in each, before breakfast every morning.

THE BALLAST-GETTERS

Of these there are two classes, viz. those engaged in obtaining the ballast by steam power, and those who still procure it as of old by muscular power.

The ballast-getters are men employed in raising ballast from the bed of the river by bodily labour. The apparatus by which this is effected consists of a long staff or pole, abouth thirty-five feet in length. At the end of this is an iron 'spoon' or ring, underneath which is a leathern bag holding about 20 cwt. The ballast is raised on board the working lighters by means of this spoon. The working-lighters cary six hands: that is, a staffsman whose duty it is to attend to the staff; a bagman, who empties the bag; a chainsman, who hauls at the chain; a heelsman, who lets go the pall of the winch; and two trimmers, who trim the ballast in the lighter as fast as it comes in.

The ballast-getters are all very powerful men; they are mostly very tall, big-boned, and muscular. Many of them are upwards of six feet high, and have backs two feet broad. 'I lifted seven half-hundredweights with one of my hands,' said one whom I saw. He was a man of thirty-nine years of age, and stood half an inch over six feet, while another was six feet two inches. They were indeed extraordinary fine specimens of the English labourer, making our boasted Life-guardsman appear almost weak and effeminate in comparison with them.

Before the steam dredging-engines were introduced, I am informed, the ballast-getters were even bigger and heavier men than they are now. The ballast-getters seldom or never fish up anything besides ballast. Four or five years back they were lucky enough to haul up a box of silver plate; but they consider a bit of old iron or a bit of copper very good luck now.

The ballast-getters usually work above the dredging-engines, mostly about Woolwich; there the cleanest ballast is to be got. The Trinity Company they speak most highly of; indeed the corporation are universally spoken of as excellent masters: the men say they have nothing to complain of. They get their money on every Friday night, and have no call to spend a farthing of their earnings otherwise than as they please. They only wish, they add,

that the ballast-heavers were as well off. 'It would be a good job
if they was, poor men,' say one and all.

The second class of ballast-labourers are

THE BALLAST-LIGHTERMEN

THESE are men engaged by the Trinity Company to carry the
ballast in the company's barges and lighters from the steam dredging-engines to the ship's side.

Some weeks the men can earn as much as 37s., but at others
they cannot get more than 12s 6d. 'I did myself only two load
last week,' said my informant. 'When there is little or no "vent,"
as we call it, for the ballast—that is, but a slight demand for it—
we have but little work. Upon an average, each lighterman makes
from 21s. to 22s. a-week. At the time of the strike among the pitmen
in the North, the lightermen, generally, only did about two load
a-week throughout the year; but then the following year we had
as much as we could do. The Trinity Company, whom I serve,
and have served for thirty years, are excellent masters to us when
we are sick or well. The corporation of the Trinity House allow the
married lightermen in their service 10s. and the single ones 7s. 6d.
a-week, as long as they are ill. I have known the allowance given
to men for two years, and for this we pay nothing to any benefit
society or provident fund. If we belong to any such society we have
our sick money from them independent of that. The superannu-
ation money is now 6l. a-year; but I understand,' continued the
man, 'that the company intend increasing it next Tuesday. Some
of the old men were ordered up to the house a little while ago, and
were asked what they could live comfortably upon, and one of the
gentlemen there promised them that no more of us should go to
the workhouse. They do not provide any school for our children;
a great many of the lightermen neither read nor write. I never
heard any talk of the company erecting a school, either for the
instruction of their men or their men's families. All I can say is,
that in all my dealings with the Trinity Corporation I have found
them very kind and considerate masters. They are always ready
to listen to the men, and they have hospitals for the sick in their
employ and midwives for the wives of the labourers; and they bury,
free of expense, most of the men that die in their service. To the

widows of their deceased servants they allow 6*l*. a-year; and if there be any children, they give 2*s*. a-month to each under fourteen years old. I never knew them to reduce the lightermen's wages; they have rather increased than lowered them. After the introduction of the steam-dredging machines we were getter off than we were before. Previous to that time the lightermen were getters as well, and then the labour was so hard that the expenses of the men for living were more than they are now.'

I now come in due order to

THE BALLAST-HEAVERS

The duty of the ballast-heaver is to heave into the holds of the ship the ballast brought alongside the vessel by the Trinity-lighters from the dredging-engines. The ships take in ballast either in the docks or in the Pool. When the ship is cranky-built, and cannot stand steady after a portion of her cargo has been discharged, she usually takes in what is called shifting or stiffening ballast. The ballast is said to stiffen a cranky vessel, because it has the effect of making her firm or steady in the water. The quantity of ballast required by cranky vessels depends upon the build of the ships. Sixty tons of cargo will stiffen the most cranky vessel.

Before the stablishment of the Coal-whippers' Office, the contractors for ballast were solely publicans; and they not only undertook to put ballast on board, but to deliver the coals from the ships as well. At this time the publicans engaged in the business made rapid and large fortunes, and soon became shipowners themselves, but after the institution of the Coal-whippers' Office, the business of the publicans, who had before been the contractors, declined. Since that period the contracts for ballasting ships have been undertaken by butchers and grocers, as well as publicans, and the number of these has increased every year, and according as the number of contractors has increased, so have the prices decreased, for each one is anxious to undersell the other. In order to do this, the contractors have sought everywhere for fresh hands, and the lodging-house-keepers in a particular have introduced labouring men from the country, who will do the work at a less price than those who have been regularly brought up to the business: and I am credibly informed, that whereas nine or ten years ago every ballast

'OLD SARAH', THE HURDY-GURDY PLAYER

A Dinner at a Cheap Lodging-House

heaver was known to his mates, now the strangers have increased to such an extent that at least two-thirds of the body are unacquainted with the rest.

In order to assure myself of the intensity of the labour of ballast-heaving, of which I heard statements on all sides, I visited a gang of men at work, ballasting a collier in the Pool. My engagements prevented my doing this until about six in the evening. There was a very dense fog on the river, and all along its banks; so thick was it, indeed, that the water, which washed the steps where I took a boat, could not be distinguished, even with the help of adjacent lights. I soon, however, attained the ballast-lighter I sought. The ballast-heavers had established themselves alongside a collier, to be filled with 43 tons of ballast, just before I reached them, so that I observed all their operations. Their first step was to tie pieces of old sail, or anything of that kind, round their shoes, ankles, and half up their legs, to prevent the gravel falling into their shoes, and so rendering their tread painful. This was rapidly done; and the men set to work with the quiet earnestness of those who are working for the morrow's meal, and who know that they must work hard. Two men stood in the gravel (the ballast) in the lighter; the other two stood on 'a stage,' as it is called, which is but a boarding placed on the partition-beams of the lighter. The men on this stage, cold as the night was, threw off their jackets, and worked in their shirts, their labour being not merely hard, but rapid. As one man struck his shovel into the ballast thrown upon the stage, the other hove his shovelful through a small porthole in the vessel's side, so that the work went on as continuously and as quickly as the circumstances could possibly admit. Rarely was a word spoken, and nothing was heard but an occasional gurgle of the water, and the plunging of the shovel into the gravel on the stage by one heaver followed instantaneously by the rattling of the stones in the hold shot from the shovel of the other.

LUMPERS

THE 'Lumpers' are, if possible, in a more degraded state than the ballast-heavers; they are not, it is true, under the same amount of oppression from the publican, but still they are so besotted with the drink which they are tempted to obtain from the publicans who employ them, as to look upon the man who tricks them out of their earnings rather as a friend than as enemy.

Let me now give a description of the lumpers' labour, and then of their earnings. The timber-trade is divided by the custom of the trade into two classes, called timber and deals.

Timber and deals require about the same time for their discharge. The largest vessels that enter into this trade in the port of London are to be found in the West India South Dock, formerly the City Canal.

The following evidence of a lumper was given unwillingly; indeed it was only by a series of cross-questionings that any approximation to the truth could be extracted from him. He was evidently in fear of losing his work; and the tavern to which I had gone to take his statement was filled with foremen watching and intimidating him. He said:

'I am a working lumper, or labourer at discharging timber or deal-ships. I have been sixteen years at the work. I should think that there are more than two hundred men at Deptford who are constantly engaged at the work; there are a great many more working lumpers living at Limehouse, Poplar, and Blackwall. These do the work principally of the West India Docks; and when the work is slack there and brisk at the Commercial, East Country, or Grand Surrey Canal Docks, the men cross the water and get a job on the Surrey side of the river. In the summer a great many Irish labourers seek for work as lumpers. They came over from Ireland in the Cork boats. I should say there are altogether upwards of 500 regular working lumpers; but in the summer there are at least 200 more, owing to the number of Irish who come to England to look for work at that time of the year. The wages of the regular lumpers are not less when the Irish come over in the summer, nor do the men get a less quantity of work to do. There are more timber and deal ships arriving at that season, so more hands are required to discharge them. The ships begin to arrive in July, and they continue coming in till January. Ater that time they lay up till March, when they sail for the foreign ports. Between January and July the regular working lumpers have little or nothing to do. During that time there are scarcely any timber or deal ships coming in; and the working lumpers then try to fall in with anything they can, either ballasting a ship, or carrying a few deals to load a timber-carriage, or doing a little "tide work."

'Our usual time of working is from six to six in the summer time and from daylight to dark in the winter. We always work under a foreman. There are two foremen lumpers to almost every ship that we discharge; and they engage the men, who work in gangs under them.

'I work under a publican. My master has only gone into the public line very lately. I don't think he's been at it more than eighteen months. He has been a master lumper I should say for these 10 or 12 years past. I worked under him before he had a public-house. Then he paid every Tuesday, Thursday, and Saturday nights, at the same house he is now proprietor of. The master-lumper always pays the men he employs at the public-house, whether they are publicans or not.

'My master employs, I should say, in the spring season, from 80 to 100 hands regularly: and most of these meet at his house on Tuesday and Thursday nights, and all of them on Saturday night, either to be settled with in full or have a part of their wages advanced. We are usually paid at 7 o'clok in the evening. I have been paid as late as 3 o'clock on Sunday morning; but that was some years ago, and I was all that time in the public-house. We go straight to the public-house after we have done our work.'

THE DOCK-LABOURERS

THE dock-labourers are a striking instance of mere brute force with brute appetites. This class of labour is as unskilled as the power of a hurricane. Mere muscle is all that is needed; hence every human locomotive is capable of working there. All that is wanted is the power of moving heavy bodies from one place to another. Dock-work is precisely the office that every kind of man is fitted to perform, and there we find every kind of man performing it. Those who are unable to live by the occupation to which they have been educated, can obtain a living there without any previous training. Hence we find men of every calling labouring at the docks. There are decayed and bankrupt master-butchers, master-bakers, publicans, grocers, old soldiers, old sailors, Polish refugees, broken-down gentlemen, discharged lawyers' clerks, suspended government clerks, almsmen, pensioners, servants, thieves—indeed, every one who wants a loaf, and is willing to work for it. The London Dock is one of the few places in the metropolis where men can get employment without either character or recommendation, so that the labourers employed there are naturally a most incongruous assembly. Each of the docks employs several hundred hands to ship and discharge the cargoes of the numerous vessels that enter; and as there are some six or seven of such docks attached to the metropolis it may be imagined how large a number of individuals are dependent on them for their subsistence. At a rough calculation, there must be at least 20,000 souls getting their living by such means.

THE LONDON DOCK

THE London Dock area accupies an area of ninety acres, and is situated in the three parishes of St. George, Shadwell, and Wapping.

The courts and alleys round about the dock swarm with low lodging-houses; and are inhabited either by the dock-labourers, sack-makers, watermen, or that peculiar class of the London poor who pick up a living by the water-side. The open streets themselves have all more or less a maritime character. Every other shop is either stocked with gear for the ship for the sailor. The windows of one house are filled with quadrants and bright brass sextants, chronometers, and huge mariners' compasses, with their cards trembling with the motion of the cabs and waggons passing in the street. Then comes the sailors' cheap shoe-mart, rejoicing in the attractive sign of 'Jack and his Mother.' Every public-house is a 'Jolly Tar,' or something equally taking. Then come sailmakers, their windows stowed with ropes and lines smelling of tar. All the grocers are provision-merchants, and exhibit in their windows the cases of meat and biscuits; and every article is warranted to keep in any climate. The corners of the streets, too, are mostly monopolised by slopsellers; their windows part-coloured with bright red-and-blue flannel shirts; the doors nearly blocked up with hammocks and 'well-oiled nor'-westers'; and the front of the house itself nearly covered with canvas trousers, rough pilot-coats, and shiny black dreadnoughts. The passengers alone would tell you that you were in the maritime districts of London. Now you meet a satin-waistcoated mate, or a black sailor with his large fur cap, or else a Custom-house officer in his brass-buttoned jacket.

As you enter the dock the sight of the forest of masts in the distance, and the tall chimneys vomiting clouds of black smoke, and the many coloured flags flying in the air, has a most peculiar effect; while the sheds with the monster wheels arching through the roofs look like the paddle-boxes of huge steamers. Along the quay you see, now men with their faces blue with indigo, and now gaugers, with their long brass-tipped rule dripping with spirit from the cask they have been probing. Then will come a group of flaxen-haired sailors chattering German; and next a black sailor, with a cotton handkerchief twisted turban-like round his head. Presently a blue smocked butcher, with fresh meat, and a bunch of cabbages in the tray on his shoulder; and shortly afterwards a mate, with green paroquets in a wooden cage. Here you will see sitting on a bench a sorrowful-looking woman, with new bright cooking tins at her feet, telling you she is an emigrant preparing for her voyage. As you pass along this quay the air is pungent with tobacco; on that it overpowers you with the fumes of rum; then you are nearly sickened with the stench of hides, and huge bins of horns; and shortly afterwards the atmosphere is fragrant with coffee and spice. Nearly everywhere you meet stacks of cork, or else yellow bins of sulphur, or lead-coloured copper-ore. As you enter this warehouse, the flooring is sticky, as if it had been newly tarred, with the sugar that has leaked through the casks; and as you descend into the dark vaults, you see long lines of lights hanging from the black arches, and lamps flitting about midway. Here you sniff the fumes of the wine, and there the peculiar fungus-smell of dry rot; then the jumble of sounds as you pass along the dock blends in anything but sweet concord. The sailors are singing boisterous nigger songs from the Yankee ship just entering; the cooper is hammering at the casks on the quay; the chains of the cranes, loosed of their weight, rattle as they fly up again; the ropes splash in the water; some captain shouts his orders through his hands; a goat bleats from some ship in the basin; and empty casks roll along the stones with a heavy drum-like sound. Here the heavily-laden ships are down far below the quay, and you descend to them by ladders; whilst in another basin they are high up out of the water, so that their green copper sheathing is almost level with the eye of the passenger; while above his head a long line of bowsprits stretches far over the quay, and from them hang spars and planks as a gangway to each ship.

He who wishes to behold one of the most extraordinary and least-known scenes of this metropolis, should wend his way to the London Dock gates at half-past seven in the morning. There he will see congregated within the principal entrance masses of men of all grades, looks, and kinds. Some in half-fashioned surtouts burst at the elbows, with the dirty shirts showing through. Others in greasy sporting jackets, with red pimpled faces. Others in the rags of their half-slang gentility, with the velvet collars of their paletots worn through to the canvas. Some in rusty black, with their waist-coats fastened tight up to the throat. Others, again, with the know-ing thieves' curl on each side of the jaunty cap; whilst here and there you may see a big-whiskered Pole, with his hands in the pockets of his plaited French trousers. Some loll outside the gates, smoking the pipe which is forbidden within; but these are mostly Irish.

Presently you know, by the stream pouring through the gates and the rush towards particular spots, that the 'calling foremen' have made their appearance. Then begins the scuffling and scrambling forth of countless hands high in the air, to catch the eye of him whose voice may give them work. As the foreman calls from a book of names, some men jump up on the backs of the others, so as to lift themselves high above the rest, and attract the notice of him who hires them. All are shouting. Some cry aloud his surname, some his christian name, other call out their own names, to remind him that they are there. Now the appeal is made in Irish blarney—now in broken English. Indeed, it is a sight to sadden the most callous, to see thousands of men struggling for only one day's hire; the scuffle being made the fiercer by the knowledge that hundreds out of the number there assembled must be left to idle the day out in want. To look in the faces of that hungry crowd is to see a sight that must be ever remembered. Some are smiling to the foremen to coax him into remembrance of them; others, with their protruding eyes, eager to snatch at the hoped-for pass. For weeks many have gone there, and gone through the same struggle —the same cries; and have gone away, after all, without the work they had screamed for.

From this it might be imagined that the work was of a peculiarly light and pleasant kind, and so, when I first saw the scene, I could not help imagining myself. But, in reality, the labour is of that heavy and continuous character that you would fancy only the best fed could stand it. The work may be divided into three classes. 1. Wheel-work, or that which is moved by the muscles of the legs and weight of the body; 2. jigger, or winch-work, or that which is moved by the muscles of the arm. In each of these the labourer is stationary; but in the truck work, which forms the third class, the labourer has to travel over a space of ground greater or less in proportion to the distance which the goods have to be removed.

The wheel-work is performed somewhat on the system of the treadwheel, with the exception that the force is applied inside instead of outside the wheel. From six to eight men enter a wooden cylinder or drum, upon which are nailed battens, and the men laying hold of the ropes commence treading the wheel round, occasionally singing the while, and stamping time in a manner that is pleasant, from its novelty. The wheel is generally about sixteen feet in diameter and eight to nine feet broad; and the six or eight men treading within it will lift from sixteen to eighteen hundred weight, and often a ton, forty times in an hour, an average of twenty-seven feet high. Other men will get out a cargo of from 800 to 900 casks of wine, each cask averaging about five hundred weight, and being lifted about eighteen feet, in a day and a half. At trucking each man is said to go on an average thirty miles a-day, and two-thirds of that time he is moving $1\frac{1}{2}$ cwt. at six miles and a-half per hour.

This labour, though requiring to be seen to be properly understood, must still appear so arduous that one would imagine it was not of that tempting nature, that 3,000 men could be found every day in London desperate enough to fight and battle for the privilege of getting 2s. 6d. by it; and even if they fail in 'getting taken on' at the commencement of the day, that they should then retire to the appointed yard, there to remain hour after hour in the hope that the wind might blow them some stray ship, so that other gangs might be wanted, and the calling foreman seek them there. It is a curious sight to see the men waiting in these yards to be hired at 4d. per hour, for such are the terms given in the after part of the day. There, seated on long benches ranged against the wall, they remain, some telling their miseries and some their crimes to one another, whilst others doze away their time. Rain or sunshime, there can always be found plenty ready to catch the stray 1*s*. or 8*d*. worth of work. By the size of the shed you can tell how many men sometimes remain there in the pouring rain, rather than run the chance of losing the stray hour's work. Some loiter on the bridges close by, and presently, as their practised eye or ear tells them that the calling foreman is in want of another gang, they rush forward in a stream towards the gate, though only six or eight at most can be hired out of the hundred or more that are waiting there. Again the same mad fight takes place as in the morning. There is the same jumping on benches, the same raising of hands, the same entreaties, and the same failures as before. It is strange to mark the change that takes place in the manner of the men when the foreman has left. Those that have been engaged go smiling to their labour. Indeed, I myself met on the quay just such a chuckling gang passing to their work. Those who are left behind give vent to their disappointment in abuse of him whom they had been supplicating and smiling at a few minutes before.

At four o'clock the eight hours' labour ceases, and then comes the paying. The names of the men are called out of the muster-book, and each man, as he answers to the cry, has half-a-crown given to him. So rapidly is this done that, in a quarter of an hour, the whole of the men have had their wages paid them. They then pour towards the gate. Here two constables stand, and as each man passes through the wicket, he takes his hat off, and is felt from head to foot by the dock-offiers and attendant: and yet, with all the want, misery, and temptation, the millions of pounds of property amid which they work, and the thousands of pipes and hogsheads of wine and spirits about the docks, I am informed, upon the best authority, that there are on an average but thirty charges of drunkenness in the course of the year, and only eight of dishonesty every month. This may, perhaps, arise from the vigilance of the superintendents; but to see the distressed condition of the men who seek and gain employment in the London Dock, it appears almost incredible, that out of so vast a body of men, without means and without character, there should be so little vice or crime. There still remains one curious circumstance to be added in connexion with the destitution of the dock-labourers. Close to the gate by which they are obliged to leave, sits on a coping-stone the refreshment man, with his two large canvas pockets tied in front of him, and filled with silver. and copper, ready to give change to those whom he has trusted with their dinner that day until they were paid.

Having made myself acquainted with the character and amount of the labour performed, I next proceeded to make inquiries into the condition of the labourers themselves, and thus to learn the average amount of their wages from so precarious an occupation. For this purpose, hearing that there were several cheap lodging-houses in the neighbourhood, I thought I should be better enabled to arrive at an average result by conversing with the inmates of them, and thus endeavouring to elicit from them some such statements of their earnings at one time and another, as would enable me to judge what was their average amount throughout the year. I had heard the most pathetic accounts from men in the waiting-yard; how they had been six weeks without a day's hire. I had been told of others who had been known to come there day after day in the hope of getting sixpence and who lived upon the stray pieces of bread given to them in charity by their fellow-labourers. Of one person I was informed by a gentleman who had sought out his history in pure sympathy, from the wretchedness of the man's appearance. The man had once been possessed of 500*l.* a-year, and had squandered it all away; and through some act or acts that I do not feel myself at liberty to state, had lost caste, character, friends, and everything that could make life easy for him. From that time he had sunk and sunk in the world, until, at last, he had found him, with a lodging-house for his dwelling-place, the associate of thieves and pickpockets. His only means of living at this time was bones and rag-grubbing; and for this purpose the man would wander through the streets at three every morning, to see what little bits of old iron, or rag, or refuse bone he could find in the roads. His principle source of income, I am informed, from such a source as precludes the possibility of doubt, was by picking up the refuse ends of cigars, drying them, and selling them at one-half-penny per ounce, as tobacco, to the thieves with whom he lodged.

The scenes witnessed at the London Dock were of so painful a description, the struggle for one day's work—the scramble for twenty-four hours' extra-subsistence and extra-life were of so tragic a character, that I was anxious to ascertain if possible the exact number of individuals in and around the metropolis who live by dock labour. I have said that at one of the docks alone I found that 1,823 stomachs would be deprived of food by the mere chopping of the breeze. 'It's an ill wind,' says the proverb, 'that blows nobody good;' and until I came to investigate the condition of the dock-labourer I could not have believed it possible that near upon 2,000 souls in one place alone lived, chameleon-like, upon the air, or that an easterly wind, despite the wise saw, could deprive so many of bread. It is indeed 'a nipping and an eager air.' That the sustenance of thousands of families should be as fickle as the very breeze itself; that the weathercock should be the index of daily want or daily ease to such a vast number of men, women, and children, was a climax of misery and wretchedness that I could not have imagined to exist; and since that I have witnessed such scenes of squalor, and crime, and suffering, as oppress the mind even to a feeling of awe.

The docks of London are to a superficial observer the very focus of metropolitan wealth. The cranes creak with the mass of riches. In the warehouses are stored goods that are as it were ingots of untold gold. Above and below ground you see piles upon piles of treasure that the eye cannot compass. The wealth appears as boundless as the very sea it has traversed. The brain aches in an attempt to comprehend the amount of riches before, above, and beneath it. There are acres upon acres of treasure, more than enough, one would fancy, to stay the cravings of the whole world, and yet you have but to visit the hovels grouped round about all this amazing excess of riches to witness the same amazing excess of poverty. If the incomprehensibility of the wealth rises to sublimity, assuredly the want that co-exists with it is equally incomprehensible and equally sublime. Pass from the quay and warehouses to the courts and alleys that surround them, and the mind is as bewildered with the destitution of the one place as it is with the super-abundance of the other. Many come to see the riches, but few the poverty, abounding in absolute masses round the far-famed port of London.

CHEAP LODGING-HOUSES

I now come to the class of cheap lodging-houses usually frequented by the casual labourers at the docks.

On my first visit, the want and misery that I saw were such, that, in consulting with the gentleman who led me to the spot, it was arranged that a dinner should be given on the following Sunday to all those who were present on the evening of my first interview; and, accordingly, enough beef, potatoes, and materials for a suet-pudding, were sent in from the neighbouring market to feed them every one. I parted with my guide, arranging to be with him the next Sunday at half-past one. We met at the time appointed, and fet out on our way to the cheap lodging-house. The streets were alive with sailors, and bonnetless and capless women. The Jews' shops and public-houses were all open, and parties of 'jolly tars' reeled past us, singing and bawling on their way. Had it not been that here and there a stray shop was closed, it would have been impossible to have guessed it was Sunday. We dived down a narrow court, at the entrance of which lolled Irish labourers smoking short pipes. Across the court hung lines, from which dangled dirty-white clothes to dry; and as we walked on, ragged, unwashed, shoeless children scampered past us, chasing one another. At length we reached a large open yard. In the centre of it stood several empty costermongers' trucks and turned-up carts, with their shafts high in the air. At the bottom of these lay two young girls huddled together, asleep. Their bare heads told their mode of life, while it was evident, from their muddy Adelaide boots, that they had walked the streets all night. My companion tried to see if he knew them, but they slept too soundly to be roused by gentle means. We passed on, and a few paces further on there sat grouped on a door-step four women, of the same character as the last two. One had her head covered up in an old brown shawl, and was sleeping in the lap of the one next to her. The other two were eating walnuts; ans a coarse-featured man in knee-breeches and 'ankle-jacks' was stretched on the ground close beside them.

At length we reached the lodging-house. It was night when I had first visited the place, and all now was new to me. The entrance was through a pair of large green gates, which gave it somewhat the appearance of a stable-yard. Over the kitchen door there hung a clothes-line, on which were a wet shirt and a pair of ragged canvas trousers, brown with tar. Entering the kitchen, we found it so full of smoke that the sun's rays, which shot slanting down through a broken tile in the roof, looked like a shaft of light cut through the fog. The flue of the chimney stood out from the bare brick wall like a buttress, and was black all way up with the smoke; the beams, which hung down from the roof, and ran from wall to wall, were of the same colour; and in the centre, to light the room, was a rude iron gas-pipe, such as are used at night when the streets are turned up. The floor was unboarded, and a wooden seat projected from the wall all round the room. In front of this was ranged a series of tables, on which lolled dozing men. A number of the inmates were grouped around the fire; some kneeling, toasting herrings, of which the place smelt strongly; others, without shirts, seated on the ground close beside it for warmth; and others drying the ends of cigars they had picked up in the streets. As we entered the men rose, and never was so motley and so ragged an assemblage seen. Their hair was matted like flocks of wool, and their chins were grimy with their unshorn beards. Some were in dirty smock-frocks; others in old red plush waistcoats, with long sleeves. One was dressed in an old shooting jacket, with large wooden buttons; a second in a blue flannel sailor's shirt; and a third, a mere boy, wore a long camlet coat reaching to his heels, and with the ends of the sleeves hanging over his hands. The features of the lodgers wore every kind of expression: one lad was positively handsome, and there was a frankness in his face and a straight-forward look in his eye that strongly impressed me with a sense of his honesty, even although I was assured he was a confirmed pickpocket. The young thief who had brought back the $11\frac{1}{2}d$. change out of the shilling that had been entrusted to him on the preceding evening, was far from prepossessing, now that I could see him better. His cheek-bones were high, while his hair, cut close on the top, with a valance of locks, as it were, left hanging in front, made me look upon him with no slight suspicion. On the form at the end of the kitchen was one whose squalor and wretchedness produced a feeling approaching to awe. His eyes were sunk deep in his head, his cheeks were drawn in, and his nostrils pinched with evident want, while his dark stubbly beard gave a grimness to his appearance that was almost demoniac; and yet there was a patience in his look that was almost pitiable. His clothes were black and shiny at every fold with grease, and his coarse shirt was so brown with long wearing, that it was only with close inspection you could see that it had once been a checked one: on his feet he had a pair of lady's side-laced boots, the toes of which had been cut off so that he might get them on. I never beheld so gaunt a picture of famine. To this day the figure of the man haunts me.

The lodging-house to which I more particularly allude makes up as many as 84 'bunks,' or beds, for which 2*d* per night is charged. For this sum the parties lodging there for the night are entitled to the use of the kitchen for the following day. In this a fire is kept all day long, at which they are allowed to cook their food. The kitchen opens at 5 in the morning, and closes at about 11 at night, after which hour no fresh lodger is taken in, and all those who slept in the house the night before, but who have not sufficient money to pay for their bed at that time, are turned out. Strangers who arrive in the course of the day must procure a tin ticket, by paying 2*d*. at the wicket in the office, previously to being allowed to enter the kitchen. The kitchen is about 40 feet long by about 40 wide. The 'bunks' are each about 7 feet long, and 1 foot 10 inches wide, and the grating on which the straw mattress is placed is about 12 inches from the ground. The wooden partitions between the 'bunks' are about 4 feet high. The coverings are a leather or a rug, but leathers are generally preferred. Of these 'bunks' there are five rows, of about 24 deep; two rows being placed head to head, with a gangway between each of such two rows, and the other row against the wall. The average number of persons sleeping in this house of a night is 60. Of these there are generally about 30 pick-pockets, 10 street-beggars, a few infirm old people who subsist occasionally upon parish relief and occasionally upon charity, 10 or 15 dock-labourers, about the same number of low and precarious callings, such as the neighbourhood affords, and a few persons who have been in good circumstances, but who have been reduced from a variety of causes. At one time there were as many as 9 persons lodging in this house who subsisted by picking up dogs' dung out of the streets, getting about 5*s*. for every basketful. The earnings of one of these men were known to average 9*s*. per week. There are generally lodging in the house a few bone-grubbers, who pick up bones, rags, iron, &c., out of the streets. Their average earnings are about 1*s*. per day. There are several mud-larks, or youths who go down to the water-side when the tide is out, to see whether any article of value has been left upon the bank of the river. The person supplying this information to me, who was for some time resident in the house, has seen brought home by these persons a drum of figs at one time, and a Dutch cheese at another. These were sold in small lots or slices to the other lodgers.

The pickpockets generally lodging in the house consist of hand-kerchief-stealers, shop-lifters—including those who rob the till as well as steal articles from the doors of shops. Legs and breasts of mutton are frequently brought in by this class of persons. There are seldom any housebreakers lodging in such places, because they require a room of their own, and mostly live with prostitutes. Besides pickpockets, there are also lodging in the house speculators in stolen goods. These may be dock-labourers or Billingsgate porters, having a few shillings in their pockets. With these they purchase the booty of the juvenile thieves. 'I have known,' says my informant, 'the speculators wait in the kitchen, walking about with their hands in their pockets, till a little fellow would come in with such a thing as a cap, a piece of bacon, or a piece of mutton. They would purchase it, and then either retail it amongst the other lodgers in the kitchen or take it to some "fence," where they would receive a profit upon it.' The general feeling of the kitchen—exepting with four or five individuals—is to encourage theft. The encouragement to the 'gonaff,' (a Hebrew word signifying a young thief, probably learnt from the Jew 'fences' in the neigh-bourhood) consists in laughing at and applauding his dexterity in thieving; and whenever anything is brought in, the 'gonaff' is greeted for his good luck, and a general rush is made towards him to see the produce of his thievery. The 'gonaffs' are generally young boys; about 20 out of 30 of these lads are under 21 years of age. They almost all of them love idleness, and will only work for one or two days together, but then they will work very hard. It is a singular fact that as a body, the pickpockets are generally very sparing of drink. They are mostly libidinous, indeed universally so, and spend whatever money they can spare upon the low prostitutes round about the neighbourhood. Burglars and smashers generally rank above this class of thieves. A burglar would not condescend to sit among pickpockets. My informant has known a housebreaker to say with a sneer, when requested to sit down with the 'gonaffs,' 'No, no! I may be a thief, sir; but, thank God, at least I'm a respectable one.' The beggars who frequent these houses go about different markets and streets asking charity of the people that pass by. They generally go out in couples; the business of one of the two

being to look out and give warning when the policeman is approaching, and of the other to stand 'shallow;' that is to say, to stand
with very little clothing on, shivering and shaking, sometimes with
bandages round his legs, and sometimes with his arm in a sling.
Others beg 'scran' (broken victuals) of the servants at respectable
houses, and bring it home to the lodging-house, where they sell it.
You may see, I am told, the men who lodge in the place, and
obtain an honest living, watch for these beggars coming in, as if
they were the best victuals in the City. My informant knew an
instance of a lad who seemed to be a very fine little fellow, and
promised to have been possessed of excellent mental capabilities
if properly directed, who came to the lodging-house when out of a
situation as an errand-boy. He stayed there a month or six weeks,
during which time he was tampered with by the others, and ultimately became a confirmed 'gonaff.' The conversation among the
lodgers relates chiefly to thieving and the best manner of stealing.
By way of practice, a boy will often pick the pocket of one of the
lodgers walking about the room, and if detected declare he did not
mean it.

LONDON WATERMEN, LIGHTERMEN, AND STEAMBOAT-MEN

Of all the great capitals, London has least the appearance of
antiquity, and the Thames has a peculiarly modern aspect. It is
no longer the 'silent highway,' for its silence is continually broken
by the clatter of steamboats. This change has materially affected
the position and diminished the number of the London watermen,
into whose condition and earnings I am now about to examine.

THE THAMES WATERMEN

THE observances on the Thames customary in the olden time still
continue, though on a very reduced scale. The Queen has her
watermen, but they have only been employed as the rowers of her
barge twice since her accession to the throne; once when Her
Majesty and Prince Albert visited the Thames Tunnel; and again
when Prince Albert took water at Whitehall, and was rowed to
the city to open the Coal-exchange. Besides the Queen's watermen,

there are still extant the dukes' and lords' watermen; the Lord Mayor's and the City Companies', as well as those belonging to the Admiralty. The above constitute what are called the privileged watermen, having certain rights and emoluments appertaining to them which do not fall to the lot of the class generally.

The Queen's watermen are now only eighteen in number. They have no payment except when actually employed, and then they have 10*s.* for such employment. They have, however, a suit of clothes; a red jacket, with the royal arms on the buttons, and dark trousers, presented to them once every two years. They have also the privileges of the servants of the household, such as exemption from taxes, &c. Most of them are proprietors of lighters, and are prosperous men.

The privileges of the retainers of the nobles in the Stuart days linger still among the lords' and dukes' watermen, but only as a mere shadow of a fading substance. There are five or six men now who wear a kind of livery. I heard of no particular fashion in this livery being observed, either now or within the memory of the watermen. Their only privilege is that they are free from impressment. In the war time these men were more than twenty-five times as numerous as they are at present; in fact they are dying out, and the last 'duke's,' and the last 'lord's' privileged watermen are now, as I was told, 'on their last legs.'

The Lord Mayor's watermen are still undiminished in number, the complement being thirty-six. Of these, eight are water-bailiffs, who, in any procession, row in a boat before the Lord Mayor's state-barge. The other twenty-eight are the rowers of the chief magistrate's barge on his aquatic excursions. They are all free from impressment, and are supplied with a red jacket and dark trousers every two years, the city arms being on the buttons.

One of these men told me that he had been a Lord Mayor's man for some years, and made about eight journeys a-year, 'swan-hopping and such-like,' the show being, as he said, a regular thing: 10*s.* a voyage was paid to each man. It was jolly work, my inform-ant stated, sometimes, was swan-hopping, though it depended on the Lord Mayor for the time being whether it was jolly or not. He had heard say, that in the old times the Lord Mayor's bargemen had spiced wine regularly when out. But now they had no wine of any sort—but sometimes, when a Lord Mayor pleased; and he did not always please. My informant was a lighterman as well as a Lord Mayor's waterman, and was doing well.

Among other privileged classes are the 'hog-grubbers' (as they are called by the other watermen), but their number is now only four. These hog-grubbers ply only at the Pelican stairs; they have been old sailors in the navy, and are licensed by the Trinity House, no apprenticeship or freedom of the Waterman's Company in that case being necessary. 'There was from forty to fifty of them, sir,' said a waterman to me, 'when I was a lad, and I am not fifty-three, and fine old fellows they were. But they're all going to nothing now.'

The Admiralty watermen are another privileged class. They have a suit of clothes once every two years, a dark-blue jacket and trousers, with an anchor on the buttons. They also wear badges, and are exempt from impressment. Their business is to row the officials of the Admiralty when they visit Deptford on a Trinity Monday, and on all occasions of business or recreation. They are now about eighteen in number. They receive no salary, but are paid per voyage at the same rate as the Lord Mayor's watermen. There was also a class known as 'the navy watermen,' who enjoyed the same privileges as the others, but they are now extinct. Such of the city companies as retain their barges have also their own watermen, whose services are rarely put into requisition above twice a-year. The Stationers' Company have lately relinquished keeping their barge.

To entitle any one to ply for hire on the river, or to work about for payment, it is provided by the laws of the City that he shall have duly and truly served a seven-years' apprenticeship to a licensed waterman, and shall have taken up his fredom at Waterman's Hall. I heard many complaints of this regulation being infringed. There were now, I was told, about 120 men employed by the Custom-house and in the Thames Police, who were not free watermen. "There's a good many from Rochester way, sir," one waterman said, 'and down that way. They've got in through the interest of members of Parliament, and such-like, while there's many free watermen, that's gone to the expense of taking up their freedom, just starving. But we are going to see about it, and it's high time. Either give us back the money we've paid for our rights, or let us have our proper rights—that's what I say. Why, only yesterday, there was two accidents on the river, though no lives were lost. Both was owing to unlicensed men.'

'It's neither this nor that,' said an old waterman to me, alluding to the decrease in their number and their earnings, 'people may talk as they like about what's been the ruin of us—it's nothing but new London Bridge. When my old father heard that the old bridge was to come down, "Bill," says he, 'it'll be up with the watermen in no time. If the old bridge had stood, how would all these steamers have shot her?' Some of them could never have got through at all. At some tides, it was so hard to shoot London Bridge (to go clear through the arches), that people wouldn't trust themselves to any but watermen. Now any fool might manage. London Bridge, sir, depend on it, has ruined us.'

Near the stairs below the bridge the watermen stand looking out for customers, or they sit on an adjacent form, protected from the weather, some smoking and some dozing. They are weather-beaten, strong-looking men, and most of them are of, or above, the middle age. Those who are not privileged work in the same way as the privileged, wear all kinds of dresses, but generally something in the nature of a sailor's garb, such as a strong pilot-jacket and thin canvas trousers. The present race of watermen have, I am assured, lost the sauciness (with occasional smartness) that distinguished their predecessors. They are mostly patient, plodding men, enduring poverty heroically, and shrinking far more than many other classes from any application for parish relief. 'There is not a more independent lot that way in London,' said a waterman to me, 'and God knows it isn't for want of all the claims which being poor can give us, that we don't apply to the workhouse.' Some, however, are obliged to spend their old age, when incapable of labour, in the union. Half or more than one-half of the Thames watermen, I am credibly informed, can read and write. They used to drink quantities of beer, but now, from the stress of altered circumstances, they are generally temperate men.

From one of the watermen, plying near the Tower, I had the following statement:—

'I have been a waterman eight-and-twenty years. I served my seven years duly and truly to my father. I had nothing but my keep and clothes, and that's the regular custom. We must serve seven years to be free of the river. It's the same now in our apprenticeship. No pay; and some masters will neither wash, nor clothe, nor mend a boy: and all that ought to be done by the master, by rights. Times and masters is harder than ever.

'Our principal customers are people that want to go across in a hurry. At night—and we take night work two and two about, two dozen of us, in turn—we have double fares. There's very few country visitors take boats now to see sights upon the river. The swell of the steamers frightens them. Last Friday a lady and gentleman engaged me for 2s. to go to the Thames Tunnel, but a steamer passed, and the lady said, "Oh, look what a surf! I don't like to venture"; and so she wouldn't, and I sat five hours after that before I'd earned a farthing. I remember the first steamer on the river; it was from Gravesend, I think. It was good for us men at first, as the passengers came ashore in boats. There was no steam-piers then, but now the big foreign steamers can come alongside, and ladies and cattle and all can step ashore on platforms. The good times is over, and we are ready now to snap at one another for 3d., when once we didn't care about 1s. We're beaten by engines and steamings that nobody can well understand, and wheels.'

THE LIGHTERMEN AND BARGEMEN

THESE are also licensed watermen. The London watermen rarely apply the term bargemen to any persons working on the river; they confine the appellation to those who work in the barges in the canals, and who need not be free of the river, though some of them are so, many of them being also seamen or old men-of-war's men. The river lightermen (as the watermen style them all, no matter what the craft) are, however, so far a distinct class, that they convey goods only, and not passengers: while the watermen convey only passengers, or such light goods as passengers may take with them in the way of luggage. The lighters are the large boats used to carry goods which form the cargo to the vessels in the river or the docks, or from the vessels to the shore. The barge is a kind of larger lighter, built deeper and stronger, and is confined principally to the conveyance of coal.

The lightermen differ little in character from the watermen, but, as far as their better circumstances have permitted them, they have more comfortable homes. I speak of the working lightermen, who are also proprietors; and they can all, with very few exceptions, read and write. They all reside near the river, and generally near the Docks—the great majority of them live on the Middlesex side. They are a sober class of men, both the working masters and the men they employ. A drunken lighterman, I was told, would hardly be trusted twice.

OMNIBUS PROPRIETORS

THE 'labourers' immediately connected with the trade in omnibuses are the proprietors, drivers, conductors, and time-keepers. Those less immediately but still in connexion with the trade are the 'odd men' and the horse-keepers.

The proprietors pay their servants fairly, as a general rule; while, as a universal rule, they rigidly exact sobriety, punctuality, and cleanliness. Their great dificulty, all of them concur in stating, is to ensure honesty. Every proprietor insists upon the excessive difficulty of trusting men with uncounted money, if the men feel there is no efficient check to ensure to their employers a knowledge of the exact amount of their daily receipts. Several plans have been resorted to in order to obtain desired check. One plan now in practice is to engage a well-dressed woman, sometimes accompanied by a child, and she travels by the omnibus; and immediately on leaving it, fills up a paper for the proprietor, showing the number of insides and outs, of short and long fares. This method, however, does not ensure a thorough accuracy. It is difficult for a woman, who must take such a place in the vehicle as she can get, to ascertain the precise number of outsides and their respective fares. So difficult, that I am assured such a person has returned a *smaller* number than was actually conveyed. One gentleman who was formerly an omnibus proprietor, told me he employed a 'ladylike,' and, as he believed, trusty woman, as a 'check;' but by some means the conductors found out the calling of the 'ladylike' woman, treated her, and she made very favourable returns for the conductors. Another lady was observed by a conductor, who bears an excellent character, and who mentioned the circumstance to me, to carry a small bag, from which, whenever a passenger got out, she drew, not very deftly it would seem, a bean, and placed it in one glove, as ladies carry their sixpences for the fare, or a pea, and placed it in the other. This process, the conductor felt assured, was a 'check'; that the beans indicated the 'long uns,' and the peas the 'short uns': so, when the unhappy woman desired to be put down at the bottom of Cheapside on a wintry evening, he contrived to land her in the very thickest of the mud, handing her out with great politeness.

One proprietor told me he had once employed religious men as conductors; 'but,' said he, 'they grew into thieves. A Methodist parson engaged one of his sons to me—it's a good while ago—and was quite indignant that I ever made any question about the young man's honesty, as he was strictly and religiously brought up; but he turned out one of the worst of the whole batch of them.' One check resorted to, as a conductor informed me, was found out by them. A lady entered the omnibus carrying a brown-paper parcel, loosely tied, and making a tear on the edge of the paper for every 'short' passenger, and a deeper tear for every 'long.' This difficulty in finding a check where an indefinite amount of money passes through a man's hands—and I am by no means disposed to undervalue the difficulty—has led to a summary course of procedure, not unattended by serious evils. It appears that men are now discharged suddenly, at a moment's notice, and with no reason assigned. If a reason be demanded, the answer is, 'You are not wanted any longer.' Probably, the discharge is on account of the man's honesty being suspected. But whether the suspicion be well founded or unfounded, the consequences are equally serious to the individual discharged; for it is a rule observed by the pro-prietors not to employ any man discharged from another line. He will not be employed, I am assured, if he can produce a good character; and even if the' 'bus he worked' had been discontinued as no longer required on that route. New men, who are considered unconnected with all versed in omnibus tricks, are appointed; and this course, it was intimated to me very strongly, was agree-able to the proprietors for two reasons—as widely extending their patronage, and as always placing at their command a large body of unemployed men, whose services can at any time be called into requisition at reduced wages, should 'slop-drivers' be desirable. It is next to impossible, I was further assured, for a man discharged from an omnibus to obtain other employ. If the director goes so far as to admit that he has nothing to allege against the man's character, he will yet give no reason for his discharge and an inquirer naturally imputes the with-holding of a reason to the mercy of the director.

OMNIBUS DRIVERS

FROM a driver I had the following statement:—

'I have been a driver fourteen years. I was brought up as a builder, but had friends that was using horses, and I sometimes assisted them in driving and grooming when I was out of work. I got to like that sort of work, and thought it would be better than my own business if I could get to be connected with a 'bus; and I had friends, and first got employed as a time-keeper; but I've been a driver for fourteen years. I'm now paid by the week, and not by the box. It's a fair payment, but we must live well. It's hard work is mine for I never have any rest but a few minutes, except every other Sunday, and then only two hours; that's the time of a journey there and back. If I was to ask leave to go to church, and then go to work again, I know what answer there would be—"You can go to church as often as you like, and we can get a man who doesn't want to go there." The cattle I drive are equal to gentlemen's carriage-horses. One I've driven five years, and I believe she was worked five years before I drove her. It's very hard work for the horses, but I don't know that they are overworked in 'busses. The starting after stopping is the hardest work for them it's such a terrible strain. I've felt for the poor things on a wet night, with a 'bus full of big people. I think that it's a pity that anybody uses a bearing rein. There's not many uses it now. It bears up a horse's head, and he can only go on pulling, pulling up a hill, one way. Take off his bearing rein, and he'll relieve the strain on him by bearing down his head, and flinging his weight on the collar to help him pull. If a man had to carry a weight up a hill on his back, how would he like to have his head tied back? Pherhaps you may have noticed Mr.——'s horses pull the 'bus up Holborn Hill. They're tightly borne up; but then they are very fine animals, fat and fine: there's no such cattle, perhaps, in a London 'bus—least-ways there's none better—and they're borne up for show. Now, a jib-horse won't go in a bearing rein, and will without it. I've seen that myself; so what can be the use of it? It's just teasing the poor things for a sort of fashion. I must keep exact time at every place where a time-keeper's stationed. Not a minute's excused—there's a fine for the least delay. I can't say that it's often levied bust still we are liable to it. If I've been blocked, I must make up for the block by galloping and if I'm seen to gallop, and anybody tells our people, I'm called over the coals. I must drive as quick with a thunder-storm pelting in my face, and the roads in a muddle, and the horses starting—I can't call it shying, I have'em too well in hand,—at every flash, just as quick as if it was a fine hard road, and fine weather. It's not easy to drive a 'bus; but I can drive, and must drive, to an inch: yes, sir, to half an inch. I know if I can get my horses' heads through a space, I can get my splinter bar through. I drive by my pole, making it my centre. If I keep it fair in the centre, a carriage must follow, unless it's slippery weather, and then there's no calculating. I saw the first 'bus start in 1829. I heard the first 'bus called a Punch-and-Judy carriage, 'cause you could see the people inside without a frame. The shape was about the same as it is now, but bigger and heavier. A 'bus changes horses four or five times a-day, according to the distance. There's no cruelty to the horses, not a bit, it wouldn't be allowed. I fancy that 'busses now pay the proprietors well. The duty was $2\frac{1}{2}d$. a-mile, and now it's $1\frac{1}{2}d$. Some companies save twelve guineas a-week by the doing away of toll-gates. The 'stablishing the three-pennies—the short uns—has put money in their pockets. I'm an unmarried man. A 'bus driver never has time to look out for a wife. Every horse in our stables has one day's rest in every four; but it's no rest for the driver.'

OMNIBUS CONDUCTORS

THE conductor, who is vulgarly known as the 'cad,' stands on a small projection at the end of the omnibus and it is his office to admit and set down every passenger, and to receive the amount of fare, for which amount he is, of course, responsible to his employers. From one of them, a very intelligent man, I had the following statement:—

'I am 35 or 36, and have been a conductor for six years. I'm a conductor now, but wouldn't be long behind a 'bus if it wasn't from necessity. It's hard to get anything else to do that you can keep a wife and family on, for people won't have you from off a 'bus. The worst part of my business is its uncertainty. I may be discharged any day, and not know for what. If I did, and I was accused unjustly, I might bring my action; but it's merely, "You're not wanted." I think I've done better as a conductor in hot weather, or fine weather, than in wet; though I've got a good journey when it's come on showery, as people was starting for or starting from the City. I had one master, who, when his 'bus came in full in the wet, used to say, "This is prime. Them's God Almighty's customers; he sent them" I've heard him say so many a time. We get far more ladies and children, too, on a fine day; they go more a-shopping then, and of an evening they go more to public places. I pay over my money every night. It runs from 40*s*. to 4*l*. 4*s*., or a little more on extraordinary occasions. I have taken more money since the short uns were established. I never get to a public place, whether it's chapel or a playhouse, unless, indeed, I get a holiday, and that is once in two years. I've asked for a day's holiday and been refused. I was told I might take a week's holiday, if I liked, or as long as I lived. I'm quite ignorant of what's passing in the world, my time's so taken up. We only know what's going on from hearing people talk in the 'bus. I never care to read the paper now, though I used to like it. If I have two minutes to spare, I'd rather take a nap than anything else. We know no more politics than the backwoodsmen of America, because we haven't time to care about it. I've fallen asleep on my step as the 'bus was going on, and almost fallen off. I have often to put up with insolence from vulgar fellows, who think it fun to chaff a cad, a they call it. There's no help for it. Our masters won't listen to complaints: if we are not satisfied we can go. Conductors are a sober set of men. We must be sober. It takes every farthing of our wages to live well enough, and keep a wife and family.'

OMNIBUS TIMEKEEPERS

ANOTHER class employed in the omnibus trade are the timekeepers. On some routes there are five of these men, on others four. The timekeeper's duty is to start the omnibus at the exact moment appointed by the proprietors, and to report any delay or irregularity in the arrival of the vehicle. His hours are the same as those of the drivers and conductors, but as he is stationary his work is not so fatiguing. His remuneration is generally 21*s.* a week, but on some stations more. He must never leave the spot. A timekeeper on Kennington Common has 28*s.* a week. He is employed 16 hours daily, and has a box to shelter him from the weather when it is foul. He has to keep time for forty 'busses. The men who may be seen in the great thoroughfares noting every omnibus that passes, are not timekeepers; they are employed by Government, so that no omnibus may run on the line without paying the duty.

HACKNEY-COACH AND CABMEN

I HAVE now described the earnings and conditions of the drivers and conductors of the London omnibuses, and I proceed, in due order, to treat of the Metropolitan Hackney-coach and Cabmen. In official language, an omnibus is 'a Metropolitan Stage-carriage,' and a 'cab' a 'Metropolitan Hackney' one: the legal distinction being that the stage-carriages pursue a given route, and the passengers are mixed, while the fare is fixed by the proprietor; whereas the hackney-carriage plies for hire at an appointed 'stand,' carries no one but the party hiring it, and the fare for so doing is regulated by law. It is an offence for the omnibus to stand still and ply for hire, whereas the driver of the cab is liable to be punished if he ply for hire while his vehicle is moving.

One of the old fraternity of hackney-coachmen, who had, since the decline of his class, prospered by devoting his exertions to another department of business, gave me the following account.

'My father', said he, 'was an hackney-coachman before me, and gave me what was then reckoned a good education. I could write middling and could read the newspaper. I've driven my father's coach for him when I was fourteen. When I was old enough, seventeen I think I was, I had a hackney coach and horses of my own, provided for me by my father, and so was started in the world. The first time I plied with my own coach was when Sir Francis Burdett was sent to the Tower from his house in Piccadilly. Sir Francis was all the go then. I heard a hackney-coachman say he would be glad to drive him for nothing. The hackney-coachman didn't like Pitt. I've heard my father and his mates say many a time "D——n Pitt!" that was for doubling of the duty on hackney-carriages. Ah, the old times was the rackety times! I've often laughed and said that I could say what perhaps nobody, or almost nobody in England can say now, that I'd been driven by a king. He grew to be a king afterwards, George IV. One night you see, sir, I was called off the stand, and told to take up at the British Coffee-house in Cockspur Street. I was a lad then, and when I pulled up at the door, the waiter ran out and said, "You jump down and get inside, the Prince is a-going to drive hisself." I didn't much like the notion on it, but I didn't exactly know what to do, and was getting off my seat to see if the waiter had put anything inside, for he let down the glass, and just as I was getting down, and had my foot on the wheel, out came the Prince of Wales, and four or five rattle-brained fellows like himself. I think Major Hanger was one, but I had hardly time to see them, for the Prince gripped me by the ankle and the waistband of my breeches, and lifted me off the wheel and flung me right into the coach, through the window and it was opened, as it happened luckily. I was little then, but he must have been a strong man. He didn't seem so very drunk either. The Prince wasn't such a bad driver. Indeed, he drove very well for a prince, but he didn't take the corners or the crossings careful enough for a regular jarvey. Well, sir, the Prince drove that night to a house in King Street, Saint James's. There was another gentleman on the box with him. It was a gaming-house he went to that night, but I have driven him to other sorts of houses in that there neighbourhood. He hadn't no pride to such as me, hadn't the Prince of Wales. Then one season I used to drive Lord Barrymore in his rounds to the brothels—twice or thrice a-week sometimes. He used always to take his own wine with him. After waiting till near daylight, or till daylight, I've carried my lord, girls and all —fine dressed-up madams—to Billingsgate, and ther I've left them to breakfast at some queer place, or to slang with the fish-wives. What times them was, to be sure! One night I drove Lord Barrymore to Mother Cummins's in Lisle Street, and when she saw who it was she swore out of the window that she wouldn't let him in—he and some such rackety fellows had broken so many things the last time they were there, and had disgraced her, as she called it, to the neighbourhood. So my lord said, "Knock at the door, tiger; and knock till they open it." He knocked and knocked till every drop of water in the house was emptied over us, out of the windows, but my lord didn't like to be beaten, so he stayed and stayed, but Mother Cummins wouldn't give way, and at last he went home.'

CHARACTER OF CABDRIVERS

AMONG the present cabdrivers are to be found, as I learned from trustworthy persons, quondam greengrocers, costermongers, jewellers, clerks, broken-down gentlemen, especially turf gentlemen, carpenters, joiners, saddlers, coach-builders, grooms, stable-helpers, footmen, shopkeepers, pickpockets, swell-mobsmen, housebreakers, innkeepers, musicians, musical instrument makers, ostlers, some good scholars, a good number of broken-down pawnbrokers, several ex-policemen, draper's assistants, barmen, scene-shifters; one baronet, and as my informant expressed it, 'such an uncommon sight of folks that it would be uncommon hard to say what they was.' Of the truthfulness of the list of callings said to have contributed to swell the numbers of the cabmen there can be no doubt, but I am not so sure of 'the baronet.' I was told his name, but I met with no one who could positively say that he knew Sir V—— C—— as a cabdriver. This baronet seems a tradition among them. Others tell me that the party alluded to is merely nicknamed the Baron, owing to his being a person of good birth, and having had a college education. The 'flashiest' cabman, as he is termed, is the son of a fashionable master-tailor. He is known among cab-drivers as the 'Numpareil,' and drives one of the Hansom cabs. I am informed on excellent authority, a tenth, or, to speak beyond the possibility of cavil, a twelfth of the whole number of cabdrivers are 'fancy men.' These fellows are known in the cab trade by a very gross appellation. They are the men who live with women of the town, and are supported, wholly or partially, on the wages of the women's prostitution.

These are the fellows who, for the most part, are ready to pay the highest price for the hire of their cabs. One swell-mobsman, I was told, had risen from 'signing' for cabs to become a cab proprietor, but was now a prisoner in France for picking pockets.

The worse class of cabmen which, as I have before said, are but a twelfth of the whole, live in Granby Street, St. Andrew's Place, and similar localities of the Waterloo Road; in Union Street, Pearl Row, &c., of the Borough Road; in Princess Street, and others,

of the London Road; in some unpaved streets that stretch from the
New Kent Road to Lock's Fields; in the worst parts of Westminster,
in the vicinity of Drury Lane, Whitechapel, and of Lisson Grove,
and wherever low depravity flourishes. 'To get on a cab,' I was
told, and that is the regular phrase, 'is the ambition of more loose
fellows than for anything else, as it's reckoned both an idle life and
an exciting one.' Whetstone Park is full of cabmen, but not wholly
of the fancy-man class. The better sort of cabmen usually reside in
the neighbourhood of the cab-proprietors' yards, which are in all
directions. Some of the best of these men are, or rather have been
mechanics, and have left a sedentary employment, which affected
their health, for the open air of the cab business. Others of the best
description have been connected with country inns, but the
majority of them are London men. They are most of them married,
and bringing up families decently on earnings of from 15*s*. to 25*s*.
a-week. Some few of their wives work with their needles for the
tailors.

Of the cabdrivers there are several classes, according to the
times at which they are employed. These are known in the trade
by the names of the 'long-day men,' 'the morning-men,' the
'long-night men,' and the 'short-night men,' and 'the bucks.'

The long-day men are the parties who mostly employ the 'bucks,'
or unlicensed drivers. They are mostly out with their cabs from
16 to 20 hours, so that their work becomes more than they can
constantly endure, and they are consequently glad to avail themselves of the services of a buck for some hours at the end of the day,
or rather night. The morning man generally goes out about 7 in
the morning and returns to the yard at 6 in the evening.

The contractors employ scarcely any short-night men, while the
better masters have but few long-day or long-night men working
for them. It is only such persons as the Westminster masters who
like the horses or the men to be out so many hours together, and
they, as my informant said, 'don't care what becomes of either,
so long as the day's money is brought to them.' The bucks are
unlicensed cabdrivers, who are employed by those who have a
licence to take charge of the cab while the regular drivers are
at their meals or enjoying themselves. These bucks are generally
cabmen who have been deprived of their licence through bad
conduct, and who now pick up a living by 'rubbing up' (that is,

polishing the brass of the cabs) on the rank, and 'giving out buck' as it is called amongst the men. They usually loiter about the watering-houses (the public-houses) of the cab-stands, and pass most of their time in the tap-rooms. They are mostly of intemperate habits, being generally 'confirmed sots.' Very few of them are married men. They have been fancy-men in their prime, but, to use the words of one of the craft, 'got turned up.' They seldom sleep in a bed. Some few have a bedroom in some obscure part of the town, but the most of them loll about and doze in the tap-rooms by day, and sleep in the cabs by night. When the watering-houses close they resort to the night coffee-shops, and pass the time there till they are wanted as bucks. When they take a job for a man they have no regular agreement with the driver, but the rule is that they shall do the best they can. If they take 2*s.* they give the driver one and keep the other for themselves. If 1*s.* 6*d.* they usually keep only 6*d.* The Westminster men have generally got their regular bucks, and these mostly take to the cab with the second horse and do all the night work. At three or four in the morning they meet the driver at some appointed stand or watering-place. Burleigh Street in the Strand, or Palace Yard, are the favourite places of rendezvous of the Westminster men, and then they hand over to the long-day man 'the stuff', as they call it. The regular driver has no check upon these men, but unless they do well they never employ them again.

It is calculated that there are at least 800 or 1,000 bucks, hanging about the London cab-stands, and these are mostly regular thieves. If they catch any person asleep or drunk in a cab, they are sure to have a dive into his pockets; nor are they particular if the party belong to their own class, for I am assured that they steal from one another while dozing in the cabs or tap-rooms. Very few of the respectable masters work their cabs at night, except those who do so merely because they have not stable-room for the whole of their horses and vehicles at the same time. Some of the cabdrivers are the owners of the vehicles they drive. It is supposed that out of the 5,000 drivers in London, at least 2,000, or very nearly half, are small masters, and they are amongst the most respectable men of the ranks. Of the other half of the cabdrivers about 1,500 are long-day men, and about 150 long-night men (there are only a few yards, and they are principally at Islington, that employ long-night men).

Of the morning-men and the short-night men there are, as near as I can learn, about 500 belonging to each class, in addition to the small masters.